WITHDRAWN

P9-CDG-764

Splendid
soups

Splendid soups

Recipes and master techniques for making the world's best soups

JAMES PETERSON

JOHN WILEY & SONS, INC.

New York, Chichester, Weinheim, Brisbane, Singapore, Toronto

sci.
Ref.
TX
757
P4823
2001

This book is printed on acid-free paper. ∞

Copyright © 2001 by James Peterson. All rights reserved.

Published by John Wiley & Sons, Inc.
Published simultaneously in Canada.

No part of this publication may be reproduced, stored in a retrieval system or transmitted in any form or by any means, electronic, mechanical, photocopying, recording, scanning or otherwise, except as permitted under Sections 107 or 108 of the 1976 United States Copyright Act, without either the prior written permission of the Publisher, or authorization through payment of the appropriate per-copy fee to the Copyright Clearance Center, 222 Rosewood Drive, Danvers, MA 01923, (978) 750-8400, fax (978) 750-4744. Requests to the Publisher for permission should be addressed to the Permissions Department, John Wiley & Sons, Inc., 605 Third Avenue, New York, NY 10158-0012, (212) 850-6011, fax (212) 850-6008, E-Mail: PERMREQ @ WILEY.COM.

This publication is designed to provide accurate and authoritative information in regard to the subject matter covered. It is sold with the understanding that the publisher is not engaged in rendering professional services. If professional advice or other expert assistance is required, the services of a competent professional person should be sought.

Library of Congress Cataloging-in-Publication Data:

ISBN: 0471-39136-0

Printed in the United States of America.

10 9 8 7 6 5 4 3 2 1

This book is dedicated to Zelik

Contents

Vegetable Soups 144

Rice Soups 280

Fish Soups 292

Bivalve Shellfish Soups 352

Crustacean Soups 386

Bread Soups **550**

Yogurt, Cheese, and Buttermilk Soups **560**

Fruit Soups and Dessert Soups **568**

Acknowledgments

FIRST AND FOREMOST I'D LIKE TO THANK PAM CHIRLS AT JOHN WILEY & SONS FOR having the commitment and enthusiasm for *Splendid Soups* to issue it in its new, enlarged form with new recipes, a new design, and photography. Special thanks must also go to the designers at Vertigo Design, including Alison Lew, who put so much energy and thought into making *Splendid Soups* appealing to look at and use.

Many of the same people who worked on the first edition of *Splendid Soups* also have worked on the revised and updated edition. Geraldine Cresci shopped for and tested all the new recipes, researched an updated source list, including on-line sources, and contributed useful input regarding which recipes would photograph best. She also drove me all around Manhattan, looking for bowls, spoons, and glasses to use for the finished photographs. For many of the photographs, we had no food stylist, and it was Geraldine's careful preparation of the soups that you see in most of the pictures. I must also thank Debré DeMers for helping me photograph the images for the new edition. She was far more than a photo assistant and contributed her keen sense of design, her friendship, and her good humor every day. Thanks also to Elizabeth Duffy and Rosemarie Spinelli for styling a number of the photographs.

My agents, Elise and Arnold Goodman, still stand behind me, as they have for the past 10 years. I have too much to thank them for to express it all here. Last, thank you Zelik Mintz for tasting thousands of dishes, some of which never made it into a book, and for always offering your love, loyalty, and support.

Introduction

WHEN I FIRST TOLD FRIENDS AND COLLEAGUES THAT I WAS WRITING A 600-PAGE book about soups, their reactions varied from incredulity to excitement. The incredulous couldn't imagine such a thing, having had no more than a dozen different soups in their lives. The excited friends already loved soup and were so eager to get their hands on more recipes that some even asked for copies of the unpublished manuscript so they could get started right away. Everyone—excited, incredulous, or somewhere in between—asked me what possessed me to undertake such a thing.

Frankly, the idea of writing a book about soups would never have occurred to me if I hadn't first written *Sauces* in the early 1990s. My work on *Sauces* led me to discover a new style of cooking that had been developing in France since the 1970s and in the United States (and no doubt elsewhere) since the 1980s. This new style consisted of replacing many of the flour-thickened sauces of French classic cooking and the rich, buttery sauces of la nouvelle cuisine with intensely flavored brothlike sauces containing no flour or fat. Because these broths contained no thickeners, they satisfied both proponents of la nouvelle cuisine, who had banished flour-thickened sauces from their kitchens, and the growing number of people who had become fearful of fats. Because these new sauces were essentially concentrated soups, it occurred to me that the difference between sauces and soups is a continuum. On one end they contain more solid than liquid (such as a red wine stew), and on the other end they contain more liquid than solid (such as a consommé with little shreds of meat or vegetables). So I started making and reading about soups (I had to buy another bookcase) and applied the insights I had gleaned while writing *Sauces* to making soups.

Since my interest in soup quickly turned into an obsession, the manuscript became a many-tentacled monster that had to be wrestled into some kind of logical organization—a process it fought bitterly. Should I organize the book according to ingredients? Techniques? Countries or regions? I finally decided to organize the book according to ingredients, such as vegetables, fish, and meat, with extra chapters devoted to recipes that didn't have a logical place in other chapters. At the same time, I've organized information about national and regional cuisine into a context by including descriptions of how ingredients work together to give soups a characteristic national or regional identity and charts that unify an infinity of soups into meaningful systems. The charts, which I've put under a heading called "Patterns for Improvising Soups," lay out the steps for making vegetable, seafood, and meat soups so that you can learn to invent soups in a systematic way instead of just following a recipe. Many of these methods cross cultural boundaries, to the extent that they are almost universal, with only the ingredients differing from place to place. Without implying that making soup is formulaic—in the boring, uncreative sense of the word—these charts make it easy to see the relationship between techniques used throughout the world so that you can take virtually any set of ingredients and turn them into a soup. Once you understand basic soup-making techniques and ingredients, you'll develop an intuitive sense for grouping ingredients that will enable you to make soups, some with a distinct ethnic identity and others perhaps more clearly your own.

While writing *Splendid Soups*, I made a couple of useful discoveries. Before *Splendid Soups*, it never would have occurred to me to make a meal out of just soup. Cooking soup at home seemed a waste of good broth that I would rather have reduced and used to make sauces. Ordering soup in a restaurant was something I never did, always opting for something flashier. But writing and testing recipes for hundreds of soups turned into an obsessive love affair and has left me a dedicated soup afficionado. One of the best things about most soups is the ease with which they can be reheated—if I'm heating a bowl or two, I use the microwave—so I always make more than I need so there's enough left over for the next day. Soup, a chunk of bread, and perhaps a little salad or cheese now make up many of the simple dinners I serve at home. I'm also amazed by the versatility of soup. Every cuisine has its own soups, and virtually any braised, sauced, or stewed dish can be converted into a soup by just increasing the proportion of liquid to solid. (One smart-aleck friend suggested that I just add water to all my sauce recipes.) Soups also run the gamut from informal, homespun meals, in which the soup is the main course, to light and sometimes elegant introductions to a multicourse dinner. Soups also can be easily digestible elixirs to help get over a flu.

One useful discovery I made was that any number of vegetables gently simmered until done makes a delicious soup, provided you include garlic or onions or some other member of the onion family, such as leeks. These simple soups are often better when made with a good homemade broth, but the best and freshest vegetables show themselves at their finest when cooked only with water. The simplest soups are made by gently simmering chopped vegetables. These same soups are easily given a bit more body by pureeing some or all of the soup using a blender—a hand-held immersion blender is great for this—or a food mill. You can also add flavor and backbone to a soup by including a small amount of meat. The best and most flavorful meats are cured pork products, such as pancetta or prosciutto, cut into cubes and sweated with aromatic vegetables (carrots, celery, onions, and sometimes garlic) before liquid is added. A smoky flavor is almost essential to relieve the flat flavor of legumes, such as beans and lentils. Bacon makes an excellent counterpoint to legumes and is easy to add at the beginning or at the end after being cooked in a pan. Smoked ham hocks work in the same way, but because they take a couple of hours to cook, I simmer them along with slow-cooking legumes or I simmer them separately and use their cooking liquid as the base for the soup. I then add the shredded meat from the ham hocks to the finished soup.

I've also come up with a formula for very flavorful main-course chicken soups. Cook a quartered chicken in a sauté pan in a little butter or oil and, when the chicken is just about done, take it out of the pan, cook aromatic ingredients in the pan (throw out most of the fat used for browning the chicken), and add broth. While the ingredients are simmering, pull the skin off the chicken parts—throw it out—and pull the meat away in shreds, and stir the meat into the soup just before serving. You can adapt this technique to almost any ethnic or regional cuisine by just using the appropriate ingredients. In the book, you'll find a Mexican-style tomatillo soup, a chicken and tomato soup with olives and capers that's inspired by a putanesca sauce, a chicken and chili soup derived from a traditional Mexican chicken mole, and a chicken soup with raisins, apricots, and almonds, modeled after a Moroccan tagine. All of these soups are made using virtually the same techniques.

I was delighted when my publisher suggested that I expand and update *Splendid Soups*, and add new recipes and information. I was appreciative that I could do so with the advantage of a decade of hindsight, a privilege not given most cookbook writers. In the last 10 years, I've traveled to, and eaten in, many wonderful places, such as Spain, Tunisia, France, and even Greenland. I've read a lot of books by others who have traveled or spent creative time in the kitchen and have benefited from their insights and passions. My editor also has allowed me to take my own photographs of some favorite soups, an opportunity to show how great a soup can look and to tempt someone casually flipping through the book to move from sofa to kitchen. I've added recipes for light consommés (one meatless), more duck soups (one of my favorites is flavored with orange), a soup made with wild rice, and information about Chinese greens so you won't be befuddled in an Asian market. You'll find more information about dumplings and other substantial garnitures for soups, including Mexican meatballs, Thai shrimp balls, fish balls, and quenelles.

Since the first edition of *Splendid Soups*, both Rick Bayless and Diana Kennedy have come out with new books about Mexican cooking, and I've been lucky enough to have several wonderful meals at both of Rick Bayless's restaurants in Chicago. The influence of all this delicious Mexican food is apparent here, as I've used new information about fresh and dried chilies (which are now easier to find) and have come up with simple soups that I hope capture the flavors of Mexican cooking at its best and most authentic. Several trips to Spain with Paula Wolfert opened my eyes to a cuisine (and to the most marvelous ham in the world) with which I had had little firsthand experience. With a little hand holding, I got to experience authentic paellas and arroces, which can be aromatic rice dishes or soups, depending on how much liquid you add. Trips to Venice revealed souplike risottos, rich with butter and seafood—soothing and elegant as soups—presentable as first or main courses. Octopus, perhaps too scary ten years ago, gets a new recipe, made by long simmering in red wine. When working on my book *Vegetables*, I learned how to get more flavor out of root vegetables and even some green vegetables by slowly roasting them instead of just chopping them and simmering them in liquid. Here you'll find some delicious new vegetable soups.

I sometimes have a hard time explaining myself when people ask me why I bother to take a perfectly good dish and turn it into a soup. I find something particularly satisfying about the balance of liquid and solid that makes a soup. Because no family of dishes surpasses the versatility of soup, I know that I can easily adapt a soup to whim, weather—a hot soup is easily turned into a cold one and vice versa—formality, and to placement in the sequence of a meal. Although many of us think of homemade soup as a rather old-fashioned undertaking in our busy world, making a pot of soup is almost always easy.

As you flip through this revised and updated edition of *Splendid Soups*, you'll see that a soup can be served at any point in the meal, even as a dessert. Hopefully, you'll discover soup's unlimited versatility and that, as you read and use *Splendid Soups*, soup-making will become for you a natural and spontaneous way to cook and eat.

Equipment

THE BEAUTY OF SOUPS IS THAT YOU DON'T NEED MUCH MORE THAN A KNIFE FOR chopping, a pot for cooking, and a bowl for eating. Even the spoon can be dispensed with if you serve your soup in cups or mugs.

In addition to these bare essentials, you might want to have on hand a wooden spoon or two for stirring and a few different kinds of bowls to grace your table. If you make pureed soups, you'll need at least a simple strainer and a ladle, but you'll be better off with a blender or food mill. If you cook often or your kitchen is spare, here are some tips about what to buy.

Soup Pots

It's helpful to have a collection of soup pots in a variety of sizes. Most of the recipes in this book call for a 4-quart pot, a useful size even if you make very small amounts of soup. It's a good idea to have at least two pots this size because a lot of soup recipes have you straining from one pot into another. I also recommend at least one 10-quart pot for making broth or for the occasional family feast. The bottom of the pot must be thick; otherwise soup will scald if it isn't stirred constantly. The thickness of the sides isn't important.

Good soup pots don't have to be expensive. I love the look and feel of heavy copper, but most of my pots are inexpensive heavy-gauge aluminum from restaurant supply stores.

The health controversy over aluminum cookware has convinced most people to switch to more costly materials—but these are not necessarily better pots. In any case, much of the early evidence linking aluminum with Alzheimer's disease is being called into question. Even if the early evidence proves correct, there is more aluminum in one antacid tablet than could be absorbed in a lifetime of eating food cooked in aluminum pots. And virtually all restaurant meals have been cooked in aluminum.

Aluminum cookware stains certain foods such as artichokes, cardoons, and fennel. These foods require a stainless-steel or an anodized aluminum pot (such as the nonreactive Calphalon brand).

Strainers

To make pureed soups, you'll need some kind of strainer. The least expensive and easiest to find is the standard variety with a handle and screen with a medium mesh. Buy the widest one you can find. If the strainer is too small, it will take you twice as long to work through semisolid ingredients, and you'll be much more likely to make a mess.

If you make a lot of clear soups or very fine pureed soups, you'll need a fine-mesh strainer. There are two types: the less expensive, shaped like a regular strainer but with a very fine screen, the other, popular with professional chefs, cone shaped. For the latter you'll probably need to go to a kitchen supply shop, perhaps one that caters to professionals. Ask for a china cap or a *chinois* (pronounced shin-wa) and be prepared to spend a surprising amount of money; they are quite expensive. A cone-shaped fine-mesh strainer is more durable and easier to use, so if you make soups regularly, it's probably worth the extra investment. Inspect the strainer carefully for tiny holes, which would defeat its purpose, before paying for it.

When you're using a fine-mesh strainer, push the mixture through with a small ladle using a gentle up-and-down motion. Don't work the ladle hard against the screen; that may damage it.

A fine-mesh strainer often leaves a pureed soup watery because only the liquid goes through. There are a couple of ways around this: you can puree the solids in a blender or food processor and strain them again, or you can force them through a drum sieve. Drum sieves are circular screens, usually about 2 feet in diameter, with a strong outer frame made of wood or stainless steel. The stainless-steel drum sieves are better because they have replaceable screens, but they cost about four times as much as wooden-framed drum sieves, which are useless once the screen wears out. To use a drum sieve, place the sieve over a sheet pan or a large bowl. Place the solids on top of the screen and work them back and forth with a rubber spatula or plastic pastry scraper. When the solids have been worked through, they can be combined with the soup.

If you make a lot of broth, you may want to invest in a coarse china cap, a heavy-duty version with relatively large holes. Because it is large and can take a lot of beating, I like to strain large pots of broth or soup through a coarse china cap and then again through a finer strainer. A coarse china cap is also useful for straining lobster or crab soups, where the shells could easily damage a fine-mesh strainer.

Equipment for Grinding and Chopping

You need at least one of these to make pureed soups.

FOOD PROCESSORS I use my food processor surprisingly little. But my students use it for doing things that I prefer to do by hand. A food processor will do a quick job of chopping vegetables, but they won't come out in very presentable shapes. So I suggest using the food processor for chopping and cutting ingredients that will be strained out of the soup or pureed. If you're leaving the chopped vegetables in the soup, you'll get a more attractive effect if you cut them by hand (see box on page 147).

Food processors are best for pureeing stiff mixtures or hard ingredients such as shrimp or crayfish shells that would get stuck in a blender or damage its more fragile blade. A blender is better for pureeing thinner mixtures.

MINIATURE FOOD PROCESSORS Very small food processors are beginning to appear in kitchen supply stores. These very inexpensive appliances are excellent for chopping small amounts of vegetables such as a single shallot, a few cloves of garlic, or a bunch of parsley.

BLENDERS These are fine for pureeing relatively thin soups.

A couple of tricks will make using a blender easier and safer: (1) Never fill a blender more than a third full of a hot mixture. (2) Always wrap a towel tightly around the lid of the blender and start on slow speed. Otherwise the hot mixture may shoot out the top of the blender and burn you or at least make a mess.

One trick that makes using a blender faster and more convenient is to puree only the soup solids. Strain the soup first—reserving the liquid—and then puree the solids along with just enough liquid to get them to move around in the blender. Then strain the solids back into the reserved liquid.

If you're shopping for a blender, buy a semiprofessional model with only two settings—slow and fast—instead of one with about 20 buttons and an equal number of synonyms for *blend*.

Don't try to puree solid or very thick ingredients in a blender, or they're liable to get stuck; use a food processor.

BLENDER ATTACHMENTS Some blenders have optional food processor-like attachments that fit on the base and are useful for grinding small amounts of vegetables, spices, and herbs.

IMMERSION BLENDERS These have the blade attached to the end of a long handle and are especially convenient for making soups, because you can stick the end of the blender right in the soup pot instead of transferring the soup to a blender and ending up with another dish to clean. If you want your soup to be perfectly smooth, it will still have to be strained after blending.

FOOD MILLS These anachronistic-looking gadgets are finally coming back into vogue. If you've never seen one, a food mill has a round metal frame with a heavy mesh plate on the bottom and a crank on top. The crank has a flat propellerlike blade, which works the food through the tiny holes on the bottom. The great advantage to using a food mill over a food processor or blender is that a food mill strains and purees at the same time. Food mills are excellent for making soups with vegetables or fruits that have seeds (tomatoes, eggplant) or a lot of fiber (asparagus, leeks).

Food mills come in various sizes. Buy the largest one you think you might ever need; the small ones are a nuisance and tend to fall apart after a few months. There are two kinds of food mills—an American type popular with our grandmothers and a French model with interchangeable disks for different textures of puree. The latter is better for making soups because it gives you some control over the final texture.

MORTAR AND PESTLE Usually found only in the kitchens of true fanatics or collectors of *objets de cuisine*, a mortar and pestle are especially useful for grinding small amounts of spices, chunks of garlic, or aromatic pastes that won't move around in a blender or food processor. A mortar and pestle also look great on the kitchen shelf.

My own mortar and pestle are old, very large, and made of marble. The size and weight help hold the mortar in place while I'm grinding away, but I was lucky enough to find the thing in an antique store, so I can't really recommend running out and buying one. A good second choice is a porcelain mortar—again a large one so it stays in place—with an unglazed inner surface that helps grind up mixtures.

If you have trouble finding a marble or porcelain mortar and pestle—or they're too outrageously expensive—look for a Mexican-style black stone mortar and pestle called a *molcajete* and *tejolote*. These are less expensive and have a rough inner surface that makes them efficient for grinding. If you find a new *molcajete* and *tejolote*, follow Diana Kennedy's advice and grind a small handful of rice to eliminate any residual black grit.

If you have access to a Japanese market, you might want to try the Japanese version of a mortar and pestle, a *suribachi* and *surikogi*. The *suribachi* has a ribbed surface on the inside, which is especially useful for breaking up seeds (namely sesame).

Whichever mortar and pestle you end up with, place the mortar on a damp towel to help hold it in place while you're grinding. If you're grinding moist roots or fibrous ingredients such as garlic, shallots, or ginger, add a good pinch of coarse salt to the mixture. The salt works as an abrasive and speeds up the grinding.

COFFEE GRINDERS A small coffee grinder is an inexpensive alternative to a spice grinder. It's perfect for grinding small batches of spices that would just rattle around in a food processor or blender. Although you're not supposed to use the same grinder for grinding spices as for grinding coffee, I can't force myself to buy a second grinder—I just wipe it out very carefully each time I grind spices.

Equipment for Slicing

MANDOLINES Most American cooks are unfamiliar with this French kitchen gadget. A mandoline looks something like a large, elongated wooden plane held up by a stand on one end. It has an adjustable blade and is used to slice vegetables to precise thicknesses. It's wonderful for slicing potatoes, zucchini, carrots, daikon, cucumbers, or any cylindrical vegetable.

The one drawback to French mandolines is that they are very expensive and you'll have to go to a fancy kitchen supply store to find one. A less expensive alternative is to buy a small plastic model from Japan, called a *benriner cutter*. The principle is almost the same except that the Japanese version has a far sharper blade and is better for very fine chopping and slicing. The Japanese model also has an attachment for cutting vegetables into julienne strips. Benriner cutters are usually sold in Asian grocery stores.

Avoid similar slicers that have insertable blades instead of the one or two (for the wide model) screws found on the back of the benriner cutter, which allow you to adjust the slices to an exact thickness. Benriner cutters are available in most cooking supply shops, but the wide model, convenient for slicing large vegetables such as cabbage, can be mail ordered (see Sources page 611).

Miscellaneous Equipment

LADLES A collection of different-size ladles is helpful for making and serving soup. Small (1- and 2-ounce) ladles are useful for pushing mixtures through strainers; medium-size (6- to 8-ounce) ladles are useful for serving; and large (12-ounce) ladles are helpful for transferring soup from one pot to another or into containers for storage.

If you live near a kitchen supply store, I recommend buying stainless-steel ladles, preferably those made from a single piece of steel. The simpler the construction, the easier the ladle will be to clean and store.

RUBBER SPATULAS These are useful for getting every last bit of soup out of a pot or container, but don't make the mistake of leaving them in hot liquids for too long. Oil and fats cling to rubber spatulas and give them a stale odor that is almost impossible to remove. If they are left sitting too long in a delicate soup, some of the stale flavor may get into the soup. They can also melt and leave specks of plastic in the soup.

WOODEN SPOONS Metal spoons are not a good substitute for wooden spoons. I can't bear the sound of a metal spoon scraping against the bottom of a metal pot when I'm stirring vegetables, and if I leave a metal spoon in the pot for more than a minute or two the handle gets too hot to hold.

BAKING DISHES These are essential for converting leftover soups into casseroles and *panades*. My favorites are the classic oval gratin dishes that the French call *plats à gratin*. They come in earthenware, porcelain, or enameled iron. Pyrex baking dishes will also do in a pinch.

Serving UTENSILS

BOWLS Many cooks labor all day over a soup and then serve it in ugly little bowls so that the natural beauty of the soup is lost. Soup bowls don't have to be expensive, but it's helpful to have several kinds to show off soups at their best.

My everyday soup bowls are relatively small—they hold about a cup—and are plain white porcelain with about a 1-inch rim. I use them mostly for serving pureed soups; a larger bowl—with a larger surface of soup exposed—does little to improve the look of a pureed soup. I also have an assortment of bowls of the same shape and size but with colored rims, which I choose according to the soup's color.

My favorite bowls are also plain white porcelain, but they are almost a foot wide, have wide rims, and hold about 2 cups of soup. I use these to show off soups that have lots of colorful solid ingredients that I like to heap up in the middle and surround with broth. They're wonderful for soups with different kinds of meat or seafood because the diners can see most of what's in the bowl. There is also enough space for me to arrange the soup ingredients as decoratively as possible.

For Japanese soups I like to use the traditional small lacquer (mine are actually plastic) bowls with lids. Be sure to select bowls that are black or a very dark color on the inside. The dark surface makes a perfect background for colored ingredients such as shrimp or tiny slices of scallions, typically Japanese ingredients. The lids keep the soup hot. I sometimes like to serve miso soup in espresso cups on chilly afternoons, the way some people serve tea.

For Chinese, Southeast Asian, and Japanese soups containing noodles, I use deep porcelain bowls with blue Chinese motifs on the outside and a plain white surface on the inside. These lidless bowls are known in Japan as *donburi*.

I serve consommé or bouillon in double espresso cups, where it stays hot; I can even serve it in the living room before we sit down to dinner.

CROCKS AND RAMEKINS For soups that are baked in the oven, don't use bowls that are fragile; bowls with rims inevitably get spattered and stained. For French onion soup or other soups finished in the oven, use 10- or 12-ounce soup crocks (without rims) or soufflé dishes.

SPOONS My all-purpose soup spoon has an elongated bowl and looks like what the British call a dessert spoon. The perfectly round spoons often encountered in restaurants are technically bouillon spoons and should be used only for broths or consommé.

Ingredients

ALMONDS In medieval cooking, almonds were used in soups and stews as an almost universal flavoring and thickener. Many recipes in fact called for milk or almond milk interchangeably. Almonds are still used in Mediterranean soups—the Spanish are very fond of them—and in Indian curries. I love the flavor of almonds with garlic, with mild curries, and in delicate pureed vegetable soups such as spinach or asparagus. The pronounced almond flavor tasted in marzipan and other candies and cookies is derived from bitter almonds, which cannot be imported into the United States because they contain a compound related to cyanide. If you want this distinct flavor in your soup, use a few drops of almond extract.

The best way to use almonds is to make almond milk—toasted almonds pureed with a little liquid and then strained (page 202). Don't cook the almond milk for too long in a soup, or you'll cook off its flavor.

BACON The smoky flavor of good bacon is a useful foil for rich soups. When you're buying bacon for soup-making, look for lean slab bacon, which often has a better flavor than presliced. Another advantage to using slab bacon is that you can slice it into any size and shape you want. Most slab bacon has a thick rind that has to be removed. The easiest way to do this is to place the bacon rind side down on a cutting board and slice along the inner side of the rind with a chef's knife while firmly holding the rind by the end.

If you can't find slab bacon, presliced bacon will also work, but be careful to buy bacon that says "naturally smoked." There are some brands of bacon now that say "smoke flavored" that are ghastly.

Bacon is used in soup-making in several ways. One method is to cut the bacon into thin strips (*lardons*), render them slowly, and then use the bacon fat to sweat vegetables or meats before liquid is added. This is an excellent method if you're cooking root or starchy vegetables such as turnips, beans, or split peas that benefit from a deep smoky flavor. If you want a more subtle smoke flavor, boil the bacon strips for a few minutes and drain them on paper towels before rendering the fat. In either case the strips of bacon can be added to the soup as a garnish just before serving.

Some soups, especially those based on traditional French red wine meat or fish stews, contain cooked strips of bacon (often in conjunction with mushrooms and pearl onions) added to the soup as a garnish and an accent. The bacon is added at the very end so none of the smoky flavor makes it into the broth itself. Ham and pancetta can also be used in this way.

My favorite bacon is lean and double-smoked and comes in a slab with the rind already removed. It keeps for a month or two wrapped in a towel in the refrigerator.

BAMBOO SHOOTS These seem to be one of the few vegetables that are better canned than fresh. Although I have seen fresh bamboo shoots in Chinese markets, I've always found them to be unpleasantly bitter. Apparently bamboo shoots must be eaten almost immediately after they're cut.

Fortunately canned bamboo shoots are readily available, even in supermarkets. Although they sometimes come already sliced, I like to buy whole ones, slice them myself, and add them to Chinese and Japanese soups.

Canned bamboo shoots should be well rinsed before they're added to a soup. Once the can is opened, they will keep in the refrigerator for up to two weeks, provided they're soaked in water that is changed every two days.

BASIL In the winter I rarely eat basil; it comes in expensive little bunches, and I don't have much desire for it. In the summer I develop a ravenous appetite for basil, and it becomes—along with tomatoes—one of my everyday foods.

I know of three kinds of basil available in the United States. The most common is the large-leaf Italian basil, which is especially useful for Italian and southern French soups such as minestrone and pistou. A second variety of Italian basil with small mint-like leaves can be difficult to find in the United States but is more common in Europe. Considering how things go, it will probably start showing up soon.

The third kind of basil is Asian basil, sometimes called "holy" basil, which is best in soups from Southeast Asia. It has a more pungent licorice-mint quality. I love combining it with fresh cilantro and adding it to a Southeast Asian-style soup just before serving.

When using basil to flavor soups, chop it, grind it in a mortar and pestle, or puree it in a blender as shortly before serving as you can. Once you add it to the soup, cook it only for a few seconds—its flavor dissipates very quickly. One tip for chopping or grinding basil is to sprinkle a teaspoon or two of olive oil over the leaves before starting. This protects the leaves from the air and prevents them from turning black.

If you can't find fresh basil, it's better to substitute another fresh herb than to use dried basil. If you have trouble finding basil, buy a lot of it when you find it, take the leaves off the stems, pack them into mason jars, and fill the jars with olive oil (if the jars are tightly packed, a cup or so of oil should do it). You can also puree the leaves with a little olive oil in a blender and freeze the mixture.

BAY LEAVES These are indispensable in a bouquet garni. As a general rule I use one whole bay leaf for 2 quarts of soup and a little bit more if the soup contains lots of meat and red wine. Be sure to use imported bay leaves and not bay leaves from California, which have a very strong eucalyptus aroma that can take over the flavor of the whole soup.

BEANS In the spring and summer you can buy (or grow) fresh beans, which are straightforward to cook in a soup. You just add them anywhere from a minute (for small, baby, twice-peeled fava beans) to 20 minutes (for older and larger cranberry beans) before the soup is finished cooking. The other options are dried beans, which can be found in gourmet stores in a lovely variety, including beans you're unlikely to ever see fresh, and canned beans. Dried beans should be soaked for 2 to 8 hours—until their skins wrinkle—before they are simmered in a soup anywhere from 30 minutes to 3 hours, depending on the variety of bean and the beans' age. I always try to buy beans from the most recent harvest but haven't yet figured out how to judge the age of a bean by looking at it through the bag. Your best bet is to buy beans from a store or mail-order company that does a lot of business so the beans haven't been sitting on the shelves for months. If you're making a long-simmered soup, soaked and drained (some cooks add the soaking liquid to the soup, but I can't tell any difference) dried beans can be cooked directly in the soup. You can also cook the beans separately with a bouquet garni and aromatic vegetables (onion, celery, garlic) and add them to the rest of the soup shortly before serving. Salt should be added to the liquid used for cooking the beans half way into the cooking. If salt is added at the beginning, it can cause the beans to toughen; if it's added at the end, it hasn't enough time to penetrate into the bean and the bean tastes flat. If you're pureeing the beans, you can add the salt at the end. Canned beans should be simply drained and rinsed. I use them only as a last resort, because they're never as flavorful as fresh beans or dried beans cooked with herbs and vegetables.

BONITO This fish, closely related to tuna, is a great delicacy in Spain and in the Basque region of France. But bonito is mentioned here because, when dried, it is the cornerstone of Japanese soup-making.

The basic Japanese broth, *dashi,* is prepared from bonito that has been dried using an elaborate process of salting and airing. To make the best *dashi,* the dried bonito fillets (katsuo-bushi) must be shaved just before they are used on a special gadget called a *katsuo-kezuri-ki.* Because katsuo-bushi can be almost impossible to find (I had to travel to another state to buy mine) and the *katsuo-kuzuri-ki* costs about $60, most cooks in this country and now even in Japan use preshaved bonito flakes (hana-katsuo or kezuri-bushi). They are easy to find and make a far better *dashi* than you're likely to find in all but the best Japanese restaurants. The flakes come in cellophane bags and weigh practically nothing. Look for flakes that are pink rather than brown. There are also packets of instant *dashi,* which contain not only finely ground bonito but the other flavor components of *dashi* as well. These mixtures are called dashi-no-moto or hon-dashi.

BUTTER I have a little trick when ordering soup in cheap restaurants: take a couple of the little pats of butter they put on the table for the bread and stir them into the soup.

Even though butter's reputation has suffered as people become more calorie and cholesterol conscious, a small amount of butter almost always enhances the flavor of a Western-style soup. It can be used in two stages—at the start, for cooking vegetables, meats, or fish before liquid is added, and just before serving by dolloping a slice of butter into the center of each bowl. Butter used in the beginning stages of cooking a soup is easy to skim off while the soup is simmering and contributes very little fat to the finished soup.

Herb butters (pages 593–594) are also excellent last-minute flavorings for vegetable, fish, and meat soups.

CALVADOS Apple brandy from Normandy, made by distilling hard cider (see box on page 477).

CAYENNE PEPPER The dried and powdered form of the cayenne chili, cayenne pepper has little flavor, but I like to add it at the last minute to soups that aren't hot enough. In fact, if you're being cautious it's better to use a small amount of hot chilies or other seasonings in the soup and then add cayenne pepper in ½-teaspoon increments until the soup has the desired hotness.

CHEESE Although cheese is cooked into several soups from the beginning of the preparation, it is used most often as a condiment, passed at the table, to be sprinkled individually into each bowl.

The cheese most often added to soups at the last minute is grated Parmesan. Unfortunately, most cheese sold as Parmesan in the United States bears little relation to the real thing. The best Parmesan comes from Italy in hard wheels and has the words *Parmigiano-Reggiano* etched into its sides. It is expensive, but a little goes a long way: it has a delicate, almost fruity flavor that is quite intense. Never buy already grated Parmesan cheese unless you plan to use it the same day and can watch the merchant grate it in front of you. To store Parmesan, wrap it tightly in several layers of plastic wrap or aluminum foil and keep it refrigerated. It should keep this way for about a month.

Soups that contain bread—*panades*—are usually sprinkled with grated cheese and then baked. The best all-purpose cheese for baking is Swiss Gruyère, which is firm and won't turn stringy; it also has a delicious, nutty flavor. Don't substitute so-called Swiss cheese, which isn't necessarily from Switzerland, or Emmanthaler, which is from Switzerland but doesn't have as full a flavor as Gruyère. Emmanthaler also has a tendency to turn rubbery when cooked. If you can't find authentic Swiss Gruyère, look for a firm, full-flavored cheese such as Cheddar, Gouda (preferably aged), or French Comté or Cantal.

CHERVIL This delicate herb has a subtle anise flavor that adds a delicate freshness to both hot and cold soups. Like parsley, it should be chopped just minutes before being stirred into a soup, or it will lose freshness. Fresh chervil is especially delicious in chicken, seafood, or vegetable soups containing cream.

Don't bother trying to use chervil in a bouquet garni. Its flavor begins to dissipate after 5 minutes of cooking, and it can be expensive. Chervil is so delicate that little sprigs or individual leaves can be used to decorate soups. Gardener friends tell me that chervil is easy to grow.

CHILIES Because chilies—often erroneously called "peppers"—have a tendency to cross-pollinate, there are hundreds of varieties, all with different shapes, colors, and degrees of hotness.

Chilies are often added to soups to give them hotness and flavor. In some parts of the United States dozens of varieties of fresh chilies can be found in the average super-market, while the rest of us may have to settle for one or two. The easiest chili to find in most of the United States is the jalapeño, which is moderately hot, flavorful, and easy to use. The small Thai chilies are also easy to find in Asian markets. The easiest way to use jalapeño or Thai chilies is to slit them lengthwise down the middle, scrape out the seeds, and chop them finely. They can then be cooked in the soup base at the beginning, usu-ally in a little vegetable oil. Some people's skin is very sensitive to chilies—their fingers may sting after the chopping and seeding—so you may want to wear rubber gloves. Whatever you do, don't touch your eyes during or soon after chopping chilies.

Some chilies are used more for flavor than for heat. Again, not everyone has access to a variety of chilies, but when I want to add the flavor of fresh chilies to a South American or Mexican soup I usually use fresh poblano, New Mexico, or Anaheim chilies, which I roast, peel, and chop in the same way as bell peppers (see page 207).

Dried chilies, which develop complex flavors of their own, can also be used to flavor soups. To use dried chilies, wipe their dust off with a damp towel and lightly toast them in a 250°F oven for about 10 minutes or by turning them around in a hot skillet for about 2 minutes. Put them in a bowl, pour over just enough boiling water to cover, and let them soak for about 20 minutes or until the flesh is soft and pliable. Taste the soak-ing water—if it's good, add it to the soup; if not, discard it. Puree the rehydrated chilies in a blender with just enough of the soaking liquid, broth, or water to get them to move around. The chili puree can then be added to a soup for flavoring.

There are as many varieties of dried chilies as fresh chilies, but the most common and best for soups are ancho chilies, chipotle chilies (also available canned), guajillos, dried New Mexicos, and pasillas. It's fun to experiment with different combinations.

CHILI SAUCES AND PASTES   There are many varieties of Asian chili sauces and pastes with different flavorings, such as black beans, ginger, and preserved radishes, but there are two basic styles: fermented, usually called pastes, and popular in China and Korea; and unfermented, usually called sauces, popular in Southeast Asia. Chinese chili paste is often used in cooking, while Vietnamese versions are usually served as condiments for dishes such as *pho. Siracha* is a bottled sweet chili sauce that often shows up in Vietnamese and Thai restaurants, again for use as a condiment. The quality of bottled chili pastes and sauces varies considerably, so you may need to experiment with different brands. Fresh chili pastes and sauces are bright red, while fermented versions have a duller brownish hue.

CHINESE BLACK MUSHROOMS   These intensely flavored dried mushrooms—actually shiitakes—are delicious in Chinese and Southeast Asian soups. Asian markets usually carry two kinds. The less expensive have smooth caps, while the better and more expensive are covered with whitish fissures. The kind with the fissures are liable to run almost $40 a pound, but only a few ounces are needed to flavor a pot of soup. I usually buy the kind with the fissures but smaller caps, which taste the same and are less expen-sive (but by no means cheap).

The quickest way to reconstitute dried black mushrooms is to pour over just enough boiling water to cover and soak for 30 minutes, but if I have the time I soak them in warm water for about 5 hours. Be sure to save the strained soaking water to add to the soup.

CHINESE PRESERVED VEGETABLES These Chinese salt-cured vegetables are sometimes called *Szechuan preserved vegetable, preserved turnips,* or *preserved radish.* The easiest way to find them is in 12-ounce cans labeled "Szechuan Preserved Vegetable," but if you live near a Chinese market you should be able to find them in tubs.

I have to admit that preserved vegetables can be scary looking and not terribly appetizing, but they do wonders when chopped and simmered in a soup. Several kinds of vegetables are used, but the most common is a knobby-looking root—usually called *mustard*—covered with a reddish paste. A second type with an entirely different flavor has wilted leaves covered with specks of salt that in Chinatown they again call *mustard* or *radish.*

Although I've included soup recipes calling for a particular kind of preserved vegetable, the best—and most interesting—approach is to go to an Asian market and see what you can find. Whatever variety you turn up, be sure to rinse it thoroughly under cold running water to eliminate excess salt before chopping it up for the soup pot.

CHINESE SPINACH (*AMARANTHUS GANGETICUS*) This herb really tastes nothing at all like spinach; to me it has a wilder taste, but it probably got its name because it's cooked in the same way as ordinary spinach. Chinese spinach has small leaves—about an inch across—and delicate little stems. Once the thicker stems near the base of the little bunches have been removed, Chinese spinach can be cooked like "Western" spinach—blanched for 30 seconds in boiling water, rinsed with cold water, and gently reheated in a little butter or cream. A more Asian approach would be to sprinkle the blanched and chilled leaves with a few drops of sesame oil. I sometimes add the leaves to Japanese or Korean soups.

CHIVES Appreciated for their delicate onionlike flavor, chives also make an elegant garnish for individual bowls of soup. Be sure to chop them very finely and uniformly within an hour of serving the soup; otherwise they will wilt and dry out. One of my favorite touches for vegetable soup is to float a tiny dollop of unsweetened whipped cream in the center of each bowl and then add a tiny pinch of finely chopped chives on top of the cream.

CHRYSANTHEMUM LEAVES (*SHUN GIKU*) The leaves from this flowering plant are popular with Japanese cooks as a last-minute addition to soups and light stews (see *shabu-shabu,* page 445). Two or three chrysanthemum leaves give a subtle and exotic flavor to soups when allowed to steep in the broth for a minute or two before serving. Don't be tempted to buy chrysanthemum leaves at a plant store—they may have been sprayed, and chrysanthemum leaves bred for eating are softer and fuller than their decorative cousins. Chrysanthemum leaves are usually sold in large bunches in Japanese and Chinese markets. The leaves will keep for a week to 10 days in the refrigerator in a glass of water.

CILANTRO (CORIANDER LEAVES, CHINESE PARSLEY) I can hardly imagine living, much less cooking, without this pungent leafy herb. Not everyone likes it; the first time I tasted it in a Chinese restaurant in San Francisco, I thought that soap had accidentally slipped into the noodles. But it does grow on you, and most people I know who've given themselves a chance to like it have become dedicated aficionados.

I especially like cilantro with hot spicy soups containing chilies and curries. It should be chopped at the last minute—so its aroma doesn't dissipate—and thrown into the soup pot just a minute or two before serving. It's hard to go wrong adding chopped cilantro to almost any soup from Southeast Asia, Mexico, or India.

The average bunch of cilantro may look like a lot, but be aware that once you remove the stems, a whole bunch might give you just ¼ cup fully chopped leaves.

COCONUT MILK Coconut milk is extracted from an infusion of grated coconut; it is not the liquid contained in a fresh coconut. It is an almost indispensable product for making tropical and Southeast Asian soups. You can make it yourself with fresh whole coconut, but that is expensive and time-consuming and little better than a good canned version.

Several brands are available, but I find the best by far come from Thailand. I can't even read the brand name on the kind I buy; I just recognize Thai lettering. There are also some acceptable Spanish brands. The main thing to avoid is coconut milk containing sugar or stabilizers such as the kind often used to make piña coladas.

Coconut cream is the rich, congealed coconut fat that settles on the top of both homemade and good canned coconut milk. For soups, the cream is added along with the milk.

You can make about 2 cups coconut milk from one fresh coconut. When you're buying coconuts, shake them to make sure you hear the liquid sloshing around inside. If there's no liquid, the coconut may have been punctured and turned rancid.

When you get the coconut home, use a hammer and a screwdriver to punch holes in two of the coconut "eyes"—the dark oval spots—near the top. Drain out the liquid—I usually just drink it as a little reward for going through all this work—and bake the coconut in a 375°F oven for 20 minutes to get the pulp to separate from the shell. Wrap the coconut in a towel and hit it with a hammer to crack it open. Pull out the pulp. Peel the thin dark peel off the sections of pulp with a vegetable peeler. Grind the pulp in a food processor for about 1 minute or grate it with a hand grater.

Put the grated pulp in a mixing bowl and pour 1 cup boiling water over it. Let the mixture sit for 10 minutes and then strain the mixture through a medium-mesh strainer over another bowl, reserving the liquid. Wrap the drained pulp in a kitchen towel and wring out any remaining liquid over the bowl. Put the wrung-out pulp in the original mixing bowl and pour another cup of boiling water over it. Repeat the straining process.

Fresh coconut milk and opened canned coconut milk can be kept in the refrigerator for 1 week or frozen indefinitely.

COGNAC, ARMAGNAC, BRANDY The term *brandy* refers to any distilled wine, while cognac and Armagnac are brandies made in relatively small French regions. Cognac and Armagnac are made according to strict laws controlling the grape types and distillation methods. Even if you buy the least expensive cognac or Armagnac, you're guaranteed a reasonably tasty product.

Most people mistakenly buy the cheapest brandy for cooking, but it rarely contributes anything worthwhile. I recommend the least expensive cognac or Armagnac (the word will appear on the bottle) rather than a nondescript generic brandy. Don't be deceived by the designation *Napoleon* on a label—it is meaningless, telling you nothing of the brandy's quality.

Recipes for crustacean soups often call for brandy to be added near the beginning and often suggest igniting the brandy to flame the shellfish. Because brandy can be expensive, my own suggestion is to add a smaller amount to the soup a couple of minutes before serving—just long enough to cook off the alcohol but not the flavor.

CORNICHONS These miniature French sour pickles are sometimes served at the table as a condiment to go with rich soups such as *pot-au-feu*. Cornichons, sometimes called *French sour gherkins*, have a delightful crunch and tang that help offset the richness of meaty dishes. They are available at specialty food stores and some supermarkets.

CREAM It's hard to imagine a more universally useful ingredient than heavy cream. Unlike milk, half-and-half, sour cream, and yogurt, when used properly heavy cream doesn't separate or curdle when heated. Its flavor is subtle enough to enhance ingredients without distorting or changing the basic flavor of the soup.

Cream's only disadvantage is that it is rich in fat and calories. Heavy cream, also called whipping cream, contains at least 37 percent butterfat, which comes to about 5 grams, or 45 calories, of fat per tablespoon. Fortunately a small amount of cream goes a long way in a soup—I tablespoon per serving is usually plenty.

Light cream is sometimes available, but it still makes more sense to buy heavy cream and use less. The effect will be the same, and heavy cream is more stable and less likely to curdle.

Once heavy cream has been added to a soup, leave the pot uncovered for any further cooking. Cream cooked in a covered pot sometimes separates. When you add cream to a soup, make sure the soup comes to a full simmer to sterilize the cream and prevent it from causing the soup to sour if stored overnight.

See also crème fraîche, yogurt, milk, and sour cream.

CRÈME FRAÎCHE French-style cream, crème fraîche has the thick texture and tanginess of sour cream and the richness and stability of heavy cream. The essential difference between American heavy cream and crème fraîche is that crème fraîche has been inoculated with a bacterial culture in the same way as yogurt or sour cream. As the bacteria act on the cream, they secrete lactic acid, which gives crème fraîche its characteristic tang and texture.

Because of its thick consistency, many cooks assume that crème fraîche is especially rich, but in fact it has the same fat content has heavy cream. In most cases heavy cream works as well in soups as crème fraîche, but crème fraîche has an advantage—it's thick enough to stay on top of the soup in decorative dollops.

For some reason—probably because it has a French name—crème fraîche is about three times the price of heavy cream. Fortunately crème fraîche is easy to make; just combine I cup heavy cream and I tablespoon buttermilk or sour cream in a mixing bowl covered with plastic wrap. (You can make as much as you want; just stretch these quantities proportionately.) Leave the cream at room temperature for 24 hours. The cream will stiffen because of the active culture in the buttermilk or the sour cream. Once the crème fraîche has stiffened, you can keep it tightly covered in the refrigerator for weeks.

CUMIN This well-known spice is actually the seed of a fruit tree. Cumin is one of the ingredients in Indian curries, in Mexican and South American fish soups, and in Moroccan *charmoula*—an herb and spice mixture used to finish *tagines* and soups. Unless I'm grinding whole spices for a batch of curry powder, I usually use ground cumin, stored in the freezer.

CURRY (INDIAN-STYLE POWDERS AND PASTES) Indian cooks rarely use commercially blended curry powder but rely instead on their own mixtures of freshly ground and roasted spices. Most of these mixtures, including the curry powder we buy in the United States, contain from five to twenty spices ground together. Although store-bought curry powder is easy to use and a delicious flavoring for soups and other dishes, the best curries are always made with freshly ground spices with the quantities of each spice varying according to the dish. The best premade curries are actually pastes rather than powders.

One of the most commonly used spice mixtures in India is *garam masala*, a mixture of six spices. Premade *garam masala* is available in specialty food stores or at Indian grocers and is a good substitute for supermarket curry powder. Daw Sen's brand is particularly good. I also use Subahdar brand "Vindaloo" curry powder, which is quite hot. Sometimes I combine Vindaloo powder with *garam masala* or commercial curry powder to give it a little extra punch.

If you want to make your own *garam masala*, you'll need a miniature food processor, coffee grinder, or blender.

Garam Masala

1 cinnamon stick, about 4 inches long

2 teaspoons cardamom seeds without pods

1 teaspoon whole cloves

1 tablespoon black peppercorns

2 tablespoons cumin seeds

2 tablespoons coriander seeds

WRAP the cinnamon stick in a towel and then smash it with a rolling pin to break it into pieces. Empty the pieces onto a cutting board and chop them into pieces no larger than ¼ inch on each side.

SPREAD the cinnamon and all the other spices in a heavy iron skillet or frying pan. Place the pan over medium heat and stir the spices until they smell aromatic and begin to brown very slightly, after about 3 minutes. Pour them immediately into a bowl to cool.

POUR the spices into a coffee grinder, blender, or miniature food processor. Grind for about 2 minutes, until you've obtained a fine powder. Store the mixture in a tightly sealed jar in the refrigerator or freezer.

Note: If you want a hot curry, add 1 teaspoon cayenne pepper to the finished *garam masala.*

Many more spices are used in Indian curries than those included in the *garam masala* recipe. I especially like to add fenugreek seeds (1 tablespoon to the recipe), which give the curry a gentle, maplelike flavor. A teaspoon of ground turmeric added to the recipe mixture won't do much for the flavor, but it will color any dish in which the *garam masala* is used an appealing yellow. Ground ginger, nutmeg (use only about ¼ teaspoon), mustard seeds, saffron threads, and fennel seeds can all be combined to produce different flavor combinations.

Curries are also prepared in Southeast Asia—especially Thailand—but different spices are used, and instead of being prepared in powder form, Thai curries are usually pastes. See curry (Thai-style pastes).

CURRY LEAVES Although curry powders and pastes are made from a combination of spices, there is an actual curry leaf used in Indian soups and stews. The leaves have a subtle spicy flavor and are best simmered in Indian soups, especially those containing beans, lentils, or split peas. When I occasionally find fresh curry leaves at Indian grocers, I buy a handful or two and store them in my freezer, where they keep for several months. Curry leaves are also available dried.

CURRY (THAI-STYLE PASTES) Thai cooks prefer freshly made pastes containing more fresh herbs and different spices than their Indian counterparts. There are several kinds of curry pastes; red, green, and Mussaman (Muslim style) are just a few used in Thai cooking. In Thailand these pastes are used in many different ways, but I've found they work as wonderful last-minute flavorings for Thai and other Southeast Asian soups.

Thai curry pastes are available in jars, but like so many products their quality rarely compares to those you make yourself.

To make Thai curry pastes you'll need a large mortar and pestle or a food processor, preferably a miniature one. If you decide to stick to tradition and use only a mortar and pestle, be prepared to spend at least an hour grinding.

Green Curry Paste

MAKES 1¼ CUPS

2 teaspoons ground coriander

1 teaspoon ground cumin

3 teaspoons freshly ground black pepper

½ teaspoon ground cloves

1 teaspoon freshly grated nutmeg

¼ cup tightly packed cilantro leaves

a ½-inch slice of ginger, peeled and grated

2 kaffir lime leaves, finely chopped, or a 1-inch strip of lime zest, finely chopped

1 teaspoon shrimp paste (optional)

1 teaspoon salt

4 garlic cloves, peeled

1 lemongrass stalk, bottom half only, finely sliced, then chopped

2 shallots, peeled and chopped

12 green jalapeño chilies or 8 Thai chilies, seeded and chopped

¼ cup peanut oil

COMBINE the spices and the rest of the ingredients in a food processor or mortar and pestle and work the mixture to a paste (for about 5 minutes in a food processor, an hour in a mortar and pestle). Store the green curry in a jar in the refrigerator. It will keep for at least a month.

Red Curry Paste

Surprisingly, red curry paste is milder than green curry paste. This isn't saying much, because green curry paste made in the traditional style (leaving the seeds in the chilies, which makes them even hotter) is about the hottest thing I've ever tasted. To make red curry paste, use the same ingredients as for green curry paste but substitute 7 dried hot red chilies such as serrano or 1 tablespoon cayenne pepper for the green or Thai chilies.

Mussaman Curry Paste

This Muslim curry has an altogether different flavor from a typical Thai curry—it contains spices more commonly found in Indian and Indonesian cooking than in Thai cooking. It is easiest to make this curry using already ground spices, but grinding them yourself in a coffee grinder or miniature food processor will give you a more aromatic paste. Traditional versions of this recipe contain shrimp paste, but I usually leave it out because it smells up the kitchen.

Whereas green and red curry are best when whisked into the hot soup shortly before serving, I like to marinate strips of chicken breasts in Mussaman curry and then sauté them in hot oil for a minute or two before adding liquids such as water or chicken or fish broth.

Because some of the ingredients in this paste are very hard, many are chopped by hand before being ground together into a paste.

MAKES ½ CUP

½ teaspoon ground cloves

4 teaspoons ground coriander seeds

2 teaspoons ground cinnamon

1 teaspoon freshly ground white pepper

1 teaspoon ground cumin

½ star anise, crushed and ground

½ teaspoon ground cardamom

2 teaspoons cayenne pepper or 7 dried hot red chilies such
    as serrano, seeded

2 tablespoons peanut oil

4 shallots, chopped (by hand)

4 garlic cloves, chopped

3 kaffir lime leaves, chopped

a 3-inch length of lemongrass, chopped

a ½-inch slice of galangal, peeled and chopped

2 teaspoons shrimp paste (optional)

COMBINE the spices and the rest of the ingredients in a food processor or mortar and pestle and work the mixture to a paste (for about 5 minutes in a food processor, an hour in a mortar and pestle). Store the Mussaman curry in a jar in the refrigerator. It will keep for at least a month.

DAIKON (ASIAN RADISH, JAPANESE RADISH) A constant presence in Asian and especially Japanese markets, daikon is a radish that looks nothing like its little red Western cousins. It's usually about a foot and a half long and two to three inches in diameter with a white or pale brown peel.

The Japanese use daikon almost the way Westerners use onions—in practically everything. Daikon doesn't have much taste but it does have a delightful and refreshing crunch. It is often used in soups, thinly sliced or cut into very fine julienne on a benriner cutter.

EGGS Whole eggs are sometimes added to soups and broths just before serving. There are three approaches to adding eggs to soup. The first is to beat the hot soup into the beaten eggs and then to gently reheat the mixture on the stove so the eggs give the soup a light creaminess and texture. The second approach, used to make egg drop soup, is to pour beaten egg in a steady stream into the simmering soup so that the egg sets in decorative strands. And third, whole eggs can be floated on top of individual bowls of soup, baked in the oven just long enough to set the eggs.

Egg yolks are sometimes used as thickeners and to enrich classic French soups. To use egg yolks as a thickener, pour the hot soup into the beaten yolks, return everything to the pot, and cook gently over low to medium heat, being careful not to let the soup boil, which will curdle the yolks (see *potage germiny*, page 212).

Egg whites are combined with vegetables and chopped meat or fish to clarify consommés (see page 72).

FENUGREEK SEEDS These small brown seeds are one of the most common spices in Indian curries and spice mixtures. Once ground, fenugreek seeds have a mild, maplelike flavor that helps soften the flavors of the other spices.

FERMENTED BLACK BEANS Familiar to lovers of Chinese food as the flavoring in black bean sauce, these black beans can also be used in surprisingly small amounts to give a full flavor to Chinese-style soups. Their flavor goes especially well with ginger, sherry, and garlic.

To use black beans, rinse them off—they're salty—and work them with a little liquid in a blender. Add the mixture a bit at a time to Chinese fish and meat soups. Usually 3 or 4 tablespoons of fermented black beans is enough to flavor 2 quarts of soup.

Look for brands that have been flavored with ginger but not with Chinese five spices. I use Yang Jiang brand, which comes in a cardboard container. Fermented black beans are usually moist but not wet. They keep for at least six months in the refrigerator.

FISH SAUCE Fish sauce is made by salting anchovies and sometimes squid or shrimp in barrels and capturing the liquid that runs out over several months. Known as *nam pla* in Thailand, *nuoc mam* in Vietnam, *nam pa* in Laos, *tuk trey* in Cambodia, *patis* in the Philippines, and *nam pya ye* in Burma, fish sauce is *the* universal condiment in Southeast Asian cooking.

At first the strong-smelling fish sauce can be off-putting to the Western palate and sensibility, but it's easy to acquire the taste, especially if you like Southeast Asian cooking.

Vietnamese fish sauce is stronger than Thai versions, though the Vietnamese-style sauces are actually made in Thailand. Tiparos brand, Flying Lion brand "Phu Quoc," and Ruang Tong brand are particularly good and available in most parts of the country. Fish sauce keeps for up to one year in the refrigerator.

When you're making Southeast Asian soups, the easiest way to know if you've added the right amount of fish sauce is to think of it as salt. When the soup is salty enough, you've added the right amount.

GALANGAL Galangal is a root (or, technically, an underground stem or rhizome) that looks somewhat like ginger. It has a slightly medicinal yet agreeable pinelike flavor that makes it particularly good in spicy Thai soups containing lemongrass.

Galangal was used along with ginger in European cooking until sometime during the 16th century, when its use died out. It is a staple in Southeast Asian cooking.

If you live near an Asian market, you should be able to find frozen whole galangal or fresh galangal, which you can store indefinitely in your freezer at home. Galangal is also sold in a less pungent powder form under the Indonesian name *laos*.

The easiest way to use fresh or frozen galangal is to peel the skin off a ½-inch section, slice it as thinly as possible, and then simmer it for at least 15 minutes in the soup. Even when simmered, it stays too hard to actually eat—but its flavor works into the soup.

GHEE *Ghee* is Indian-style clarified butter used for cooking curry mixtures that in turn are added to soups for flavoring and enriching. (See recipe, page 592.) French cooks also use *ghee* or *beurre noisette* in certain pastries and sauces.

GINGER To use fresh ginger, peel the skin off as much as you need with a sharp paring knife. Then grate the peeled section as finely as you can with a hand grater. The grated ginger can then be added to the soup with other flavorings, vegetables, meats, or fish. Slices of fresh ginger can also be simmered in broth and strained out so that a subtle ginger flavor remains in the background.

If you use ginger only once in a while but want to keep it on hand, it will keep for months in the freezer (its texture will suffer, but for making soup this is usually not important). Just be sure to wrap it tightly in plastic wrap and then again in aluminum foil.

HAM Gently sautéing little cubes or strips of ham with aromatic vegetables such as onions, carrots, garlic, and turnips before any liquid is added is one of my favorite tricks for preparing a flavorful base for a soup. Unless you or your guests are completely vegetarian, this is a perfect method for giving a delicate savor to a vegetable soup. Ham, cut into fine shreds, is also a traditional flavoring for many Chinese soups.

It's important to buy the best ham you can find or afford. If your soup contains delicate flavors or young vegetables, use a raw cured ham (prosciutto), preferably one that hasn't been smoked. If the soup is more robust or contains split peas, cabbage, or root vegetables, you may want to use smoked ham or smoked ham hocks. Tasso is a very spicy smoked ham from Louisiana used for gumbos. Westphalian ham and Black Forest ham are also smoked; Parma ham, Smithfield ham, and Serrano-style hams are not. Parma ham (prosciutto) is my favorite, but it's expensive, and I use it only if I can convince the shop to sell me the end piece for half price. If you can find a prosciutto end, I recommend buying a whole chunk (a pound or so) and keeping it wrapped in a cloth towel in the refrigerator. It will keep for months. If you're stuck buying something more expensive, ¼-inch slices are usually the most useful, because once you get them home you can slice them again into thin strips.

If you find prosciutto ends on the bone, trim off any rind, use the meat as you need it, and when you get down to the naked bone, simmer it in slow-cooking broths. Ham hocks are ham ends that usually have been smoked. They are wonderful simmered in assertively flavored soups such as gumbos. (See also bacon and pancetta.)

HOISIN SAUCE This sweet bottled sauce is based on soybeans, but unlike miso (another soybean derivative), it tends to be sweet (often cloyingly so) and is usually flavored with five-spice mixture. It's often served as a condiment with Chinese foods, but I prefer to use it as a glaze—often thinned with water—for grilled foods such as chicken and ribs. It is sometimes served as a condiment with *pho*.

HOMINY (POZOLE) These are the dried kernels of field corn that Mexican and Southwestern cooks like to include in long-cooking soups and stews. Traditionally hominy is cooked for a short time with slaked lime, well rinsed, and the tiny germ at the end of each kernel removed. The partially precooked kernels are then cooked along with the other ingredients in the soup or stew. When the hominy is finished cooking, it opens up into an attractive "flower" and contributes a delicious corn flavor to the soup.

Precooked, canned hominy is also available, but it doesn't flower, and it contributes little if any flavor to the soup.

KAFFIR LIME Kaffir lime rind and leaves are used in Thai and other Southeast Asian cooking. Kaffir lime (*Citrus hystrix*) is closely related to our common lime (*Citrus aurantifolia*), but the flavor of kaffir lime is slightly subtler and more lemony. Kaffir lime leaves can be added whole to soups or can be finely chopped or ground as an ingredient in Thai curry pastes. The zest of the kaffir lime can also be grated and used as a flavoring.

To find kaffir lime leaves and fruit, you'll need to shop at a Thai or Asian market. The leaves and fruit will keep frozen for several months, and the fruit can be kept in the refrigerator for a couple of weeks. Regular lime leaves and grated zest can be substituted.

KIMCHEE Pickled cabbage, *kimchee*, is as universal a condiment on Korean tables as ketchup or mustard in the West. It is eaten as an accompaniment to almost all Korean foods and is also sometimes used directly in cooking. *Kimchee* comes in many different styles, but most varieties fall into one of two categories, winter and summer. Winter *kimchee* has a stronger flavor, while the summer version is comparatively light and refreshing.

Kimchee is usually found in jars in the refrigerator section of a Korean grocery, or you can make it yourself. Both homemade and commercial *kimchee* will last for several weeks in the refrigerator.

Kimchee

MAKES 1½ TO 2 QUARTS

1 3- to 4-pound Chinese (Napa) cabbage
3 tablespoons coarse salt
2 tablespoons hot red pepper flakes
3 teaspoons sugar
5 garlic cloves, finely chopped
3 tablespoons finely grated fresh ginger

REMOVE and discard the outer leaves of the cabbage and quarter the cabbage lengthwise. Remove the core. Slice the quarters crosswise into 2-inch-wise strips. Put the cabbage strips in a stainless-steel bowl and sprinkle with the salt. Rub the salt into the cabbage strips, cover the bowl with plastic wrap, and let sit overnight.

THE next day, drain the cabbage in a colander, but don't rinse it. Toss the cabbage with the rest of the ingredients and pack into mason jars. Stored in the refrigerator, it will be ready to eat in 5 to 7 days.

KOCHUJANG This Korean red chili paste, made from red chilies, Korean soybean paste (*twoenjang*), and rice flour, is used as a spicy flavoring in Korean soups and stews. Although it's almost essential in some recipes to contribute a characteristically Korean flavor, a homemade version can be made using Chinese chili paste.

KONNYAKU (DEVIL'S TONGUE JELLY) These Japanese-style gelatinous cakes are made from the starch of a particular kind of yam. *Konnyaku* doesn't have much taste but if simmered long enough will absorb flavor from the surrounding broth. I like to tear it into 1-inch sections and add it to long-simmered Japanese soups, especially those containing vegetables.

Konnyaku is sometimes made into noodles, called *shirataki*, which is one of the traditional ingredients in a *sukiyaki*.

Konnyaku can be found in Japanese groceries in both "refined" (white) and "unrefined" (gray) forms. *Konnyaku* will keep in the refrigerator for 2 weeks if kept covered in water that is changed daily.

LEMONGRASS Lemongrass comes in stalks about 18 inches long that look a bit like elongated miniature ears of corn. To use lemongrass the fibrous outer sheath is pulled away—again like corn—and only the bottom half is used. Because lemongrass is hard and fibrous, it must be sliced very thinly or chopped and worked to paste in a food processor or with a mortar and pestle.

Lemongrass has a soft lemon flavor with none of the sourness of lemon juice. If you can't find lemongrass, cut a strip of lemon zest into julienne and boil it for a minute in water (to eliminate its bitterness) as a replacement for one stalk of lemongrass.

Lemongrass is most often used in soups from Southeast Asia. It can be kept tightly wrapped in the freezer for several months.

LIMES Many soups need a certain amount of sourness to bring out their flavor, especially soups from Mexico and Thailand that contain cilantro and hot spices. In Thailand tamarind is used to give a subtle tartness to soups, but I usually substitute lime juice, which is fresher and easier to find. I also add lime juice to gazpacho and spicy cold soups.

MACADAMIA NUTS Pureed into nut butter and then used as a light thickener and flavoring in soups, macadamia nuts are used as a substitute for kemiri nuts (also called *candlenuts*), which are a staple in Indonesian soups and stews.

MARJORAM Even though they taste nothing alike, people often confuse marjoram with oregano, probably because the two herbs are sometimes used together in Italian cooking. Marjoram has a forthright flavor and an alluring subtlety that make it irresistible in soups, especially those with Italian or southern French ingredients such as tomatoes, fish, saffron, fennel, beans, garlic, and olives.

Fresh marjoram can be used in a bouquet garni with or instead of thyme—about 5 sprigs for 2 quarts of soup—or better yet, a teaspoon or two of the leaves can be chopped and stirred into the soup a few minutes before serving.

If you can't find fresh marjoram, you can use dried as long as it isn't stale. Smell it to make sure it has some aroma left, then chop it to release more of its fragrance.

MILK Sometimes called for in chowders or traditional French cream soups, milk must be cooked with some kind of starch such as flour or potatoes to stabilize the proteins in the milk and prevent it from curdling. Don't try to substitute milk in recipes that call for cream. If you're concerned about the richness of cream, it's better just to use less or to dilute it with water.

MINT Several varieties of mint appear in food stores at different times of the year, so out of necessity I'm not terribly fussy about which to use when. Although mint is well known (unlike some neglected herbs), most cooks rarely think to use it. Coarsely chopped or torn into little pieces, it's wonderful as a finish in Vietnamese soups (along with basil and cilantro). Italian cooks—especially those from Rome—are especially fond of chopping it and adding it to vegetable soups just a minute or two before serving. (Its flavor dissipates after a few minutes.) Northern Italian cooks also make a wonderful mint sauce to serve with *bollito misto* (page 438).

One of my favorite ways to use mint is to convert it into a mint butter (page 593) and then dollop it into bowls of vegetable soups, especially those made from cucumbers, peas, and green beans.

MIRIN A very sweet, sakelike cooking wine, mirin is often used as a marinade for Japanese grilled fish. I also like to use it, along with soy sauce, to flavor a basic Japanese *dashi*. Mirin can be found in small bottles in Japanese specialty stores. It's inexpensive and keeps indefinitely in the refrigerator.

MUSTARD SEEDS Other than as a component of curry, ground mustard is rarely used to make soups. However, mustard seeds, particularly the black Indian variety that resembles poppy seeds, are used as a decorative flavoring in Indian soups and stews.

Whole black mustard seeds should be cooked for a minute or two in *ghee* or vegetable oil before being added to a soup shortly before serving.

OLIVE OIL I like to have two kinds of olive oil: so-called pure olive oil and extra virgin olive oil. "Pure" olive oil is inexpensive because it comes from the second pressing of the olives and has relatively little flavor. Extra virgin olive oil is relatively expensive, usually cold pressed (check the label), and has a lively, fruity flavor. I use the "pure" oil for sautéing and preliminary cooking of vegetables (the heat dissipates the delicate flavor of extra virgin oil), and I reserve the extra virgin oil for dribbling on toasted bread, for making *aïoli*, and as an all-purpose condiment passed at the table for dribbling into bowls of Mediterranean fish and vegetable soups.

ONIONS While onions come in various sizes and colors, almost any onion will work in a recipe that calls for them. So-called yellow onions are the least expensive and are easy to find in decent shape, with no soft or dark patches. White onions, popular in Mexican cooking, have a gentler flavor (making them good to serve raw as a condiment or last-minute addition) but are more perishable and slightly more expensive than yellow onions. Because red onions, sometimes called Bermuda onions, have a deeper flavor and delicate sweetness and are less harsh than yellow onions, I use them in most recipes calling for onions. So-called sweet onions, named after where they are grown—Vidalia, Walla Walla, and Maui onions are a few examples—are best used, chopped or thinly sliced, as condiments, because they're too expensive to use in a soup and their delicate flavor is lost. Scallions, sometimes called green onions, make a lovely garniture for many Asian soups when thinly sliced. Authentic green onions—round (or at least bulbous)—with part or all of the greens left attached are best used in hearty meat soups in which the onions are left whole. So-called boiling onions, which are about the size of walnuts, can be used in the same way. Pearl onions, usually about the size of marbles, are sold in pint boxes and make a beautiful garniture in a hearty soup, but they're time-consuming to peel.

ORANGE ZEST In the south of France, dried orange zest is sometimes included in a bouquet garni. Whereas Provençal cooks always seem to have a jar of dried orange zest on hand, I usually make do with a 2-inch strip of fresh zest, blanched for a minute in boiling water, for 2 quarts of soup. The subtle flavor of the orange zest is especially good with tomatoes, fennel, and saffron.

OREGANO This is one of the few herbs I prefer dried to fresh; drying seems to intensify its flavor. Oregano is used widely in Italian and Mexican cooking, but when I buy dried oregano—usually at the supermarket—I opt for so-called Mexican oregano, which seems to have a brighter, more convincing flavor.

It's not worth paying high prices for fresh oregano, but because oregano dries so well it's worthwhile to plant it in the garden and dry it in bundles at the end of the summer. The bundles can then be kept in jars and used year-round.

PANCETTA In France and Italy, smoked bacon—the kind we use in the United States—is less common than unsmoked bacon. In the United States it's almost impossible to find unsmoked bacon (pork breast). The only version readily available is salt pork, which has very little lean and not much flavor. The Italians use pancetta—lightly salted pork breast rolled into a large sausage shape. When it cooks, it has a lovely rich pork flavor that contributes to the soup without taking over. Pancetta makes a wonderful substitute in recipes calling for bacon and ham.

To use pancetta, unroll it and slice it into thin strips or dice. It will keep in the refrigerator for 3 or 4 weeks, wrapped in a cloth towel or napkin.

PARSLEY It's hard to imagine a more useful herb for soup-making than parsley. Finely chopped parsley can be added to almost any soup at the last minute to give it freshness and color.

Fortunately, unlike so many fresh herbs, parsley can be found fresh in almost any supermarket. Two types are available—the curly parsley we all grew up with and Italian parsley, which has flat, wide leaves and a slightly more pungent flavor. Both types can be used, but if I have a choice I buy the Italian variety. When you're checking to see whether you have enough parsley in the refrigerator to prepare a certain recipe, keep in mind that parsley chops down considerably. An average bunch will give you about ¼ cup finely chopped leaves; a small bunch, about the size of a fist, gives about 2 tablespoons.

There is only one important trick to remember when using parsley—chop it as close to the last minute as you can. Chopped parsley that has been sitting around for more than an hour loses flavor and ends up smelling like grass clippings. Dried parsley is useless.

Chopped parsley should be added to soups just seconds before serving so that its bright fresh flavor doesn't have time to cook off.

PEANUTS Ground into peanut butter, shelled roasted peanuts are used to thicken and flavor in South American soups such as *vatapa* (page 325) and in some African-style soups. They are delicious when combined with coconut milk, tomatoes, cilantro, and curries. Smooth peanut butter, the kind with no additives, can be used in recipes calling for whole peanuts. Substitute ⅓ cup peanut butter for ½ cup of shelled peanuts.

PEPPER I rarely use pepper in soups because I find that it loses its flavor and takes on an unpleasant harshness after it has cooked for more than 5 or 10 minutes. I much prefer to have a pepper mill on the table and let my guests help themselves. (Sometimes I make a point of seasoning my own bowl of soup at the table so my guests won't hesitate and think they're hurting my feelings.)

As to the often asked question about which to use, white or black pepper, my own preference is for black except that it sometimes spoils the look of a perfectly white soup.

PERNOD, PASTIS, RICARD Each of these is a brand name for an alcoholic, liqueurlike drink made from fennel. They are all popular as aperitifs in the south of France, and because of their heady aroma and flavor of fennel they are often used to flavor Mediterranean fish soups. You don't need much—a tablespoon in a pot of soup added a few minutes before the end of cooking is usually enough to give an extra dimension to a soup already containing tomatoes, olive oil, and maybe saffron. Pernod or one of the others is good to have around in a pinch as a substitute for fresh fennel.

RICE When making soup, I use rice in one of four ways: I add leftover cooked rice to a pot of reheated soup to turn last night's first course into something more substantial; I add raw rice directly to a soup early enough for the rice to cook; I sometimes use rice as a thickener for pureed soups and bisques in the same way as potato, pureed beans, or flour, and I sometimes cook rice in a small amount of fat or flavorful vegetable mixture before adding liquid, such as when making risotto- or paellalike soups.

When adding rice to a soup to give it a substance, I use long-grain rice. The best long-grain rice is genuine basmati rice from India or American-grown basmati rice, called *texmati*. Basmati rice has a wonderful nutty flavor and aroma, and the grains won't fall apart and turn sticky, even if you overcook it. Unless I'm cooking the rice directly in the soup, I cook rice the same way as pasta—in a large pot of water—and then drain it in a colander. Instead of first bringing the water to a boil and throwing in the rice, I soak the rice for 30 minutes in cold water and then bring it to a boil in its soaking water. In this way the grains are fluffy and separated with no gumminess. After simmering the rice for about 10 minutes, I reach in with a spoon and start testing the grains for doneness. When it's done, I drain the rice in a colander and add it to the soup. If the soup needs to be thinned, some of the rice-cooking water can also be added. If you're making a paella- or arrocelike soup, medium-grain Spanish rice works best, because it keeps its texture and yet absorbs the flavors of the surrounding liquids. (See page 282 for more information about Spanish rice, and Sources page for where to buy it.)

If you're using rice to thicken pureed soups, you may want to use regular American long-grain rice or Italian Arborio short-grain rice, which releases its starch as soon as it's completely cooked. Add the raw rice to the soup about 30 minutes before it's going to be pureed. I also use risotto rice for making the risotto like recipes on pages 286 and 287. (See also Wild Rice.)

ROSEMARY   Perhaps it's because of its distinctive flavor and because it is easy to identify that rosemary is more popular in the United States than thyme or marjoram, which are both far better known in Europe. When used correctly, rosemary is a delicious herb that goes particularly well with garlic, olive oil, tomatoes, and beans. But rosemary can also be aggressive and take over the flavor of a soup. Its sharp pointed leaves are annoying to eat if left floating around in the soup. The best way to use rosemary is to tie it up into a bouquet garni and simmer it with the soup, tasting the soup occasionally to make sure the rosemary flavor doesn't grow too strong. If it does, the bouquet garni can be fished out of the soup in time.

Rosemary takes very well to drying. If you buy rosemary in jars, buy whole leaves, never ground. If you're using rosemary leaves in a bouquet garni, you'll need to wrap them in cheesecloth to keep the sharp leaves out of the soup.

SAFFRON   Many cooks are intimidated by saffron because it's supposedly very expensive. Although by weight saffron is more expensive than gold, a tiny bit goes a long way—50¢ worth is usually enough to transform a pot of soup. Buy saffron in threads rather than powder, which is often adulterated. Avoid light-colored threads.

Saffron threads—actually crocus stamens—are best soaked in a tablespoon of water for 20 minutes to soften and release their flavor before being added to a soup. Sometimes saffron that has been sitting around for a month or more becomes brittle—with no loss of flavor—so that it can be easily crushed to a powder with your fingers and just stirred into the soup a couple of minutes before serving.

The flavor of saffron is especially wonderful in Indian curries and in Mediterranean fish and shellfish soups. It has a lovely affinity for fennel and tomatoes.

SAKE (JAPANESE RICE WINE) AND SHAOXING (CHINESE RICE WINE)   Along with miso and soy sauce, sake is one of the principal flavorings for *dashi* and Japanese soups. When you're using sake, it's a good idea to simmer it for about 5 minutes in a saucepan to burn off the alcohol. Unfortunately, I don't have sake sitting around the house in the same way as wine, so I frequently substitute a small amount of mirin instead. But be careful when substituting mirin; it is sweet—sake is not— and should be added in small increments to taste.

Chinese rice wine, also called *Shaoxing wine,* is also made with rice but using a different process from that used for making sake. Rice wine is fairly alcoholic with a deep amber color that makes it more like sherry than sake or white wine. Sherry can be used as a substitute in recipes calling for Chinese rice wine.

SALT   My favorite salt is sea salt from France. Sea salt has a more delicate and more satisfying flavor than ordinary table salt and comes in various forms. I have noticed that the best-tasting sea salt is gray or even violet and is slightly damp because it contains no additives to keep it from absorbing moisture from the air. The most luxurious sea salt is *fleur de sel*, made by skimming off the first salt that crystallizes as salt water is allowed to dry in the sun. Because it is very expensive, I only use it in elegant soups in which it remains visible on something solid. I sometimes pass it at the table when serving *pot-au-reu*. (See Sources, page 611.)

SAUSAGES Adding a good sausage to a hearty vegetable or meat soup is a fast and simple way to transform the soup into a satisfying meal. The best sausages for soup-making are fresh sausages, which can be simmered directly in the soup during the last 30 or 40 minutes of cooking.

There are several types of sausages that can be found in most parts of the country. Kielbasa—Polish garlic sausage—is usually easy to find, but some brands have a strong "hot dog" taste that I like to avoid. If you have access to French-style sausages, *saucisse de campagne, saucisse de Toulouse,* and *saucisse à l'ail* are all good choices.

Chorizo is a peppery Spanish sausage that is sometimes smoked. The *chorizo* found in the United States varies a lot in quality, so you will probably want to experiment with the different kinds available in your area. *Chorizo* is particularly good in soups containing beans.

The Italians, like the French, have dozens of regional sausages. In the United States the best known is simply called *Italian Sausage,* but it has little to do with the best sausages found in Italy. In Italy one of the favorite sausages is *cotechino,* which when made correctly contains garlic, spices, and pork rinds. *Zampone* is probably the most famous and easiest to spot because instead of being stuffed into a sausage skin *zampone* is made by stuffing a pig's foreleg. Either *cotechino* or *zampone* is excellent when simmered in a *bollito misto* (page 438) or other hearty soup during the last 30 minutes of cooking.

The most distinctive American sausages are Creole or Cajun sausages from Louisiana. Even though they have French names, they are usually far spicier than a sausage with the same name bought in France. *Andouille* from New Orleans is a reddish spicy pork sausage, whereas an *andouille* bought in France is gray-black and made from tripe. An American *boudin blanc* is spicy and made with pork; in France a *boudin blanc* is usually made with chicken or veal, contains cream, and is very mild.

SEAWEED Konbu is a dried seaweed sold in 3-foot-long strips that have been folded over themselves for easy packaging. The best konbu comes from the northern Japanese island of Hokkaido and is usually covered with a white, delicate, saltlike dust. Konbu is the basis—along with dried bonito—for the basic broth *dashi* (page 87) common to most Japanese soups.

Wakame is a delicate black-green seaweed that is delicious added to a pot of simmering soup a minute or two before serving. In Japan, wakame is available fresh, but in the United States we have to make do with dried, which must be soaked in warm water for 20 minutes before it is used. Wakame sometimes has tough sections still attached that must be cut away.

Nori is the dried paperlike seaweed used for wrapping sushi. It's rarely used in soup making except when thinly shredded and floated on top as a last-minute garniture.

SESAME OIL The extract of toasted sesame seeds, sesame oil is a potent flavoring used in Chinese and Korean soups. As little as ½ teaspoon will give a pot of soup a distinctive flavor. I especially like to use sesame oil in soups containing ginger and soy sauce. Be sure to buy a dark-colored Asian brand made from toasted seeds and preferably one in a glass bottle or tin rather than in plastic. Kadoya brand from Japan is especially recommended.

SEVEN-SPICE MIXTURE (SHICHIMI) This Japanese mixture of powdered flavors is sprinkled on soba and udon noodles or stirred directly into soups. I place a small container of the mixture on the table whenever I'm serving Japanese soups with noodles.

The mixture contains red pepper flakes, sansho pepper pods, dried mandarin orange peel, white poppy seeds, white sesame seeds, black sesame seeds, and ground nori seaweed.

SHIITAKE MUSHROOMS These Japanese mushrooms are now available fresh in most parts of the country and—at least compared to other exotic mushrooms—are relatively inexpensive. Shiitake mushrooms can be sautèed first or added directly to a pot of simmering soup. They have a lovely delicate mushroom flavor and look very elegant floating in a bowl of clear Japanese soup.

Usually the tough stems on shiitake mushrooms need to be removed. I always save them to add to broths.

Shiitake mushrooms are available dried—confusingly labeled "Chinese black mushrooms."

SHRIMP, DRIED Dried shrimp, which come in lengths varying from ¼ inch to 1 inch, can be added whole to Asian or South American soups to give them a bit of crunch or ground to a powder and used as a seasoning.

I rarely use whole dried shrimp—probably because it's easy to find good fresh shrimp—but I do like to grind ½ cup or so in a blender to keep in the freezer and then add a teaspoon or two to Asian and South American soups for an extra dimension of flavor. The size of the shrimp for grinding isn't important, so I usually use the inexpensive small ones that come from Thailand in small cellophane bags. Look for bright pink shrimp. Both the powder and the shrimp will keep indefinitely in the freezer.

SHRIMP PASTE A popular condiment in Southeast Asian and Indonesian cooking, shrimp paste—made by fermenting shrimp in the sun—is not to most Westerners' taste. But if you begin using it in Thai, Indonesian, or Vietnamese soups, you'll start to miss it when it isn't there. It gives Asian soups body and another layer of complexity in much the same way as fish sauce.

If used in the way most recipes recommend—cooked in oil before liquid is added—shrimp paste will smell up the house for days. I learned this the hard way, and now when I use any fish paste I stir in small amounts near the end of the cooking time. My favorite brand is Trachang from Thailand. Shrimp paste keeps for several months in the refrigerator.

SORREL Sometimes called *sour grass* (not to be confused with lemongrass), sorrel is unfortunately in season only during the summer and can be difficult to find even then. When it's available, I cook with it almost every day. It has a clean sour taste that makes it especially delicious with fish or shellfish, but it can also be used to make a delicious vegetable soup.

Sorrel is easy to cook—just add it directly to a soup. If you're cooking it by itself, heat it in a pot (you don't need any butter or oil), and in about 2 minutes it will melt into a sort of puree. Alas, nothing can be done to prevent it from turning a sad grayish green. If you're making a pureed sorrel soup, you don't need to remove the leaves from the stems because the stems will be strained out anyway, but if you're leaving the leaves whole, you'll need to pull the stems away from each leaf.

Sometimes I combine sorrel with blanched spinach, cook the raw sorrel with the blanched and drained spinach in a tablespoon or two of heavy cream, and then use this tangy vegetable base to prop up pieces of fish or chicken and then surround them with the soup.

Try to buy sorrel by the pound and avoid places that sell it by the bunch—it melts to nothing when you cook it, so you'll need about a pound for six servings.

SOUR CREAM Unlike crème fraîche, which is made from heavy cream, sour cream is manufactured by inoculating a mixture of milk and cream with lactic acid-producing bacteria. Sour cream contains approximately 18 percent butterfat, while heavy cream and crème fraîche contain at least twice that much.

Sour cream is served as a condiment for dolloping in the center of bowls of hot soup, especially Mexican soups and Eastern European soups such as borscht or *shchi*. Unlike heavy cream or crème fraîche, sour cream cannot be stirred into a hot soup, or it will curdle.

SOYBEAN PASTES AND FERMENTED SOYBEANS Called *miso* in Japan, *twoenjang* in Korea, and *jiang* in China, fermented soybeans come in different strengths, degrees of saltiness or spiciness, and textures ranging from smooth pastes to whole beans. All of these preparations are easy to use. Usually they are thinned with a little of the soup broth and then stirred directly into the soup, but in some soups the solid ingredients are stir-fried with fermented soybean paste before any liquid is added.

For soup-making, the most useful fermented soybean product is miso, which most Japanese eat every day of their lives. There are subtle differences among all brands of miso, but you need to be familiar with only three or four types to make soup. The most commonly found miso in this country is shinshu miso, which has a pale tan color and is relatively inexpensive. It's a good all-purpose miso for soup-making. Shiro miso, which contains a large proportion of rice, is very pale yellow and relatively sweet. It is excellent in soups, but I usually like to combine it with a saltier, more savory miso to offset its sweetness. Of the darker, more savory misos, inaka miso, or "red" miso, and hatcho miso (the more expensive of the two) are the best for soups. They come in both smooth pastes and slightly chunky styles.

While miso is a mild product, rarely offensive to the Western nose and palate, the

Korean equivalent, *twoenjang*, is a bit more feisty and may take some getting used to. Even though it's an acquired taste, *twoenjang* is an essential condiment and flavoring in Korean soups. It's easy to find in big cities, but if you have limited access to exotic products, substitute miso or order *twoenjang* from one of the sources listed in the back of this book.

The oldest version of fermented soybeans is Chinese bean sauce, which is the predecessor to modern soy sauce. Chinese bean sauce comes in both whole bean form and ground form, but the ground form is extremely salty, so I always try to buy the whole bean version. I've found two brands I like in Chinese markets, Koon Chun "Bean Sauce" and Sze Chuan brand "Szechuan Bean Sauce." These bean sauces are best added to soups that are stir-fried before liquid is added.

Fermented soybean products keep for a year in the refrigerator.

SOY SAUCE There are so many brands, colors, and varieties of soy sauce that finding the right one for a soup can seem like a daunting project. The first thing to look for is an authentic sauce that has been naturally brewed. Authentic soy sauce is made by fermenting roasted soybeans with wheat for at least 4 months and up to 2 years. Synthetic soy sauces, such as the La Choy brand found in supermarkets, are only slightly less expensive and have an entirely different flavor from slow-fermented versions. If you're unsure whether a soy sauce is authentic, check the label. A traditionally made sauce will usually say "naturally fermented" or "naturally brewed." If none of this is mentioned, check the ingredients. Natural soy sauce should contain water, soybeans, wheat, and salt. Occasionally even the natural brands contain sodium benzoate as a preservative (if I have a choice, I avoid these too). If the label is a long list of suspect ingredients such as hydrolyzed vegetable protein, steer clear.

To add to the confusion, Japanese and Chinese soy sauces are not interchangeable. Japanese sauces are usually softer and slightly sweeter than Chinese versions. So if you cook both Chinese and Japanese soups, it's best to have both. Fortunately, even the best soy sauce is inexpensive, unless you buy it in a health food store, where the same sauce—called *tamari*—is likely to sell for twice as much as in a Japanese or Chinese market. Authentic tamari, made using traditional techniques, is rarely found in Japan, much less here.

For Japanese cooking, Kikkoman and Yamasa brands are my favorites. Japanese soy sauce comes in both light and dark styles. The light style is, surprisingly, somewhat saltier, so if you're substituting light for dark in a Japanese recipe, use half as much of the light and then add more as needed to taste. Light soy sauce is somewhat harder to find and may mean a trip to a Japanese market.

Both dark and light soy sauces are also used in Chinese cooking, although I rarely have need for the light version. A good middle ground for both Japanese and Chinese cooking is Kikkoman brand dark soy, but if you cook a lot of Chinese food and want to be authentic, Pear River Bridge and Koon Chun brands both make good versions of both light and dark soy sauce. Be careful; both of these contain more salt than Japanese brands. All soy sauce will keep in the refrigerator for at least a year.

STAR ANISE This spice is well named because it looks like a miniature star. It has a distinct licorice taste but shouldn't be confused with so-called anise or fennel seeds, which have a milder flavor.

Star anise is sometimes used in combination with cinnamon in Chinese or Vietnamese soups. It's very strong; half of a single star, crushed under a pot, is enough to impart a licorice flavor to 2 quarts of soup. Star anise is also one of the ingredients in Chinese five-spice powder.

Star anise will keep for months in a tightly sealed jar away from heat.

SZECHUAN PEPPERCORNS Szechuan peppercorns neither look nor taste like black pepper, but they've been used in Chinese cooking for centuries. They are almost invariably roasted before they are used (I roast them by stirring them in a skillet over medium heat for about 20 minutes until they release their fragrance) and release a rather beguiling aroma, again nothing like black pepper, that reminds me vaguely of burning leaves but with a distinct spicy note. (See recipe for Chinese Duck and Orange Soup on page 502).

TABASCO SAUCE Tabasco is made by macerating tabasco chilies to extract both their heat and flavor. I often add it to soups at the last minute for an extra jolt of heat. It can also be passed at the table for people who want more spice. Tabasco has a distinct flavor that might not be appropriate in some hot soups such as those from China or Southeast Asia. For these I use cayenne pepper instead.

TAMARIND (TAMARINDO) The first time I saw these lumpy brown pods in a Chinese market I brought some home and tried to eat the little beans on the inside of the pods—not a success. It's the sticky pulp that surrounds the beans that Asian and South American cooks use to give a sour tang to cold drinks, jams, and soups. I've since figured things out, and tamarind has become one of my favorite flavorings for Thai soups.

Extracting tamarind pulp from fresh tamarind pods can be a nuisance, and since fresh tamarind isn't always available I usually rely on tamarind paste because it's easy to find in Asian markets (or to order by mail) and keeps for months in the refrigerator. To use tamarind paste, dissolve a walnut-size chunk by working it around with a wooden spoon in ½ cup boiling water, strain it through a fine-mesh strainer, and add it to the soup.

If you can't find tamarind or don't have it on hand, substitute lime juice.

TARRAGON Anyone I know who has tasted fresh tarragon for the first time is instantly converted by its clean licoricelike flavor. Tarragon is a natural with chicken and seafood, especially shellfish.

To use tarragon in soups, chop the leaves at the last minute with a teaspoon of olive oil to prevent them from turning black. Add them to the soup about 2 minutes before serving so their flavor has time to infuse. You can also include sprigs of fresh tarragon in a bouquet garni, but this uses up a lot of tarragon, so if you're buying tarragon by the sprig—it can be expensive—chopping it and adding it at the end is more efficient. I never bother with dried tarragon.

If you decide to grow your own tarragon, be sure you buy French tarragon and not the Russian variety, which looks similar but has no flavor. Taste a leaf or be sure of your seeds before planting.

THYME If I had to use only two herbs for the rest of my life, I'd choose thyme and parsley. There is hardly a soup that thyme doesn't improve by blending subtly and enhancing the flavor of the other ingredients.

Because thyme releases its flavor slowly into a surrounding liquid, it should be added to a soup near the beginning of cooking—usually in the bouquet garni. When composing a bouquet garni, I use about 5 sprigs of fresh thyme (or one teaspoon dried leaves) for 2 quarts of soup.

I prefer fresh thyme to dried, but if you can't find it fresh, it is still worthwhile to use dried thyme. The best dried thyme is sold with the leaves still on the branches, but this can be hard to find, so you may have to settle on the little jars of thyme leaves. Don't bother buying ground thyme.

TIGER LILY STEMS, LILY BUDS, GOLDEN NEEDLES Despite all the confusing names, all of these are dried unopened day lily flowers. Although I rarely use lily buds except when making hot and sour soup, I've read that they're a popular flavoring in Chinese vegetarian dishes. I don't think they have much taste, but this might be because they're easily overshadowed by other ingredients.

Tiger lily buds are sold in small plastic bags. They should be moist and flexible when you buy them and not at all dried out. They should be soaked for 30 minutes in warm water to soften them and then shredded before being added to a pot of soup.

TOFU (SOYBEAN CURD) One of Asia's staples, soybean curd is tasty, nutritious, and an easy-to-use addition to clear Asian broths and soups. A couple of cubes added to a cup of miso soup add enough substance to make it a small meal. (This is one of my favorite breakfasts.)

Often called *tofu*—its Japanese name—soybean curd is prepared by boiling roasted and crushed soybeans with water, straining out the pulp, and adding a coagulant—usually a natural mineral such as gypsum—to the strained soybean "milk." The curd is then drained and, depending on the final style, pressed to extract excess water. The process is almost exactly analogous to cheese-making.

Soybean curd is available in several different styles. The best type to use for soup-making is Japanese-style tofu, which is the softest and most delicate and fortunately the easiest to find. Excellent tofu can be found in most supermarkets in little plastic containers. Check the date on the containers—look in the back or on the bottom of the stack of containers to find the freshest batch. If possible, don't use tofu that's more than a week old. To use Japanese-style tofu, cut it into cubes—usually about 1 inch— and just add them to the soup a minute or two before serving so they have time to heat through.

If you shop in an Asian market, you're likely to find Japanese "grilled bean curd" (yakidofu). Yakidofu has been pressed and broiled so it has a much firmer texture. I like to use grilled bean curd when it's going to be exposed to rambunctious treatment such as stir-frying or for dishes where the diners cook their own and have to hold it firmly between two chopsticks.

Chinese-style bean curd (pronounced doe-foo in Chinese) is firmer than Japanese tofu and like yakidofu is best for stir-fried dishes or one-pot meals where it can be cut into relatively thin strips without falling apart. Chinese bean curd usually comes in pillow-shaped squares while Japanese tofu comes in squares.

Store bean curd at home submerged in water, which should be changed every day.

TREE EARS, CLOUD EARS, WOOD EARS I could never figure out why the Chinese are so fond of tree ears until I began to cook with them and realized that despite their lack of flavor they have an intriguing, squeaky, semicrunchy texture unlike any food I've ever tasted.

Tree ears aren't really mushrooms but dark leafy growths that attach themselves to fallen trees and rotting wood. They're usually sold dried in cellophane bags. Small tree ears—which look like irregular black flakes—are the best even if not the most impressive to look at.

Reconstitute tree ears by pouring over enough boiling water to cover and soaking for 30 minutes. Rinse the reconstituted tree ears thoroughly and pull off or cut away any sections that didn't soften.

TREFOIL (MITSUBA) Trefoil looks a little like cilantro or Italian parsley, but it has a distinct celerylike flavor that sets it apart from any other herb. Apparently it is sometimes used in Chinese cooking, but I've found it only in Japanese dishes. A sprig or two added to a Japanese broth during the last minute of cooking will give the broth a distinctive Japanese look and flavor.

TURMERIC I've read that turmeric is available fresh in some markets, but I've been unable to track it down in even my favorite out-of-the-way places in Chinatown. Fresh turmeric looks somewhat like ginger except that it has a distinct orange tint. According to Bruce Cost (*Bruce Cost's Asian Ingredients*), Indian and Southeast Asian cooks slice or chop turmeric to use in stews (and presumably soups).

Even though it has no detectable flavor, I use ground turmeric to give an appealing orange color to soups containing curry. If you're stuck with an Indian or Southeast Asian soup that looks drab, whisk in a teaspoon of ground turmeric.

VEGETABLE OILS Many soup recipes call for preliminary sautèing of meats or vegetables before liquid is added. The fat (usually oil) used for the sautèing is poured off after the browning (in the case of meat) or skimmed off once liquid is added (in the case of vegetables).

Because the vegetable oil used in soups is removed, the kind of oil you use isn't terribly important. I use "pure" olive oil for Mediterranean soups and peanut oil for Asian dishes. I find that corn oil and so-called vegetable oil have an unpleasant "fishy" smell when I heat them in a sauté pan, so I usually avoid them, more because I dislike the smell they leave in my kitchen—in fact, they don't affect the taste of the soup very much.

VINEGAR Some people may wonder what place vinegar has in a bowl of soup, but most meat or fish soups as well as soups made with beans and lentils need a little tartness to wake up their flavor. I often add lime juice to Mexican or South American soups; for French or Italian soups I often add a teaspoon or two of wine vinegar to bring the soup's flavor into focus. In Chinese soups I use black rice wine vinegar (Gold Plum brand "Chinkiang vinegar"), and in soups containing apples or other fruits I use cider vinegar.

Taste your vinegar before you use it. You may have to work through a couple of brands until you find one you like—sometimes the vinegar in the fanciest bottles is the least tasty. Other than rice wine and cider vinegar, I keep several wine vinegars around, including Champagne vinegar, sherry vinegar, balsamic vinegar, and homemade vinegar. Never use distilled white vinegar in cooking—it has a harsh chemical taste.

WATER SPINACH This leafy vegetable usually appears in Chinese markets in the late winter. Water spinach has long stems and narrow pointed leaves and no physical resemblance to common spinach, although it can be cooked in the same way. It tastes somewhat like ordinary spinach with a slightly "wilder" vegetable flavor. I sometimes use water spinach in Chinese vegetable soups, when I want to use something typically Chinese. When cooked, water spinach has a slightly slimy consistency that not everyone likes.

WILD RICE Despite its name, wild rice isn't really rice but only a distant relative, more closely related to certain grasses. Wild rice has long grains—much longer than even the longest grained white rice—with a shiny brown coating. It takes much longer to cook than regular rice, at least 30 minutes, and ends up with a nutty flavor and a texture reminiscent of barley. I like it best in soups pared with smokey ingredients such as smoked duck which balances its nutty flavor. Wild rice is priced according to the length of the grains and whether or not it has been harvested by hand (traditionally by American Indians in canoes) or by machine.

WINE In one form or another, wine is used throughout the world for making soups. The Japanese rely on sake, the Chinese on rice wine, and European cooks on an assortment of red, white, and fortified wines. Most of the time using wine in cooking is simple; the wine is added and cooked just long enough—10 minutes or so—to cook off its alcohol.

Wine contains natural acids that add a gentle tang and subtle lightness to soups containing fish, meat, or vegetables. Usually a small amount of wine is added along with other liquids to give character to a soup, but occasionally wine comprises most or all of the liquid.

Wine does have a couple of quirks that can make cooking with it unpredictable. White wine sometimes slows down the cooking of beans and other starchy vegetables, so it's a good idea to add wine to these soups only after the vegetables have softened. Red wine can be harsh and acidic unless cooked for several hours. For this reason most recipes recommend adding the wine practically from the start.

Sherry and Madeira are also useful in soups for their slightly sweet, nutty flavor. I particularly like the flavor of these wines with root vegetable soups such as carrot, turnip, or celeriac. They can also be used in fish soups to give them a distinctive Spanish character. Use only authentic Madeira and Spanish sherry.

YOGURT   Yogurt can be used as a refreshing finish for cold soups such as leek and potato, watercress, cucumber, or tomato. Freshly chopped herbs can be stirred into the yogurt for both flavor and color before it is swirled into or dolloped over a soup.

The main advantage to using yogurt over heavy cream or crème fraîche is that yogurt is less rich and has a pleasant refreshing tang.

The biggest disadvantage to using yogurt in soups is that it curdles if allowed to boil. If you decide to substitute yogurt for heavy cream in a hot soup, be sure to add the yogurt just before serving and don't allow it to boil for even a second. However, if the soup contains a lot of starch—bean, lentil, or split pea soups or soups that have been thickened with a fair amount of flour—the starch will stabilize the yogurt so that it *can* be boiled.

YUZU (JAPANESE CITRUS)   This Japanese citrus fruit is used primarily for its colorful and aromatic rind. The rind is cut into tiny shreds and used to flavor and decorate clear Japanese soups. The zest from western lemons has a somewhat different flavor but can be used as a substitute.

Ethnic
SOUPS

I RARELY PREPARE DISHES ACCORDING TO AN EXACT RECIPE BECAUSE I NEVER LIKE TO cook the same thing twice—I need to invent as I go along, or I get bored. Whether your dishes are authentic or not, you'll have more fun playing around with flavors and ingredients, adding things here and there, than you will by methodically following a recipe. On the other hand I always adhere to a set of ingredients—a sort of national or regional idiom—so that I don't come up with a hopeless potpourri of flavors.

Starting with Basic Flavors: An Almost Universal Technique

Although the ingredients that cooks choose to flavor their soups vary throughout the world, certain techniques are almost universal—for instance, the preparation of a flavor mixture lightly cooked in oil or fat before any liquid ingredients are added. Because onions, carrots, celery, garlic, sweet peppers, ham, spices, and certain herbs release a more pungent and forthright flavor when gently cooked in fat than when simmered directly in liquid, this is often the first step in soup-making.

In southern European soups, this flavor base—*soffrito* in Italian, *mirepoix* or *matignon* in French, and *sofregit* in Catalan—is likely to include garlic, onions, carrots, celery, fennel, and herbs such as thyme or marjoram, lightly cooked in olive oil. Each country has its own variations; Moroccan cooks are likely to include cinnamon and turmeric, the Provenáaux may add dried orange peel, and the Spanish will include ham. Northern and Eastern European cooks as well as New Englanders are likely to prepare a simple flavor base of onions gently stewed in a little butter or bacon fat.

Asian cooks make a flavor base by gently stewing pungent mixtures of spices and often chilies in a small amount of peanut or palm oil. Thai and Vietnamese cooks usually include shallots, garlic, ginger, and hot chilies in the flavor base, while the Indonesian equivalent—called a *bumbu*—is likely to contain kemiri (or macadamia) nuts, ground galangal (laos), cloves, and shrimp paste. Indian cooks start out with a mixture of well-browned onions.

Although the most important function of the flavor base is to give the soup additional savor, some recipes include thickeners such as flour (in European cooking) or kemiri nuts (in Indonesian cooking) that are best cooked before being combined with liquid.

Here are some brief descriptions of the national cuisines that form the basis for the recipes in this book.

CHINA Chinese cooking is almost impossible to characterize because it encompasses such a huge area. It's a bit like being asked to describe European cooking. Still, there are certain flavors and characteristics that make Chinese cooking different from the cuisines of Korea, Japan, and Southeast Asia.

Chinese soups are striking in their simplicity. Unlike Southeast Asian soups, which rely heavily on certain herbs and condiments such as lemongrass, kaffir lime leaves, and fish sauce, Chinese soups are often made by simmering one or two vegetables in a ginger-scented chicken broth. Frequently the only seasoning is soy sauce, used the way Europeans use salt. Ginger is used almost universally in much the same way that European cooks use onions. Although a large number of Chinese soups are seasoned only with ginger and soy sauce, other flavorings are used to give soups depth and a special character. Sesame oil—also used in Korea but rarely in Southeast Asia—often makes its way in minute amounts (it's very strong) into a wide range of Chinese dishes. Chinese cooks are also fond of ham—they have their own variety of smoked ham, unavailable here—which they shred and add to soups near the end of cooking to give them body and a light smoky flavor. American cooks can use a smoked and cured ham such as Smithfield, Westphalian, or Black Forest.

The Chinese, as in other parts of Asia, use noodles to add substance to their soups, but they are also fond of dumplings such as wontons. Tofu, more popular in North Asian countries, is also used in Chinese soups.

There's a particular fondness for eggs: the best known is of course egg drop soup, which contains beaten eggs stirred in at the last minute, but there are also egg flower soups where the eggs are allowed to set in decorative flower shapes just before serving.

Rice wine is often called for in Chinese recipes, but many Americanized versions substitute good dry sherry because authentic rice wine (Shaoxing) can be hard to find.

The Chinese use an incredibly wide range of ingredients and flavorings in their cooking, but certain of these are used only rarely while others are almost everyday staples. Mushrooms—including the dried "Chinese" mushrooms, straw mushrooms (also popular in Southeast Asia), cloud ears, and Cantonese tree ears—are all used for flavor and texture. Preserved vegetables—mostly mustard greens and radishes—are sometimes used to give a distinctive and surprisingly full flavor to soups. Black beans—about 3 tablespoons per quart of soup—rinsed and crushed, will give a soup a delicious winy flavor.

Although almost any vegetable can be simmered into a Chinese-style fish soup, water chestnuts, Chinese mushrooms, snow peas, Chinese or water spinach, bok choy, Chinese cabbage, tofu, and watercress leaves help give a Chinese feel to the soup.

Chinese cooks often use cornstarch to give their soups sheen and a thicker consistency, but I usually leave it out because I like thin brothy soups and I've developed an aversion for the overly thickened soups that often appear in Chinese restaurants. If you want to experiment with cornstarch, start by using just a little at a time; 1 tablespoon combined with 2 tablespoons water whisked into a quart of simmering soup just a minute before serving is usually adequate.

Although the Chinese use relatively few spices compared to cooks in neighboring India and Southeast Asia, they do like to use certain pungent flavorings such as star anise, dried orange or tangerine peel, and five-spice mixture, which doesn't always contain exactly five spices but various combinations of star anise, cloves, cinnamon, ground ginger, Szechuan peppercorns, licorice root and fennel or anise seed.

FRANCE Because of the importance of cooking in the upper classes the French have simultaneously developed two cuisines. Regional cooking—the everyday food eaten by all—evolved spontaneously, while on a more rarefied level the so-called *cuisine classique* painstakingly developed over centuries, first at the royal court and later in restaurants.

Soup is so important to French dining that few French people can imagine dinner without it. Except in restaurants, where a meal is likely to start with a salad or something more elaborate, a family dinner in France always starts with soup. Soup is a staple at the French dinner table, but is never served at lunch.

The French housewife's ability to throw together a simple and delicious soup from a few fresh ingredients or leftovers has taken on almost mythic proportions. Part of this magical ability is probably the result of a long oral tradition—alas, one that is ending—passed on from mother to daughter.

Soups from the classic tradition are carefully stratified in an elaborate system of *broths, veloutés, crèmes, bisques, consommés,* and *purées,* which are prepared and served according to rigid criteria. Although these soups are served around the world and are representative of what most people think of as French cuisine, only occasionally are they eaten by the French. Far more typical of native French cooking are regional specialties that have come about as a natural result of the availability of certain foods.

Mediterranean cooking is based on local seafood and vegetables that flourish in the hot climate. Because of the millennia-old history of trade along the Mediterranean, cooks in these regions use a diversity of herbs and spices not found farther north. Soups from Provence are likely to contain saffron, olive oil, fennel, garlic, and certainly tomatoes. Southern French recipes often have more in common with the cooking of other Mediterranean countries than they do with those of their northern French neighbors. One exciting and characteristically Mediterranean technique is to finish a pot of soup with one of several pungent sauces, such as the Provençal *aïoli*—a pungent garlic mayonnaise. *Rouille,* a thick paste made of garlic, bread, chilies, and sometimes saffron, is used as a thickener and final flavoring for a classic *bouillabaisse.*

One almost universal component of French cooking is a mixture of chopped vegetables—onions, carrots, and celery—called *mirepoix. Mirepoix* is gently cooked in butter or oil to give a flavorful and aromatic background to soups and stews.

In cold mountainous regions traditional soups often contain rich meat broths, wine, root vegetables, and cheese and are likely to be served over plenty of stale bread. Cabbage and pork products—especially sausages—are also widely used in colder regions.

In France's northernmost regions, soups are made from the abundant shellfish caught or cultivated along the Atlantic coast and the channel. In Normandy, Dover sole and other flatfish as well as oysters, shrimp, and scallops are likely to be combined with cream and perhaps cider (wine grapes don't grow this far north) to make fish soups and stews.

The French Southwest is known for hearty cooking based on the farming of ducks and geese and the production of foie gras. Ducks and geese—often cooked in their own fat to produce *confit*—along with beans, cabbage, and onions, make for some of the heartiest and most satisfying soups in France.

Because of the sophistication of French classic cooking, many people are surprised to discover that most French cooks also prepare very simple dishes. One of the cornerstones of French cooking is a vegetable soup made with a few herbs, chopped vegetables, and water. Leek and potato soup is one of the best loved of Parisian soups.

Until the 16th century French cooking and the cooking of most of Europe was dominated by spices. Gradually a change took place; more emphasis was placed on drawing out the natural flavors of foods rather than masking them with strong-tasting ingredients. French cooks began to flavor their foods with subtle ingredients such as herbs, mushrooms, and truffles. This reverence for the natural flavors of foods and for subtle seasoning with local ingredients is what continues to distinguish French cooking to this day.

INDIA I've always admired the way Indian cooks make the most out of a few lean and simple ingredients. In skillful hands the most humble foods are transformed through the masterful use of spices and spice mixtures. When I started making my own curry powder I was amazed by the versatility and subtlety of Indian spices.

In addition to elaborate curry mixtures, Indian cooks usually start out with a flavor base of very finely chopped onions, garlic, ginger, and hot peppers cooked slowly in oil or butter. The powdered curry is then added and the mixture cooked for a minute or two more to wake up its flavor. Liquid ingredients—usually vegetable, fish, or chicken broth—are then added to the flavor base. Another popular method is to prepare a flavorful spice mixture—called a *tadka*—made by cooking ground spices and flavorings such as onions and garlic in the Indian-style butter called *ghee* and whisking this mixture into the soup just before serving.

Probably because so many Indians are vegetarians, Indian cooks work wonders with vegetables. Lentil soup was always something I settled for in cheap restaurants, but when I started experimenting with Indian recipes I was amazed to see this humble legume become the focal point of a satisfying meal.

I was also delighted to discover *ghee*, which I had always thought was simply clarified butter but is really much more flavorful (see recipe, page 592). *Ghee* is rich—even richer than whole butter—but it has such an intense flavor that very little is needed to give a buttery suaveness to a soup.

Indian cooks also finish their soups with yogurt, which gives them a delicate tang and lightness, and is magical in combination with Indian spices.

To finish a fish soup, Indians are fond of the creamy texture and subtle sweetness of coconut milk—a lovely vegetable equivalent of the heavy cream Europeans use, and a perfect foil for hot and powerful spices. You can buy good coconut milk in cans or make it yourself.

A number of curry powders can be purchased, but the real fun begins when you start making your own. I sometimes just stand over a pot of simmering soup and add tiny pinches of ground spices until I come up with a flavor I like. Spices sometimes impart a murky gray color to soups, which is easily corrected by adding a teaspoon or two of turmeric worked to a paste in a little water.

When I'm cooking for myself or for diet-oblivious guests (a rare breed), I cook the ground spices in a few tablespoons of *ghee* for a minute or two and then stir the mixture into the soup just before serving.

When you're buying spices for Indian cooking, try to find an Indian or Middle Eastern market that sells spices in bulk; they will be much cheaper and usually much fresher. I also recommend using ground spices unless you become truly fanatical and want to grind the spices yourself minutes before you use them—in which case you'll need a small coffee grinder. Buy spices in small quantities and keep them in the freezer.

Indians also rely on a variety of herbs. Most often, I run into cilantro—at least in Indian restaurants in New York—but basil and mint also pop up from time to time. Instinctively I've always used thyme when making Indian soups even though I've never seen any mention of it in Indian cookbooks. But recently I discovered that Indians use ajowan seeds, which have a thymelike flavor.

When making Indian soups, I make sure to have enough for leftovers. Then the next day I heat cooked rice and sometimes bits of leftover meats, fish, or vegetables in the soup to turn it into a light stew, perfect for lunch or a light dinner.

It's surprising that in a country as hot as India so few soups are served cold. Though it's untraditional, I sometimes serve "hot" Indian soups chilled. Because soups thicken as they cool, they may need to be thinned with a little water or broth.

INDONESIA Although Indonesian cooking shares much with the cuisines of Thailand and the rest of Southeast Asia, it has a few interesting quirks of its own.

Whereas Southeast Asian cooks rely on fish sauce and Chinese and Japanese cooks on their own versions of soy sauce, the most distinctive component of Indonesian cuisine is a dark, rather sweet soy sauce called *kecap manis* and a lighter version, *kecap asin*. Indonesians are also fond of galangal, but unlike Thai cooks, who use it freshly sliced, Indonesians use it in its powdered form, laos.

When Indonesian cooks prepare soups, they start out with a mixture of flavorful ingredients and spices called a *bumbu*. The exact ingredients depend on the recipe, but a typical *bumbu* contains shallots, garlic, turmeric, ginger, laos, cumin, coriander, cinnamon, cardamom, nutmeg, and cloves. Traditionally a *bumbu* is prepared in a mortar and pestle, but a food processor does a good job in a minute or two. The *bumbu* is cooked in a little vegetable oil—or, more traditionally, coconut oil—and liquids such as broth and *kecap manis* are added. Other flavorful ingredients such as lemongrass, tamarind, or *trassi*—fermented shrimp paste—are often added at this point, as are meats, fish, or vegetables.

One particularly Indonesian ingredient is the kemiri nut, which is ground to a paste and used as a thickener for soups and stews. Fortunately, macadamia nuts make a good substitute; kemiri nuts can be hard to track down. Another Indonesian oddity are salam leaves, which are apparently similar to bay leaves, but I've never been able to find them in the United States.

Indonesian cooks are also fond of peanuts—roasted, ground, and whisked into soups as a thickener, often in conjunction with coconut milk.

ITALY Italy has been a nation only since 1861, when only a small minority spoke the common language. French chefs are proud that French classic cooking is consistent around the world, but Italian cooks emphasize the individuality of each of their dishes. The diversity of Italy's regions is still apparent today, with each tiny province making its own contribution. Waverley Root, in his book *The Food of Italy*, tried to give some order to Italian cooking by grouping regions according to the major ancient influences—Etruscan, Greek, and Saracen. Each of these ancient groups had an important influence on modern Italian cooking. The Etruscans were fond of a kind of porridge that evolved into today's polenta; the Greeks contributed the first fish soups to the Italian peninsula; the Saracens contributed rice, tarragon, exotic fruits, and spices that had been used under Roman rule but were lost and forgotten once the empire crumbled. But what Italian soups do have in common is the quality of the ingredients. Italians insist on impeccably fresh ingredients and shop at least once a day for the best vegetables, meats, and seafood.

Italian soups fall into several broad categories. *Minestre*—sometimes called *minestre in brodo*—are light soups that usually contain rice or pasta and one or two vegetables in water or broth; minestrone are relatively thick soups that contain starch such as pasta, rice, or beans and a rich collection of herbs and vegetables; *zuppe* are soups that either include bread or are served with sliced stale bread, toasted bread, or *crostini*—fried bread sometimes sprinkled with cheese. Although Italians are less fond of pureed soups than the French, they make their own version called *passati*.

The basis for Italian soups is often a *battuto* (when cooked, called *soffrito*), which is a mixture of carrots, onions, celery, parsley, garlic, and sometimes ham or pancetta. The *battuto* is cooked for 10 to 15 minutes in olive oil or butter before the first liquids, often seeded and chopped tomatoes, are added.

Italian cooks like to use fresh basil (often ground into pesto sauce), rosemary, oregano, wild mint (especially in Rome), and sage, while their more restrained French neighbors are more likely to use tarragon, thyme, chives, or chervil.

Another characteristic that separates Italian soups from those of the rest of Europe is the widespread use of cheese—especially Parmesan—as a condiment to be sprinkled into the soup at the table or just before serving.

The Italians are blessed with plenty of seafood from both the Mediterranean and the Adriatic, which they put to good use in a variety of fish soups and stews. There are several *bouillabaisse*-like soups—*burrida* and *brodetto*—made with a *battuto* containing garlic, tomatoes, and basil or a little oregano and occasionally some squid ink. Plenty of soups are made with shellfish, which Italian cooks like to combine with beans, parsley, and tomatoes. The combination of beans with shellfish is surprisingly good—both hot and served cold the next day.

JAPAN In Japan, *dashi*, made from seaweed and dried bonito flakes, is the broth most commonly used not only for fish soups but for meat and vegetable soups as well. Other flavorings such as miso (fermented soybean paste), mirin (a kind of sweet sake), and soy sauce are all used by Japanese cooks to flavor a basic *dashi*, sometimes with great subtlety. Once you master a basic *dashi*, it's easy to finish it with tidbits of seafood, vegetables, or meats to come up with elegantly simple Japanese soups.

Japanese cooks also like to use chopped scallion, toasted seaweed (nori), prickly ash leaves (kinome), grated yuzu rind (a citrus fruit), bonito shavings, and chrysanthemum leaves as understated and subtle flavorings and garnishes for their fish soups. Obviously these are not ingredients you can run out and find at the last minute at the corner supermarket, but it's easy to capture the spirit and style of Japanese cooking with a carefully placed parsley or watercress leaf, a tiny sliver of lemon zest or carrot, or a carefully sliced mushroom. In fact, because many of the basic ingredients used for making Japanese soups—seaweed (konbu), bonito flakes, soy sauce, and miso—will keep almost indefinitely, it's easy to put together an authentic Japanese soup with these staples and perhaps a run to the corner grocery for some scallions and tofu.

The Japanese soup best known to Westerners is *sukiyaki*. *Sukiyaki* is made by simmering thinly sliced meats and vegetables at the table in a light broth. Although the Japanese do not eat *sukiyaki* often (it's usually reserved for special guests), it's representative of the light touch typical of Japanese cooking. The sliced meats and vegetables are cooked quickly, and the communal pot creates a convivial atmosphere of quick-dunking chopsticks and rapid-fire conversation.

Noodles are a continuous presence in Japanese kitchens and at inexpensive noodle stands. There are dozens of varieties of Japanese noodles, most of which can be used in soups. Udon, a white flour noodle, and soba, made from buckwheat flour, are the most popular Japanese noodles.

QUICK-COOKED VERSUS LONG-SIMMERED SOUPS

Most Asian cooks, who prefer quick-cooking dishes, make their soups with highly flavored ingredients that release their flavor immediately. Fish sauce is as much a staple in Thai and Vietnamese kitchens as salt is in Europe and America. Chinese cooks will often opt for soy sauce, sesame oil, tiny slivers of Smithfield ham, and dried mushrooms, while the Japanese add subtle herbs and greens such as grated yuzu rind or chrysanthemum leaves to their simmering *dashi*. When Asian cooks prepare meat soups, the meat is usually shredded or very finely chopped so it will cook quickly.

Americans and Europeans, who have a tradition of long-simmered dishes, usually include relatively long-cooking ingredients such as potatoes, carrots, large chunks of meat, tomatoes, tomatillos, and chilies as flavors for their soups.

Second to soy sauce, tofu is Japan's most popular soybean product. The Japanese enjoy eating it alone—chilled with a little scallion and soy sauce—and tofu is also a frequent addition to a light soup.

KOREA Although Korean cooking is similar in many ways to Chinese and Japanese cuisine, it uses its own distinctive ingredients. Unlike Southeast Asian cooks, who rely on fish sauce as an almost universal flavoring and condiment, Koreans, like the Chinese and Japanese, use soy sauce as their basic seasoning. Also like the Japanese, Koreans are fond of fermented soybean sauce. Whereas Japanese miso is relatively mild, the Korean version—*twoenjang*—has a gamier, more assertive aroma and flavor. Even though Japanese miso is an acceptable substitute for *twoenjang*, you'll never capture the distinctive flavor of Korean cooking without it. If you live outside a major city, you'll have to order *twoenjang* by mail, but fortunately, once you have it on hand, it keeps in the refrigerator for up to a year.

Koreans are also fond of a garlic-flavored chili paste called *kochujang*, which is often stirred into soups as a basic flavor. I like to marinate strips of meat in 2 or 3 tablespoons of *kochujang*, then lightly stir-fry the meat before adding broth. *Kochujang* is so flavorful that little additional seasoning is needed.

As in Chinese cooking, sesame oil is often used in Korean soups and other dishes. Koreans don't limit themselves to the oil or even the seeds; they also enjoy sesame leaves, which they eat raw or use as a wrapper for tasty fillings served deep-fried.

No Korean meal would be complete without *kimchee*, Korean pickled cabbage flavored with ginger, garlic, and hot peppers. Although crunchy *kimchee* is typically served as a condiment to accompany literally every Korean meal, it is also sometimes shredded and cooked along with *twoenjang* or *kochujang* to form the flavor base to which broth is added for making soup.

MEXICO Mexican cooking is startlingly sophisticated and diversified. Few American cooks have access to the foods they need to make authentic Mexican dishes, but it is possible to give soups and other dishes a distinctly Mexican character if you know how to use a few basic products.

Chilies are of course nearly universal in Mexican cooking and enter into soups in almost bewildering variety—fresh, dried, and pickled. The variety of chilies available in the United States rarely matches that of Mexico, but it's still possible to make do with dried chilies or the more common varieties of fresh chilies such as jalapeños and serranos or even sweet peppers spiced up with a little cayenne or Tabasco.

Mexican cooks are especially fond of corn, used both dried and fresh. Several of Mexico's most famous soups, including *pozole verde* and *pozole rojo*, are made with dried corn (*pozole*)—called *hominy* in English. Mexican cooks also make a variety of chowder-style fresh corn soups that usually contain chilies, garlic, and onions. Naturally these soups are best made with freshly picked corn, but frozen corn kernels make an acceptable substitute. I don't recommend canned corn, which can be sickeningly sweet. Fresh or frozen corn kernels can be pureed or simmered whole with broth, water, milk, or cooked tomato puree and the whole thing livened up with finely chopped chilies. Corn puree gives a natural creaminess to chowders even when no milk or cream is used. A typical Mexican touch is to pass more chopped chilies, some grated (such as Monterey Jack or Cheddar) or crumbled cheese (such as pot cheese), lime wedges, and some deep-fried tortilla triangles at the table. It's probably heretical, but I like to stir in a good amount of roast garlic puree and finely chopped cilantro and finish the corn soup with a dollop of sour cream.

Tomatoes are another important Mexican ingredient that have a natural affinity for other Mexican flavors. It's hard to miss by putting a cup or two of peeled, seeded, and chopped tomatoes into almost any Mexican soup. The Mexicans grill or roast them for extra flavor. Tomatillos, sometimes mistakenly called green tomatoes, are actually related to gooseberries. They are sometimes included in Mexican soups in the same way as tomatoes and give them a delightful sour tang.

Mexicans are also great aficionados of beans, which they use in soups, sometimes pureed and combined with cooked tomatoes. Garlic, onions, chilies, chopped cilantro, and sometimes bacon can all be used as flavorings. Cheese can also be sprinkled on these soups in the same way as corn soups.

Of all Mexican seasonings, cilantro is my favorite, not only because it's delicious but also because it's easy to find fresh. Mexican cooks are also fond of epazote—which Diana Kennedy says grows wild in New York's Central Park—but it's usually very difficult to find. Oregano is also a popular Mexican seasoning that dries well and can be found on the spice rack in any supermarket. (Look for *Mexican* oregano.)

Another interesting ingredient that Mexican cooks use to flavor soups is dried shrimp. A variety of large dried shrimp is sold in Mexico but is hard to find in the United States; the small dried shrimp found in Asian markets make a good substitute. The shrimp can be left whole or ground into a powder and stirred into the soup.

Mexicans are also fond of fresh seafood from both the Pacific and Gulf coasts and like to prepare stewlike soups from fresh fish, oysters, clams, and crabs. The *chilpachole* is a crab soup from Veracruz prepared in the same way as seafood soups from all over the world except that it's flavored with chilies, epazote, and a generous amount of garlic. Lime wedges, served at the table, give it a sprightly tang.

I had never been a big fan of tripe until I tasted a Mexican *menudo*—long-simmered tripe with chilies, cumin, sometimes hominy, and oregano.

MOROCCO   Moroccan food uses an amazing blend of typically Mediterranean ingredients and combines them with spices that are used only rarely in other Mediterranean countries.

Many of the spices that were popular in medieval Europe were gradually abandoned and displaced by local herbs and a less exotic style of cooking. In Morocco, this change never took place, and today many of the same combinations of ingredients that were popular more than 500 years ago are still used.

Moroccan cooks like to combine fruits such as dates, raisins, and apricots with savory meats. Some of these dishes are also sweetened further with honey. Another characteristic Moroccan flavor is preserved lemon, chopped and added to a number of soups and stews. Nuts, especially almonds, are also used in Morocco to make stews. I sometimes add toasted slivered almonds to Moroccan-style soups to give them an exotic flavor and a delightful crunch.

The Moroccan fondness for lamb accounts for the large number of lamb-based soups, including the best-known Moroccan soup, *harira*. Harira is made by first cooking lamb, celery, and onions in *smen* (the Moroccan equivalent of the Indian *ghee*) and then flavoring the mixture with turmeric, ginger, and cinnamon. Tomatoes and lentils are added, and the whole dish is served with lemon wedges and dusted with cinnamon.

While cooks in other Mediterranean countries like to finish their soups with flavorful sauces such as *aïoli*, *picada*, or *rouille*, Moroccan cooks have their own distinctive herb mixture, called *charmoula*. *Charmoula* is made by grinding together cilantro, parsley, garlic, vinegar, lemon juice, paprika, and cayenne into a pestolike paste. *Charmoula* is also sometimes used as a marinade for fish.

SOUTH AMERICA   I hope that lovers of South American cooking will forgive me the presumptuousness of trying to describe the cooking of an entire continent in a couple of paragraphs. South American cooking is a diverse mixture of European and native cooking that includes an array of *cocidos* (hot soups and stews), *ceviches* (marinaded fish and shellfish), and *chupes* (chowders). Many South American soups are reminiscent of traditional Spanish and Portuguese versions—they often even have the same names—but flavored with typically South American ingredients.

Chilies, both fresh and dried, are a frequent component in South American cooking, and many of the same varieties are used that are popular in Mexico and Latin America. South American cooks combine chilies with cilantro, tomatoes, and a wide assortment of herbs including oregano, thyme, dill, mint, and parsley.

Coconut milk is used in much the same way as in Southeast Asia—as a finish for soups and stews. The first time I tasted a *vatapa*—a Brazilian stewlike soup made with peanuts, ginger, tomatoes, and coconut milk—I thought I was tasting Thai food.

Many of the foods that are now popular all over the world are native to South America. Potatoes are of Peruvian origin, and varieties are still available there that are seen nowhere else. South American cooks are also fond of corn, which according to Felipe Rojas-Lombardi, in his book *The Art of South American Cooking*, has kernels the size of cherry tomatoes.

South Americans *chupes* are prepared all along the coasts of Chile, Peru, and Ecuador. A typical *chupe*—similar to a North American chowder but likely to be more highly seasoned—will probably be made with potatoes but may also contain chilies, spices such as mace, cumin, and ginger, herbs such as mint, oregano, or cilantro, and starches such as beans and hominy. Any seafood can enter into a *chupe*, but South Americans are especially fond of shellfish such as clams, shrimp, and crab.

Cooks from all over South America have come up with their own versions of meat soups adapted from the Spanish and Portuguese settlers. Many of these hearty soups are similar (many have the same names) to soups found in Spain and Portugal today. Most of them contain an assortment of meats, sausages, and typically South American vegetables simmered together for at least several hours. *Olla podrida* (originally Spanish but nowadays rarely found in Spain), *sancocho* from Ecuador (made with plantains and cabbage), *hervido* from Venezuela (made with corn, plantains, leeks, and mint), the Brazilian *vatapa*, and *puchero* from Argentina (made with hot pepper and the local chorizo) are just a few examples.

SPAIN Spanish soups are often hearty stewlike affairs made with an assortment of meats and sausages, beans, lentils, and sometimes fish and seafood. What a healthy Spanish peasant is likely to eat as an opener to a meal would probably suffice as a main course in a generous American dinner.

Although the best-known Spanish soups are elaborate and often require long cooking, the principles are simple; meats are simmered in water or broth with beans or chick-peas (garbanzos) until the meats are tender and the beans have absorbed most of the surrounding liquid. Faster-cooking meats such as sausage or chicken are added during the last hour of cooking.

FLAVORFUL FINISHES
FOR INTERNATIONAL SOUPS

In many countries soups are flavored by whisking pungent sauces and mixtures into the soup just before serving. Sometimes these sauces are also served at the table for guests to help themselves. The intense aroma of garlic and herbs so characteristic of Mediterranean fish soups comes from these special sauces. In France, *aïoli* or *rouille*—pungent mixtures of garlic or red peppers and saffron—are added to the soup and also served at the table. In Spain the elaborate *picada* or *romesco* is used as a flavorful thickener. In Morocco, *charmoula*, a mixture of cilantro, parsley, garlic, and cumin, is used both as a marinade and a finish for fish soups and stews.

Asian cooks stir heady spice mixtures into their soups just before serving. Thais make pungent curry pastes redolent with cilantro, hot chilies, and spices, while Indian cooks like to gently sauté freshly ground spices in Indian-style clarified butter (*ghee*) to make a rich and spicy finish called a *tadka*.

Some soups are finished with gentler and more delicately flavored ingredients such as a dollop of butter or sour cream or a dribble of olive oil. Herb butters—which can be made in advance and stored for months in the freezer—are also elegant finishes.

Some soups include ingredients designed to give them extra subtlety and finesse. Europeans use heavy cream, crème fraîche, and egg yolks; in Southeast Asia, coconut milk gives soups a satisfying delicacy and sweetness.

Except for gazpacho, the most famous Spanish soup is the stewlike *cocido*. An authentic *cocido* is prepared in much the same way as a French *potée;* meats including chicken, beef, and an array of sausages are simmered with chick-peas. Any broth that remains is then served first—in the same way as a French *pot-au-feu*—followed with a groaning platter of beans, vegetables, and meats to finish everyone off.

Another famous Spanish dish, the *fabada* from Asturias, reminds me of a soupy version of a French cassoulet. Sausages including *morcilla* (blood sausage) and *chorizo* are simmered with white beans and smoked pork and are presented in a white bean soup.

Although based on pork and beans as are so many Spanish soups, the *caldo gallego* is a lighter, more brothy version containing kale or Swiss chard and new potatoes.

Like the Italians, Spanish cooks often combine beans with seafood but with distinctive Spanish additions like a little hot chili pepper and a generous pinch of saffron.

While the Basques are known for their *marmitako*—fresh bonito or tuna simmered in a hearty mixture of tomatoes, garlic, chilies, and potatoes—the Catalans have developed a distinctive cuisine that takes advantage of Mediterranean seafood. One of its cornerstones is the *picada*, a heady paste made by grinding together almonds, garlic, olive oil, fried bread, and any number of fresh herbs. The paste is then swirled into seafood soups just before serving (see blue crab soup with *picada*, page 406). Catalonia's most famous soup is the *suquet*, made in much the same way as a Provençal *bouillabaisse* but finished with *picada* instead of *rouille*. The Catalan seafood soup/stew called *romesco* (page 314) is finished with a mixture containing not only almonds, fried bread, and garlic like a *picada*, but also hot peppers, hazelnuts, and tomatoes.

Spanish rice dishes, such as paellas and arroces (see page 282), can also be adapted for making into soup.

THAILAND Some people are intimidated by the idea of cooking Thai food, but once you get familiar with a few semiexotic ingredients, Thai soups are easy to improvise.

While European soups get much of their flavor from a basic broth made from meat or fish bones and trimmings, cooks in Southeast Asia rely on a variety of potent flavorings to give character to their soups. An almost universal flavoring is bottled fermented fish sauce, which ends up in practically everything, including meat dishes. Fish sauce is prepared by packing anchovies in barrels and capturing the liquid that runs out over a period of several months. Although to Western ears fish sauce does not sound appealing, you'll be amazed at how it improves the flavor of Thai and Vietnamese soups.

When Thai cooks prepare a soup, they make a flavor base in the same way as Western cooks, but instead of onions, carrots, and perhaps tomatoes, Thai cooks typically start out with finely chopped shallots, garlic, ginger, and hot peppers lightly browned in oil. To this is added light broth—usually chicken—or water and herbs such as lemongrass, kaffir lime leaves, galangal, mint, and basil. Sometimes Thai soups are finished with fairly elaborate curry pastes made by grinding together spices, chilies, and other flavorful ingredients in a mortar and pestle (see page 4).

European and American cooks often finish their soups with heavy cream, but Thai cooks use the Eastern equivalent, coconut milk. Tamarind—a sour paste taken from the tamarind pod—is often stirred into soups to give them a delightful sour tang. Lime juice makes a good substitute.

Two of Thailand's most popular soups are *tom yam gung*, a hot and sour shrimp soup flavored with fish sauce, lemongrass, kaffir lime leaves, and coriander; and *gaeng tom yam gai*, a chicken soup flavored with galangal, lemongrass, fish sauce, and coconut milk.

VIETNAM Although Vietnam has a distinct and lovely cooking of its own, many of the basic flavors are the same as those used in Thailand.

Vietnamese fish sauce (*nuoc mam*) has a stronger flavor than Thai fish sauce, but since authentic Vietnamese fish sauce cannot be imported into the United States, everyone uses the Thai version anyway. Look for a brand labeled *Phu Quoc* (an island off the coast of Vietnam once famous for its fish sauce). The term is now used simply to mean best quality. The best brand I've found is Flying Lion. Lemongrass and lime leaves are used in the same way as in Thai cooking, but Vietnamese cooks make more liberal use of mint and Asian "holy" basil—usually coarsely chopped and added to soups just before serving.

Vietnamese soups are also more likely to contain pineapple and tomatoes than their Thai counterparts. Bean sprouts are also used more often, best added to soups a minute or two before serving.

Several Vietnamese recipes include spices such as cinnamon, cloves, and star anise, while these ingredients are relatively uncommon in Thai cooking. Shrimp paste—made from fermented shrimp—is used throughout Southeast Asia, but it's only for the fearless: it will smell up the kitchen for days.

Both Thais and Vietnamese are very fond of noodles, but the best-known Thai soups contain no noodles, while most Vietnamese soups contain either rice noodles or cellophane (mung bean) noodles. *Pho*, which can mean any of many varieties of noodle soup, is so popular it might qualify as Vietnam's national dish. Typically eaten for breakfast, *pho* starts out with a spicy beef broth (or sometimes chicken broth) flavored with ginger, cinnamon, cloves, star anise, fennel seeds, and at times a little sugar. Rice noodles and thinly sliced beef are then simmered in the broth just before serving. Assorted condiments and garnishes such as lime wedges, basil, chopped chilies, bean sprouts, fish sauce, hoisin sauce, and pepper are then served at the table (or noodle stand) (see recipe, page 538).

Cutting Out
THE FAT

I ADMIT IT. I LOVE CREAM, BUTTER, COCONUT MILK, BACON, DUCK FAT, OLIVE OIL, and almost any other tasty fatty thing. I was trained in Paris restaurants, where tubs of Norman butter and crème fraîche were set out for the cooks to whisk into the sauces. I loved the cooking in those places, and I've resisted every teaspoon I've since had to cut out.

But I've had to face the music. Sometime during the early 1980s my students started looking at each other incredulously—with horror and, yes, a certain delight—every time I'd casually throw in a hefty amount of cream or butter. So I've cut back and gradually become satisfied with much less fat.

Fortunately, after such a long romance with cream and butter I still fit into the same size clothes I've been wearing for years, but I have less tolerance for fatty foods. If the food is too rich, I quickly get full—and when I get up from the table I just want to go to sleep.

On the other hand, I'm surprised by and perhaps a little resentful of the way some people eat. I've been out with people who tremble at the idea of a tablespoon of butter in a bowl of healthy vegetable soup but who spread three times that much on bread before dinner or who order a slice of cheesecake for dessert.

My recommendation is moderation without abstinence, but here are a few more concrete suggestions:

1. Don't allow meat broths to boil. If the broth is allowed to boil, the fat will be churned back into the broth rather than floating to the top, not only making the broth fattier and more caloric but also giving it a greasy taste and feel in the mouth.

2. Carefully skim any fat off the soup. Because butter, oil, and animal fats are lighter than water, most of the fat used to prepare a soup will float to the top as the soup is cooking so that you can skim it off. Do so as you see it accumulate during simmering and then, if you have time, store the soup overnight in the refrigerator so the fat congeals on top and can then be easily removed with a spoon.

3. Don't precook the vegetables in fat. Most soup recipes, including those in this book, suggest cooking some of the ingredients, especially vegetables, in fat (usually butter, olive oil, or rendered animal fat) before any liquid is added because the fat helps to bring out the flavor of the vegetables. Most of this fat will float to the top of the soup and can be skimmed off with a ladle, but if you're being very careful about fat, just combine the vegetables directly with the liquid and simmer them until they soften.

4. Thicken soups with vegetable purees. **Many soups contain heavy cream and butter—usually added at the end—to give them a rich flavor and a silky texture. You can accomplish almost the same effect by using finely pureed vegetables such as waxy potatoes and root vegetables (boil until soft, then puree in a food mill or ricer), garlic (roast whole heads or blanch individual unpeeled cloves, then push through a medium-mesh strainer), spinach and green vegetables (blanch in boiling water until soft, puree in a blender or food processor, or work through a food mill), or mushrooms (puree raw in a blender or food processor, cook down until thick, then strain through a medium-mesh strainer).**

5. Use fats judiciously. **Many traditional soups are finished with cream, butter, or coconut milk or sprinkled with croutons cooked in olive oil or butter. A little bit of a rich ingredient will go a long way; 2 tablespoons of heavy cream is often enough though the recipe calls for a whole cup; a tiny dollop of butter swirled into the finished soup will give it a buttery flavor and smooth texture. Remember also that even 1/2 cup of heavy cream used in a recipe for 8 servings comes out to only 1 tablespoon per serving.**

6. Substitute lighter ingredients. **Cooks are often confused about when and where it's appropriate to substitute lighter ingredients for rich ones such as cream, butter, or olive oil. Here are some guidelines for substituting ingredients.**

Yogurt: **Often yogurt can be swirled into a soup shortly before serving as a substitute for heavy cream, but because of its sour tang it doesn't work with all ingredients. I especially like yogurt in Indian-style bean and lentil soups or in fish soups. Once you've added yogurt to a soup, don't let the soup boil, or the yogurt will curdle. Low-fat and nonfat yogurt work as well as whole-milk yogurt.**

Sour Cream: **Sour cream is especially wonderful when dolloped on a bowl of black bean soup or on hot Mexican-style soups. Sour cream certainly doesn't qualify as diet food, but it has half the fat of heavy cream or crème fraîche. If you decide to whisk sour cream into a soup as a substitute for heavy cream, don't let the soup boil, or the sour cream will separate.**

Vegetable Oils: **Many cooks like to substitute light—and flavorless—vegetable oils for more saturated fats such as olive oil, butter, or rendered animal fats. It's certainly possible to make perfectly good soups using these oils, but unless you're being very strict (and remember, the calorie and fat count is the same), the flavor trade-off isn't worth the small saving in saturated fat. Mass-produced vegetable oils contribute nothing to the soup. Sometimes the kind of oil you use is of little importance because its flavor won't come through in the finished soup anyway. For instance, if you're sautéeing meat in oil and the soup is then simmered for a long time the flavor of the oil will disappear in the process. My own standby for sautéing is pure olive oil (not extra virgin, which would lose its delicacy) except for Asian soups, where olive** oil doesn't seem appropriate. My favorite oil for Asian soups is peanut oil but vegetable oil will work in a pinch.

7. Pass rich ingredients at the table so your guests have a choice. Many of the ingredients recommended in this book as last-minute finishes and garnishes can be passed at the table so your guests can add what they want. My guests love passing things around at the table—and if they don't know each other, it gets them chatting. Depending on what kind of soup I'm serving, I pass croutons, whipped or sliced herb butters, sour cream, créme fraîche, lightly whipped cream, olive oil, finely chopped hot peppers, Tabasco, Thai fish sauce, and innumerable little dipping sauces.

8. Make lighter soups to begin with. Many soups contain very little or no fat. A simple, well-skimmed broth is a good place to start. Asian cooks are experts at getting a lot of flavor out of their ingredients without using fat. Japanese *dashi* and Thai soups—those without coconut milk—contain virtually no fat.

What to Drink
WITH SOUP

I'VE HEARD IT SAID THAT SERVING ANOTHER LIQUID WITH A BOWL OF SOUP IS REDUN-
dant, because soup satisfies one's need for both liquid and solid. This might be logical,
but it's certainly not much fun.

My first thought at any meal after "What are we having?" is "What are we drinking?" This almost always means wine, but occasionally in the summer or with a hot
Asian or Mexican soup, beer enters the choices.

I take a haphazard approach to choosing wine, based more on whim and a sudden
craving for certain flavors rather than on predetermined rules and concepts.

I prefer red wine to white, and unless I'm serving my soup as the first course of a
dinner where red wine is being served with one of the upcoming courses, I almost always
opt for red—even with fish soups. Cold soups and shellfish soups are the one exception—I always serve them with a dry white wine.

If I'm being fancy and serving a meal with a couple of courses, I'm likely to buy
more expensive wine, and I'm a little more careful about matching it up with the food so
that neither the wine nor the food takes over. I won't serve a French Chablis with a hearty
bowl of black bean soup—the wine's delicacy and complexity will be completely overwhelmed. On the other hand, I don't want to serve a wine that's heavy or too alcoholic.
A Chardonnay from California might have the body and flavors to compete with the
soup, but may be a bit too rich to serve as the first wine of a meal. I more likely would
serve a crisp Alsatian Pinot Blanc or Sylvaner—at the risk of overwhelming the wine's
flavor somewhat. The freshness of these wines makes them a perfect counterbalance to
rich and hearty soups. One reliable guideline for selecting wine for a meal is to stick to a
particular country or region and then limit your wines to that place. I'm often amazed
by how wines from a particular country or region are a perfect match for foods from that
place. It also makes an interesting meal for your guests to have wines from places other
than France or California.

Be sure to serve wine well chilled when serving it with cold soups; otherwise the
soup will be colder than the wine and the wine will taste flat. One approach for special
dinners is to serve champagne to the guests when they arrive and then keep serving the
same champagne through the soup course. The sparkle in champagne is a perfect foil for
cold soups or for soups that are somewhat sour, such as the cream of sorrel soup on
page 212.

Although I almost invariably serve red wine with full-meal soups, I'll decide on the
type of wine largely depending on the style and formality of the meal. In the winter I
like to serve *pot-au-feu* for an informal Sunday lunch. There should be plenty of wine but
a wine that's light—so people can drink without getting knocked out or wanting to go

to sleep in half an hour. For a dinner like this I put out a light, inexpensive French Chardonnay such as a Mâcon-Villages or a St.-Véran for people who like white and then bottles of cool Beaujolais. Each of these wines has enough body to hold up to the *pot-au-feu* but is light enough for people to drink freely.

At more formal dinners, where a main-course soup is being served, I serve more serious wines that require a little more attention and that people will sip more slowly. If I'm serving a luxurious soup such as the medallions of beef with caramelized onions and red wine broth on page 98, I'll likely serve a French Bordeaux or a California Cabernet; with duck or a full-flavored chicken soup, French Burgundy or a good California Pinot Noir.

If I'm serving a hearty peasant soup such as a *garbure*, I may try to seek out a wine from the region where the dish originated (the French Southwest) such as a Cahors, a Côtes de Buzet, or a Madiran. Most of the wines from these little-known French regions are amazingly inexpensive, and even the most jaded guests are unlikely to have sampled them.

Pairing wines with Asian soups can be complicated because there is little tradition of drinking wine at Asian meals. With European dishes we can be almost sure that a dish from a particular region will go reasonably well with a wine from that same region. But with Asian foods we must base our decision purely on flavor. When I used to go out for Chinese food with French friends in Paris, the only wine that was considered acceptable drinking was Gewürztraminer or, with a little luck, Riesling. I enjoy both of these wines, but limiting my choices to these two with something so diverse as Chinese cooking takes away half the fun. I've since gotten more adventurous and found that red wines—especially from the Rhône valley and Rhône-style wines from California—match the bold but subtle flavors of Chinese and Southeast Asian cooking.

I love Japanese soups—miso soup is one of the few soups I can imagine having for breakfast—but I've never grown fond of sake. It's not that I dislike it, but I'm always wishing I could have a glass of white wine instead. Most Japanese soups contain *dashi*, whose delicate smokiness goes well with French white Burgundy or California Chardonnay. With miso soups, a French Sauvignon Blanc (Sancerre) works very well.

Dessert soups are a perfect match for dessert wines. Because dessert wines are expensive, I serve them only occasionally, so they are always a special treat. It can sometimes be hard to pair a dessert with a dessert wine because the dessert must be less sweet than the wine, the dessert mustn't be too cold, and chocolate is a disaster. Fruit soups are a perfect match for sweet wines, provided the dessert isn't too sweet. French Sauternes, late-harvest California Riesling, late-harvest German Riesling (Beerenauslese, trockenbeerenauslese), Muscat wines such as Muscat de Beaumes de Venise, and Hungarian Tokay are just a few examples of dessert wines that go well with fruit soups.

Dessert soups can also be served with champagne, but I wouldn't use a great champagne at this stage, because its delicacy is liable to be overwhelmed by the soup's sweet and fruity flavors. If I'm serving one of my "serious" dinners, I like to keep a bottle of champagne in reserve to serve *after* coffee, when my guests are starting to feel tired and need a little refreshment. And champagne at this point is so unexpected that everyone is delighted and surprised.

The only time I hesitate to serve wine with soup is if the soup is fiery hot. It's not that the wine doesn't taste good—although any subtlety is annihilated—but that my guests and I end up guzzling just to cool our mouths, with obvious results. I must admit that I approach a wineless meal with diminished enthusiasm, but sometimes a gathering around a hot pot of Thai or Vietnamese soup is best accompanied with ice cold beer. When I'm serving beer with Asian soups, I always try to find beer from that country; these beers aren't better than good European or American microbrewery beers, but they contribute to the adventure of trying foods that may be new or excitingly foreign.

"There are a few tricks for making broth delicious . . ."

Broths, Consommés, and Simple Broth-Based

SOUPS

Many cooks who gladly spend hours in the kitchen baking or preparing elaborate dinners are thrown into a panic when it comes to preparing a simple chicken broth. Although there are a few tricks for making broth clear and especially delicious, slowly simmering meat, fish, or bones are all that is needed. Once you get the broth going, you can set it on the back of the stove and, except for occasional skimming of fat and froth, forget about it. The actual time spent working in the kitchen is 15 or 20 minutes, and the result is well worth it.

Methods for Making Broth: White and Brown

The easiest way to make broth is to combine meat or fish trimmings and bones with flavorful vegetables such as carrots, onions, garlic, and celery, plus a bouquet garni, and then add enough cold water to cover. Professionals call broth made in this way *white stock* because none of the ingredients is browned ahead of time. White stock is best used as a backdrop for other flavors and in pureed soups or pale soups, where a deeply colored broth would interfere with the soup's appearance.

For most soups, use a clear broth with an appetizing deep brown color. For this broth, you need to brown the meat or bones before putting them into a pot with the water. If you're making more than a quart or two of broth, it is easiest to spread the bones and vegetables (leave the skin on the onions; they provide color) on a sheet pan and bake them in a 400°F oven for about 45 minutes, until well browned. Pull the pan out of the oven—let it cool for a few minutes so it's easier to work with—and scrape the cooked bones, vegetables, and any juices in the pan into a pot. Cover it with cold water and finish it in the same way as white stock.

If you're making only a small amount of broth, it's usually easier to brown the bones and vegetables with a tablespoon of vegetable oil in a small pot on top of the stove before adding water. This usually takes about 20 minutes.

SIMMERING VERSUS BOILING

Despite what many recipes say, it's essential to cook broth at a slow simmer. Broth that is allowed to boil will not cook any faster, and any fat rendered by the meat or bones will be churned back into the broth instead of floating to the top where it can be skimmed off. Broth that has been boiled is cloudy and has a greasy taste and feel in the mouth.

Broth should always be cooked uncovered so that it can be easily skimmed of fat and froth. Certain long-cooking soups, however, are cooked covered; because it is sometimes difficult to maintain these at a slow simmer on top of the stove, you may find it easier to cook covered soups in a 275°F oven.

Broth Made from Poultry, Beef, or Fish

The methods for making broth are the same regardless of the ingredients; the only difference is simmering time. Fish bones fall apart and give up their flavor to the surrounding liquid in about 20 minutes, while beef knuckle bones take about 12 hours to give their all. Chicken parts fall in between—about 3 hours.

Using Meat Versus Bones

Unlike their 19th-century counterparts, which were made with whole hens or slabs of meat, most contemporary broths are made from bones and trimmings. If broth is being used as a backdrop for other flavors (technically, this is called *stock*)—as in vegetable soups—it isn't necessary to use meat. When broth is being served alone or as the basis for a consommé, the flavor depends entirely on the ingredients used to make the broth—which will benefit from using meat instead of bones.

Using meat does not have to be as extravagant as it sounds. A flavorful stewing hen costs little more than the price of a chicken, and beef chuck and other stewing cuts are usually quite reasonable. You can also use leftover cooked meat—well seasoned with chopped fresh herbs—in salads or as ravioli filling.

Making a Bouquet Garni

A traditional bouquet garni is a collection of fresh herbs tied up in a bundle with string so they don't float around in the broth and interfere with skimming. In the United States, where until recently fresh herbs except parsley were almost impossible to find, most recipes recommend making a little packet of dried herbs and fresh parsley in cheesecloth. This is still the best method if you don't have access to fresh thyme or other herbs you may want to include in the bouquet garni.

If you have fresh herbs, simply bundle the herbs together with string. Although parsley, thyme, and bay leaves are the traditional components of a bouquet garni, you can substitute herbs to come up with different nuances. I often use rosemary or marjoram in broths for Italian soups and sometimes fresh tarragon in chicken broth.

Most cooks make their bouquet garnis so small that they couldn't possibly improve the flavor of the broth. The size of the bouquet garni should be adjusted according to how much soup you're making. For 4 quarts of broth I use the following:

MAKING BROTH FROM
LEFTOVER ROAST MEATS

Although the best meat broth is made from raw meats and bones, very decent broth can be made from bones and trimmings of leftover roasts, turkey, chicken, and duck carcasses, and even leftover stews. When you're making broth from leftover chicken or turkey, be sure to break up the carcasses so they will take up less room in the pot. Otherwise you'll end up having to add too much water, and the broth will be too weak. Because bones and trimmings from roasts have already been cooked, there is no need for preliminary browning—the meat and vegetables can go straight into the pot. Just a few things to watch out for: don't add chunks of fat or skin to the broth, don't let the broth boil, and regularly skim off fat and scum.

for a fresh bouquet garni (tied together with string):

10 fresh thyme sprigs

1 large bunch of parsley

1 bay leaf

for a dried bouquet garni (in a cheesecloth packet)

2 teaspoons dried thyme leaves (never ground thyme)

1 bunch of parsley, including stems, coarsely chopped

1 bay leaf, crumbled

Storing Broth

It makes more sense to prepare a pot of broth on a rainy Sunday and keep it around for throwing together last-minute soups than it does to wait around for a broth to cook every time you want to make a simple soup.

Broth is easy to freeze, but not everyone has freezer space for more than a couple of recipes' worth. If you don't have room, you can refrigerate the broth for 5 days without its spoiling. To keep it longer, just bring it to a simmer on top of the stove for 10 minutes, let it cool, and then refrigerate it for up to another 5 days. You can repeat this trick indefinitely.

If you do decide to freeze broth, store it in quantities that you're likely to need; don't freeze it in gallon containers, or you'll have to thaw the whole thing when you need only a few bowlfuls of soup. I freeze broth in 1-quart containers; square containers take up less room in the freezer than round ones.

Put the hot broth into heat-resistant freezer containers and let it cool to room temperature. Then refrigerate for a few hours or overnight before putting it into the freezer. Putting warm broth directly into the freezer may cause other frozen foods to spoil.

CONCENTRATED BROTHS
AND GLAZES

A number of high-quality concentrated broths have appeared on the market in recent years, including my favorite, Demi-Glace Gold, from More-Than-Gourmet (see Sources, page 611). This company also makes concentrated glazes and broths from chicken, duck, and seafood, which, when thinned with water, rival homemade broths and are certainly better than canned broth. The only disadvantage to these concentrated broths is their cost, which tends to be high.

Fast Broths

Canned or instant broth is never going to taste homemade, but if you need broth fast and don't have any in the refrigerator or freezer, commercial broth will do. Use it only with flavorful vegetables or meats, though, never when the flavor of the broth is the primary flavor of the soup—not, for instance, for consommé or brothlike soups with just a few tidbits floating in them.

The best approach to choosing among the brands of commercial broth available in your area is to experiment with them. The biggest problem with commercial broth used to be excess salt, but in the last couple of years several manufacturers have come up with better-tasting low-sodium versions. (I have found low-sodium versions of only chicken broth, not beef broth.) Even these are still somewhat salty, so add salt (or salty ingredients such as fish sauce) to any commercial broth only to taste. To improve the flavor of canned broth, see the box on this page.

Even though recipes often call for them, I've had no luck using bouillon cubes. They seem to add only a stale vegetable flavor with none of the meaty richness that makes broth satisfying. Rumor has it that European bouillon cubes are better tasting than their American counterparts, but I've experimented with both and haven't been able to tell the difference.

Chinese restaurants will usually sell homemade chicken broth that you can use in your soups. Although this broth is sometimes a little light in flavor, it is authentic and better tasting than canned. And you can even have it delivered!

IMPROVING

COMMERCIAL BROTH

Canned broth always has a distinctive taste—not necessarily unpleasant but one that I always recognize. (Try ordering French onion soup in a cheap restaurant.) If all you have is commercial broth, you can greatly improve it and give it a fresh flavor with a few herbs and vegetables. Coarsely chop a small onion, $1/2$ a carrot, and $1/2$ celery rib for each quart of broth. Make a bouquet garni (preferably with fresh herbs) and simmer everything together slowly, partially covered, for 45 minutes. Strain.

Double and Triple Broth

Occasionally, if you want an extra-rich, deeply flavored broth, or if you're stuck with more bones or meat trimmings than you know what to do with, you can make a double or triple broth. A double broth is simply a broth made with another broth instead of water. A triple broth is made using double broth to moisten another set of bones or meat trimmings.

Making double and triple broth sometimes makes sense if you don't have a lot of storage space. Because these broths are so concentrated, you can use less in recipes that call for ordinary broth and make up the difference with water. (Add equal parts water to a double broth and two parts to a triple broth.)

What to Do with Meats Left Over from Making Broth

As mentioned earlier, sometimes generous seasoning can make meat used for broth usable in salads or ravioli. Generally, though, it will be dried out and short on flavor. Chop it up and serve it to the family pet.

An alternative is to simmer the meat or fish in the broth just long enough to cook it through and then serve it right away or have it cold the next day. Obviously, however, broth made this way will be very light, because the meat or fish won't have released all its flavor into the surrounding liquid.

Basic Brown Chicken Broth

This simple broth is the cornerstone for many a delicious soup. Even though it involves an extra step—browning the bones and vegetables—it comes out perfectly clear and an appetizing brown.

MAKES 3 ½ QUARTS

6 pounds chicken backs, necks, or bones
1 medium-size onion, coarsely chopped
1 medium-size carrot, coarsely chopped
1 celery rib, chopped
4½ quarts cold water or enough to cover
1 bouquet garni

PREHEAT the oven to 450°F. Trim extra fat off the chicken parts and spread them in a heavy-bottomed roasting pan or large skillet with the chopped vegetables. Roast them until they are well browned, usually 45 minutes to an hour. Do not let the bottom of the roasting pan burn.

REMOVE the roasting pan from the oven, transfer the chicken and vegetables to an 8- to 10-quart pot, and pour off or ladle off any grease in the bottom of the roasting pan. Discard the grease. Pour 2 cups water into the roasting pan and scrape the bottom with a wooden spoon to dissolve the juices adhering to the bottom.

PUT the bouquet garni into the pot with the chicken and vegetables and pour over the contents of the roasting pan. Add the rest of the water or slightly more or less if necessary to barely cover the chicken parts.

HEAT over medium heat until the water comes to a simmer. Turn the heat down low enough to keep the broth at a slow simmer and cook for about 3 hours. Every 30 minutes, skim off any fat or froth that comes to the surface.

WHEN the broth is done, strain it into a clean pot or heat-resistant plastic container. Let it cool, uncovered, for an hour before putting it in the refrigerator. The next day, when the broth is cold, spoon off and discard any fat that has congealed on its surface.

Basic White Chicken Broth

This is the simplest of all broths to make. You simply simmer chicken parts and vegetables with water. White chicken broth is better for pale soups, where the color of brown chicken broth would interfere.

MAKES 3½ QUARTS

6 pounds chicken backs, necks, or bones or a 6-pound
    stewing hen, cut into 8 pieces
1 medium-size onion, coarsely chopped
1 medium-size carrot, coarsely chopped
1 celery rib, chopped
1 bouquet garni
4½ quarts cold water or enough to cover

TRIM excess fat off the chicken parts. If you're using a stewing hen, trim off the fat and the skin. Put the chopped vegetables and the bouquet garni in the bottom of a 10- or 12-quart pot (these are added first so they don't float to the top and interfere with skimming), add the chicken parts, and pour over enough water to barely cover.

HEAT over medium to high heat until the water comes to a simmer. Turn the heat down low enough to keep the broth at a slow simmer and cook for about 3 hours. For the first 30 minutes, occasionally skim off any fat or froth that comes to the surface.

WHEN the broth is done, strain it into a clean pot or heat-resistant plastic container. Let it cool, uncovered, for an hour before putting it in the refrigerator. The next day, when the broth is cold, spoon off and discard any fat that has congealed on its surface.

BROTH FOR CHINESE SOUPS

Chinese soups require a broth with a different backdrop of flavors than Western-style broth. If you're going to make chicken broth to use in Chinese recipes, leave out the onion, carrot, celery, and bouquet garni and add instead a ½-inch chunk of finely sliced fresh ginger and 3 crushed garlic cloves when you add the water.

If you already have chicken broth on hand and want to use it in a Chinese soup, simmer it for 20 minutes with a slice or two of fresh ginger.

Turkey Broth

I always make a delicious soup from the turkey carcass left over from holiday feasting. Although the broth is perfectly satisfying as a soup, I usually add diced vegetables, little strips of cooked turkey, or noodles, just to make it more substantial. Turkey broth can also be clarified and used as the base for an elegant consommé.

MAKES 3 TO 5 QUARTS

the leftover carcass from a cooked 12- to 20-pound turkey

1 medium-size onion, coarsely chopped

1 medium-size carrot, coarsely chopped

1 celery rib, chopped

1 bouquet garni

3 to 5 quarts cold water, just enough to cover

BREAK up the main part of the turkey—the back and breastbone—so it will fit into the soup pot without taking up too much room. Put the chopped vegetables and the bouquet garni in a 12-quart pot and add the broken-up turkey bones. Add enough cold water to barely cover the bones.

HEAT over medium heat until the water comes to a simmer. Turn the heat down low enough to keep the broth at a slow simmer and cook for about 3 hours. Every half hour, skim off any fat or froth that floats to the top with a ladle.

WHEN the broth is done, strain it into a clean pot or heat-resistant plastic container. Let it cool, uncovered, for an hour before putting it in the refrigerator. The next day, when the broth is cold, spoon off and discard any fat that has congealed on its surface.

Pork Broth

Although Asian cooks frequently use pork broth as a soup base, it rarely occurs to Western cooks to use it. In my opinion it's the most savory and satisfying of all meat broths. Because pork is relatively inexpensive, you can use meat instead of relying on bones alone.

Whole pork shoulder is the most economical cut to use for broth, but since there is little call for the whole shoulder it usually has to be ordered in advance. A quicker solution is to use shoulder pork chops from the local butcher or supermarket.

Although the easiest method for making pork broth is to simmer the pork directly in water, you'll get a deeper colored and more savory broth by browning the pork in a sauté pan in a little oil before adding the water or by browning the meat in the oven for large quantities.

Depending on how you're going to use the broth, you can flavor it with the usual aromatic vegetables such as carrots and onions and a bouquet garni, or, for Chinese or other Asian recipes, you can simmer ginger and garlic with the broth for flavoring.

MAKES 2 QUARTS

3 tablespoons canola or safflower oil

4 pounds shoulder pork chops or pork shoulder cut into
   1-inch cubes

for western-style soups:

1 medium-size onion, coarsely chopped

1 medium-size carrot, coarsely chopped

1 celery rib, chopped

1 bouquet garni

for asian-style soups:

1 medium-size onion, coarsely chopped

2 garlic cloves, crushed

2 ¼-inch slices of fresh ginger

STOVETOP METHOD Carefully dry the shoulder chops or cubes with paper towels to help them brown. Heat 1½ tablespoons of the oil over high heat in a 4-quart pot until it begins to smoke. Brown the shoulder chops or cubes on all sides. With a slotted spoon, transfer the browned pork to a mixing bowl.

POUR the burned oil out of the pot and add the remaining fresh oil. Lightly brown the chopped vegetables (whichever style you have chosen) over medium heat for about 5 minutes. Return the meat to the pot and add just enough water to cover.

OVEN METHOD Preheat the oven to 400°F. Spread the meat and vegetables (except the ginger if you're using it) in a heavy-bottomed roasting pan. Bake until the meat is well browned, about 30 minutes. If the vegetables start to burn, add a cup of water to prevent further burning.

TRANSFER the meat and vegetables to a 4-quart pot. Add a cup of water to the roasting pan, scrape up any juices, and pour the liquid over the meat. Add just enough water to cover.

HEAT over medium heat until the water comes to a slow simmer. Turn the heat down low enough to keep the broth at a slow simmer and cook for about 3 hours, skimming every half hour. With a ladle, skim off any fat or froth that floats to the top.

WHEN the broth is done, strain it into a clean pot or heat-resistant plastic container. Let it cool, uncovered, for an hour before putting it in the refrigerator. The next day, when the broth is cold, spoon off and discard any fat that has congealed on its surface.

Lamb Broth

Because lamb broth has a distinctive flavor that can easily take over a delicate soup, it doesn't have the universal appeal of chicken or pork broth. But in some soups, especially those from the Middle East or North Africa, there is no substitute.

Lamb shanks make the best broth, but they can be a nuisance to track down. Lamb shoulder chops make a good substitute.

MAKES 2 QUARTS

4 pounds lamb shanks, cut in half crosswise, or 4 pounds shoulder lamb chops
I medium-size onion, coarsely chopped
I medium-size carrot, coarsely chopped
I celery rib, chopped
I bouquet garni

PREHEAT the oven to 425°F. Spread the meat and vegetables in a single layer in a roasting pan or heavy-bottomed skillet. Roast them until well browned, about 40 minutes.

TRANSFER the meat and vegetables to a 4-quart pot and add the bouquet garni. Add a cup of water to the roasting pan, scrape up any juices, and pour the liquid over the meat. Add just enough water to cover, about 2 quarts.

HEAT over medium heat until the water comes to a slow simmer. Turn the heat down low enough to keep the broth at a slow simmer and cook for about 3 hours. With a ladle, skim off any fat or froth that floats to the top.

WHEN the broth is done, strain it into a clean pot or heat-resistant plastic container. Let it cool, uncovered, for an hour before putting it in the refrigerator. The next day, when the broth is cold, spoon off and discard any fat that has congealed on its surface.

Veal Broth

Veal broth was the almost universal liquid base for French classic *velouté* and cream soups. Nowadays most cooks find veal too expensive to use for making broth and use chicken broth instead. But if you use an inexpensive cut—breast is surprisingly cheap—a good full-flavored veal broth is not as expensive as you might think. And a well-made veal stock gives an extra dimension and depth of flavor to delicate vegetable soups.

Because veal comes from young animals, the meat contains a large amount of albumin, which can cloud the broth and make it an unpleasant gray. There are two ways around this: make brown stock (roast the veal and vegetables before adding water) or blanch the meat by putting it in a pot with enough cold water to cover, bring to a simmer, and then rinse the meat in cold running water.

MAKES 2 QUARTS

4 pounds veal breast, including bones
I medium-size onion, coarsely chopped
I medium-size carrot, coarsely chopped
I celery rib, chopped
I bouquet garni

TRIM any large chunks of fat off the veal breast and slice it into pieces by cutting between the ribs.

FOR WHITE BROTH Put the veal breast in a pot and add enough cold water to cover. Bring to a boil over high heat and let boil for 2 minutes. Drain in a colander and rinse the bones and meat thoroughly under cold running water.

PLACE the vegetables in a 4-quart pot and add the blanched meat, the bouquet garni, and enough cold water to cover. Bring to a slow simmer. Simmer gently for 4 hours, skimming off fat and froth as needed and adding water from time to time to keep the bones covered.

FOR BROWN BROTH Preheat the oven to 425°F. Spread the meat and vegetables in a single layer in a roasting pan or heavy-bottomed skillet. Roast them until well browned, about 40 minutes.

TRANSFER the meat, vegetables, and bouquet garni to a 4-quart pot. Add a cup of water to the roasting pan, scrape up any juices, and pour the liquid over the meat. Add just enough water to cover.

HEAT over medium heat until the water comes to a slow simmer. Turn the heat down low enough to keep the broth at a slow simmer and cook for about 4 hours. Every half hour, skim off any fat or froth that floats to the top with a ladle.

WHEN the broth is done, strain it into a clean pot or heat-resistant plastic container. Let it cool, uncovered, for an hour before putting it in the refrigerator. The next day, when the broth is cold, spoon off and discard any fat that has congealed on its surface.

Vegetable Broth

The strong flavor of meat sometimes interferes with the delicate flavor of certain vegetables, and more people than ever are reducing the amount of meat in their diet. Vegetable broth is a light and delicate alternative to meat broth. It is also a good way to use leek greens, mushroom stems, the juices squeezed out of seeded tomatoes, fennel branches, even turnip trimmings. This recipe includes a good balance of vegetables, but don't feel like you have to follow it exactly—you're probably not going to have all the vegetables it calls for anyway. I just use what I have around.

If you like to add wine to your broth—which is a good idea especially if you're using the broth to make fish soup—don't add the wine until the vegetables have cooked for at least 20 minutes. If the wine is added too soon, the vegetables won't soften and release their flavor into the surrounding liquid.

MAKES ABOUT 2 QUARTS

2 unpeeled carrots, sliced

2 leeks, both white and green parts, washed and sliced

greens from 1 fennel bulb or the bulb itself, sliced

2 turnips, peeled and sliced

1 large onion, sliced

3 unpeeled garlic cloves, cut in half

1 bunch of parsley or the stems from 2 bunches

4 fresh thyme sprigs or 1 teaspoon dried

I bay leaf

I cup mushroom stems

I tablespoon black peppercorns

I cup dry white wine

COMBINE all the ingredients except the peppercorns and wine in a 4-quart pot. Pour over just enough water to cover and heat on high heat until the liquid comes to a boil. Turn the heat down, cover the pot, and keep the broth at a slow simmer.

WHEN the vegetables have simmered for 30 minutes, add the peppercorns and white wine and simmer for 10 minutes more. Strain through a medium-mesh strainer and into a clean pot or heat-resistant plastic container. Let it cool, uncovered, for an hour before putting it in the refrigerator.

SUGGESTIONS AND VARIATIONS | This broth is a great backdrop for vegetable and fish soups because it has a neutral vegetable flavor—no particular vegetable or flavoring stands out and takes over. Sometimes, however, you may want a broth with the distinct flavor of one particular vegetable or herb. You may want a garlic broth to poach a piece of fish or to drink by itself (just simmer 3 broken-up garlic heads in a quart of water and strain after 30 minutes), or if you're lucky enough to have lots of mushroom stems left over from the stuffed mushrooms served at last night's cocktail party, you can make a delicious broth flavored with mushrooms alone. Add a little salt and pepper, perhaps a bit of cream, and you have a delicious mushroom soup. Simple pureed soups such as corn or tomato can also be used as the base for more elaborate vegetable soups.

FRESH herbs can also be used to make distinctively flavored broths. Because fresh herbs are expensive to buy in large quantities, you'll most likely want to make these broths if you grow your own herbs and have a lot left over when the winter sets in.

SIMMER a handful of fresh thyme or marjoram in a quart of water for 30 minutes, strain it, and then use it to simmer 4 or 5 zucchini or summer squash or maybe a few handfuls of mushrooms. Serve the soup with French bread toasts and good Parmesan cheese passed at the table.

HOW MUCH LIQUID FOR THE BROTH?

To make rich and flavorful broth, you should add only enough liquid to barely cover the solid ingredients. The exact amount of liquid you need will of course depend on how tightly packed are the meat and vegetables, but as a general rule figure on a pint of liquid to a pound of solid ingredients.

If as the broth cooks the liquid evaporates so that solid ingredients are sticking out above the surface, add just enough cold water to cover.

Dried Porcini Broth

This is one of my favorite answers to the need for a quick and easy broth to use as a base for delicate soups including the herb soup on page 188. Its only drawback is that dried porcini can be expensive; it pays to shop around. They keep indefinitely, though, and I always make sure to have some around. This broth also freezes well. This recipe is made with a little chopped Italian ham, but if you don't eat meat or don't have any, just leave it out.

MAKES 2 QUARTS

¼ pound dried porcini
10 cups cold water
1 small onion, finely chopped
1 garlic clove, finely chopped
2 ounces prosciutto, cut into ¼-inch dice
2 tablespoons unsalted butter or olive oil

SOAK the porcini in 2 cups cold water for 30 minutes. Drain the porcini and save the soaking liquid. Check the porcini and, if necessary, rinse them quickly to eliminate dirt and grit.

COOK the rest of the ingredients in a 4-quart pot over medium heat for 5 minutes. Add the drained porcini and cook for 5 minutes more. Add the soaking liquid— pour it in slowly, leaving any grit behind (or if necessary strain it through a cloth napkin or coffee filter)—and the remaining 8 cups water. Cover the pot, bring to a boil, and simmer slowly for 30 minutes. Strain through a fine-mesh strainer and discard the porcini.

Clear
BROTHS

FOR SOME SOUPS YOU WILL NEED TO USE A PERFECTLY CLEAR BROTH. ODDLY ENOUGH, white broth—if it's made with bones—will stay cloudy no matter how carefully you skim it and keep it at a slow simmer. If you need a clear broth, make a brown broth or a white broth made from whole chicken parts with the skin removed.

Even brown broth that is carefully skimmed and prevented from boiling will remain slightly cloudy because of minute particles of protein that get stirred up when you strain it. The only way to eliminate these particles is to strain the broth through a triple layer of cheesecloth or a cloth napkin. Any broth, white or brown, can of course be clarified with egg whites, but I always avoid this extra step if I can.

Straining Through Cheesecloth or a Napkin

Line a wide strainer with a triple layer of cheesecloth or a cloth napkin. Be sure to rinse the cheesecloth or napkin thoroughly to get rid of any residual soap or bleach. Place the strainer over a large bowl or pot and ladle in the broth. After a couple of minutes, you'll notice that the broth is going through the cloth very slowly. Gently pull the cloth to one side so the broth is sitting over an unused section. Keep doing this until all the broth has been strained.

WHY MEAT CLARIFIES

The protein in meat slowly coagulates in broth and binds with free-floating fat particles. These aggregates of fat and protein float to the top of the pot and get skimmed off. Bones don't release enough protein to clarify a white broth while it cooks.

Consommé

CONSOMMÉ IS DOUBLE (SOMETIMES TRIPLE) BROTH THAT HAS BEEN CAREFULLY skimmed of fat and made perfectly clear by straining it through cheesecloth or a cloth napkin. Authentic consommé is expensive and time-consuming to prepare because meat or fish instead of bones is used to prepare a concentrated broth, which is then further enriched and clarified with more meat or fish.

It's not surprising that Americans show little interest in drinking consommé—most of us remember the stuff out of a can served on a tray in a sickroom. A real consommé is deep flavored, delicious, and free of fat and cholesterol.

The first step in making any consommé is to prepare a rich broth from meat or fish, vegetables, and a bouquet garni. Once this broth is ready, it is strained and then combined with more meat or fish and egg whites—or sometimes egg whites alone—and simmered a second time. The broth cooks gently until the egg whites coagulate and simultaneously remove free-floating particles of fat and protein from the broth. When this double broth is ready, it is strained through cheesecloth or a cloth napkin, then seasoned and flavored.

Basic Chicken Consommé

MAKES 10 SERVINGS

the basic broth:

> 1 recipe (3½ quarts) basic brown chicken broth made with 6 pounds chicken thighs or drumsticks instead of the necks and backs called for.

to clarify the broth:

> the basic broth
>
> 2 pounds boneless and skinless chicken meat, cut into 1-inch cubes (boneless chicken breasts are easier but expensive; a cheaper method is to buy 2 3½- to 4-pound whole chickens and remove the meat and skin yourself)
>
> 3 egg whites
>
> 1 small carrot, finely chopped
>
> 1 small onion, finely chopped
>
> ½ celery rib, finely chopped
>
> 1 garlic clove, crushed and peeled

1 teaspoon fresh or dried thyme leaves
¼ cup chopped parsley leaves
salt

GENTLY warm the chicken broth if it is cold.

COMBINE the chicken meat, egg whites, vegetables, and herbs in a 6-quart pot. The easiest way to do this is to work them together with your hands.

WHISK the lukewarm chicken broth into the pot with the chicken and vegetables. Beat the mixture with a large whisk to make sure the vegetables and egg whites are well distributed in the broth.

BRING the broth with the chicken and vegetables to a slow simmer over medium heat. Turn down the heat slightly and move the pot to one side of the burner so that it boils gently on one edge. After about 5 minutes, take a long wooden spoon and gently scrape along the bottom of the pot to make sure the solids don't stick and burn. Leave the broth at a gentle simmer for 40 minutes more, positioning the pot differently over the burner every 10 minutes so it boils in a different place.

BY this time a thick layer of coagulated froth (professional chefs call this the *raft*) should be floating on top of the soup. Poke a hole in the froth with a wooden spoon so that the soup simmers up through the hole. Simmer for 10 minutes more or until the broth is completely clear except for little specks of egg white and vegetable.

LINE a wide strainer with a triple layer of cheesecloth or a cloth napkin. Be sure to rinse the cloth thoroughly to get rid of any residual soap or bleach. Place the strainer over a pot and ladle in the consommé. To do this you have to break through the layer of coagulated egg, but be careful not to break up the vegetable/egg white mixture too much or you will cloud the consommé. To strain the last bit of consommé, you'll have to tilt the pot over the strainer. If after a few minutes the consommé starts to drain very slowly, gently pull on one side of the cheesecloth or napkin so the liquid can drain through an unused section of cloth.

ADD salt to taste. Garnish and flavor the consommé according to your own whims or follow some of the suggestions on page 76.

TO THICKEN CLEAR BROTHS

Cornstarch: Cornstarch is sometimes used to thicken clear broths, consommés, and Chinese clear soups to give them a richer, more concentrated appearance. To lightly thicken a clear broth or consommé, stir 1 tablespoon cornstarch with 2 tablespoons water until the mixture is smooth. Whisk into 2 quarts of simmering soup. Allow a minute or two for the soup to thicken.

Arrowroot: Very similar to cornstarch and usually found on the supermarket spice rack, arrowroot is also used to thicken soups lightly. Use the same ratio of arrowroot to water as for cornstarch and mix as described.

Basic Beef Consommé

Beef consommé is prepared exactly the same way as chicken consommé except that the basic broth takes longer to cook.

the basic broth:

4 pounds beef shank, cut into 1-inch-thick rounds, or
    chuck, round, or rump steak, cut into 1-inch cubes

1 medium-size onion, coarsely chopped

1 medium-size carrot, coarsely chopped

1 celery rib, chopped

2 tablespoons vegetable oil for stovetop browning

1 bouquet garni

2 quarts water or broth or enough to cover by 1 inch

to clarify the broth:

1½ pounds round or rump steak, carefully trimmed of all
    fat and ground or finely chopped

3 egg whites

1 small carrot, finely chopped

1 small onion, finely chopped

½ celery rib, finely chopped

1 garlic clove, crushed and peeled

1 teaspoon fresh or dried thyme leaves

¼ cup chopped parsley leaves

salt

PREPARING THE BASIC BROTH Preheat the oven to 450°F. Spread the beef shanks or cubes in a heavy roasting pan with the chopped vegetables. Bake for 45 minutes to an hour, until the meat is thoroughly browned. If at any point the vegetables start to burn, add a cup of water to the roasting pan. The meat and vegetables can also be browned in vegetable oil in a sauté pan on top of the stove.

TRANSFER the meat and vegetables to a 4-quart pot and add the bouquet garni. Pour 2 cups water into the roasting or sauté pan. Heat the pan over the stove and scrape the bottom with a wooden spoon to dissolve the coagulated meat juices. Pour this liquid over the meat and vegetables, then add the water or broth.

PLACE the pot over medium heat until the liquid reaches a simmer. Turn the heat down low enough to keep the liquid at a slow simmer. Cook for 4 hours, skimming off fat and scum as needed. If necessary, add more broth or water to keep the meat completely covered. Strain the broth through a medium-mesh strainer. Let cool. Refrigerate if you're not going to finish the consommé the same day.

CLARIFYING THE BROTH If the broth has gelled, warm it on the stove to melt it.

COMBINE the ground meat, egg whites, chopped vegetables, and herbs in a 4-quart pot. The easiest way to do this is to work everything together with your hands.

WHISK the beef broth into the pot with the ground meat and vegetables. Beat the mixture with a large whisk to make sure the vegetables and egg whites are well distributed in the broth.

BRING the broth with the beef and vegetables to a slow simmer over medium heat. Turn down the heat slightly and move the pot to one side of the burner so that it boils gently on one edge. After about 5 minutes, take a long wooden spoon and gently scrape along the bottom of the pot to make sure the solids don't stick and burn. Leave the broth at a gentle simmer for 40 minutes more, positioning the pot differently over the burner every 10 minutes so it boils in a different place.

BY this time a thick layer of coagulated froth should be floating on top of the soup. Poke a hole in the froth with a wooden spoon so that the soup simmers up through the hole. Simmer for 10 minutes more or until the broth is completely clear except for little specks of egg white and vegetable.

LINE a wide strainer with a triple layer of cheesecloth or a cloth napkin. Be sure to rinse the cloth thoroughly to get rid of any residual soap or bleach. Place the strainer over a pot and ladle in the consommé. To do this you have to break through the layer of coagulated egg, but be careful not to break up the vegetable/egg white mixture too much or you will cloud the consommé. To strain the last bit of consommé, you'll have to tilt the pot over the strainer. If after a few minutes the consommé starts to drain very slowly, gently pull on one side of the cheesecloth or napkin so the liquid can drain through an unused section of cloth.

ADD salt to taste. Garnish and flavor the consommé according to your own whims or follow some of the suggestions on page 76.

Flavoring Consommé

Although a well-made consommé should already have a full, rich flavor, a few tablespoons of good fortified wine such as sherry or Madeira will usually round out and enhance its flavor. Choose sherries or Madeiras that have a little sweetness and slowly add them to taste to the finished consommé. Don't get carried away and add the wine too fast, or it may cloud the consommé.

Don't add ground pepper to a finished consommé, or the little specks will float around in the soup and spoil its appearance. If you want to flavor a consommé with pepper, crush about 20 peppercorns with the bottom of a saucepan and wrap them in cheesecloth. Soak the packet in the hot consommé for about 10 minutes before serving.

Garnishes for Consommé

Although a plain bowl of perfectly clear consommé is an impressive sight, most consommé is served with decorative vegetables cut into different shapes, thin pasta noodles, shredded crêpes, cubed tomatoes, herbs, or even tiny dumplings. Older recipes recommend even more elaborate garnishes such as quenelles and miniature custard cutouts, but today most cooks and diners are more impressed by the authentic shapes of untampered-with foods than complicated contrivances. Here are a few suggestions:

FRESH TARRAGON Not only is tarragon a delicious flavoring for both meat and fish consommés, but the bright green leaves floating in the perfectly clear soup are striking and elegant. Fresh tarragon is also effortless to prepare.

For 8 bowls of consommé, plunge three fresh tarragon sprigs into 2 cups boiling water for 10 seconds. Rinse the sprigs in cold water and remove and reserve the leaves. Just before serving, put the leaves into each of the hot bowls and pour the consommé over.

VEGETABLES CUT INTO JULIENNE OR CHIFFONADE One of the most beautiful garnishes for consommé is a mixture of leeks, carrots, or turnips cut into julienne. You can cut the vegetables into long and very thin strips—chefs call these "angel hair"—or into thicker pieces the size of matchsticks so they form geometric patterns in the soup.

Although vegetables can be cut into julienne with a good chef's knife, it's much easier with an inexpensive Japanese gadget called a *benriner cutter.*

Unlike carrots and other root vegetables, leeks must be cut into julienne by hand. The easiest way to do this is to wash them thoroughly and finely slice the leaves one at a time with a chef's knife. If the leaves are too long to slice evenly, fold them over themselves so they fit more easily under the knife.

Leafy vegetables such as spinach or sorrel cut into thin strips are called *chiffonade.* The easiest way to chiffonade leafy vegetables is to roll up three or four of the leaves and slice them thinly with a chef's knife.

Once you've cut the vegetables (you should have about 1 cup, loosely packed, for eight servings of consommé), you need to thoroughly cook them. Put 1 cup of the consommé in a small saucepan, add the vegetables, cover the pan, and gently simmer the vegetables. Root vegetable julienne should be simmered for about 10 minutes; leafy vegetables, about 1 minute. Reach in and taste one to make sure it's tender and return the cooking liquid to the rest of the consommé. Distribute the vegetables in the hot bowls just before serving.

WILD MUSHROOMS AND TRUFFLES Because of their shape and color, wild mushrooms and truffles are magnificent floating in a bowl of clear brown consommé.

They also contribute a subtle and irresistible flavor to the soup. Mushrooms for consommé should be small so they can be left whole in the soup. Morels and chanterelles are especially flavorful and beautiful.

For eight bowls of consommé, rinse about ⅓ pound fresh wild mushrooms to eliminate sand and dirt and then simmer them for about 10 minutes in a cup of the consommé. Distribute the mushrooms in the hot bowls just before serving. Stir the cooking liquid from the mushrooms back into the consommé.

If you're lucky or extravagant enough to have a black truffle, slice it into thin rounds or into julienne with a sharp knife or a benriner cutter. Simmer it in a cup of consommé in a small covered saucepan for about 5 minutes. Arrange the truffle in the serving bowls, return the cooking liquid to the rest of the consommé, and serve immediately.

CRÊPES Tiny shreds of crêpes, well flavored with fresh herbs, make an elegant and old-fashioned consommé garnish. Although I never make a batch of crepes just to use for consommé, it's easy when you're preparing crêpes to make two or three extra and freeze them.

CRÊPES WITH HERBS Whisk together 3 eggs and 1 cup flour in a mixing bowl to make a smooth paste. Slowly stir in 1½ cups milk—or more if necessary—until the batter has the consistency of heavy cream. Add a pinch of salt and ¼ cup chopped fresh herbs such as chives or tarragon. Ladle as little of the batter as possible into a hot buttered skillet or crêpe pan to cover the bottom.

Set the pan over medium heat. When the batter sets and barely begins to brown around the edges, after about 3 minutes, carefully turn over the crêpe with a spatula. Cook 1 more minute on the second side.

When the crêpes are done, arrange them on a sheet pan so they overlap—don't stack them or they may stick.

To freeze the crêpes, separate each crêpe with a sheet of wax paper and then wrap the whole stack in a sheet of aluminum foil. They freeze well for several months.

To shred the crêpes, roll them and slice them as thinly as you can.

COLD CONSOMMÉ Unlike the French, who love aspics and meat jellies, Americans' only experience with such things is often the green or red Jell-O of childhood. This is a pity, because lightly jelled consommé is delicious, delicately flavored, and absolutely free of fat. It has all the flavor of hot consommé but is a light and refreshing soup for summer dining.

The important thing when serving cold consommé is to make sure that it is not too gelatinous—eating rubbery jelly is indeed revolting—but barely holds together so that it melts the instant it's in your mouth. Serving it cool but not ice-cold will usually give it the right texture.

If the cold consommé is at all stiff, turn it out while it is set onto a cutting board and chop it before distributing it in cold bowls.

I rarely serve chilled consommé by itself; I like to top it with chopped herbs, chopped tomatoes, chilled pieces of shellfish (crayfish tails are especially dramatic), or heavy cream with herbs. Another trick is to pour small amounts of cold soups over a mound of cold consommé. This is especially wonderful with chilled sorrel soup (*potage germiny*, page 212) or crustacean soups.

Beef Tea

This soup, really more a delicate infusion of beef—hence the name tea—is made by very gently cooking perfectly lean beef in a small amount of water for several hours. The proportion of water to beef is up to you, but the idea is to come up with something light, delicious, and digestible for someone who's been ailing with an upset stomach. Earlier versions (from the 17th century) of meat teas were called "restaurants" and were supposed to revitalize and restore anyone who drank them. Unlike modern versions, these 17th-century recipes contained no water at all and consisted only of the natural juices released by a combination of meats sealed up in a jar and poached for hours in a water bath. Even with the water used here, beef tea is expensive because you'll need a pound of beef to make 1 cup of tea. You'll need four 1-quart mason jars to make 1 quart of tea.

MAKES FOUR 1-CUP SERVINGS

5 pounds very lean beef such as round or rump

4 cups water

2 teaspoons salt

additional salt as needed

IF you're buying the meat from a butcher, have him strip away any pieces of fat and grind the meat on the finest setting. If you're buying meat at a supermarket, trim the fat off yourself and grind it in a food processor meat grinder to the consistency of fine hamburger meat.

DIVIDE the meat evenly into four 1-quart mason jars and pour a cup of water into each jar. Add ½ teaspoon salt to each jar and seal the jars tightly.

PUT a folded kitchen towel in a large pot or roasting pan with high sides large enough to hold the jars upright. The towel protects the jars from the direct heat of the stove. Pour enough water into the pot or roasting pan to come one-third up the sides of the jars and place the pot or pan on the stove over medium heat. When the surrounding water comes to the simmer, turn the heat down to maintain at a gentle simmer. Simmer in this way for 3 hours, adding hot tap water to the surrounding water to make up for evaporation. Take the jars out of the water and let cool at room temperature for an hour. Strain the liquid through a fine-mesh strainer or through a regular strainer lined with a well-rinsed out muslin kitchen towel. Don't push on the solids or you'll cloud the broth. If the strainer or cloth gets clogged so no more liquid is draining through, discard what's in the strainer or cloth and rinse them out or pull the cloth to one side so that the beef is draining through a clean patch. Strain the tea in batches, discarding the meat, and thoroughly rinsing the strainer or cloth between batches. Refrigerate the tea until you're ready to serve it (you can also freeze it for emergencies, it will keep up to a year) and then bring it to a simmer. Serve in tea cups.

Smoked Chicken or Duck Consommé

Smoked meats perfectly accent the flavor of a delicate consommé. In this recipe smoked chicken or duck and a chiffonade of fresh spinach are added to a clear chicken broth or consommé just minutes before serving.

MAKES 6 SERVINGS

I smoked chicken or duck breast, skin removed

6 cups basic chicken consommé or clear chicken or duck broth

I large bunch of spinach or sorrel, stems removed, about 50 leaves, sliced into ⅛-inch chiffonade

salt

pepper

THINLY slice the chicken or duck breast and then slice the slices into matchstick-size slivers.

BRING the consommé to a simmer in a 4-quart pot and add the slivered meat and the chiffonade. Simmer for 2 minutes. Season to taste with salt and pepper. Ladle into hot bowls.

SUGGESTIONS AND VARIATIONS | This soup is also excellent served cold. Place the pot on a bowl of ice as soon as you add the chiffonade and stir to chill the soup as quickly as possible. Ladle into chilled bowls and serve.

Seafood Consommés

Consommé can be prepared with fish, shellfish, and crustaceans using almost the same methods used to make meat consommés, with fish broth usually used instead of meat broth for the consommé base. For some consommés, however, such as those made from shellfish, brown chicken stock can also be used.

When using fish to make consommé, it's important to start out with a concentrated, full-flavored broth made from very fresh whole fish or bones. Whenever I decide to make fish consommé, I go to Manhattan's Chinatown and look over the fish stalls for very fresh and inexpensive local fish.

The best fish to use are small flatfish such as flounder and nonoily round fish such as sea bass. On the East Coast I often use small porgy. Have the fishmonger clean the fish. When you get them home, make sure the gills have been removed and the fins snipped off. If not, follow the directions on pages 307–308.

If I can't find small whole fish, I buy larger fish, have them filleted, and then make a fish broth with the bones and heads. I then use the fillets to clarify the broth.

Fish Consommé

Usually a plain fish broth, especially one made with bones alone, is neither clear nor full-flavored enough to be served as fish consommé. A lot of parsley is added to freshen the flavor.

MAKES 2 QUARTS

the basic broth:

8 round fish such as red snapper or sea bass, gutted, gills
and fins removed, fillets and bones and heads reserved

I large onion, chopped

I bouquet garni: I bunch of parsley, 3 fresh thyme sprigs or
I teaspoon dried, and I bay leaf

2 cups dry white wine

3 quarts water or enough to cover

to clarify the broth:

I onion, chopped

I carrot, chopped

I celery rib, chopped

¼ cup coarsely chopped parsley leaves

5 egg whites

PREPARING THE BASIC BROTH Put the fish bones and heads in a large mixing bowl and cover them with cold water. Stir them around and change the water. Repeat this several times during an hour to eliminate blood, which will discolor the broth. Drain in a colander.

COMBINE the fish bones and heads, the onion, the bouquet garni, and the white wine in a 6-quart pot and add enough water to cover barely. Heat over medium heat until the liquid comes to a boil. Turn the heat down low enough to keep the broth at a slow simmer and cook for 40 minutes.

STRAIN the broth and let cool.

CLARIFYING THE BROTH Cut the fish fillets into ½-inch chunks and combine them with the remaining vegetables, parsley, and egg whites in a 4-quart pot. Knead the mixture for a minute or two with your hands to make sure the egg white is well broken up and coats the fish and vegetables.

WHISK the warm (but not hot) fish broth into the clarification mixture. Make sure that the egg white and vegetables are well distributed in the broth.

POUR the mixture into a clean pot and bring to a slow simmer over medium heat. Turn down the heat slightly and move the pot to one side of the burner so that it boils gently on one edge. After about 5 minutes, take a long wooden spoon and gently scrape along the bottom of the pot to make sure the solids don't stick and burn. Leave the broth at a gentle simmer for 40 minutes more, positioning the pot differently over the burner every 10 minutes so it boils in a different place.

BY this time a thick layer of coagulated froth should be floating on top of the soup. Poke a hole in the froth with a wooden spoon so that the soup simmers up through the hole. Simmer for 10 minutes more or until the broth is completely clear except for little specks of egg white and vegetable.

LINE a wide strainer with a triple layer of cheesecloth or a cloth napkin. Be sure to rinse the cloth thoroughly to get rid of any residual soap or bleach. Place the strainer over a pot and ladle in the consommé. To do this you

MAKING A BOUQUET GARNI

A bouquet garni is a small bundle of herbs tied up in cheesecloth so the herbs don't come loose and float around in the soup. Depending on what kind of soup you're making, almost any combination of herbs can be used, but a traditional bouquet garni contains only thyme, parsley, and bay leaves.

A bouquet garni is best made by tying fresh herbs together in a little bundle with a short length of string. The size of the bouquet garni will depend on the amount of soup you're making but most people make them too small. For 3 quarts of soup I use about 10 thyme stems, a medium bunch of parsley, and a whole bay leaf. If you don't have fresh thyme use 1 teaspoon dried thyme.

have to break through the layer of coagulated egg, but be careful not to break up the vegetable/egg white mixture too much or you will cloud the consommé. To strain the last bit of consommé, you'll have to tilt the pot over the strainer. If after a few minutes the consommé starts to drain very slowly, gently pull on one side of the cheesecloth or napkin so the liquid can drain through an unused section of cloth.

ADD salt to taste. Garnish and flavor the consommé according to your own whims or the following suggestions.

SERVING SUGGESTIONS | Unlike meat consommé, which can be served alone or with a few slivers of vegetable julienne, fish consommé needs something more substantial, or it will taste monotonous. I like to use fish consommé as a backdrop for more elaborate shellfish soups made with scallops, crayfish, or lobster. Fish consommé is striking when served with small shrimp, crayfish tails, lobster medallions, or even oysters. I also like to add finely chopped chives for color.

Scallops in Clear Broth

To make this soup, you need fish or chicken consommé or Japanese bonito broth (*dashi*). Once you have the consommé, all you have left to do is simmer the vegetables and lightly poach the scallops at the last minute. I like to serve this soup in those little Japanese lacquer bowls used to serve miso soup.

MAKES 8 FIRST-COURSE SERVINGS

I small leek, white part only, washed and sliced into fine
    julienne

I small carrot, cut into fine julienne

2 quarts fish or chicken consommé or *dashi*

1¼ pounds sea scallops, about 5 small scallops or slices per
    serving

salt

IN ADVANCE Prepare the vegetable julienne and simmer in a cup of the consommé in a 1-quart saucepan for about 10 minutes, until tender. Reserve both broth and vegetables.

IF the scallops are large, slice them crosswise into halves or thirds—you should have about 5 small scallops or scallop slices per serving. Rinse them in cold water and keep them in the refrigerator until needed.

AT THE LAST MINUTE Bring the remaining consommé to a slow simmer.

ARRANGE the scallops in a single layer in a small pot or sauté pan with a tight-fitting lid. Pour in just enough fish consommé to come halfway up the sides of the scallops. Cover the pan and set it over high heat. Start checking it after 1 minute; when the broth reaches a simmer, replace the lid, turn down the heat, and cook the scallops for a minute or two more, until they're firm to the touch.

WHILE the scallops are cooking, heat the vegetables in their original liquid.

DISTRIBUTE the scallops among hot bowls. Arrange the hot vegetables over the scallops. Combine the liquid used to heat the vegetables with the rest of the consommé. Season the consommé with salt and ladle it into the individual bowls.

SUGGESTIONS AND VARIATIONS | This is just one simple example of how a clear broth or consommé can be garnished with cooked shellfish and vegetables. This simple dish is suitable as the first course of an elaborate dinner, but you can make it as complex as you like with pieces of peeled shrimp, lobster, fish, and leafy vegetables such as spinach, sorrel, or watercress.

THE SCALLOP-POACHING LIQUID

Although the liquid used for poaching the scallops will be intensely flavored, it may be cloudy. If it is cloudy, it might spoil the appearance of the soup when combined with the rest of the consommé. You might want to freeze it and use it in your next fish soup instead.

Lobster Consommé

This rich and elegant consommé is the perfect opening soup for an elegant dinner served with the best china and silver.

Lobster consommé is time-consuming because you need a full-bodied beef or chicken broth to start with. You can also use fish or vegetable broths as shortcuts, but the flavor of the soup will be less complex and luxurious. Fortunately, you can make the basic broth a couple of days ahead and the finished consommé the day before.

Buy female lobster culls if you can find them. Culls are less expensive—because they're missing a claw—and the females contain roe, which turns orange and looks great floating in the clear consommé.

MAKES 8 SERVINGS

2½ quarts basic beef broth, basic brown chicken broth, fish
    broth for consommé, or vegetable broth
4 1¼ to 1½-pound female lobsters, preferably culls
4 egg whites
1 small onion, chopped
½ celery rib, chopped
¼ cup coarsely chopped parsley leaves
1 fresh tarragon sprig, coarsely chopped (optional)

BRING the broth to a boil in a 6-quart pot.

RINSE the lobsters under cold running water to rinse off stale water from the lobster tank. With kitchen string, tie the lobsters together in pairs so they are facing each other, to prevent the tails from curling while the lobsters are cooking.

PLUNGE the lobsters into the boiling broth. They probably won't fit, but this isn't a problem—the parts sticking out will steam. Cover the pot and simmer the lobsters for 4 minutes. Wrap your hand in a towel, reach into the pot with a long wooden spoon, and move the lobsters around to submerge any parts that were sticking out. Cover the pot and simmer for 4 minutes more.

MAKE sure the lobsters have turned completely red before taking them out of the pot. If they're still brown in sections, cook them for 2 or 3 minutes more.

AFTER the lobsters have cooled, take the meat out of the shells following the directions on page 391. Save the lobster shells. Slice each lobster tail into 6 medallions. Slice the meat from each claw in half. Cover the sliced lobster meat with plastic wrap and store in the refrigerator.

LIGHTLY break up the lobster shells with a rolling pin and put them back in the broth. Bring the broth to a slow simmer and continue breaking up the lobster shells with the end of a cleaver or large wooden spoon. Cover the pot and simmer for 30 minutes. Strain the broth into a 4-quart pot and let it cool to lukewarm; discard the shells or freeze them to use for making lobster butter.

COMBINE the egg whites, vegetables, and herbs in a small mixing bowl. Work the mixture with your hands to make sure the egg whites have completely broken up and are coating the vegetables. Thoroughly whisk the egg white/vegetable mixture into the broth and bring to a slow simmer over medium heat. Turn down the heat slightly and move the pot to one side of the burner so that it boils gently on one edge. After about 10 minutes, take a long wooden spoon and gently scrape along the bottom of the pot to make sure the solids don't stick and burn. Leave the broth at a gentle simmer for 40 minutes more, positioning the pot differently over the burner every 10 minutes so it boils in a different place.

WHEN a thick layer of coagulated froth has formed on top of the soup, poke a hole in the froth with a wooden spoon so that the soup simmers up through the hole. Simmer for 10 minutes more or until the broth is completely clear except for little specks of egg white and vegetable.

LINE a wide strainer with a triple layer of cheesecloth or a cloth napkin. Be sure to rinse the cloth thoroughly to get rid of any residual soap or bleach. Place the strainer over a pot and ladle in the consommé. To do this you have to break through the layer of coagulated egg, but be careful not to break up the vegetable/egg white mixture too much or you will cloud the consommé. To strain the last bit of consommé, you'll have to tilt the pot over the strainer. If after a few minutes the consommé starts to drain very slowly, gently pull on one side of the cheesecloth or napkin so the liquid can drain through an unused section of cloth.

ADD salt to taste. Garnish and flavor the consommé according to your own whims or the following suggestions.

TO serve the soup, arrange the sliced lobster in porcelain or Japanese lacquer bowls. If you're using porcelain bowls, heat them in a 200°F oven and pour over the simmering consommé. If you're using lacquer bowls, heat the lobster first in a little of the consommé and heat the bowls by filling them with boiling water.

SERVING SUGGESTIONS AND VARIATIONS | Lobster consommé is delicious served cold. This is especially true if you've used a full-bodied, slightly gelatinous broth as the consommé base, which will set into a light jelly when served chilled. When serving cold consommé, arrange the lobster in a decorative pattern in chilled bowls and ladle the consommé over.

I sometimes decorate bowls of hot or cold consommé with blanched tarragon leaves or, in summer, finely chopped yellow and red tomatoes.

Tomato Consommé

Growing up in the fifties, I found certain foods epitomized elegance and sophistication. Tomato consommé and its close relative, tomato aspic, were often served at the most formal dinners—the kind of pretentious affairs that often started out with a finger bowl. These consommés were made in the classic fashion, with beef and, of course, tomatoes. Recently, the tomato consommé has reappeared, but under a different guise—in versions containing no meat, just the pure essence of the tomatoes themselves. If you use the poblano chili, this consommé has a bit of a bite.

MAKES 6 FIRST-COURSE SERVINGS

6 pounds medium-size, very ripe tomatoes, cored and coarsely chopped

1 medium-size onion, peeled and finely chopped

1 bunch of parsley, stems and leaves coarsely chopped

1 poblano chili, charred and peeled (see page 207–208 for more about how to peel bell peppers and chilies), coarsely chopped, or 1 large bunch of fresh tarragon, including stems, coarsely chopped

3 large eggs with shells

salt

COMBINE the tomatoes—seeds, peels, and all in a blender (you'll have to work in batches, since they won't all fit at once) with the onion, parsley, and chili or tarragon. Puree for about 1 minute. Separate the eggs, save the yolks for something else or discard them, and work the egg whites and the egg shells into the tomatoes by crushing everything together with your fingers in a medium pot.

PUT the pot on the stove over medium heat, repositioning it every 5 minutes so the burner is under another part of the pot and the mixture heats through evenly. When the mixture comes to the simmer, turn the heat down to keep the mixture at a gentle simmer. Simmer for 30 minutes. Every 10 minutes, gently run a long wooden spoon along the inside bottom of the pot to detach any egg white that may have sunk down and could scald.

USE a ladle to gently transfer the mixture to a fine-mesh strainer set over a clean pot. Unless you have a very large fine-mesh strainer, the mixture will have to be done in batches. When liquid from one batch stops dripping out of the strainer, discard the contents of the strainer and fill it again. Don't be tempted to push down on the mixture or you'll cloud the consommé. I like to serve this soup in double espresso cups with little strands of julienned vegetables as a garniture.

Grilled or Sautéed Salmon Fillet in Consommé, Clear Broth, or *Dashi*

This is one of those dishes I serve to guests who like something a bit more elaborate and elegant than a piece of grilled fish but who are jaded or scared off by rich sauces. The salmon is served surrounded by a savory broth speckled with fresh herbs, then topped with a julienne of vegetables simmered in the broth. Guests are always startled by the dramatic look of this soup; I always underplay it when they ask what we're having: "Oh, I hope you like fish soup?"

If you decide to serve the salmon in consommé, this dish will take you some time, but *dashi* takes only a minute. Once you have the broth, all you have to do is grill or sauté the salmon and simmer the vegetables.

You can prepare this dish using salmon fillet or steaks. If you decide to use fillets, cut them into squares or rectangles. If you use steaks, cut the steaks through the back so they separate into two halves. This is easier than it looks; just make sure you keep the knife in the center of the steak until you get to the backbone and then keep the knife against the bone. Cut off the skin and remove any stray bones. Any little bones sticking out of the sides of the steaks can be pulled out with a pair of pliers or a good thumbnail. When it comes time to grill or sauté the steak halves, fold the thin flap of flesh under so the halves are the same thickness while they cook.

I serve this dish as a light but elegant main course or sometimes, in smaller portions, as a fish course for a more elaborate dinner.

MAKES 6 LIGHT MAIN-COURSE SERVINGS

2¼ pounds salmon fillets (6 ounces per serving) cut into
    6 squares, or 3 1½-inch-thick salmon steaks, cut in half

salt

pepper

3 tablespoons dark Japanese soy sauce if you're using dashi

4 teaspoons mirin if you're using dashi

3 medium-size carrots, cut into fine julienne

2 medium-size turnips, cut into fine julienne

2 medium-size leeks, sliced into fine julienne

6 cups consommé, clear broth, or *dashi*

3 tablespoons chopped parsley leaves

3 tablespoons chopped fresh chervil (optional)

2 tablespoons chopped chives

1 tablespoon unsalted butter if you're sautéeing the salmon
    or 1 tablespoon olive oil for grilling

IN ADVANCE Season the salmon with salt and pepper. If you're using *dashi*, combine it with the soy sauce and mirin.

PUT the vegetables and 1 cup of the consommé in a 2-quart saucepan. Cover and simmer for 10 minutes, until the vegetables are tender but not mushy. Transfer the cooked vegetables to a plate with a slotted spoon; transfer the cooking liquid to a bowl. Reserve both until needed.

AT THE LAST MINUTE Bring the consommé to a simmer. Reheat the vegetables in their cooking liquid in a separate saucepan and add the chopped herbs.

IF you're grilling the salmon fillets, brush them with olive oil and season with salt and pepper. Place them on a grill about 6 inches away from a bed of hot coals. Be sure the grill is hot before putting on the salmon or the fish may stick. Grill them for about 4 minutes on the first side and slightly less on the second side (about 7 minutes total cooking time per inch of thickness because you want to leave the fillets slightly undercooked).

IF you're sautéing the fillets, sauté them in a tablespoon of butter, preferably in a nonstick pan. Arrange the vegetables on top of each fillet in hot bowls and ladle the herb-flecked broth into each bowl. Ladle over the rest of the hot consommé or *dashi*.

SUGGESTIONS AND VARIATIONS | Try topping the fish with medallions of lobster, scallops, or shrimp and surrounding the whole thing with grilled baby vegetables (skewer the vegetables so they don't fall through the cracks in the grill). Sometimes I put a large spoonful of cooked spinach under the salmon to help prop it up in the bowl and to make the dish more complete.

GRILLED or sautéed salmon is also delicious with a red wine broth. Salmon bones are usually considered too strong as a base for fish broth, but when cooked with red wine they produce a hearty broth. To prepare a red wine/salmon broth, ask the fishmonger for a salmon head and use it to prepare the red wine fish broth on page 308. Be sure to take the gills out of the salmon by cutting them on each side with scissors and giving a tug. Don't bother chopping the salmon head—not easy in any case—because it will fall apart as it's cooking with the vegetables.

THIS dish is very similar to Russian *ukha*, which is salmon served in consommé with diced carrots and potatoes.

SERVING GRILLED OR SAUTÉED FOODS IN BROTH

Instead of serving grilled or sautéed foods with rich sauces or completely unadorned, try serving them in bowls surrounded with a tasty broth. You can flavor the broth as you like—with chopped fresh herbs, pieces of cooked vegetables, chunks of tomatoes—and then ladle it around a piece of grilled fish, meat, or vegetables in a wide bowl. The effect is striking, and of course the broth is completely fat-free.

Sautéed or Grilled Duck Breast in Savory Broth

This elegant, almost fat-free soup is the perfect way to serve duck without resorting to rich or heavy sauces. It can be served as a striking opener to a formal dinner or in more generous servings as a main course.

The duck breast is set on a bright tangle of vegetable julienne and surrounded by a clear brown broth flecked with green herbs. The soup is best served in wide soup bowls to show off the colors of the vegetables and the broth.

Although this soup may seem elaborate, the broth and the vegetables can all be prepared in advance; only the final assembly needs to be done at the last minute.

MAKES 4 MAIN-COURSE OR 8 FIRST-COURSE SERVINGS

2 Long Island ducks, 5 pounds each

1 medium-size onion, chopped

1 medium-size carrot, chopped

2 quarts chicken broth or water

1 bouquet garni: 3 fresh thyme sprigs, 1 bay leaf,
    and 5 green leek leaves

salt

3 medium-size carrots, cut into fine julienne

2 medium-size turnips, cut into fine julienne

3 medium-size leeks, white parts only, cut into fine
    julienne

3 tablespoons chopped parsley

3 tablespoons chopped fresh chervil (optional)

2 tablespoons chopped chives

pepper

IN ADVANCE—PREPARING THE DUCK BROTH Remove the boneless breasts and thighs from the ducks (see box on page 494 or have the butcher do it). Refrigerate the breasts until needed. Break up the duck wings, back, and breastbones with a heavy knife or cleaver.

PUT the duck thighs, skin side down, in a 4-quart pot over medium heat. Cook them gently for 10 minutes, until they begin to render their fat. Add the chopped onion and carrot and the broken-up duck bones. Stir the mixture every few minutes until the duck thighs, vegetables, and bones are well browned, about 20 minutes. Add the chicken broth and bouquet garni. Bring to a slow simmer. Simmer the duck broth slowly for 2 hours, skimming every 30 minutes to eliminate fat or froth.

USES FOR DUCK BROTH

I serve duck quite often because it seems the perfect compromise between chicken and red meat and because it's tasty and relatively inexpensive. As a result I'm often left with duck bones, wings, and sometimes thighs, which I turn into broth. Duck broth can be used in almost any soup as a substitute for chicken broth, but it is especially good in Asian-style soups that include red meat or of course duck.

STRAIN the duck broth into a clean 3- or 4-quart pot. Bring it back to a simmer and cook it for about 45 minutes, until it reduces to half its original volume—down to about 1 quart.

STRAIN the reduced duck broth through a fine-mesh strainer. If it seems cloudy, strain it again through a cloth napkin or a triple layer of cheesecloth. Season with the salt.

IN ADVANCE—COOKING THE VEGETABLE JULIENNE Put the vegetable julienne and 1 cup of the strained duck broth into a 2-quart saucepan. Cover and simmer for 10 minutes, until the vegetables are tender but not mushy. Transfer the cooked vegetables to a plate with a slotted spoon. Reserve both broth and vegetables until needed.

AT THE LAST MINUTE—SAUTÉING THE DUCK BREASTS With a sharp paring knife, lightly score the skin on the duck breasts both lengthwise and crosswise, without cutting all the way through to the meat. Each breast should have about 20 slashes in each direction. This helps render the fat quickly in the sauté pan so the skin will be crispy but the meat still rare.

PLACE the duck breasts skin side down in a hot sauté pan. You don't need to use any oil—the breasts will provide their own. Cook the breasts for 8 to 10 minutes over medium heat. Turn them over and cook them on the other side for 2 minutes more, until rare.

SERVING While the duck breasts are cooking, heat the duck broth in a saucepan with the cooked vegetable julienne and the chopped herbs. When the duck breasts are ready, distribute the vegetables among hot soup bowls. Slice the duck breasts crosswise on an angle and arrange them over the vegetables.

SPRINKLE the duck breasts with salt and pepper. Pour hot broth into the bowls—it should come just below the top of the sliced duck breasts.

SUGGESTIONS AND VARIATIONS | Many cooks like to remove the fat from the duck breasts—a good idea if you want a lean and fat-free soup—but I like the flavor of the crispy skin. If you do remove it, cook the duck breasts in a small amount of butter or oil for only about 3 minutes on each side.

I sometimes don't want to bother with the vegetable julienne and instead prop the duck on a mound of freshly cooked spinach. I also like to add small mushrooms, even wild mushrooms, to the broth. If you want to give the broth an Asian flavor, simmer a star anise in the broth along with the vegetables.

THIS soup style—sliced meat served in a broth with vegetables and herbs—can be used for practically anything. A more casual version of this dish might be chicken in a simple broth—even a commercial broth would do—flecked with fresh herbs such as tarragon or cilantro.

Red Wine, Onion, and Duck Thigh Soup

I often serve duck breasts because they're simple to cook—they're just sautéed like steak—which leaves me with a lot of duck carcasses, wings, and thighs that accumulate in the freezer. When the freezer reaches its limit and I can no longer get at the ice cubes, I make duck stock with the carcasses, which I reduce to a glaze and use later in sauces for the duck breasts, and I make duck confit (see page 454) with the thighs. I also like to make this soup, which uses both the thighs and the carcasses and several bottles of red wine. It's a delicious and rich (although not fatty) soup for a winter meal—as either a substantial first course or main course.

MAKES 6 FIRST-COURSE SERVINGS OR 4 MAIN-COURSE SERVINGS
BY ADDING NOODLES OR OTHER GARNITURES (SEE SUGGESTIONS AND VARIATIONS)

Thighs, wings and carcasses from 2 Long Island ducks
1 medium-size onion, peeled and quartered
1 large carrot, peeled and cut into ½-inch sections
3 garlic cloves, peeled
3 bottles full-bodied red wine (see box, page 96)
salt
pepper
bouquet garni containing 1 bunch of parsley, 5 thyme sprigs
    (or ½ teaspoon dried thyme leaves), and 1 bay leaf
3 tablespoons butter or olive oil
3 large red onions, peeled and sliced as thin as possible
    (a plastic vegetable slicer works great for this)
1 teaspoon sugar
¼ cup port wine (optional)

PREHEAT the oven to 450°F. Break up the carcasses into small pieces with a cleaver or heavy knife and spread them and the quartered onion, carrot, and garlic in a heavy-bottomed roasting pan (or a couple of skillets) just large enough to hold everything in a single layer. Slide the roasting pan in the oven and bake the bones and vegetables, turning them around in the pan every 15 minutes to prevent burning, until they are well browned, from 45 minutes to 1½ hours. Spoon out and discard any fat that has accumulated in the pan. Pour half a bottle of wine into the roasting pan and place it over the stove over high heat for about 5 minutes while scraping against the bottom of the pan with a wooden spoon to dissolve any caramelized juices. Transfer the contents of the roasting pan to a narrow pot. Nestle in the bouquet garni and pour over the rest of the wine. Bring to a boil over high heat and then turn down the heat to maintain at a gentle simmer. Simmer for 3 hours, skimming off fat and froth with a ladle.

SEASON the duck thighs on both sides with salt and pepper and brown them, starting with the skin side down, in a tablespoon of butter over medium heat, for about 15 minutes on the skin side (to get the fat to render) and 10 minutes on the flesh side. Take them out of the pan with tongs and put them in the pot with bones no later than an hour after the broth came to the simmer so the thighs simmer for at least 2 hours.

WHILE the broth is simmering, melt the rest of the butter in a pot over medium heat and add the red onions. Stir the onions every couple of minutes until they soften and release a lot of liquid, about 20 minutes. Turn the heat up to high to evaporate the liquid—this takes about 10 minutes—and then turn the heat back down again and stir the onions continuously to caramelize them without letting them burn. Ladle about 2 cups of the red wine broth and the optional port over the onions and boil it down until there's nothing left and the onions start to caramelize a second time. Set the pot with the onions aside.

USE a slotted spoon to take the thighs gently out of the red wine broth and reserve on a plate. Strain the broth through a fine-mesh strainer into the pot with the onions. Discard the rest of the bones and wings. Bring the broth back to a simmer and simmer it gently for about 20 minutes more to reduce it slightly and so you can skim off additional fat and froth.

PEEL the skin off the thighs and discard. Pull the meat away from the bones—don't shred it too much, but leave it in chunks—and add it to the simmering soup. Season the soup to taste with salt and serve in heated bowls.

VARIATIONS | You can add croutons—cubes of bread about ½ inch on each side and sautéed in butter to this soup to give it crunch. If you want to get luxurious, truffles or wild mushrooms are nice, as is a slice of quickly sautéed duck foie gras set on a fried slice of crusty bread in the middle of each bowl. You can also turn this soup into a luxurious main course by sautéing duck breasts (score the breasts as described on page 90) almost entirely skin side down until the skin is crispy and then slicing them and serving them, again on a crusty slice of fried bread (the bread keeps them out of the broth so they don't poach and lose their pink color) set in the middle of each bowl. Adding noodles (see box, page 107) is simple and an inexpensive way to turn this soup into a substantial main course.

Japanese Clear Broth

DASHI

Dashi is to Japanese cooking what clear broth or consommé is to Western cooking. Once you track down the ingredients, *dashi* is easier to prepare, less expensive, and at least as satisfying as a well-made consommé. Master a simple *dashi*, and other Japanese soups—including authentic miso—take almost no effort.

Dashi is made with only three ingredients—strips of giant seaweed (konbu), shaved dried bonito (hana-katsuo), and water. Unlike Western-style broth, which takes hours to prepare, making *dashi* is akin to making tea—the ingredients are infused for 5 or 10 minutes, and the broth is done.

The best konbu (giant seaweed) comes from Japan's northernmost island, Hokkaido—a source that may be hard to establish when you're wandering around a store where all the labels are in Japanese. Konbu comes in 18-inch strips that look like very dark, brown leather, covered with white mold. (It's not really mold but a kind of natural sea salt.)

Though *dashi* is easy to prepare, today many Japanese cooks use instant *dashi* (see box on page 94), which is surprisingly good.

MAKES 4 SERVINGS

1 18-inch length of giant seaweed (konbu), about 1 ounce

5 cups water

1 ounce shaved bonito (hana-katsuo), 4 cups unpacked

FOLD the konbu over itself and place it in a 2-quart saucepan. Pour the water over the konbu and put the saucepan over low heat so that it takes about 15 minutes to come to a simmer. Remove the konbu as soon as the water comes to a simmer.

INCREASE the heat so the broth comes to a full boil. Pour in the bonito flakes and immediately take the saucepan off the heat. Let the bonito flakes sit in the broth for 1 minute and immediately strain the soup through a fine-mesh sieve or through an ordinary sieve lined with a single layer of cheesecloth.

THE *dashi* can now be used as a base for other clear soups. *Dashi* keeps for 2 weeks in the refrigerator and will keep indefinitely in the freezer.

USING LEFTOVER BONITO FLAKES AND KONBU

Leftover bonito flakes and konbu can be used a second time to make *dashi* for strong-tasting soups. To make *dashi* a second time, simmer the used konbu and the bonito flakes from this recipe in 1 quart water for 20 minutes. Then add 1/3 ounce of fresh flakes and strain the mixture in the same way. Discard the twice used bonito flakes and konbu.

Miso Soup

Miso soup is one of the most satisfying foods in the world. Although the Japanese seem to enjoy it most at breakfast, beginning a dinner with a bowl of miso soup always seems to put people in good humor.

In the best Japanese restaurants miso soups are made by carefully blending several types of miso paste to come up with a distinctive "house" style. This recipe uses half white miso and half red, but as you start playing around you'll come up with your own favorite brands and blends.

Once you have the *dashi* and the miso paste, miso soup takes only a few minutes to prepare.

MAKES 4 SERVINGS

I quart *dashi*

1½ tablespoons red miso

1¼ tablespoons white miso

BRING the *dashi* to a slow simmer. Combine the two kinds of miso in a mixing bowl and slowly whisk in several tablespoons of the *dashi* until the miso is a smooth paste. Stir the miso into the simmering *dashi*. Ladle into Japanese lacquer bowls with lids.

GARNISHES FOR MISO SOUP Vegetables, shellfish, and meat can all be used to decorate a bowl of miso soup. Although any of the garnishes used for consommé will work equally well in a bowl of miso, I always like to stick to a Japanese theme. And I always use Japanese lacquer bowls with lids to hold in the flavor of the soup and to give a Japanese feel to the whole thing.

TRADITIONALLY, Japanese clear soups are garnished with three solids. The central ingredient is usually a piece of shellfish such as a clam or shrimp (in Japan, my breakfast miso had little limpets), a strip of meat, or a small fish head. The second ingredient should be some kind of vegetable and have a contrasting shape. I like to use daikon or carrot, finely shredded with a Japanese mandoline called a benriner cutter, or a slice of shiitake mushroom. The last ingredient is some kind of Japanese herb such as trefoil or Japanese citrus rinds or *yuzu*, but since these can be hard to track down, especially at the last minute, I often use finely chopped chives or a leaf or two of watercress.

INSTANT DASHI

Unlike so many convenience foods, which rarely capture the flavor of the real thing, instant *dashi* is surprisingly subtle and satisfying. It's available in most grocery stores where there is even a small Asian clientele.

Called *dashi-no-moto* or *hon-dashi*, instant *dashi* comes in granulated form in small packets or jars. In case there's no English on the packet, instant *dashi* is surprisingly strong; 1 teaspoon is usually enough to make 1 quart of full-flavored stock. Be careful when using instant dashi, because some brands are very salty.

CUBES of tofu provide an especially nutritious and satisfying garnish for miso or other *dashi*-based soups. Simply cut the tofu into ½-inch cubes, rinse them off, and arrange them in the soup bowls before pouring the soup over.

Thai Hot and Spicy Broth

GAENG PRIK

This soup is a great beginning to a Thai meal. It's also the perfect foil for a bowl of jasmine or basmati rice as a light but very satisfying dinner. It's very hot, so if you want something a little tamer, use half the number of chilies called for here and then adjust the hotness upwards by adding cayenne a little at a time.

You can make this soup 20 minutes in advance or up to 3 days in advance if you keep it refrigerated.

MAKES 6 SERVINGS

6 cups chicken or pork broth

3 small red Thai chilies or 4 jalapeño chilies, seeded and finely chopped

3 garlic cloves, chopped

2 shallots, chopped

a ¼-inch slice of galangal or ginger

4 kaffir lime leaves, cut into very thin shreds

a 6-inch length of lemongrass, finely sliced

3 tablespoons tamarind paste dissolved in ½ cup hot water, strained, or juice of 2 limes

¼ cup Thai fish sauce (*nam pla*) or more to taste

10 grinds of white pepper

cayenne pepper if needed

1 scallion, finely chopped, both green and white parts

¼ cup finely chopped cilantro

½ cup coconut milk (optional)

IN a 4-quart pot, simmer the broth with the chilies, garlic, shallots, galangal, lime leaves, and lemongrass for 10 minutes. Stir in the rest of the ingredients and simmer for 2 minutes more.

SUGGESTIONS AND VARIATIONS | Although this broth is great to drink alone, it also makes a perfect backdrop for fish, shellfish, and meats. Just toss in cubes or strips of fish, chicken, or pork or pieces of whole shellfish such as shrimp or scal-

CHOOSING A RED WINE

Select the wine for this broth carefully. I like to use Spanish Rioja, red Zinfandel from California, or Dão from Portugal—all have a deep color and a rich flavor and won't break the bank. Avoid light fruity red wines such as Beaujolais, which are pleasant to drink but don't have enough body for cooking.

lops 5 to 10 minutes before serving. I sometimes cook basmati or jasmine rice directly in the soup to make it substantial enough for a light meal.

THIS broth is also used in the Shrimp Balls in Hot and Sour Thai Broth on page 132.

Red Wine Broth for Meat

Red wine broth is a delicious backdrop for soups that contain lightly sautéed, grilled, or roasted meats. Made in almost the same way as red wine sauce, but neither as concentrated nor as rich, it makes it possible to serve elaborate meat dishes without the excess calories and fat.

MAKES 1 QUART

The trick for making a savory red wine broth is to cook pieces of meat with aromatic vegetables such as carrots, onions, and turnips until both the meat and vegetables are thoroughly browned. Then, instead of adding the red wine all at once, add a small amount and cook it all the way down until the pan is completely dry. This reinforces the color of the broth and also removes some of the wine's bitterness.

Be prepared to use a lot of red wine—it's essential to the color and flavor of the broth—but if you're using the red wine broth as part of a more elaborate soup, you can get by using only ½ cup per serving.

Red wine broth has a very light texture. If you want it to be slightly thicker, whisk in the optional flour and butter paste.

    2 tablespoons unsalted butter
    1 medium-size carrot, chopped
    1 medium-size onion, chopped
    1 small turnip, peeled and chopped
    2 garlic cloves, crushed and peeled
    6 ounces lean raw beef or pork trimmings or ¼ pound
        pancetta or unsmoked raw cured ham such as
        prosciutto trimmings, cut into ½-inch cubes
    2 cups chicken, beef, or pork broth (optional)
    3 fifths of dry red wine

1 bouquet garni

salt

pepper

beurre manié (optional):

2 tablespoons unsalted butter

2 tablespoons all-purpose flour

MELT 2 tablespoons butter in a 4-quart pot over medium heat. Add the vegetables and meat and stir every few minutes. After about 10 minutes the mixture should start to brown. If it starts to brown earlier, turn down the heat. Cook the mixture for 20 minutes, until both the meat and vegetables are thoroughly browned.

ADD the broth if you're using it and 2 cups of the red wine. Boil the mixture until all the red wine and broth have evaporated. Only a small amount of transparent fat should appear on the bottom of the pot. Don't cook beyond this point, or the mixture will burn.

ADD the rest of the red wine and bouquet garni to the caramelized meat and vegetables. Bring the liquids to a boil and turn the heat down low enough to keep the liquid at a slow simmer. Cook until reduced to 1 quart, about 30 minutes, using a ladle to skim off any fat or froth that floats to the top. Strain the mixture into a clean 2-quart saucepan and season with salt and pepper.

FOR a thicker broth, use the *beurre manié*. Work the butter and flour to a smooth paste on a plate with a fork, then whisk the paste into the hot broth. Bring the broth to a full boil for 15 seconds and then remove it from the heat.

THE broth freezes well and will keep up to 3 days in the refrigerator.

BEURRE MANIÉ

Beurre manié (kneaded butter) is the traditional thickener for French country soups and stews, especially those containing red wine. *Beurre manié* contains the same ingredients as roux-flour and butter—but instead of being cooked, the flour and butter are left raw and worked into a smooth paste with the back of a fork. *Beurre manié* should be stirred into a hot soup just a minute or two before serving and the soup brought to a full boil for the thickening to take effect.

Medallions of Beef with Caramelized Onions and Red Wine Broth

This is a delicious and elegant way to serve beef, and the broth is as satisfying as a rich sauce but without the fat. You can make the broth weeks ahead and freeze it; then all you have to do is caramelize the onions and roast the beef.

MAKES 4 MAIN-COURSE SERVINGS

2 tablespoons unsalted butter

8 medium-size onions, 3 pounds, peeled and thinly sliced

2 teaspoons chopped fresh thyme leaves or 1 teaspoon dried

salt

pepper

1½ pounds beef tenderloin, preferably center cut

2 tablespoons olive oil

1 quart red wine broth

10 medium-size mushrooms, quartered

2 tablespoons chopped chives or parsley

CARAMELIZING THE ONIONS Up to a day in advance, melt the butter over medium heat in a 4-quart pot. Add the onions and thyme. Cook for about 20 minutes, stirring every few minutes to prevent sticking and burning, until the onions are thoroughly softened. Cook for another 10 to 15 minutes, stirring constantly, until the onions caramelize and turn a deep brown. Season with salt and pepper. Transfer the onions to a mixing bowl and keep covered. Refrigerate them if you're working a day in advance.

BROWNING AND ROASTING THE BEEF Thirty minutes before serving, preheat the oven to 500°F. Season the tenderloin with salt and pepper and brown over high heat in olive oil in a small sauté pan or small heavy skillet (make sure it doesn't have plastic handles). Roast in the same pan for about 15 minutes, until it browns and you see blood forming on its surface. Tenderloin is best served very rare.

TAKE the tenderloin out of the oven and cover it loosely with aluminum foil to keep it warm while you're setting up the rest of the soup.

ARRANGING THE BOWLS Bring the red wine broth to a slow simmer, add the mushrooms, and simmer for about 3 minutes. Add the chives and simmer for 1 minute more. Reheat the caramelized onions in a small saucepan and arrange them in an elongated mound across the center of each bowl.

SLICE the beef tenderloin into 12 thin slices. Arrange 3 slices over the onions in each bowl.

LADLE the hot red wine broth and the mushrooms around the meat, sprinkle the slices of meat with salt and pepper, and serve.

SUGGESTIONS AND VARIATIONS

| Almost any method can be used to cook the meat. If you don't want to roast the tenderloin, try barbecuing it whole or slicing it into thin steaks, which can then be quickly sautéed.

YOU don't have to restrict yourself to using just onions as the vegetable base for the meat. Combinations of fine vegetable julienne such as carrots, leeks, turnips, and string beans cut into fine strips, or a mound of fresh spinach can be used. You can also place a large slice of toasted French bread in the middle of each soup plate and use it to prop up the slices of meat.

THIS technique can be used for presenting almost any kind of meat or fish.

BUYING TENDERLOIN

The center section of the tenderloin is the best part to use for this dish because it makes perfectly even, round medallions, but you may have a hard time getting the butcher to give it to you. You might find it more economical to buy a whole tenderloin, cut out the center section for this soup, and then freeze the rest to use for steaks.

Combining Broth
WITH EGGS,
CHEESE, AND HERBS

IN MANY COUNTRIES EGGS, EITHER RAW OR COOKED, ARE USED AS A QUICK AND SAT-isfying finish for a simple broth. In some recipes the hot broth is whisked into the beaten eggs to give the broth extra body. Often the eggs are combined with herbs or spices and sometimes cheese, as in the following *stracciatella* recipe. Other recipes add pieces of cooked egg to the broth or add raw egg in a steady stream so it cooks instantly and holds its shape in the soup—as in egg drop soup.

Although most of the recipes for these soups are backed by long traditions with the ingredients carefully spelled out, I like to improvise by adding different herbs and cheeses, spices such as cayenne pepper or Tabasco, and lemon or lime juice.

Hot Broth with Eggs and Parmesan Cheese

STRACCIATELLA

The secret to this soup is to use only authentic Parmigiano-Reggiano and a generous amount of freshly chopped parsley. I also like to float small croutons cooked in butter in the soup. *Stracciatella* means "little rags," a fairly accurate description of how this soup looks once the eggs have set.

MAKES 4 SERVINGS

1 quart chicken or beef broth

2 large eggs

3 tablespoons finely grated Parmigiano-Regiano cheese

3 tablespoons finely chopped parsley

2 or 3 gratings of nutmeg or a tiny pinch of ground nutmeg

salt

freshly ground white pepper

small croutons sautéed in butter (page 594)

BRING the broth to a simmer. Beat together the eggs, cheese, parsley, and nutmeg with a fork. Beat the egg mixture into the simmering broth with a fork. Give the egg about 45 seconds to set—it should set into tiny threads in the same way as Chinese egg drop soup.

SEASON the soup with salt and pepper. Ladle into hot bowls, then sprinkle croutons over each bowl and serve.

SUGGESTIONS AND VARIATIONS | Try replacing the nutmeg with a pinch of ground cinnamon or cloves. Instead of using parsley, try chervil, tarragon, or marjoram (with no spices).

Greek Lemon Soup

AVGOLEMONO

One of the things I like about this soup is that I can serve it any time of the year—hot with rice in winter, and cold without the rice in summer. This recipe reflects my own tastes and contains more lemon and parsley than traditional versions. Be sure to chop the parsley within an hour before serving—its freshness is essential to this soup.

MAKES 4 SERVINGS

1 quart chicken broth
½ cup raw rice or 1½ cups leftover cooked (optional)
2 eggs
juice of 3 lemons
5 tablespoons freshly chopped parsley
salt
freshly ground white pepper

IF you're using raw rice, bring the broth to a simmer with the rice, partially cover the pot, and simmer until the rice is done, in about 20 minutes. If you're using cooked rice, just bring the broth to a simmer and add the rice a minute or two before serving. Whisk together the eggs, lemon juice, and parsley. Pour the simmering broth into the egg mixture and stir for a minute or two to make sure the eggs are well combined with the broth. If you've included rice, you can whisk the soup, which will break the grains of rice and thicken the soup.

SEASON the soup with salt and pepper and serve either hot or cold.

SUGGESTIONS AND VARIATIONS | I sometimes make a wonderfully rich winter version of this soup by replacing the 2 eggs with 6 egg yolks and a cup of heavy cream and adding a teaspoon of grated lemon zest to the mixture to accentuate the lemon flavor. Pour the simmering broth into the egg yolk mixture as directed, return the soup to a saucepan, and cook it gently while stirring to thicken it, but don't allow it to boil. (For a full explanation of thickening soup with egg yolks, see page 212.) Then strain the soup through a fine-mesh sieve.

THERE are several well-known *avgolemono* variations, including an elegant variation by James Villas that includes orzo and oysters. One of my favorite variations is made with lamb broth—I make it when I have leftover roast leg of lamb—a little chopped tomato, and a good pinch of saffron threads. Sometimes I peel little pieces of cooked lamb off the bone and add them to the soup. One Moroccan version flavors this soup with cinnamon and finishes it with chopped cilantro. I haven't heard of it, but a little saffron would also be a typical Moroccan touch.

ANYA von Bremzen and John Welchman in their book *Please to the Table* have a somewhat more complicated version from Georgia in the former Soviet Union called *chikhirtma*, which contains saffron, garlic, ground coriander seeds, ground fenugreek, red pepper, chopped cilantro, basil, and mint, and shredded chicken breast. Here's a simplified version of their original recipe:

SIMMER 1 quart chicken broth with ½ teaspoon crushed coriander seeds, ⅛ teaspoon ground fenugreek, and ¼ teaspoon hot red pepper flakes for 5 minutes. Combine the juice of 3 lemons with 2 eggs as directed. Instead of adding parsley to the egg mixture, stir in a pinch of saffron, 2 tablespoons finely chopped cilantro, 2 tablespoons finely chopped fresh basil, and 2 tablespoons finely chopped fresh mint. Whisk the simmering stock into the egg mixture as described. You can also fill out this soup with a cup of shredded chicken breast.

Egg Drop Soup

This is a soup you can whip up at the last minute with easy-to-find ingredients. Although egg drop soup can be made by swirling beaten egg into almost any hot broth, the two best-known versions come from China and Japan. I sometimes end up making a cross between the two versions based on what I have in the refrigerator.

The Japanese version uses *dashi* as the basic broth, while the Chinese version uses a simple chicken broth flavored with ginger and garlic. Other than preparing a few simple garnishes, the techniques for preparing the two versions are the same.

MAKES 4 SERVINGS

chinese version:

1 quart Chinese chicken broth (see box on page 63)
1 tablespoon plus 2 teaspoons dark soy sauce or to taste
salt
1 tablespoon cornstarch
3 tablespoons cold water

2 scallions, both white and green parts, finely chopped

3 tablespoons finely chopped cilantro leaves

2 eggs, beaten

BRING the broth to a simmer. Add soy sauce and salt to taste.

COMBINE the cornstarch and water and work them to a smooth paste. Whisk the paste into the hot broth. Simmer the broth for 1 minute, until it thickens slightly. Add the scallions and cilantro.

USE a small pitcher to pour the eggs in a steady stream over the simmering broth. Swirl the broth so it's moving in a circle as you're pouring in the beaten egg. Don't stir the broth for about 45 seconds so the eggs have a chance to set. Once the egg has set, lightly break up the threads with a fork.

SERVE in hot bowls.

japanese version:

1 quart *dashi*

1 tablespoon plus 1 teaspoon light soy sauce

2 tablespoons sake or 1 tablespoon plus 1 teaspoon mirin

salt

½-inch section of fresh ginger, peeled

2 eggs, beaten

4 trefoil stalks, cut into 1-inch lengths, or 2 tablespoons chopped chives or scallions

BRING the *dashi* to a simmer and add the soy sauce and sake. Add salt to taste if necessary.

PUT the ginger into a garlic press (cut it up if you need to) and squeeze out the juice over the soup. Taste the soup as you add the juice. As soon as the ginger flavor is barely perceptible, stop adding the juice.

USE a small pitcher to pour the eggs in a steady stream over the simmering broth. Swirl the broth so it's moving in a circle as you're pouring in the beaten egg. Don't stir the broth for about 45 seconds so the eggs have a chance to set. Once the egg has set, lightly break up the threads with a fork.

ADD the trefoil and serve immediately.

Hot and Sour Soup

A word of warning: once you've tasted this soup, you'll never be satisfied with restaurant versions again. And your friends—even Chinese food aficionados—will be amazed by it. What makes this version of hot and sour soup so wonderful is the quality of the ingredients and the use of much less cornstarch than usually encountered in restaurants. Other than the obvious hot and sour tastes, most of the flavor comes from the Chinese mushrooms.

Don't panic at the list of ingredients. First, consult the Ingredients chapter for more information on anything unfamiliar. Second, be aware that even though you'll need to make a trip to a large Chinese market or mail-order some ingredients, they last a long time, and once you have them on hand it will be easy to throw this soup together on short notice. If you run out and want to avoid a shopping trip, just use regular button mushrooms and leave out the tree ears and the tiger lily stems.

Most sweet and sour soups I encounter in New York Chinese restaurants are made with chicken or pork. Barbara Tropp, in her excellent book *The Modern Art of Chinese Cooking*, includes a Moslem version made with beef. The techniques for using different meats are the same, so I leave the choice to you. This soup can be made entirely in advance.

Hot and sour soup loses some of its hotness and sourness if it sits overnight in the refrigerator, so you may need to add more pepper and vinegar to reheated soup.

MAKES 6 SERVINGS

6 large or 12 small dried black Chinese mushrooms or 6
    medium-size cultivated mushrooms, cut into quarters

¼ cup dried tree ears

20 dried tiger lily stems

1 small cake of Japanese tofu, cut into ¼-inch cubes

2 skinless and boneless chicken breast halves or 2 6- to
    8-ounce pork rib chops or 10 ounces round or
    chuck steak

2 tablespoons dark soy sauce

½ teaspoon sugar

½ teaspoon dark sesame oil

5 cups chicken broth, preferably flavored with ginger and
    garlic (see page 63)

1 tablespoon cornstarch

3 tablespoons cold water

6 tablespoons excellent wine vinegar, preferably Chinese rice
    vinegar or sherry vinegar, or more to taste

1 tablespoon freshly ground white or black pepper or more
    to taste

salt

1 egg, beaten

4 scallions, both white and green parts, finely chopped

IN ADVANCE Put the Chinese mushrooms, tree ears, and tiger lily stems in separate bowls. Pour over just enough boiling water to cover the Chinese mushrooms (regular mushrooms need no soaking; just wash and dry them) and the tree ears. Pour over just enough warm water to cover the tiger lily stems. Let them soak for 30 minutes, until all have softened. (The Chinese mushrooms and the tree ears can also be soaked overnight in cold water.) Save the soaking water from the Chinese mushrooms.

CUT off and discard any hard pieces from the mushrooms (you may need to cut off the stems) and cut the caps into quarters.

DISCARD the tiger lily soaking water and cut off the hard stem end. Shred the rest with your fingers and cut them in half crosswise.

DRAIN the tree ears, discarding the soaking water, and rinse them several times, working over them with your fingers to get rid of any grit. Tear off and discard any hard pieces. Some of the tree ears will have grown very large, so you'll need to tear them into pieces no more than an inch in diameter.

IF you're using pork or beef, take the meat off the bone and trim off any fat. With a sharp knife, cut the meat or chicken in half horizontally and then cut each half across the grain into thin 1-inch-long strips. In a mixing bowl, combine the meat strips with the soy sauce, sugar, and sesame oil and marinate for at least 30 minutes but as long as overnight, refrigerated.

RESERVE all these ingredients in covered bowls in the refrigerator until you're ready to cook the soup.

AT THE LAST MINUTE Bring the chicken broth to a simmer and add the mushrooms, tree ears, tiger lily stems, and soaking water from the mushrooms (leave any grit behind). Simmer for 2 minutes, then stir in the meat with its marinade. Bring the soup back to a simmer and simmer for 2 minutes more.

WORK the cornstarch and cold water to a smooth paste. Stir the paste into the simmering broth, then stir in the vinegar and pepper. Taste the soup to see if it needs additional soy sauce, vinegar, sesame oil, pepper, or some salt.

POUR the egg in a thin stream into the simmering soup while stirring gently. Give it a minute or two to set into thin strands.

SERVE the soup with a little chopped scallion sprinkled over each bowl.

SUGGESTIONS AND VARIATIONS | Because freshly ground pepper, mushrooms, and vinegar transform a simple broth into a savory soup, I don't like to limit this magical combination to the traditional Chinese version. For a simple soup for dining alone or with a close friend or two, I sometimes simmer dried morels or porcini in a cup or two of broth, grind in some fresh pepper, and sprinkle in wine vinegar. The same technique will also transform a simple vegetable or mushroom soup.

Noodles,
WONTONS, STUFFED PASTA, AND DUMPLINGS

Noodles

Noodles are used all over the world to give substance to soups. In France, tiny vermicelli are sometimes served with the broth from the *pot-au-feu;* in Asia, noodles made from wheat, rice, and beans help transform a cup or two of spicy broth into a hearty meal; the Italians have a whole family of soups, *minestre in brodo,* that contain different kinds of pasta and occasionally rice served in broth; and of course there is the beloved American staple, chicken noodle soup.

All of these soups are easy to prepare once you have the broth. Most supermarkets carry an array of dried Italian noodles, and more are beginning to carry fresh fettuccine and linguine.

NOODLES:
HOW MUCH TO SERVE?

Add 1 ounce dried noodles per serving if you want the noodles to float around in the soup along with the other ingredients. If the noodles are the focal point for a miniature soup meal, use 2 ounces.

For fresh Italian or Chinese egg noodles, use about 50 percent more by weight than dried: 1½ ounces for a light soup, 3 ounces for a main-course soup.

Chicken Noodle Soup

Chicken noodle soup may have been a pleasure when I was growing up, but I admit to being more jaded now. I rarely serve chicken noodle soup without sneaking in some chopped herbs (basil, shredded or ground into *pistou;* a leaf or two of fresh sage simmered with the broth; some finely chopped mint; even freshly chopped parsley) or, in summer, a bit of chopped fresh tomato. Sometimes I heap up the noodles in the broth and sprinkle the whole thing with Parmesan.

This soup is wonderfully economical—if you make your own broth you can take the cooked chicken off the bone and add it to the soup just before serving. You can make an extraspecial version of this soup by cooking whole cut-up chickens in chicken broth instead of water.

Vermicelli or spaghetti noodles are the old standbys for chicken noodle soup, but I sometimes use macaroni or whatever shape I spot that seems interesting. Sometimes I use fresh fettuccine or linguine and heap them up in wide plates surrounded with broth.

Although the easiest way to cook the noodles is to throw them into the simmering broth just long enough before serving to cook them through (about 3 minutes for fresh noodles and 10 minutes for dried), this sometimes clouds the broth. So, if you're being fussy, your best bet is to cook the noodles in a separate pot of boiling water along with a tablespoon of olive oil to keep the noodles from clumping, drain them, and add them to the broth just before serving.

MAKES 8 SERVINGS

6 cups chicken broth

2 medium-size carrots, peeled, halved lengthwise, and sliced

1 tablespoon olive oil (optional)

1 tablespoon salt

6 ounces dried noodles such as vermicelli or spaghetti
or 9 ounces fresh noodles such as linguine or
fettuccine

1 cup shredded chicken from making the broth or 2 skinless
and boneless chicken breasts, cut into 1- by ¼-inch
strips (optional)

salt

pepper

BRING the broth to a simmer in a 4-quart pot and add the carrots. Simmer until the carrots are soft, about 15 minutes.

COOKING THE NOODLES SEPARATELY (OPTIONAL) Fill a 4-quart pot three-quarters full of water and add a tablespoon of salt; cover and bring to a rapid boil. Add the olive oil and noodles and cook for 3 to 10 minutes, depending on whether the pasta is dried or fresh and what the directions on the package say. Drain the noodles in a colander and slide them into the simmering chicken broth. Add the raw or cooked chicken to the broth 3 minutes before serving. Season with salt and pepper and serve in hot bowls.

COOKING THE NOODLES IN THE BROTH Just slide the noodles into the simmering broth and cook until done. Add the raw or cooked chicken to the broth 3 minutes before serving. Season with salt and pepper and serve.

Chicken Broth with Noodles, Chicken Livers, and Peas

PASTA IN BRODO CON FEGATINI

This is an example of a classic *minestre in brodo* I found in Elizabeth David's *Italian Food*, first published in 1954. Her original recipe calls for fresh peas, but I use frozen. (Peas are one of the few vegetables I prefer frozen; fresh peas always seem overgrown.)

MAKES 4 SERVINGS

2 quarts water

1 tablespoon salt

¼ pound dried vermicelli, broken into 3-inch lengths

1 quart basic brown chicken broth

8 chicken livers, about ½ pound

1 tablespoon unsalted butter

salt

pepper

1 10-ounce package frozen peas

½ cup freshly grated Parmesan cheese

BRING the water to a rapid boil with the tablespoon of salt and cook the vermicelli in it until soft, about 10 minutes. Meanwhile, bring the chicken broth to a simmer. When done, drain the vermicelli in a colander.

COOK the chicken livers in the butter in a small sauté pan over medium heat until they feel firm to the touch. Transfer them to a cutting board and chop coarsely. Season with salt and pepper.

PUT the peas into the simmering chicken broth—they don't need to be thawed—and wait for the broth to come back to a simmer. Stir in the chopped chicken livers, the Parmesan, and season to taste with salt and pepper.

Asian Noodles

When I started working with Asian noodles, I was amazed by how many types there are. In one Chinese grocery I found almost 60 varieties, but there has been no need to scour New York looking for exotic stores that sell them—my corner grocery has more than 15 different kinds of Japanese noodles alone.

Asian noodles provide a delightful and inexpensive way to turn a simple broth into a filling and satisfying meal. They're easy to prepare, when dried they keep indefinitely, and some types, such as soba, are extremely nutritious.

JAPANESE NOODLES: It's surprising that Japan's more exotic fare—raw fish (sashimi) and sushi—became popular in the United States long before the Japanese everyday staple: a bowl of hot noodles in broth.

The Japanese make a wide array of noodles, each served in its own traditional way. I have to admit to using a more casual approach, mixing and matching broths, noodles, and garnishes, coming up with combinations I like and then using different noodles for variety. I love shopping for Japanese noodles; they're so beautifully wrapped that I sometimes end up buying three or four different kinds.

Japanese noodles are cooked in rapidly boiling water before they are added to broth; they are never cooked directly in it. After the first cooking, which can last from 30 seconds to several minutes, they are thoroughly rinsed with cold water to eliminate starch that would cloud the broth. They are then reheated in some of the broth before serving.

Soba: These brownish buckwheat noodles are just slightly thinner than spaghetti but not as thin as vermicelli. They have a delightful texture, a rich color, and a full flavor. These are my favorite Japanese noodles. One of my favorite lunches is a bowl of soba noodles served with *dashi*, a sprinkling of chopped scallions, and the Japanese seven-spice mixture called *shichimi*.

Udon: Japan's most popular noodles. They are easy to recognize because they are relatively thick, have squared edges, and are perfectly white. They are usually folded in half before they are dried and packaged. Udon can be served in the same way as soba.

Kishimen: Almost identical to udon but wider. I sometimes use them in *sukiyaki*like soups served in large bowls that have lots of ingredients floating around.

Somen: These are very fine white noodles. There is also a yellow-tinted somen—enriched with eggs—called *tamago somen*.

Hiyamugi: These very thin white noodles look a lot like somen. Although the Japanese prefer them cold with dipping sauce, they can also be served in broth.

Cha-soba: Soba with a pale green tint that has been flavored with green tea. Any noodle whose name starts with *cha* has been flavored in this way. I often use these noodles instead of plain soba noodles.

Shirataki: These are thin noodles made from the starch of yams. The only time I use them or have seen them called for is in *sukiyaki*. I've found them dried in Japanese groceries under the name *saifun*. From time to time shirataki are also available fresh. (To cook shirataki, see the recipe for *sukiyaki*, page 448.)

NOODLES FROM CHINA, SOUTHEAST ASIA, AND KOREA:

Cellophane Noodles: These shiny transparent noodles are made from mung bean starch. They have little flavor of their own, but they are appreciated for their texture and the fact that they quickly take on the flavor of the surrounding broth. Unlike rice or wheat noodles, which have to be cooked in boiling water and rinsed before being added to a broth, cellophane noodles need only to be soaked for about 30 minutes in warm water and then cooked directly in the broth for only a minute. In Vietnam, cellophane noodles are usually cut into shorter lengths—a heresy in China, where long noodles are associated with longevity.

Cellophane noodles have many names depending on where they are made or sold. In English they are also called *bean threads, mung bean vermicelli, glass noodles, transparent noodles*, or *shining noodles*. In Vietnamese they are called *mien* or *bun tau*, and in Thailand *wun sen*. The Koreans have a thick version made from potatoes and yams called *tangmyon*.

Rice Noodles: If you're going to an Asian grocery looking for rice noodles, be prepared—there are at least a dozen different kinds—and depending on where you go, they will be sold under different names.

The best rice noodle for soups is a dry thin variety that looks vaguely like a nest. These noodles are usually called *rice vermicelli* or sometimes *rice sticks*. Thicker noodles, usually called *rice sticks* or *river rice noodle* (*sen yai, sen lek*, or *sen mee* in Thai; *banh pho* or just *pho* in Vietnamese) are among the most common and versatile rice noodles. They are sold dry and come in three different sizes. The thinnest of the three are best to use in soups. Thin dried rice noodles don't need to be precooked, just soaked in warm water until soft and pliable, about 20 minutes, before being added to soup. Many recipes, however, suggest a 30-second simmering in boiling water just to heat the noodles through before they are added to broth.

The Chinese use a thick spaghettilike noodle called *lai fen*. This noodle is also used by the Malaysians under the name *laksa* and in the Philippines as *pancit luglug*.

Chinese Egg Noodles: Egg noodles—made with wheat flour in much the same way as Italian noodles—are popular throughout China. If you live near an Asian market, it's easy to find fresh noodles. In Chinese the thin noodles are sometimes sold under the name *don mein*, and the wider noodles, more often used in soups, under the name *fu don mein*. In Vietnamese they are called *mi*, and in Thai *ba mee*. Chinese egg noodles should be precooked for about 4 minutes (until completely cooked, not *al dente*), thoroughly rinsed with cold water, and tossed with a teaspoon of vegetable oil (to prevent clumping) before being added to a soup.

Italian fettuccine or linguine noodles can be substituted in recipes calling for Chinese egg noodles.

Chicken or Duck Broth with Cellophane Noodles

I first saw a recipe similar to this one in Nicole Routhier's book *The Foods of Vietnam*. Hers was the first Vietnamese recipe I had seen that uses Chinese preserved vegetables—a delicious and simple way to give a full flavor to a broth.

This soup is a simple way to turn a few cups of broth into a full meal. While the broth gets its flavor from Vietnamese-style fish sauce, preserved vegetables, and cilantro, it gets its bulk from cellophane noodles. If you can't find cellophane noodles, substitute another type of thin rice noodle.

MAKES 6 SERVINGS

¼ pound dried cellophane noodles

3 ounces Chinese preserved vegetable

5 cups chicken or duck broth

2 skinless and boneless chicken or duck breast halves, cut into 2- by ¼-inch strips

3 tablespoons Vietnamese-style fish sauce (*nuoc mam*)

3 scallions, both white and green parts, finely sliced

¼ cup chopped cilantro leaves

SOAK the cellophane noodles in a bowl of warm water for about 30 minutes. When they have softened, cut them into 5-inch lengths with scissors.

RINSE and drain the preserved vegetable. Slice it and cut the slices into pieces the size of matchsticks; you should end up with about ¼ cup.

BRING the broth to a full boil and add the noodles. Cook for 1 to 3 minutes, until the noodles are completely soft (bite into one; they should not be *al dente*). Quickly arrange the noodles in hot bowls. Put the strips of chicken, preserved vegetables, fish sauce, scallions, and cilantro into the hot broth. Simmer gently for 2 minutes.

ARRANGE the cooked chicken on top of the noodles in each bowl. Ladle the hot broth over the noodles and chicken.

Thai-Style Chicken and Cellophane Noodle Soup

> I like this intriguing soup because, although it's exotic, I don't have to worry about scaring my guests with strong or unusual flavors. The basic broth is very mild but served with a pungent sauce, so guests can flavor it to their own taste. The least adventurous don't have to add any sauce at all.

MAKES 8 SERVINGS

3 skinless and boneless chicken breasts, cut crosswise into strips about 2 inches by ¼ inch

6 tablespoons Thai fish sauce (*nam pla*)

5 tablespoons light soy sauce

pinch of sugar

½ pound cellophane noodles

2 quarts chicken broth

5 scallions, both white and green parts, finely sliced

¼ cup chopped cilantro leaves

the sauce:

3 garlic cloves, finely chopped and crushed to a paste

½ cup fresh lime juice

3 teaspoons cayenne pepper

3 tablespoons Thai fish sauce (*nam pla*)

5 teaspoons dark soy sauce

5 teaspoons sugar

MARINATE the sliced chicken breasts in a tablespoon each of the fish sauce and soy sauce and the pinch of sugar for 30 minutes.

SOAK the cellophane noodles in warm water for 20 minutes and drain.

PREPARE the sauce by whisking together all of the ingredients.

BRING the chicken broth to a simmer and add the noodles. Cook for 1 to 2 minutes, until the noodles are soft. Divide the noodles among 8 hot bowls.

ADD the chicken with its marinade to the hot broth. Simmer gently for 2 minutes and skim off the froth that floats to the top. Add the scallions, cilantro, and remaining fish and soy sauces to the hot broth. Simmer for 2 minutes more. Distribute the chicken over each bowl with a slotted spoon. Ladle the broth over all.

SERVE the sauce at the table with a small spoon.

Udon or Soba Noodles in Broth

This is one of the simplest and most satisfying of all Japanese noodle soups. I like to make it for lunch on a cold winter day—it warms me up, and I usually have all the ingredients on hand, saving me a trip out into the cold. I never try to get fancy with this soup—it doesn't need it—but I do like to vary it with strips of leftover meat or fish or pieces of fresh shrimp.

The broth is made by seasoning *dashi* with both light and dark soy sauces, mirin, and a little sugar. Although this recipe spells out exact quantities, you should play with the ingredients until you come up with a style you like. Use a larger quantity of noodles for a light main course, less for a first course.

MAKES 6 SERVINGS

4 quarts water
8 to 18 ounces dried udon or soba noodles
5 cups *dashi*
2 tablespoons dark soy sauce
2 tablespoons light soy sauce
2 teaspoons sugar
2 tablespoons mirin
4 scallions, both white and green parts, finely sliced
seven-spice mixture (*shichimi*)

BRING the water to a rapid boil and cook the noodles in it until they are *al dente*—completely cooked but with a little bit of texture and no rawness in the middle, about 10 minutes. (Check every minute or two.) Drain the noodles in a colander and rinse with cold water to eliminate starch.

BRING the *dashi* to a simmer and add the soy sauces, sugar, and mirin. Slide in the noodles and heat them in the *dashi* for about 2 minutes.

DISTRIBUTE the noodles among hot Japanese noodle bowls and pour the hot *dashi* over them. Sprinkle with the sliced scallions.

SERVE the seven-spice mixture at the table with a small spoon so guests can help themselves.

SUGGESTIONS AND VARIATIONS | You can add almost anything to this soup to vary it or make it more substantial. Shrimp is a favorite of the Japanese, but since I rarely have shrimp just sitting around, I often add leftover meat such as thinly sliced chicken or duck.

ONE charming and particularly Japanese approach is to form a nest out of the noodles in each bowl and place a raw egg yolk in the center of each one. Although the Japanese love to eat raw eggs, Americans worried about salmonella may want to stir the egg into the soup before eating so the yolk ends up completely cooked.

Chinese Pork Noodle Soup

This flavorful soup is easy to prepare and doesn't contain so many exotic ingredients that you'll have to spend half the day shopping. The only unusual ingredient is the preserved vegetable, which gives the soup an exciting flavor; if you can't get it, the soup is still worth making.

MAKES 8 SERVINGS

½ pound pork loin or 2 ½-inch-thick pork chops

I tablespoon dry sherry or Chinese rice wine (Shaoxing wine)

I teaspoon cornstarch

4 teaspoons dark soy sauce

½ teaspoon dark sesame oil

freshly ground pepper

3 ounces Chinese preserved vegetable, preferably leafy mustard greens

4 quarts water

I quart chicken or pork broth

1½ pounds fresh Chinese egg noodles or fettuccine

2 scallions, both white and green parts, finely sliced

IN ADVANCE Remove the bones and any large sections of fat from the pork loin or chops. Slice the meat into ¼-inch strips about 1 inch long. Combine the pork strips with the sherry, cornstarch, soy sauce, and sesame oil. Add 3 grinds of pepper. Work the mixture with your fingers to eliminate any lumps of cornstarch. Pinch hard on the pork strips to flatten them slightly. Marinate for 1 or 2 hours or overnight, refrigerated.

RINSE the preserved vegetable and cut it into fine shreds about an inch long. If you're not making the soup right away, keep these covered in a bowl in the refrigerator.

AT THE LAST MINUTE Bring the water to a rapid boil. Bring the broth to a simmer.

PLUNGE the noodles into the boiling water and cook until *al dente*, about 2 minutes. Drain them in a colander and divide them among 4 soup bowls.

STIR the pork, its marinade, the preserved vegetable, and the sliced scallions into the hot broth. Simmer for 1 minute while stirring. Season the soup to taste with fresh pepper and the remaining soy sauce (or more if needed).

POUR the soup over the noodles in each bowl.

CHINESE GREENS

Unless you live in an area with a large Asian population, the only Chinese vegetable you're likely to encounter at your local supermarket is bok choy. If you live in a more cosmopolitan place or you venture into a Chinatown, you'll not only find an additional two or three varieties of bok choy but also a collection of closely related mustards and cabbages. The most common bok choy has beautiful pure white stalks and dark green leaves that hold loosely together in elongated bunches. In a Chinese market you'll also find a winter variety of bok choy called Shanghai bok choy. Shanghai bok choy is more squat than common bok choy and has pale green spoon-shaped stalks. Shanghai bok choy is usually sold in relatively small bunches, 6 to 8 inches long. Another variety of bok choy looks like Shanghai bok choy except that it has white stalks instead of green, or you may spot smallish bunches of "bok choy sum" with little yellow flowers and irregularly shaped leaves. Bok choy sum, also called "choy sum" or "flowering cabbage," has much the same flavor as regular bok choy, but the little edible yellow flowers look so good in stir-fries that, given the choice, you may want to buy bok choy sum when you see it. In some places—such as New York's Chinatown—there are so many varieties of bok choy that it's almost impossible to figure them all out, much less learn how to pronounce their Chinese names.

Fortunately, most Chinese vegetables are cooked the same way—quickly stir-fried or simmered directly in broth. To prepare bok choy for cooking, gently fold back and separate the branches as you would celery. After washing, you can then just slice the bok choy, but I usually cut the leaves off the white stalks so I can simmer or stir fry the stalks for a few minutes before adding the greens. Once you get everything separated, all you need to do is slice the stalks and cut the leaves into strips.

Other Chinese vegetables include Chinese broccoli, which has the full-flavor of broccoli rabe but without the bitterness. A bunch of Chinese broccoli has more leaves than both broccoli and broccoli rabe, and the leaves are larger. It often has the familiar dark green buds that we see on broccoli rabe, but much of the time the buds have blossomed into pretty little white flowers. Chinese broccoli has dark green stalks, so it's easy to distinguish it from bok choy, which has white or pale green stalks. Simmer every part of Chinese broccoli, except for the thick central stem, directly in a soup.

Oil seed rape is another delicious soup vegetable, easy to recognize by its yellow flowers, oval leaves, and diminutive stalks. It's usually sold in 6- to 8-inch-long bunches and is completely edible except for the largest central stalk at the base. Oil seed rape should be simmered in broth for about 10 minutes.

Bamboo mustard cabbage looks similar to other mustard greens but nothing like what we usually think of as cabbage. It's easy to recognize because its leaves have sawtooth edges. It's usually sold in small bunches of about 8 inches long and has thin, very pale green stalks. Bamboo mustard cabbage can be added to soups and simmered for 5 to 10 minutes.

Wrapped heart mustard cabbage looks like an elongated cabbage—slightly bulbous at one end but with dark green leaves opening at the other. Mustard cabbage is most often pickled, but it can also be shredded and added to soups in the same way as regular cabbage and simmered for 5 to 10 minutes.

Chinese-Style Short Rib Soup with Chinese Vegetables

Because I live in New York, I see immigrants from all over the world, and in my forays, largely on foot, to or from the subway, I often get a quick peek of people eating lunches behind store counters or on park benches. I'm most impressed by Asians who always seem to be slurping some combination of broth, noodles, and green leafy vegetables—a possible explanation for why so few Asians are overweight. Since I've written a book called *Vegetables*, a number of people assume I'm a vegetarian. But in fact I don't care for vegetables without meat anymore than I care for meat without vegetables. The trick, I think, is to reverse the ratio and eat plenty of vegetables but to use meat to provide savor. This soup has plenty of savor, from slowly simmered short ribs, plenty of flavor from spices, chilies, ginger, and sesame oil, and lots of greens, the choice of which is up to you (see box, page 117).

You first must make the broth by simmering roasted short ribs. Short ribs come in two forms, the so-called English cut, which contains one piece of rib running its length and is usually about 4 inches long, and "flanken"-style short ribs, which are 1-inch-wide pieces made by cutting across the ribs so each piece has several pieces of bone. Since you're going to be taking the meat off the bone anyway, it doesn't matter which kind you buy, but given the choice I prefer the English cut because it's easier to separate the meat from the ribs.

Because short ribs contain a lot of fat, brown them in the oven so they release the fat, which you can then pour off before putting the short ribs in the pot with water. The ribs will continue to release fat as you simmer them, so you must be careful not to let the broth boil (which, of course churns the fat into the broth) and you should skim the broth regularly with a ladle. If you have the forethought, make the broth a day or two ahead, refrigerate it, and remove the congealed fat in one solid piece.

MAKES 8 MAIN-COURSE OR 12 FIRST-COURSE SERVINGS

for the broth:

> 5 pounds short ribs, preferably English style
>
> 2 medium-size onions, halved but not peeled
>
> 2 large carrots, peeled and cut into 1-inch sections
>
> bouquet garni containing 1 bunch of parsley, 5 fresh thyme sprigs (or ½ teaspoon dried), and 1 bay leaf
>
> reserved mushroom stems (see below)

for finishing the broth:

> 1 medium-size onion, peeled, and finely chopped
>
> 3 garlic cloves, peeled and finely chopped

1-inch piece of fresh ginger, peeled and grated

1 tablespoon peanut or canola oil

1 teaspoon red pepper flakes or 1 fresh Thai chili, stem and
   seeds removed, finely chopped

¾ pound shiitake mushrooms, stems removed (added to
   broth above), caps thinly sliced

¼ cup balsamic vinegar or more to taste

¼ cup Japanese dark soy sauce

the greens:

1 pound spinach, chard, bok choy, or other Chinese
   vegetables (see box), stems cut out and sliced into
   ½-inch-wide sections, leaves cut into ½-inch-wide
   strips, or, if the greens have flowers, clusters separated
   from stems

4 scallions, both white and green parts, finely chopped

1 teaspoon freshly ground black pepper

1 teaspoon Asian (preferably Japanese) dark sesame oil or
   more to taste

PREPARING THE BROTH Preheat the oven to 425°F. Spread the short ribs and vegetables in a high-sided (to catch the fat), heavy-bottomed roasting pan (or a couple of heavy skillets) just large enough to hold them in a single layer. Slide the roasting pan into the oven and bake until the short ribs and vegetables are well browned. Turn the short ribs and vegetables over with tongs and continue baking until they're well browned on all sides. The total baking time will be about 1 hour. Carefully remove the roasting pan from the oven—it will contain a lot of fat—and use tongs to transfer the ribs and vegetables to a tall narrow pot. Discard the fat and pour about a quart of water into the roasting pan. Set the pan over high heat on the stove and scrape the bottom with a wooden spoon to dissolve the caramelized juices. Pour the liquid over the short ribs. Nestle the bouquet garni in the ribs and add the stems from the shiitake mushrooms. Pour over enough water to cover, bring to a boil over high heat, and turn down heat to maintain at a gentle simmer. Simmer until the meat is falling off the bone, about 3 hours. Use a ladle, throughout the simmering, to skim off the fat and scum that float to the top. Gently take the short ribs out of the broth with a large slotted spoon or skimmer and reserve. Strain the broth. Don't push down on the vegetables in the strainer or you'll cloud the broth. (It's better to just let them drain for 10 to 15 minutes.) Reserve the broth. Discard the vegetables and, when the short ribs have cooled slightly, pull away and discard the bones and any large chunks of fat and connective tissue. Cut the meat into strips 1 or 2 inches long and about ½ inch wide. (The exact size isn't important and will be partially determined by what kind of ribs you bought.) You can also pull the meat apart in shreds. Reserve the meat, covered with plastic wrap or sealed in zip-lock bags (braised meat quickly dries out and turns dark when left uncovered).

FINISHING THE BROTH In a pot large enough to hold the soup, cook the chopped onion, garlic, and ginger in the oil for about 5 minutes over medium heat, until they release their fragrance. Pour in the broth and add the pepper flakes, mushrooms, vinegar, and soy sauce. Bring to a simmer.

THE GREENS If you're using the stems from the greens, add them to the broth first and simmer them for about 5 minutes before adding the greens. Simmer the greens for 2 to 5 minutes—reach in to taste a piece to determine when it's done. Stir in the scallions, pepper, sesame oil, and the reserved meat.

SUGGESTIONS AND VARIATIONS | This is a model for an infinite number of soups that, once you have the broth, you can toss together at the last minute. As marvelous as it is, it isn't necessary to braise short ribs to provide the meat and broth for the soup. Pieces of leftover cooked or thinly sliced raw beef, pork, chicken, or duck can be simmered in any full-flavored broth, the broth finished in the same way as above—which takes only 10 minutes—and green vegetables added at the end. The soup can be made more substantial—it can even be turned into a whole dinner—by adding noodles such as Chinese egg noodles (or, for that matter, regular pasta noodles), soba noodles, or rice noodles (see box on page 107).

Stuffed Pasta

Stuffed squares or rounds of pasta are delicious served in a simple broth that stays in the background and doesn't interfere with the tasty filling.

Wonton Soup

Twenty years ago, after discovering wonton wrappers in a San Francisco supermarket, I realized that the possibilities for different fillings were infinite and went on a wonton binge. The wonton soup of Chinese restaurant tradition contains a simple pork and spinach stuffing flavored with garlic, but once you have a stack of wrappers on hand it's easy to improvise stuffings with leftovers and a few seasonings.

After stuffing the wontons, just heat them in chicken or pork broth or *dashi* and add some chopped scallions or spinach leaves for color and contrast.

STUFFING WONTONS Wonton wrappers are thin square sheets of raw dough, a form of fresh pasta. They're easy to work with, but be careful to keep them moist. When you open a package of wonton wrappers, quickly take out what you need and wrap the rest in plastic wrap and keep them in the refrigerator. Tightly wrapped, they keep for several weeks in the refrigerator and indefinitely in the freezer.

TO stuff wontons, coat the surface of the wrapper with beaten egg using your finger or a small brush. Place a teaspoon of stuffing in the middle of each casing and then fold the wonton in half, away from you. Press firmly on the outside of the wrapper to seal the stuffing inside. Take the 2 corners nearest you and bring them together so that the wonton curls around like tortellini. Moisten the corners with a little beaten egg and pinch them together.

LET the wontons dry for about 20 minutes before simmering in the soup. Once you add them to the simmering soup, they will take 3 minutes to cook. If you want to make the wontons in advance (you can keep finished wontons in the refrigerator for up to 2 days and in the freezer for several weeks), cook them for 3 minutes in boiling water containing a tablespoon of peanut oil (to prevent them from sticking) and drain them in a colander. Rinse them with cold water, drain them well, and wrap them tightly in plastic wrap.

traditional pork filling (makes 1 cup, enough for about 50 wontons):

> 2 quarts water
>
> I large bunch of spinach, stems removed and leaves washed,
>   2 cups tightly packed leaves
>
> ¾ cup cooked or raw pork—leftover roast pork or
>   I 6-ounce pork chop—trimmed of fat and bones
>   and cut into cubes
>
> ¾ teaspoon finely chopped fresh ginger
>
> I garlic clove, finely chopped
>
> 4 teaspoons soy sauce
>
> ¾ teaspoon freshly ground white or black pepper
>
> ¾ teaspoon dark sesame oil
>
> I teaspoon freshly ground pepper
>
> I teaspoon salt

BRING the water to a rapid boil and cook the spinach in it for I minute. Drain in a colander and rinse quickly in cold water to prevent overcooking. Gently wring out the spinach in your hands to eliminate excess water.

Count from four to seven wontons per serving and a teaspoon of filling per wonton. There are 48 teaspoons to a cup. Hence for eight bowls of wonton soup with seven wontons per bowl, you'll need 56 teaspoons—or about 1 1/4 cups of filling.

IN a food processor, combine the cooked spinach with the rest of the ingredients except the salt. Process for about 30 seconds; the mixture shouldn't be so finely ground that it loses all its texture. Taste for salt and pepper.

Salmon-filled wontons are especially delicious when served in a bowl of *dashi* flavored and decorated with sliced scallions.

salmon filling (makes 1 1/2 cups, enough for about 70 wontons):

1/2 pound fresh salmon fillet, cut into 1-inch cubes

1 small onion, finely chopped

1 garlic clove, finely chopped

1 teaspoon finely chopped fresh ginger

1 teaspoon salt

4 teaspoons dark soy sauce

1 teaspoon freshly ground pepper

1 tablespoon chopped cilantro

WORK the salmon with the chopped vegetables and herbs in a food processor for 30 seconds. You can chop the onion and garlic in the food processor before adding the salmon, but the ginger must be chopped by hand, or it will escape the processor blades.

The smoky flavor of leftover barbecued meats and fish makes a perfect wonton filling. You'll probably have fun just rummaging around in the refrigerator looking for leftovers, adding as you go along. This recipe is something I devised doing exactly that.

barbecued meat or fish filling (makes 1 1/2 cups, enough for 70 wontons):

2 to 3 pieces of leftover barbecued chicken, pork, salmon, etc.

1 small onion, finely chopped

1 garlic clove, finely chopped

1 teaspoon finely chopped fresh ginger

1 ½ tablespoons dark soy sauce

2 tablespoons finely chopped fresh herbs such as cilantro,
    parsley, chives

cayenne pepper or Tabasco sauce

salt

freshly ground pepper

CHOP the leftover meat or fish in a food processor or by hand. Combine it with the onion, garlic, ginger, soy sauce, and herbs. Add the cayenne and salt and pepper to taste.

Stuffed Pasta

Stuffed squares or rounds of pasta are delicious served in a simple broth that stays in the background and doesn't interfere with the tasty filling.

Ravioli and Tortellini

Although ravioli and other pasta are stuffed in almost the same way as wontons, you're likely to use Italian or French flavors in pasta stuffings and Asian flavors when making wontons. A ginger-flavored ravioli might taste odd in an Italian-style dish; a wonton stuffed with Swiss chard and Parmesan cheese is also likely to taste out of place floating in a ginger-scented broth.

The broths for an Italian soup are also going to have different flavors from those for an Asian soup even though the basic techniques for making the broth are almost identical. An Asian soup may be a simple flavored *dashi* or a chicken broth flavored with scallions and ginger. In an Italian-style dish, the broth is more likely to be flavored with thyme, marjoram, or rosemary and may have little bits of tomato, chard, or spinach floating amid the pasta.

Ultimately, the choice of stuffing is yours—stuffings are such last-minute improvised things that it would be a pity to limit yourself with a strict set of rules. Here are a few ideas.

Before you begin, sprinkle thin sheets of pasta dough thoroughly with flour so they don't stick together, then arrange them on a sheet pan. Cover them with plastic wrap so they don't dry out.

CUTTING AND ASSEMBLING PASTA DOUGH If you want to make tortellini, cut the pasta into 2-inch circles with a fluted cookie cutter or with a paring knife and a small glass. Brush each cutout with cold water and then place a small amount of stuffing in the center of each circle. One by one, fold the circles over themselves to make half-moons, pressing firmly around the edges to create a seal. Next, pull back the two corners around your finger and pinch them together.

IF you want square shapes for ravioli (with less waste), you can cut the sheets of pasta into squares with a knife and then assemble the ravioli one by one. A much easier method is to arrange the stuffing in rows—using a pastry bag or small spoon—on a long rectangular sheet of pasta, brush between the rows with water, lay another sheet on top, and then cut out the finished ravioli with a ravioli cutter. A ravioli cutter is similar to a circular pizza cutter, with two fluted blades that seal the ravioli with a decorative fluted edge.

AN even easier method for making ravioli is to use a ravioli mold, which will make a dozen at a time. To use the mold, cut a sheet of pasta an inch larger than the form on all sides. Lightly flour the pasta and set it over the mold. Make indentations in the pasta with the top part of the mold and fill the indentations with stuffing. Wet the pasta between the indentations and place another sheet of pasta over the mold. Roll over the mold with a rolling pin and turn the mold over so the finished ravioli fall out.

COOKING RAVIOLI OR TORTELLINI The easiest way to cook stuffed pasta for soup is to simmer it in the broth about 10 minutes before serving. Do not let stuffed pasta come to a full boil, or the stuffing will expand and the pasta will burst open in the soup.

FOR pasta in a perfectly clear broth, or when the stuffing contains cream, which could cloud the broth if it escaped, simmer the pasta in a pot of simmering water and then drain it before distributing it among the soup bowls. Add a tablespoon of olive oil to the simmering water to help prevent the pasta from sticking together.

STUFFINGS FOR PASTA You can make a pasta stuffing out of almost any flavorful ingredient. I especially like to use leftover vegetables and meats or fish well seasoned with onion and garlic. Wonton skins will also work if you have no fresh pasta dough.

One principle that even professional cooks often forget is that the flavor of the pasta filling is best when it contrasts with the flavor of the surrounding broth. If, for example, you're using broth that has been scented with smoked ham or ham hock, don't put these ingredients in the pasta stuffing.

One way to make a broth containing stuffed pasta more exciting is to leave the broth itself relatively bland so the flavor of the pasta is even more dramatic once your guests bite into the stuffing.

Ultimately the choice of stuffing is yours—stuffings are such last-minute improvised things that it would be a pity to limit yourself with a strict set of rules. Here are a few ideas.

Spinach and Ricotta Stuffing

This simple traditional stuffing is especially good when flavored with garlic and fresh marjoram.

MAKES 1 CUP, ENOUGH FOR 40 TO 50 SMALL RAVIOLI OR TORTELLINI

2 quarts water

1 large bunch of spinach, stems removed and leaves washed,
    2 cups tightly packed leaves

2 garlic cloves, finely chopped

2 tablespoons olive oil

½ cup ricotta cheese

½ cup grated Parmesan cheese

1 teaspoon chopped fresh marjoram or thyme leaves, or
    ½ teaspoon dried

1 large egg

salt

pepper

BRING the water to a rapid boil and cook the spinach leaves in it for 1 minute. Drain the spinach in a colander and rinse in cold water to prevent overcooking. Gently wring out the spinach in your hands to eliminate excess water. Chop finely.

COOK the garlic in olive oil in a 1-quart saucepan over medium heat for 2 minutes.

IF the ricotta seems wet, drain it for 30 minutes in a fine-mesh strainer.

COMBINE all of the ingredients in a mixing bowl and season to taste.

Improvised Leftover Meat Stuffing

This is just one idea for converting leftover meats into a delicious pasta stuffing.

MAKES 1½ CUPS, ENOUGH FOR ABOUT 60 SMALL RAVIOLI

I small onion, finely chopped

I garlic clove, finely chopped

2 tablespoons olive oil

I cup leftover meat such as stewed beef, lamb, or barbecued
    chicken, ½ cup leftover or freshly cooked vegetables
    such as carrots, onions, garlic, spinach, mashed
    potatoes, beets, or tomato sauce

I teaspoon chopped fresh herbs such as thyme, marjoram,
    oregano, basil, tarragon

salt

pepper

COOK the onion and garlic in the olive oil in a small sauté pan over medium heat until the onion turns translucent, about 10 minutes.

COMBINE the onion/garlic mixture with the rest of the ingredients in the bowl of a food processor and process for about 1 minute, until you've obtained a smooth paste.

Smoke-Scented Broth with Ravioli

I once had a soup similar to this one at Bradley Odgen's restaurant, The Lark Creek Inn in Larkspur, California. It made a perfect main course for an outdoor lunch because the broth was full of flavor but had virtually no fat. My brother and I left the table so energized that we took a hike in the surrounding mountains in spite of the bottle of red wine we had downed with lunch.

The smoky broth is the perfect backdrop for vegetables and ravioli. This version contains chopped fresh tomatoes and a whopping 24 whole garlic cloves, but once you have the basic broth—which takes about an hour and a half to cook—you can add almost any vegetable. Some of my favorites are blanched spinach or chard leaves (cut into thin shreds—chiffonade), pearl onions, carrots cut into cubes, and wild mushrooms.

MAKES 8 SERVINGS

2 small ham hocks, about 1 pound

1 medium-size onion, coarsely chopped

1 medium-size carrot, coarsely chopped

2 tablespoons unsalted butter

2 quarts chicken or beef broth

1 bouquet garni: 2 fresh sage leaves or 1 teaspoon dried,
    3 fresh thyme sprigs or 1 teaspoon dried, 1 small bunch
    of parsley or 2 tablespoons leaves

24 garlic cloves, peeled

24 or more ravioli or other stuffed pasta, 3 to 5 per person

3 medium-sized tomatoes, peeled, seeded, and coarsely
    chopped

2 tablespoons Italian parsley leaves or a small handful of
    basil leaves, torn into small pieces

salt

pepper

IN ADVANCE Up to 3 days ahead, put the ham hocks in a 4-quart pot with enough cold water to cover. Bring the water to a simmer. Simmer the ham hocks for 5 minutes, pour off the water, and rinse the ham hocks with cold water.

COOK the onion and carrot in the butter in a 4-quart pot over medium heat until they begin to soften, about 10 minutes. Add the ham hocks, pour the broth over, and add the bouquet garni. Simmer slowly, partially covered, for 1½ hours. Add extra broth or water from time to time to replenish the liquid. Make sure the ham hocks are covered at all times.

REMOVE the ham hocks and strain the soup into a clean pot. Discard the cooked vegetables and bouquet garni. Bring the broth to a simmer, skim off any fat that floats to the surface, and add the garlic cloves. Keep the broth at a slow simmer until the garlic cloves are completely soft, about 20 minutes.

LET the ham hocks cool slightly, then remove and discard the rind and bone. Pull away the cooked meat and shred it with a fork or your fingers.

AT THE LAST MINUTE Add the ravioli to the simmering broth and simmer for 8 to 10 minutes. With a slotted spoon, transfer them to hot soup bowls. Add the shredded ham, the tomato, and the parsley or basil leaves to the broth and simmer for 1 minute more.

ADJUST the salt—the broth usually won't need any because of the ham hock—and ladle the broth into the bowls. Grind fresh pepper on top of each serving.

SUGGESTIONS AND VARIATIONS | The magical part of this soup is the smoke-scented broth. If you don't have ham hocks or you don't want to eat pork, you can make a smoke-scented chicken broth by first barbecuing 2 cut-up chickens or the equivalent number of chicken parts—making sure the fire doesn't smell like liquid fire starter—putting them in a pot with some vegetables, and simmering them into a broth.

IF you want to make this broth spicy, add 1 or 2 seeded and chopped chilies at the same time as the garlic cloves. You can also experiment using different herbs to finish the soup—tarragon and chervil are just two possibilities.

YOU may want to serve this soup with slices of toasted bread on the side so guests can smear the cooked garlic cloves on them.

Dumplings

Dumplings are another one of those universal preparations that people all over the world have made for centuries to keep body and soul together. It's amazing how a few tasty homemade dumplings can turn a simple bowl of broth into something interesting and substantial.

Dumplings are almost like pasta, except they contain more liquid, have a looser consistency, and—ideally—are lighter once cooked. They are necessarily a last-minute, homemade kind of thing—no doubt one reason I find them so appealing.

Italians are the all-time experts on dumplings. It seems they have a type of dumpling for practically every region: *canederli* made with liver, ham, and dried fruit from Trentino; spinach *gnocchi* from Tuscany; *passatelli* from Bologna; *chenelle* made from rice and chicken livers from Bologna; *palline* from Mantua. Many of these Italian dumplings are similar to spaetzle from Alsace, a light noodlelike dumpling made by pushing batter through a sort of colander over a pot of simmering broth.

Chicken Broth with Cheese and Bread Crumb Dumplings

PASSATELLI

I first read about *passatelli* in Elizabeth David's *Italian* Food—one of the first books to make Italian cooking accessible to English and American cooks. What intrigued me was her remark that traditional cooks from Modena and Bologna replace the pasta in their *pasta in brodo* with a lighter paste made from Parmesan cheese, eggs, and bread crumbs. The paste is pushed through the holes of a colander—or, better yet, a potato ricer—over the simmering broth, in which it forms delicate strands.

Don't try to use stale or packaged bread crumbs, which will give the noodlelike strands an unpleasant sandy texture and a stale taste. It's easy enough to make your own bread crumbs with a few slices of white bread—crusts removed—zapped for 30 seconds in a food processor or dried out ever so slightly in the oven and pushed through a medium-mesh strainer.

MAKES 6 SERVINGS

6 cups clear beef or chicken broth

¼ cup fine white bread crumbs made from 2 slices white bread, crusts removed

4 eggs

6 tablespoons finely grated Parmesan cheese

pinch of freshly grated nutmeg

4 tablespoons unsalted butter, softened to room temperature

salt

pepper

BRING the broth to a slow simmer in a 4-quart pot.

COMBINE the rest of the ingredients in a 2-quart saucepan and work them into a paste over medium heat for about 1 minute.

PUT the paste in a potato ricer or colander set over the simmering broth. Push the paste through into the broth. Simmer for a minute or two and serve in hot, wide bowls. Pass extra cheese at the table.

THE *passatelli* paste can also be rolled by hand in grated Parmesan cheese or flour into thin sausage shapes and simmered in the soup for 5 minutes. You can also pipe the *passatelli* mixture into the simmering broth with a pastry bag, cutting it into 1-inch lengths with a paring knife as it comes out the tip.

Meatballs
AND SHRIMP BALLS

IT'S EASY TO TURN A SIMPLE BROTH INTO A SUBSTANTIAL SOUP BY ROLLING UP MIX-tures of chopped meat or seafood into balls and then deep-frying them or poaching them in salted water before adding them to the soup. (I don't poach them directly in the soup, because they cloud it.) I prefer to chop meat or fish myself in a food processor, being careful not to overwork the mixture, so the meatballs or shrimp balls have some texture instead of being turned into a smooth paste. If they're pasty when raw, they'll be dense and heavy once they're cooked. You can flavor meatballs or shrimp balls, using your own imagination. My favorite flavors are aromatic vegetables, such as cooked or raw onion or garlic, ginger, Asian sesame oil, and herbs such as tarragon, thyme, or chives. Because meatballs should contain some fat to keep them moist, I like to make them out of pork shoulder chops, which contain more fat (and are less expensive) than center-cut or loin pork chops. The meatballs and tomatoes can be prepared ahead of time and reheated in the soup.

Diced Tomato Soup with Chicken or Beef Broth and Marjoram-Flavored Meatballs

MAKES 6 FIRST-COURSE SERVINGS OR 4 MAIN-COURSE SERVINGS

for the broth:

4 cups basic brown beef broth (see step I of Basic Beef Consommé, page 74) or basic brown chicken broth page 62)

bouquet garni containing I small bunch of parsley, 5 thyme leaves sprigs (or ½ teaspoon dried thyme leaves), and I bay leaf

2 pounds ripe tomatoes, peeled

for the meatballs:

I medium onion, peeled and finely chopped

I tablespoon unsalted butter

12 ounces pork shoulder meat (or I pound pork shoulder chops)

2 garlic cloves, peeled, finely chopped, and crushed to a
    paste with the side of a chef's knife

1 tablespoon fresh marjoram leaves, finely chopped, or
    1 teaspoon fresh chopped thyme leaves or ½ teaspoon
    dried thyme

1 teaspoon salt

½ teaspoon freshly ground pepper

2 tablespoons salt for poaching the meatballs

¾ cup finely grated Parmigiano-Reggiano

GENTLY simmer the broth with the bouquet garni for 30 minutes.

CUT each of the tomatoes vertically into 6 or 8 wedges, depending on their size, and seed and cut the pulp out of each of the wedges so you're only left with the outer red flesh of the tomato. Cut the pulp into dice about ¼ inch on each side. Reserve. If you're in a hurry, cut the tomatoes crosswise, squeeze the seeds out of each half and discard. Chop the tomatoes coarsely.

COOK the onion in the butter for about 15 minutes, until it turns fragrant and translucent but without letting it brown. Reserve.

IF you're using pork shoulder chops, take the meat off the bones. Cut away any obvious pieces of gristle or sinew from the meat but leave the fat attached. Pulse the meat in a food processor or chop it by hand until it has the consistency of hamburger meat. Stir the onion, garlic, marjoram, salt, and pepper into the meat mixture. Chill the mixture, covered with plastic wrap, in a bowl in the refrigerator. Roll the meat into 24 meatballs about the size of small walnuts.

BRING about 2 quarts of water to a simmer with 2 tablespoons salt. Gently lower the meatballs into the simmering liquid, partially cover the pan (so the parts of the meatballs that aren't submerged will cook), and poach the meatballs at a very gentle simmer for 10 minutes.

HEAT the tomato cubes in the broth and arrange the meatballs in heated bowls. Ladle over the hot broth and sprinkle parmigiano over each serving.

Shrimp Balls in Hot and Sour Thai Broth

Fried shrimp balls give a crunchy and savory accent to virtually any broth. In this version, the shrimp balls are flavored with Asian ingredients—ginger and sesame oil—and are floated in a tangy Thai broth. You can poach the shrimp balls in simmering water in the same way as the meatballs on page 130, but I like to coat them with Japanese bread crumbs (*panko;* see Sources) and deep-fry them to give them a little extra crunch. If you can't have *panko*, use dried regular bread crumbs instead. The broth can be prepared a day or two ahead of time and the shrimp balls earlier the same day. Don't, however, coat the shrimp balls with the bread crumbs until just before frying or the crumbs will get soggy.

MAKES 6 FIRST-COURSE SERVINGS

for the shrimp balls:

1¼ pounds shrimp in the shell or 1 pound shelled shrimp

1 large garlic clove, peeled, finely chopped, and crushed to a paste with the side of a chef's knife

2 scallions, including about half the green, finely chopped

1½ teaspoons Asian dark sesame oil (preferably Japanese)

1½ tablespoons finely grated fresh ginger

1 egg white from a large egg

1¼ teaspoons salt

1¼ cups Japanese bread crumbs (*panko*) or 1¼ cups regular, dried bread crumbs

2 cups pure olive oil or vegetable oil for deep-frying

1 recipe Thai Hot and Spicy Broth, without coconut milk (page 95)

PEEL and devein the shrimp if they're still in the shell and combine them with the garlic, scallions, sesame oil, and ginger in the bowl of a food processor. Lightly beat the egg white with the salt and add it to the food processor. Pulse the shrimp mixture, a couple of seconds per pulse, scraping down the inside walls of the processor with a rubber spatula between pulses. Continue until the shrimp have the consistency of ground meat. If you don't have a food processor, chop the shrimp by hand with a chef's knife and combine it in a mixing bowl with the same ingredients. Refrigerate the mixture, covered with plastic wrap, for at least 4 hours or preferably overnight.

DIVIDE the shrimp mixture into 36 equal portions—about a tablespoon for each ball—and roll each one, between both hands, into balls. Roll the balls in the bread crumbs.

PREHEAT the oven to 200°F.

HEAT the oil in a 2-quart saucepan until it begins to ripple, about 350°F. Fry the shrimp balls, six at a time, in the hot oil for about 1½ minutes, turning them around in the oil after 45 seconds so they brown evenly. Place them on a sheet pan covered with a double layer of paper towels and keep them warm in the oven while you're making the rest.

BRING the broth to a simmer, ladle it into heated bowls, and place six shrimp balls in each bowl.

Mexican Meatball or Shrimp Ball or Fish Ball Soup

SOPA DE ALBONDIGAS

Albondigas are meat, fish, or shrimp balls—shrimp or fish in places near the sea, meatballs inland—and can be served surrounded with a broth (usually a simple fish or chicken broth containing chilies and tomatoes) in a soup or, as a main course, with a substantial sauce. The principles behind making albondigas are universal—meats or seafood are more or less finely chopped, the mixture is held together with a bit of egg and lightened with bread crumbs, crackers, rice, or cooked vegetables such as zucchini. The albondigas are flavored in various ways, but every recipe I read contains Mexican oregano; Diana Kennedy, in her book *The Cuisines of Mexico*, calls for mint and cumin. My own interpretations often include cilantro (unless I also include it in the surrounding broth) and garlic (probably heretical, but too good to leave out), and soaked and finely chopped dried chiles—again, unless I've included them in the broth. Most recipes serve albondigas in a relatively simple broth flavored with tomatoes and chilies. Rick Bayless, in *Authentic Mexican*, flavors his broth with fresh poblanos; Diana Kennedy, with chipotles; I, with whatever's in the cupboard or at the corner greengrocer.

The broth for this soup can be made a day or two ahead, and the albondigas can be made earlier the same day.

MAKES 6 GENEROUS FIRST-COURSE SERVINGS

for the albondigas:

1¼ pounds shrimp in the shell (or 1 pound out of the shell) or 1 pound ground pork shoulder

2 slices dense crumb white bread (such as Pepperidge Farm), crusts removed

½ cup milk

1 large egg, beaten

½ teaspoon dried oregano, preferably Mexican oregano

2 tablespoons chopped cilantro

2 tablespoons chopped mint or parsley

¼ teaspoon ground cumin (optional)

2 tablespoons onion, finely chopped

1 small garlic clove, peeled, finely chopped, and crushed to a
 paste with the side of a chef's knife

1 teaspoon salt

for the broth:

2 dried ancho, mulato, gaujillo, or other chilies, stemmed,
 halved, seeded, and soaked for 30 minutes in 1 cup
 boiling water, drained, or 2 chipotle chilies in adobe
 sauce, rinsed and seeded, or 2 poblano chilies, skin-
 charred, peeled, and seeded

1 medium-size onion, peeled, and finely chopped

2 garlic cloves, peeled and finely chopped

1 tablespoon olive oil

6 ripe medium-size tomatoes, coarsely chopped (don't
 bother seeding or peeling)

3 cups chicken, beef, pork, or fish broth (the broth will
 depend on what kind of balls you're making)

salt

PREPARING THE ALBONDIGAS If you're using shrimp, chop it fine—but not
to a paste—in a food processor or by hand. Soak the bread in the milk until soft
and then squeeze out the excess milk and discard. Work the shrimp or pork, the
soaked bread, and the rest of the meatball ingredients together with your hands.
Don't work them any longer than necessary to combine them or you'll make the
mixture heavy. Chill the mixture, covered, and roll it into 36 balls.

PREPARING THE BROTH Chop the chilies fine. Heat the onion and garlic in the
olive oil over medium heat, stirring every couple of minutes until the onion turns
translucent, about 10 minutes. Add the chilies, stir for a minute or two to get them
to release their flavor (stand back or the fumes can knock you over), and add the
tomatoes and broth. Simmer gently until the tomatoes are mushy and falling apart,
about 20 minutes. Work the soup through a food mill or use a ladle to push it
through a strainer. Season to taste with salt.

FINISHING THE SOUP Just before serving, bring about 3 quarts of water to a
gentle simmer in a wide pot with a tablespoon of salt and add the albondigas. Poach
the albondigas in the barely simmering salt water with the pot partially covered for
about 10 minutes. Bring the broth to the simmer. Ladle six albondigas into each of
six heated bowls and ladle over the broth.

Singapore-Style Pork Broth with Noodles, Fish Balls, and Chinese Greens

MEE SWA

I first read about this soup in *Saveur*, a beautifully illustrated and informative magazine that combines cooking and travel. *Mee swa* is another one of those delightful and savory soups that you can turn into a substantial and healthy meal by just serving more of the soup or adding more ingredients. I like to serve this soup as a main course, usually after serving some light Asian hors d'oeuvre, such as Vietnamese spring rolls or Japanese Kebabs, *yakitori*. The fish ball mixture should be made at least an hour before rolling the fish balls and refrigerated to help the balls hold their shape. Once formed, the fish balls can be kept for up to a day in the refrigerator. You can also poach the fish balls in advance and gently reheat them in a 200°F oven before serving.

MAKES 4 MAIN-COURSE SERVINGS

for the fish balls:

I pound lean skinless, white fish fillets such as red snapper, sea bass, or cod

I garlic clove, peeled, finely chopped, and crushed to a paste with the side of a chef's knife

I scallion, both green and white parts, finely chopped

I teaspoon Asian dark sesame oil (preferably Japanese)

I tablespoon finely grated fresh ginger

I egg white

I teaspoon salt

for the soup:

6 large tree ears or ¼ cup smaller tree ears

salt

½ pound fresh Chinese egg noodles or ⅓ pound dried egg noodles, soba, or udon noodles (see page 107 for more about noodles)

4 cups Asian-style pork broth (see page 512) or chicken broth

2 Thai chilies or 4 jalapeño chilies, seeded and stemmed, finely chopped

2 tablespoons Thai fish sauce or more to taste

½ pound Asian greens (see box, page 117) washed, trimmed of hard stems, and cut into manageable pieces

2 heaping tablespoons coarsely chopped cilantro

4 scallions, both green and white parts, finely chopped

PREPARING THE FISH BALLS Cut the fish fillets into cubes about ½ inch on each side and combine them with the garlic, scallion, sesame oil, and ginger in the bowl of a food processor. Lightly beat the egg white with the salt and add it to the food processor. Pulse the fish mixture, a couple of seconds per pulse, scraping down the inside walls of the processor with a rubber spatula between pulses. Continue until the fish mixture has the consistency of ground meat. If you don't have a food processor, chop the fish by hand with a chef's knife and combine it in a mixing bowl with the same ingredients.

DIVIDE the fish mixture, a tablespoon at a time. Roll between both hands into 30 balls. Reserve in the refrigerator until needed, but for least an hour, covered with plastic wrap.

PREPARING THE SOUP Pour 2 cups of boiling water over the tree ears and let soak for 30 minutes. Cut off and discard any pieces of the tree ears that didn't soften during soaking.

PREHEAT the oven to 200°F.

BRING about 2 quarts of water to the simmer with 2 tablespoons of salt in a wide pot for cooking the fish balls and another 3 quarts of water to the simmer with 2 tablespoons of salt for cooking the noodles.

SIMMER the fish balls in the simmering water in two batches for about 3 minutes for each batch. Remove from the simmering water with a slotted spoon or skimmer and reserve on a sheet pan in the oven.

BRING the broth to the simmer and add the tree ears, chilies, and fish sauce. Add the noodles to the water and simmer for about 3 minutes, until soft when you bite into one. Drain in a colander.

ADD the greens and simmer for 1 to 5 minutes to cook the greens (the time will depend on the greens and how small you cut the pieces). Add the scallions and cilantro to the broth, and simmer about 1 minute more.

DISTRIBUTE the noodles and fish balls evenly among each of six heated bowls and ladle over the soup.

Matzo Ball Soup

Matzo balls—or *kneidlach*—are made in much the same way as any dumpling except that matzo meal replaces flour and, in keeping with Jewish tradition, no butter or dairy products are allowed in the batter. There are at least as many matzo ball recipes as Jewish grandmothers; some insist the matzo balls should be firm and chewy, while others, who claim lightness the ultimate goal, include seltzer water or even beaten egg whites to contribute the essential airiness. This recipe falls between the two schools; the beaten egg whites seem a bit recherché and are left out, but plenty of whole eggs are used so the matzo balls puff up when they're poached. Since I'm not a fan of chicken fat, I suggest duck or goose fat as a tastier alternative.

Matzo balls in chicken broth are served as part of the traditional Passover seder. Because most of the flavor comes from the broth itself, you must have a good broth. If you're willing to spend the time, your best bet is to make a double brown broth—broth cooked with broth instead of water. The first broth can be made with chicken bones, but the second broth should be made with chicken legs or wings for the fullest flavor. If you have the time, make the broth the day before so it will be easier to remove any congealed fat.

MAKES 12 SERVINGS

the double chicken broth:

> 5 pounds chicken legs or wings
>
> 1 medium-size onion, coarsely chopped
>
> 1 medium-size carrot, coarsely chopped
>
> 1 bouquet garni
>
> 3½ quarts brown chicken broth

the matzo balls (makes about 36):

> 1 medium-size onion, finely chopped
>
> 1 cup duck, goose, or chicken fat
>
> 2 cups water
>
> ⅛ teaspoon freshly grated nutmeg
>
> 4 teaspoons salt
>
> 2 cups matzo meal
>
> 6 eggs
>
> pepper

PREPARING THE DOUBLE CHICKEN BROTH Preheat the oven to 450°F. Spread the chicken legs or wings in a heavy-bottomed roasting pan or large skillet with the chopped vegetables. Roast until the meat and vegetables are well browned, usually in about 45 minutes. Add a cup or two of water to the roasting pan if you notice the vegetables or the bottom of the pan starting to burn.

REMOVE the roasting pan from the oven, transfer the chicken and vegetables to an 8- to 10-quart pot, and pour or ladle off any grease in the bottom of the roasting pan. Discard the grease. Pour 2 cups of the broth into the roasting pan and scrape the bottom with a wooden spoon to dissolve the juices sticking to the bottom.

PUT the bouquet garni in the pot with the chicken and vegetables and pour the contents of the roasting pan over them. Add the rest of the broth or slightly more or less if necessary to barely cover the chicken parts.

PUT the pot on the stove over medium heat until the broth comes to a simmer. Turn the heat down low enough to keep the broth at a slow simmer and cook for about 3 hours. Every 30 minutes, skim off any fat or froth that comes to the surface.

IF you're using the double broth the next day, strain it into a clean pot or heat-resistant plastic container. Let it cool, uncovered, for an hour before putting it in the refrigerator. The next day, remove any congealed fat with a spoon.

PREPARING THE MATZO BALLS Cook the onion in 1 tablespoon of the fat until it softens, about 10 minutes.

COMBINE the water, remaining fat, nutmeg, and 1 teaspoon salt and bring to a simmer in a 4-quart pot. Stir in the matzo meal and work the mixture over medium heat for about 1 minute, until it pulls away from the sides of the pan.

TURN the mixture out into a mixing bowl and work the eggs into the mixture one by one with a wooden spoon. Because the size of eggs varies, you may need to add slightly more or less. To know when you've added the right amount, dip a wooden spoon sideways about an inch into the batter, then pull it to one side to make a crevice. The crevice should slowly close in on itself. If it remains rigid, add more egg. Season the batter to taste with salt and pepper.

FILL a wide pan or pot with about 6 inches of water. Add the remaining salt to the water and bring it to a simmer. Shape the balls into egg or ball shapes by dipping two soupspoons into a bowl of cold water and forming the batter with them. Slide the matzo balls into the simmering water. Simmer them gently for about 25 minutes, then turn them over and simmer for 25 minutes more. Transfer them to an oiled sheet pan and cover them with a damp kitchen towel. (You can keep them this way overnight.) When it comes time to serve, heat the matzo balls (still covered with the damp kitchen towel) in a 250°F oven for 15 minutes.

BRING the broth to a simmer, season with salt and pepper, and ladle it into hot bowls. Arrange 3 matzo balls in each bowl.

SUGGESTIONS AND VARIATIONS | I know that matzo ball soup is one of those things that should not be toyed with; tradition is tradition and is best left alone. However, I never leave anything alone and in all honesty never really cook the same thing twice; every time I have a recipe at hand I think of myriad little changes and variations. For instance, it's hard for me to resist putting herbs in the broth, especially chopped parsley, chives, and/or tarragon. I don't mean to sound heretical, but since Passover is such a celebration of good food and drink, mightn't this be the time to splurge on a black truffle to slice thinly and simmer for a minute in the hot broth?

Rich Chicken Broth with Tarragon

Although this soup is nothing more than an intensely flavorful chicken broth with fresh tarragon and thin slices of chicken breast, keep in mind that simplicity can be deceiving. The soup tastes more like chicken than chicken itself and is supremely elegant to look at and taste.

To make this soup, you prepare a brown chicken broth twice, using the first batch of broth to moisten the second batch of browned chicken parts to create what's called a double broth. You can even go crazy and keep repeating the process, making a triple broth or a quadruple broth.

Once you have your double broth, which will be as clear as consommé (provided you carefully skimmed the broth and didn't let it boil) but with a more forthright flavor, you simply add fresh tarragon (and/or parsley or chives). If you want to make the soup richer, you can add heavy cream. This soup can also be served cold with the chicken suspended in the chopped *gelée* so each serving looks like a mound of topaz. I like to serve the soup in tea cups or coffee cups with straight sides—like double espresso cups.

The most time-consuming part of this dish—making the broth—can be done several days ahead of time or even months ahead of time and the broth frozen.

MAKES 6 FIRST-COURSE SERVINGS

5 pounds chicken legs or wings or whole cut-up chicken

1 medium-size onion, peeled and quartered

1 large carrot, peeled and cut into 1-inch sections

3½ quarts basic brown chicken broth (one batch of the recipe on page 62)

bouquet garni containing 1 bunch of parsley, 5 thyme sprigs, the stems from the tarragon, and a bay leaf

leaves from 15 sprigs of fresh tarragon

> 3 boneless chicken breasts (one side only, not the whole "double" breast)
>
> salt
>
> pepper
>
> 2 tablespoons butter or olive oil

PREHEAT the oven to 450°F.

SPREAD the chicken parts, onions, and carrots in a heavy-bottomed roasting pan (or a couple of skillets) just large enough to hold them in a single layer. Bake for 45 minutes to 1½ hours, stirring the mixture every 15 minutes to prevent burning, until the chicken and vegetables are well browned. Transfer the chicken and vegetables to a clean narrow pot, using tongs so you leave the fat behind in the roasting pan. Pour off and discard the fat and deglaze the pan with 2 cups of the broth. Pour the deglazing liquid and the rest of the broth over the chicken parts and vegetables. Nestle the bouquet garni into the pot, bring to a simmer, starting over medium heat, and then turn the heat down to maintain at a low simmer. Simmer for 3 hours, using a ladle to skim off fat and froth that floats to the top. Strain the broth through a fine-mesh strainer or a regular strainer lined with a triple layer of cheesecloth.

SHORTLY before you're ready to serve, bring the broth to a simmer and stir in the tarragon leaves.

PULL off the small tenderloin that runs along one side of each of the breasts. Remove the small tendon from each of the tenderloins by holding it against the cutting board with one of the fingers of your left hand (if you're right-handed) and sliding a knife along its surface while pressing against the cutting board with the knife. Gently pound the chicken breasts on the thick side, but don't overdo it— pound them just enough so they end up being of even thickness. Season the chicken breasts and tenderloins with salt and pepper and brown them on both sides in butter over medium-high heat (if you're using oil, you can use high heat) until they feel firm to the touch, 5 to 7 minutes on each side. Pat the cooked fat off the breasts with a paper towel and slice the breasts crosswise into ¼-inch-thick strips. Arrange the strips, keeping them together, in the center of heated soup bowls.

SEASON the broth with salt and ladle it around the chicken in each bowl. Serve immediately.

VARIATIONS | I already mentioned using heavy cream, which makes this soup more filling. You can turn the soup into a little *pot-au-feu* (see recipe, page 426) by simmering baby carrots, turnips, and onions in a little of the broth and then spooning them over and around whole chicken breasts. A mound of cooked spinach, placed under the chicken breast to prop it up, adds substance to the dish, as do slices of French bread sautéed in olive oil and rubbed with garlic. If you're serving this soup as a main course, offer a whole breast—the breast meat from half the chicken—per person. Similar methods work with duck and squab (see recipe page 507). As I mentioned above, you can serve this soup cold (it will need a bit more salt since the saltiness recedes when the broth is chilled). If you want to go all out, add a packet of gelatin to the broth or, better yet, reduce the broth by half to make it more gelatinous (don't add the tarragon until after reduction), and then layer the broth and the thinly sliced chicken in a terrine and serve it sliced as a first course. Other ingredients—cooked artichoke bottoms, mushrooms, foie gras, and truffles—can, of course, be included among the layers of chicken.

Quenelles

Until the days of the food processor, a quenelle was something you only ate at the fanciest French restaurants. This wasn't because quenelles were particularly tricky to make, but because they were very labor intensive—fish had to be first ground and then laboriously worked through a drum sieve—usually by the lowliest apprentice. Nowadays quenelles are a snap to make because you only need to grind the fish (you can also make them out of chicken or veal) to a paste in a food processor and work cream and seasonings into the mixture over a period of several hours. You can shape the mixture with two spoons, held in opposing directions, or even easier, with a special quenelle-shaped (quenelles are egg-shaped) scoop like one used for ice cream. In classic French cooking, quenelles are (or were) served covered with a rich sauce (a sauce Nantua, made with crayfish was a favorite), covered with sauce and baked like a gratin, or made miniature and served as a garnish for consommé.

Chicken Soup with Chicken Quenelles

This is the rich, French, and decidedly nonkosher version (chicken is combined with cream) of matzo ball soup. I use the white chicken breast meat to make the quenelles themselves and the rest of the chicken to make the broth. You can make the broth several days ahead and the quenelles a day or two ahead and reheat them in the broth.

MAKES 6 FIRST-COURSE SERVINGS

for the quenelles:

I tablespoon fresh tarragon leaves

I tablespoon butter

I pound boneless chicken breasts

I teaspoon salt or more as needed

I teaspoon finely ground white pepper

2 cups heavy cream, or more as needed

I teaspoon butter (for poaching the quenelles)

for the broth:

½ recipe double chicken broth on page 72 or 6 cups of other full-flavored broth salt (if needed)

pepper

CHOP the tarragon leaves with the butter, continually scraping the mixture off the sides of the knife, until the tarragon is finely chopped. (The tarragon is chopped with the butter to prevent the leaves from turning dark.)

TRIM any pieces of fat or sinew off the chicken breasts, including the small tendon that runs along the tenderloin, the long thin strip of meat attached to the side of each breast. Pull away the tenderloin and slide a small knife under the tendon. Slide the knife along, under the tendon, while holding the tendon against the cutting board with a finger, until it pulls away. Cut the breasts into chunks about I inch on each side and put them in a food processor with the tarragon, butter, salt, and pepper. Puree the mixture for about 3 minutes, scraping down the inside walls of the food processor every 30 seconds so none of the chicken escapes.

TRANSFER the pureed chicken to a medium stainless steel or glass mixing bowl, cover with plastic wrap (make sure the wrap is pressed onto the surface of the puree so a crust doesn't form), and refrigerate for 2 hours or overnight. Work I cup of cream into the puree, ¼ cup at a time, until smooth and refrigerate again for I hour. Work in the last cup of cream in the same way.

BRING a cup of water to a simmer in a saucepan and drop in a dollop of the quenelle mixture. Simmer the mixture for about 5 minutes and then taste it. Add more salt and pepper to the mixture as needed to taste. If the mixture falls apart in the simmering water, work 2 lightly beaten egg whites into the mixture to hold it together. If the mixture seems dry or rubbery, work in more cream.

RUB a heatproof baking dish with high sides with butter.

WHEN the cooked quenelle mixture has the texture and flavor you like, shape the quenelles into 24 small egg shapes by taking two elongated tablespoons, dipping them in a glass of cold water to keep the mixture from sticking, and then, with the spoons facing each other—one held in the right hand, the other in the left—shape the mixture.

ARRANGE the quenelles in rows in the buttered baking dish. Bring about 3 quarts of water to a boil—I use a tea kettle—and pour the hot water gently down along one side of the baking dish. Place the dish on the stove—use a flame tamer if the dish is glass—and place a sheet of aluminum foil loosely over the baking dish. Simmer the quenelles gently for about 5 minutes. Cut into one to make sure they're cooked all the way through—simmer them more if they're not—and transfer to a sheet pan lined with a dish towel (don't use paper towels or they'll stick and tear).

JUST before you're ready to serve, bring the broth to a simmer in a wide pan—large enough to hold the quenelles—and simmer the quenelles for 3 minutes to heat them through. Use a slotted spoon to place three quenelles in each of six heated bowls. Season the broth to taste and ladle it over the quenelles.

"Vegetable soups can be almost ridiculously simple to make . . ."

Vegetable SOUPS

Vegetable soups can be almost ridiculously simple to make; a sliced leek and a handful of chopped potato can be boiled in a cup or two of water, a dollop of butter tossed in, and the whole thing slurped up with a few good slices of crusty bread. A last-minute vegetable soup along with a salad and a wedge of cheese make up many of my weekday dinners at home. Vegetable soups can also be hearty meals in themselves; some are elaborate concoctions groaning with sausages, meats, rice, pasta, beans, and a dozen kinds of vegetables. Most vegetable soups fall somewhere in between these two extremes and contain three or four vegetables and maybe a few cubes of leftover meat.

Because there are so many kinds of vegetable soup, it's helpful to understand a few basic principles instead of trying to remember a stack of recipes. Once you see how a vegetable soup is put together, it's easy to improvise based on what you find in the refrigerator or the local supermarket.

Although a few soups are made with a single vegetable—onion soup is one example—most vegetable soups contain more than one vegetable, usually added at different stages during the cooking. Even in soups where one flavor predominates, garlic, onion, or other root vegetables are usually added to round out the soup's basic flavor.

Almost any vegetable can be used in a soup; it's important to know only at what stage in the cooking it should be added. Root vegetables such as turnips, carrots, or onions are best cooked at the beginning in a little fat, while green vegetables—green beans, peas, spinach—are best added at the end so they retain their color and texture. Some vegetables, such as artichokes, need to be cooked separately and added near the end, or their sometimes bitter flavor will take over. Watery vegetables such as tomatoes or squash are best added to the soup at the same time as the liquids. Herbs can be added at several stages. Some, such as thyme or bay leaves, release their flavors slowly, so they are best added near the beginning and cooked along with the first vegetables in fat or tied together in a bouquet garni and added with the liquid. Delicate herbs such as chervil, parsley, basil, or chives should be added almost at the very end, or their delicate flavor will cook off.

Many vegetable soups are improved by adding a small amount of flavorful meat near the beginning. Cubes of prosciutto, pancetta sliced into thin strips, bacon cut into thin strips and gently rendered, and confit of duck or goose will enhance a soup, especially if you cook them at the beginning along with the aromatic vegetables.

One of the most reliable tricks for flavoring a soup is to whisk in a flavorful finish. Sometimes this is as simple as a dribble of olive oil or a pat of butter, but more complicated mixtures such as pesto, *aïoli*, *picada*, or compound butters will produce more dramatic results.

Pasta, rice, or beans can be added to a vegetable soup to give it more bulk and make it a satisfying main course. Although pasta can be added to the soup a few minutes before serving, rice and especially beans need longer cooking and can be cooked separately in advance or added at the beginning if the soup requires long cooking.

Although most vegetable soups are prepared by cooking the vegetables together in one pot, especially beautiful and elegant versions of vegetable soup can be prepared by cooking each vegetable separately, combining the cooking liquids, and then arranging the vegetables in the middle of the bowl and serving the broth around them.

Serving Vegetable Soups

One problem with serving soup is that it sometimes cools off by the time you get it to the dining room. One way to avoid this is to use heavy bowls and heat them in a 200°F oven before ladling out the soup. But don't forget to warn your guests. Or serve the soup from a tureen at the table.

Garnishing Vegetable Soups

When a vegetable soup contains whole or chopped vegetables, additional garnishing usually isn't needed, because the soup will look striking on its own. Pureed soups, though, have one color and the same consistency and usually need some kind of garnish. The obvious garnish for most purees is a piece of the vegetable that went into the soup, placed on top of each serving in the middle of the bowl. If you're making an asparagus soup, for instance, save some of the tips, cook them in boiling salted water, and place one or more in the center of the bowls.

One annoying problem when garnishing vegetable soups is that the garnish tends to fall to the bottom of the bowl, out of sight. To avoid this, float a small crouton or thin slice of French bread in the soup and then place the garnish on top.

A swirl of heavy cream also makes a decorative touch on top of each bowl. Because cream will sometimes sink below the surface out of sight, a good trick is to whip the cream ever so slightly to get it to float. The cream can also be used to support very light garnishes such as herbs or vegetable julienne.

CUTTING VEGETABLES:

CHOPPING VERSUS DICING

There are several ways to cut vegetables for soup. For pureed soups the exact size of the vegetables isn't important because everything is going to be pureed anyway. You do, however, want the vegetables to be *approximately* the same size so they cook at the same time.

For soups in which the appearance of the vegetables is important, dice them into even cubes. This involves a certain amount of waste because round vegetables such as turnips must be sized off into square shapes before being diced.

Some recipes call for vegetable julienne. First, thinly slice the vegetables. This is easiest to do with a mandoline. Then slice each slice again into thin strips.

Some vegetables such as fennel or turnips are occasionally cut into wedges. This is a good method for long-cooking soups when you want the vegetables to maintain their shape and texture.

Leafy vegetables such as spinach or Swiss chard often need to be shredded before they are added to a soup. French cooks refer to this as *chiffonade*. The easiest way to make a chiffonade of vegetables is to roll the leaves over themselves and then thinly slice the rolls.

A pat of butter can also be placed at the center of each soup or, if you want to get fancy, use some of the compound butters in the Basic Preparations chapter.

Small croutons cooked in butter are pretty and give the soup a little crunch. They can be combined with any of the other garnishes.

Patterns for Improvising Soups

STEPS FOR MAKING VEGETABLE SOUP	INGREDIENTS/EQUIPMENT
Melt fat for cooking vegetables (optional).	Butter, oil, rendered bacon fat, goose fat, duck fat
Gently cook flavorful meats in fat (optional).	Ham (thinly sliced, cut into strips) Bacon (cut into 1- by ¼-inch strips) *Pancetta* (unrolled, thinly sliced, cut into 1- by ¼-inch strips) Confit of duck or goose (shredded) Raw pork (cut into cubes or strips) Leftover roast meats (cut into cubes or shredded)
Gently cook aromatic vegetables in fat until they soften or simmer directly in liquid.	Carrots (chopped, diced, or julienne) Onions (chopped) Garlic (chopped, or peeled and left whole) Turnips (chopped, diced, julienne, or cut into wedges) Leeks (chopped or julienne) Fennel (chopped or cut into wedges) Celeriac (chopped, diced, julienne, or cut into wedges)
Fresh or dried herbs that can be added to the soup near the beginning (chopped or tied into a bouquet garni).	Thyme Oregano Marjoram Savory Bay leaf
Add starch or starchy vegetables. These can provide substance to a soup containing whole or chopped vegetables or can function as thickeners in pureed soups.	Flour Rice Beans (soaked, sometimes precooked) Potatoes (chopped)
Add liquid; simmer soup until vegetables soften.	Broth (chicken, beef, vegetable, etc.) Wines (white wine, sherry, Madeira, etc.) Cooking liquids (from beans, rice, or potatoes) Water
Vegetables best added at the same time as the liquid.	Zucchini (sliced, diced, or julienne) Squash (sliced, diced, or julienne) Tomatoes (peeled, seeded, chopped) Mushrooms (left whole, quartered, or sliced) Cabbage (shredded, blanched/optional)
Add thickener (pureed soups only)	Cooked bread Precooked rice Mashed potatoes

STEPS FOR MAKING VEGETABLES SOUP	INGREDIENTS/EQUIPMENT
	Leftover vegetable purees (spinach, sorrel, garlic, etc.) Precooked beans Cornstarch Flour worked to a paste with butter
Add quick-cooking green vegetables and other ingredients.	Spinach (stems removed, shredded) Green beans (chopped or cut into ½-inch lengths) Swiss chard (stems removed, shredded) Peas Broccoli Sorrel (stems removed, shredded) Dried pasta Precooked rice Fresh pasta
Puree soup.	Blender, food processor, food mill
Strain puree.	Medium-mesh strainer, fine-mesh strainer, or drum sieve
Add flavorful finishes and enrichment.	Tender herbs (tarragon, chervil, parsley, chives) Butter Herb butters Cream Pesto/pistou (basil and garlic puree) *Aïoli* (garlic mayonnaise) *Picada* (Spanish garlic and almond puree) Extra virgin olive oil Coconut milk Yogurt Curry Hot chili purees *Tadka* (Indian spice mixture) Grated Parmesan, Gruyère
Garnish.	Croutons Chopped fresh herbs Strips or cubes of vegetables Noodles

Improvising Vegetable Soups

When you're improvising, you don't need to adhere to any particular formula, but the chart above is a guide to help you keep your options in mind.

Suppose, for example, that a neighbor has given you a bucket of turnips and you want to turn them into a soup. You must first decide if you want the turnips to remain whole or chopped in the soup or if you want to make a pureed soup. If the turnips are to remain chunky, you might want to round out the flavors and texture of the soup by adding chopped or diced complementary vegetables such as potatoes, parsnips, carrots, or celeriac. A good tip to remember also is that smoked or cured meats go well with root vegetables; you may want to render a little bacon, pancetta, or ham at the beginning.

If you decide to make a puree, the first step is to peel and chop the turnips and cook them in a little fat such as butter or rendered bacon fat, which will complement the soup with its smoky flavor. I usually add chopped onion at this point to round out the flavors.

Because turnips don't have enough starch to thicken the soup on their own, you'll need to use additional thickener such as potato, rice, bread, or flour.

If you decide to use potato or rice, cook them with the turnips and puree the whole soup when the potato or rice is completely soft. If you're using precooked rice or leftover mashed potatoes, add them to the soup just before pureeing.

If you decide to use cooked bread as a thickener, add it to the soup 5 minutes before pureeing.

You can also thicken your soup with flour by adding it to the turnips while they're gently cooking in fat and then add milk or broth.

When the soup has been pureed and strained, you can adjust its consistency by adding more broth or milk or by straining it through a finer-mesh strainer. You can then finish the soup with butter, cream, and egg yolks, either alone or in any combination.

A Note on Reheating Soups

One of the great advantages of making soups is that they are easy to reheat the next day and are often better for having spent a night in the refrigerator. Starchy soups that contain potatoes, beans, corn, or other legumes tend to thicken as they sit, so reheated soups may need to be thinned with water, broth, or milk. Be careful when reheating soups that contain egg yolks; they must not come to a boil, or the egg yolks will curdle.

Using Fats

Traditional pureed soup recipes call for fats at practically every stage of the cooking, although the total amount of fat per bowl is not as horrifying as it may seem when you read some of the recipes. If you make a pureed soup in the richest way—cook the vegetables in butter, thicken it with bread cooked in butter, and then use butter as a finish—it all adds up to only slightly more than 2 tablespoons of butter per bowl.

If you want to use less fat, don't bother with cooking the vegetables in fat at the beginning—just simmer them in a little bit of broth or milk. If you're using bread as a thickener, toast it lightly instead of cooking it in butter. And don't whisk in butter or cream at the end. Serve the soup with dollops of sour cream (which has much less fat than heavy cream) or if you're really watching it, yogurt. For additional suggestions, see Cutting Out the Fat.

Soups Containing Whole or Chopped Vegetables

For these soups the ingredients are simply combined with hot liquid, cooked until they are done, and served.

Pureed Soups

In these soups one or more vegetables are lightly cooked in butter or fat, liquid is added, the mixture is simmered, and the soup is then pureed in a food mill, blender, or food processor. The consistency of the soup is adjusted—usually by adding broth, milk, or water—and butter, cream, sour cream, or coconut milk is often added as a final finish. Simple pureed cream soups can also be made by simmering flavorful ingredients such as tomatoes, corn, or mushrooms in heavy cream, with or without broth and water, and then pureeing in a blender.

HOW PUREED SOUPS ARE THICKENED While some starchy vegetables—beans, potatoes, corn, even garlic—act as their own thickeners, some vegetables don't have enough natural starch to give a soup the desired body and consistency, so an additional thickener is needed.

Flour, gently cooked with vegetables in butter or fat, is one of the most common thickeners. Usually I try to use the vegetable as its own thickener, because flour doesn't add any flavor and can give the soup a gluey consistency like the clam chowder in cheap restaurants. But flour is very convenient—you can sprinkle a little into the vegetables to give the soup extra body without anyone knowing it's there. If your finished soup is too thin, you can whisk flour in at the end by working it to a paste with an equal amount of butter and then whisking it into the simmering soup.

Cornstarch, arrowroot, and potato flour can also be used as last-minute thickeners. They are best used for clear soups because they won't cloud them. They are especially popular in Chinese recipes. Work either of these into a thin paste with water and whisk into the simmering soup shortly before serving.

Another common thickener—and a very satisfying one—is potato puree. The easiest way to use potato as a thickener is to add chopped potatoes to the other vegetables near the beginning of the cooking so they soften by the time the rest of the vegetables are cooked. The vegetables and potatoes are then pureed together.

Cooked rice can also be used as a thickener (see puree of carrot soup, page 164). There are two ways to use it: you can add it to the soup at the same time as the liquid and cook it along with the vegetables, or you can cook it separately in water or broth and then puree it with the vegetables.

Bread cooked in butter or oil has been used as a thickener since the Middle Ages and is still used in Mediterranean soups and bisques. Older recipes suggest removing the crusts from white bread and cooking the slices gently in butter on both sides until the slices are pale brown and crispy. The bread slices are then added to the liquid to soften them and are pureed along with the vegetables. This method produces delicious results, but the slices absorb so much butter that the soup ends up being very rich. Another method is to brush the slices lightly with melted butter before browning them in a pan or simply toast the bread slices and leave the butter out altogether.

Beans can also be used to thicken vegetable soups with natural starch. They are best soaked, drained, cooked separately in fresh water and added to the soup just before it is pureed (see pages 235 and 236 for information about cooking beans).

Classic French recipes sometimes call for egg yolks to thicken pureed soups. Most of these recipes come from the days when richer supposedly meant better even when the extra richness did little for taste or texture. But there is one recipe—a classic *potage germiny* made with sorrel (page 212)—that is so delicious I had to include it here.

LIQUID INGREDIENTS FOR PUREED SOUPS The main liquid ingredient in most soups made from vegetable purees is broth, but milk or even water can also be used.

FRENCH CLASSIC NAMES
FOR PUREED SOUPS

French classical chefs categorize pureed soups according to thickener, liquid, and finish. Although it's of little importance nowadays whether you remember their names, understanding how these soups are made makes it easier to invent a soup with whatever vegetables you have on hand or find at the market.

Although most people think of a pureed soup as any soup that contains pureed vegetables, in the classical French system, a pureed soup is thickened with the pureed vegetable itself and usually an additional starchy element such as rice, potatoes, or bread. A classic pureed soup contains no flour. Traditionally, butter and sometimes egg yolks are added to these soups just before serving.

A classic cream (*crème*) soup contains pureed vegetables but also flour to thicken and give a smooth texture. The liquid used is always milk, and the soup is finished with heavy cream.

A classic *velouté* is prepared in almost the same way as a cream soup except that broth is used instead of milk. Traditionally, cream and egg yolks are added to *velouté* soups just before serving.

Some soups benefit from some white wine being added along with the other liquids—I love sherry with carrots or squash—but be careful; sometimes the acid in white wine will clash with certain vegetables, such as turnips and green vegetables.

HOW TO PUREE THE SOUP When the vegetables in the soup have softened, the soup is ready to be pureed. The easiest method is to strain it through a food mill, which strains and purees at the same time. Depending on the consistency you want for the finished soup and whether your food mill has different disks, you may want to do this twice—once with the coarse disk and then again with the fine.

Nowadays many cooks have a blender or food processor but not a food mill. Either a blender or a food processor can be used for pureeing soup, but be careful not to overwork the puree, or the soup will end up gluey.

It's easier to strain the soup through a regular kitchen strainer and then just puree the solids than it is to try to puree the whole soup with all its liquid. If the solids get stuck in the machine, add just enough of the cooking liquid to get them moving. The pureed solids are then combined with the strained liquid.

When you're using a blender or food processor, don't fill it more than one-third full with hot soup or the hot liquid will expand and shoot out the top, at best making a mess and at worst causing a burn. Wrap a towel around the blender lid and hold it down firmly. If the soup is cold, you can fill the blender three-quarters full.

Green vegetable soups should be served immediately or chilled quickly; otherwise they'll lose their bright color.

ADJUSTING THE SOUP'S TEXTURE If the soup is too thick, obviously you can easily thin it by adding more broth, water, milk, or cream. Because thickening a soup is more difficult—you'll have to prepare more of the puree base or add flour or cornstarch—when you're improvising a soup or using an unfamiliar recipe, add less liquid than you think you'll need or than the recipe calls for and then thin the soup to the right consistency at the end.

Another way to thin a soup and at the same time give it a smoother texture is to strain it through a fine-mesh strainer. Although ordinary kitchen strainers have a fine enough mesh for most soups, if you want a very fine, smooth texture, you'll have to buy a fine-mesh strainer.

Occasionally you may want a very smooth soup, but when you strain it through the fine-mesh strainer none of the solids go through and the liquid ends up being too thin. Trying to force the solids through the strainer will not only drive you crazy but may also damage the strainer. You can try pureeing the solids a second time in a blender, food processor, or food mill, but in really stubborn cases you will need another, somewhat expensive gadget called a drum sieve.

Single-Vegetable
SOUPS

ALTHOUGH MOST OF THESE SOUPS ACTUALLY INCLUDE MORE THAN ONE VEGETABLE, they are designed so that the flavor of a single vegetable predominates.

Virtually all of them can be made days in advance and refrigerated or frozen. Just be sure the soup comes to a boil first, chill it quickly, and don't add cream if you're freezing it until just before it's served.

ARTICHOKES

It wasn't too long ago that Americans outside of California had never seen an artichoke, to say nothing of knowing how to eat one. Some people like the flavor of artichokes but are still somewhat mystified about how to approach them—especially when they get down to separating the choke from the heart. This soup solves all such problems.

Puree of Artichoke

Most recipes for artichoke soup use only the bottoms and have you throw out the leaves. This recipe uses everything; you don't have to cut off the leaves, and there is no need to remove the choke because everything gets strained carefully.

Don't use an aluminum pot, or the artichokes will turn a miserable gray. Stainless steel or enamel works best.

MAKES 8 SERVINGS

4 quarts water
6 medium-size or 4 large artichokes
juice of 1 lemon
1 tablespoon olive oil
4 tablespoons unsalted butter
7 cups chicken or vegetable broth
6 slices of white bread, crusts removed
4 tablespoons unsalted butter, melted (optional)
½ to 1 cup heavy cream
salt
white pepper
lightly whipped cream or crème fraîche

BRING the water to a rapid boil in an 8-quart pot.

CUT the top two-thirds off the artichokes and discard. Cut the artichokes into quarters and toss them with the lemon juice and olive oil in a 4-quart mixing bowl. Dump the contents of the bowl, including the lemon juice and oil, into the pot and boil for 10 minutes. Drain the artichokes in a colander.

MELT 4 tablespoons butter in a 4-quart pot and add the artichokes. Stir them around in the butter over low heat for about 10 minutes. Be careful not to let the butter burn. Pour in the broth and turn up the heat until the broth comes to a slow simmer. Simmer the artichokes for 20 minutes, until soft.

DIP the bread slices in the melted butter on both sides and lightly sauté them over medium-low heat until they turn golden brown, about 3 to 4 minutes on each side. Add the cooked bread to the pot with the artichokes and simmer for 5 minutes more. You can also just lightly toast the bread and leave the butter out.

PUREE the soup in a food processor and then work it through a food mill. (If your food mill has several disks, use the one with the largest holes.) Strain the soup a second time through a fine- or medium-mesh strainer or through a food mill with the finest disk.

ADD the heavy cream to the soup, bring it to a simmer, and season with salt and pepper.

SERVE the soup with a dollop of lightly whipped cream or crème fraîche.

SUGGESTIONS AND VARIATIONS | The cooked bread gives this soup a very satisfying flavor and texture, but instead you can sprinkle 6 tablespoons flour over the blanched artichokes while you're cooking them in butter.

IF you want to give this soup a little texture, cook and slice three artichoke bottoms and add them to the soup just before serving:

CUT off the leaves on the lower third of the artichoke. If you're right-handed, hold the artichoke in your left hand, the paring knife in your right and rotate the artichoke against the knife, trimming the green off the base as you go. When you've trimmed all the green off the base, rub the bottoms with a lemon half and cook them in 4 quarts boiling water with a tablespoon of olive oil.

WHEN the artichokes are done—poke them with a knife, they should have the texture of barely cooked new potatoes—drain them and let them cool. Scrape inside each artichoke with an ordinary kitchen spoon and pull out the choke. Cut into slices about ¼ inch thick.

IF you're not using the slices right away, toss them in a tablespoon of wine vinegar to keep them from turning gray.

AN interesting variation—Escoffier wrote about it in 1902—is to roast a dozen hazelnuts and puree them along with the other ingredients before straining.

OTHER finishes include a teaspoon of chervil butter (page 594) or a sprinkling of small croutons (page 594) in the center of each bowl.

ASPARAGUS

Asparagus lovers are split into two camps—those who like it thin and those who like it thick. I for one am firmly planted among the lovers of the thickest stalks possible. When it comes to making soup, the texture of the asparagus isn't important, but thick stalks always have more flavor.

The best time of year to buy asparagus is May and April, when it is the least expensive and has the best flavor. In Europe you can't even find asparagus out of season. I still dream of the giant white asparagus we used to get in France at the end of April—at the price of filet mignon.

Puree of Asparagus

I always get frustrated when I serve asparagus. I laboriously peel the stalks so that my guests can eat the whole thing, and then they only eat the tips anyway. When I make this soup, I can be sure nothing will be wasted because the stalks are pureed and the tips are left whole.

MAKES 8 SERVINGS

4 quarts water
2 pounds asparagus
4 tablespoons unsalted butter
2 medium-size onions, finely chopped
1 medium-size waxy potato, peeled and sliced
6 cups chicken or vegetable broth
1 bunch of parsley, about 12 stems, tied up with string
½ to 1 cup heavy cream
salt
pepper

BRING the water to a boil in a 6-quart pot.

CUT off and discard 2 inches of the asparagus at the base. (This section is usually woody and fibrous and will make the soup difficult to puree.) Cut off the asparagus tips and reserve them. Chop the remaining stalks into 1-inch segments and reserve.

WHEN the water comes to a boil, put the asparagus tips in a strainer and submerge them in the water for 2 or 3 minutes, until they are tender but not mushy. Take them out—don't throw out the water—and immediately rinse them under cold running water. Set them aside.

NEXT, put the stalks in the boiling water and simmer them for 5 minutes to eliminate bitterness. Pour the water with the stalks into a colander and rinse them under cold running water.

HEAT the butter in a 4-quart pot over medium heat. Add the onions and potato and stir every 2 minutes for about 10 minutes, until the onions turn translucent (don't let them brown) and the potatoes soften slightly.

ADD the broth, the cut-up asparagus stalks, and the parsley. Simmer for about 15 minutes, until the asparagus and potatoes have softened thoroughly.

PUREE the soup in a food mill, food processor, or blender. Strain it through a medium-mesh strainer.

HEAT the soup, add the heavy cream, and season it with salt and pepper. You can add the asparagus tips directly to the soup or heat them at the last minute in a little water and arrange them on top of the soup.*

SUGGESTIONS AND VARIATIONS | This soup is even more dramatic when made with white asparagus. Your guests will be surprised by the flavor because the soup will be perfectly white. But be careful; some white asparagus is very bitter, so be sure you boil the stalks long enough (taste them as you go along).

THE flavor of this soup is quite delicate. The only herbs I ever risk using are parsley and chervil. A nice touch is to garnish each bowl with a tablespoon of parsley or chervil butter (page 594) just before serving. Small croutons cooked in butter also create a nice effect.

AVOCADOS

Once in a while—usually during annual visits to California—I taste an avocado with the buttery texture and nutty flavor that recall the tree-ripened avocados of my childhood. Although such perfection is rare, decent avocados can be found year-round throughout the United States. The best are the ones with the rough, pitted skin—the small Hass avocados from California—but smooth-skinned Florida avocados are certainly worth using.

*If the asparagus tips fall to the bottom of the soup, float a thin slice of buttered and toasted bread on top of each bowl and prop the asparagus tips on top.

Buying avocados takes forethought, because in the markets they're usually rock hard and you'll need to leave them outside the refrigerator for a day or two to let them ripen. Try not to cut open an avocado any sooner than you need to, or it will turn brown. A good amount of lemon or lime juice—which is often included in avocado preparations anyway—will also help keep the avocado green.

Avocado Soup

I once served this cold soup in a Paris bistro where I worked. The Parisians, completely unused to Mexican flavors and not jaded by bowls of indifferent guacamole wolfed down with a couple of stiff margaritas at cheap Mexican restaurants, loved it.

There are of course a number of recipes for avocado soup, usually pureed and then thinned with broth or cream. These recipes are often good, but I find that half the enjoyment of eating avocado comes from its rich, buttery texture, so my avocado soup isn't a puree.

I also like avocado with hot, spicy flavors as well as the lemon or lime that helps prevent discoloring. This recipe is a cross between guacamole and gazpacho and is best after sitting for an hour. Serve it with tortilla chips.

MAKES 6 SERVINGS

2 garlic cloves, peeled

1 small onion, minced

2 jalapeño chilies, seeded and very finely chopped

juice of 4 limes

1 bell pepper, preferably yellow, roasted, peeled (page 207), and chopped

4 large or 6 medium-size tomatoes, peeled, seeded, and finely chopped

¼ cup finely chopped cilantro leaves

2 ripe avocados

1 cup ice water

salt

pepper

tortilla chips

sour cream

IN ADVANCE Up to 8 hours ahead, crush the garlic to a paste in a mortar and pestle or by chopping it and crushing it on a cutting board with the side of a chef's knife. Stir the garlic paste, onion, jalapeños, lime juice, and bell pepper into the chopped tomatoes in a mixing bowl.

ADD the cilantro leaves to the soup.

AT THE LAST MINUTE Peel the avocados, remove the pits, and dice them into ½-inch cubes. Combine with the rest of the soup and the ice water. Adjust the seasoning with salt and pepper to taste and serve in chilled bowls. Pass tortilla chips and sour cream.

SUGGESTIONS AND VARIATIONS | Try substituting yellow tomatoes for red or, better yet, make two different versions—one with red tomatoes and one with yellow—and serve them together in the same bowl.

IF you want a more substantial soup, barbecue or sauté some shrimp or chicken and add the whole shrimp or the chicken (taken off the bone and cut into chunks) to the soup just before serving.

YOU can pass croutons cooked in olive oil or toasted slices of French bread instead of chips.

BEETS

People are never indifferent to beets—they either love or loathe them. I grew up on canned beets and grew to love them only when I started eating them fresh.

Cream of Beet Soup

This recipe contains a fair amount of vinegar—I think beets need to be tangy—but you may want to add it a bit at a time; not everyone likes things as sour as I do.

MAKES 6 SERVINGS

I pound (about 3 medium-size) beets, peeled and coarsely chopped

I large onion, coarsely chopped

I fresh marjoram sprig or 1 teaspoon dried or chopped fresh thyme

3 tablespoons unsalted butter

I quart chicken or vegetable broth

2 tablespoons good red wine vinegar or to taste

½ cup heavy cream

salt

pepper

½ cup heavy cream, lightly whipped

small croutons (page 594)

¼ cup chopped fresh herbs such as dill or marjoram

COOK the beets, onion, and marjoram in the butter in a 4-quart pot over medium heat until the onions begin to soften slightly, about 10 minutes. Add the broth, partially cover the pot, and simmer slowly for about 30 minutes, until the beets are completely soft. Check them by trying to crush one against the side of the pot with a wooden spoon. Simmer longer if necessary.

PUREE the soup in a blender or food processor. If you want the soup to have a smoother texture, strain it through a medium-mesh strainer. Add the cream and vinegar and bring the soup back to a simmer. Season with salt and pepper.

YOU can decorate each bowl with the whipped cream, croutons, and herbs or let your guests help themselves.

MAKING A BASE FOR VEGETABLE SOUPS

Many vegetable soups are made by combining vegetables with a liquid base of broth or milk thickened with flour. Broth thickened with flour is called a *velouté;* milk thickened with flour is a *béchamel.* Once you know how to make these bases it becomes a simple matter of adding vegetables and pureeing the mixture to come up with a soup.

To prepare 2 quarts of *velouté* base, cook 1 finely chopped medium onion in 4 tablespoons of butter over medium heat for about 10 minutes. Add 3 tablespoons of flour to the onions and stir over medium heat for 2 minutes more. Whisk in 2 quarts of chicken, veal, or fish broth and bring the base to a simmer. Simmer for 10 minutes, skimming off any froth or fat that floats to the top.

For a *béchamel,* simply replace the broth with milk.

SUGGESTIONS AND VARIATIONS | You can look at this soup as a simplified borscht. Scandinavian and Russian cooks often serve seafood with beets. Alan Davidson, who's written several excellent books on seafood, describes a Russian version with squid.

FOR the Scandinavian version, simmer fish fillets or salmon cubes in the soup just long enough before serving to cook them through.

BROCCOLI

It took me a long time to appreciate broccoli after having it so often in restaurants as the ubiquitous overcooked accompaniment to meat or fish. Making a pot of soup is an excellent way to capture broccoli's sometimes fleeting flavor. Cooking broccoli into a soup allows to use not only the delicate flowers but also the stems.

If you want to make a puree of broccoli soup with a bright green color, cook it for a very short time in boiling salted water before pureeing it in a blender or food processor. There is one problem with this method: the broccoli florets cook in about 15 seconds, while the stems take about 5 minutes. The obvious way around this is to add the stems—cut into ½-inch sections—to the water 5 minutes before adding the florets.

Once you've prepared the basic broccoli puree, add it to a classic cream or *velouté* soup base (onion cooked in butter with a little flour, milk or cream added, page 160) or a leek and potato base (page 190) just before serving so the broccoli doesn't overcook and turn gray.

Broccoli can also be cooked slowly with garlic and olive oil to prepare the full-flavored Italian version that follows.

Slow-Cooked Broccoli Soup with Garlic and Olive Oil

When I first studied cooking in the 1970s, chefs in France had just started undercooking vegetables so they still had a slight crunch. For years after that it was de rigueur in the United States to serve vegetables practically raw, and the slow-cooked vegetable recipes of the past were—mostly for the best—forgotten.

It wasn't until I saw a recipe for long-cooked broccoli in Paul Bertholli and Alice Waters's *Chez Panisse Cooking* that I began to experiment with some of these old fashioned methods. This soup is best in the winter, when full flavor is more important than freshness and delicacy.

MAKES 8 SERVINGS

2 large bunches of broccoli, about 3 pounds

½ cup virgin olive oil

8 garlic cloves, thinly sliced

2 teaspoons chopped fresh thyme or marjoram or
    ½ teaspoon dried

6 cups chicken or vegetable broth

1 tablespoon fresh lemon juice

salt

pepper

toasted slices of French bread

finely grated Parmesan cheese

CUT the florets off the broccoli and again into smaller pieces so that each floret is about an inch in diameter. Cut off and discard the bottom 2 inches of the stems. Peel the remaining stems and slice them as thinly as you can.

COMBINE all the ingredients except for the salt, pepper, and cheese in a 4-quart pot. Bring the soup to a simmer, cover it, and turn the heat down low enough to keep the soup at a slow simmer. Simmer for 1 hour.

STIR the soup with a spoon to break up the broccoli and season it with salt and pepper.

SERVE slices of toasted bread at the table and pass the grated cheese. I like to make garlic bread and put a slice in the center of each bowl before pouring the soup over.

CARDOONS

Cardoons look like giant bunches of celery except a bit more rough-and-tumble, with scraggly leaves and discolored ends. Although the cooked stalks have a flavor reminiscent of artichokes, cardoons have a subtle and distinctive flavor all their own.

I first read about them in *Remembrance of Things Past* when Marcel sits down to a plate of *cardons à la moelle*—cardoons with beef marrow. Years later I saw cardoons in an Italian market in Manhattan and dragged off a huge bundle to my restaurant to be served as the evening special, *cardons à la moelle*. Alas, I found *cardons à la moelle* a bit disappointing—cardoons have an understated flavor, and the béchamel sauce called for in *Larousse Gastronomique* didn't help matters much.

This recipe is more Italian than Proustian, and at the risk of overpowering the gentle cardoons I've included lots of garlic, herbs, and olive oil.

Italian-Style Cardoon, Bean, and Tomato Soup

MAKES 8 SERVINGS

¼ pound pancetta or prosciutto end

1 medium-size onion, finely chopped

3 tablespoons olive oil

3 pounds cardoons

juice of 1 lemon

24 garlic cloves, peeled

1 bouquet garni—1 sage leaf and 3 fresh marjoram
    sprigs—or 1 teaspoon dried thyme

5 cups chicken broth or water

½ cup cannellini, borlotti, or Great Northern beans, soaked,
    drained, and cooked until tender (see pages 235 and
    236 for information about cooking beans)

2 medium-size tomatoes, peeled, seeded, and coarsely
    chopped, or 1 cup drained and seeded canned
    tomatoes, coarsely chopped

¼ cup finely chopped Italian parsley

salt

pepper

slices of crusty bread

grated Parmesan cheese

IF you're using pancetta, unroll it. Cut it into ⅛- by 1-inch strips. Over medium heat, cook the pancetta and onion in the olive oil in a 4-quart pot until the onion starts to turn translucent, about 10 minutes.

PEEL the cardoon stalks with a vegetable peeler in the same way as for celery. Cut the stalks into ½-inch-thick slices and toss them in the lemon juice in a mixing bowl to prevent them from turning dark.

PUT the cardoons in the pot with the pancetta and add the garlic cloves, bouquet garni, and broth. Simmer until the cardoons and garlic have softened thoroughly and can be crushed easily against the inside of the pot, about 20 minutes.

ADD the cooked beans, along with their cooking liquid, the tomatoes, and parsley and simmer for 5 minutes more. Season with salt and pepper and serve with the bread and cheese.

CARROTS

It's hard for me to imagine cooking without the reliable carrot—always there, never expensive, rarely bad or unusable. But carrots weren't always orange—in old French cookbooks they're described as pale yellow.

I always buy fresh carrots with the greens still attached instead of the ones that come wrapped in plastic bags. I can't swear there's a difference in taste, but certainly the carrots with tops are fresher. If you buy carrots with tops, remove them before storing.

Whatever carrots you do buy, make sure they don't have cracks running along one side; this is a sign that they're old. And don't worry if the carrots are big and fat—these seem to have more flavor than the chic and expensive baby versions.

Cooks sometimes argue about whether carrots should be peeled or scraped. I usually recommend scraping baby carrots and peeling older fat ones.

Puree of Carrot Soup

PURÉE CRÉCY

This is one of those classics that the French have named in their inimitable way—after one of two towns, but no one knows which. Few people dining today are likely to recognize that *crécy* indicates carrots, so just call it carrot puree.

This delicious soup lends itself to a lot of variation. It is traditionally thickened in several ways, so it's a good candidate for play in the kitchen; experiment with different techniques and see how each contributes its own nuances to the soup.

All three versions that follow begin with gently cooking sliced carrots and an onion in butter until they soften. In the first version raw rice (basmati gives the soup a lovely flavor but is by no means essential) is cooked along with the carrots; in the second potatoes—ideally, Yukon Golds or other waxy potatoes—are used; and in the last version toasted bread is added.

Just before serving, each of the soups is strained and finished with a small amount of heavy cream. Once you get a feel for how the different thickeners work, the recipe variations given here can be used as models for other pureed soups.

Serve the soup in piping hot bowls with tiny croutons floating on top.

MAKES 6 SERVINGS

1½ pounds (about 7 medium-size) carrots, peeled and
    sliced

4 tablespoons unsalted butter

2 teaspoons sugar

3 fresh thyme sprigs or 1 teaspoon dried

version 1:

½ cup long-grain rice, preferably basmati, rinsed

version 2:

2 medium-size potatoes, peeled and chopped

version 3:

7 slices of white bread, crusts removed, toasted

5 cups chicken or vegetable broth

½ cup heavy cream or more to taste

salt

pepper

small croutons (page 594)

COOK the carrots with the butter, sugar, thyme, and rice or potatoes (if you're using them) in a 4-quart pot over medium heat until the carrots begin to soften, about 10 minutes. Add the broth and bring to a simmer. Simmer the soup until the rice is puffed up and soft or until the potatoes can be crushed easily with a spoon, about 15 minutes.

IF you're using the bread, you'll need to simmer it only for about 5 minutes in the soup—just long enough for the bread to soften.

STRAIN the soup through a food mill with the coarse disk and then again with the fine disk or puree the soup in a blender or food processor and strain it through a medium-mesh strainer and again through a fine-mesh strainer if you want it even finer.

WHISK the cream into the soup and bring the soup back to a simmer. Season with salt and pepper. Serve immediately with the croutons.

SUGGESTIONS AND VARIATIONS | If you want this soup to have a little more piz-zazz, try adding a teaspoon of grated fresh ginger to the soup just before straining.

CARROT soup is also delicious with curry. For one batch of soup I use one teaspoon of "Vindaloo" curry, which is hot and strong. If you're using a milder curry pow-der, you may need to add more. Cook the curry powder in a tablespoon of butter over medium heat for about 30 seconds and then whisk this paste into the finished soup. If you're adventurous, you may also want to experiment with your own spice mixtures. The *garam masala* recipe on page 245 is a good place to start. Curry-flavored carrot soup is especially delicious when you've used basmati rice to thicken the soup. Try replacing the heavy cream with coconut milk if you have some around.

MADEIRA or a sweet sherry also adds a lovely nuance to carrot soups. A half cup added with the broth is a good amount for 6 servings.

YOU might also want to experiment with a Mexican version—minced hot peppers are added along with the carrots, and finely chopped cilantro is added to the soup just before it is served.

CARROT soup can also be served cold.

CASHEWS

It only recently occurred to me that I'd never seen a cashew in its shell. A little research revealed why. The cashew "nut" is actually a fruit that grows on the end of a fruitlike "apple," which, according to Alain Davidson in *The Oxford Companion to Food*, isn't a fruit but a fruit receptacle, in some places more prized than what we call the nut. To further complicate matters, what we call the nut is difficult to peel and defends itself by surrounding itself with a shell that contains corrosive and irritating compounds. Usually, cashews in the shell are roasted to destroy some of these compounds and to make the shell brittle and easier to remove.

Brazilian-Style Cashew Nut Soup

In my teens, I used to go backpacking every summer with my brother Dick and his wife Susan, often for more than a week at a time in California's High Sierra. The memories of working our way to the base of glaciated peaks and camping next to icy blue lakes remain among the happiest of my life. The only damper on those lovely trips, other than the occasional thunderstorm, was the food. Because our staples had to be light and energy packed, we'd fill our packs with ghastly freeze-dried dinners, instant pancake mixes, and peanut butter. Later, we discovered cashew butter, which when spread on a cracker became the highlight of our day. I've since found more luxurious dishes, from India and Brazil, that call for cashew butter and other nut butters to thicken and give a silky richness to soups and stews. This recipe is adapted from a Brazilian soup *(sopa de castanha do para)* made with Brazil nuts. You can buy cashew butter already made and whisk it into this soup, but it's just as easy to puree whole roasted cashews right into the soup.

MAKES 6 FIRST-COURSE SERVINGS

1 medium-size onion, chopped

1 garlic clove, peeled and finely chopped

2 tablespoons olive oil

4 cups chicken broth (preferably homemade basic brown chicken stock, page 62)

2 cups roasted cashews (or, if you're using raw, see below)

1 15-ounce can unsweetened coconut milk (preferably a brand from Thailand)

2 tablespoons chopped cilantro

salt

pepper

½ cup sour cream or créme fraîche (optional)

GENTLY cook the onion and garlic in the olive oil in a heavy-bottomed pot over medium heat for about 10 minutes, until the onion turns translucent and smells fragrant.

IF you're using raw cashews, preheat the oven to 350°F and roast them on a sheet pan for 15 minutes.

COMBINE the onion-garlic mixture with the cashews in a food processor and puree for about 3 minutes, scraping down the sides every minute with a rubber spatula.

COMBINE the chicken broth with the cashew mixture and work it through a food mill or use a ladle to work it through a strainer into a pot. Whisk in the coconut milk, add the cilantro, and season to taste with salt and pepper. Ladle into heated bowls. Put a dollop of sour cream in the center of each bowl.

CAULIFLOWER

Cauliflower tends to fall apart in soup, so it's best cooked into a puree. Because cauliflower doesn't have much starch of its own, it needs to be cooked with something starchy such as potato or flour to hold it together.

Puree of Cauliflower Soup

The French call this soup *crème du barry*, which dates back to the 17th century, when cauliflower was still a rarity only the nobility could afford.

This version is thickened with potatoes, but 300 years ago *crème du barry* was thickened with flour—the French had yet to discover the potato.

To prepare the cauliflower, cut around the central core from the bottom so that the little flowerlike sections fall away. Discard the core.

MAKES 6 SERVINGS

I head of cauliflower, core removed
2 medium-size waxy potatoes, sliced
I quart milk
½ cup heavy cream (optional)
salt
white pepper
small croutons sautéed in butter (page 594)

COMBINE the cauliflower, potatoes, and milk in a 4-quart pot. Bring the mixture to a simmer. Leave it at a slow simmer until the potatoes are soft and the cauliflower is easy to break up with a fork, about 20–25 minutes. Be careful not to let the milk boil over.

PUREE the soup through a food mill or in a blender or food processor. Strain it through a regular kitchen strainer or a fine-mesh strainer if you want an even finer texture.

ADD the cream if desired and bring the soup back to a simmer. Season with salt to taste. Serve in hot bowls with croutons.

SUGGESTIONS AND VARIATIONS | This is a very delicately flavored soup, and I must admit I always want to jazz it up with herbs (thyme or sage is especially tempting) or a little grating of nutmeg. The problem with these flavorings is that the taste of cauliflower is easy to lose, so if you decide to play around, be careful.

YOU can also make this soup with broccoli—cut the broccoli in the same way—but add it to the milk and potato mixture only when the potatoes are already soft. Otherwise it will overcook, and the soup will turn gray. When you're using broccoli, chill the soup as soon as it's done or serve it right away.

THE most exciting cauliflower soup I ever tasted was at lunch at Jamin, Joël Robuchon's three-star restaurant in Paris. It was called *crème de choufleur au caviar*. When it arrived, chilled in a deep soup bowl, I carefully tasted it, and although it had just the right creamy texture, I couldn't taste the caviar. A little disappointed, I tasted again, digging a little deeper, and discovered that the cauliflower soup comprised only the top ½ inch—underneath that layer lay a thick bed of Beluga caviar. The cauliflower soup functioned mostly as a delicate sauce for spoonfuls of caviar. Happy afternoon.

EVEN if you don't have caviar, cauliflower soup is delicious served cold with a dollop of whipped cream and a pinch of chopped chives in the center of each bowl. Or try a spoonful of chervil or parsley butter (page 594 or 593) or some tiny cauliflower florets cooked until soft in boiling water.

CELERIAC

Celeriac is one of the great underrated vegetables. Although its flavor is similar to that of celery, it has an ineffable subtlety that makes it delicious in soups and purees. It's also delicious cooked and pureed into mashed potatoes.

Don't try to peel celeriac with a vegetable peeler; use a sharp stainless-steel paring knife instead. And once you've peeled it, unless you're going to use it right away, rub it with lemon to prevent it from browning.

Cream or Velouté of Celeriac Soup

Don't be confused by the title of this soup. Almost any pureed soup can become a *velouté* or a cream soup, depending on whether you use broth or milk as the liquid. While most traditional cream soups and *veloutés* are thickened with flour, this version is held together with potato cooked along with the celeriac.

MAKES 6 SERVINGS

I large celeriac, about I pound, peeled with a sharp paring
    knife and coarsely chopped
I medium-size waxy potato, coarsely chopped
I medium-size onion, finely chopped
6 cups chicken or vegetable broth, milk, or water
I bouquet garni
¾ cup heavy cream
salt
pepper
small croutons
herb butter (pages 593–594) with mint, chervil, or parsley

COMBINE the celeriac, potato, onion, broth, and the bouquet garni in a 4-quart pot. Bring to a slow simmer and cover the pot. Simmer the soup for about 30 minutes, until the potatoes and celeriac are easy to crush against the side of the pot with a spoon.

STRAIN the soup through a food mill with the finest disk or puree it in a blender or food processor and strain it through a regular kitchen strainer.

ADD the heavy cream. If you want the soup to have a finer or smoother texture, strain again through a fine-mesh strainer. Season with salt and pepper and serve with croutons and herb butter.

SUGGESTIONS AND VARIATIONS | This is a subtle and delicate winter soup. If you want something more robust, gently cook three ¼-inch-thick slices of bacon cut into little strips (*lardons*) in a 4-quart pot. When the bacon starts to turn crisp, take it out of the pot with a slotted spoon and gently sweat the celeriac and the potatoes in the rendered fat. Add the liquids and the bouquet garni, finish the recipe as directed, and garnish the individual bowls with the bacon strips.

IF you don't want to bother with the croutons, pass thinly sliced and buttered baguette toasts at the table with the soup.

CELERIAC soup is delicious served cold, but you may want to thin it slightly—it thickens as it chills.

CHESTNUTS

Puree of Chestnut

I always associate the smell of roasting chestnuts with fall feasting and like to serve this soup as a prelude to a holiday meal. If you decide to make it at Thanksgiving, be sure to make enough so you can have it hot the next day with cold leftover turkey.

Depending on how adventurous (or masochistic) you are, this soup can be thrown together in a few minutes or can take most of an afternoon. You can start with whole unpeeled chestnuts, peeled chestnuts in jars or cans (broken pieces are cheaper and just as good), or unsweetened chestnut puree. To be honest, the results are almost the same, but you never know when someone is going to give you a 20-pound bag of chestnuts, and there is something satisfying about converting a recalcitrant natural product into something smooth and effortless to eat.

If you start with raw chestnuts, you must peel them. Make a slit in the concave side of each chestnut with a paring knife. This is important; otherwise they may blow up in the oven. Roast them on a sheet pan in a 450°F oven for about 15 minutes, until the slit you made curls open slightly. Take them out and peel them while they are still hot by holding them in a kitchen towel and pulling on each side.

Once you've removed the tough outer peel, boil the chestnuts for 5 minutes, drain them, and, while they are still hot, rub them vigorously in a wet towel. This should remove most of the inner peel. Don't panic if you can't get all of this membrane off, most of it will be strained out of the soup anyway.

Even though this soup contains very little fat, it is amazingly rich.

MAKES 8 SERVINGS

I celery rib, finely sliced

I medium-size onion, sliced

3 tablespoons unsalted butter

1½ pounds peeled chestnuts or 2½ cups chestnut puree

2 quarts chicken broth or milk

1¼-inch-thick slice of prosciutto or Smithfield ham, diced
    into ¼-inch cubes, about ½ cup

salt

pepper

small croutons (page 594)

COOK the celery and onion in the butter in a 4-quart pot over medium heat until soft, about 10 minutes (don't let them brown). Add the chestnuts and broth and bring to a simmer.

IF you're using chestnut puree, simmer the soup for 5 minutes and strain the soup through a regular kitchen strainer.

IF you're using whole chestnuts, simmer the mixture until the chestnuts are easy to crush against the side of the pot with a fork, usually 30 minutes.

STRAIN the soup through a food mill—first the coarse and then the fine disk—or puree it in a blender or food processor. Check the soup's consistency. If you want it finer, strain it through a medium-mesh strainer or even through a fine-mesh strainer.

ADD the ham cubes to the soup, bring it back to a simmer, and season it with salt and pepper. Sprinkle with croutons or a dollop of herb butter such as parsley, chervil, or tarragon (pages 593–594).

SUGGESTIONS AND VARIATIONS | You may find that the soup needs a little sweetness. If so, sprinkle in 1 or 2 teaspoons sugar or, for a more sophisticated touch, ½ cup port.

I find that chestnuts go well with smoky-flavored foods, so I sometimes use bacon fat instead of butter for cooking the onions and celery at the beginning. Cut 3 ¼-inch-thick slices of bacon crosswise into ¼-inch-wide strips. Gently cook them in the pot you're using to make the soup. When they just start to turn crisp, take them out with a slotted spoon and start cooking the onion and celery in the rendered fat. You can then use the bacon strips as garnish for the finished soup.

CHILIES

Even though they're closely related, I call any pepper that isn't a bell pepper a chili. While the variety of fresh chilies in most parts of the United States is limited (unless you're lucky enough to live in New Mexico), an assortment of dried chilies is easy to find in specialty food stores, and chilies are easy and inexpensive to mail order because they're light and don't require refrigeration.

What's most exciting about chilies—especially dried chilies—are their subtle differences in aroma, flavor, and heat that allow you to give your soups a completely different character by changing the chilies or using them in different combinations.

CORN

I hate to say it, but fresh corn really is best when cooked within a few hours after it has been picked. When corn sits, the natural sugars that give it its sweetness start to turn to starch. If you find perfectly fresh corn but you don't plan to serve it for a few days, it's better to make the soup in advance and keep it in the refrigerator than to keep the corn waiting. Although I make these soups only when corn is in season, frozen corn is an acceptable alternative if you're in a pinch. Don't try to make these soups with canned corn.

The corn soups that follow are all pureed and have a smooth, creamy texture. If you want to leave the kernels in the soup, just skip the pureeing and straining.

Creamed Chili Soup

This soup is based on a light tomato soup well flavored with garlic. Virtually any chili or chili combination can be used to give this soup its own special flavor.

MAKES 8 SERVINGS

I medium-size onion, peeled and chopped

4 large garlic cloves, crushed, peeled, and chopped

2 tablespoons olive oil

6 medium-size tomatoes, stemmed and coarsely chopped (don't bother with seeding or peeling)

3 cups chicken broth or water

I or 2 (depending on how much heat you want) hot smoked dried chilies such as chipotles (smoked jalapeños) or pasillas de Oaxaca

4 mild to medium hot dried chilies such as anchos, chilhuacle negros, guajillos, mulatos, or pasillas

I½ cups heavy cream

juice of I lime

salt

lime wedges (optional)

sour cream or crème fraîche (optional)

finely grated Monterey Jack or Cheddar cheese (optional)

COOK the onion and garlic in the olive oil in a heavy-bottomed pot over medium heat until they smell fragrant and the onion turns translucent, about 10 minutes. Add the tomatoes and the chicken broth or water; cover the pot and simmer gently, stirring every couple of minutes—scrape against the bottom of the pot so the tomatoes don't stick—until the tomatoes are completely soft, 20 to 30 minutes.

WHILE the tomatoes are cooking, wipe the dust off the chilies with a damp towel and toast them in a hot skillet for about a minute on each side, until you smell their fragrance. Cut off the stems, cut the chilies in half lengthwise, and brush out their seeds. Put the chilies all together in a bowl and cover with about 2 cups of boiling water. Let soak for 20 minutes and discard the water. Chop the chilies fine.

ADD the chilies and heavy cream to the tomato soup base, simmer for 2 minutes, and work through a food mill or a large strainer with the back of a ladle. Stir in the lime juice and season to taste with salt. Bring back to the simmer and ladle into heated soup bowls.

PASS one, two, or all three of the optional garnitures at the table for guests to help themselves.

Creamed Puree of Fresh Corn

This soup is essentially creamed fresh corn that has been pureed and strained. You can leave out the jalapeño pepper and the thyme and just cook the corn with a little broth and finish it with cream, but the thyme and hot chilies give it a lovely Mexican accent and do wonders for its flavor.

MAKES 6 SERVINGS

4 tablespoons unsalted butter

1 medium-size onion, finely chopped

4 garlic cloves, chopped

1 jalapeño chili, seeded and finely chopped

1 teaspoon fresh thyme leaves or ½ teaspoon dried

4 cups corn kernels, from 6 to 8 ears of fresh corn, or 2 10-ounce packages frozen

1 quart chicken or vegetable broth

½ cup heavy cream

2 tablespoons finely chopped cilantro

1 teaspoon sugar or more to taste

2 tablespoons fresh lime juice or more to taste

pinch of cayenne pepper (optional)

salt

pepper

sour cream or grated Cheddar or Monterey Jack cheese

Tabasco sauce or finely chopped jalapeño peppers

MELT the butter over medium heat in a 4-quart pot and add the onion, garlic, jalapeño chili, and thyme leaves. Stir this mixture until the onion turns translucent, about 10 minutes.

ADD the corn kernels and *half* the broth. Partially cover the pot and simmer the soup for about 15 minutes, until the corn kernels have softened thoroughly.

PUREE the soup in a blender or food processor and strain it through a food mill with a medium disk or force it through a medium-mesh strainer. Add the rest of the broth—slightly more or less, depending on the texture you want. If you want the soup to have an even smoother texture, strain it again through a fine-mesh strainer.

ADD the cream, bring the soup back to a simmer, and add the cilantro. Add the sugar, lime juice, and cayenne to taste. Season the soup with salt and pepper. Pass a bowl of sour cream or grated cheese at the table. I also make a bottle of Tabasco or some chopped chilies available for those who want the soup hotter.

SUGGESTIONS AND VARIATIONS | This soup is particularly good with barbecued foods. Sometimes I put barbecued shrimp or chicken—taken off the bone and cubed—right into the soup. The spiciness of the soup is incredible with the smoky flavors from the grill.

Indian-Style Corn Soup

This soup is part of my new obsession with Indian food, especially vegetarian food, which is amazingly flavorful and satisfying—and I've always been a big meat eater.

The recipe starts out like any French puree soup; the corn kernels are added to a base of lightly cooked aromatic vegetables, water or broth is added, and the soup is simmered for a few minutes before it is pureed and strained. But the finishes for this version are different. Instead of being finished with heavy cream and maybe some chopped herbs, the soup is finished with coconut milk and curry powder cooked in a little butter. I rely on a spicy "Vindaloo" curry powder, but you should feel free to fool around with the spices or to try making a curry blend of your own.

This soup can be made completely in advance.

MAKES 6 SERVINGS

1 medium-size onion, finely chopped

2 garlic cloves, finely chopped

1 teaspoon fresh thyme leaves or ½ teaspoon dried

3 tablespoons unsalted butter

4 cups corn kernels, from 6 to 8 ears of fresh corn, or 2 10-ounce packages frozen

3 cups water or vegetable or chicken broth

1 teaspoon curry powder

1 cup coconut milk

1 teaspoon sugar

2 teaspoons fresh lime or lemon juice

2 tablespoons finely chopped cilantro leaves

salt

COOK the onion, garlic, and thyme in 2 tablespoons butter in a 4-quart pot over medium heat until the onion turns translucent, about 10 minutes.

ADD the corn and half the water, cover partially, and simmer until the kernels are soft, about 15 minutes.

HEAT the remaining tablespoon of butter in a small saucepan over low to medium heat. Stir in the curry powder and heat gently for 1 minute to wake up its aroma, but be careful not to let it burn. Remove the pan from the heat.

PUREE the corn mixture in a blender or food processor and then strain it through a food mill with a medium disk or a medium-mesh strainer. If you want a smoother texture, strain it again through a fine-mesh strainer. Add the rest of the water or broth (slightly more or less, depending on the texture you want) to the strained mixture.

WHISK the cooked curry, coconut milk, sugar, lime or lemon juice, and cilantro into the soup a minute or two before serving. Season with salt.

SUGGESTIONS AND VARIATIONS | I like to use this soup as the liquid base for more elaborate vegetable soups and stews. One of my favorite additions is chopped peeled and seeded tomatoes, but I also sometimes add cooked spinach, potatoes, cauliflower, broccoli, and green beans. Each of these vegetables, except the tomatoes, should be cooked separately in boiling water rather than being cooked directly in the corn soup.

USING FRESH CORN

Taking the kernels off fresh corn is easier than it looks. Just husk the ears and remove the kernels by standing each ear in a large bowl and then cutting down the sides with a sharp paring knife.

Chinese Corn and Shrimp Soup

This soup is delicious and a snap to prepare; the corn kernels are simmered directly in broth with Chinese flavorings, and the whole soup is strained. The shrimp is added just before serving.

18 medium-size shrimp, peeled and shells reserved, deveined, and cut into ½-inch dice

4 cups corn kernels, from 6 to 8 ears, or 2 10-ounce packages frozen

a ¼-inch slice fresh ginger, peeled and finely chopped, or 1 teaspoon ground

5 cups chicken broth

2 teaspoons sugar

½ cup dry sherry

1½ teaspoons dark sesame oil

3 tablespoons balsamic or Chinese rice wine vinegar

COMBINE the shrimp shells with the corn, ginger, and half the chicken broth in a 4-quart pot. Partially cover the pot and bring the soup to a slow simmer. Simmer slowly for 15 minutes.

PUREE the soup in a blender and strain it through a food mill with a medium disk or through a medium-mesh strainer. If you want an even smoother consistency, strain it again through a fine-mesh strainer.

ADD the rest of the broth along with the sugar, sherry, sesame oil, and vinegar. Simmer the soup for about 3 minutes to cook off the alcohol in the sherry. Add the shrimp cubes to the hot soup about 2 minutes before serving, just long enough to turn them orange.

Mexican Corn, Tomato, Chili, and Chicken Soup

I don't know if this soup is served in Mexico, but certain ingredients form such a perfect alliance that, at the risk of sounding cocky, it should be. My own trick is to deconstruct the elements in the soup—a puree of fresh corn, a spicy tomato soup, and a chili sauce—so they look great in the bowl and allow the guests to take spoonfuls that combine varying amounts of each soup so no spoonful ends up tasting the same.

for the chili sauce:

>   4 dried chilies such as anchos, chilhuacle negros (or
>   chilhuacle rojos or amarillos, but negros are best),
>   guajillos, mulatos, or pasillas, alone or in combination
>
>   1 cup heavy cream
>
>   salt

for the tomato soup:

>   5 garlic cloves
>
>   1 medium-size red onion, peeled and halved
>
>   4 medium-size tomatoes (about 1½ pounds)
>
>   1 cup basic brown chicken broth (page 62)
>
>   salt
>
>   pepper

for the corn soup:

>   1 4-pound chicken, quartered (see box, page 472)
>
>   salt
>
>   pepper
>
>   2 tablespoons olive oil
>
>   1 medium-size onion, finely chopped
>
>   2 garlic cloves, finely chopped
>
>   2 dried chipotle chilies, stemmed and seeded, soaked in
>   warm water for 30 minutes, drained, finely chopped, or
>   2 chipotle chilies in adobo sauce, rinsed, seeded, finely
>   chopped, or 2 jalapeño chilies, stemmed, seeded, finely
>   chopped
>
>   3 cups chicken broth
>
>   2 cups corn kernels, from 3 to 4 ears of fresh corn, or one
>   10-ounce package frozen corn

the condiments:

>   1 cup sour cream
>
>   lime wedges from 2 limes
>
>   leaves from 1 small bunch of cilantro, coarsely chopped
>
>   8 jalapeño chilies, stemmed and seeded, finely chopped

PREPARING THE CHILI SAUCE Wipe the chilies with a damp paper towel to
eliminate dust. Cut the stems off the chilies and cut the chilies in half lengthwise.
Brush out the seeds and put the chilies in a heatproof bowl. Pour over about

2 cups of boiling water and let sit, for about 30 minutes, until the chilies become soft and pliable. Bring the cream to a simmer. Drain the chilies—discard the soaking water—and put them in the blender with the cream. Puree the chilies with the cream—start out with short pulses on the lowest speed while holding the blender lid firmly to the base with a towel—for about 2 minutes until the mixture is smooth. Use a ladle to work the sauce through a strainer. Season to taste with salt and reserve.

PREPARING THE TOMATO SOUP Place an iron skillet on the stove over high heat for about 5 minutes—if you can avoid it, don't use a well-seasoned pan because the high heat without oil will destroy the seasoning. Add the garlic and onion and stir about every minute until the onion falls apart and blackens on the edges and everything smells fragrant. Take the onion and garlic out of the pan and reserve in a bowl. Put the tomatoes in the pan and gently stir them around until their skins wrinkle and blacken in places and the tomatoes start to sizzle and pop, about 8 minutes. Do your best to get the tomatoes in contact with the hot skillet on all sides. Take the tomatoes out of the pan, turn off the heat, and let cool.

PUT the garlic and onion in a blender with two of the tomatoes and puree until smooth. Pour this mixture into a food mill or a strainer set over a bowl and work it through (with a ladle if you're using a strainer), eliminating peels and seeds. Puree the rest of the tomatoes, working in batches, and work them through the food mill or strainer into the bowl with the first batch. Stir the chicken broth into the strained tomato mixture and season to taste with salt and pepper. Reserve.

PREPARING THE CHICKEN AND CORN SOUP Season the chicken parts with salt and pepper and brown them for about 8 minutes on the skin side and 5 minutes on the flesh side, over high heat, in olive oil, in a heavy-bottomed pot just large enough to hold them in a single layer. Transfer to a plate and reserve.

POUR all but I tablespoon of fat out of the pan, and stir in the onion, garlic, and chilies. Cook over medium heat, stirring every couple of minutes until the onion turns translucent but doesn't brown. Be careful of the fumes from the chilies—sniff carefully. Pour in the broth, stir in the corn, and put back the chicken. Cover the pot and bring to a gentle simmer over medium heat. Simmer the chicken for 15 minutes after the broth has reached the simmer—once the chicken pieces feel firm to the touch, don't cook them any more. Take the chicken out of the broth with tongs to let cool. Use a ladle to skim off any fat that has risen to the top of the soup. Work the corn broth through a food mill or puree it in a blender and use a ladle to work it through a strainer. (You can also leave the kernels in the soup, but I prefer them pureed.) Take the chicken off the bones in strips, discard the bones and skin, and reserve. Season the broth to taste with salt and pepper.

ASSEMBLING THE SOUP If the chicken meat has cooled off, warm it in a 300°F, covered with aluminum foil so it doesn't dry out. Bring the corn and tomato soups and the chili sauce, separately, to a gentle simmer. Place a mound of chicken in the center of heated soup plates. Use two ladles or measuring pitchers to ladle the corn and tomato soups into the soup plates at the same time, so one soup is on one side and the other soup on the other. Swirl the chili sauce on top of each serving. Pass the condiments at the table.

CUCUMBERS

Cucumbers are a refreshing ingredient in gazpacho and cool summer soups. Two kinds of cucumbers are sold in American food markets—the short version we all grew up with and the longer European-style cucumbers sometimes called "gourmet" or "hothouse" cucumbers. The long cucumbers have less water and a somewhat firmer texture than short cucumbers, but for most soups this isn't important. The long cucumbers are more expensive, but when deciding which to buy, remember you'll get about twice as much usable pulp from a long cucumber.

The trick to using cucumbers—too often ignored—is to take out the seeds. This is easy; just cut the cucumber down the middle and scrape the seeds out with a tablespoon.

You may find when working with cucumbers that the soup seems dry. Don't thin the soup with liquid until you've added the salt. Cucumbers contain a lot of water that the salt draws out into the soup.

Spicy Cold Cucumber Soup with Yogurt

MAKES 6 SERVINGS

3 medium-size or 2 long cucumbers, about 1½ pounds

2 jalapeño or other small hot chilies, halved, seeds removed, finely chopped

1 medium-size onion, finely chopped

2 garlic cloves, finely chopped and crushed to a paste with the side of a chef's knife

2 tablespoons finely chopped cilantro leaves

1 tablespoon olive oil

1½ teaspoons salt

2 cups yogurt, 1 tablespoon per serving reserved for garnish

1 to 1½ cups cold water

chopped chives

PEEL the cucumbers, slice them lengthwise, and remove the seeds with a spoon. Chop the cucumbers by hand or in a food processor using the pulse mechanism. They should be finely chopped, but don't overdo it and puree them.

COMBINE the chopped cucumbers, chilies, onion, and garlic in a mixing bowl. Sprinkle the cilantro leaves with the olive oil and chop them finely; you should end up with about 2 tablespoons. Add the chopped leaves to the soup along with the salt and yogurt. Stir the soup thoroughly. Thin the soup with cold water until it has the desired consistency.

CHILL the soup for at least an hour and serve it in cold bowls. Dollop the reserved yogurt on each serving. Sprinkle the yogurt with chives.

SUGGESTIONS AND VARIATIONS | There are dozens of variations for cucumber soups and salads from all over the world. One of my favorites is Indian *raita*. Although raita is a salad rather than a soup, the same ingredients—chopped tomatoes, hot peppers, ground cumin, and chopped mint or cilantro—can be used to flavor a cucumber soup.

TARATOR is a Yugoslavian cucumber soup made with walnuts and flavored with garlic and olive oil. A similar version, the Turkish *cacik*, is flavored with vinegar, olive oil, mint, and dill. Another Indian version, *salata*, is flavored with vinegar, ginger, garlic, hot chilies, and mint. Any cucumber salad can become a refreshing cold soup—just add yogurt, broth, water, or even ice cubes.

COOKED cucumber soups are unusual, probably because cold cucumber is so refreshing and makes such delicious cold soups in the hot climates where it is popular. Cooked cucumber soups were popular in 18th-century France—the cucumbers were simmered in broth and the whole mixture strained and finished with a little cream.

ONE last trick: add ½ cup of the almond milk from page 202 to give the yogurt soup a delicious and indescribable flavor that will mystify and delight your guests.

EGGPLANT

Several varieties of eggplant are available in the United States. The most common is the large round eggplant that most of us grew up with. Less bitter and less seedy is the long and thin Italian-style eggplant. The best eggplants—with the fewest seeds and mildest flavor—are the thin purple Chinese eggplants or the miniature Japanese eggplants usually found in Asian food markets. These are the eggplants I always use if I have a choice.

Because I find eggplant seeds unpleasant to eat and almost impossible to remove, I usually turn the eggplant into a puree and strain them out. The easiest way to do this is to poke the eggplants a couple of times with a fork and bake them in a 350°F oven for about 30 minutes, until they look like partially collapsed hot-air balloons. Slit them lengthwise down the middle and let them cool. Scrape out the pulp with a spoon and work it through a medium-mesh strainer or drum sieve to eliminate the seeds.

Strained eggplant puree can be whisked into soups to give them additional flavor and as a light thickener. It is especially wonderful stirred into garlic soup or miso soup.

Miso and Eggplant Soup

Roasted and pureed eggplant is excellent for adding body and a slightly richer consistency to miso soup. When cooked alone, eggplant has a surprisingly delicate flavor that doesn't interfere with the flavors of the miso base.

MAKES 4 SERVINGS

I pound Japanese, Chinese, or Italian eggplant
I quart miso soup (page 94)

PREHEAT the oven to 375°F. Poke the eggplants in 3 or 4 spots with a sharp paring knife to prevent them from exploding in the oven. Put them on a baking sheet and bake for 20 minutes. Give them a quick squeeze; if they're not thoroughly softened, continue baking, checking them every 10 minutes.

REMOVE the eggplants, let them cool, and slit them lengthwise down the middle. Scrape the pulp out with a spoon and work it through a fine-mesh strainer. You should end up with about a cup of pulp.

BRING the miso soup to a slow simmer just before serving and whisk in the eggplant puree to taste—you may not want to use all of it, in which case cover the rest tightly and freeze it.

SERVE in Japanese lacquer (or lacquerlike plastic) bowls. Garnish the bowls according to your own whim—a slice or two of shiitake mushroom, a watercress leaf, a cube of tofu, perhaps a single shrimp.

FENNEL

Growing up in California, I was surrounded by wild fennel. It grew wherever there was a bit of space, even along city streets. My great aunt, who grew up in San Francisco, remembered chewing on it as a little girl before the 1906 earthquake. She and her classmates called it "ladies' chewing tobacco."

In the United States fennel isn't in season in the summer, which is unfortunate because its flavor goes so well with summery Mediterranean things like tomatoes, garlic, and fresh basil. But if you want fennel in the summer, you'll have to buy it imported from Italy.

Preparing Fennel

Most fennel comes with at least a small section of stalk, which should be removed at a level with the top of the bulb. Save the fuzzy green leaves for a decorative garnish and chop the hard stalks for broth.

The easiest way to use fennel is to simply chop it by cutting it vertically into quarters, cutting off the section of core that runs along each wedge, and then slice the quarters as finely as possible.

I sometimes like to cut fennel into decorative wedges and then serve it in vegetable or fish soups. To prepare fennel wedges, pull off and discard the outermost section of the fennel bulb (if it is cracked and browning); if it looks in good shape, leave it on and peel it with a vegetable peeler to remove the outer stringy membrane.

Cut the fennel bulb into 8 wedges by first cutting it in half from top to bottom. Cut 4 wedges from each half starting in the center of the core; it's important to leave a section of core attached to each wedge, or the wedges will fall apart. Put the wedges in a small pot and simmer them in just enough broth to cover. Simmer them until they soften—they should have the texture of a ripe apple when poked with a knife—for about 20 minutes.

Fennel, Tomato, and White Bean Soup

This soup is light, easy, and amazingly good. Try using different herbs in the bouquet garni (rosemary and marjoram are worthwhile experiments) or substituting chopped chervil for the parsley.

MAKES 8 SERVINGS

1 fennel bulb

1 medium-size onion, finely chopped

18 garlic cloves, peeled

1 quart chicken broth or water

1 bouquet garni, preferably containing a fresh marjoram
  sprig

4 medium-size tomatoes, peeled, seeded, and chopped, or
  2 cups drained and seeded canned tomatoes, chopped

I cup cannellini, borlotti, or Great Northern beans, soaked,
    drained, and cooked until tender (see pages 235 and
    236 for information about cooking beans)

¼ cup finely chopped parsley

salt

pepper

garlic toast (page 195)

olive oil

REMOVE the fuzzy green tops from the fennel, chop coarsely, and reserve. Remove
and discard the stalk or save it for broth.

CHOP the fennel bulb by first cutting it in half (lengthwise from top to bottom) and
then slicing each half. Chop the slices into ¼-inch chunks. Combine the fennel,
onion, garlic, broth, and bouquet garni in a 4-quart pot. Simmer gently for 15 minutes, until the vegetables soften slightly, then add the tomatoes. Simmer for 10 minutes more.

STIR in the beans and their cooking liquid, the parsley, and reserved fennel leaves.

SUGGESTIONS AND VARIATIONS | If you want a slightly more assertive fennel
taste, add a teaspoon of anise liqueur such as Pernod or Ricard. A tiny pinch of saffron is also a nice touch.

THIS soup is very similar to the base for Mediterranean fish soups. To convert it into
a fish soup, just simmer the fish in the soup just before serving.

SERVE garlic toast at the table. I also like to put a small pitcher of virgin olive oil on
the table for guests who want to drizzle a little into their soup.

GARLIC

It's hard to think of a more versatile flavor than garlic. Used in small quantities, roasted
or boiled, garlic is surprisingly mild. It is the central flavor in several wonderful soups;
used more sparingly it enhances other soups' basic flavors from the background.

When you're buying garlic, inspect it carefully. The heads should be perfectly white
or purple, not brown. Look at the cloves, especially where they attach at the base, to
make sure there is no browning or mold. The freshest garlic has papery skin that adheres
tightly and feels slightly moist, even sticky. Avoid elephant garlic, which has a peculiar
taste.

Peeling

A good trick for breaking heads of garlic into cloves is to hold the garlic in a bowl of water. Once you've separated the individual cloves, crush them with the side of a chef's knife on a cutting board; the peel will then slip right off.

Chopping and Crushing

Chop garlic by first slicing it very thinly with a paring knife and then finely chopping the slices with a chef's knife. Some recipes call for garlic that has been ground to a paste in a mortar and pestle. If you don't have a mortar and pestle, work the chopped garlic back and forth on the cutting board with the side of a chef's knife. Lean on the knife as you go; in a minute or so you'll have an almost perfectly smooth paste.

Cooking Methods

Most recipes containing garlic have you chop it and cook it for a minute or two in olive oil or butter, usually along with other vegetables before any liquid is added. This causes it to release its flavor quickly and give the soup a strong garlic flavor.

Whole garlic cloves can also be cooked in a broth or soup until soft. They're so mild that people rarely guess one of the central ingredients in their soup is whole cloves of garlic. One of the easiest methods for making a quick garlic soup is to throw 2 or 3 broken-up heads' worth of unpeeled garlic cloves into a quart of boiling water, simmer them for about 30 minutes, and strain the mixture—pushing firmly on the garlic so the pulp ends up in the soup.

Garlic can also be roasted. Break the heads into cloves (don't peel them), wrap them tightly in aluminum foil, and roast them for 30 minutes in a 350°F oven—the garlic will be very soft. Squeeze the pulp out of the cloves with your fingers or—if you're making a lot—push them through a drum sieve to get rid of the skin. The resulting puree is delicious and surprisingly mild. It can be spread on croutons at the table or whisked into soups as a last-minute flavoring. It's worth roasting extra garlic to keep on hand; it lasts for about 5 days in the refrigerator and for months in the freezer.

Fresh Thyme and Garlic Soup

This is the easiest of all the garlic soups to make. I like to throw it together for a lean, simple dinner when the refrigerator is almost bare and I don't want to go out to shop. You can serve it as a light opener or the main course in an impromptu dinner of salad, some cheeses, and maybe a little fruit. Be sure to have enough crusty bread on hand for dunking.

Very fresh spring garlic and fresh thyme are best for this soup, but don't give up if you have only summer or winter garlic. If you don't have fresh thyme or at least thyme that has been dried on the branches, substitute another fresh herb such as marjoram, sage, tarragon, or even parsley.

MAKES 4 SERVINGS

4 heads of garlic

I bunch of fresh thyme, about 12 sprigs, or 4 fresh sage leaves, or 3 fresh tarragon sprigs, or I small bunch of fresh marjoram, about 6 sprigs, or I large bunch of parsley

I quart chicken broth, water, or dashi

juice of I lemon or lime

salt

pepper

4 slices of stale or lightly toasted French bread plus extra slices for passing

BREAK up the heads of garlic into cloves. Throw out the papery membrane that comes off while you're breaking up the heads, but don't bother peeling the cloves.

TIE the thyme or other herbs into a small bundle and put it into a 4-quart pot with the garlic. Pour in the stock, cover the pot, and bring the soup to a slow simmer. Cook for about 30 minutes, until the garlic cloves are very soft and can be crushed easily against the inside of the pot.

STRAIN the soup through the fine disk of a food mill or puree it in a blender and push it through a medium-mesh strainer with the back of a ladle. Add the lime juice and season the soup with salt and pepper.

PLACE a slice of stale bread in each bowl and pour the soup over it. You can top each bowl of soup with a spoonful of virgin olive oil or dollop of butter, but this isn't essential. Pass toasted slices of French bread brushed with olive oil in a basket.

SUGGESTIONS AND VARIATIONS | You can make a spicy version of this soup by combining 2 Thai or jalapeño chilies, sliced down the middle, with the garlic. A pinch of saffron added to the soup 10 minutes into the cooking is also a nice touch.

This soup is also nice lightly creamed by adding ½ cup heavy cream after the soup is strained.

IF you and your guests can never get enough garlic, try finishing the soup by whisking it into ½ cup garlic and saffron mayonnaise (page 350) just before serving. Garlic soup can also be finished by whisking in eggplant puree (page 180).

Spanish-Style Garlic Soup

SOPA DE AJO

Even though this soup doesn't contain as much garlic as some recipes, it's particularly pungent because the garlic is cooked before liquid is added. I adore this soup and so will you if you don't mind the fragrance of garlic lingering in the atmosphere. The soup is also delicious without the eggs.

MAKES 4 SERVINGS

I head of garlic, broken into cloves

5 tablespoons olive oil

4 slices of country bread

I tablespoon paprika

½ teaspoon ground cumin

I quart chicken broth or water

4 eggs (optional)

LIGHTLY brown the unpeeled garlic in 5 tablespoons of olive oil over medium heat for about 10 minutes. Remove the garlic from the pot with a slotted spoon and brown the country bread slices on each side in the garlic-scented oil. Take the bread out and set aside. Sprinkle the bottom of the hot pot with the paprika and cumin. Return the garlic to the pot along with the broth. Cover the pot and simmer until the garlic cloves soften, about 30 minutes. Strain the soup through the finest disk of a food mill or puree it in a blender and strain it through a medium-mesh strainer.

PREHEAT the oven to 350°F. Bring the soup back to a simmer and ladle it into ovenproof bowls or soup crocks. Place a browned bread slice on top of each one, then break an egg into each bowl on top of the bread if you're using the eggs. Bake the soup until the egg white sets but the yolk is still runny; start checking after about 6 minutes.

GREEN BEANS

Green beans are often cut into ½-inch lengths and used in mixed vegetable soups. They should be added only during the last 15 minutes of cooking, or they will overcook and turn gray.

Puree of Green Bean and Mint

Green beans make wonderful pureed soups. This recipe uses a simple leek and potato soup as a base and includes a handful of mint leaves. You can also flavor green bean soup with a little grated nutmeg or ground cloves.

MAKES 8 SERVINGS

3 medium-size potatoes, cut into ½-inch dice

4 medium-size leeks, tough greens removed, cleaned and finely sliced, 4 cups

4½ cups water, milk, or vegetable or chicken broth

4 quarts water

salt

2 pounds green beans, ends removed, finely chopped

1 cup heavy cream

1 bunch of fresh mint, stems removed, ½ cup tightly packed leaves (optional)

pepper

lightly whipped cream or sour cream

COMBINE the potatoes, leeks, and 4½ cups water in a 4-quart pot. Bring to a simmer and cook gently until the potatoes are easy to crush against the side of the pot, about 20 minutes. Meanwhile, bring the 4 quarts of water to a boil, add salt, and cook the beans in it for 5 minutes. Drain and refresh under cold running water.

ADD the blanched beans, heavy cream, and mint to the soup and puree in a blender or food processor. Strain the soup through a medium-mesh strainer. Season with salt and pepper.

THIS soup can be served hot with a dollop of lightly whipped cream or cold with sour cream.

Herb Soup

I save this rich and elegant soup for special dinners, because it never fails to impress. My guests are always intrigued and full of questions about which herbs I've used, and they're usually fascinated when I tell them. Invariably they've never heard of one or two and usually leave wanting to make this soup at home.

Try the soup with different combinations of your favorite fresh herbs. Always remember when cooking with fresh herbs to chop them at the last minute; otherwise their flavor will fade.

MAKES 6 SERVINGS

1 quart dried porcini broth

6 egg yolks

1½ cups heavy cream

1 large bunch of fresh chives, finely chopped, about ¼ cup

2 bunches of fresh chervil, finely chopped, about 5 tablespoons

¼ cup finely chopped parsley

12 large sorrel leaves, cut into thin shreds

juice of 1 lemon or more to taste

salt

white pepper

WORKING WITH EGG YOLKS

Egg yolks are sometimes used to give soups a rich, silky texture.

Soups containing egg yolks must be cooked carefully, because if allowed to boil for even a second they curdle. Always pour some of the hot broth into the egg yolks before adding them to the rest of the soup. Sometimes called *tempering*, this method prevents the eggs from curdling as soon as they come in contact with the hot broth.

If the soup curdles, remove it immediately from the heat and quickly whisk it to cool it slightly. This sometimes reverses the curdling. If it doesn't work, puree the soup in a blender.

BRING the broth to a simmer in a nonaluminum 4-quart pot. (Aluminum turns egg yolks gray.)

WHISK together the egg yolks and cream in a mixing bowl. Whisk about 2 cups of the simmering broth into the egg yolk/cream mixture. Stir that mixture back into the broth and add the herbs. Stir the soup with a wooden spoon over low to medium heat. Be sure to reach into the corners of the pot to prevent the egg yolk from curdling. Continue stirring until the soup thickens slightly and coats the back of the spoon. (The soup should be at 175°F.) The soup must *not* boil. Remove the pan from the heat and stir for 1 minute more. Otherwise, heat retained in the pan may cause the soup to curdle.

ADD the lemon juice and season with salt and white pepper. Serve immediately.

SUGGESTIONS AND VARIATIONS | You can make this soup lighter and eliminate any worry about overcooking the egg yolks by just leaving them out. But it won't have such a luxurious texture.

LEEKS

Although similar in taste to onions, leeks have a subtle earthy flavor all their own. They are used in many kinds of soups either by themselves or along with other vegetables.

Leeks vary considerably in price from season to season, so if you get to the market and find they're outrageously expensive, substitute onions or make a different soup.

To tell if leeks are fresh, look at the greens, especially the upper part where they've been trimmed. The greens should be fairly stiff and bright green. Avoid leeks whose greens are limp or gray.

Most recipes use only the white part of the leek with maybe an inch or two of the green. The tough green leaves can be used for making broth.

Trimming and Cleaning

When you're cutting off the leek greens, save as much of the white as you can. Sometimes there are white leaves running underneath the first several inches of green, so don't just chop the green off at the base—trim away the leaves to see if they reveal any white that can go into the soup.

Leeks can be treacherous to clean because of sand hidden between the leaves. To get rid of the sand, remove the greens, trim off the hairy roots, and cut the white lengthwise down the middle. Hold each half under running water with the green end facing down. Flip through the leaves and rub them with your thumb to loosen any stubborn sand. Once they're washed, give them a shake. Check your cutting board for sand before chopping the leeks.

Chopping

Place the leek halves cut side down on the board and slice them with a chef's knife.

Cooking Methods

Chopped leeks are added directly to a simmering soup or are first gently cooked in a little butter before liquids are added.

Leek and Potato Soup

This soup has all the characteristics of simple, comforting food. It is easy and inexpensive to make, it lends itself to a happy-go-lucky approach in the kitchen, and it's deeply satisfying to eat. Exact ratios don't seem to matter much, so the soup always turns out well.

The easiest way to make leek and potato soup is to chop the leeks and potatoes, simmer them in water until the potatoes are soft, throw in a tablespoon or two of butter, grind in a little pepper, and serve.

Leeks can also be used to prepare the traditional cock-a-leekie from Scotland. Prepare a chicken broth, but simmer the chicken for only 1½ hours. Gently cook chopped leeks in a little butter; add the broth and the meat from the chicken cut into bite-size pieces. Some versions of cock-a-leekie also call for two or three pitted prunes per serving.

You can also use leek and potato soup as a base for other vegetable soups. Watercress, sorrel, and pea soups are excellent when made with a leek and potato soup base (see the variations on this page).

MAKES 6 SERVINGS

3 medium-size waxy potatoes, peeled and cut into
    ½-inch dice

4 leeks, 3 pounds, tough greens removed, washed, and finely
    sliced, 4 cups

4½ cups water, milk, or vegetable or chicken broth

salt

unsalted butter or herb butter such as parsley, chervil, or
    mint (pages 593–594)

COMBINE the potatoes, leeks, and water in a 4-quart pot. Bring to a simmer and cook gently until the potatoes are easy to crush against the side of the pot, about 20 minutes.

ADD salt to taste, ladle the soup into hot bowls, put a slice of butter or herb butter on each serving, and pass the pepper mill at the table.

SUGGESTIONS AND VARIATIONS | This soup can be converted into a cream soup by adding a cup of heavy cream when the potatoes have finished cooking and bringing the soup back to the simmer.

IF you want a smooth pureed soup, just push the finished soup through a medium-mesh strainer or food mill; alternatively, puree it in a blender or food processor, but don't process it for any longer than you have to—30 seconds will usually do—or the soup will become gluey.

Vichyssoise

When I was first trying to teach myself French cooking in California in the 1960s, vichyssoise—along with quenelles and lobster bisque—epitomized style and elegance. I assumed that such a thing must be terribly difficult to make before I realized that it was a simple leek and potato soup pureed with a little cream and served cold. It *is* elegant, but it isn't complicated.

MAKES 8 SERVINGS

> 1¼ cups heavy cream
> 7 cups Leek and Potato Soup (preceding recipe)
> salt
> 1 tablespoon finely chopped chives

COMBINE ¾ cup of the cream with the soup while it is still hot. Bring it back to a simmer to sterilize the cream. Strain the soup through the fine disk of a food mill or puree it in a blender or food processor. Strain it again through a fine-mesh strainer.

CHILL the soup, making sure the soup is covered with plastic wrap, or a crust will form on its surface. Beat the remaining cream until it barely starts to stiffen. Keep it cold and covered with plastic wrap.

LADLE the soup into chilled bowls, dollop a little of the whipped cream into the center of each bowl, and sprinkle the chopped chives on the cream.

SUGGESTIONS AND VARIATIONS | Watercress, sorrel, spinach, peas, and green bean purees are prepared using the same method. The additional vegetables are simply added shortly before the soup is strained. For green beans, use only ¾ cup cream.

POTATO AND WATERCRESS PUREE Remove the leaves from 2 bunches of watercress. Cook them for 2 minutes in 2 quarts of boiling salted water to eliminate bitterness, pour the water out into a colander, and rinse the leaves with cold running water.

PUT the leaves in a blender with just enough water—about ½ cup—to help them move around. Blend on high speed for 2 minutes. Add this puree to 1 recipe of vichyssoise. Simmer the soup for 2 or 3 minutes. If you want to eliminate the specks of watercress, strain the soup through a medium-mesh strainer.

WATERCRESS soup can be served either hot or cold. If you decide to serve it hot, don't keep it waiting for more than 15 or 20 minutes, or its beautiful green hue will start to turn gray. Garnish both hot and cold soup with a dollop of lightly whipped cream and a watercress leaf.

POTATO AND GREEN PEA PUREE Add 2 cups (I package) frozen peas to the vichyssoise along with the heavy cream. Bring the soup to a simmer—this will take a few minutes, especially if the peas are frozen—and puree it in a food processor or blender. Straining is up to you; I don't mind the little bits of pea. Season with salt and pepper and serve hot or cold. Several small croutons sprinkled in the center of each bowl create a nice effect.

POTATO AND SORREL PUREE This tangy soup is my favorite of all the leek and potato soup derivatives. You can serve it hot or cold, but I usually serve it cold because sorrel is in season in the summer and this soup works so well in hot weather.

TO make 6 servings, add 2 well-packed cups sorrel leaves to the vichyssoise along with the cream. Simmer the soup for about 2 minutes and strain it through a medium-mesh strainer or food mill. Adjust the salt. Don't panic about the color— it's not your fault. Because it has so much natural acidity, sorrel always turns a sad army green the instant it gets hot. Fortunately its taste makes up for the dreary color.

SERVE the soup in chilled bowls with a dollop of lightly whipped cream in the center of each. You can also sprinkle the cream with a few shreds of sorrel.

POTATO AND SPINACH PUREE Cook 2 tightly packed cups spinach leaves (about I bunch) in boiling salted water for about I minute. Drain them in a colander and rinse them immediately in cold water.

PUREE the cooked spinach in a blender or food processor with just enough vichyssoise to get them to spin around. Add this puree to the rest of the vichyssoise. If you want the soup to have a finer texture, strain it through a food mill or a medium-mesh strainer. Garnish each bowl with a dollop of whipped cream and a shredded spinach leaf.

Lettuce Soup

This recipe is a quick thrown-together soup with lettuce leaves, a little rice, some garlic, and some good olive oil. Feel free to elaborate according to what you have around or how much energy you have. I sometimes throw in cooked beans, chopped tomatoes, chopped and stewed zucchini, even artichoke hearts. You might also want to play around with a little saffron.

MAKES ABOUT 6 SERVINGS

½ outermost leaves from 2 heads of romaine, escarole, or
  chicory or leaves from 1 whole head of either, 1 pound
  leaves

1 medium-size onion, finely chopped

6 garlic cloves, finely chopped

1 teaspoon finely chopped fresh marjoram or ½ teaspoon
  dried oregano or marjoram

2 tablespoons olive oil

5 cups chicken or vegetable broth

½ cup long-grain rice, preferably basmati

garlic toast (page 195)

grated Parmesan cheese

toasted slices of French bread

WASH the lettuce carefully, bunch it up, and shred it into strips about ⅛ inch thick.

IN a 4-quart pot over medium heat, cook the onion, garlic, and marjoram in the olive oil until the onion turns translucent, about 10 minutes. Add the broth and rice. Partially cover the pot and simmer the soup for about 15 minutes. Uncover the pot, add the lettuce, and simmer for 10 minutes more.

PLACE a slice of garlic toast in each bowl and pour the soup over it. Pass the Parmesan cheese and toasted bread.

MUSHROOMS

Because I love the distinctive woodsy taste of mushrooms, I rarely combine them with other vegetables but prefer to cook them alone so nothing interferes with their flavor. Ordinary cultivated mushrooms make wonderful soups, but wild mushrooms offer a completely different dimension.

The best way to learn about wild or exotic varieties of cultivated mushrooms is to buy them as you see them appear in the markets and take them home and experiment. While I've never had a mushroom I didn't like, some are distinctly better than others.

If you can't find fresh wild mushrooms, dried mushrooms are often worthwhile. Morels, Chinese black mushrooms, and porcini (*cèpes*) seem to take best to drying, but the quality varies considerably among brands. Look for whole large mushrooms instead of little broken pieces.

Dried mushrooms are often sandy and need to be rinsed off—but do it quickly, or you'll rinse out a lot of their flavor. Once the mushrooms are rinsed, they need to be soaked for from 15 minutes to an hour (depending on the kind of mushroom) to soften them for cooking. Although you can soak them in water, sherry or Madeira will enhance their flavor. Whatever liquid you use, be sure to include it in the soup.

Mushroom Velouté

Almost any combination of mushrooms and heavy cream is going to be delicious no matter what you do to it, but there is one trick that works magic—puree the mushrooms raw and add them to the rest of the soup just before serving.

MAKES 8 SERVINGS

> 1 medium-size onion, finely chopped
> 4 tablespoons unsalted butter
> 3 tablespoons all-purpose flour
> ½ cup Madeira or dry sherry
> 1 quart chicken, vegetable, or dried porcini broth
> 14 ounces fresh cultivated white or cremini mushrooms, rinsed and dried
> 1 cup heavy cream
> salt
> pepper
> ½ cup heavy cream, lightly whipped

PREPARE a *velouté* base by cooking the onion in butter in a 4-quart pot over medium heat, stirring almost continuously to prevent browning. When the onion turns translucent, after about 10 minutes, add the flour and stir over medium heat for 5 minutes more to cook out the starchy taste.

ADD the Madeira and broth, whisk the soup to get rid of any lumps, and bring it to a simmer. Simmer for 5 minutes.

PUT the mushrooms in a blender and add 1 cup of the hot soup base. Blend the mushrooms on high speed for about 2 minutes. Add a little more of the soup base if necessary to get them moving.

PUT a strainer over the pot and pour the contents of the blender through it into the pot with the rest of the base. Add the cream. If you want the soup perfectly smooth, strain it through a medium or fine-mesh strainer. Bring the soup back to a simmer and season it with salt and pepper. Ladle it into hot bowls and put a dollop of whipped cream on each serving.

SUGGESTIONS AND VARIATIONS
| This soup takes on a new dimension of flavor with wild or specially cultivated mushrooms. If you want to use dried mushrooms such as morels or porcini, soak a handful of the dried mushrooms in the Madeira or sherry used in the soup. When the mushrooms have softened, put them into the blender with the regular cultivated mushrooms.

YOU can also use dried mushrooms or mushroom stems to make a mushroom broth to use as the base for mushroom soup.

IF you have fresh wild mushrooms such as morels, porcini, portobellos, or chanterelles, rinse them thoroughly and use them to replace any proportion of the regular cultivated mushrooms in the recipe. Save some of the whole mushrooms to decorate the bowls.

GARLIC TOAST

Garlic toast makes a wonderful accompaniment to hearty soups. The easiest way to prepare it is to toast the bread—I like sourdough or a good crusty French bread best—then rub each slice thoroughly with a peeled garlic clove. One clove is enough for about five slices. If you like, brush the toasted slices with melted butter or virgin olive oil but the garlic toast is also fine without the extra fat.

Morel Soup

Morels are so special that they deserve a soup all their own. They also take very well to drying, so you can use them dried when fresh morels are out of season.

Fresh morels are usually available in the spring and early summer. They are sometimes very expensive, but often they have dried out somewhat—which does them no harm—and a nice bagful weighs surprisingly little. Don't buy morels that are wet or smell damp. When you get the morels home, inspect them carefully for dirt and sand. Rinse them off quickly in cold running water and dry them on paper towels. Store them in a paper bag—not plastic—to prevent them from getting moldy.

If you're using dried morels, don't be horrified by the price; they're sold by the ounce, but an ounce goes a long way. It's best to quickly rinse dried morels to eliminate grit and sand, but don't let them absorb too much water, or they'll lose flavor. After rinsing, soak them in just enough water—or, better yet, sherry or Madeira—to cover. They should be soft enough to use in 20 minutes. Be sure to save the soaking liquid.

This version uses the light cream of mushroom soup as the liquid base. The morels are then added whole or split lengthwise down the middle and simmered in the soup a few minutes before serving.

MAKES 4 SERVINGS

6 ounces fresh morels, 7 to 9 per serving, or I ounce dried
mushrooms, rinsed (soak dried in I cup Madeira or
sherry)

3 tablespoons unsalted butter if you're using fresh morels

I shallot, finely chopped if you're using fresh morels

I quart mushroom *velouté* (preceding recipe)

FOR FRESH MORELS If the morels are large, cut them in half lengthwise; otherwise leave them whole. Sauté the morels in butter over high heat for 5 minutes. Sprinkle with the chopped shallot and sauté for I minute more. Stir the sautéed morels into the hot soup.

FOR DRIED MORELS In a saucepan, simmer the morels for 5 minutes in the soaking liquid. Carefully lift them out and transfer them to a bowl with a slotted spoon so that any sand stays on the bottom of the pan. Keep them warm.

CAREFULLY pour the soaking liquid into the mushroom velouté so that any sand stays behind in the saucepan.

WHICHEVER method you use, reserve 8 of the morels for garnishing the soup and stir the remainder into the hot soup. Simmer for about 5 minutes.

SERVE the soup in hot bowls. Decorate with 2 morels on each bowl.

SUGGESTIONS AND VARIATIONS | It's hard to improve on this soup, but sometimes I get carried away and cook with delicious extravagant things. For one decadent little trick you'll need about an ounce per serving of foie gras—the whole block kind, not the mousse, and fairly large fresh morels; the dried usually won't work because they're too small.

CUT the foie gras into strips and push the strips inside the morel stems with a chopstick or the back of a pencil so the hollow mushrooms are filled with the foie gras. Then serve them whole in the soup without breathing a word!

THIS is also a good way to show off a black truffle if you're lucky or extravagant enough to get your hands on one. Slice or cut the truffle into julienne and simmer it in the soup for about 5 minutes before adding the morels.

DRIED PORCINI

Depending on where you live, these wonderful mushrooms go by different names. In America they are easiest to find under their Italian name, *porcini*, but in a French market they will be called *cèpes*. Eastern European markets also carry this wild mushroom, under the name *borowiki*, *prawdziwki*, or simply *Polish mushrooms*. In Germany the name is *steinpilz*.

Mixed Wild Mushroom Soup

This is a wonderfully dramatic way to show off wild mushrooms. It's almost a mushroom stew except that the mushrooms are sitting over a shallow layer of flavorful broth instead of being bound together with a thick sauce.

In this recipe the mushrooms are sautéd with shallots, garlic, and parsley in olive oil. There are no hard and fast rules, so feel free to play around with different herbs or different cooking fats, such as butter or, best of all, goose or duck fat.

This soup is best served in the spring or fall, when you have the best selection of mushrooms.

MAKES 6 SERVINGS

2 pounds assorted fresh wild or specially cultivated
    mushrooms: morels, porcini (cèpes), hedgehogs, bear's
    heads, portobellos, chanterelles, oyster mushrooms,
    pleurottes, shiitake

2 shallots, finely chopped

2 garlic cloves, finely chopped and crushed into a paste

2 tablespoons finely chopped parsley leaves

I quart consommé, full-flavored broth, *dashi,* or mushroom
    velouté (page 194)

salt

pepper

6 tablespoons olive oil

CHECK the mushrooms carefully for sand and grit. If they need washing, rinse them quickly under running water and drain them immediately. Don't let them sit in water, or they'll get soggy.

IF the mushrooms are small, leave them whole. Larger mushrooms may need to be sliced or cut into smaller pieces, but do your best to show off the natural shapes of the mushrooms, which make this soup so visually striking.

STIR together the shallots, garlic, and parsley in a small mixing bowl. (The French call this mixture a *persillade.*)

BRING the broth to a slow simmer and season it with salt and pepper.

MAKE sure the mushrooms are perfectly dry and sauté them in the olive oil over high heat. Don't put more than one layer of mushrooms in the pan at once, or they will release water and stew in their own juices.

WHEN the mushrooms begin to brown and shrink slightly, after about 7 minutes, sprinkle the *persillade* over them and sauté for 1 minute more. Season with salt and pepper.

LADLE the broth into wide soup bowls and arrange the mushrooms over the broth.

Porcini Soup

ACQUACOTTA CON FUNGHI

There are many variations of this well-known Tuscan soup, with different vegetables playing major or minor roles. By definition, *acquacotta* (literally, "cooked water") is made with water instead of broth. Even though it's good with water, I use broth if I have any around.

This version is traditionally made with fresh porcini, so if they're in season (in the fall) and you feel like splurging (porcini are never cheap), this is a wonderful way of savoring them. Otherwise you can use dried porcini or other fresh wild or cultivated mushrooms, such as chanterelles, portobellos, morels, and shiitakes.

Be sure to use authentic Parmigiano-Reggiano—lesser substitutes detract from the flavor of the mushrooms.

MAKES 6 SERVINGS

1 pound fresh porcini, portobellos, chanterelles, or other wild mushrooms or ¼ pound good-quality dried porcini

¼ cup olive oil

2 garlic cloves, finely chopped

¼ pound prosciutto, preferably *di parma*, cut into ¼-inch cubes

½ teaspoon fresh or dried thyme or marjoram leaves

2 tomatoes, peeled, seeded, and chopped or 1 cup canned, seeded and drained

1 quart chicken, beef, or vegetable broth

4 eggs

½ cup finely grated Parmesan cheese

salt

pepper

4 1-inch-thick slices of crusty bread from a wide loaf, toasted

QUICKLY rinse off the mushrooms and immediately dry them with paper towels. If you're using porcini, check them carefully for worms. (The worms are harmless and usually appear after the mushrooms have been at room temperature for a few minutes.) Cut the stems and caps into 1-inch slices.

IF you're using dried mushrooms, soak them in just enough warm water to cover (about a cup) until they soften, about 30 minutes. Feel them with your fingers and cut off and discard any pieces of hard stem that won't soften. Drain the mushrooms, saving the soaking liquid. Strain the soaking liquid or pour it off carefully into another container to eliminate sand.

HEAT the olive oil in a 4-quart pot over medium heat. Add the garlic and prosciutto and stir for about 5 minutes, until the garlic softens, but don't let it brown.

ADD the mushrooms and turn up the heat. Sprinkle the thyme leaves over the mushrooms. Stir the mushrooms almost constantly for about 5 minutes, until they release liquid.

ADD the tomatoes and the soaking liquid if you've used dried mushrooms and simmer the soup for 5 minutes more. Add the broth.

WHISK the eggs with the grated Parmesan in a 4-quart mixing bowl.

JUST before serving, pour the simmering soup into the egg/cheese mixture while whisking. Season with salt and pepper. Place a slice of toast in the bottom of each soup bowl. Reach into the soup with a slotted spoon and distribute the mushrooms equally among the bowls. Ladle the broth over them.

SUGGESTIONS AND VARIATIONS | As an ultimate extravagance, grate fresh white truffles over the soup at the table.

THIS is another soup that appears in similar guises around the world, especially in Russia and Eastern Europe. In their book *Please to the Table*, Anya von Bremzen and John Welchman list three variations from the former Soviet Union. One version from Byelorussia—*su lapsha s gribami*—contains potatoes, carrots, noodles, and a last-minute sprinkling of dill and a dollop of sour cream. Another version, from Moscow, includes cheese, barley, and potatoes, while a Latvian version contains bacon, cream, and paprika in addition to the ubiquitous potatoes.

RATHER than tracking down these recipes and following them exactly, it's probably best to think of wild mushrooms as a flavoring that can be added to almost any vegetable soup. You can also use dried porcini broth (page 70) as the base for vegetable and other soups.

ONIONS

It's hard to imagine cooking without onions. Even though they're strong when raw, their flavor softens and melds with other ingredients after just a few minutes of cooking.

All of the many kinds of onions—large Spanish onions, red Bermuda onions, and little white onions—can be used for making soup. In addition to these basic types, the sweet onions—Maui, Vidalia, and Walla Walla—are becoming more widely available.

Peeling and Chopping

There are no easy answers to the age-old problem of tearing eyes. Wearing contact lenses or glasses helps somewhat, but the only certain way of avoiding tearing is to peel onions under water. When you're chopping onions, sprinkling a tablespoon or two of wine vinegar on the cutting board seems to help. If you're painfully sensitive, it might be worthwhile to pick up a pair of work goggles.

Cooking Methods

Most soup recipes use onions in combination with other vegetables. Usually the onions are cooked in olive oil or butter for about 10 minutes, until they turn shiny and translucent. This releases their flavor and softens them before any liquid is added. Once the liquid is added, relatively little cooking is needed to extract the onions' flavor.

Using Pearl Onions

Whole pearl onions are sometimes added to soups for decorative effect. If you're using a lot of them, peeling them can be a bit tedious. A good trick: plunge them into boiling water for 1 minute, drain them, and rinse them with cold water. Once peeled, all they need is 10 or 15 minutes of simmering in the soup to finish cooking.

French Onion Soup

A good onion soup is easy to make, but there are a few secrets to making it extraordinary: authentic Swiss Gruyère, good broth, and plenty of onions. French onion soup is best made with homemade beef broth, but canned low-sodium beef broth will work. I sometimes use fresh turkey or duck broth.

When you put the onions into the pot, you're going to think you've sliced too many; but as you stir them over the heat they will shrink down to about one-eighth of their original volume. Use the sweetest onions you can find. I usually use large red Bermuda onions because they're inexpensive and easy to find, but Vidalia or Maui onions will give the soup an even sweeter flavor.

MAKES 10 SERVINGS

5 pounds onions, peeled

4 tablespoons unsalted butter

10 cups beef, turkey, or chicken broth

1 bouquet garni: 3 fresh thyme sprigs, 3 parsley sprigs, and
    1 bay leaf

salt

pepper

2 cups finely grated Swiss Gruyère, about ½ pound

8 thick slices of French bread cut from a large loaf, toasted

IN ADVANCE Slice the onions as finely as you can. Melt the butter in a wide, heavy-bottomed 4-quart pot and add the onions. Stir the onions every few minutes over medium heat until they soften and begin to brown, about 40 minutes. When they start to brown, pour in ½ cup broth and turn the heat to high. Stir the onions, scraping off any caramelized juices that have clung to the bottom and sides of the pan. When the broth has completely evaporated and forms a brown glaze on the bottom of the pan, add another ½ cup broth and repeat. Continue doing this until you've used up 2 cups of the broth.

ADD the remaining broth and the bouquet garni to the onions and gently simmer the soup for 15 minutes. Be sure to scrape the pan so the caramelized juices dissolve in the soup. Season to taste with salt and pepper and remove the bouquet garni.

AT THE LAST MINUTE Preheat the oven to 400°F. Ladle the hot soup into deep bowls. Sprinkle half the cheese over the soup and place a slice of toast in each bowl. Sprinkle with the remaining cheese. Put the bowls on a sheet pan and bake until the cheese bubbles and turns light brown, about 10 minutes.

SUGGESTIONS AND VARIATIONS | This recipe is a rich winter version of the traditional French onion soup. If you want something lighter, make small French bread toasts, sprinkle a little cheese on each one, and bake them for a few minutes to melt the cheese. Serve the soup in wide bowls instead of crocks. Float a cheese toast on each bowl before serving.

YOU can also experiment with adding ½ cup port, Madeira, or sherry to the onions when you've added the last of the broth, which will give the broth a little additional sweetness and complexity. It's also fun to try different cheeses—Camembert is wonderful (be sure to trim off the rind).

IF you want to make a Spanish version, called *cebollada con almendras*, substitute olive oil for butter; cook the onions until they are completely soft and translucent, but don't allow them to brown. A minute before you add the broth to the onions, sprinkle in a teaspoon of ground cumin. Finish the soup with almond milk. Serve this version in the same way as French onion soup.

ALMOND MILK For 10 servings, toast ½ cup (¼ pound) blanched whole or slivered almonds in a 300°F oven until they turn pale brown, in about 15 minutes (check them every few minutes). Grind the toasted almonds in a blender or food processor for 2 or 3 minutes with ½ cup broth or water. Strain the almond mixture through a fine-mesh strainer. Pour the almond milk into the simmering soup just before ladling the soup into bowls.

A wonderful Italian variation is a Renaissance soup called *carabaccia*; in addition to the almond milk used in the Spanish version, this one contains sugar, cinnamon, and lemon juice. A *carabaccia* is pureed in a food mill, food processor, or blender and contains no bread or cheese.

CARABACCIA cook the onions in butter the same way as when making the French version. Add the broth, simmer for 15 minutes, and then puree the mixture. If you want it smoother, strain it through a medium-mesh strainer.

PREPARE the almond milk and whisk it into the soup just before serving along with the juice of a lemon, 2 teaspoons sugar, and I teaspoon ground cinnamon.

Pureed Roasted Onion and Garlic Soup

Root vegetables develop a different flavor when roasted in the oven instead of being gently cooked on the stove. In this recipe, onions and garlic are roasted together and then pureed. The roasting accentuates the flavor of both vegetables. This soup is meant to be served as a relatively light (but full-flavored) first course, but, if you like, bake it in the oven as you would a classic French onion soup, with croutons and cheese.

MAKES 8 FIRST-COURSE SERVINGS

4 to 6 large red onions (3½ pounds total weight), peeled,
    hairy root end cut off, quartered or cut into 6 wedges
    each if very large

cloves from 1 large head of garlic, peeled

2 tablespoons olive oil

2 leaves fresh sage (optional)

I quart beef, chicken, or turkey broth

½ to 1 cup heavy cream (optional)

salt

pepper

I tablespoon balsamic vinegar, or more to taste

PREHEAT the oven to 425 F. Toss the onions and garlic with the olive oil in a roasting pan just large enough to hold them in a single layer. If you have to pile the onions up a bit, don't worry, but by no means leave any space on the roasting pan exposed or the onion will burn.

ROAST the onions and garlic for about 1½ hours, stirring around every 15 minutes with a wooden spoon so the onions break apart and brown evenly. If the onions aren't completely browned and caramelized, roast them longer but watch them closely so they don't burn.

PUT the roasting pan on top of the stove, put in the sage and pour in about 2 cups of broth. Scrape the bottom of the pan with a wooden spoon to dissolve any caramelized juices. Transfer the onions, garlic, and broth to a blender—you'll have to work in batches—and puree the mixture about I minute, or until smooth. If you want the soup to be perfectly smooth (my own preference), work it through a food mill or use a ladle to work it through a strainer. Add the optional cream and season to taste with salt, pepper, and balsamic vinegar.

PEANUTS

Although they originated in the Andes and are widely used all over South America, peanuts were not popular in the United States until the 20th century, and even then usually in peanut butter or as a snack. Peanuts have taken better hold in Africa—where they are called *groundnuts*—and are used to make soups and meat stews.

To make peanut soup, it is easiest to use old-fashioned peanut butter without stabilizers to keep it from separating. Health food stores are a good source.

Senegalese Peanut Soup

This soup is simple to make, and the natural sweetness of the peanuts works beautifully with the curry and the cayenne pepper.

MAKES 8 SERVINGS

1 large onion, finely chopped

2 garlic cloves, chopped

1 teaspoon cayenne pepper or more to taste

2 tablespoons peanut or vegetable oil

2 tablespoons curry powder such as *garam masala* (page 245)

3 cups chicken broth

10 medium-size tomatoes, cut in half crosswise, seeds squeezed out, coarsely chopped or 5 cups drained and seeded canned tomatoes, chopped

⅔ cup smooth peanut butter

salt

pepper

sour cream

lime wedges

IN a 4-quart pot over medium heat, cook the onion, garlic, and cayenne pepper in the oil until the onion turns translucent, about 10 minutes. Stir in the curry powder and stir the mixture over medium heat for 1 minute more.

ADD the chicken broth and tomatoes, simmer for 10 minutes more, and strain the soup through the fine disk of a food mill or push it through a medium-mesh strainer with a ladle.

BRING the soup to a simmer and whisk in the peanut butter. Season with salt and pepper and more cayenne if you want it hotter.

SERVE sour cream and lime wedges at the table.

SUGGESTIONS AND VARIATIONS | You can give this soup extra richness and a velvety texture by adding a cup of coconut milk or heavy cream. Sometimes I add a few tablespoons of chopped cilantro.

THE same combination of ingredients is also used to make chicken *à la senegalese,* so if you want to turn this soup into a substantial main course, brown a cut-up chicken in peanut oil, then simmer it in the soup for 15 or 20 minutes.

Georgia Peanut Soup

This traditional Southern soup is similar to the Senegalese version (page 204), except that no tomatoes are used and hot pepper sauce such as Tabasco is used instead of curry. A small amount of roux is used as a thickener. I serve small portions—¾ cup—because this soup is very rich.

MAKES 8 FIRST-COURSE SERVINGS

I medium-size onion, peeled and finely chopped

2 tablespoons unsalted butter

2 tablespoons all-purpose flour

6 cups basic brown chicken broth (page 62)

I cup heavy cream

1½ cups natural peanut butter (the only ingredients should be peanuts and salt)

2 teaspoons Tabasco sauce or more to taste

salt

2 tablespoons sour cream or crème fraîche

2 tablespoons coarsely chopped peanuts or I tablespoon finely chopped chives, parsley, or cilantro

HEAT the onion in the butter in a heavy-bottomed pot over medium heat until the onion turns fragrant and translucent, about 10 minutes. Add the flour, stir until smooth, and whisk in the broth. Bring to a simmer while whisking.

WHISK the cream and peanut butter into the soup. Stir in the Tabasco sauce and season to taste with salt or more Tabasco sauce. Ladle into heated bowls and top each bowl with a dollop of sour cream and a pinch of chopped peanuts on top of the sour cream (the sour cream keeps the peanuts from sinking in the soup).

PEAS

Peas are the only vegetable that I prefer frozen to fresh. But then I've never had perfectly fresh *little* peas. The fresh peas that I find in the markets are always too large and don't have a very sweet taste. Peas seem to take better to freezing than most vegetables and retain their bright color and sweetness.

When you're using frozen peas—get the tiniest ones, usually called "petite"—don't follow the directions on the package; just dump them into the soup as they are—you don't even have to thaw them. (Incidentally, if you're serving peas as a vegetable, just heat them in a little butter without the preliminary boiling recommended on the package.)

Cooking Methods

Don't cook peas for more than 5 or 10 minutes, or their flavor and color will suffer. For this reason they should be added to soups 5 minutes before serving.

One of the easiest and most satisfying pea soups is prepared by making a leek and potato soup, pureeing it with peas at the end, and then straining (page 190). You can also make a light split pea soup by simmering split green peas in broth and, as soon as they are tender, adding frozen peas and then pureeing and straining the whole thing together.

You can also prepare a pea soup as a classic cream soup or *velouté*: Make a roux by cooking 3 tablespoons all-purpose flour and 3 tablespoons unsalted butter in a 4-quart pot over medium heat for 5 minutes, add a quart of broth or milk, and simmer for 15 minutes. Add 2 10-ounce packages of frozen peas, simmer for 10 minutes more, puree in a blender, and strain. Finish the soup with ½ cup heavy cream or 4 tablespoons unsalted butter.

Fresh chervil and mint—chopped and added before straining or made into herb butters and swirled into the soup at the end—are excellent flavors for pea soups.

Medieval Pea Soup with Ginger, Saffron, and Almonds

CRETONNÉE DE POIS NOVIAUX

I came across this recipe in a reproduction of a 14th-century manuscript written by Guillaume Terel, better known as Taillevent. Taillevent's cooking—nothing like what's served at the present-day Taillevent restaurant in Paris—was characteristic of medieval Europe because the dishes almost always contained spices.

Taillevent's recipes don't give quantities, so it's hard to imagine exactly how the food tasted. Most writers about medieval cooking assume that the cooks of the era were heavy-handed with the spices and that medieval dishes would have little appeal to people today. I'm not so sure, and in any case, I've come up with my own spice quantities for this delicious soup.

MAKES 6 FIRST-COURSE SERVINGS

> 2 10-ounce packages of frozen petite peas or 2 pounds
>   fresh peas, 2 cups shelled
> 1 medium-size onion, chopped
> a ¼-inch slice of fresh ginger, peeled and chopped
> 2 tablespoons unsalted butter
> ¾ cup blanched almonds

3 cups chicken broth or water

¼ teaspoon saffron threads, soaked in 1 tablespoon water
for 20 minutes

6 drops almond extract

salt

pepper

PREHEAT the oven to 350°F. If you're using frozen peas, don't bother to thaw them. If you're using fresh peas, cook them for 5 minutes in a large pot of boiling salted water, drain them in a colander, and rinse them with cold water.

COOK the onion and ginger in the butter in a 4-quart pot over medium heat until the onions turn translucent, about 10 minutes.

BROWN the almonds by toasting them on a baking sheet for about 15 minutes. Watch them carefully and stir them around every few minutes so they brown evenly and don't burn.

ADD the almonds, peas, and 1 cup of the broth to the onion/ginger mixture. Stir the mixture over medium heat until it comes to a simmer and the peas soften slightly. Puree in a blender for 2 minutes.

PUSH the pea mixture through a medium-mesh strainer with the back of a ladle or large wooden spoon. Combine the strained pea mixture with the remaining broth, the saffron with its soaking water, and the almond extract. Season to taste with salt and pepper.

BELL PEPPERS

Until a few years ago you were lucky to find green and red sweet peppers at the same market. Now peppers come in all colors—bright orange, yellow, and even purple. Even though the different-colored peppers have a similar taste—and anything other than green is sold at a premium—I can never resist getting a few of each just to brighten things up.

Since most recipes using peppers—though not the one that follows—have you roast and skin them, always look for peppers with smooth sides. Peppers that curl up on themselves in funny shapes are hard to roast evenly.

Peeling

The only way to remove the peel from a pepper is to burn it off, which also cooks the pepper and improves its flavor. The easiest way to do this is to put the pepper directly over a gas flame turned on high, turning it every minute or so with tongs until it is completely charred. If you don't have a gas stove, blacken the peppers under the broiler or, better yet, on the barbecue.

Once the pepper is charred, set it on a plate for 5 minutes to cool. Then pull off as much of the charred peel as you can. Quickly scrape off the remaining peel with a paring knife under cold running water. Cut the pepper in half lengthwise, remove the stem, and pull out the seeds.

Chopping

Cut the stem out of the pepper. Slit one side of the pepper and fold the whole thing open. Pull out the seeds and the strips of white pulp that run along the inside of the pepper. Cut the pepper into strips. For some soups it is best to leave the different-colored peppers in strips for a more dramatic effect, while for others they should be cut into small cubes.

Cooking Methods

Because sweet peppers have a strong flavor, they will easily take over the flavor of a mixed vegetable soup. If you want to add them to a soup—strips of different-colored peppers in a tomato or summer fish soup are beautiful to look at—do so near the end of cooking so their flavor doesn't have a chance to work its way into the rest of the soup.

Roasted peppers can also be pureed in a mortar and pestle or in a food processor and combined with bread crumbs and garlic to make *rouille* (page 350) wich can be used to finish fish and vegetable soups.

Red Pepper Soup

The base for this Mexican-style soup is made with red bell peppers, which have no heat, but dried and soaked chilies are added to give it a more complex flavor and a bit of fire. If you don't have dried chilies, the easiest way to spice up this soup is with a little Tabasco—which also has a nice flavor—or a pinch of cayenne.

If you want to get fancy, make this soup twice—once with red peppers and once with yellow peppers. Then ladle the two soups into the bowls simultaneously using two ladles, one in each hand.

In the summer I like to thin this soup with a little extra broth and serve it ice-cold. Hot or cold, it's delicious served with a dollop of sour cream.

This soup can be made entirely in advance.

MAKES 8 SERVINGS

¼ cup olive oil

6 large red bell peppers, seeded and chopped into
    ½-inch cubes

1 large onion, chopped

6 garlic cloves, chopped

leaves from 3 fresh thyme sprigs, stems removed, or
    ½ teaspoon dried

5 guajillo or pasilla chilies

3 cups chicken or vegetable broth

1 cup heavy cream

3 tablespoons white wine vinegar or more to taste

salt

Tabasco sauce or cayenne pepper

sour cream

tortilla chips

PREHEAT the oven to 250°F. Heat the olive oil over medium heat in a 4-quart pot. Add the sweet peppers, onion, garlic, and thyme. Stir the mixture from time to time until the chopped onions turn translucent, about 10 minutes.

REMOVE the stems and seeds from the dried chilies and toast them in the oven for about 10 minutes. Place them in a bowl and pour over just enough boiling water to cover. Let the chilies sit in the water until they have completely softened, about 10 minutes. Taste the chili-soaking water; if it's sweet and tasty, save it for the soup. Chop the chilies very finely or puree them with a little of the broth in a blender until they have the consistency of a paste.

ADD 2 cups of the chicken broth to the bell pepper mixture, cover the pot, and gently simmer the soup for 15 minutes. Puree in a blender or food processor until smooth.

COMBINE the puree with the rest of the broth and strain the soup through a medium- or fine-mesh strainer. Stir in the chopped dried chilies, cream, and vinegar. Simmer the soup for 5 minutes. Season to taste with salt, Tabasco, and vinegar. Pass sour cream and tortilla chips at the table.

SUGGESTIONS AND VARIATIONS | In addition to the bicolor soup idea, sweet pepper soup can be garnished with different-colored sweet peppers that have been roasted, peeled, and cut into small dice. To prevent the dice from sinking, unseen, to the bottom of the bowl, float a small slice of toasted French bread on the top of each bowl and place the dice on top.

IT'S also worth playing around with different varieties and amounts of dried chilies. The flavors of the chilies are also good with corn. If you have access to good corn, simmer 2 cups kernels with the soup before straining. Shelled pumpkin seeds can also be used to give the soup a distinctive Mexican flavor and texture. Lightly toast I cup of the seeds in the oven at 350°F, puree them in a blender with just enough of the soup to get them to move around, and strain the mixture into the soup.

HUNGARIAN cooks are also fond of using chilies—not only in their dried and ground form, paprika, but also fresh. One typical Hungarian dish, *letcho*, is a simple stewlike soup of chopped peppers and onions first cooked in a little fat and then simmered with chopped tomatoes. Ground paprika is then added as a final flavoring. The Hungarians also make a soup called *paloc* that is actually a lamb goulash—redolent with hot and sweet paprika and fresh green peppers—to which are added extra broth, sour cream, and green beans.

THE Italians—especially the Abruzzesi—are fond of adding dried hot red peppers—*diavolilli* (little devils)—to vegetable and fish soups and stews. Many of the soups from this region are likely to contain no tomatoes but instead a generous sprinkling of the powdered *diavolilli*. Cayenne pepper makes a suitable substitute.

Roasted Red Bell Pepper, Garlic, and Onion Soup

In this soup, the sometimes domineering flavor of cooked bell peppers is balanced with that of roasted onions and garlic. Bell peppers also develop a more complex flavor when they are roasted rather than stewed or sweated. I like to garnish this soup with a sauce made with *crème fraîche* or sour cream, and roasted and peeled poblano chilies, but if you like, just use a dollop of sour cream or *crème fraîche*.

MAKES 6 FIRST-COURSE SERVINGS

4 large red bell peppers (2 pounds)

I head of garlic, broken into cloves, cloves left unpeeled

2 medium red onions, peeled and cut into 6 wedges each
(I pound total)

2 tablespoons olive oil

4 medium-size tomatoes, stemmed and coarsely chopped
(don't bother seeding or peeling)

I quart chicken broth

½ teaspoon dried oregano, preferably Mexican

2 fresh poblano chilies (optional)

1 cup sour cream or crème fraîche

salt

pepper

PREHEAT the oven to 425°F.

CUT the stems out of the bell peppers and discard. Cut the peppers in half length-wise and swat them together to get rid of their seeds. Cut out any strips of white pulp. Chop the pepper halves coarsely and toss them with the garlic, onions, and olive oil in a roasting pan or sheet pan just large enough to hold them in a single layer. Slide the pan into the oven and bake the mixture, stirring every 15 minutes, for 45 minutes to 1 hour, or until the peppers are browned on the edges, the onions have browned and come apart, and the bottom of the pan is covered with a light caramelized glaze.

TAKE the pan out of the oven and transfer the peppers, garlic, and onions to a heavy-bottomed pot. Add the tomatoes, half the broth, and oregano to the pot, and bring to the simmer. Add the remaining broth to the roasting pan and scrape the bottom of the pan for a couple of minutes with a wooden spoon so the caramelized glaze dissolves into the broth. Add this liquid to the pot. Simmer for 20 minutes more, until the tomatoes are falling apart. Puree the mixture in a blender and then strain it, pushing it through the strainer with a ladle, or work it through a food mill.

IF you're using the poblanos, char the skin on top of the stove by turning the chilies around in the flame until they are thoroughly charred—if you see white ash, how-ever, you're overdoing it. (If you have an electric stove, see page 208.) Put the hot poblanos in a plastic bag for 10 minutes so the steam loosens the blackened skin. (I don't bother with this when peeling bell peppers, but the skin on poblanos is a little more stubborn.) Scrape the blackened skin off the chilies with a small knife and quickly rinse them under cold water. Cut out the stems and cut the chilies in half lengthwise. Rinse out the seeds, cut out any white pulp, and chop the chilies fine.

STIR the chopped chilies with the sour cream or crème fraîche and season the mix-ture to taste with salt.

SEASON the red pepper soup to taste with salt and pepper and ladle it into heated bowls. Swirl the top of each serving with the poblano mixture or the plain sour cream or crème fraîche.

SORREL

It's a mystery why sorrel is so little known or appreciated in the United States. It's easy to grow, and it has an irresistible tang that makes it perfect for light summer soups.

Sorrel is in season in summer. It should be dirt cheap—it grows like a weed—but sometimes fancy food stores jack up the price because it's unusual and people think it's rare and exotic. I asked a friend to grow some in her garden, and before long it completely took over.

If you can't find fresh sorrel, commercial cooked sorrel in jars isn't bad. Cooked sorrel, whether fresh or out of a jar, is a sad-looking gray-green, but there's nothing you can do about it—it turns this color after about 5 seconds of cooking.

If you want to add fresh sorrel to a soup containing other vegetables, just cut it into strips (chiffonade) or chop it and add it to the soup just a minute or two before serving.

Cream of Sorrel Soup
POTAGE GERMINY

This is one of those classic soups so full of rich things people love that perhaps it's against my better judgment to include it. But I can't resist—the texture and flavor are so satisfying.

This version contains egg yolks, which give it a smooth and silky texture, but if you want a less rich version, try the potato-thickened recipe on page 192.

Don't use an aluminum pot to cook this soup, or the egg yolks will turn gray.

MAKES 6 SERVINGS

I pound fresh sorrel, stems removed and leaves washed, or I 12-ounce jar cooked

I quart chicken or vegetable broth

6 egg yolks

1½ cups heavy cream

4 tablespoons unsalted butter

salt

white pepper

¼ cup heavy cream, very lightly whipped

6 chervil leaves or 2 fresh sorrel leaves, finely shredded

IN ADVANCE In a 4-quart saucepan, combine the sorrel leaves or cooked sorrel with 2 cups of the broth. Bring the broth to a simmer over high heat and stir for I minute. If you're using fresh sorrel, stir the leaves in the hot broth until they turn gray. Strain the mixture through the fine disk of a food mill or puree it in a blender or food processor. Strain it again through a medium-mesh strainer. Work through as much of the pulp as you can with the back of a ladle or wooden spoon.

AT THE LAST MINUTE Combine the rest of the broth with the sorrel puree and bring it to a slow simmer in a 4-quart pot.

BEAT the egg yolks with a whisk in a mixing bowl for about 2 minutes, until they are smooth. Stir the cream into the yolks. Stir the simmering sorrel mixture into the egg yolk/cream mixture. Make sure the liquids are well combined and then pour the mixture back into the pot used to cook the sorrel.

PUT the soup back on the stove over low to medium heat. At this stage you must be careful not to let the soup boil, or the egg yolks will curdle. Continuously stir the soup with a wooden spoon. Reach into the corners of the pot while stirring, or the egg yolk will stick there and curdle.

AS soon as you notice the soup thickening (at 175°F), turn off the heat, add the butter, and stir the soup for a minute more. Strain the soup through a fine-mesh sieve. Season to taste with salt and pepper.

SERVE the soup in hot bowls—not scalding hot, or the egg yolk will curdle around the edges of the soup.

DECORATE the soup with a spoonful of the lightly whipped cream and the chervil.

SUGGESTIONS AND VARIATIONS | This soup is wonderful served cold. It thickens as you chill it, so you may want to thin it with a little vegetable broth, milk, or water.

I sometimes reinforce the tanginess of the sorrel by adding the juice of a lemon, but some people don't like things too sour, so use your own judgment.

YOU can add some small croutons sautéed in butter (page 594) to the garnish.

SPINACH

Because it is one of my favorite vegetables, I try to sneak spinach into soup whenever I can. For a delicate soup like this one, the spinach needs to be cooked in boiling water for a minute first. If a relatively small amount of spinach is going into the pot with lots of other ingredients, the whole or shredded leaves can be thrown in as they are—after a careful washing.

Of course spinach can also be used as the focal point of a soup. The following Indian-style recipe is flavored with garlic, onion, and spices, thickened with cooked rice. Spinach soup can also be prepared using potato and leek soup as a base (page 190) or as a cream soup, using béchamel and heavy cream (see box, page 160).

The only time-consuming part of preparing spinach is removing the leaves from the stems and washing. Unless you're using spinach in a puree, where everything is strained, you'll need to pull the leaves off the stems. Don't just break the leaf off at the base. Hold the leaf between the thumb and forefinger of your left hand and peel back the stem so it comes off the back of the leaf.

Indian-Style Spinach Puree

Although this soup is derived from one in Julie Sahni's wonderful book about classical Indian food, the techniques are actually those used in classical French cooking; only the Indian flavors are different. This recipe is not only delicious but also has a special texture because it's thickened with rice.

MAKES 6 SERVINGS

3 pounds or 4 10-ounce bags spinach, stems removed and
    leaves washed

4 tablespoons unsalted butter

1 large onion, chopped

2 garlic cloves, chopped

1 teaspoon ground cumin

¼ teaspoon ground cloves

⅛ teaspoon freshly grated nutmeg

1 quart chicken or vegetable broth

½ cup cooked rice, preferably basmati

1 cup milk

½ cup heavy cream

salt

pepper

COOK the spinach leaves in boiling salted water for 1 minute, rinse until cool, and drain. (In a pinch, you can substitute 4 10-ounce packages frozen spinach.)

MELT the butter in a 4-quart pot. Add the onion and garlic and stir over medium heat until the onion is soft and translucent, about 15 minutes.

TURN off the heat and immediately stir in the cumin, cloves, and nutmeg. Transfer this mixture to a food processor and add 2 cups of the broth, the rice, and the spinach. Puree until smooth. Add more broth if needed to get the mixture to churn around. If you want the soup to be smoother, work it through a food mill with a medium disk.

COMBINE the puree with the rest of the broth, the milk, and the cream. Season with salt and pepper. Check the consistency of the soup. If you want an even smoother texture, strain it through a fine-mesh sieve.

SUGGESTIONS AND VARIATIONS | Try playing around with different spice combinations: ground coriander, cardamom, fennel seeds, and homemade or commercial curry powders. A lovely and exotic variation is to substitute coconut milk (either canned or homemade) for the heavy cream. Yogurt is another possibility. One of my favorite tricks is to stir in ½ cup almond milk (page 202) just before serving.

I like this soup best served hot, but obviously it can be served cold too. If you serve it hot, heat it at the last minute and serve it immediately so it doesn't turn gray.

IF you make this soup ahead of time—it keeps for 2 or 3 days in the refrigerator— quickly chill the pot in a bowl of ice as soon as the soup is ready. Otherwise the soup stays hot for too long and will turn gray.

SQUASH (WINTER) AND PUMPKIN

Winter squash and pumpkin are among my fall and early winter staples. I sometimes peel and cut them into chunks to add to mixed vegetable soups, but more often I like to turn them into buttery purees.

Puree of Squash or Pumpkin

Soups made with pumpkin seem to be more popular than soups made with other kinds of squash. I can't account for this, since squash has a sweeter taste than pumpkin. I usually use a small local squash such as butternut or acorn.

This version is thickened with lightly toasted bread, but you can also use potato or sweet potato; just cook 2 medium-size peeled and sliced potatoes or sweet potatoes along with the squash at the beginning.

MAKES 6 SERVINGS

2 butternut or acorn squash, about 1½ pounds peeled and
   seeded
1 quart milk
pinch of freshly grated nutmeg
2 teaspoons sugar
8 slices of white bread, crusts removed, lightly toasted
½ cup heavy cream
½ cup medium-dry sherry
salt
pepper
parsley butter (page 593)
small croutons (page 594)

PEEL and seed the squash and cut it into 1-inch cubes. Combine it with the milk, nutmeg, and sugar in a 4-quart pot. Heat the pot over medium heat, partially cover, and simmer slowly—be careful the milk doesn't boil over—for 20 to 30 minutes, until the squash is soft and can be crushed easily against the side of the pot with a fork. Add the bread to the soup and simmer for 5 minutes more.

STRAIN the soup through a food mill first with the coarse disk and then again with the fine disk or puree the soup in a blender or food processor and strain it through a medium-mesh kitchen strainer. If you want the soup to have a finer texture, strain it again through a fine-mesh strainer.

ADD the cream and sherry to the soup and bring it back to a simmer. Season it with salt and pepper. If it seems too thick, thin it with more milk or broth. Top with a spoonful of parsley butter and some croutons.

Roasted Garlic and Acorn Squash Soup

Unlike many vegetable soups in which the vegetables are simmered directly in liquid or gently sweated in butter or oil, the vegetables in this recipe are all roasted. Acorn squash and garlic predominate, but onion and carrots are also used to add sweetness and aromatic support. (Roasting squash also makes irregularly shaped varieties easier to peel. The pulp is just scooped out and the peels discarded.) Another method is to poke three or four small holes in the squash with a knife and then cook it in the microwave until it begins to soften, about 10 minutes. The pulp can then be scooped out of the squash, combined with the milk/nutmeg/sugar mixture, and simmered for only a minute or two before the bread is added.

MAKES 8 FIRST-COURSE SERVINGS

3 acorn squash, about 1 pound each (or a total of 3 pounds)

4 heads of garlic

2 medium-size red onions, peeled and halved

3 medium-size carrots, peeled and halved lengthwise

¼ cup olive oil

5 fresh thyme sprigs or 3 fresh sage leaves or ½ teaspoon dried thyme leaves

4 cups basic brown chicken broth or more as needed (page 62)

salt

pepper

PREHEAT the oven to 375°F.

CUT the squash crosswise in half and scoop out the seeds. Break the garlic into cloves but don't bother peeling the cloves. Toss the onions, carrots, and garlic in the olive oil and put everything in a heavy-bottomed roasting pan with the squash halves flat side up. The pan should just be large enough to hold the vegetables in a single layer. Roast for about 1½ hours, stirring the vegetables (except the squash) every 20 minutes so they brown and cook evenly. Near the end of cooking, after about 1 hour and 20 minutes, add the thyme to the roasting pan.

WHEN the squash is soft—it's easily penetrated with a knife or skewer—let it cool and scoop the pulp out into a mixing bowl and discard the peels. Combine the squash with the roasted vegetables and herbs, or, if you've used herbs on the stem, discard them, and enough of the broth to get it to turn around, in a blender or food processor and, working in batches, puree until smooth. Work the puree through a food mill or strainer (use a ladle to work it through a strainer) into a clean pot. Add the rest of the broth—add a little more as needed to thin the soup to the consistency you like—and season to taste with salt and pepper. If you want the soup to be silky smooth, strain it again through a fine-mesh strainer. Ladle into heated bowls.

Roasted Pumpkin Soup

This dramatic soup was inspired by a recipe from Paul Bocuse, who loads an entire pumpkin with heavy cream and bakes it. His version is delicious but so rich that when I prepared it one fall I truly horrified some health-conscious relatives visiting from California. In this version some of the cream is replaced by chicken, turkey, or vegetable broth; it isn't quite as rich as eating bowlfuls of heavy cream, but it's still very rich.

Don't do what I did and buy a pumpkin too large for your oven.

MAKES 8 SERVINGS

I pumpkin, about 12 inches in diameter
I quart chicken, turkey, or vegetable broth
2 cups heavy cream
I thick round loaf of French bread, sliced ½ inch thick
2 teaspoons fresh thyme leaves or I teaspoon dried
1½ cups grated Gruyère cheese, about ½ pound
salt
pepper

PREHEAT the oven to 350°F. Cut the top off the pumpkin and scrape out the seeds as though making a jack-o'-lantern.

COMBINE the broth and heavy cream in a mixing bowl.

TOAST the bread slices. Arrange a slice in the bottom of the pumpkin, sprinkle with thyme leaves and grated cheese, and ladle over just enough of the broth/cream mixture to cover the bread. Sprinkle with salt and pepper.

REPEAT this process until the pumpkin is three-quarters full. Don't try to fill the pumpkin all the way, because the filling expands and will ooze out the top. Replace the lid on the pumpkin.

PLACE the pumpkin on a baking sheet (this is important in case any of the filling does ooze out) and bake for 2 hours.

TAKE the pumpkin to the table on the baking sheet or on a platter, but be careful—it's fragile. Remove the lid. Carefully reach in with a large metal spoon and scrape around the insides to detach the pulp and mix it with the other ingredients. Ladle (or scoop; the soup is quite thick) into hot bowls.

SUGGESTIONS AND VARIATIONS | This makes a wonderful main course—served along with a salad—for a fall luncheon. The soup is great left over the next day, sprinkled with more cheese and baked as a casserole.

Sweet Potato, Chili, and Lime Soup

For years the only time I ate sweet potatoes was at Thanksgiving, well doused with butter and occasionally scented with cloves or cinnamon. Although I always enjoyed the Thanksgiving version, the first time I tasted this soup I was amazed that it was made from a vegetable I had always thought so stodgy.

MAKES 6 SERVINGS

2 medium-size onions, chopped

2 garlic cloves, chopped

2 tablespoons unsalted butter

2 pounds sweet potatoes, about 4, peeled and sliced ½ inch thick

I quart chicken broth

2 jalapeño chilies, cut in half lengthwise, seeded, and finely chopped

3 poblano chilies, roasted, peeled (page 172), and chopped

½ cup corn oil

4 corn tortillas, cut into I- by ¼-inch strips

juice of 2 limes or more to taste

salt

pepper

3 tablespoons finely chopped cilantro leaves

2 tablespoons olive oil

¾ cup sour cream

sour cream

lime wedges

GENTLY cook the onions and garlic in the butter in a 4-quart pot over medium heat until the onions turn translucent, about 10 minutes.

ADD the sweet potatoes and broth to the onion mixture; bring to a simmer, cover the pot, and keep at a slow simmer until the sweet potatoes have softened and are easy to crush against the side of the pot with a fork, about 20 minutes.

ADD the jalapeño and roast poblano chilies to the soup and simmer, covered, for 5 minutes more.

HEAT the corn oil over high heat in a medium-size skillet until its surface ripples. Turn the heat down to medium-low and fry the tortilla strips for about I minute. Drain them on paper towels.

FIXING THE SOUP

Sometimes, after carefully tracking down all the best ingredients and dutifully following a recipe, your soup, while not a total disaster, comes out just so-so. You wonder if it was worth all the effort.

A dull-tasting soup is often easy to bring around. Sometimes a tablespoon or two of butter or heavy cream swirled in just before serving will add exactly the note of luxuriousness that was missing. Chopped herbs such as parsley, basil, or cilantro will give the soup freshness and vitality—qualities that are easily lost if the soup sits too long on the stove. One of my favorite tricks is to add a couple of tablespoons of good wine vinegar or fresh lemon juice to give the soup enough of a discreet tang to bring the other flavors into perspective. When vegetable soups taste flat or almost heavy, I sometimes add a half cup of white wine or dry sherry and cook the soup for just a minute to get rid of the alcohol. The raw fruitiness and tartness of the wine often lighten the soup.

Some soups, especially root vegetable soups, need a smoky accent to balance their earthy taste. If one of these soups seems to lack something, try slicing a strip of bacon or pancetta into little strips and cooking them until just slightly crispy before stirring them into the soup.

These days people are very timid with salt. And while it's a good idea to undersalt soup (put a salt shaker on the table for guests who want more), salt is often just what a flat-tasting soup lacks. And don't forget a grind of fresh pepper.

PUREE the soup in a blender or put it through the fine disk of a food mill and strain it through a medium-mesh strainer. Stir in the lime juice to taste and season with salt and pepper.

COMBINE the chopped cilantro with the olive oil.

LADLE the soup into hot bowls and drizzle the top of each one with the cilantro/olive oil paste, sour cream, and the tortilla chips. Serve with extra sour cream and lime wedges.

SWISS CHARD

Although Swiss chard is often ignored in the United States, it's very popular in Italy and the south of France. Its distinct earthy taste—it reminds me of beets—makes it perfect in dishes containing garlic. I have no idea what makes Swiss chard Swiss. I've never encountered it in Switzerland; on the contrary, I associate it with hot climates, robust cuisine, and dishes made with garlic and olive oil.

Like spinach, Swiss chard can be precooked or added directly to a soup. The choice is yours—some people find that its beetlike flavor takes over if it isn't precooked, but if matched with other full-flavored ingredients such as garlic this is rarely a problem. Swiss chard is a bit tougher than spinach, so I add the leaves to a soup 10 to 15 minutes before serving, whereas spinach is best added just a minute or two before.

I like to add shredded chard leaves to vegetable soups and soups containing whole beans. When I'm home alone and there's not much in the refrigerator, I sometimes make a little garlic soup by boiling a whole head of garlic in a quart of water with a little thyme or sage, maybe adding some tomatoes if they're around, plus some blanched and shredded chard leaves and a good splash of olive oil, and pouring the mixture over a thick slice of bread in a wide pasta bowl. I then sprinkle the whole dish with Parmigiano-Reggiano.

Swiss Chard, Parsley, and Garlic Soup

I first made this soup one lazy afternoon—inventing as I went along. When I added the hot peppers, I wasn't sure whether the soup was going to come out Italian or Mexican, but the result is distinctly Italian. Whatever its nationality, this soup is delicious and satisfying.

MAKES 8 SERVINGS

1 large bunch of Swiss chard, stems removed—about
    2 pounds; 12 ounces after trimming

3 garlic cloves, finely chopped

2 medium-size onions, finely chopped

2 fresh hot chilies such as jalapeños, seeded and finely
    chopped

3 tablespoons olive oil

1 teaspoon fresh chopped thyme, marjoram, or oregano or
    ½ teaspoon dried

6 cups chicken broth

4 medium-size tomatoes, peeled, seeded, and chopped or
    2 cups canned, seeded and drained

½ cup finely chopped parsley leaves

salt

pepper

slices of French or Italian bread, lightly toasted

olive oil

grated Parmesan cheese

SHRED the Swiss chard by cutting the stems out of the leaves, rolling up each leaf into a small sausage shape, and then slicing the rolls as thinly as possible—⅛ to ¼ inch thick is a good width. You should have about four tightly packed cups.

COMBINE the garlic, onions, chilies, and olive oil in a 4-quart pot. Stir over medium heat for about 10 minutes or until the onions turn translucent but don't brown. Add the thyme and cook for 2 minutes more.

ADD the broth and tomatoes and bring to a slow simmer. Simmer gently for 5 minutes, add the chard, and simmer for 10 minutes more. Add the parsley to the simmering soup a minute or two before serving. Season with salt and pepper.

IF you like, place a slice of stale or toasted French or Italian bread in the bottom of each bowl—or, if you want to keep things light, leave out the bread and let the guests help themselves at the table. Pass the olive oil—I like to drizzle it over this soup—and the grated cheese.

SUGGESTIONS AND VARIATIONS | If you want to make this soup more substantial, add a cup or two of cooked white beans such as cannellini, borlotti, or navy white beans. I also sometimes add leftover cooked rice if I'm throwing this together for a last-minute lunch or light supper. Basil leaves, finely chopped with a tablespoon of olive oil, whisked in at the end, make a lovely finish.

TOMATOES

When you're making tomato soup, your approach and style should depend most of all on the quality of the tomatoes. When tomatoes are at their end-of-summer best, you don't need to do much more than peel them, chop them, and sprinkle them with a little salt and pepper. The only accompaniment can be a slice or two of toasted French bread for occasional dipping and smearing.

Throughout the year and alas even at the end of summer, we rarely have access to perfect tomatoes. Even when bright red and at the height of the season, they are usually picked before fully ripened and have most likely been overwatered. Fortunately tomatoes adapt themselves well in the kitchen, and cooks have developed techniques to bring out and enhance their flavor. Usually the better the tomatoes, the less flavoring and manipulation they require; as we move away from perfection we need to toy with them more to make them interesting.

For soups, use the juiciest tomatoes you can find. Plum tomatoes are excellent for sauces but don't contribute much liquid to a soup—you'll end up needing to thin it with tomato juice, stock, or water and thus weaken its flavor. The best tomatoes for soup are big and fat and seem ready to burst out of their skins. Sometimes the skin is wrinkled and feels as though it might slide right off the tomato. Fat juicy tomatoes can hardly ever be found in supermarkets or at greengrocers because they would have fallen apart on their way in from the farm. City dwellers, unless they have access to an authentic farmer's market, have to content themselves with the greengrocer's shelves and mediocre tomatoes. Cherry tomatoes often have a surprisingly good flavor and make good soup—just strain the soup before serving to eliminate the skins and seeds.

Most people select tomatoes based on color. Although color tells something about the tomatoes' flavor, other indicators are sometimes more reliable. Look for tomatoes with a matte appearance; this is caused by natural yeasts that will cling to the tomato's skin only if the sugar content of the tomato is high enough to be tempting. Pick up the tomato. A flavorful tomato often feels sticky. And finally, good-tasting tomatoes often have a short section of stem still attached. Most supermarket tomatoes have only a hollow indentation where the stem was removed.

Tomatoes for soups are prepared in one of two ways. In the first method, for rustic chunky-style soups, the tomatoes are peeled and cut in half crosswise, and the seeds are squeezed out of each half. They are then chopped to the desired fineness. For the second method, the tomatoes—skins, seeds, and all—are chopped and cooked with flavorful ingredients. The whole soup is then strained at the end.

If you can find only less than perfect tomatoes, don't despair. Regular store-bought tomatoes—although not the pink ones that show up in December—will make excellent soups but require extra flavor to make them interesting. You can

CANNED TOMATOES

Being a purist and aficionado of fresh vegetables, I usually resist anything that comes out of a can. But for much of the year canned tomatoes are better than fresh.

Canned tomatoes usually contain a lot of juice and seeds, so when you use them in a recipe, drain off the juice and squeeze the seeds out of each tomato. When canned tomatoes are called for in this book, the measurements are based on drained and seeded tomatoes. To substitute canned tomatoes for fresh, use $1/2$ cup canned (after draining and seeding) for each medium-size fresh tomato. I never bother using the juice in the can—it often tastes metallic and has little tomato flavor in any case.

add flavor to a tomato soup at different stages during the preparation. The most common method is to prepare a flavor base by gently stewing various combinations of onions, garlic, peppers, or sometimes bacon or ham in an appropriate fat such as olive oil. The coarsely chopped unpeeled tomatoes are then added to the flavor base and stewed just long enough to soften and release their juices. The soup is then strained through a food mill to eliminate seeds and pieces of peel and to give the soup a smooth texture. You can make the soup easier to strain by pureeing it first in a blender once it's cooled down a little. Don't leave the soup in the blender for more than 5 or 10 seconds, or the tomatoes will turn pink and frothy and your soup will look bizarre.

Besides using cooked aromatic vegetables, tomato soups can be flavored by adding herbs to the flavor base or along with the tomatoes. Provençal herbs such as thyme, marjoram, or savory should be added near the beginning so their flavor has a chance to infuse into the soup. Other, more delicate herbs such as basil, tarragon, or parsley should be added near the end, or their flavor will cook off.

Many cooks add sugar to tomato soups and sauces. If used carefully, sugar can enhance the natural sweetness of the tomatoes. Although it may sound contradictory, a few teaspoons of good wine vinegar stirred into a tomato soup just before serving will often sharpen its flavors and bring them into focus.

You can give tomato soups a decorative flourish and an exciting flavor by swirling in a simple flavorful sauce just before serving. Try flavoring homemade mayonnaise with garlic and saffron (page 350) or freshly chopped herbs or use a small amount of yogurt or heavy cream combined with freshly chopped herbs such as tarragon or cilantro.

Perfect Summer Tomato Soup with Tarragon Sauce

This is the soup for the perfect tomato. It is best served from the height of summer to the end of September, when the best tomatoes are in season. If you can find them, try it with yellow tomatoes; or, if you want something more elaborate, make both a yellow and a red version and ladle them out next to each other in the bowl.

The tarragon sauce is wonderful but certainly not essential, so don't give up on the soup if you don't want to deal with it or can't find the herbs.

This soup is thick, and you may want to thin it with a little water or an ice cube or two (anything else takes away from its delicacy), but I like it almost the consistency of a stew so I can scoop it up onto slices of crusty bread. Serve hot or cold.

MAKES 8 SERVINGS

the soup:

6 large or 10 medium-size perfect tomatoes, 4 to 5 pounds

1 tablespoon salt*

pepper

the sauce:

3 large fresh tarragon sprigs

2 teaspoons olive oil

½ cup heavy cream or yogurt

salt

pepper

6 slices of country-style French bread, toasted

BRING a pot of water large enough to hold the tomatoes to a rapid boil. While the water is heating, put a colander in the sink. Plunge the tomatoes into the boiling water for about 20 seconds and pour the tomatoes and water into the colander. Quickly rinse them off with cold water. Keep rinsing until they have completely cooled. Gently peel away the skin with your fingers or a small paring knife. Slice the tomatoes in half crosswise and gently squeeze the seeds out of each half over a strainer set over a bowl. Strain the liquid. Save the liquid and discard the seeds.

CHOP the tomato halves on a cutting board until they have the texture you like—I recommend leaving the texture on the chunky side. Put the chopped tomatoes in a glass or stainless-steel bowl and sprinkle with the salt and pepper. If the soup seems too thick, thin it with the strained juice from inside the tomatoes or add a little water.

*Although this may seem like a lot, the salt not only functions as a seasoning but also draws the water out of the tomatoes and gives the soup a thinner consistency. Of course you can use less salt, but the soup may be thicker as a result.

PREPARING THE SAUCE Remove the tarragon leaves from the stems and put them on a cutting board with the olive oil, which will prevent them from turning black once they are chopped. Chop the leaves coarsely so their color remains and contrasts with the soup. Combine the chopped tarragon with the heavy cream and season the sauce with salt and pepper. Let the sauce sit for 30 minutes to allow the flavors to infuse in the cream. If you're serving the soup cold, chill it in the refrigerator.

SERVING Heat the soup if you're serving it hot. Stir half the tarragon sauce into the soup and pass the rest of the sauce at the table for guests to swirl into their soup. Serve the soup in wide bowls. Pass the French bread toasts.

SUGGESTIONS AND VARIATIONS | Eat outside if you can; this is great *al fresco* fare. The tarragon sauce is wonderful, but basil, marjoram, and cilantro can all be used for unique variations. You can also try more elaborate sauces such as the mayonnaises and vinaigrettes. Or try serving the soup with a bottle of extra virgin olive oil on the table as the only sauce.

THIS soup is also delicious served hot. If the weather suddenly turns cold and you want something a little richer, stir the tarragon sauce directly into the hot soup and add an extra ½ cup or more of heavy cream and you'll have the ultimate cream of tomato soup.

Roasted Tomato Soup

For some reason I don't fully understand, the flavor of tomatoes develops far more dramatically when the tomatoes are roasted than it does when they are slowly stewed, as when making a traditional tomato sauce. I discovered the magic of roasted tomatoes when I was developing recipes for my book *Vegetables*, and I have essentially converted that recipe to a soup by pureeing the tomatoes and thinning them with a little broth and/or cream. You can also take advantage of less than perfect tomatoes by slow roasting, which dramatically improves their flavor.

MAKES 10 FIRST-COURSE SERVINGS

15 pounds ripe tomatoes

⅓ cup extra virgin olive oil

12 large garlic cloves, peeled, finely chopped, and crushed to a paste with the side of a chef's knife

3 teaspoons chopped fresh marjoram, or 2 teaspoons chopped fresh thyme, or 1 teaspoon dried thyme or marjoram leaves

4 cups basic brown chicken broth (page 62)

1 cup heavy cream (optional)

salt

pepper

CUT the tomatoes in half crosswise and squeeze out the seeds.

PREHEAT the oven to 400°F.

POUR the olive oil into a large, heavy-bottomed roasting pan or into a sheet pan with sides and arrange the tomatoes in a single layer, flat side facing down. Roast the tomatoes for about 45 minutes, until you see that they've released a lot of liquid. Gently tilt the roasting pan and ladle off the liquid into a small saucepan. Keep roasting the tomatoes, ladling off the liquid and reducing it, until the tomatoes stop releasing liquid and they barely begin to brown around the edges. This may take as long as 2 hours. An hour into the roasting, sprinkle over the garlic and herbs and stir the tomatoes around in the roasting pan—the garlic and herbs should roast for at least 30 minutes. Boil down the liquid released by the tomatoes to about ¾ cup.

COMBINE the reduced tomato liquid with the tomatoes and work through a food mill or a strainer, pushing the tomatoes through with the back of a ladle. Skim off any olive oil that has floated to the top of the puree. Combine the puree with the broth and the optional heavy cream, and bring to a simmer. Season to taste with salt and pepper.

VARIATIONS | You can lightly beat the heavy cream and swirl it on top of each serving. I sometimes turn the cream into a chili sauce by stemming and seeding one or two dried chilies (such as anchos, chipotles, guajillos, mulatos, pasilla de Oaxcas) and soaking them in a cup of boiling water for about 30 minutes to soften them. I then chop the chilies very fine and combine them with the cream in a saucepan. I bring the cream to a simmer and let it cool for 15 minutes to infuse it with the flavor of the chilies. I then chill the cream, lightly beat it, and swirl it over each serving or (especially if it's hot) pass it for the guests to help themselves. Croutons—cubes of bread about ½ inch on each side—sauteed in olive oil until golden brown provide a delightful crunch.

Tomato Soup with Saffron and Garlic Mayonnaise

So much flavor is worked into this delicious soup during each stage of cooking that by the time it reaches the table it seems ready to ignite. The finish for the soup—a southern French garlic- and saffron-flavored mayonnaise—is the same one used to finish Mediterranean fish soups. Extra garlic and saffron mayonnaise can be passed at the table with crusty French bread. Try serving the soup with a simple baby artichoke salad—some diners will cheat and use the mayonnaise on the artichokes—and you'll have a complete summer lunch or light dinner.

MAKES 6 SERVINGS

2 tablespoons olive oil

1 medium-size onion, chopped

3 garlic cloves, chopped

1 small fennel bulb or the green tops, chopped (optional)

4 fresh thyme or marjoram sprigs or 1 teaspoon dried

a 1-inch strip of orange zest (optional)

8 medium-size tomatoes, about 3 pounds

2 cups chicken broth, vegetable broth, or water

salt

pepper

sugar and red wine vinegar

1 cup saffron and garlic mayonnaise (page 350)

slices of French bread, toasted

HEAT the olive oil in a 4-quart pot over medium heat and add the onion, garlic, and fennel. Cook the mixture, stirring every few minutes with a wooden spoon. After about 5 minutes, put the herbs, including their stems, and the orange zest into the pot. Continue cooking until the vegetables soften and the onion turns shiny and translucent, about 10 minutes.

WHILE the vegetables are cooking, wash the tomatoes and cut them in half crosswise. (The peels and seeds will be strained out later.) Add the tomato halves and broth to the hot vegetables. Simmer gently for about 20 minutes more, until the tomato halves have completely softened.

STRAIN the soup through a food mill with the finest disk or push it through a strainer with the back of a ladle. You can also work it for a few seconds in a blender to make it easier to strain, but be careful not to overwork it, or the soup will be pale. Season the soup with salt and pepper. If it tastes flat, alternately add a teaspoon of sugar and a teaspoon of wine vinegar until it has the desired taste.

FINISH the soup by bringing it back to a simmer and whisking it into 6 tablespoons of the mayonnaise in a large mixing bowl. Ladle the soup into hot bowls. Decorate the top of each serving with a swirl of mayonnaise. Serve the rest of the mayonnaise at the table—leaving it in the mortar is a nice touch—along with slices of toasted French bread.

SUGGESTIONS AND VARIATIONS | Tomato soup can be used as a base for delicious shellfish soups by steaming open clams, mussels, or cockles in a little white wine and then adding the liquid they release during steaming to the tomato soup base. The steamed shellfish is then added to the soup just before serving. Steam open the mussels, clams, or cockles with a cup or two of white wine (see *moules à la marinière*, page 361 and remove the top shells. Add the wine/shellfish liquid to the soup—straining it to eliminate sand—and reheat the shellfish in the soup just before serving. You can finish the mussel or clam soup with the garlic and saffron mayonnaise as directed. For an even simpler seafood and tomato soup, just simmer some peeled shrimp or scallops in the soup about 3 minutes before serving.

BECAUSE I associate tomato soup with summer, I rarely add cream, which can make the soup too rich for a hot summer day or evening. Occasionally in mid-September, when the weather turns unexpectedly cool, I'll replace the garlic and saffron mayonnaise with a cup of heavy cream.

Mexican Tomato Soup with Assorted Condiments

This soup gets a special toasty character by first charring the onion, garlic, and tomatoes in a heavy cast-iron skillet (Mexicans use a heavy flat iron skilletlike plate called a *comal*) before they are pureed. This method contrasts with the approach used in most parts of the world, where aromatic vegetables are chopped and gently cooked in some kind of fat before the tomatoes are added. But the drama and delight of eating this soup comes not so much from the basic tomato broth but from the assortment of condiments you serve with it. The convivial passing back and forth of various bowls brings guests together and initiates conversation. I serve this soup at informal dinner parties where people are meeting for the first time.

MAKES 8 FIRST-COURSE SERVINGS

for the broth:

10 garlic cloves, peeled

2 medium-size or 1 large red onion, peeled and halved

8 medium-size tomatoes, about 3 pounds

4 cups basic brown chicken broth (page 62)

salt

pepper

the condiments:

6 dried chilies such as anchos, chipotles, guajillos, mulatos,
pasillas, pasillas de Oaxaca

15 6-inch corn tortillas (1 8-ounce package)

½ cup corn oil or canola oil

2 ripe avocados, preferably Hass (the kind with the rough
skin)

2 tablespoons lemon juice

8 small jalapeño chilies, stemmed, seeded, and finely
chopped

2 limes, cut into wedges

2 cups grated sharp white Cheddar cheese or Monterey Jack

leaves from 1 bunch of cilantro

1 14-ounce container sour cream

PREPARING THE BROTH Place in an iron skillet or grill pan on the stove over high heat for about 5 minutes—if you can avoid it, don't use a well-seasoned pan because the high heat will destroy the seasoning. Add the garlic and onion and stir about every minute until the onion falls apart and blackens on the edges and everything smells fragrant. Take the onion and garlic out of the pan and reserve in a bowl. Put the tomatoes in the pan and gently stir them around until their skins wrinkle and blacken in places and the tomatoes start to sizzle and pop. Do your best to get the tomatoes in contact with the hot skillet on all sides—this will take about 8 minutes. Take the tomatoes out of the pan, turn off the heat, and let cool.

PUT the garlic and onion in a blender with two of the tomatoes and some broth and puree, in small batches (to prevent the mixture from shooting out of the blender), until smooth. Pour this mixture into a food mill or a strainer set over a bowl and work it through (with a ladle if you're using a strainer), eliminating peels and seeds. Puree the rest of the tomatoes, working in batches, and work them through the food mill or strainer into the bowl with the first batch. Stir the broth into the strained tomato mixture and season to taste with salt and pepper.

PREPARING THE CONDIMENTS Cut the stems off the chilies and cut the chilies lengthwise in half. Open the chilies and brush out the seeds. Soak the chilies for 20 minutes in 2 cups of boiling water to soften them. Drain the chilies and cut them into strips about ⅛ inch wide and 2 inches long (whether you need to cut them crosswise or lengthwise will depend on the size of the chilies) by rolling them up and slicing the rolls—this technique is called cutting in chiffonade.

CUT the tortillas in half and slice them into ¼-inch-wide strips.

HEAT the oil in a sauté pan over high heat until it ripples and sauté the chili strips, stirring them around with a slotted spoon until they sizzle and you smell their fragrance, 30 seconds to a minute. Scoop them out with the spoon and spread them out on paper towels. Add the tortilla chips, about a fourth at a time, to the hot oil and stir them around until they turn crispy, about 30 seconds. Drain them on paper towels.

PEEL and pit the avocados and cut them into ¼-inch dice. Gently toss the dice with lemon juice and season to taste with salt and pepper.

BRING the soup to the simmer and ladle it into heated bowls.

PASS the chilies, tortilla strips, avocados, and other condiments in decorative bowls at the table.

SUGGESTIONS AND VARIATIONS | You can make this soup more substantial—enough for a main course—by including shredded cooked chicken (you can even use the chicken used for making the broth) or other leftover cooked meats along with the other condiments.

TURNIPS

The poor turnip has such a bad public image that many cooks are scared off by the very idea of eating it, much less making a soup out of it. I don't know where turnips got this reputation, because they not only make wonderful soup by themselves; they're also delicious cooked with other vegetables—in minestrone, for instance. They have a great affinity for smoked meats, so if you're using turnips as the main ingredient in a soup, it's a good idea to include bacon, smoked ham, or a smoked ham hock. It is true that if they're too old they're often a little bitter.

Good fresh turnips are heavy; older turnips turn spongy in the middle and feel light. The easiest way to peel turnips is with a paring knife.

Cream or Velouté of Turnip Soup

The secret to this soup is the ham or bacon. The smoky flavors give the soup an extra dimension of flavor. You can also make this a rutabaga soup; replace the turnips with an equivalent weight of rutabagas.

Turnips have fairly thick skins, which should always be removed with a sharp paring knife instead of a vegetable peeler.

MAKES 8 SERVINGS

10 medium-size turnips, 2½ pounds, thinly sliced

4 tablespoons unsalted butter or bacon fat

¼ pound Westphalian, Black Forest, or other smoked ham
     or bacon, cut into 1- by ¼-inch strips

1 medium-size onion, finely chopped

3 cups chicken or vegetable broth or milk

½ cup heavy cream

salt

pepper

freshly grated nutmeg

small croutons (page 594)

TASTE one of the turnip slices. If it tastes bitter, bring 4 quarts water to a boil and slide in the turnip slices. When the water returns to a simmer, drain the turnips in a colander to eliminate the bitterness.

IF you're using ham, melt the butter in a 4-quart pot over medium heat and add the ham strips. Cook the ham for 10 minutes, then remove half of it with a slotted spoon and reserve.

IF you're using bacon, omit the butter and cook the strips in a 4-quart pot over medium heat until they render their fat and start to turn crisp. Remove half the strips with a slotted spoon and reserve.

ADD the turnips and onion to the butter or bacon fat. Stir the mixture over medium heat for 10 minutes, until the onion turns translucent. Add the broth and gently simmer until the turnips are completely soft, about 15 minutes.

PUREE the soup through the fine disk of a food mill, food processor, or blender. Strain the soup through a medium-mesh strainer into a clean pot. Add the cream to the soup, season it with salt, pepper, and nutmeg, and bring it to a simmer.

SPRINKLE each serving of soup with the remaining ham or bacon strips and croutons.

SUGGESTIONS AND VARIATIONS | You can also use this soup as the liquid base for a more complicated soup and add cooked pearl onions, cooked potatoes, or shredded spinach.

WATER CHESTNUTS

I've never thought much of the water chestnuts I've had in Chinese restaurants, probably because they've come out of a can and much of their delightful texture and flavor has been lost. But recently I've become much more adventurous about shopping in Chinese markets, so I've been finding fresh water chestnuts to use in soups. Water chestnuts have a cool crispness and a slightly sweet taste like apples, which makes this soup wonderfully light and refreshing.

Don't bother to make the soup unless you can get your hands on fresh water chestnuts. Check their texture; they should be rock hard. When you get them home, wash them thoroughly—they grow in the mud on the edge of swamps—and peel them with a very sharp paring knife. Toss the peeled water chestnuts with a tablespoon of lemon juice to prevent them from browning.

Water Chestnut and Watercress Soup

MAKES 6 SERVINGS

18 fresh water chestnuts, peeled and quartered
1½ quarts chicken broth
2 bunches of watercress, stems removed
1 tablespoon dark soy sauce or more to taste
½ teaspoon dark sesame oil or more to taste

SIMMER the water chestnuts in the chicken broth for 10 minutes, then add the rest of the ingredients. Add more soy sauce or sesame oil to taste if needed and serve.

SUGGESTIONS AND VARIATIONS | Peeled and sliced jícama has a similar texture and flavor to water chestnuts and makes a delicious substitute.

WALTER chestnuts can be simmered in almost any Asian-style soup for about 10 minutes before serving.

PREVIOUS PAGE Poached Salmon with Fermented Blackbean-Scented Broth, *page 347*

FACING PAGE Chicken Soup with Garlic, Saffron, Basil, and Tomatoes, *page 478*

CLOCKWISE FROM TOP LEFT Vietnamese Spicy Soup with Rice Noodles (Pho Bo), *page 538*; Goulash Soup (Gulyásleves), *page 533*; Chicken Tagine with Apricots, Raisins, and Almonds, *page 495*; Chicken and Tomatillo Soup, *page 482*

CLOCKWISE FROM TOP LEFT Oyster Stew, *page 376*; Medallions of Beef with Caramelized Onions and Red Wine Broth, *page 98*; Rich Chicken Broth with Tarragon, served cold, *page 139*

FACING PAGE Clam or Cockle Soup with Borlotti Beans (Zuppa di Vongole), *page 372*

CLOCKWISE FROM TOP LEFT French Boiled Beef
and Vegetables (Pot-au-Feu), *page 426*;
Chinese Rice Soup (Congee), *page 290*;
Fruit Soup with Spice Broth, *page 584*

PREVIOUS PAGE Bellini Soup, *page 580*

FACING PAGE Southern French Vegetable Soup (Soupe au Pistou), *page 258*

CLOCKWISE FROM TOP LEFT Shrimp Balls in Hot and Sour Thai Broth, *page 132;* Roasted Red Bell Pepper, Garlic, and Onion Soup, *page 210;* Simple Version of Borscht, *page 465;* Miso Soup (with scallions), *page 94*

CLOCKWISE FROM TOP LEFT Light Cream of Lobster Soup, *page 394;* Diced Tomato Soup with Chicken or Beef Broth and Marjoram-Flavored Meatballs, *page 130;* Cream or Velouté of Sweet Pea Soup, *page 206*

FACING PAGE Gazpacho, *page 251*

FACING PAGE Chicken and Tomato Soup with Olives, Capers, and Anchovies, *page 480*

CLOCKWISE FROM TOP LEFT Foie Gras and Truffle Soup, *page 546*; Perfect Summer Tomato Soup with Tarragon Sauce, *page 224*; Mixed Shellfish Pot-au-Feu, *page 383*; Cold Rhubarb and Strawberry Soup (with vanilla ice cream), *page 576*

CLOCKWISE FROM TOP LEFT Thai-Style Hot and Sour Blue Crab Soup, *page 405*; Fennel, Tomato, and White Bean Soup, *page 182*; Shrimp, Mussel, Chorizo, and Spanish Rice Soup in the Style of an Arroce, *page 283*

WATERCRESS

Watercress has such a lovely and distinctive flavor that it's best used by itself with a few mildly flavored vegetables (onions, leeks, or potatoes) in the background. It makes wonderful pureed soups that can be served either hot or cold.

To eliminate bitterness, cook watercress in rapidly boiling water for 2 minutes and then rinse it in cold water before using it to make soup. If you're using watercress in a puree, you don't have to bother removing the little stems that hold together the clusters of leaves; the preliminary cooking will eliminate their bitterness and they'll be strained out.

My favorite watercress soup is made with a leek and potato base (page 190), but you can also prepare it as a classic cream soup or thicken it with egg yolks as for *potage germiny* (page 212), substituting 3 bunches of watercress (blanched) for the sorrel. Puree the blanched watercress with 1 cup of the broth in a blender or food processor. Strain the puree through a medium-mesh strainer and reserve. Meanwhile, cook the egg yolks with the broth until the soup thickens, and just before you're ready to serve the soup add the cream and the puree. This method prevents the watercress from cooking too long and turning gray.

Watercress Soup

This soup is similar to the leek- and potato-based soup, but because it isn't pureed it can be put together in 10 or 15 minutes. I sometimes throw the whole thing together after the guests have arrived. It's delicious and doubly impressive because it's so informal and effortless. You can also use this recipe as a model for last-minute improvised soups—just substitute other vegetables for the watercress, keeping in mind that the cooking times for some vegetables will be much longer.

MAKES 4 SERVINGS

2 large leeks, white part only, washed and finely sliced,
2½ cups
2 medium-size waxy potatoes, peeled, quartered, and finely
chopped
1 quart chicken or vegetable broth, milk, or water
2 bunches of watercress, stems removed
salt
pepper
unsalted butter

SIMMER the leeks and potatoes with the broth until the potatoes are soft and can be crushed easily against the inside of the pot, about 15 minutes.

WHILE the soup is simmering, cook the watercress leaves for 2 minutes in a small pot of boiling water to eliminate bitterness. Pour the water with the leaves into a colander and rinse them with cold water.

STIR the watercress leaves into the soup and season with salt and pepper. Ladle the soup into hot bowls and put a pat of butter on each one.

SUGGESTIONS AND VARIATIONS | This little base of potatoes and leeks can be finished with almost any fresh and tasty vegetable. Spinach is great, and you don't have to precook it as you do the watercress. Chard is also good, but since it can be quite strong, shred it and drop it into boiling water for a minute or two before adding it to the soup.

YOU'LL find that your soups evolve around your shopping habits and what you have left in the refrigerator. I often add a couple of ribs of chopped celery to the base. I also like to use the shredded outer leaves from romaine or butter lettuce that are too tough to go into a salad.

IF you want a richer version—especially if you've used water as the cooking liquid— add ½ cup heavy cream to the soup before serving. Or dollop a spoonful of sour cream, crème fraîche, butter, or herb butter (pages 593–594) onto each bowl.

ZUCCHINI AND SUMMER SQUASH

I never bother making a soup out of just zucchini or summer squash because the flavor isn't assertive enough to give a soup a distinctive character. On the other hand, they're wonderful in combination with other vegetables such as tomatoes, garlic, and beans.

In most recipes zucchini and summer squash are sliced and added to other vegetables along with the liquid. When they're used this way of course they add body to the soup, but they don't add much flavor. Nor do zucchini and summer squash benefit from a gentle cooking in fat the way onions and garlic do—they just turn mushy, especially if they are stirred too much.

The way to bring out the flavor of zucchini and summer squash is to slice them and sauté the slices over high heat in olive oil or something tasty like duck or goose fat. In this way the squash browns slightly and its flavor is concentrated and enhanced. Try sprinkling zucchini or summer squash with chopped thyme, marjoram, or oregano before adding it to your soup. If you cook zucchini or squash this way, don't add too many to the pan at once, or it will steam instead of brown.

Another trick for enhancing the flavor of zucchini or squash is to cut it into ¼-inch-thick slices, coat them with olive oil and chopped fresh thyme, marjoram, or garlic, and grill them over a wood fire before adding them to the soup. They'll give a mixed vegetable soup a gentle and remarkable smoky flavor. (See recipe for grilled vegetable soup, page 274.)

Beans,
LENTILS, DRIED PEAS

BEANS, LENTILS, AND DRIED PEAS—THE LEGUMES—ARE WONDERFULLY VERSATILE AND nutritious. Their gentle flavors make them a perfect backdrop for more assertive tastes such as herbs, spices, olive oil, and smoked meats. They also have the advantage of being available in several forms and are almost ridiculously cheap. You'll find the largest variety in dried form—your best bet is an Indian or Middle Eastern grocer. I like to have three or four bags of different varieties in the cupboard so I can whip up a hearty and flavorful soup on a chilly afternoon.

Interesting fresh beans—like favas and borlotti (cranberry) beans—are also available, especially if you have access to Italian and Latin markets. They take a little time to peel—especially fava beans, which have to be peeled twice—but they cook in just a few minutes and have a delicate flavor and texture missing in dried beans.

Dried Beans

Because dried beans usually take almost 2 hours to cook, cook them separately before adding them to the soup so the other ingredients don't end up overcooked.

Although most recipes recommend soaking dried beans overnight in cold water, I find that 3 hours is usually enough—with the exception of chickpeas, which need overnight soaking. To tell if they've soaked long enough, look at their skins—the outer skin on all the beans should be shriveled. Some cooks simmer beans in the same liquid in which the beans were soaked. I prefer to drain them and cook them in fresh water or, occasionally, directly in the soup.

Beans are marvelous cooked with pork. Cured pork products such as prosciutto and pancetta give beans the best flavor, but fresh pork, even trimmings from a leftover roast, will enhance their flavor. Smoked ham hocks can also be used for cooking beans, but their smoky flavor is very strong. Keep cured pork

TIPS FOR COOKING LEGUMES

- Check carefully for pebbles and debris.
- Soak beans until their skins have shriveled, usually about 3 hours, but occasionally as long as 8. Don't soak beans any longer or they may sprout. Split peas and lentils don't need soaking. Chick-peas should be soaked overnight.
- Drain beans after soaking and cook them in fresh water or directly in the soup.
- Add salt 30 minutes into the cooking.
- Cook beans partially covered in a heavy-bottomed pan to minimize evaporation; the lid should be about an inch off to the side.
- When you're adding whole beans to a vegetable soup, cook the beans separately and add them, along with their cooking liquid, near the end.

products in the refrigerator wrapped in a cloth towel, not in plastic wrap or wax paper, which doesn't allow moisture to evaporate and may cause the meat to turn rancid.

It's also a good idea to cook beans with a bouquet garni and a few garlic cloves. Some recipes suggest adding other vegetables, but if you're going to use the beans in a vegetable soup anyway, the flavor of these extra vegetables will be lost. Don't add tomatoes, wine, or other acidic ingredients to beans until they are completely cooked. The acid contained in these ingredients prevents the beans from softening.

The amount of liquid needed for cooking dried beans depends on the kind of bean, but four times as much water as beans is a good general formula. The important thing is to keep your eye on the beans; if the liquid runs dry, just add more. If you've added too much liquid, just add it to the soup along with the beans. Remember when cooking beans to stir them every 30 minutes, or they may stick to the bottom of the pot and burn.

Precooking Dried Beans for Soup

If beans are the main ingredient in the soup, cook about ⅓ cup raw beans per serving—they'll expand to almost a full cup. If beans are only one of many ingredients, figure half as much per serving.

MAKES ABOUT 5 CUPS

2 cups dried beans such as cannellini, borlotti, navy, flageolets, etc.

¼ pound pancetta, prosciutto, or unsmoked raw-cured country ham such as Smithfield*

3 garlic cloves, peeled

1 small bundle of fresh herbs such as thyme, marjoram, or rosemary

¼ cup olive oil

1 tablespoon salt

SOAK the beans in enough cold water to cover them by several inches (this is because they expand and soak up the water) in a large bowl for 3 to 8 hours, until their skins are well wrinkled. Drain the beans, put them in a pot with enough water or other liquid to cover by about an inch.

BRING the beans to a simmer and use a ladle to skim off any froth that floats to the surface. Cover the pot and turn the heat down to keep the liquid at a very slow sim-

---

*If you're using the beans in a soup that already calls for pork products such as prosciutto or pancetta, you can leave out the ham when cooking the beans.

mer. After 30 minutes, add the salt* and continue cooking until the beans are thoroughly softened, usually 1½ hours (old beans may take considerably longer, up to 3 hours). Depending on the beans, you may need to add water from time to time to keep them from drying out. The best way to see if they're done is to just pull one out with a spoon and taste it. It should be very soft and not at all mealy.

WHEN the beans are done, drain them (save any liquid to add to the soup) and let them cool. Pull out the pieces of pork and the herbs.

Fresh Beans

Fresh beans cook fairly quickly, so they can be added raw to a vegetable soup 10 to 15 minutes before serving. If fresh beans are one of the main ingredients in the soup, use about ¾ cup per serving. If they are one ingredient among many, figure ⅓ cup per serving.

It takes about ¾ pound fresh beans (in the shell) to yield 1 cup shucked beans. Fava beans are an exception because they have to be peeled twice. Figure about a pound of fava beans in the shell for 1 cup shucked beans.

Bean and Pasta Soup

MINESTRA DI FAGIOLI

MAKES 6 SERVINGS

6 tablespoons olive oil

¼ pound pancetta or prosciutto trimmings, preferably from
a Parma ham, cut into ¼-inch cubes

2 medium-size onions, chopped

1 celery rib, chopped

4 garlic cloves, chopped

4 medium-size tomatoes, peeled, seeded, and chopped, about
2 cups, or 2 cups drained and seeded canned tomatoes

5 cups chicken or vegetable broth

about 2 cups cannellini or navy beans, soaked and cooked (see
pages 235 and 236 for information about cooking beans)

---

*Many cooks insist that salt should not be added until the beans are completely cooked or they will never soften. However, if you don't add salt until the very end, the beans will taste underseasoned as you bite into them. Adding the salt 30 minutes into the cooking prevents both problems.

¾ cup macaroni or little shells

½ cup fresh basil leaves, tightly packed

salt

pepper

HEAT half the olive oil in a 4-quart pot over medium heat and add the pancetta, onions, celery, and garlic. Stir gently for about 15 minutes, until the pancetta releases its fat and the vegetables begin to color slightly.

ADD the tomatoes and broth and simmer for about 10 minutes.

WORK the cooked beans through the fine disk of a food mill or puree them in a blender or food processor and add them to the soup. You'll need a cup of the bean cooking liquid or the broth from the soup to get them to move around in a blender or food processor. Add this puree to the rest of the soup. Add the macaroni or shells to the soup and simmer for 5 to 10 minutes, until the pasta is soft.

SPRINKLE the basil leaves with two tablespoons of the remaining olive oil and chop them so finely that you end up with a paste. In a bowl, combine the paste with the remaining olive oil.

CHECK the consistency of the soup. If it is too thick, thin it with some broth or water. Season it with salt and pepper. Stir the basil paste into the soup just before ladling the soup into hot bowls.

SUGGESTIONS AND VARIATIONS | This is one of those simple vegetable soups that can feature virtually any vegetable. I especially like to add chard or spinach, blanched and coarsely shredded, to the soup a minute or two before serving.

WHAT makes this soup distinctive is the cooked bean puree, which gives body and a satisfying creamy consistency. Try experimenting with fresh beans such as fava, lima, or borlotti beans.

White Bean and Vegetable Soup

This is one of my favorite bean soups because it's full of flavor and yet thin enough so that I can serve it hot in winter and cold in the summer. It's also a convenient catchall for vegetables I have around and feel like throwing in—the beans seem to hold everything together. Don't worry if you don't have all the vegetables listed in the ingredients; just figure on a total of 2 cups mixed chopped vegetables.

This soup is pureed, but if you like, just leave the vegetables whole in the soup.

MAKES 8 SERVINGS

¼ pound bacon, pancetta, or prosciutto trimmings, cut into
cubes

3 tablespoons olive oil (if you're using pancetta or
prosciutto)

1 medium-size onion, coarsely chopped

1 carrot, coarsely chopped

4 garlic cloves, peeled

1 turnip, peeled and chopped

1 celery rib, sliced

2 cups dried white beans such as cannellini, borlotti, or Great
Northern, soaked and cooked, 5 cups (see pages 235 and
236 for information about cooking beans), or 4 cups
fresh beans such as cranberry, fava (peeled twice), or lima

1 bouquet garni: 1 bunch of parsley, 1 bay leaf, and 3 fresh
thyme sprigs

6 cups chicken or vegetable broth

½ cup heavy cream

salt

pepper

chervil or basil butter (optional; page 594 or 593)

small croutons (page 594)

COOK the cubes of bacon in a 4-quart pot over medium heat until they render their fat and just begin to turn crisp. If you're using pancetta or prosciutto, cook it in the olive oil for 10 minutes.

ADD the vegetables and beans to the pot. Stir every few minutes until they soften, about 15 minutes.

ADD the bouquet garni and broth and simmer until the vegetables are very soft, about 20 minutes more.

REMOVE the bouquet garni and puree the soup in a blender, food processor, or through the fine disk of a food mill. Strain it through a medium-mesh strainer into a clean pot.

ADD the heavy cream and bring the soup back to a simmer. Season with salt and pepper and place a dollop of the herb butter, if you're using it, in the center of each bowl. Sprinkle with the croutons and serve.

SUGGESTIONS AND VARIATIONS | This soup has a lovely delicate flavor that I like to contrast with thick slices of garlic bread either placed in the bowls before the soup is poured in or passed in a basket at the table.

Black Bean Soup

Like most beans, black beans are best when cooked with something smoked. This recipe uses both bacon and a ham bone or ham hocks, as well as sherry to give it a rich, smoky flavor.

Give yourself a lot of time to cook this soup; black beans take longer to cook than most—at least 3 hours but often as long as 5.

Some people like black bean soup to be almost solid, with the consistency of chili, while others like a thinner, more souplike puree. This depends on how much broth or water you add at the end—it's completely up to you.

The soup is great served with fresh corn bread.

MAKES 8 SERVINGS

2 cups dried black turtle beans, soaked
1 quart beef broth or water, or more as needed
1 bouquet garni
1 ham bone or 2 ham hocks
1 tablespoon salt
½ pound bacon, preferably slab
1 large onion, chopped
2 garlic cloves, chopped
4 jalapeño chilies, seeded and finely chopped (optional but
    recommended)
1 cup dry sherry
2 tablespoons finely chopped cilantro leaves
4 tablespoons unsalted butter (optional)
salt
pepper
Tabasco sauce
sour cream

DRAIN the beans and put them in a 4-quart pot with the broth, the bouquet garni, and the ham bone. Cover the pot and simmer very slowly for 30 minutes. Add the salt, then simmer for 1½ to 3½ hours more, until the beans are soft. If the broth starts to run dry, add more broth or water during cooking to keep the beans covered.

WHILE the beans are cooking, slice the bacon into ¼-inch thick slices—remove the rind if you're using slab bacon—and slice each of these into 1- by ¼-inch strips (called *lardons*). Cook the bacon strips in a 4-quart pot over medium heat until they just start to turn crisp. Remove them with a slotted spoon and reserve.

ADD the onion, garlic, and jalapeños to the bacon fat and cook until the vegetables soften and smell fragrant, about 10 minutes.

WHEN the beans are finished cooking, take out the ham bone or hocks, trim and discard any rind, pull the meat away from the bones, and cut it into ½-inch cubes. Remove and discard the bouquet garni.

ADD the cooked beans and their cooking liquid, the ham, and the sherry to the vegetables in the pot.

BRING the soup to a slow simmer and simmer for about 5 minutes to cook the alcohol out of the sherry. Whisk in the cilantro and butter, if desired, just before serving. Season the soup with salt and pepper. Sprinkle the cooked bacon strips over each bowl of soup before serving. Leave a bottle of Tabasco on the table to accommodate guests who like their black bean soup hot and spicy and pass a bowl of sour cream.

SUGGESTIONS AND VARIATIONS | If the soup comes out thin, beat it for a minute or two with a whisk to break up some of the beans, which will thicken the soup. Or you may want to puree part of the beans in a blender or food processor and then add them to the rest of the soup, or you can puree all and convert this soup into a smooth puree.

Indian-Style Black Bean Soup

This soup is modeled after a luxurious and traditional Indian *dal* I read about in Julie Sahni's book *Classic Indian Cooking*. Whereas the original recipe is thick and chililike, this version can be served as a soup with the rich and delicate spice flavors of the original still coming through.

To make this soup, you'll need tiny beans called *black gram beans*, which you can find in fancy food stores or in Indian markets, where they're called *sabut urad dal* or *kali dal*. Black gram beans take 3 to 5 hours to cook, so it pays to make a lot of this soup at once and freeze it or serve it over the next few days. The genius of this soup is the spice mixture—called *tadka*—which gives it an incomparable suavity and depth of flavor. This soup is quite rich. Unlike many bean soups, this recipe includes the soaking liquid from the beans.

MAKES 8 SERVINGS

the soup:

1 cup black gram beans

7 cups water

2 medium-size onions, finely chopped

1 garlic clove, finely chopped

a 1-inch slice of fresh ginger, peeled and finely chopped

4 medium-size tomatoes, peeled, seeded, and chopped, or
    2 cups drained and seeded canned tomatoes, chopped

I tablespoon salt

I teaspoon ground cardamom

2 tablespoons ground coriander

the tadka:

½ cup *ghee* (page 592)

2 medium-size onions, finely chopped

2 teaspoons ground cumin

½ to I cup heavy cream

I½ cups yogurt

¼ cup finely chopped cilantro leaves

IN ADVANCE In a 4-quart pot, soak the beans in the water for 2 hours. Add the onions, garlic, and ginger and bring to a boil over medium heat. Cover the pot and turn down the heat so the beans cook at the slowest possible simmer. Check every hour over the next 3 to 5 hours to prevent them from sticking to the bottom of the pot and to replenish the water if needed.

AFTER the beans have cooked for I hour, add the tomatoes, salt, cardamom, and coriander. Cook for 2 to 4 hours more, until the beans are completely tender. Be sure to taste one—if the beans are slightly undercooked, they'll be soft but mealy on the inside.

WORK the soup through a food mill, first with the coarse disk and then the fine, or puree in a blender or food processor and then strain through a medium-mesh strainer. Thin the soup with a little water if necessary.

AT THE LAST MINUTE Combine the *ghee* with the onions and cumin in a 2-quart saucepan. Heat the mixture over medium heat, stirring every minute or two, for about 10 minutes—the onions should sizzle, but if they start to brown, turn down the heat.

SLOWLY whisk the *tadka* into the hot soup. (If you pour too fast, the soup won't absorb the *ghee* and will look and taste greasy.) When all the *ghee* is incorporated into the soup, stir in the rest of the ingredients. Adjust the salt.

SUGGESTIONS AND VARIATIONS | Many recipes for *dal* and Indian-style soups call for red pepper. If you want a spicier version, stir in cayenne pepper to taste about I5 minutes before adding the *tadka*.

IN northern India, *dal* is usually served with a flat bread called *chapati*; in southern India, it is usually served with rice. The closest thing I've found to *chapati* in the United States—outside Indian restaurants—is whole wheat pita bread, which can be heated in the oven and served in a stack on the table. This soup is too thin to serve over rice, but you can serve rice (preferably basmati) in a bowl at the table and people can add it *to* the soup. You could of course serve this soup with French bread, but I always find that mixing up cultures detracts somehow. Best of all, serve this soup as the first course of an Indian meal.

IF you want to give the soup a rounder, fuller flavor, stir in ½ can of coconut milk. If you want to make it less rich, eliminate the cream and add an extra cup of yogurt.

Lentil Soup

Lentil soup is easier to make than most bean soups because you don't have to soak the lentils beforehand and lentils cook very quickly—in 45 minutes to an hour or even less.

Even though you can make a lentil soup with just a little onion and some broth, I always like to include something smoky such as bacon or ham. If I have it, I also like to add confit of duck. Although I prefer pureed lentil soup, it's also fine with the lentils left whole.

The most commonly available lentils are the regular brown lentils sold in plastic bags in supermarkets. These are perfectly good, but the next time you get to a fancy food store, buy a bag of tiny *de puy* lentils from France or the bright orange Indian or Egyptian lentils. Different lentils take different cooking times, so start checking them after 20 minutes— take a nibble; they should be completely soft.

Although most packaged lentils are free of debris, it's a good idea to pour them out on a baking sheet and check them for pebbles. Remember when cooking lentil soup to stir it every once in awhile to prevent sticking and scalding.

MAKES 6 SERVINGS

3 ¼-inch-thick slices of bacon, sliced into ¼- by 1-inch strips, or a ¼-inch-thick slice of prosciutto or raw-cured country ham, cut into ¼-inch dice, or confit from 3 duck legs pulled into coarse shreds

2 tablespoons unsalted butter if you're using prosciutto or ham

2 tablespoons duck fat if you're using confit

1 medium-size onion, finely sliced

1 carrot, finely sliced

1 celery rib, finely sliced

2 cups lentils, checked for pebbles, rinsed

1 bouquet garni

2 quarts chicken, turkey, pork, or duck broth

4 tablespoons unsalted butter

COOK the meat in a 4-quart pot over medium heat. If you're using bacon, cook the strips until they just start to turn crisp; if you're using prosciutto, cook it in 2 table-spoons butter because it doesn't have much fat of its own; if you're using confit, cook the shreds in 2 tablespoons duck fat. Take the meat out with a slotted spoon, reserve, and leave the fat in the pot.

ADD the onion, carrot, and celery to the pot and cook over medium heat until the vegetables brown slightly, about 15 minutes.

ADD the lentils, bouquet garni, and broth. Simmer until the lentils are tender, 45 minutes to an hour. Discard the bouquet garni and puree the soup through the fine disk of a food mill, blender, or food processor. Strain it through a fine-mesh sieve if you want a finer consistency or add broth or water if you want it thinner.

SWIRL the 4 tablespoons butter into the hot soup and add the reserved meat.

SUGGESTIONS AND VARIATIONS | In her book *The Foods and Wines of Spain*, Pene-lope Casas gives a recipe similar to this one that contains potatoes and a little garlic and is garnished with Spanish blood sausages, *morcilla*. If you can't find blood sausages, other sausages such as French *saucisse à l'ail* or kielbasa could be used to turn this soup into a winter meal.

Indian-Style Lentil Soups

The Indians are especially adept with lentils which they convert into *dal* and seem to eat constantly in little bowls with rice. The *dal* I remember finding in the little street stalls in India was usually thick, while the *dal* served in Indian restaurants in the United States often has the texture of thin soup.

In addition to regular brown lentils, the Indians use yellow lentils (*toovar dal/Cajanus cajan*), which have a flavor reminiscent of split peas, or pink lentils (*masoor dal/Lens culi-naris*), which have a subtle, almost meaty taste. Either of these can be used for making Indian-style lentil soups. They can be cooked as regular brown lentils but take only about half the time. I also like to use the red Egyptian lentils.

While European cooks are likely to finish their soups with a dollop of butter or a drizzle of olive oil, the Indians prepare a spice-flavored butter or oil called a *tadka*, stirred into the soup just before serving.

Dal is best served with rice—preferably Indian basmati rice.

Red Lentil Soup with Coconut Milk and Moghul Garam Masala

This soup captures the magic of Indian spices as well as any Indian dish I know. The trick is the mixture of spices called Moghul *garam masala*, which, unlike the more common "regular" garam masala, contains saffron and is unavailable commercially; you have to combine the spices yourself. This is no big deal especially if you use ground spices as I do. I keep my ground spices in the freezer so they stay fresh.

MAKES 8 SERVINGS

the soup:

2 medium-size onions, finely chopped

3 garlic cloves, finely chopped

1 teaspoon fresh or dried thyme leaves

½ teaspoon ground turmeric

2 tablespoons unsalted butter

2 cups pink, yellow, or red Egyptian lentils, checked for pebbles and rinsed

6 cups water or vegetable broth

¼ teaspoon saffron threads, soaked in 2 tablespoons warm water for 15 minutes (optional but recommended)

1¾ cups coconut milk or 1½ cups yogurt

salt

the tadka:

¼ cup *ghee* (page 592)

¾ teaspoon ground cardamom

¼ teaspoon ground cinnamon

¼ teaspoon ground cloves

¼ teaspoon freshly ground pepper

⅛ teaspoon freshly grated nutmeg

IN a 4-quart pot over medium heat, cook the onions, garlic, thyme, and turmeric in the butter until the onions soften and turn translucent, about 10 minutes.

ADD the lentils and water and bring to a boil. Cover the pot, turn the heat down low enough to keep the liquid at a slow simmer, and cook until the lentils are very soft, about 30 minutes.

WORK the soup through a fine- or medium-mesh strainer with a ladle and stir in the saffron and its soaking liquid. (The lentils will be so soft that pureeing in a blender or food processor isn't necessary.)

TO make the *tadka*, melt the *ghee* in a 1-quart saucepan and stir in the spices. Continue to stir the *tadka* over medium heat until you can smell the ingredients. Whisk the *tadka* into the soup.

WHISK the coconut milk or yogurt into the hot soup just before serving and bring the soup back to a simmer. Coconut milk gives the soup a wonderful delicate sweetness, but it also makes the soup quite rich. Yogurt makes the soup lighter and tangier. The choice is yours.

SUGGESTIONS AND VARIATIONS | Play around with the *tadka* by adding different spices and flavorings such as chopped fresh or ground ginger, ground cumin, ground coriander, fenugreek, chopped onions, garlic, or even good-quality commercial curry powder such as *garam masala.*

INDIAN cooks sometimes use this lentil soup or one of its variations as a basis for vegetarian soups and stews. Just add different cut-up vegetables (green vegetables should be cooked separately in boiling water) and cook them in the soup for 10 to 15 minutes.

IN his book *Sephardic Cooking,* Copeland Marks describes an Egyptian recipe for red lentil soup similar to the version given here, except that the Egyptian version contains a small potato to give it texture. And instead of Moghul *garam masala,* the Egyptian version is flavored with ground cumin, turmeric, and chopped cilantro.

IN *Please to the Table,* Anya von Bremzen and John Welchman describe an Armenian lentil soup—*vospapur*—in which red lentils are simmered with vegetables, tomatoes, and dried apricots. Another *vospapur* is prepared by simmering brown lentils with spinach and tomatoes.

Split Pea Soup

I never liked split pea soup until I started experimenting with lighter recipes—not the por-ridgelike interpretations I remember from my childhood. This version is quite lovely even though I cheat a bit by adding some frozen peas to give it a bright color and a fresher taste.

Before you use split peas, spill them out on a sheet pan and check them for pebbles. Then rinse them in a large strainer and let them drain.

MAKES 8 SERVINGS

½ pound slab bacon or pancetta (unrolled), rind removed,
    cut into 1- by ¼-inch strips
¼ cup olive oil if you're using pancetta
2 large onions, chopped
2 cups green split peas
2 quarts chicken broth or water
1 clove
1 bouquet garni
2 10-ounce packages frozen peas
1 cup heavy cream
salt
pepper
small croutons (page 594)

COOK the bacon in a 4-quart pot over medium heat until it just begins to turn crisp, about 10 minutes. If you're using pancetta, cook it in olive oil, because it doesn't provide enough fat of its own. Remove the strips with a slotted spoon and reserve.

COOK the onions in the fat left in the pot until they soften and turn translucent, about 15 minutes. Add the split peas, broth, clove, and bouquet garni, cover the pot, and simmer for about 1 hour, until the split peas are completely soft.

ADD the frozen peas and heavy cream and bring the soup to a simmer. Simmer for 5 minutes and puree, a bit at a time, in a blender or food processor. Strain the puree through a medium-mesh strainer. If you want to thin the soup, strain it through a fine-mesh strainer or simply thin it with extra broth or water.

SEASON with salt and pepper, ladle into individual bowls, and garnish with the reserved bacon or pancetta and, if you like, croutons sizzled in butter.

SUGGESTIONS AND VARIATIONS | Yellow split peas can also be used to make split pea soup, but if you use these you won't be able to freshen the soup with the frozen peas, or the colors will clash and the soup will come out looking a nasty army green.

Quebec Split Pea Soup

This Quebec version of split-pea soup differs from our more familiar "American" soup in that yellow split peas are used, the peas aren't pureed, and the vegetables used to give the soup additional flavor are left whole and chunky right in the soup. Most recipes call for salt pork, but because I've never been satisfied with the salt pork I find in the United States, I substitute ham hocks, simmered in the broth until they fall apart, the meat taken off the bone and added to the soup at the end. Traditional recipes call for adding a salted herb mixture (a 19-century preserving technique somewhat the equivalent of our freezing pesto), but I use fresh herbs, since they're now easy to find year-round (in my garden in summer; at the supermarket in winter). If you want to make your own salted herbs, a combination that develops its own distinctive flavor, see box on page 249.

MAKES 10 FIRST-COURSE SERVINGS

1 pound (2½ cups) yellow split peas

3 8-ounce smoked ham hocks or 1½ pounds total if the
    ham hocks are larger

8 cups chicken broth (don't use canned broth because its
    saltiness combined with that of the ham hocks will
    make the soup too salty)

2 tablespoons butter (if you're using ham hocks)

2 medium-size onions, peeled, finely chopped or 2 large
    leeks, halved, washed, and finely sliced

3 medium-size carrots, peeled and cut into ¼-inch dice

2 celery ribs, cut into ¼-inch dice

4 garlic cloves, chopped

4 tablespoons chopped fresh marjoram or 2 teaspoons
    chopped fresh thyme or ½ teaspoon dried thyme or
    4 tablespoons salted herbs (see box, page 249)

salt

pepper

RINSE the peas in a colander and drain.

PUT the ham hocks in a pot with enough water to cover and bring to a simmer over high heat. Drain in a colander and rinse the ham hocks with cold water. (This is to eliminate some of their salt.) Combine the ham hocks with the chicken broth and peas and simmer gently for 2 hours, in a pot with the cover ajar, adding water from time to time to make up for evaporation of the broth. Take the ham hocks out of the broth, peel away the meat, and chop it coarsely.

Put the meat in the soup and discard any bones and sinew.

COOK the vegetables in a heavy-bottomed pot in butter, over medium heat, until the onions turn translucent and all the vegetables have completely softened, about 15 minutes. Stir the vegetables into the soup.

STIR the herbs into the soup and season to taste with salt and pepper. Thin the soup, if necessary, with more broth or water.

SALTED HERBS

Even though most of us are able to find fresh herbs year-round, salted herbs, like many preserved foods, develop a distinctive flavor of their own. If you want to try it, combine 1/4 cup each of finely chopped scallions (including the green), chives, parsley, thyme, and 1/4 cup of coarse salt in a mixing bowl. Stir the mixture thoroughly and put it in a jar. Refrigerate for 2 weeks or up to 2 months before using.

SUGGESTIONS AND VARIATIONS | You can give the soup a creamy consistency by pureeing some of the beans and combining them with the rest of the soup. This soup can also be made with pancetta instead of the ham hocks. If you want to use pancetta, cut 1/2 pound of 1/4-inch-thick slices into 1/4-inch cubes. Cook the beans in the broth just as described above, but without the ham hocks. Cook the pancetta cubes with the vegetables and stir the mixture into the soup near the end of cooking. Simmer the soup gently for 15 minutes to infuse the flavor of the pancetta.

Creamed Puree of Fresh Fava Beans

Even though fresh fava beans have a more delicate flavor and give soups a smoother texture than most beans, they've never been very popular in the United States. In the years I've been buying fava beans at a fancy grocer in Manhattan, I've met only one other person filling up her plastic bag at the same time—an elderly Italian lady. We looked at each other in amazement and compared notes. Hers were going into a salad; mine were going into this soup.

No doubt one reason for the fava bean's unpopularity is that it has to be peeled twice: once to get the big beans out of their lovely padded shells and then again, individually. I recommend scheduling the bean peeling for sitting around with friends (who can join in).

Fresh fava beans are usually in season starting in April and into the late fall. If you can't find fresh fava beans, try substituting fresh borlotti beans or fresh or frozen lima beans. Don't use dried fava beans, which have too strong a flavor.

Although this soup is pureed, if you like seeing whole vegetables in your soup, use the same ingredients and just skip the straining.

MAKES 4 SERVINGS

I small onion, finely chopped

I small waxy potato, peeled and finely chopped

3 cups chicken or vegetable broth

2 pounds fresh fava beans, shelled and peeled, 2 cups; or
1¼ pounds shucked borlotti beans, 2 cups; or 2 cups
shucked lima beans

½ cup heavy cream

salt

pepper

small croutons (page 594)

COMBINE the onion, potato, and broth in a 4-quart pot. Bring to a slow simmer and cover the pot. Keep at a very slow simmer until the potatoes have softened and can be crushed easily against the side of the pot with a spoon, about 15 minutes. Add the fava beans and simmer gently for about eight minutes more.

STRAIN the soup through a food mill with the finest disk or puree in a blender or food processor.

ADD the cream, bring the soup back to a simmer, and strain it through a medium-mesh strainer. If you want it even smoother, strain it again through a fine-mesh strainer. Season with salt and pepper. Serve with croutons.

SUGGESTIONS AND VARIATIONS | French cooks like to cook fava beans with a sprig or two of winter savory. If you have some fresh savory, try adding 2 sprigs to the soup along with the potatoes and onions.

WHISK 3 tablespoons mint or chervil butter (page 593 or 594) into the soup just before serving or whip it and pass it at the table so guests can help themselves.

Mixed
VEGETABLE SOUPS

Gazpacho

I always think of gazpacho as a wonderful vegetable salad with all the ingredients so finely chopped that you can drink it instead of eating it. It's also one of those soups that people never completely agree on; some insist on including bread, others vinegar, still others yogurt, or cream. I don't think any of this is terribly important; I just throw in ingredients, tasting as I go along, guided by my own whims and what's sitting in the refrigerator.

But with due respect to spontaneity, a few guidelines are helpful. I'm sorry to report that gazpacho is always better when the ingredients are chopped by hand. If you really must use a food processor, at least process the ingredients separately so they have slightly different sizes and textures. The easiest and least appealing method for making gazpacho is just to put everything in the blender. The action of the blender turns the tomatoes an unappetizing shade of pink, and the other vegetables are reduced to a puree. You may wish you'd just made a Bloody Mary instead.

Most gazpacho in the United States is served with all the ingredients already mixed into the soup, but you can also serve it Spanish style with some of the chopped ingredients—onions, cucumbers, peppers—held back and passed at the table for guests to help themselves.

If you want to make gazpacho in advance, add all the ingredients except the ice cubes. Gazpacho will keep in the refrigerator for several days.

MAKES 8 SERVINGS

8 large or 12 medium-size tomatoes, peeled, seeded, and chopped

3 garlic cloves, peeled

2 large onions, preferably Bermuda, Maui, or Vidalia, finely chopped

2 regular or 1 hothouse cucumber, peeled, seeded, and finely chopped

2 bell peppers, preferably yellow or green, seeded and finely chopped

2 jalapeño chilies, seeded and very finely chopped

juice of 3 lemons or limes or 3 tablespoons sherry vinegar

cayenne pepper (optional)

salt

pepper

1 cup small ice cubes

small croutons (page 594)

Tabasco sauce

CRUSH the garlic to a paste in a mortar and pestle or by chopping it and crushing it on a cutting board with the side of a chef's knife. Stir the garlic paste into the chopped tomatoes in a mixing bowl.

PREPARE the remaining vegetables and stir them into the tomato mixture or reserve some of the vegetables to pass at the table. Stir in the lemon juice, a pinch of cayenne if you want the soup hotter, season with salt and pepper, and add the ice cubes. If the soup is too thick, thin it with a little water.

LADLE the finished soup into bowls and sprinkle a few croutons on each serving. I like to leave the Tabasco bottle on the table for people who want extra spice.

SUGGESTIONS AND VARIATIONS | If you make gazpacho regularly, you'll probably start altering the proportions to suit your own taste. Some people like their gazpacho burning hot and full of garlic, while others prefer tamer versions.

FRESH herbs are also good for giving the soup an individual character. Chopped fresh marjoram is both common and delicious. Even though it's more Mexican than Spanish, I often add freshly chopped cilantro. Another Mexican touch is to add some cooked, pureed, and strained tomatillos to the tomato base and to pass a bowl of sour cream at the table.

MANY cooks like to add extra virgin olive oil—about a tablespoon per bowl—for an extra note of flavor before serving. You can also stir in 2 cups yogurt or heavy cream for a richer, almost wintry variation. Gazpacho can be converted into a wonderful saladlike soup by tossing it with large cubes of toasted French bread that have been brushed lightly with olive oil (see summer basil and tomato bread soup, page 554).

A light and elegant version combines the gazpacho with an equal part of cold beef or chicken consommé (page 74 or 72).

Gazpacho Scented with Smoked Fish

One exciting way to flavor gazpacho is to stir small strips of carefully sliced smoked fish into the soup several hours before serving. The smoky marine flavors of the fish are irresistible—especially when the soup contains enough hot peppers to have a little bite. Almost any smoked fish will do, but sable is the least expensive and has an excellent flavor.

MAKES 6 SERVINGS

1 quart gazpacho (preceding recipe)

6 ounces smoked fish such as sable, sturgeon, or salmon

SLICE—or have the purveyor slice—the smoked fish into thin sheets. Cut the sheets into strips about 1 inch long and ⅛ inch wide. Save about a quarter of the strips for decoration and add the rest to the gazpacho. Let the gazpacho steep for 3 to 4 hours. Adjust the seasoning and serve in chilled bowls. Arrange the decorative strips in the center of each bowl.

White Gazpacho from Málaga with Almonds and Grapes

Although most gazpacho lovers think first of the iced tomato version, tomatoes weren't popular in Europe until the 19th century. Gazpacho was originally a Moorish invention made with bread, oil, and nuts.

This is an easy recipe to prepare, except perhaps for peeling 48 grapes, which isn't essential anyway. But if you're a perfectionist, plan the grape peeling for a long phone conversation or a half interesting TV show. Unfortunately I don't know any little tricks to make the peeling easier (plunging the grapes into boiling water doesn't work).

Originally the ingredients were ground in a mortar and pestle, but this is a long job and the results are as good with a food processor, provided you work in the olive oil by hand. For some mysterious reason, extra virgin olive oil turns bitter when beaten too hard.

MAKES 4 SERVINGS

¾ cup blanched almonds, lightly toasted in the oven
(10 to 15 minutes at 350°F)

3 garlic cloves, peeled

5 slices of country French bread, crusts removed, lightly toasted

1 quart cold vegetable or chicken broth or water

2 tablespoons extra virgin olive oil

¼ cup good white wine vinegar

salt

cayenne pepper (optional)

48 seedless grapes, peeled (optional) and cut in half

small croutons sautéed in olive oil (page 595)

COMBINE the almonds and garlic in the bowl of a food processor or in a mortar. Soak the bread in the broth. If you're using a mortar and pestle, grind the almonds and garlic to a paste and then add the bread. Continue working the mixture to a smooth paste. If you're using a food processor, combine the bread with the almonds and garlic and process the mixture for about a minute until smooth.

TRANSFER the mixture to a mixing bowl. Work in the olive oil with a wooden spoon and then stir in the remaining broth and the vinegar.

STRAIN the soup through a food mill with a medium disk or through a medium-mesh strainer. If you're using a strainer, push firmly on the solids in the strainer with a ladle to extract as much liquid as possible.

SEASON the soup with salt and, if you like, a little cayenne. Chill the soup in the refrigerator for an hour or two or overnight. Sprinkle each bowl with the peeled grapes (24 halves per person) and the croutons.

White Gazpacho with Peppers and Cucumbers

This tangy tomatoless gazpacho is a delight on a hot afternoon. It is extremely light in both texture and richness.

This recipe contains raw eggs; if you're unsure of your eggs, see the note at the end of the recipe.

MAKES 8 SERVINGS

2 red bell peppers, roasted and peeled (page 207)

3 garlic cloves, peeled

2 regular or 1 hothouse cucumber, peeled and cut into 1-inch sections

2 eggs

5 slices of country French bread, crusts removed, lightly toasted

1 quart vegetable or chicken broth or water

¼ cup extra virgin olive oil

¼ cup good white wine vinegar

salt

cayenne pepper or Tabasco sauce

small croutons sautéed in olive oil (page 595)

FINELY chop the pepper for the soup and cut the pepper for the garnish into ¼-inch dice. Combine the garlic, finely chopped pepper, cucumbers, and eggs in a blender. Blend for about 1 minute, until the mixture is smooth.

SOAK the bread in 2 cups of the broth and add it to the blender. Process the mixture for 1 minute more, until smooth.

TRANSFER the mixture to a mixing bowl and gradually stir in the olive oil with a wooden spoon as though making a mayonnaise. Stir in the vinegar.

STRAIN the mixture through a food mill with a medium disk or through a medium-mesh strainer. Season with salt and cayenne or Tabasco.

CHILL the soup for a couple of hours or overnight. Serve it in chilled bowls and sprinkle with small croutons and cubes of roasted red pepper.

Note: If you don't want to use raw eggs, cook the eggs in simmering water for 5 minutes. Let them cool and scoop them out of their shells. Puree the soft-cooked eggs in the blender with the other ingredients. Combine this mixture with the vegetables and bread in the blender.

Puree of Mixed Vegetables

This is just one example of a vegetable soup that you can probably make with vegetables you already have in the refrigerator. Feel free to leave out ingredients here and there and to substitute others. If you don't have leeks, use onions; if you have carrots, chop one or two and add them; if you have some frozen peas, add them near the end of cooking.

In this version the vegetables are cooked in fat, butter, or oil before water or broth is added; you can also add the chopped vegetables directly to the simmering water or broth.

MAKES 8 SERVINGS

¼ cup olive oil, unsalted butter, or rendered fat such as
    bacon, duck, or goose
2 leeks, washed and finely sliced, white and 1 inch of green
2 celery ribs or 1 small celery root—1 pound before
    trimming; 10 ounces after trimming—chopped
2 medium-size waxy potatoes, peeled and thinly sliced
2 quarts broth or water
1 cup tightly packed chopped spinach leaves or 1 10-ounce
    package frozen
1 tightly packed cup chopped sorrel leaves (optional)
¼ cup chopped parsley leaves
1 large handful of green beans, chopped
¾ cup heavy cream
salt
pepper
olive oil or unsalted butter

IMPROVISED VEGETABLE SOUPS

One of my favorite ways to clean out the refrigerator and at the sametime save myself a trip to the store is to make a mixed vegetable soup. Almost any combination of vegetables simmered in water or broth and pureed or left whole will make a spontaneous and satisfying soup.

One easy way to turn a mixed vegetable soup into something more substantial is to add raw or cooked pasta or rice to the soup just long enough before serving to ensure they cook. Count about 20 minutes for raw rice, 8 to 10 minutes for dried pasta, and 2 minutes for fresh pasta or cooked rice.

It's up to you to decide whether to leave whole chopped vegetables in the soup or to puree the whole thing in a blender or food processor. I sometimes leave the vegetables in pieces and thicken the soup with leftover mashed potatoes or pureed roast garlic. The Italians, who call their purees *passati*, usually sprinkle the finished soups with Parmesan cheese, maybe a little olive oil, and small croutons. The French are more likely to put a dollop of plain or flavored butter on each soup.

HEAT the fat in a 4-quart pot over medium heat. Add the leeks, celery, and the potatoes. Stir the vegetables for about 10 minutes, until the leeks and celery soften. Don't let any of the vegetables brown.

ADD the broth and simmer until the potatoes are soft, about 10 minutes more. Add the spinach, sorrel, parsley, and beans. Simmer for 10 minutes more to cook the green vegetables.

THE soup is ready, unless you want to puree it. Puree the soup in a blender or food processor, strain it through a food mill with a medium disk, and then again through a medium-mesh sieve or food mill with a fine disk. Stir in the cream and season to taste with salt and pepper. Thin the soup if necessary with a little extra broth, water, milk, or cream. If you want a smoother texture, strain it through a fine-mesh sieve.

SERVE the soup with a drizzle of olive oil or a pat of butter on each bowl.

SUGGESTIONS AND VARIATIONS | You can pass grated Parmesan at the table or finish the soup with a spoonful of herb butter (pages 593–594). Top each serving with croutons. This soup also can be served with the vegetables left chunky. Stir in the heavy cream as a finish, if desired.

Mulligatawny Soup

Until recently I never really thought much of this soup. Versions tasted in New York always seemed insipid compared to other Indian food. The few times I tried it in India—usually when I was feeling out of sorts and wanted something safe—it was pallid and uninteresting.

But this version, flavored with almond milk, is marvelous. The kinds of vegetables you use aren't terribly important—in fact you can use almost any vegetable puree as a base.

MAKES 6 SERVINGS

4 tablespoons unsalted butter

2 medium-size carrots, chopped

2 medium-size onions, chopped

2 garlic cloves, chopped

2 medium-size waxy potatoes, peeled and thinly sliced

7 cups chicken or vegetable broth or water

1 cup tightly packed spinach leaves

1 cup blanched almonds

1 cup water

¼ teaspoon saffron threads, soaked in 1 tablespoon water
    for 15 minutes

2 tablespoons *ghee* (page 592) or unsalted butter

4 teaspoons curry powder

½ cup heavy cream or coconut milk

2 tablespoons finely chopped cilantro leaves

salt

pepper

MELT the butter in a 4-quart pot over medium heat and add the carrots, onions, garlic, and potatoes. Cook for about 10 minutes, stirring every few minutes, until the onions start to turn translucent.

ADD the broth and bring the soup to a medium simmer. When the vegetables are soft and can be crushed easily against the side of the pot with a spoon, about 20 minutes, add the spinach leaves and simmer for 2 minutes more.

WHILE the vegetables are cooking, use the almonds and water to make almond milk as directed on page 202.

PUREE the soup in a blender or through the fine disk of a food mill. If you want the soup to have a smoother texture, strain it through a medium-mesh strainer. Add the almond milk and the saffron with its soaking liquid.

COMBINE the *ghee* and curry in a small sauté pan. Stir over medium heat for about 2 minutes, until you can smell the curry. Add this mixture to the soup.

STIR in the cream or coconut milk and the cilantro. Season with salt and pepper. Bring the soup to a simmer and serve.

Southern French Vegetable Soup

SOUPE AU PISTOU

A *soupe au pistou* is a simple vegetable soup that the guests elevate to lofty heights by dolloping a French-style pesto—called a *pistou*—into each of their bowls.

Although this version is traditional, don't limit yourself to any particular recipe. I for one am not always up to waiting for beans to soak (canned beans won't work here) and sometimes leave them out when the summer craving for fresh basil strikes and I want a quick version of this soup. If I'm not trying to show off, I simply combine five or six peeled and seeded tomatoes, a few sliced zucchini, some garlic, and maybe a handful of dried macaroni. The soup then simmers just until the vegetables and pasta are soft.

MAKES 12 SERVINGS

the soup:

> ¼ cup extra virgin olive oil
>
> 2 leeks, washed, white and tender green parts, sliced
>
> I large onion, coarsely chopped
>
> 3 medium-size carrots, chopped
>
> I cup dried white beans such as navy or cannellini, soaked
>   for 2 hours and cooked until tender, about 2½ cups
>   cooked
>
> 4 medium-size zucchini, cut into ¼-inch slices
>
> 2 quarts chicken or vegetable broth or water
>
> I bouquet garni
>
> I cup miniature dried macaroni (ditalini)
>
> ½ pound green beans, preferably small French type, cut into
>   I-inch lengths
>
> salt
>
> pepper
>
> slices of French bread, toasted

the pistou:

> 8 garlic cloves, peeled
>
> 2 large bunches of fresh basil, stems removed, 2 cups tightly
>   packed leaves
>
> 2 teaspoons coarse salt
>
> 2 cups finely grated Parmesan cheese
>
> 2 medium-size tomatoes, peeled, seeded, and coarsely
>   chopped
>
> I½ cups extra virgin olive oil

IN ADVANCE To make the soup base, heat the olive oil in a 4-quart pot over medium heat. Add the leeks, onion, and carrots. Stir until the leeks and onion turn translucent, about 10 minutes.

ADD the beans, zucchini, broth, and bouquet garni. Bring the soup to a simmer, simmer for about 5 minutes, and add the macaroni and green beans. Continue simmering for about 5 to 10 minutes, until the zucchini and macaroni have softened.

DON'T season the soup until you've added the pistou, which is very salty. If you're not serving the soup right away, chill it as quickly as you can so the vegetables don't overcook.

MAKE the pistou by hand or in a blender.

HAND METHOD If you have a mortar and pestle, combine the garlic, basil, and coarse salt in the mortar. Grind the mixture to a paste and add the cheese. Gradually work in the chopped tomato and then the olive oil.

IF you don't have a mortar and pestle, chop the garlic finely and crush it into a paste with the side of a chef's knife. Put the basil leaves on the cutting board with the garlic and sprinkle them with a few tablespoons of the olive oil (to prevent them from turning black during chopping). Chop the basil very finely.

COMBINE the basil and garlic in a bowl with the cheese and the chopped tomato. Add the salt.

BLENDER METHOD Put the tomatoes and then the rest of the ingredients except the olive oil in the blender. (The tomatoes go in first to provide liquid to get the mixture moving around.) Blend at high speed for about 1 minute, until the mixture turns into a paste. Transfer the pistou to a mixing bowl and stir in the olive oil. (The olive oil must be added by hand, or it will turn bitter.)

AT THE LAST MINUTE To serve, whisk half of the pistou into the hot soup, then season with salt if needed and pepper. Immediately ladle the soup into hot bowls. Serve the French bread toasts in a basket. Pass the remaining pistou at the table—in a bowl or mortar—and let guests help themselves.

SUGGESTIONS AND VARIATIONS | Although basil wilts quickly in the refrigerator, pistou will hold up for weeks if tightly sealed and for months if frozen. If you have the refrigerator or freezer space, making a quart of pistou (double the quantities given here) is a worthwhile project. You can use it not only to finish vegetable and fish soups but also as pasta sauce.

PESTO *(pesto genoese)* is almost identical to pistou and works perfectly here. Make pesto as directed but replace the tomatoes with 3 tablespoons toasted pine nuts.

Minestrone

There are so many different kinds of minestroni that it's safe to say they have only one thing in common: they contain mostly vegetables. The combinations are almost limitless, and each region of Italy has its own traditions. In Genoa a minestrone is likely to be finished with pesto (much like the *soupe au pistou* in the preceding recipe), in Rome a bit of wild mint will probably enter into the concoction, in the South oregano and marjoram are added with a heavy hand, and in the Abruzzi hot peppers are added.

Most but not all minestroni contain cannellini or borlotti beans, but if you can't find these, use white navy or Great Northern beans. Sometimes I find fresh borlotti or fava beans in New York markets; when I do, I choose them over any type of dried bean.

Tuscan-Style Minestrone

This version of minestrone contains beans in two forms: whole, as one of the vegetables, and pureed to give the soup body and texture. Traditionally this soup is ladled into a soup tureen with alternating layers of stale bread just before serving. The result is a soup so thick that a spoon will stick straight up when plunged in.

Most minestroni are made with water—preferably the cooking water from the beans—but I like to use chicken stock if I have any around.

For a lighter version, add a couple more cups of broth or water to thin the soup and dispense with the layers of bread. Just serve the soup in bowls and pass little croutons sautéed in olive oil.

The Italians prize leftover minestrone, which they combine with bread and serve cold or reheated by the name *ribollita*.

MAKES 12 SERVINGS

3 quarts water

½ head of cabbage, preferably Savoy

1 large red onion, chopped

1 celery rib, chopped

4 garlic cloves, peeled

1 large carrot, sliced

¼ cup olive oil

½ bunch of kale, stems removed and leaves cut into strips,
    about 3 cups tightly packed

1 large waxy potato, peeled and cut into ½-inch cubes

6 cups chicken broth, bean-cooking water, or fresh water

4 medium-size tomatoes, peeled, seeded, and chopped or 1
    cup drained and seeded canned tomatoes

1 bouquet garni: 1 fresh rosemary sprig, 1 fresh thyme
    sprig, and 1 bunch of parsley

1 cup dried cannellini or borlotti beans, soaked and cooked,
    about 3 cups

1 bunch of spinach, stems removed and leaves cut into
    strips if large, about 1 cup packed

salt

pepper

slices of French bread, either stale or lightly toasted (for
    traditional version) or small croutons sautéed in olive
    oil (for lighter version; page 595)

Grated Parmesan cheese

BRING the water to a rolling boil. Cut the cabbage into quarters through the core. Cut the core out of two of the quarters and slice them as thinly as possible. Boil the sliced cabbage for 5 minutes and drain it in a colander. Rinse it with cold water. (This preliminary cooking eliminates some of the strong taste and prevents it from taking over the flavor of the soup.)

IN a 4-quart pot, cook the onion, celery, garlic, and carrot in the olive oil over medium heat until softened, about 10 minutes. Add the blanched cabbage, kale, potato, broth, tomatoes, and bouquet garni. Bring the soup to a gentle simmer and cook for 10 to 15 minutes, until the potatoes are soft.

STRAIN half the cooked beans through a food mill with the finest disk or puree them in a blender or food processor. Add the puree and the whole beans to the simmering soup. Simmer the soup for about 5 minutes more—reach in with a spoon and taste a few of the vegetables; make sure the cabbage and kale are completely soft.

ADD the spinach. Simmer the soup for 1 minute more. Add salt and pepper to taste.

THE soup can now be ladled into hot bowls, but if you want to present it in the traditional style (and make it suitable for a next-day *ribollita* or casserole), layer it in a tureen with the bread slices—alternating a ladle of soup with a slice of bread—and let it sit for 10 minutes before serving. Pass the cheese at the table.

SUGGESTIONS AND VARIATIONS | If you make the thick layered-bread version of this soup, it is delicious the next day served as a casserole with a light salad. Spread the cold congealed soup in a porcelain or glass casserole; sprinkle it with grated Parmesan cheese and some olive oil. Bake the casserole at 350°F for 20 to 30 minutes.

Milanese-Style Minestrone

The Milanese, of course, make their minestrone a little differently from the Tuscans (see preceding recipe). Both soups contain many of the same vegetables, but the Milanese don't thicken theirs at the end with the pureed beans. In the summer the Milanese sometimes serve this soup at room temperature.

Don't worry about following this recipe exactly; think of it more as a model for using summer vegetables. This soup calls for both fresh and dried beans, but if you can't find fresh, use all dried.

This recipe is for a crowd, but it's worth making for a smaller gathering so you have leftovers the next day.

MAKES 12 GENEROUS SERVINGS

5 tablespoons unsalted butter

1 large onion, chopped

2 leeks, white part only, chopped, about 1½ cups

1 celery rib, chopped

¼ pound pancetta, prosciutto, or raw pork, cut into ¼-inch
   cubes

2 carrots, quartered lengthwise and chopped

4 medium-size tomatoes, peeled, seeded, and chopped or
   2 cups canned, seeded and drained

1 bouquet garni: 1 bunch of parsley, 1 fresh rosemary sprig,
   and 1 bay leaf

10 cups chicken or vegetable broth

1 medium-size waxy potato, peeled and cut into ½-inch
   cubes

¾ cup long-grain rice, preferably basmati

2 zucchini, quartered lengthwise and sliced

1½ cups shucked fresh beans such as borlotti (1 pound
   unshucked) or fava beans (1½ pounds unshucked)

1 cup dried cannellini, Great Northern, or navy beans,
   soaked and cooked, about 3 cups, or 1½ cups
   uncooked if you're using dried beans alone

½ head of cabbage, preferably Savoy, shredded, cooked in
   boiling water for 5 minutes, and drained

6 garlic cloves, chopped and crushed to a paste

1 tightly packed cup fresh basil leaves, shredded

salt

pepper

MELT the butter in a 6-quart pot. Add the onion, leeks, celery, pancetta, and carrots. Stir the vegetables over medium heat until they turn shiny and start to smell good, about 15 minutes.

ADD the tomatoes, bouquet garni, broth, potato, and rice. Simmer the soup for 15 minutes.

ADD the rest of the ingredients except the garlic, basil, and salt and pepper. Simmer the soup for 10 to 15 minutes more, long enough to finish cooking the rice and potatoes. Season with salt and pepper.

STIR in the garlic paste and basil a minute before serving. Season with salt and pepper to taste.

PASS grated Parmesan and sliced French bread or garlic toast at the table.

SUGGESTIONS AND VARIATIONS | The garlic and basil added to the soup at the end are really a kind of primitive pesto. If you want to make an authentic pesto and pass it at the table, use the recipe on page 258.

MINESTRONE is great served the next day. You can simply reheat it—you'll need to add a little more broth or water—and serve it as a soup, or you can spread it out in a casserole, sprinkle it with some Parmesan cheese, and bake it into a traditional *ribollita*.

French Farmer's Vegetable Soup

SOUPE CULTIVATEUR

This is a French country soup *par excellence*. It's not the dramatic kind of soup you'd serve when the boss is coming to dinner (unless he or she happens to be French) but a comforting and savory mixed vegetable soup. The chopped vegetables (don't worry if they're not cut exactly the same size) are cooked gently in bacon fat, broth is added, and the whole thing is simmered until the vegetables are soft. This country soup is perfect for a light dinner *à deux* or an impromptu gathering of close friends when you don't want to deal with a filling dinner.

MAKES 8 SERVINGS

2 cups water

¼ pound slab bacon, rind removed, cut into ¼-inch cubes

1 medium-size carrot, cut in half lengthwise and sliced

1 medium-size turnip, peeled and cut into ¼-inch cubes

2 leeks, white part only, washed and thinly sliced

1 medium-size onion, chopped

1 medium-size waxy potato, peeled and cut into ¼-inch cubes

1 quart chicken, turkey, or beef broth

salt

pepper

½ cup unsalted butter

French bread

BRING the water to a boil and cook the bacon in it for 5 minutes. Drain it in a colander.

COOK the bacon in a 4-quart pot over medium heat for about 10 minutes, until it renders its fat and barely starts to turn crisp. Add the vegetables to the pot and stir them around every 3 or 4 minutes for about 15 minutes, until they soften slightly and start to smell good. Add the broth and simmer until the vegetables have softened thoroughly. Season with salt and pepper.

SERVE this soup in hot bowls. Put a tablespoon of butter on each serving if desired and pass a basket of crusty French bread at the table.

SUGGESTIONS AND VARIATIONS | This is a soup that can be changed around by substituting what's available. If you have leftover roast meats, you can make a more filling version by cutting the meat into cubes and adding it along with the vegetables at the beginning.

Chinese Mixed Vegetable Soup

There are no doubt strict rules governing what combinations of vegetables go into certain regional Chinese soups, but I've never cooked by the book. I like to play around with a few recipes until I get a feel for a style of cooking. So review the section on China in Ethnic Soups and take off from there.

The best place to start experimenting with Chinese cooking is in an Asian market. I'm lucky enough to live in New York, with its large Chinatown, where I can wander from store to store and where, with a little luck, I'll find a friendly English-speaking grocer who will explain things to me. Whenever I shop in Chinatown I try to buy a few things I've never used before so when I get home with my bag of vegetables I can experiment. I always feel proud of myself if I've come up with something completely unrecognizable and then figure out what it is and how to cook it.

This soup contains a lot of ingredients to give you a sense of all the options, but the soup will still be good with a minimalist approach. Consult the Ingredients chapter if there's something you don't recognize.

MAKES 8 SERVINGS

7 cups Chinese-style chicken broth or vegetable broth

12 medium-size dried Chinese mushrooms, soaked in just enough boiling water to cover for 30 minutes or in cold water for 3 hours, or 12 fresh shiitake mushrooms

2 ounces Chinese preserved vegetables

¼ cup dried tree ears, soaked in enough water to cover for
      30 minutes, hard parts removed, torn into 1-inch
      pieces

2 cups tightly packed Chinese spinach, water spinach,
      regular spinach, or watercress leaves

2 shallots, finely chopped

3 garlic cloves, thinly sliced

1 cake of tofu (preferably Chinese-style), cut into
      ¼-inch dice

¼ cup medium-dry sherry

3 tablespoons dark soy sauce

1 teaspoon dark sesame oil

¼ pound Smithfield ham, cut into ⅛- by 1-inch shreds

BRING the broth to a simmer in a 4-quart pot.

CUT off any hard parts—these may include the stems—from the mushrooms. Slice the mushrooms into about 4 slices each.

RINSE off the preserved vegetable and cut it into thin strips the size of matchsticks. Eliminate excess salt by soaking the matchsticks in warm water for 20 minutes. Drain off and discard the water.

ADD the mushrooms, soaking liquid, tree ears, greens, shallots, preserved vegetable, and garlic to the simmering broth. Simmer gently for 5 minutes.

ADD the rest of the ingredients and simmer for 5 minutes more. Add more soy sauce or sesame oil to taste.

Japanese Mixed Vegetable Soup

What makes Japanese soups distinct from all others is the use of *dashi* as the cooking liquid. *Dashi* is one of the easiest and certainly the quickest of all broths to make. The basic ingredients, although they may require a trip to an Asian grocery or a mail-order wait, are easy to store and use.

Although the Japanese use many of the same vegetables as Western cooks, certain vegetables and starchy ingredients are peculiar to Japanese cooking. At least one of these should be used to give a soup a recognizable Japanese character.

Daikon, also called *giant white radish*, is one of Japan's most popular vegetables and is becoming easier to find in the United States. Use a benriner cutter to cut it into julienne. Bamboo shoots, easy to find in cans and occasionally available fresh in Asian markets, are also a popular Japanese (and Chinese) vegetable. Shiitake mushrooms can be found both fresh and dried and go well in almost any Japanese soup.

The Japanese are very fond of tofu, which is easy to find and use. In addition to tofu, Japanese cooks also use konnyaku—sometimes called *devil's tongue jelly*—which comes in both cake and noodle form.

MAKES 12 SERVINGS

2 quarts *dashi*

2 bamboo shoots, quartered lengthwise and thinly sliced

8 medium-size shiitake mushrooms, stems removed, sliced

2 medium-size carrots, halved lengthwise, thinly sliced

2 medium-size turnips, peeled, cut into 10 wedges, and boiled for 3 minutes

1 8-ounce cake konnyaku, torn into ½-inch pieces

1 small cucumber, peeled, cut in half lengthwise, and seeds removed with a spoon

1 4-inch length of daikon, ½ pound, peeled and cut into fine julienne

1 cake of Japanese tofu, cut into ½-inch cubes

2 tablespoons light miso

2 tablespoons dark miso

2 tablespoons light soy sauce or more to taste

BRING the *dashi* to a simmer in a 4-quart pot. Add the bamboo shoots, mushrooms, carrots, turnips, and konnyaku. Simmer the soup, partially covered, for about 30 minutes, until the vegetables have softened. Add water or more *dashi* as needed to make up for evaporation.

ADD the cucumber, daikon, and tofu and simmer gently for 5 minutes more.

WHISK together the 2 types of miso in a small bowl with ¼-cup of the simmering soup broth to obtain a smooth paste. Whisk the paste back into the soup.

STIR in the soy sauce or slightly more to taste. Serve in hot bowls.

Indonesian Vegetable Soup

SAJUR TERUNG ATAU LABU

Although this spicy soup is traditionally made with squash or eggplant, I sometimes prepare the spicy base—called a *bumbu*—and add whatever vegetables I have around. Yellow squash and zucchini are especially good, but I also like mushrooms and green vegetables such as spinach or green beans. If you're using a combination of vegetables, keep them separate so they can be added to the soup in stages according to their cooking times.

This soup contains some exotic ingredients. Laos powder may be easier to find, but fresh or frozen galangal has a much better flavor; look for it at a Thai market. Curry leaves and shrimp paste add an exotic Asian flavor but are not essential to the soup.

If you're using whole seeds to make the spice mixture, the best way to grind them is in a small coffee grinder or in a mortar and pestle. The nuts should be ground in a mortar and pestle or in a food processor (don't use the coffee grinder). Unfortunately, it's almost impossible to grind 10 nuts in a food processor, so you'll have to make more than the recipe calls for and freeze it to use in something else.

MAKES 6 SERVINGS

¼ cup peanut oil

2 large onions, chopped

2 garlic cloves, finely chopped

2 Thai or jalapeño chilies, seeded and finely chopped

a ¼-inch slice of fresh ginger, peeled and finely chopped

1 teaspoon coriander seeds, freshly ground, or ground coriander

¼ teaspoon cumin seeds, freshly ground, or ground cumin

½ teaspoon ground turmeric

½ teaspoon laos powder or a ¼-inch slice of fresh or frozen galangal

10 macadamia nuts or peeled almonds, ground to a paste

3 cups chicken or vegetable broth or water

2 curry leaves (optional)

4 cups vegetables either alone or in combination: zucchini,
    sliced or diced; yellow squash, sliced or diced;
    mushrooms, sliced, quartered, or left whole; green
    beans, cut into 1-inch lengths; spinach, whole or
    shredded leaves

1 teaspoon shrimp paste

2 teaspoons water

2 teaspoons ground dried shrimp

1 cup coconut milk

juice of 2 limes

salt

pepper

HEAT the peanut oil in a 4-quart pot. Add the onions, garlic, and chilies. Cook over medium heat until the onions turn translucent, about 10 minutes.

ADD the ginger, ground spices, laos, and nut paste. Stir the mixture for 5 minutes over medium heat to release the flavor of the spices.

ADD the broth, curry leaves, and vegetables. Simmer until the vegetables are soft— about 10 minutes for zucchini and squash, 8 minutes for green beans, 5 minutes for mushrooms, and 2 minutes for spinach.

WORK the shrimp paste with the water to thin it and stir it into the soup. Stir in the ground dried shrimp.

ADD the coconut milk and lime juice. Simmer the soup for 1 minute and season with salt and pepper.

Moroccan Vegetable Soup

I'm always amazed by the similarities of vegetable soup recipes from around the world. Usually the basic ingredients and techniques are the same; what's different is a few special ingredients that give the soup the unmistakable character of a particular country's cooking.

This soup is prepared almost like a minestrone but with a few Moroccan touches. Instead of chicken broth, lamb broth is used; chick-peas replace the cannellini beans; and instead of parsley and a bouquet garni, saffron, cayenne pepper, and chopped cilantro are added near the end.

If you can't find lamb stew meat or lamb shanks, buy 3 pounds lamb shoulder chops and trim off the bones. The bones can be cooked in the soup to contribute their flavor or saved for making stock.

The entire soup can be made in advance or in stages, the broth made one day and the soup finished the next.

MAKES 12 GENEROUS SERVINGS

the lamb broth:

2 pounds lamb stew meat, cut into ½-inch dice, or
3 1-pound lamb shanks, trimmed of excess fat

¼ cup olive oil

1 medium-size onion, coarsely chopped

1 medium-size carrot, coarsely chopped

the soup:

1 cup dried chick-peas, soaked in 2 cups water overnight

2 medium-size onions, finely chopped

¼ cup olive oil

4 medium-size tomatoes, about 1½ pounds, peeled, seeded, and chopped

4 garlic cloves, peeled

2 medium-size waxy potatoes, peeled and cut into ½-inch dice

2 medium-size carrots, halved lengthwise and sliced

2 zucchini, halved lengthwise and sliced

6 ounces fresh or 2 ounces dried mushrooms, soaked and sliced

¼ teaspoon ground turmeric

½ teaspoon finely chopped fresh ginger or ¼ teaspoon ground

¼ teaspoon saffron threads

¼ teaspoon ground cinnamon

¼ teaspoon cayenne pepper or more to taste

I small bunch of fresh cilantro, stems removed, about
    3 tablespoons finely chopped

salt

pepper

PREPARING THE LAMB BROTH In a 4-quart pot, brown the lamb and lamb bones (if any) in the olive oil over high heat. Remove the meat and bones with a slotted spoon and pour out the burned fat. Add the chopped vegetables to the pot and return the meat and bones. Add enough water to cover, about I quart.

BRING to a slow simmer and simmer the broth for about 3 hours, skimming off fat and scum as needed. If necessary, add water from time to time to make up for evaporation. Strain the broth and discard the bones and vegetables. If you're using lamb shanks, peel off the meat and discard the bones. Reserve the meat and broth.

PREPARING THE SOUP Place the chick-peas and their soaking water in a 4-quart pot. Add more water if necessary to cover by I inch. Cover the pot and simmer until the chick-peas are soft, about an hour.

COOK the chopped onions in the olive oil in another 4-quart pot over medium heat until the onions turn translucent, about 10 minutes. Add the tomatoes, garlic, potatoes, carrots, zucchini, mushrooms, lamb broth, and reserved meat. Simmer until the potatoes and carrots have softened, about 20 minutes. Add the chick-peas along with their cooking liquid.

STIR in the spices and simmer the soup for 5 minutes. Add the cilantro and simmer for I minute more. Season with salt and pepper.

Indian Mixed Vegetable Soup

I've always been a bit wary of vegetarian food—so much of it has left me yearning for the full flavors of meat and fish—but Indian cooks are such masters of spices and flavors that a good vegetarian dish in an Indian restaurant rarely leaves me wanting anything more.

It's little wonder that Indian cooks work such miracles with vegetables; a large part of the population is completely vegetarian, and they've had millennia to work out some of their magical combinations. In addition to their talent with spices, Indians are unrivaled in the use of legumes. Besides the many bean soups (*dal*) that the Indians flavor with fragrant spice mixtures, they also make soups—some of them rather thick and stewlike—with chunks of vegetables simmered in legume broth. With this in mind, Indian-style black bean soup (page 241) or red lentil soup (page 245) can be used as the liquid base for more substantial soups containing a variety of mixed vegetables. The bean puree base in this recipe can also be used.

Typically, peas, lentils, or dried beans—mung beans are an Indian favorite—are simmered with aromatic vegetables and fragrant spices, the legumes are pureed or left alone, and chunks of potato, cauliflower, cucumber, green beans, spinach, or mushrooms are simmered in the bean mixture until they soften. The soup (or stew) is then flavored at the end with various spice mixtures—called *tadka*—gently cooked in *ghee* or butter.

This soup can be cooked entirely in advance, but you may need to thin it with a little extra water or broth; it thickens as it sits.

MAKES 6 MAIN-COURSE SERVINGS

the bean puree base:

I cup dried yellow split peas or yellow lentils or split mung beans or red lentils

I medium-size onion, finely chopped

4 garlic cloves, peeled and finely chopped

I teaspoon grated fresh ginger or ground ginger

½ teaspoon ground turmeric

I teaspoon ground cumin

I½ tablespoons ground coriander

3 medium-size tomatoes, cut in half crosswise and seeds squeezed out, or I cup drained and seeded canned tomatoes

6 curry leaves (optional)

5 cups water

salt

pepper

the vegetables:

> 2 cups trimmed vegetables, alone or in combination: waxy
>> potatoes, peeled and cut into approximately 1-inch
>> cubes (about 20 minutes' cooking time)
>
> cauliflower, trimmed into florets about 1 inch wide
>> (10 minutes' cooking time)
>
> green beans, cut into 1-inch lengths and cooked in boiling
>> water until slightly soft, about 5 minutes (2 minutes'
>> additional cooking time)
>
> spinach leaves (1 minute's cooking time)
>
> peas, frozen or fresh (1 minute's cooking time for frozen,
>> 5 to 10 minutes for fresh)
>
> carrots, cut into ½-inch lengths (20 minutes' cooking time)
>
> eggplant, peeled and cut into 1-inch dice (15 minutes'
>> cooking time)
>
> squash, sliced or cut into 1-inch dice (10 minutes' cooking
>> time)
>
> zucchini, sliced (10 minutes' cooking time)
>
> mushrooms, whole or quartered (5 minutes' cooking time)

tadka:

> ½ cup *ghee* (page 592) or unsalted butter
>
> 2 teaspoons black mustard seeds
>
> 1 teaspoon ground cumin
>
> ½ bunch of cilantro, stems removed and leaves finely
>> chopped
>
> rice, preferably basmati, optional

RINSE the legumes and combine them with the rest of the ingredients for the bean puree base in a 4-quart pot. Bring the mixture to a slow simmer and cover the pot. Simmer gently until the legumes are completely soft, depending on the type of bean or lentil, from 30 minutes to 2 hours.

PUREE the mixture in a blender or work it through a food mill with a medium disk and again through a medium-mesh strainer. Season the puree to taste with salt and pepper.

BRING the puree back to a simmer and add the vegetables in order of their cooking times—potatoes and carrots first, spinach last, and so forth.

PREPARE the *tadka* by heating the *ghee* or butter over low heat. When the *ghee* starts to smell fragrant or the whole butter froths, add the mustard seeds and cumin. Stir the

Ghee is not only a rich and delicious flavoring for Indian-style soups but is also useful for browning meats, fish, and vegetables when high heat and a buttery flavor are needed.

Because whole butter contains almost one-quarter water and a small amount of protein, it burns at a comparatively low temperature. This low burning temperature makes butter useless for browning foods over high heat. Many recipes suggest combining butter with a small amount of oil for hot sautéing, but even with the oil the butter burns. *Ghee*, in contrast, contains no milk solids, so it can be used over high heat.

Ghee differs from clarified butter in that it is cooked until the milk solids caramelize and impart a characteristic nutty flavor to the butter. Clarified butter is simply butter with the milk solids and water removed.

mixture with a wooden spoon for about 1 minute until you can smell the spices. Stir in the cilantro and immediately stir the spice mixture into the hot soup. The soup is particularly good served with basmati rice.

SUGGESTIONS AND VARIATIONS | I sometimes stir a cup of yogurt or coconut milk into this soup along with the spice mixture.

Grilled Vegetable Soup

I always include grilled vegetables as part of my many summer barbecues, partly because I'm lazy—I can cook everything outside and don't have to clean the kitchen—but mostly because I love the gently smoky flavor of grilled foods. One evening last summer I grilled too many vegetables, and the next day I converted the leftovers into a soup.

Like so many vegetable soups, you're best off improvising this one, using the best-looking vegetables in the markets or homegrown ones. It's hard to go wrong with grilled vegetables, but there are a couple of tricks for getting the best flavor from your fire.

Don't let any flame touch the vegetables, or they'll be covered with soot, which will end up in the soup. Avoid putting too much oil on the vegetables, or it will drip into the coals and cause the fire to flare up. Whatever you do, don't cover the grill or your vegetables will be covered with a fine layer of soot.

During the last decade a great deal of fuss has been made over exotic woods for grilling. Mesquite wood, fruit woods, and vine cuttings all impart a delicious flavor to grilled foods, but I hate to see people paying as much for wood as they should for vegetables. The best way to use exotic woods is to build a fire with something cheap—like charcoal briquets—and wait for the flame to die down. Then add a few wood chips, soaked in water first so they smolder and make a lot of flavorful smoke, and then put on the vegetables.

MAKES 10 FIRST-COURSE SERVINGS

1 large Bermuda or other sweet onion, peeled and sliced
   lengthwise ½ inch thick

1 fennel bulb, cut into 10 wedges

12 medium-size mushrooms, threaded on a skewer

2 small eggplants, preferably Chinese or Japanese, peeled
   and cut lengthwise into ¼-inch-thick strips, about
   12 ounces

1 zucchini, cut lengthwise into ¼-inch-thick strips

½ cup extra virgin olive oil

1 tablespoon freshly chopped or dried herbs such as thyme,
   marjoram, or oregano

1 garlic clove, peeled and finely chopped

1½ pounds tomatoes, peeled, seeded, and chopped, about
   4 medium-size

6 cups chicken or vegetable broth or water

1 large bunch of fresh basil, stems removed, about 1 tightly
   packed cup leaves

salt

pepper

slices of French bread, toasted or grilled

LIGHTLY brush all the vegetables—except the garlic and tomatoes—with all but a tablespoon of the olive oil and sprinkle them with the chopped herbs. Grill the vegetables over hot wood coals (about 8 inches from the coals, but adjust it if need be) until they soften and have light brown grill marks on each side, usually in about 10 minutes. You may have to work in stages, taking the vegetables off the grill one by one as they are ready.

FINELY chop the grilled onions, coarsely chop the grilled fennel wedges, slice the mushrooms, and cut the eggplant and zucchini into ½-inch dice. In a 4-quart pot, combine the grilled vegetables, garlic, tomatoes, and the broth. Bring to a simmer and simmer slowly for about 8 minutes.

FINELY chop the basil leaves with a tablespoon of olive oil (the oil prevents the basil from turning black).

WHEN the vegetables are done—push a few against the side of the pot with a wooden spoon to see if they crush

GRILLING BONUS

I sometimes use the extra heat of still-hot coals to grill extra vegetables, which I marinate in a little olive oil and vinegar and then use in salads or as antipasti during the week. Mushrooms, strips of zucchini, and sliced onions are particularly good.

easily—whisk in the chopped basil, season with salt and pepper, and serve immediately.

SUGGESTIONS AND VARIATIONS | You may also want to whisk some saffron and garlic mayonnaise (page 350) into this soup, which will work wonders with the basil. Pass extra mayonnaise at the table.

ONE refinement is to sprinkle each vegetable with a different herb. It's unlikely that anyone will notice this (at least consciously), but the result is that the soup keeps changing flavor while it's being eaten, so its flavor never grows tiresome.

Elaborate Mixed Vegetable Soup

I made this soup for the first time one summer afternoon in California when I was fixing dinner for my brother's family and a few friends. I had gone to the market looking for fish—thinking I'd experiment with some West Coast varieties—but was so impressed by all the vegetables that I wanted to cook something that used as many of them as possible.

This soup is time-consuming to prepare because instead of throwing all the vegetables into one big pot you cook them all separately. The vegetables are then arranged in deep, wide bowls over a creamy red tomato broth flavored with pancetta. Chopped yellow tomatoes and a light basil sauce are added at the end as dramatic garnishes. The effect is unexpected and striking—especially if you do what I did and tell your guests, "Oh, we're just having a little vegetable soup."

When you make this soup, don't feel you have to adhere to this recipe exactly. The idea is to go to a good greengrocer and buy little bits of all the best things and make soup out of them.

Although this soup is best made the same day you serve it, you can get by preparing the vegetables, the broth, and the basil cream the day before and storing them in the refrigerator.

MAKES 8 FIRST-COURSE OR 4 MAIN-COURSE SERVINGS

the vegetables:

8 baby artichokes

5 tablespoons olive oil

1 fennel bulb, cut into 8 wedges

juice of ½ lemon

8 baby carrots, peeled or scraped

2 tablespoons unsalted butter

2 teaspoons sugar

24 pearl onions, peeled

1 head of garlic, broken into cloves, peeled

1 medium-size bunch of spinach, stems removed and leaves
cooked in simmering water for 30 seconds, drained,
and rinsed with cold water

1 pound wild mushrooms, preferably ½ pound each of two
kinds, quickly rinsed, drained in a colander, and dried

1 pound fava beans, peeled twice, cooked for 2 minutes in
boiling water, rinsed in cold water, and drained

¼ pound small French-style green beans, ends snapped off,
cooked in boiling water until barely tender, drained,
and rinsed in cold running water

salt

pepper

the broth:

¼ pound pancetta, prosciutto, or raw-cured ham, cut into
⅛- by 1-inch strips

1 tablespoon olive oil

4 large tomatoes, peeled, seeded, and chopped

½ cup Madeira or dry sherry

1 cup heavy cream

1 bunch of parsley, finely chopped

salt

pepper

the basil cream sauce:

1 bunch of basil, stems removed, 1 cup tightly packed
leaves, washed and dried

½ cup heavy cream

salt

pepper

additional garnish:

3 large yellow tomatoes, peeled, seeded, and chopped

PREPARING THE VEGETABLES Cut the stems off the artichokes and then cut
off the outer leaves with a sharp paring knife. The easiest way to do this is to hold
the artichoke firmly in one hand and rotate it against the blade of the knife. Be careful not to cut into the white flesh in the center of the artichoke. Cut off and discard
the top half of the artichoke.

SIMMER the artichoke hearts in a quart of boiling water containing I tablespoon olive oil in a nonaluminum pot (aluminum would turn them gray) until they soften to the texture of a barely cooked boiled potato. Drain them—discard the cooking water—and place them on an ovenproof platter or baking sheet.

SPREAD the fennel wedges in a pan with I cup water, a tablespoon of olive oil, and the lemon juice. Cover the pan and cook the fennel over medium heat for about 20 minutes, until the wedges can be pierced easily with a fork; don't overdo it, or they will turn mushy. Transfer the fennel wedges to the platter with the artichokes. Reserve any leftover cooking liquid from the fennel in a mixing bowl.

PLACE the carrots with I tablespoon butter, a teaspoon of sugar, and ½ cup of water in a 2-quart covered saucepan. Cover the saucepan and cook over medium heat until soft, about 15 minutes. Check every few minutes; if the water starts to run dry, add more as needed. Place the carrots on the pan with the fennel wedges. If there is any leftover cooking liquid, pour it into the reserved fennel-cooking liquid.

SPREAD the pearl onions in the bottom of a small pan so they form a single layer. Pour over enough water to come halfway up their sides, add a tablespoon of butter, and sprinkle with a teaspoon of sugar. Partially cover the pan and cook the onions over medium heat until they soften and become lightly glazed, about 15 minutes. Put the onions on the platter with the other vegetables.

COOK the garlic cloves in 2 cups simmering water for about 20 minutes, until soft. Drain them in a colander, discard the cooking liquid, and place the garlic on the pan with the other vegetables.

GENTLY squeeze the excess water out of the cooked spinach, sprinkle it with a tablespoon of olive oil, and place it on the pan with the other vegetables.

SAUTÉ the mushrooms in 2 tablespoons olive oil over high heat until they soften, about 10 minutes. Drain them in a colander and place them on the pan with the other vegetables.

PLACE the fava beans and green beans on the platter with the other vegetables. Sprinkle all the vegetables with salt and pepper and cover the platter with aluminum foil. Refrigerate the vegetables until needed.

PREPARING THE BROTH In a 2-quart saucepan, cook the strips of pancetta in the olive oil over medium heat for 5 minutes. Add the tomatoes, any reserved cooking liquid from the vegetables, the Madeira, the cup of cream, and the parsley. Simmer the mixture for 10 minutes to soften the tomatoes and cook off the alcohol. Season with salt and pepper. Reserve off the heat.

PREPARING THE BASIL CREAM SAUCE Puree the basil with ½ cup water in a blender at high speed for I minute. Strain. Reserve the liquid and discard the solids that don't go through. Add the ½ cup cream to the reserved liquid and season to taste with salt and pepper. (Don't try to puree the basil with the cream, or it will turn to butter.)

SERVING Place the tray of vegetables in a 275°F oven for about 15 minutes. Bring the broth to a slow simmer. Bring the yellow tomatoes to a simmer in a small saucepan and season them with salt and pepper. Heat the sauce just a minute or two before serving.

DISTRIBUTE the broth among hot wide bowls and arrange the vegetables in a decorative pattern in each bowl.

ARRANGE the yellow tomatoes on each bowl with the vegetables.

SPOON the sauce over the vegetables or drizzle it on vegetables à la Jackson Pollock.

SUGGESTIONS AND VARIATIONS | Save the fennel stalks to make broth; use the fronds to decorate the soup if they're pretty and not tired.

"Rice can be added to
virtually any soup . . ."

Rice

SOUPS

Rice can be added to virtually any soup to make it more substantial and to contribute starch. Rice turns many a simple soup into a complete one-pot meal. In addition to its versatility in a supporting role, rice is the base for many of the world's greatest soups and souplike dishes. Rice dishes—paella, risotto, and congee—are easily converted to soups by adding flavorful liquids, pieces of meat, seafood, or vegetable, and various condiments.

Paellas and Arroces

Paella normally doesn't qualify as a soup, but I make tasty soupy versions simply by using more liquid. Like so many legendary dishes—cassoulet and clam chowder come to mind—paella is a dish people argue about. The importance of each component, even the water, is fiercely debated, and most versions encountered in the United States (which unlike so-called authentic versions are usually made with seafood) are declared travesties by paella aficionados.

I have never quite understood what all the fuss is about and have never liked rigidly following a recipe anyway, preferring to add ingredients that I like, using a traditional recipe as a model instead of a dictate. Paula Wolfert knows more about Spanish rice dishes (including paella, of course) than anyone else I've ever encountered, so if you want to understand them in depth, I highly recommend her book *Mediterranean Greens and Grains*. There, Ms. Wolfert not only explains the traditional paella Valenciana but also discusses similar rice dishes, called *arroces,* from the Alicante. These lesser-known paella-like dishes provoke less argument than paella and allow far more freedom in the kitchen.

I admit to being careless about fine distinctions between the various paellas and arroces, but instead keep in mind basic techniques, ingredients, and concepts that give these dishes their special character. First is the *sofrito* (*sofregit* in Catalan), a mixture of onions, tomatoes, dried (Spanish cooks use *ñora* chilies—see Sources—but I usually substitute anchos) and fresh chilies (I often omit the fresh chilies because of their domineering flavor), and garlic cooked in olive oil before liquid is added. (My own system consists of slow, gentle cooking and then letting the ingredients caramelize.) Next comes the liquid, in Spain often water, but in my own kitchen usually stock made from trimmings and bones (such as fish or shrimp heads, rabbit bones and forequarters, chicken wings). Then comes the rice. Spanish rice absorbs a lot of liquid (like Italian risotto rice) but without becoming mushy, like long-grain rice, or releasing too much starch, like short-grain rice. Spanish rice is a medium-grain rice sold as Calasparra rice or the more luxurious (and more absorbent) Bomba (see Sources for both kinds). Paellas and arroces are often flavored with saffron and a kind of powdered and smoked paprika called *pimentón.*

Ideally, rice soups should be made at the last minute because as they sit the rice tends to get soggy and lose its texture. If you do want to make them advance, cook the rice only partially and then finish cooking it at the last minute. If you have leftover rice soups or soups that have been sitting for a while, you'll see that they will have gotten considerably thicker. You can thin them with water or broth to bring them back to the consistency you like.

Shrimp, Mussel, Chorizo, and Spanish Rice Soup in the Style of an Arroce

You can make this soup with the headless shrimp you find at any fish store, but it will be far more flavorful if you can find shrimp with the heads still on, usually in an Asian market or by ordering them in advance. You can also save shrimp shells in the freezer and when you have about a pound, use them to make the broth.

The tastiest (and most expensive) shrimp are pink or white shrimp from the Gulf of Mexico. You can also make this soup with other crustaceans such as lobster or crayfish by lightly pre-cooking them, taking the meat out of the shells, breaking up the shells with the front of a cleaver or rolling pin, and simmering the shells in the same way the shrimp shells are simmered here. The mussels, cooked directly in the liquid, release their briny juices into the soup.

MAKES 4 MAIN-COURSE SERVINGS

16 extra large or jumbo shrimp, preferably with heads
(or more if the shrimp are smaller)

2 pounds small cultivated mussels

⅓ pound cured and/or smoked chorizo sausages
(optional)

for the broth:

2 tablespoons olive oil

1 medium-size onion, peeled and finely chopped

2 garlic cloves peeled and finely chopped

2 tomatoes, coarsely chopped, (don't bother peeling or
seeding)

bouquet garni containing 5 fresh thyme sprigs
(or ½ teaspoon dried), 1 bunch of parsley,
1 bay leaf

for the sofrito:

  2 tablespoons olive oil

  3 medium-size onions, preferably sweet onions such as
      Vidalia or Maui or Walla Walla, peeled and finely
      chopped

  1 dried ancho or ñora chili, dust wiped off with a damp
      towel, stemmed, seeded, soaked for 30 minutes in hot
      water, and drained

  2 garlic cloves peeled and finely chopped

  4 medium-size tomatoes, peeled, seeded, and finely
      chopped, or 1 28-ounce can, drained, seeded (by
      pushing your thumb into the side of each tomato and
      squeezing), and chopped

the rice:

  1 cup Spanish Calasparra or Bomba rice, or risotto rice such
      as Violone Nano or Arborio

final flavorings:

  1 large pinch of saffron

  2 teaspoons hot Hungarian paprika or Spanish pimentón

  salt

  pepper

IF you have shrimp with heads, twist them off and peel and devein the bodies, reserving both heads and shells in the refrigerator. Otherwise, just peel and devein the shrimp and reserve the shells in another bowl in the refrigerator. Scrub and rinse the mussels, pull off any beards sticking out the sides, and reserve in the refrigerator until needed. Slice the chorizos into rounds between ⅛ and ¼ inch thick.

PREPARE the broth: Heat the olive oil in a heavy-bottomed pot over medium heat and stirring in the onion and garlic. Cook until the onion turns translucent but doesn't brown, about 5 minutes, and stir in the shrimp heads (if you have them), the shells, and, if you don't have heads, any shells you've saved up in the freezer. Break up the heads and shells with the end of a European-style rolling pin (the kind without the handles) or the front end of a cleaver with the handle held sticking straight up. Continue breaking up the heads and/or shells for about 5 minutes and stirring them around until they turn orange and smell fragrant. Add the tomatoes, bouquet garni, and 6 cups of water (you could also use chicken broth) and simmer for 30 minutes. Work through a food mill or strainer (if you're using a strainer, push hard with a ladle or wooden spoon to extract the juices) and reserve. Discard the heads and/or shells.

PREPARE the *sofrito*: Heat the olive oil over medium heat in a heavy-bottomed pot and stir in the onions. Stir the onions until they soften and begin to caramelize. If the onions start to brown before 15 minutes, turn down the heat—they should only caramelize after they've completely softened and the sweet juices are released into the pan. Chop the chili very fine, into a paste. Stir the chili and garlic into the caramelized onions and stir over medium heat for 3 minutes more. Stir in the tomatoes and reserved broth.

BRING the mixture to a simmer and pour in the rice (Spanish cooks insist it shouldn't be rinsed). Stir the rice only once or twice during the cooking (too much stirring will cause it to release too much starch), moving a wooden spoon along the bottom of the pot to make sure the rice isn't sticking. Stir in the saffron and paprika and return to a simmer. Simmer the rice, covered, for about 15 minutes— bite into a grain to make sure it is very close to being done—and add the mussels. Simmer, covered, until the mussels open, about 5 minutes, then add the shrimp and chorizo. Simmer for 2 minutes more. Adjust the seasoning with salt and pepper and ladle into heated bowls, making sure everyone gets an equal share of shrimp and mussels.

SUGGESTIONS AND VARIATIONS | Spanish rice soups are great made with fish (the broth made with the heads and bones, the fish filets added minutes before the soup is done) and poultry (broth made with chicken stock, chicken parts browned separately and almost completely cooked in olive oil before a 5-minute simmering in the soup). Green vegetables—peas, green beans, spinach, and chard (shredded)— can be stirred into and cooked directly in the soup, essentially turning it into a one-pot meal.

Risotto

Before my first trip to Venice it would never have occurred to me that a risotto could be a soup. But ever since that initial Venetian risotto, I've preferred risotto on the soupy side. Like paella, risotto can be flavored with just about anything and made more or less rich by adding varying amounts (or none at all) of butter. *Risotto à la milanese* remains one of my all-time favorites (although, unlike Venetian versions, it's relatively thick) and is simple to make because the only flavorings are onions, saffron, Parmigiano-Reggiano, chicken broth, a little wine, and plenty of butter. In soupy versions I cut back on the butter and, of course, just use a higher proportion of liquid. Risottos (*risotti* if you're being

Italian) are best made at the last minute. If you're reheating risotto, it will have thickened as it sat so you'll need to add broth or water to thin it.

Soup in the Style of *Risotto à la Milanese*

I medium-size onion, peeled and chopped finely

½ cup unsalted butter

I cup short-grain Italian rice such as Vialone Nano, Romeo, Ribe-Ringo, Arborio, or Carnaroli (do not rinse)

6 cups basic brown beef broth (see step I of Basic Beef Consommé, page 74) or basic brown chicken broth (page 62)

½ cup dry white wine

I large pinch of saffron threads

2⅓ cup finely grated Parmigiano-Reggiano

salt

HEAT the onion in 2 tablespoons of butter in a heavy-bottomed pot over medium heat. Stir the onion until it turns translucent and fragrant, about 10 minutes, without letting it brown. Stir in the rice and continue stirring for about 2 minutes. Stir in a cup of the broth and the white wine and stir the rice until all the liquid has been absorbed. Add the rest of the broth and the saffron threads and simmer, covered, for about 15 minutes until the rice is soft—but not mushy—when you bite into a grain. Bring back to the simmer, stir in the rest of the butter and add the cheese, and immediately remove from the heat. Season to taste with salt. Serve immediately in heated bowls.

Soup in the Style of *Risotto di Frutti di Mare*

My first seafood risotto, *risotto di seppie,* tasted in Venice, arrived as a frighteningly black soupy mound that I later found out was colored with cuttlefish ink. Cuttlefish ink is far darker—and there's more of it—than squid ink, but cuttlefish are hard to find in the market, especially with their ink sac intact. The equally well-known *risotto di frutti di mare* is easier to put together with clams and mussels, which are easier to find in the United States.

MAKES 6 FIRST-COURSE SERVINGS

3 pounds cultivated mussels

18 littleneck clams

1 cup dry white wine

½ cup unsalted butter

1 medium-size onion, peeled and finely chopped

1 cup short-grain Italian rice such as Vialone Nano, Romeo,
   Ribe-Ringo, Arborio, or Carnaroli (do not rinse)

4 cups basic brown chicken broth (page 62), basic fish
   broth (page 307), or shrimp head broth (contained in
   the recipe on page 284)

1 large pinch of saffron threads

salt

SCRUB the mussels—pull off any beards if they have them—and clams under running water. Sort through them, pushing against the two shells in opposite directions, to eliminate any dead ones. (A dead mussel or clam will come apart in your hand when you push the shells.)

PUT the white wine in a pot large enough to hold both the mussels and clams with plenty of room leftover (for when they open) and bring it to a boil over high heat. Put in the clams and cover the pot. Turn the heat down to medium and steam the clams until most have opened, 10 to 12 minutes. Wedge a knife into the front of any unopened clams—they should snap right open. Scoop the clams out of the pot with a skimmer or slotted spoon and take them out of their shells (or, if you like, leave a few in the shell to decorate the soup), reserve the clam meats, and put the mussels in the pot with the same wine used to steam open the clams. Steam the mussels in the same way, until they've all opened, about 5 minutes. Take the mussels out of the shells and reserve. (Unlike clams, which are usually good even if you have to nudge them open, discard any unopened mussels.)

HEAT 2 tablespoons of butter in a heavy-bottomed pot over medium heat and stir in the onion. Stir the onion around until it turns translucent and smells fragrant, about 10 minutes. Add the rice and stir it around for about 2 minutes. Pour the briny wine juices from steaming the clams and mussels over the rice, being careful to leave any grit or sand behind in the pot used for the clams. Pour over the broth, add the saffron, and give the rice a quick stir. Simmer for about 15 minutes, covered, until the rice is tender but not mushy when you bite into a grain. Stir in the remaining butter, the reserved mussels and the clams, and serve immediately in heated soup plates or bowls.

SUGGESTIONS AND VARIATIONS | Crustaceans such as shrimp, lobster, and crayfish can be lightly cooked, the meat taken out of the shell, and a broth made with the shells (see paella recipe on page 282). The meat can then be stirred into the soup just before serving. If you want to use squid, braise the squid for about 45 minutes in red wine (with the usual aromatic vegetables) and then make the risotto with the braising liquid and a little extra broth and add the cooked squid just before serving. The same trick works with octopus; see page 320.

Venetian Rice and Fresh Pea Soup

RISI E BISI

I admit that the chances of finding a decent fresh baby pea are slim—in New York they're available for a two-week period in June—but this soup is worth knowing about anyway since you can use the same method for virtually any green vegetable. You can also make it with frozen baby peas (see page 205 for more about peas). When I do find fresh baby peas I eat them every day, so I'm eager to know about as many different ways to cook them as possible—usually just boiled for a minute and tossed with butter or in one of the soups described on pages 205 and 206.

MAKES 6 FIRST-COURSE SERVINGS

2½ pounds fresh baby peas (in the pod) or two 10-ounce
    packages frozen baby peas

¼ pound pancetta or prosciutto end, finely chopped

1 medium-size onion, peeled and finely chopped

2 tablespoons butter (if you're using pancetta) or
    4 tablespoons (if you're using prosciutto, which
    renders less fat), plus 3 tablespoons for finishing
    the soup (optional)

1 cup short-grain Italian rice such as Vialone Nano, Romeo,
    Ribe-Ringo, Arborio, or Carnaroli (do not rinse)

7 cups basic brown chicken broth (page 62)

2 tablespoons finely chopped parsley (chopped at the
    last minute)

salt

pepper

1 cup finely grated Parmigiano-Reggiano

SHUCK the peas if they're fresh; thaw them if they're frozen.

HEAT the pancetta and onion in butter over low to medium heat in a heavy-bottomed pot, stirring every couple of minutes, for about 10 minutes until they release their aroma. Don't allow the pancetta or onion to brown.

ADD the rice and stir it over medium heat for about 2 minutes. Pour over the broth and bring to a simmer. Simmer for about 15 minutes, covered, and bite into a grain of rice—it should be almost, but not completely, done. Add the peas and simmer for 1 or 2 minutes more. Stir in the parsley and optional butter and season to taste with salt and pepper. Serve in hot soup plates. Pass the cheese at the table.

SUGGESTIONS AND VARIATIONS | You can make this soup with any vegetable (or combination of vegetables) you like. Just keep in mind the cooking times for the vegetables and add them to the rice-broth mixture accordingly. Diced or sliced root vegetables such as carrots or turnips should be added at the beginning—even sweated with the pancetta—while delicate green vegetables such as fresh fava beans, sections of French string beans, or spinach should be added almost at the end. A handful of dried porcini, soaked first in a little water and chopped, works wonders stirred in about halfway through the cooking. Freshly grated white truffles (maybe use cardoons or artichokes as the vegetables, since they're in season at the same time) shaved over each serving at the table are magnificent.

Chinese Rice Soup

CONGEE

Many of my books and Chinese friends describe congee as more a porridge than a soup. I think of it as a soup, since the word *porridge* has an unpleasant *Oliver Twist* sound about it and conjures up images of low-end British boarding schools.

I'm drawn to this soup by the assortment of garnitures rather than the soup itself. Since the soup contains only rice and water, its real function is as a soothing backdrop for sometimes fiery condiments. I use congee as a medium or slices or strips of leftover roast meats, thinly sliced raw meats, and leftover or fresh vegetables. This soup can, of course, be made with broth instead of water—in fact, Chinese-American Grace Young, in her lovely book *The Wisdom of the Chinese Kitchen*, describes a version made with the broth from the leftover Thanksgiving turkey carcass.

MAKES 6 FIRST-COURSE OR LIGHT MAIN-COURSE SERVINGS,
DEPENDING ON WHICH CONDIMENTS YOU USE.

1½ cups Jasmine or Carolina rice (this is one of the few instances where Basmati isn't an appropriate long-grain variety)

2 quarts broth or water, or more as needed

1 teaspoon salt or more to taste

optional condiments (as many or as few as you like; if you're only using one or two, double the amounts):

4 ounces pickled Chinese vegetables (see page 12), rinsed and finely chopped

1 bunch of scallions, both green and white parts, finely chopped

leaves from 1 bunch of cilantro

3 tablespoons finely chopped hot fresh chilies, such as Thai chilies or serrano chilies, or 5 tablespoons milder (but still hot) chilies such as jalapeños

soy sauce (even though this dish is Chinese, I prefer Japanese dark soy sauce)

1 pound pork tenderloins, the thin end of a beef tenderloin, lean steaks, or leftover meats

2 tablespoons peanut oil or more as needed (if you're sautéing raw meat as a condiment)

salt

pepper

RINSE the rice by putting it in a strainer and running cold water through it, then combine it with the broth or water in a heavy-bottomed pot. If you're using water, add the salt. If you're using broth, taste it first and only add salt to taste. Bring to a simmer and simmer gently for about 20 minutes. Let the rice sit—don't cover it— for about 30 minutes more. Reheat the soup just before serving—you may also need to thin it with more broth or water because it thickens as it sits. Taste the soup and add more salt if it needs it.

ARRANGE the condiments in separate bowls. If you're using raw meats, slice them into thin strips about 2 inches long. The shape isn't terribly important because the cuts suggested here are very tender. Heat the oil in a wok or iron skillet over high heat until it ripples and just begins to smoke, then add half the meat. Stir rapidly, working over high heat, until the meat is lightly browned, 1½ to 2 minutes. Season the meat with salt and pepper. Repeat with the remaining meat, adding more oil to the wok if needed. If you're using leftover meats, cut them into bite-size cubes or strips and serve them cold. Arrange the meats, hot or cold, in bowls along with the other condiments. Ladle the soup into hot soup plates and set the condiments in the middle of the table.

"Fish is so versatile that it can be simmered in almost any liquid . . ."

Fish

SOUPS

Fish is so versatile that it can be simmered in almost any liquid to make a great soup. Every culture seems to have thought of cooking fish in a pot with some liquid and local vegetables, herbs, and spices, in infinite variety.

Fish soups are much appreciated in Asia and Europe, where they are served at different stages in a meal or as meals in themselves. Americans, who used to think of fish as a cheap substitute for meat, are now eating it more because it's light and nutritious. Now that better, fresher, and more varied fish is appearing in markets, Americans are sampling fish dishes they didn't even know existed a decade ago.

Perhaps it is the increased popularity of fresh fish or widespread pollution that has caused the price of fresh fish to skyrocket over the last 10 years, but many of the fish that used to be popular and inexpensive because they were caught in local waters are now scarce or nonexistent. Farm-raised fish is becoming more common and is often available very fresh. Unfortunately, it can still be quite expensive, and it often doesn't have as much flavor as its wild cousins.

One way to enjoy fish more—and save money—is to cook with lesser-known varieties. New kinds of fish are constantly appearing in fish markets as people become more adventurous, well traveled, and willing to experiment. Ethnic markets are good sources for unusual varieties of seafood, much of it surprisingly fresh and delicious.

If you don't know a lot about fish, it might pay to go first to a fancy fish store where everything is clearly labeled and get a sense of what looks good and what things cost before setting out for an ethnic market.

Selecting and Buying Fish

Always approach fish shopping with an open mind and make your selections based on freshness rather than limiting yourself to a particular kind of fish. Most of the recipes in this chapter call for a *style* of fish—firm-fleshed, thick fillets, and so on—so that you have some flexibility when you get to the fish market.

Buy whole fish instead of fillets and have the fishmonger fillet them for you or take them home and do it yourself. There are several reasons why: it's always easier to judge the freshness of a whole fish than of fillets; fishmongers tend to fillet fish that is starting to look a little stale; and you'll usually want to use the head and bones to make a basic broth.

HOW MUCH FISH TO BUY You'll need to gauge the amount of fish to buy on your guests' or family's appetite and if the fish soup is being served as one of many courses or as a first or main course. Usually I count on 3 to 4 ounces of fish fillets (buy 6 to 8 ounces whole fish) per person for a light opening soup and 6 to 8 ounces (buy 12 to 16 ounces whole fish) for a main-course version. Whole fish is usually half bones, head, and guts, so buy twice the weight you would of fillets.

FRESH VERSUS FROZEN Because commercial fishing boats often spend weeks at sea without coming into port, so-called fresh fish has often been out of the water for many days before it reaches the fish market.

Although no frozen fish will compare with a fish cooked the same day it is caught, techniques for freezing fish have been much improved in recent years so that a fish that has been quickly gutted and immediately frozen will retain more flavor and a better texture than so-called "fresh" fish.

If you end up buying frozen fish or friends give you fish they have caught and frozen themselves, use it within a week or two. The flavor and texture of frozen fish slowly deteriorates in a home freezer. Defrost frozen fish in the refrigerator or in a microwave, never in warm water, which can damage its texture.

STORING FISH Once you get your fish home, cook it the same day even if this means making the soup in advance. Soup containing cooked fish holds better than raw fish, so it's better to make the soup right than to keep the fish waiting.

If you need to store the fish for a few hours or overnight before making the soup, it's

There are many ways to tell if a fish is fresh, but it takes a little practice to get the knack:

- Because of rigor mortis (not a common cookbook term, but it's important to know this), fish that is very fresh is stiff and may even curl up on itself. Fish still in rigor mortis will be completely stiff and stick straight out when you hold it horizontally by the head. Rigor mortis usually lasts for only 2 to 24 hours, so when you find fish this fresh—which may be rare—buy it, whatever the variety, and adapt your cooking plans accordingly.

- Fresh fish is firm to the touch. If the fishmonger will let you, press firmly on the side of the fish; if there is an indentation when you pull your finger away or if the flesh feels soft, look for another fish.

- Look at the eyes. Many very fresh fish have cloudy eyes, so clarity is less accurate as an indication of freshness than most people think. Look instead for eyes that protrude and, as silly as it sounds, have some kind of expression such as cynicism or indignation. Old fish looks dead; fresh fish still look surprised at having been caught.

- Lift up the base of the head and look at the gills. They should be rosy pink or red, never brown or gray. This test isn't completely reliable because the gills are sometimes caked with mud, but with a little practice you'll learn to see the difference.

- Fresh fish is shiny. Most very fresh fish is coated with a thin layer of transparent slime that makes it slippery to the touch. As fish deteriorates, the slime will either dry out or turn white and thick.

- Don't buy fish that seems dried out. Look at the end of the tail, which will be dry and curled at the very end if the fish is stale or hasn't been stored properly.

- Fresh fish should not smell fishy. Lift up the flap under the base of the head and give the gills a sniff. There should be a fresh sealike smell.

essential to gut the fish as soon as you get it home if the fishmonger hasn't done it already. Keep the fish in the coldest part of the refrigerator or, better yet, covered in ice in the refrigerator. Be sure not to let the ice melt so that a few hours later the fish is submerged in water. A good system is to put the ice with the fish in a colander placed over a pot to catch the water.

The Best Fish for Soups

One secret to good fish soup is to use more than one kind of fish. Although certain fish have more taste and a better texture than others, no one kind of fish is best. The best flavor comes from having as many different kinds of fish in the pot as possible. Try to select several kinds of fish without sacrificing freshness.

The best fish for soups are round fish with thick fillets and firm flesh that won't fall apart in the broth.

Some of the best and least expensive of this type on the East Coast are black sea bass, striped bass, and red snapper. Monkfish (lotte) is also excellent for soup-making.

On the West Coast, try rockfish, butterfish, and white sea bass. Although so-called true cod is found only on the Atlantic coast, West Coast varieties such as Pacific cod and lingcod are also excellent.

Tilapia fillets have a lean, mild flavor which makes them good for chowders and delicately flavored soups. The fish take well to aquaculture, so they're often available in areas where truly fresh fish is a rarity.

Avoid oily fish such as mackerel, bluefish, sardines, and fresh anchovies, which will give the soup too strong a taste. Be careful of salmon, which also gives soups and broths a strong flavor that can be unpleasant. The bones from flatfish such as sole and flounder make an excellent basic broth, but flatfish fillets are expensive, don't give much flavor to the broth, and fall apart once they are cooked through.

Kinds of Fish

ANCHOVIES: It's unusual to find fresh anchovies in American fish markets, and when they are available they are rarely suitable for soup-making because of their oiliness and strong flavor. Salted or canned anchovies are sometimes ground to a paste and used as a substitute for shrimp paste in Asian fish soups. A similar paste can also be used to prepare the French *anchoïade*—a strong-flavored puree of anchovies and olive oil best spread on croutons and eaten *with* the soup, not in it.

BASS: There are many types of bass, including fresh- and saltwater varieties. The most common bass on the East Coast is the black sea bass. It usually can be found very fresh, it's inexpensive, and it provides pure white firm-fleshed fillets. It's perfect for making soup. White bass, found on the West Coast, is also excellent in soups but is quite expensive.

Until about 10 years ago, striped bass was the most popular bass on the East Coast, but since then commercial fishing of striped bass has been restricted and now it's available only farm-raised. When you do find it, use it.

BLACKFISH: Sometimes called *tautog*, blackfish is often found in East Coast fish markets. It is excellent for soup-making because it has very firm, lean, white flesh. Because it lends itself poorly to large-scale commercial fishing, it is often found very fresh and sometimes even alive (in Chinese markets).

BLOWFISH: Until recently, fishermen used to throw blowfish back into the water, but the public is gradually beginning to discover that these fish are delightful to eat. Blowfish are small—usually about 4 inches long—but since they have only one central bone, which is easy to remove, each fish provides two tasty little fillets. At the fish market they are usually sold with the skin and heads removed, ready to fillet and cook.

BUTTERFISH: There are two kinds. The fillets found in West Coast supermarkets, labeled *butterfish fillets,* are usually taken from the sablefish, a round fish that grows up to

15 pounds. Whole butterfish—the authentic Pacific butterfish—are usually under a pound and look like miniature pompano. Unless you're just using them to make broth, Pacific butterfish are more trouble than they're worth. Butterfish fillets don't have much flavor, but they're convenient in soups where you don't need the head and bones to make a broth.

CATFISH: Years ago, catfish had a questionable reputation (at least among northerners) as a bottom dweller and a garbage fish, but times have changed, and catfish has attained a certain culinary chic. It's very adaptable to farming, so it often shows up very fresh or even alive in Chinese markets. It has firm flesh that holds together well when cut into chunks or strips. Farmed catfish doesn't have a great deal of flavor, so unless I have access to a specimen caught in the wild, I try to use catfish along with other kinds of fish.

COD, FRESH: Many varieties of cod and unrelated fish go by that name, but fortunately all of them work well in the soup pot. Other than varieties of true cod, which can be found on both the Atlantic and Pacific coasts, haddock, hake, and pollack are similar and can be prepared in the same way. So-called rock cod and lingcod from the Pacific coast are not true cod, but both have excellent firm flesh that makes them good in soups.

One disadvantage to cooking with cod is that it tends to fall apart when even slightly overcooked. Time the cooking carefully when you add it to the pot.

COD, SALT (ITALIAN, BACCALÀ; SPANISH, BACALAO; FRENCH, MORUE): Salt cod is cod that has been cured in brine or directly in salt and then allowed to dry slowly. To use it, simply soak it in cold water in the refrigerator for between 24 and 48 hours, changing the water every 6 hours. To know when it's been soaking long enough, just bite into a corner and taste. When it's no longer salty, it's ready to use.

Once you've soaked the dried cod, you can use it in the same way you would fresh fish, but it's especially good in Mediterranean-style dishes. Of course you may be wondering why one should bother with salt cod in this age of the airplane and deep freeze. Aficionados claim—and I agree—that salt cod develops a quality all its own in the same way as other preserved foods such as ham, sausage, and pickles.

The best salt cod—and the easiest to deal with—comes already filleted from Canada or Norway. Of the Canadian salt cod, that from Quebec or Nova Scotia—especially the "Gaspé" variety—is the best. When you're selecting salt cod, look for thick rectangular chunks called *middles,* which are firm and thick enough to hold up in a soup. A second choice is the so-called loin, which usually has pieces of skin and bone still attached. Avoid thin strips or fillets, which are meant to be flaked or pureed and don't have as good a flavor.

CONGER EEL: This is one of those creatures that have long been popular in European fish soups but haven't caught on in America. Admittedly it looks a bit daunting— it has a large pointed jaw with little jagged teeth—but it has good, firm, white flesh and a full flavor that makes it excellent for soups and fish stews. It's plentiful on the East

Coast—fishermen I talk to are always running into it but usually throw it back. When you find it, buy it.

DOLPHINFISH (MAHIMAHI): Don't worry; this isn't dolphin the mammal but a completely unrelated fish. It's most common in Hawaii but can also be found in markets on the West Coast. It has firm, white flesh that holds up well in soups and stews.

EELS: Even though eels are eaten in huge quantities throughout the world, Americans have all but ignored them. In fact the mere thought of having eel for dinner often inspires nothing more than a bone-tingling chill. This is not surprising considering their resemblance to snakes and the fact that you need to buy them alive; like lobster, they deteriorate quickly when dead. Eels can be wonderful to eat—provided you have a coop-erative fishmonger who will skin them for you—or you have a certain love for the macabre and want to do it yourself.

To get your live eel you'll probably have to go to Chinatown. Ask the fishmonger to skin and gut it for you. He'll probably want to chop it up, but if you're fussy and want all the pieces the same size, do this yourself. If you're adventurous and want to clean the eel yourself—I always like to try these things at least once—you'll have to go through a couple of grisly processes to get the creature ready for the pot.

To clean an eel, grab it at the base of the neck with a towel and whack its head on the kitchen counter (you need the towel; eels are slippery and may get loose and end up hiding under the stove). This first step, presumably to kill it or at least stun the eel into docility, makes no visible change in its behavior; an eel with its head bashed in will still wrap firmly around your arm as you grip its neck.

Next, make a slit around the base of its neck and first pull the skin away with a pair of pliers; then peel it off like a glove using a towel. Gut the eel starting at the base of the head by slitting into the cavity that runs along its underside and pulling out the guts. Rinse the cavity under cold running water. Be forewarned: none of this does anything to slow down the eel. And last, cutting the skinless eel into inch-long segments still does nothing to abate its electrical energy—each of the pieces continues to twitch, including the head, with the mouth continuously opening and closing. Still interested?

Once you get the eel in segments, the rest is easy. The only difference in the treat-ment of eel and other fish is that because eel can be a bit oily it's a good idea to season and flour it and brown it in butter or olive oil before putting it in the soup pot. You may also want to remove the bones by slicing along the back of each 3- or 4-inch segment and using only the fillets.

Eel is especially good in red wine soups and in Thai and Vietnamese soups.

FLATFISH: Although flatfish such as fluke and flounder give a full, sealike flavor to a basic broth, the flesh itself is fragile and tends to fall apart. Halibut, the largest of all flatfish, is an exception. Its flesh is thick enough to cut up into good-sized meaty chunks that will hold together in a soup. It also has an excellent flavor. If you have access to small, very fresh flatfish without paying a premium price, it may be worthwhile to use these fish to prepare a basic fish broth, but use fillets of firmer fish for the chunks.

GROUPER: Although I've had good luck finding very fresh grouper in New York markets, I haven't seen it in my sporadic travels to other places. Because the fillets are very thick and very white, I sometimes cut them into very large chunks and make a dramatic presentation by serving only one piece of fillet per serving, surrounded by the flavorful broth.

MACKEREL: When very fresh, mackerel is one of my favorite fish, but it can be too strong if thrown haphazardly into a pot of soup. The best way to cook it is to lightly marinate it, grill it, and serve atop some noodles in a Japanese *dashi*.

MONKFISH (LOTTE): Twenty years ago there was no market for this fish in the United States, and when you were able to find it, it cost practically nothing. Now monkfish, long a favorite of Mediterranean cooks, has caught on in America, and although it is no longer a bargain, it is an excellent fish for soup-making. It is easy to fillet—there is only one central backbone, which once removed leaves two meaty fillets with absolutely no bones. There is only some unsightly coloration on the fillets, which is easy to trim off. Although most fish stores sell monkfish with the skin taken off, it's easy to skin yourself. Just pull on the skin and cut it away from the flesh before filleting.

OCTOPUS: As a child I'd sit for hours flipping the pages of one of my favorite books, a colorful tome about life in the sea. But one page I dared only look at during the day—the fascinating, dreadful page was filled with the image of an octopus awaiting its prey. Had I known that years later I'd be sitting in some trattoria happily wolfing down big meaty tentacles while quaffing red wine, I would never have wanted to grow up. Most of us who enjoy octopus encounter it in Italian or Greek restaurants, either in salads or grilled. But unlike other seafood (except the octopus's cephalopod relatives, squid and cuttlefish), octopus shares many of the characteristics of tougher cuts of meat—it needs to be tenderized and cooked lightly, or it needs to be braised for a good hour or two. Everyone has his or her own method of tenderizing it. The Greeks beat it against rocks, the Japanese marinate it with shredded daikon, some cooks dip it repeatedly in boiling water, and somewhere I read that freezing it, thawing it, and freezing it again does the trick. But when making soup (or stew), you don't have to worry about tenderizing the octopus, because it will soften and yield a rich gelatinous broth in the same way as stewing cuts of meat. I like it best braised in red wine, like the Octopus and Red Wine Soup on page 320.

POMPANO: These elegant-looking fish have lovely firm flesh and are delicious no matter how you cook them. They work fine in soups but are usually quite expensive.

PORGY: These small round fish have very fragile flesh, and fishmongers are rarely willing to fillet them, but because they're so inexpensive I sometimes use them whole to make fish broth.

RED SNAPPER: Because of its bright red skin, I like to use red snapper for fish soups where I can show it off by arranging the fillets skin side up in wide bowls. Red snapper is usually more expensive than most round fish, but, in New York at least, it is sold already gutted, so you're actually getting a better yield of fish for a given weight.

ROCKFISH: There seem to be dozens of varieties of rockfish, mostly from the West Coast. Sometimes called *rock cod* or *Pacific snapper*, they vary considerably in price, and as usual when on uncertain ground I opt for the most expensive. The bolina is the best for soup-making. The thickest varieties seem to have the firmest flesh, best for making soup.

SALMON: Even though salmon has a delicate flavor when eaten alone, it develops a strong taste when simmered in a soup. Reserve it for soups made with red wine or soups that already contain full-flavored shellfish.

SEA ROBIN: Very popular in Europe, this peculiar-shaped fish (it's red and looks like it has wings) is one of the traditional ingredients of a *bouillabaisse*. Although sea robin is very abundant on the American side of the Atlantic, most fishermen throw it back. It is just now gradually beginning to be appreciated and to appear in eastern markets. It has an excellent flavor but a lot of bones, which need to be pulled out carefully with pliers.

SHAD: Shad comes into season in the early spring and disappears during the summer. Because the roe is more popular than the flesh, the rest of the fish is usually quite inexpensive. It's also delicious. The main drawback to shad is that even when filleted by an expert, it contains lots of hard-to-find little bones; so go over the fillets carefully and pull out any remaining bones with a pair of pliers. Or use it in a puree-type soup where the bones will be strained out. (See *soupe de poisson niçoise*, page 313.)

SHARK: This much-maligned fish is still an excellent bargain when you can find it. On the East Coast, mako shark is the most common. It comes in thick white steaks looking something like swordfish and holds up well in soups. I also had good luck cooking sand shark a friend bought at the wholesale fish market and a rather frightening creature (probably a leopard shark) I found once in a Parisian fish stall. Although I've never cooked it, I've heard that thresher shark, available on the West Coast, is also excellent.

SQUID: Because squid has a lot of flavor, it's best in full-flavored Mediterranean-style soups made with lots of herbs, garlic, and red wine, which hold up to its taste.

To clean squid, give the tentacles a yank. Most of the insides will come out of the hood, but reach under and pull out the plasticlike feather that runs up the inside of the hood. Rinse out the inside of the hood. Cut the tentacles off just under the eyes and save them. If you want to use the ink, it will color a soup and give it a wonderful sealike flavor. Carefully transfer the ink sac (inside the hood) to a small bowl. Puncture the sac with a knife and squeeze out the ink. Whisk the ink into a fish soup 2 minutes before serving. Discard all the other insides of the squid. Pull the thin purple skin off the hoods or scrape it off with a paring knife. Cut the hoods into ½-inch rings and rinse thoroughly.

TILEFISH: This is an excellent soup fish with thick, white fillets. However, be careful to not overcook it, or it will flake and fall apart.

TROUT: Perhaps because trout are farmed and kept alive until just before they are marketed, they are one of the few freshwater fish that are available year-round. Unfortunately, farmed trout have a very delicate flavor that easily gets lost in an assertively flavored soup. I sometimes use them instead of eel to prepare the *anguille au vert* on page 321.

TUNA/SWORDFISH/STURGEON/YELLOWTAIL: These fish all have firm, dense flesh that makes them more suitable for grilling and sautéing than for cutting up to make soup. But one marvelous trick is to lightly grill or sauté slices of any of these, place them in wide soup bowls, and then ladle over a small amount of full-flavored, light-textured soup such as clam or mussel broth.

Tips for Cooking Fish

Unless you're making a pureed soup, where the texture of the cooked fish is of no importance, it is best to prepare the soup almost completely before adding the fish. In this way the pieces of fish—usually filleted and cut into manageable pieces—can be added to the soup just before serving so they don't overcook.

REMOVING BONES FROM FILLETS

Even though fish fillets are not supposed to have any bones, they usually have a set running along the front two-thirds of the fillet. Most recipes recommend pulling these out with a pair of pliers, but this is a nuisance. It's easier just to cut a thin strip out of the fillet by cutting along each side of the strip of bones and just pulling it out. This leaves the front part of the fillet cut in half, but since fish for soups is cut into chunks this rarely matters.

CUTTING UP FISH FOR SOUP

Keep the pieces the same size and shape so they cook evenly and look better in the bowl. The size of the pieces is up to you, but they will shrink by almost half once cooked, so cut them accordingly. You may want to try cutting them on the bias into strips or triangles. For dramatic effect I

WHAT LIQUID TO USE FOR FISH SOUP?

The best European-style soups are made with freshly made fish broth. If you want to flavor a fish soup with vegetables but don't want the vegetables floating around in the finished soup, cook the vegetables in the fish broth and strain them along with the fish bones before adding the broth to the soup. If you do want vegetables in the finished soup, put the vegetables directly into the soup and leave them out of the fish broth.

If you don't want to bother making fish broth, be assured that water works perfectly well for most fish soups. Most already contain many flavorful ingredients, such as herbs, tomatoes, garlic, Pernod, saffron, and so on. Chicken broth makes a good substitute for fish broth, but don't use bottled clam juice; it has a strong taste and will spoil your soup.

Japanese cooks rarely bother making fish broth but use a flavorful *dashi* instead.

sometimes leave the pieces of fish very large—perhaps one large piece in each bowl—and then I serve the soup with a fork, knife, and spoon. You may even want to practice positioning the fish fillets in decorative patterns in the bowls so you'll know exactly what you're doing when it comes time to serve.

REMOVING THE SKIN   Whether or not to leave the skin on fish fillets is mostly a matter of taste. If I'm presenting a fish soup in wide bowls with the fillets carefully arranged and the broth poured around, I usually leave the skin on, especially if I'm using brightly colored fish. In soups where the fish is cooked along with the other ingredients, I remove the skin because it has a tendency to come off in the broth—and not everyone likes having a piece of fish skin left dangling at the end of a fork.

When you're leaving the skin on, watch out for a couple of things. One is the tendency for the skin to contract in contact with hot liquid, which causes the fillet to curl. There are two ways around this—lightly scoring the fillets with a sharp knife and poaching the fillets skin side up with just enough liquid to cover. This way the flesh contracts before the skin, and curling is avoided.

If you're leaving the skin on the fillets, be careful that the fish have been scaled thoroughly. Fishmongers are often a bit careless about this. It's a good idea to scrape the fillets with a sharp knife and then rinse them to eliminate any scales that might have been left.

COOKING TIMES   Fish needs to cook for about 8 minutes per inch of thickness, so time adding the fish as well as you can before serving the soup. Keep in mind also that it will continue to cook in the hot bowls.

If you're making a soup with a variety of fish, the fillets will likely have different thicknesses, so you may have to add them in stages. Thin fillets may need to cook for only a minute.

SERVING FISH SOUP   One of the prettiest and least formal ways to serve a fish soup is to ladle it out of a large tureen at the table. The host or hostess can serve from one end of the table, or someone can walk around with the tureen and let the guests serve themselves.

If you don't like the idea of serving soup in the dining room—dealing with the tureen can be cumbersome—ladle the soup out in the kitchen. This way you can place the fish in the bowls yourself and make sure that each one looks beautiful before taking them out to the guests.

If you want to make an attractive arrangement of fish in the individual soup bowls, a good plan is to simmer the fish fillets at the last minute in a wide pan in a little bit of the soup. This makes the fish easier to distribute into the bowls—you're not left searching through a large pot of soup for pieces of fish.

Methods for Cooking and Presenting Fish Soups

SOUPS MADE WITH WHOLE FISH VERSUS SOUPS MADE WITH FILLETS: Traditional recipes for fish soups often suggest boiling the fish whole or cutting it into chunks so bones are left in the individual pieces. Contemporary diners don't want to pick through bones while they're eating soup, so the recipes here use the fish bones and head to make a broth and add the fillets at the end.

Some soups, such as *bouillabaisse*, are traditionally served in two courses—first the broth itself, followed by the whole fish presented on a platter. In updated versions using fillets, the fillets are presented in the bowl of broth, all as one course.

If you decide to serve a soup containing whole fish—admittedly a dramatic sight— know your guests. They may not know how to eat a whole cooked fish with a knife and fork without turning it into a hopeless mess.

STEWLIKE SOUPS: Some of the most delicious fish soups were originally stews. Because these soups contain a high proportion of fish to broth, they actually fall some- where in the middle between soups and stews. There are many different types—the French alone have dozens—and most contain either white or red wine, while some are made with beer, cider, or a basic fish broth. Because these soups contain relatively small amounts of liquid, they lend themselves to dramatic presentations, with the fish arranged in wide bowls and surrounded by broth, unlike most fish soups, in which the fish ends up submerged and invisible in the liquid.

Most recipes for stewlike fish soups suggest poaching the fish directly in some kind of flavorful liquid. Although this method will work, it requires a large amount of poach- ing liquid to cover the fish completely. The finished broth is then cooked down (to con- centrate its flavor) while the fish—and the guests—is kept waiting.

Instead of poaching the fish, try steaming it over a small amount of the flavorful liquid such as a fish broth made from the bones and heads of the fish. Because less liq- uid is needed for steaming, the soup base can be cooked down in advance and used at the last minute as a steaming liquid for the fish. In this way there is no waiting around for either guests or fish. If you cook a lot, a steamer might be a worthwhile investment, but you can improvise one by putting a cake rack or a metal trivet in the bottom of a wide pot. You then add just enough of the liquid you're using to come up to the bot- tom of the rack, arrange the fish on the rack, and cover the pot. Just before serving, bring the broth to a rolling boil so that the fish is steamed and any juices it releases fall into the hot liquid. Arrange the fish in hot soup bowls and ladle the hot liquid right out of the steamer.

Another method is to prepare the soup using the fish bones and heads and then bake the cut-up fish on an oiled sheet pan in a 400°F oven for 5 to 10 minutes (depend- ing on the thickness of the fish) just before serving. It's then a simple matter of distrib- uting the fish among bowls and pouring the broth over it.

Many traditional recipes for fish stews call for specific fish. Since it isn't always easy to find a large assortment of fresh fish, don't hesitate to substitute different varieties—including saltwater fish in stews that originally contained only freshwater varieties.

PUREE-TYPE SOUPS: Pureed fish soups are strained through a food mill so that the flesh from the fish ends up pureed in the soup and helps thicken it and improve its flavor. Like bisques, pureed fish soups usually have some kind of starchy binder such as rice or bread crumbs to help keep the minute particles of fish in suspension.

When you're making pureed soups, you don't have to worry about overcooking the fish—since it's all being pureed, texture is unimportant. The only laborious part is working the soup through a food mill.

If you don't have a food mill, you can puree the soup in a blender or food processor and then strain it through an ordinary kitchen strainer. The problem with this method is that a blender or food processor breaks the bones into tiny bits, which are difficult to strain out and may end up in the soup. The best way around this is to fillet the fish, make a broth with the heads and bones, strain it, use it to cook the fillets, and then puree the broth and cooked fish in the blender or food processor.

CREAM SOUPS AND CHOWDERS: Even though cream soups and chowders are made all over the world, they all use similar techniques and many of the same ingredients. Chowders are simply cream soups (sometimes made with milk) that contain starchy ingredients such as potatoes or corn.

To prepare a cream soup or chowder, make a fish broth with the fish heads and bones, a little onion, and herbs bundled into a bouquet garni.

Prepare a flavor base by gently cooking vegetables such as leeks, celery, onions, garlic, hot peppers, and potatoes in butter or oil. Add the fish broth to this vegetable mixture and simmer the soup for 10 or 15 minutes to soften the vegetables and extract their flavor.

Once this flavorful soup base is ready, add the cut-up fish just before serving the soup. Finish the soup with heavy cream, milk, or sour cream.

Making Fish Soups: A Step-by-Step Guide

Almost every country has its own fish soups. Although the kinds of fish and the ingredients that go into these fish soups vary enormously, most of the techniques for making fish soups are the same throughout the world. Once you understand the logical progression of steps, preparing a fish soup from even the most exotic place is a simple matter of substituting different ingredients at various stages during the cooking.

Because most fish cooks quickly and loses its texture and flavor if overcooked, adding the fish to the soup is often the last step. A skillful cook will prepare a basic soup independent of the fish—except perhaps the fish head and bones—before adding the filleted fish.

STEP ONE: PREPARING THE FLAVOR BASE The first step in making most fish soups is to cook a flavorful mixture of ingredients in a small amount of oil or fat before adding any liquid. This brings out the flavor of certain ingredients such as onions, garlic, sweet peppers, ham, spices, and certain herbs. Each country has its own mixtures, but feel free to improvise on your own.

Bumbu (Indonesian mixture of kemiri nuts or macadamia nuts, hot chilies, shallots, cloves, ginger, shrimp paste, and garlic)
Sofregit (Catalan onion and tomato mixture cooked in olive oil)
Soffrito (Italian mixture of aromatic herbs and vegetables cooked in olive oil or with ham or pancetta)
Sofrito (Spanish mixture similar to *sofregit* but containing ham)
Mirepoix or *Matignon* (French mixtures of carrots, celery, and onion sometimes combined with ham or pork)
Onions (used alone for northern European and American soups such as chowders)
Indian curry pastes
Thai curry pastes

Olive oil (for cooking Mediterranean mixtures)
Peanut oil (used in Asia and South America)
Palm oil (used in South America)

STEP TWO: ADDING LIQUID When the ingredients in the flavor base have softened and released their flavor, usually in about 20 minutes, liquid is added. Asian cooks are likely to use water or chicken broth (in Thailand, Vietnam, or Indonesia, it will be flavored with fish sauce or shrimp paste), while European cooks prefer fish broth made fresh from the fish bones and heads. Here are a few liquids that make good soups:

Water
Fish broth (made from the heads and bones of the fish)
Wine (white or red, cooked in advance with the fish heads and bones)
Tomatoes
Cider
Dashi

STEP THREE: ADDING FLAVORFUL INGREDIENTS While some ingredients best release their flavor when cooked in a small amount of fat, others such as tomatoes, squash, and mushrooms are best simmered directly in the soup before the fish is added. Quick-cooking vegetables such as spinach and snow peas may need to be added to the hot soup just a minute or two before serving.

Fish sauce (Southeast Asian, Indonesian)
Sesame oil (Southeast Asian, Chinese)
Soy sauce (Chinese, Japanese, Korean)
Tamarind (Southeast Asian, Indonesian)
Lemongrass and kaffir lime leaves (Southeast Asian, Indonesian)
Miso (Japanese)

Twoenjang (Korean)
Bouquet garni (European, American)
Preserved vegetables (Chinese, Vietnamese)
Fermented black beans (Chinese)

Vegetables Added for Variety:
Leafy greens (spinach, watercress, mustard greens, etc., added near the end of cooking; typical in Asian soups)
Corn (North and South American chowders)
Root vegetables (North and South America, eastern and northern Europe)
Mushrooms (Chinese mushrooms, straw mushrooms—Thailand—enokidake—Japan)

STEP FOUR: ADDING FINAL FLAVORINGS AND THICKENERS Many ingredients will break down or lose their flavor if cooked for more than a few minutes. Finely chopped delicate herbs such as basil, mint, parsley, or chervil lose their fragrance; cream or coconut milk may turn grainy; egg yolks will curdle; green vegetable purees will turn gray; and garlic will lose its pungency. Thickeners such as cornstarch or vegetable purees should also be added during the last 10 minutes of cooking, or they will break down. Here are some examples of ingredients that are best added shortly before the soup is served.

Final Finishes:
Enricheners:
Cream
Coconut milk
Egg yolks
Butter (plain or herb)

Thickeners:
Cornstarch
Vegetable purees
Egg yolks

Flavorings:
Picada (Catalan garlic and almond mixture, page 348)
Romesco (similar to *picada*)
Aïoli (Provençal garlic mayonnaise, page 349)
Rouille (Provençal mixture of bread crumbs, garlic, and saffron or red peppers, page 350)
Thai-style curry pastes (page 17–18)
Flavored butters (pages 593–594)
Indian *tadka*

STEP FIVE: ADDING THE FISH Because fish cooks very quickly, it is often the last thing to be added to a fish soup. Provided the fish is already filleted and the bones removed, it needs only to be simmered in the soup for a few minutes before serving. In most cases this is a simple matter of sliding the filleted and cut-up fish into the simmering soup and cooking it for about 8 minutes per inch of thickness. In some soups, where the fish is carefully filleted and presented in wide bowls surrounded with broth, the fish should be poached in only enough of the soup base to come up its sides so that it can be retrieved easily for arranging in the bowls.

STEP SIX: SERVING OPTIONAL ACCOMPANIMENTS (IN THE SOUP OR ON THE SIDE) Many soups are enhanced by sprinkling in condiments, bread, croutons, or other ingredients on them at the last minute or by passing these ingredients at the table for guests to help themselves. These ingredients can provide contrast, additional richness, or bulk. Here are a few possibilities:

Croutons (cubes or heart-shaped, page 595)
Bread (passed at the table, or stale slice put in the bowl before ladling over soup)
Rice (cooked rice added to the soup to make it more filling or passed at the table)
Noodles (simmered in brothlike soups shortly before serving)
Mustard (passed at the table for meaty soups such as pot-au-feu)
Cornichons (passed at the table to contrast with rich meaty soups)

Basic Fish Broth

In most cases you'll make the basic fish broth out of the bones and heads of the fish you buy for the soup, but in some situations—shellfish soups, for instance—you'll have to buy fish heads and bones separately to make the broth. In Chinese markets good fresh fish heads are available at very little cost, but in some parts of the country you may need to buy inexpensive whole fish such as porgy or undersized bass to make the broth.

This is a simple, classic fish broth. When fish broth is prepared for Mediterranean soups or full-flavored versions from around the world, it usually contains other vegetables such as fennel, garlic, and peppers in addition to the leeks and onions included here.

MAKES 2½ QUARTS

4 pounds fish bones and heads, from about 6 pounds whole
    fish, or 4 pounds whole fish, gutted and scaled
2 medium-size onions, peeled and sliced
3 leeks, green part only, washed (optional)
4 fresh thyme sprigs or I teaspoon dried leaves
I small bunch of parsley
1¼ cups dry white wine (optional)

FISH bones and heads need to be rinsed thoroughly before they are used to make broth, or traces of blood will cloud the broth and make it gray.

IF the fishmonger has not removed the gills from the base of the head, you'll have to take them out yourself. The easiest way to do this is to reach under the base of the head with a pair of scissors and cut the gills on each end and then just pull them out with your fingers.

BREAK the bones into several pieces with a cleaver or an old knife. Put them in a large bowl and cover them with cold water. Let them soak for about 30 minutes, change the water every 10 minutes, rinse them thoroughly one last time, and drain.

COMBINE the sliced onions, leek greens, fish bones, thyme, and parsley in a 4-quart pot. Add the white wine if desired and enough cold water to barely cover the bones. Bring the water to a slow simmer, skimming off any froth that floats to the top with a ladle. After the broth has simmered slowly for about 30 minutes, strain it and throw out the bones.

Red Wine Fish Broth

Some of the most delicious soups in the world are made with red wine. The French are masters at cooking fish in red wine, and almost every region has its own version of red wine fish soups and stews. Making a basic red wine broth is an easy shortcut for more elaborate red wine soups. Although traditional recipes often call for simmering the whole cut-up fish in the wine with herbs and aromatic vegetables and then serving the mixture, bones and all, it is more convenient to fillet the fish and use the bones to prepare a red wine fish broth in advance. The fish fillets are then poached in the broth just before serving.

You'll need a lot of red wine—it takes more than 2 bottles to prepare a quart of broth—or the flavor will be weak and the soup will be an unappetizing pink instead of a rich purple-brown.

The kind of wine to use is also important. The same kinds that work well for a broth for meat work in a broth for fish (see page 96).

MAKES 1 QUART

2 pounds fish bones and heads
2 tablespoons unsalted butter
1 medium-size onion, coarsely chopped
4 garlic cloves, crushed but not peeled
5 fresh thyme sprigs or 2 teaspoons dried
2 quarts full-bodied, low-tannin red wine, about 2½ fifths)

BREAK the fish heads and bones into pieces with a cleaver or heavy knife and soak them in cold water for at least 30 minutes, changing the water at least twice.

MELT the butter in a heavy-bottomed 4-quart pot and add the fish heads and bones, vegetables, and thyme. Cook over low to medium heat for 20 to 30 minutes, until the bones fall apart and the juices have formed a browned, caramelized layer on the bottom of the pot. Be careful not to burn the bottom of the pot. Add 2 cups of the red wine, turn up the heat, and reduce it while scraping the bottom of the pot with a wooden spoon until the wine completely evaporates and a caramelized layer forms a second time on the bottom of the pan. Again, be careful not to let the bottom or sides of the pot burn. Add the rest of the wine, and turn the heat down low enough to keep the wine at a slow simmer. Partially cover the pot so there is only a ½-inch crack to one side of the lid and leave the broth at a simmer for 30 minutes. Strain the broth through a fine strainer. The broth freezes well.

French Mediterranean-Style Fish Soup

BOUILLABAISSE

Because *bouillabaisse* is arguably one of the world's greatest soups, food cognoscenti love to argue the relative merits of their favorite versions in restaurants in Marseilles, Toulon, and Paris. I hesitate to call this soup a *bouillabaisse*. People are more or less dogmatic on this subject, the most resolutely purist insistent that *bouillabaisse* can be made only within sight of Mediterranean shores, moderates able to enjoy a *bouillabaisse* as far away as Paris. Any American rendition will certainly be a far cry from an authentic Mediterranean version but no less pleasurable. Many of the ingredients are the same, except for the kinds of fish. A strictly authentic *bouillabaisse* contains only fin fish and no shellfish but even in France this rule is often broken, so feel free to include mussels and clams or even lobster.

Cooks in the south of France always try to search out seven essential varieties of Mediterranean fish (unavailable elsewhere) but usually have to make do with fewer. Mediterranean cooks also have access to little fresh fish that they use to make a basic broth, which is in turn used to cook the large fish. In the United States sea bass, red snapper, and other lean varieties work best. Since tiny soup fish are rarely available here, the best method is to make a basic broth with the fish bones and heads.

Any fish soup is best made the day you buy the fish, but the fish broth for *bouillabaisse* can be made earlier the same day and the fish itself cooked shortly before serving.

MAKES 6 MAIN-COURSE SERVINGS

the fish broth:

8 pounds assorted whole fish, filleted, heads and bones
    reserved

3 tablespoons olive oil

6 garlic cloves, chopped

1 fennel bulb, coarsely chopped (optional)

1 medium-size onion, coarsely chopped

6 fresh thyme or marjoram sprigs or 1 teaspoon dried

a 2-inch strip of orange zest

for the soup base:

3 medium-size leeks, including 1 inch of the green,
    washed and finely chopped

3 tablespoons olive oil

8 medium-size tomatoes, peeled, seeded, and chopped

¼ cup Pernod or Ricard

½-inch slices of French baguette, about 5 per person

2 cups *rouille* (page 350) or saffron and garlic mayonnaise
    (page 350)

PREPARING THE FISH Cut out the strip of bones that runs along the front end of the fillets and cut the fillets in half lengthwise. If the fillets are large enough, these in turn can be cut in half; each guest should have at least 3 pieces.

IF you want to leave the skin on the fish, make several parallel cuts into the skin side of the fillets with a sharp knife to prevent them from curling during cooking.

PUT the fish bones and heads in a pot and cover with cold water for at least 30 minutes. Change the water every 10 minutes and drain.

MAKING THE FISH BROTH Heat 3 tablespoons of the olive oil in a 4-quart pot. Add the garlic, fennel, onion, herbs, and orange zest. Cook over medium heat, stirring occasionally with a wooden spoon, for about 10 minutes, until the vegetables start to soften.

BREAK up the fish bones with a cleaver or an old kitchen knife and add them to the cooking vegetables along with the heads. Stir them around with a wooden spoon for about 10 minutes more, until they start to break apart. Add just enough water to cover—about 5 cups—and leave the broth at a slow simmer for 30 minutes more. Strain through a medium mesh strainer. Discard the bones and vegetables.

PREPARING THE SOUP BASE Cook the leeks gently in the olive oil until they soften and turn slightly translucent, about 10 minutes. Don't let them brown. Add the tomatoes, Pernod, and fish broth. Simmer for about 10 minutes, until the tomatoes have softened. If you're not serving the soup right away, refrigerate this mixture until just before serving.

PREPARING THE BREAD Just before serving the soup, toast the bread slices under the broiler. Take 2 slices per person, smear them with a little *rouille* or mayonnaise, and reserve. Keep the remaining slices warm to pass in a basket at the table.

FINISHING AND SERVING THE BOUILLABAISSE Arrange the fillets skin side up in a pan large enough to hold them in a single layer. Bring the soup base to a simmer and ladle enough over the fillets to barely cover them. Heat the fillets over medium heat until the liquid returns to a slow simmer. The fillets are usually done as soon as they lose their sheen and take on a matte appearance. In any case, remember that they'll continue to cook in the soup bowls, so don't overcook them.

AS soon as the fish is ready, place 2 of the sauce-coated bread slices in each hot, wide soup bowl and arrange the fillets in the bowls with the largest piece on top of the bread.

PUT ½ cup of the *rouille* or mayonnaise in a large mixing bowl and whisk in the poaching liquid from the fish. Return this mixture to the rest of the hot soup, stir thoroughly, and ladle it over the fillets in the bowls. Serve immediately. Pass the remaining sauce and the crusty bread slices in a basket at the table.

Poached Fish in Garlic-Flavored Broth

BOURRIDE

A *bourride* is a kind of simplified *bouillabaisse* that often calls for only one kind of fish. It is thickened at the last minute with aïoli, a pungent mayonnaise made with olive oil and garlic. *Bourride* is one of my favorites among all soups—partly because I love aïoli and can add as much as I want to the broth. *Bourride* is also a simple soup to make for a last-minute dinner for a small gathering of friends.

This version contains Swiss chard, whose earthy flavor is a perfect foil for the garlic and is consistent with the rustic character of the soup. If you can't find Swiss chard or you don't like it, use spinach.

The fish broth, the Swiss chard, and the *aïoli* can all be prepared in advance, with only the final assembly of the soup done at the last minute.

MAKES 6 FIRST-COURSE OR 4 MAIN-COURSE SERVINGS

4 pounds firm-fleshed round fish, ideally 3 whole fish
    so each person gets one whole fillet
I large onion, coarsely chopped
I cup dry white wine (optional)
I bouquet garni

4 quarts water

1 bunch Swiss chard (about 1½ pounds)

salt

2 leeks, white part only, washed and finely chopped

¼ cup olive oil

2 cups *aïoli* (page 349)

slices of French bread, lightly dried out in the oven

IN ADVANCE Have the fishmonger gut and fillet the fish, remove the gills, and save the bones.

PREPARE the broth by combining the fish bones, the head, onion, wine, and bouquet garni in a 4-quart pot and adding just enough water to cover. Bring to a slow simmer over medium heat, simmer for 30 minutes, skimming off any froth that floats to the surface, and strain.

BRING the water to a boil and cut the white stems out of the chard. Rinse off the leaves and shred them: roll them over themselves and then thinly slice the rolls about ⅛ inch thick. Blanch the shredded leaves for 2 minutes in the boiling salted water. Drain them in a colander and rinse them off with cold running water so they don't overcook. When the leaves have drained, gently bunch them up and squeeze out the water.

GENTLY cook the leeks in the olive oil in a heavy-bottomed sauté pan for about 10 minutes, until they soften. Add the chard and stir it for 2 minutes to heat it through.

AT THE LAST MINUTE Ten minutes before you're ready to serve the soup, poach the fish fillets in the broth for about 8 minutes per inch of thickness. If you've decided to leave the skin on the fillets, spread them skin side up in a single layer in a wide pan; don't let the hot liquid cover the skin or it will curl.

DISTRIBUTE the hot leek and chard mixture in mounds in hot bowls and arrange the fish fillets next to or on top of the chard.

PUT 1 cup of the aïoli in a large bowl and whisk in half the hot broth. Combine this with the rest of the fish broth and pour the finished broth into the bowls over the fillets.

PASS the sliced bread and the rest of the *aïoli* at the table.

Saffron-Scented Fish Broth from Nice

SOUPE DE POISSON NIÇOISE

Think of this soup as a *bouillabaisse* with all the fish pureed into the broth. Which is better, *bouillabaisse* or *soupe de poisson*, remains a long-standing argument among the French. They're both incredible soups, with similar flavors but different styles.

Traditional recipes for *soupe de poisson niçoise* usually recommend boiling cut-up fish and vegetables until the vegetables soften and the fish falls apart—about 30 minutes. This version starts with a fish broth made from the fish bones and heads. The strained broth is then added to the fillets and the mixture cooked until the fillets start to fall apart. Eliminating the bones at the beginning makes it easy to puree the soup in a food processor or blender.

MAKES 8 FIRST-COURSE SERVINGS

4 pounds assorted whole fish
1 bouquet garni
1 small fennel bulb, stalk removed and chopped
¼ cup olive oil
2 medium-size onions, chopped
8 garlic cloves, peeled
6 tomatoes, seeded and coarsely chopped
1 pinch of saffron threads, soaked in 1 tablespoon water for
    20 minutes
1½ cups *rouille* (page 350)
salt
pepper
slices of French bread, lightly toasted

HAVE the fishmonger gut and fillet the fish and remove the gills and the skin from the fillets. Be sure to save the fish head and bones. When you get the fillets home, check them carefully and remove any bones. Put the fish bones and head in a bowl covered with cold water for 30 minutes. Change the water at least once during the soaking.

MAKE a fish broth by combining the bones and heads with the bouquet garni, chopped fennel stalk, and enough water to cover (about 5 cups) in a 4-quart pot. Bring the broth to a slow simmer and simmer for 30 minutes, skimming off any froth that floats to the top. Strain the broth through a medium-mesh strainer.

CHOP the rest of the fennel bulb and put it in a 4-quart pot with the olive oil, onions, and garlic. Put the pot over medium heat and stew the vegetables, stirring every few minutes with a wooden spoon, until tender, about 15 minutes altogether. Don't let the vegetables brown.

ADD the fish broth, tomatoes, and fish fillets to the vegetable mixture. Simmer the mixture until the fish is ready to fall apart, after about 30 minutes.

STRAIN the broth into a bowl and puree the solid ingredients in a food processor or blender for about 2 minutes. If the mixture gets too stiff and won't turn around, thin it with some of the broth. After pureeing the fish mixture, work it through a food mill, first through the coarse disk and then through the fine, adding broth from time to time to loosen the mixture.

COMBINE the pureed fish mixture with the remaining broth and add the saffron threads and their soaking water. Whisk ½ cup of the *rouille* into the soup. Bring the soup to a simmer, season it with salt and pepper, and serve it immediately in hot bowls. Pass the remaining *rouille* and the bread at the table.

SUGGESTIONS AND VARIATIONS | In Spain there is a low-fat version of fish soup, *caldo de perro gaditano*, that is similar to *soupe de poisson niçoise* and is flavored with Seville orange juice (regular orange juice combined with a little lime juice will also work) instead of *rouille*. To make it, prepare the soup as directed but include a 2-inch strip of orange zest in the bouquet garni. Then stir the juice from 2 oranges and the juice of 1 lime into the finished soup or use the juice of 2 Seville oranges and leave out the lime juice.

Spanish Fish Soup with Chilies, Almonds, and Garlic

ROMESCO

It would be hard for me to beat Colman Andrews's description of *romesco* in his marvelous book, *Catalan Cuisine:* "The word *romesco*, in fact, has three meanings in the region [Catalonia]: It is a variety of dried pepper, small, ruddy-red, and medium-mild, also called the *nyora* . . . ; it is a sauce; and it is a great seafood dish—perhaps the most interesting of all Catalan fish soups and stews."

The nyora peppers can quickly be put to rest because they are unavailable in the United States (anchos are the best substitute). The sauce is almost identical to the *picada* on page 348, and that is what we use here. As for the seafood soup, here it is.

MAKES 8 MAIN-COURSE SERVINGS

8 pounds assorted whole fish

the fish broth:

2 medium-size onions, sliced

3 leeks, green part only, washed (optional)

4 fresh thyme sprigs or 1 teaspoon dried leaves

1 small bunch of parsley

2 cups dry sherry or white wine

to finish the soup:

1 tablespoon extra virgin olive oil

1 cup picada (page 348)

salt

pepper

IN ADVANCE For the fish broth, have the fishmonger gut and fillet the fish and remove the gills and the skin from the fillets. Be sure to save the fish head and bones. When you get the fillets home, check them carefully and remove any bones.

SOAK the bones for 30 minutes. Thoroughly rinse the bones in cold water and combine them with the rest of the broth ingredients and enough water to cover in a 4-quart pot. Bring the broth to a slow simmer and simmer for 30 minutes, skimming off any froth that floats to the top. Strain the broth through a medium-mesh strainer.

AT THE LAST MINUTE To finish the soup, heat the olive oil in a 4-quart pot over medium heat until it ripples but hasn't started to smoke. Add the *picada* and stir with a wooden spoon for 2 minutes. Pour in 2 cups of the hot fish broth and whisk the mixture until smooth. Gently slide the fish fillets into the simmering liquid, adding more broth if necessary to barely cover the fillets.

POACH the fish fillets in the simmering broth for 5 to 10 minutes, about 8 minutes per inch of thickness. When the fillets are cooked, take them out with a slotted spoon or spatula and arrange them in hot bowls. Add the rest of the fish broth to the broth in the pot; bring it to a full simmer while whisking, season it with salt and pepper, and ladle it over the fish in the bowls.

SUGGESTIONS AND VARIATIONS | Most recipes for *romesco* suggest flouring the fish fillets and browning them in oil before adding them to the broth. The *picada* is then added to the pan used for browning the fillets. This is an excellent method if you have firm, thick fillets, but if the fillets are thin (an inch or less), they are likely to overcook by the time you brown them and then transfer them to the simmering broth.

French Country Red Wine Fish Soup

MATELOTE À LA BOURGUIGNONNE

A traditional *matelote* is a French soup or stew made from a mixture of freshwater fish and wine. The Burgundian version given here originally called for red Burgundy and the local freshwater fish, but I've Americanized it somewhat so it can be made with both freshwater and ocean fish—freshwater fish can be hard to find in some parts of the country—and California wine. A well-made red wine *matelote* is almost the same as a *coq au vin or a boeuf à la bourguignonne* except that fish is used instead of chicken or beef.

MAKES 6 FIRST-COURSE SERVINGS

Most *matelotes*—judging from those I've tasted in the French countryside—are made by quickly simmering cut-up whole fish in wine and then rapidly boiling down the poaching liquid to concentrate its flavor. The problem with this method is that you're stuck with a lot of last-minute cooking and the red wine isn't cooked enough, so the *matelote* ends up tasting harsh and acidic.

In this version the red wine broth is made in advance to soften the flavors of the wine and get the time-consuming work out of the way. The fish is then poached at the last minute in the simmering red wine broth, and the broth is thickened with *beurre manié* (see box).

This soup looks and tastes best with at least three types of fish, but freshness is more important than variety; if you find only one variety in perfect shape, leave it at that.

This recipe is served with the classic garnish of glazed pearl onions, bacon, and mushrooms.

> 3 pounds assorted firm-fleshed fish such as red snapper, sea bass, or trout, filleted, bones and heads reserved
>
> red wine fish broth (page 308), made from the reserved fish bones and heads

the garnish:

> 30 pearl onions or 18 small shallots
>
> 2 teaspoons sugar
>
> 2 tablespoons unsalted butter
>
> salt
>
> pepper
>
> ¼ pound bacon, preferably slab with the rind removed
>
> 18 small mushrooms, wild or cultivated

to finish the soup:

2 tablespoons unsalted butter

2 tablespoons all-purpose flour

salt

pepper

2 tablespoons finely chopped parsley, chervil, or chives

1 to 2 tablespoons cognac, marc, or grappa (optional)

6 slices of country-style French bread, toasted

IN ADVANCE To prepare the fish, cut into 1-inch chunks so there are 3 or 4 pieces per serving. Cut along the bones so none are left attached to the pieces of fish. Reserve the fish in the refrigerator. Prepare the broth as directed in the recipe and reserve.

TO prepare the garnish, peel the pearl onions by first plunging them into boiling water for about 1 minute and rinsing them with cold water. Put them in a pan that holds them in a single layer. Sprinkle them with sugar, 1 tablespoon of the butter, salt and pepper, and enough water to come halfway up their sides. Cook over medium heat until they soften and are lightly browned and glazed, about 20 minutes.

IF you're using slab bacon, cut it into ¼-inch slices. Cut the bacon slices crosswise into ¼-inch strips (*lardons*). Cook the strips in a small pan until just slightly crisp. Drain on a paper towel.

SAUTÉ the mushrooms in the remaining butter over high heat for 5 minutes.

COMBINE the onions, bacon, and mushrooms in a sauté pan for last-minute reheating.

AT THE LAST MINUTE Arrange the fillets in a pan just large enough to hold them in a single layer. Bring the broth to a simmer and ladle over just enough to cover the fillets. Keep the broth at a slow simmer, allowing about 8 minutes per inch of thickness. If the fish varies in thickness, you will need to figure out the approximate cooking times for each piece and add them in stages.

REHEAT the mushrooms, onions, and bacon over medium heat or in a 300°F oven for 10 minutes.

BEURRE MANIÉ:
A LAST-MINUTE THICKENER

French cooks sometimes work flour and butter into a paste called *beurre manié* that is used as a last-minute thickener for soups, stews, and sauces.

Beurre manié is especially useful because it can be made in a minute or two and whisked into a hot soup just before serving. To make *beurre manié*, take equal parts of butter and flour and knead them into a smooth paste with the back of a fork. Whisk the *beurre manié* into the simmering soup a minute before serving. Four tablespoons of *beurre manié* are usually required to lightly thicken a quart of soup.

WORK the butter and flour to a paste on a small plate to make *beurre manié*.

WHEN the fish is done, arrange the fillets in wide soup plates and season with salt and pepper. Add the remaining broth (if you haven't used it all) to the broth in the pan and stir in the herbs. Season with salt and pepper and the cognac if you're using it. For marc or grappa, bring the broth to a simmer for 10 seconds to cook off the alcohol. Whisk the *beurre manié* into the simmering broth and maintain the simmer for 30 seconds.

CAREFULLY ladle the broth into the bowls around the fish and arrange the mushrooms, onions, and bacon over each bowl.

THE toasts can be placed in bowls first and the fillets arranged over them, or they can be simply passed at the table.

SUGGESTIONS AND VARIATIONS | Glazed baby carrots and baby turnips both look wonderful against the purple background of the broth, and the juxtaposition of flavors and textures is irresistible.

YOU can also cook green vegetables and, instead of serving them on the side, add them directly to the soup at the end. Try fennel wedges gently stewed in a little butter, leeks braised in water or broth, or tiny green beans blanched for 4 or 5 minutes in boiling water. A few quickly blanched spinach leaves intertwined between the pieces of fish also create a lovely effect.

Squid Soup with Red Wine

This is one of those messy, rough-hewn dishes that I revel in. There's something about the almost purposely messy look of bowls filled with squid—tentacles sticking out of mudlike broth—and the aroma of garlic that awakens a wonderful instinct that perks up the appetite and makes eating (and drinking) a joy. I always imagine eating this dish outside— in fact I never bother with it unless it's a beautiful day and I'm devoting the afternoon to food and wine and being with friends.

Unlike most fish, which is cooked as soon as it's heated through, squid is best when simmered for almost an hour. When cooked in red wine with a generous bouquet garni of fresh herbs, it develops the depth of flavor of a well-made *coq au vin* or red wine meat stew. Like meat stews, squid soups and stews taste even better the day after they're made.

The *aïoli* is listed as optional but is a wonderful accompaniment. This heady soup— almost a stew—is not for timid eaters.

MAKES 8 FIRST-COURSE OR 4 MAIN-COURSE SERVINGS

4 pounds squid, cleaned (page 300)

5 tablespoons all-purpose flour

¼ cup olive oil

18 whole garlic cloves, peeled

1 large bouquet garni, preferably including a few fresh
    marjoram sprigs

1 fifth full-bodied, deep-colored red wine

4 medium-size tomatoes, peeled, seeded, coarsely chopped
    or 2 cups canned, seeded and drained

18 large mushrooms, quartered

2 tablespoons chopped parsley

salt

pepper

slices of French bread, lightly toasted

1 cup *aïoli*

SLICE the squid hoods into ½-inch rounds. Cut off the tentacles just below the eye-like ink sac and reserve.

DREDGE the squid in the flour. Heat the olive oil in a 4-quart pot and stir the squid and garlic cloves around for 2 to 3 minutes, until the squid browns slightly.

ADD the bouquet garni, wine, and tomatoes. Bring the liquids to a slow simmer, cover the pot, and simmer slowly for 45 minutes on the stove or in a 300°F oven.

TAKE the bouquet garni out of the soup and discard it. Distribute the squid and whole garlic cloves in hot soup bowls with a slotted spoon. Skim off any fat that floats to the surface of the broth with a ladle.

ADD the mushrooms and parsley to the broth and simmer for 2 minutes. Divide the mushrooms among the bowls, season the broth with salt and pepper, and pour it over the squid.

PASS the bread and the *aïoli* at the table.

SUGGESTIONS AND VARIATIONS | For a more elaborate or elegant soup, or if your friends are squeamish about squid, save the squid itself—it's delicious in a salad—and use the full-flavored red wine broth for last-minute simmering of more "presentable" kinds of seafood. You can also cook additional seafood such as shrimp or scallops in the red wine broth and present it in the soup along with the squid. I sometimes poach a small slice of salmon in the broth and use it as a prop for the squid.

YOU can also convert this soup into a vegetable and squid stew—magnificent as the main course for a summer lunch. Try sliced zucchini (sautéed in olive oil and sprinkled with finely chopped garlic and parsley), wild mushrooms (sautéed in the same way as the zucchini), olives or capers (added at the end), whole basil leaves (simmered in the hot broth 30 seconds before serving), or blanched French green beans sprinkled over the bowls at the last minute.

Octopus and Red Wine Soup

This soup is almost identical to the Squid Soup with Red Wine on page 318 except that the octopus is prepared for cooking differently from squid and the cooking time is longer. The same accompaniments—little French bread toasts and aïoli—also work with octopus. You can make this soup a day or two in advance and reheat it just before serving.

Most octopus comes frozen and cleaned, but if you find a fresh creature, cut off the head just above the eyes and turn it inside out. Pull out any organs or viscera and rinse the head, which you can cut up and cook with the octopus tentacles. Cut the eyes off the rest of the octopus and remove the small hard little beak by turning the octopus upside down and pressing against the opposite side of the "base" where all the tentacles meet. Push the beak through the opening in the middle. Give the octopus a thorough rinsing, kneading it with your hands in a sink full of cold water, being sure to rinse out any mud that may be clinging to the inside of the suckers. If the tentacles have a lot of mud clinging to them, scrub them with a plastic kitchen brush.

MAKES 6 FIRST-COURSE OR 4 MAIN-COURSE SERVINGS

2 2-pound octopuses or the equivalent, cleaned

3 bottles full-bodied red wine

6 garlic cloves, peeled, cloves left whole

2 medium-size onions, peeled and quartered

2 medium-size carrots, peeled and cut into 1-inch sections

1 bouquet garni, made with 3 fresh thyme sprigs
      (or ½ teaspoon dried), 1 medium bunch of
      parsley, and 1 bay leaf

3 tablespoons finely chopped parsley

2 cups aïoli (optional; recipe on page 349)

crunchy French bread or miniature toasts (which can be
      spread with aïoli)

BLANCH the octopus by submerging it in a large pot of boiling water for 5 minutes. Drain, rinse with cold water, and cut the tentacles into 1-inch lengths and the center section into 1-inch chunks.

PUT all the ingredients except the parsley and aïoli into a heavy-bottomed pot, bring to a gentle simmer, and simmer, covered, very gently on the stove (or in a 325°F oven) for about 1½ hours or until the octopus pieces feel tender when you stick a fork into one or take a bite of one.

STRAIN the soup into a clean saucepan and bring it to a gentle simmer. Skim off fat and froth with a ladle and continue simmering for about 10 minutes over gentle heat. Pick the pieces of octopus out of the strainer and add them to the soup. Press down on the bouquet garni and vegetables in the strainer to extract as much liquid as you can and then discard them. When you're ready to serve, heat the soup, stir in the chopped parsley, simmer for 30 seconds, and pass the aïoli and the toasts.

Eel or Other Fish with Fresh Green Herbs

ANGUILLE AU VERT

Although it's meant to be prepared with fresh river eels, this soup is too good for it to be limited to when you find (or are brave enough to use) live eels. The method—cooking with a little fish broth and finishing with a handful of freshly chopped herbs—can be used with any fish. I even made it once with sand shark.

The trick to this soup is to throw in handfuls of fresh herbs that have been finely chopped at the last minute. The fish can be cut up and the fish broth made ahead of time, but the herbs must be chopped and the fish poached just before serving. It doesn't matter so much which herbs you use as long as they're fresh. Even with parsley alone, the soup is bright green and has a fresh and complex flavor.

Originally a stew, this version of *anguille au vert* uses more fish broth than traditional recipes. If you want a more stewlike version, just use half as much broth as called for here.

If you use eels instead of fish, you won't have any fish heads and bones to make a fish broth. You can buy some fish heads and throw together a quick broth or just use a 50/50 mixture of water and white wine instead.

Fish stews are traditionally served with heart-shaped croutons—the tips dipped in chopped parsley—surrounding the platter. These still provide a decorative touch when arranged around each bowl.

MAKES 6 FIRST-COURSE SERVINGS

3 pounds whole fish, filleted and skinned, bones and heads
reserved, or

3 pounds fresh eel, skinned, cleaned, and cut into 3-inch
lengths (page 298)

the fish broth:

2 medium-size onions, coarsely chopped

2 cups dry white wine

I bouquet garni

to finish the soup:

4 egg yolks

½ cup heavy cream

2 tablespoons finely chopped parsley

2 tablespoons finely chopped chives

2 tablespoons finely chopped chervil leaves

30 fresh mint leaves, finely chopped

20 fresh sorrel leaves, shredded

juice of 2 lemons

salt

freshly ground white pepper

heart-shaped croutons, 3 per serving (page 595)

French bread slices

IN ADVANCE When you get the fillets home, check them carefully and remove
any bones.

MAKE a fish broth by thoroughly rinsing the bones in cold water and combining
them with the onions, wine, bouquet garni, and enough water to cover (about 3
cups) in a 4-quart pot. Bring the broth to a slow simmer and simmer for 30 minutes, skimming off any froth that floats to the top. Strain the broth through a
medium-mesh strainer.

CUT the fish fillets into I-inch chunks so that you end up with 3 chunks per person.*

AT THE LAST MINUTE Whisk together the egg yolks, cream, and herbs in a
2-quart mixing bowl.

*If you're using eels, lightly season them with salt and pepper and lightly flour them. Shortly before serving, brown them
lightly in butter, throw out the butter, and simmer the eel sections in fish broth or a light broth made by simmering 2
cups water, 2 cups wine, I onion, and a bouquet for 30 minutes and then straining.

SPREAD the chunks of fish in a pan just large enough to hold them in a single layer. Pour the simmering fish broth over them and poach the fish for 8 minutes per inch of thickness.

WHEN the fish is done, distribute it among 6 hot bowls with a slotted spoon. Whisk the broth used to poach the fish into the bowl with the egg mixture and return the soup to the pan used to poach the fish. Gently heat this mixture to cook the egg yolks. Stir the mixture constantly until it thickens slightly—if you have a thermometer, it will be at 175°F. Be very careful not to let the mixture boil, or the egg yolks will curdle. Add the lemon juice and salt and pepper to taste. Decorate each bowl with the heart-shaped croutons.

SUGGESTIONS AND VARIATIONS | This dish is a marvelous way to use greens and fish together. I use whatever I have or can find—spinach (boiled briefly and shredded), sorrel (shredded), basil (finely chopped), chard (blanched and shredded)—and often simplify and lighten the dish by leaving out the egg yolks and sometimes even the cream.

Hearty Fish Soup with Cider, Leeks, and Mushrooms

MATELOTE NORMANDE

A *matelote normande* is made in almost the same way as a red wine fish *matelote* (see *matelote à la bourguignonne*, page 316) except that cider and cider vinegar are used instead of wine. It's hard to go wrong with this soup since the flavors of leeks, mushrooms, and cider finished with heavy cream make a delicious base for just about anything—the fish becomes almost superfluous.

SERVES 6

3 pounds whole fish

the fish broth:

I medium-size onion, coarsely chopped

3 leeks, green part only but whites reserved, coarsely chopped

5 cups hard cider or 3 cups apple cider combined with 2 cups water

I bouquet garni

the soup:

>2 tablespoons unsalted butter
>
>18 small mushrooms, quartered
>
>½ cup heavy cream
>
>1 tablespoon chopped parsley or chervil
>
>2 tablespoons Calvados
>
>⅓ to ½ cup cider vinegar
>
>salt
>
>white pepper

IN ADVANCE To prepare the fish broth, have the fishmonger gut and fillet the fish and remove the skin. Be sure to save the fish head and bones. When you get the fillets home, check them carefully and remove any bones.

MAKE a fish broth by thoroughly rinsing the head and bones in cold water and combining them with the onions, leek greens, cider, and bouquet garni in a 4-quart pot. Bring the broth to a slow simmer and simmer for 30 minutes, skimming off any froth that floats to the top. Strain the broth through a medium-mesh strainer.

AT THE LAST MINUTE To finish the soup, slice the white parts of the leeks finely and put them in a 4-quart pot with the butter. Cook them gently until they soften, for about 10 minutes. Add the mushrooms and cook gently for 3 minutes more.

JUST before serving, arrange the fish in one layer in the pot with the leeks and mushrooms. Pour the simmering fish broth over the fish. Poach the fish fillets for about 8 minutes for each inch of thickness and distribute them among soup bowls with a slotted spoon.

ADD the cream, parsley, Calvados, and a tablespoon of the cider vinegar to the broth. Taste it, adjust the vinegar, and season with salt and pepper. Ladle the broth with the mushrooms and leeks over the fish.

APPLE CIDER AND HARD CIDER

In the United States, the terms *apple juice* and *apple cider* are often used interchangeably to refer to the non-alcoholic juice of the apple. In France *cidre* always means hard cider—apple juice that has been fermented so that its natural sugar has changed to alcohol. Hard cider is sometimes difficult to find, so in recipes that call for it I sometimes substitute American apple cider, which I dilute with water because nonalcoholic cider tends to be very sweet, especially when cooked in a soup.

SUGGESTIONS AND VARIATIONS
Apple wedges lightly sautéed in butter make a lovely additional garnish for the soup.

Spicy Brazilian Fish Soup with Coconut Milk

VATAPA

I first tasted a stewlike version of *vatapa* in a Brazilian restaurant in Manhattan. *Vatapa* combines so many of the flavors I love in soups—a delicate sweetness from peanuts; the spicy flavors of hot peppers, ginger, and cilantro; and the suave creaminess of coconut milk.

In traditional versions an intensely flavored sauce is made in advance and chunks of cut-up whole fish (or chicken) are simmered in it at the last minute. This lighter soup is made with filleted fish so there is no sorting through bones while eating the soup.

You can make the most complicated part of this recipe—the saucelike broth—ahead of time and keep it in the refrigerator for several days. Then you just add the fish to the hot broth before serving.

Authentic Brazilian recipes call for dende oil (palm oil), taken from the fruit of a South American palm, but it's loaded with cholesterol and I've had no trouble getting by with a little safflower oil.

MAKES 10 FIRST-COURSE SERVINGS

2 pounds fish fillets, bones and skin removed

1 pound large shrimp, peeled and deveined

½ cup shelled raw peanuts or cashews or ⅓ cup peanut or cashew butter

3 tablespoons safflower oil

1 large onion, finely chopped

3 garlic cloves, finely chopped

a ½-inch slice of fresh ginger, peeled and finely chopped

3 Thai chilies or 6 jalapeño chilies, cut in half lengthwise, seeds removed, finely chopped

6 medium-size tomatoes, peeled, seeded, and coarsely chopped or 3 cups canned, seeded, and drained

juice of 2 limes

¼ cup dried shrimp, ground to a powder, 2 tablespoons (optional)*

1 quart chicken broth

2 cups coconut milk

*Because it's difficult to grind so little dried shrimp in a blender or food processor, I prepare ½ cup and keep the powdered shrimp in the freezer.

2 tablespoons finely chopped cilantro leaves

salt

pepper

CUT the fish fillets into 1- or 2-inch cubes. Keep the fish and shrimp refrigerated until just before serving.

IF you're using whole nuts, grind them in a food processor until they have the consistency of smooth peanut butter. This takes about 3 minutes, and you may have to scrape the sides of the food processor with a rubber spatula once or twice to get the mixture moving.

HEAT the safflower oil in a 4-quart pot over medium heat and cook the onion, garlic, ginger, and chilies until the vegetables shine and the kitchen fills with their aroma, about 10 minutes. Add the tomatoes, lime juice, ground shrimp, and pureed nuts. Whisk in the chicken broth a cup at a time to keep the mixture smooth. Add the coconut milk and cilantro.

JUST before you're ready to serve the soup, arrange the fish in a straight-sided sauté pan large enough to hold it in a single layer. Put the shrimp in a 2-quart saucepan. Pour the soup over the fish and the shrimp, making sure both are completely covered. Slowly bring the fish and shrimp to a simmer and cook until they are done— they may need slightly different cooking times. The fish will take about 8 minutes per inch of thickness and the shrimp about 3 minutes. The shrimp is done as soon as it turns completely red.

DISTRIBUTE the fish and shrimp among hot bowls. Season the broth with salt and pepper and pour it over the fish.

SUGGESTIONS AND VARIATIONS | In traditional Brazilian cooking a *vatapa* is usually served as a stew or as a piece of fish or chicken with a sauce. If you want a thicker version, use half as much broth as called for in this recipe.

Spanish Cod Soup with Spinach and Chick-Peas

POTAJE DE VIGILIA

When I first saw this dish on a Spanish menu in New York, I was disconcerted. I had never really liked chick-peas—the first time I had them was in college, when I boiled them in water in a failed attempt at an economical meal—and combining them with seafood sounded contrived. Despite my skepticism, this soup is delicious, and a little research has revealed that it's not contrived at all—Spanish and Italian cooks have been combining chick-peas with fish for centuries.

Although cod—either fresh or salted—is traditionally used to make this soup, I buy whatever looks freshest at the fish market. If I end up buying a fillet instead of a whole fish, I ask the fishmonger to throw in fish heads for making the fish broth.

Although most of the work for this soup—making the fish broth and cooking the chick-peas—can be done in advance, it is best to make and serve this soup the day you buy the fish.

MAKES 8 GENEROUS FIRST-COURSE SERVINGS

2 pounds fish bones or heads

1 onion, peeled and thinly sliced

1 bouquet garni

1 cup dry white wine

2 pounds cod, grouper, or tilefish fillets, cut into 8 pieces

1 cup dried chick-peas, soaked overnight

2 tablespoons olive oil

½ cup slivered almonds

3 garlic cloves, finely chopped

3 medium-size tomatoes, peeled, seeded, and chopped or
    1½ cups canned, seeded and drained

1 large bunch of spinach, stems removed, 2 tightly packed
    cups, leaves torn in half if large

2 tablespoons finely chopped parsley leaves

salt

pepper

IN ADVANCE Remove gills from the fish heads. Soak the bones and heads for 30 minutes. Make a fish broth by thoroughly rinsing the fish bones and heads in cold water and then combining them with the onion, bouquet garni, wine, and enough water to cover in a 4-quart pot. Bring the broth to a slow simmer and simmer for 30 minutes, skimming off any froth that floats to the top. Strain the broth through a medium-mesh strainer.

REMOVE any bones that are still attached to the fish fillet. Reserve the fish in the refrigerator.

DRAIN the chick-peas and combine them with the fish broth in a 4-quart pot. Bring to a simmer, cover the pot, and simmer gently until the chick-peas can be crushed easily against the inside of the pot, about 1½ hours. Add water or extra fish broth from time to time to keep the chick-peas covered.

HEAT the olive oil in a 4-quart pot over medium heat. Add the almonds and stir for about 5 minutes, until they start to smell toasty. Add the garlic and stir for 3 minutes more. Add the tomatoes, spinach, and parsley and simmer for 5 minutes. Stir this mixture into the chick-peas.

AT THE LAST MINUTE Place the pieces of fish in a straight-sided pan or pot just large enough to hold them in a single layer. Add just enough cold water to barely cover the fish. Bring to a simmer over medium-high heat, then turn the heat down to low and simmer the fish for about 4 minutes per inch of thickness.

TRANSFER the fish to a hot plate and pour the poaching liquid into the chick-pea mixture. Season the chick-pea mixture to taste with salt and pepper and ladle it into hot bowls. Place a piece of fish in the center of each bowl.

Ceviche

Every country in Central and South America seems to have its own version of *ceviche*. Despite each country's assertion that its version is the best, many of the recipes are similar. Once you're familiar with a basic recipe it's easy to substitute ingredients here and there to come up with your own original interpretations.

Ceviche is made by "cooking" seafood in lime or lemon juice and then seasoning it with herbs (usually cilantro), chilies, onions, garlic, and other flavorings. Traditionally it is served as an hors d'oeuvre but here is presented as a tangy and refreshing summer soup.

Although the underlying principle of *ceviche* is that none of the seafood be exposed to heat, certain shellfish, such as shrimp or lobster, must be cooked lightly before being combined with the other ingredients.

Some fish and shellfish are no longer safe to eat raw. Be sure to check the origin of any seafood you buy for this dish and ask your fishmonger if it's safe to eat raw.

MAKES 6 FIRST-COURSE SERVINGS

¾ pound squid, cleaned (page 300)
¾ pound medium-size shrimp, peeled and deveined
4 tablespoons extra virgin olive oil

¾ pound fresh tuna or swordfish steaks or flounder fillets,
   cut into ½-inch cubes

½ pound bay scallops

3 jalapeño chilies, seeded and finely chopped

1 garlic clove, finely chopped and crushed to a paste

1 small Bermuda onion, finely chopped

1 tablespoon finely chopped cilantro leaves

½ cup fresh lime juice, from about 4 limes

6 medium-size tomatoes, peeled, seeded, and finely chopped
   or 3 cups canned, seeded and drained

salt

pepper

finely chopped jalapeño chilies

Tabasco sauce

AFTER cleaning the squid, cut the bunch of tentacles in half if large. Cut the cone into ¼-inch-thick slices.

SAUTÉ the shrimp in 2 tablespoons of the olive oil in a sauté pan over high heat until they turn orange, after about 3 minutes. Take them out with a slotted spoon and sauté the squid in the same pan for about 1 minute.

COMBINE the shrimp and squid with the remaining olive oil and the scallops, jalapeños, garlic, onion, cilantro, and lime juice in a mixing bowl in the refrigerator. Marinate for 30 minutes to an hour. Stir in the chopped tomatoes and salt and pepper to taste. Pass the Tabasco and the jalapeños at the table.

SUGGESTIONS AND VARIATIONS | I sometimes make this soup with tomatillos, cooked for about 15 minutes in a little oil with onion and garlic. Stir in the chilled tomatillo mixture instead of the tomatoes and serve the soup with sour cream and tortilla chips. A coarsely chopped avocado is another good addition.

Cold Trout Soup with Herbs, White Wine, and Vinegar

The inspiration for this soup came from reading about *escabeche* in books about Mexican, Catalan, South American, and French cooking. *Escabeche* is a method of preserving cooked fish in a marinade of olive oil, vinegar, wine, and herbs and then serving it as a cool hors d'oeuvre or first course. Whenever I've eaten *escabeche*—I especially remember one French version made with cider vinegar—I've always enjoyed soaking up the marinade with French bread as much as eating the fish itself.

This soup version is designed so there's plenty of liquid to soak up with bread. It can be made 2 or 3 days in advance.

The right olives here are *picholines*—not Californian or very large olives.

MAKES 8 SERVINGS

4 trout, about 1 pound each, gutted

salt

pepper

all-purpose flour for dredging trout

1 cup extra virgin olive oil

1 cup water

2 cups dry white wine

1 cup good wine vinegar such as sherry, champagne, or balsamic

1 large Bermuda onion, thinly sliced

8 garlic cloves, peeled

1 large carrot, thinly sliced

1 teaspoon fresh thyme leaves or ½ teaspoon dried

3 tablespoons finely chopped parsley leaves

2 tablespoons drained capers

½ cup green olives, pitted and coarsely chopped

SEASON the trout with salt and pepper and dredge them in flour. Cook the trout in ¼ cup of the olive oil in a skillet over medium-high heat until cooked through and well browned, about 4 minutes on each side. To make sure the trout is done, insert the tip of a paring knife where the 2 fillets join on the back of the trout; the flesh should be easy to separate from the bones. Transfer the trout to a plate and let cool.

COMBINE the remaining olive oil, the water, the white wine, vinegar, vegetables, and thyme in a 4-quart pot. Bring to a simmer, cover the pot, and keep at a slow simmer for 30 minutes or until the vegetables have softened but aren't mushy. Remove the pot from the heat, add the parsley, capers, and olives, and let cool.

FILLET the trout by sliding a long flexible knife along each side of the fish's back, pulling the fillets away from the rib bones as you go. Once you've removed both fillets, discard the head and bones and pull the tiny bones remaining in the fillets with a pair of tweezers, needlenose pliers, or your thumbnail.

ARRANGE the fish in a glass or porcelain bowl or casserole and pour the cooled vegetable mixture over it. Cover with plastic wrap and refrigerate for at least three hours.

TO serve, transfer the vegetables to a bowl, arrange the trout fillets in wide chilled bowls, and ladle the cold vegetables and cooking liquid over the fish.

SUGGESTIONS AND VARIATIONS | A Mexican version of this dish might include hot chilies, cilantro, and lime juice, while an Italian or Spanish interpretation might include tomatoes and be a bit heavier-handed with the capers and olives.

SELECTING WINE VINEGAR

Wine vinegar is often used in soups to wake up their flavor and give them a refreshing tang. White and red wine vinegars can usually be used interchangeably but the quality of the vinegar you use is important. My favorite all-purpose vinegar is sherry vinegar, which has a rich nutty flavor and a nice tang. Balsamic vinegar is also good but the less expensive brands are often not acidic enough and the color is so dark that it isn't appropriate for some soups. Avoid raspberry vinegar, which has a cloying flavor inappropriate for soups.

Thai Fish Soup with Tamarind

Even though you may need to shop around for some of the ingredients used in Thai soups, almost any combination of Thai ingredients or even substitutes makes wonderful soup. I never let a missing ingredient or two stop me when I'm in the mood for something tart and spicy (which is often). If you don't know where to shop for Thai ingredients, go into a local Thai restaurant and ask them where they buy their ingredients or order from some of the sources listed in the back of this book.

The tamarind gives this soup a lovely clean, tart flavor, but if you don't have any, use lime juice instead. The recipe starts out with dried shrimp—which may mean a trip to a Thai market or to Chinatown—but they're not essential, so you can leave them out. If you want the flavor of shrimp, add ½ pound fresh peeled shrimp along with the fish.

You can also get by without the galangal (ginger will work), but if you're going to a Thai market anyway, it's worth picking some up. It has a lovely pine resin flavor that makes it worth the trouble. Tightly wrapped in plastic and aluminum foil, galangal freezes indefinitely.

MAKES 8 FIRST-COURSE SERVINGS

2½ pounds firm-fleshed white fish fillets, skin and bones removed

6 tablespoons tamarind paste or juice of 3 limes

1 cup boiling water if you're using tamarind paste

2 shallots, finely chopped

2 garlic cloves, finely chopped

2 tablespoons dried shrimp, ground to a powder, 1 tablespoon

¼ cup Thai fish sauce (*nam pla*)

2 tablespoons finely chopped cilantro leaves

2 Thai chilies or 4 jalapeño chilies, cut in half lengthwise, seeds removed, finely chopped

2 tablespoons safflower oil

6 ⅛-inch slices of peeled fresh galangal or ginger

1 quart chicken broth

3 kaffir lime leaves or a 2-inch strip of lemon zest, chopped

a 2-inch length of lemongrass, finely sliced, or 3 scallions, both white and green parts, finely sliced

IN ADVANCE Cut the fish into 1½ inch cubes and keep it in the refrigerator until just before serving.

COMBINE the tamarind paste with the boiling water. Work the mixture with a wooden spoon to dissolve the tamarind.

MAKE a paste with the shallots, garlic, ground shrimp, fish sauce, cilantro, lime leaves or lemon zest, and chilies. This is traditionally done in a large mortar and pestle, but a food processor will work, provided you add a little chicken broth to loosen the mixture enough and get it to move around.

HEAT the paste in the safflower oil in a 4-quart pot over medium heat for about 2 minutes. Add the galangal and the rest of the broth. Strain the tamarind mixture into the soup, discarding the solids that stay in the strainer, or add the lime juice.

AT THE LAST MINUTE When you're ready to serve the soup, bring the broth to the simmer and add the fish. Poach the fish until done, about 5 minutes, and use a slotted spoon to distribute it among hot bowls, then pour the broth on top.

SUGGESTIONS AND VARIATIONS | Peeled shrimp or strips of skinless and boneless chicken breast are easy substitutes for the fish.

Vietnamese-Style Hot and Sour Fish Soup

Although the name is similar, this hot and sour soup tastes nothing like the Thai version. The combination of Asian basil, mint, and pineapple gives the soup a lovely subtlety that's hard to imagine until you've tasted it. When this soup is served in Vietnamese restaurants in the United States, it is most often made with shrimp and sometimes with eels, but my favorite version, given here, is made with fish.

The sourness comes from tamarind, which is available as a paste, but the soup is still delicious—if less authentic—made with lime juice.

MAKES 10 FIRST-COURSE SERVINGS

2 pounds firm-fleshed fish fillets, skin and bones removed

½ pineapple, peeled, core removed, cut into wedges or
    I 14-ounce can, drained

I tablespoon sugar

6 tablespoons tamarind paste or juice of 3 limes

I cup boiling water if you're using tamarind paste

2 tablespoons safflower oil

3 shallots, thinly sliced

4 garlic cloves, finely chopped

2 Thai chilies or 4 jalapeño chilies, cut in half lengthwise,
    seeds removed, finely chopped

¼ cup fish sauce, preferably Vietnamese-style Phu Quoc

2 medium-size tomatoes, peeled, cut into thin wedges, and
    seeds removed or I cup canned, seeded and drained

I quart chicken broth or water

24 small fresh mint leaves, coarsely chopped

24 fresh Asian basil leaves or regular sweet basil leaves,
    coarsely chopped

½ cup bean sprouts

IN ADVANCE Cut the fish into 20 equal-size pieces. Toss the pineapple wedges in a bowl with the sugar.

COMBINE the tamarind paste with the boiling water and soak it for about 15 minutes, stirring once in a while with a wooden spoon, until it is soft.

IN a 4-quart pot, heat the safflower oil over medium heat and lightly brown the shallots, garlic, and chilies for about 5 minutes. Add the fish sauce, tomatoes, and broth. Strain the tamarind into the soup, discarding the pulp left in the strainer, or add the lime juice. Add the herbs and simmer the soup for 2 minutes.

AT THE LAST MINUTE If you're serving this soup in one large bowl at the table, just add the fish to the soup and simmer it for about 3 minutes, until done.

IF you're serving the soup in individual bowls, ladle some of the broth into a wide pan and poach the fish separately, so you're not left searching through the pot for the pieces of fish. Arrange 2 pieces of fish in each bowl and combine the poaching liquid with the rest of the soup. Add the bean sprouts to the hot soup about 20 seconds before serving just to heat them through.

SUGGESTIONS AND VARIATIONS | In the summer, when I have guests over for evening dinners outdoors, I like to turn this soup into a kind of tropical fish stew by adding slices of mango and papaya, shrimp, and occasionally some lobster. The colors alone get everything off to a good start, and I don't need to serve much else. This soup will also make 4 main-course servings if you include ½ pound (4 bunches) of cellophane noodles, soaked in cold water for 10 minutes and then simmered in the soup 5 minutes before serving. Rice is also an excellent accompaniment.

LIKE most fish soups, Vietnamese hot and sour fish soup has to be made the day it is served or the fish will fall apart. If you want something that will hold up better, substitute shrimp.

Indian-Style Curry and Coconut Fish Soup

You can make this elegant soup with a good commercial spice mixture such as garam masala or curry powder. Better yet, make your own blend of spices (pages 16–17). This soup is purposely on the mild side; if you want it hotter, stir in cayenne powder to taste.

MAKES 10 FIRST-COURSE SERVINGS

4 pounds firm-fleshed fish

3 medium-size onions, 1 chopped and 2 just peeled

a 1-inch slice of fresh ginger, peeled

4 garlic cloves, peeled

2 Thai chilies or 4 jalapeño chilies, cut in half lengthwise, seeds removed, finely chopped

3 tablespoons unsalted butter

2 tablespoons garam masala

2 teaspoons ground turmeric

4 medium-size tomatoes, peeled, seeded, and coarsely chopped or 2 cups canned, seeded and drained

2 cups coconut milk

2 tablespoons cilantro leaves, chopped

salt

pepper

cayenne pepper (optional)

IN ADVANCE Have the fishmonger gut and fillet the fish and remove the skin from the fillets. Be sure to save the fish heads and bones. When you get the fillets home, check them carefully and remove any bones.

MAKE a fish broth by soaking the fish heads and bones in cold water for 30 minutes and then combining them with the chopped onion and enough water to cover in a 4-quart pot. Bring the broth to a slow simmer and simmer for 30 minutes, skimming off any froth that floats to the top. Strain the broth through a medium-mesh strainer.

CUT the fillets into 20 equal-size pieces (2 pieces per bowl). Refrigerate the pieces of fish.

WORK the ginger, peeled onions, garlic, chilies, and butter to a smooth paste with a food processor, a mortar and pestle, or by chopping them together very finely with a chef's knife.

COOK the vegetable/butter mixture in a 4-quart pot over medium heat for about 5 minutes. Add the garam masala and the turmeric and cook for 2 minutes more. Add the fish broth, tomatoes, and coconut milk and bring the soup to the simmer.

AT THE LAST MINUTE When you are ready to serve the soup, reheat the broth and add the fish. Cook the fish for 5 or 10 minutes, about 8 minutes per inch of thickness. Add the cilantro a minute or two before serving. Distribute the pieces of fish among hot bowls with a slotted spoon, season the broth with salt, pepper, and cayenne if desired, and ladle it over the fish in the bowls.

SUGGESTIONS AND VARIATIONS | You can make this soup more substantial by adding cooked rice (preferably basmati) to the broth just before serving. It will lose some of its elegance, but there will be plenty to go around if you want to serve it as the main course for 4 to 6 at a family dinner.

THE flavor of this soup can be varied almost endlessly by playing around with your own blend of spices. I sometimes add a pinch of saffron when I add the liquid ingredients to give the soup a different nuance.

Medieval Fish Soup with Peas and Spices

CRETONNÉE À POISSON

Even though this recipe is taken from a 14th-century manuscript—the first cookbook written in French—it specifies the strikingly modern technique of using pureed peas as a
thickener. The original recipe suggests garnishing the finished soup with slices of hard-
boiled eggs sautéed in lard, a medieval touch I've left out. What makes this dish especially unusual and delicious is the combination of spices, almond milk, parsley, and fresh
marjoram.

   This soup—except for the last-minute cooking of the fish—can be prepared early the
same day.

3 pounds firm-fleshed fish such as red snapper, striped bass,
   or sea bass

I medium-size onion, sliced

2 ¼-inch-thick slices of fresh ginger

I cup dry white wine

2 10-ounce packages frozen petite peas or 2 pounds fresh
   peas, shucked

2 teaspoons chopped fresh marjoram or thyme

½ teaspoon ground cumin

¾ cup blanched almonds, lightly toasted in a 350 °F oven
   for 15 minutes

¼ teaspoon saffron threads, soaked in I tablespoon water
   for 20 minutes

salt

pepper

IN ADVANCE To prepare the basic broth, have the fishmonger gut and fillet the
fish and remove the skin from the fillets. Be sure to save the fish heads and bones.
When you get the fillets home, rinse them and remove any bones.

SOAK the fish heads and bones for 30 minutes. Thoroughly rinse the fish heads and
bones in cold water and combine them with the onion, ginger, wine, and enough
water to cover in a 4-quart pot. Bring the broth to a slow simmer and simmer for 30
minutes, skimming off any froth that floats to the top. Strain the broth through a
medium mesh strainer.

CUT the fillets into 12 equal-size pieces (2 pieces per bowl). Refrigerate the pieces of
fish.

TO prepare the soup base, if you're using frozen peas, let them thaw. If you're using fresh peas, cook them in a pot of boiling salted water for 5 minutes, drain them in a colander, and rinse them with cold water.

COMBINE the peas, 1 cup of the fish broth, the marjoram, and the cumin in a blender and process for 2 minutes. Work the mixture through a food mill or, if you want a smoother texture, directly through a medium-mesh strainer with a ladle or wooden spoon.

PREPARE a batch of almond milk by pureeing the almonds in a blender with 1 cup of the fish broth for about 1 minute. Strain the almond milk through a fine-mesh strainer. Discard the solids in the strainer and add the almond milk to the pea mixture.

ADD the remaining fish broth and the saffron threads with their soaking water to the pea mixture. Season to taste with salt and pepper.

AT THE LAST MINUTE Bring the soup to a slow simmer in a 4-quart pot and add the fish fillets. Simmer gently for about 5 minutes, 8 minutes per inch of thickness of the fillets. Transfer the fish to hot soup bowls with a slotted spoon and pour the hot soup over it.

Fish Chowder

When people think chowder, they usually think clams. True, clam chowder is a hard thing to improve on, but why limit such a delicious soup to clams alone? Chowders are simple to make and, except for the seafood, require just some onions, potatoes, and a little cream and butter.

Although there are many variations, fish chowders are all based on a few fundamental ingredients and principles. All chowders contain onions, and most contain potato or some other starchy ingredient such as corn. Many recipes use salt pork or blanched bacon to provide fat for cooking the onions, but I usually end up using butter, not only because it's good but also because it's always on hand. Sometimes milk is the only liquid used, but I prefer to make a fish broth and finish it with heavy cream or crème fraîche.

Almost any firm-fleshed white fish can be used for chowder, but cod is traditional.

New England Fish Chowder

4 pounds firm-fleshed fish

1 medium-size onion, coarsely chopped

1 large bouquet garni

3 large onions or 4 leeks, white part only, thinly sliced

3 medium-size waxy potatoes, cut into ½-inch cubes

3 tablespoons unsalted butter

1 cup heavy cream or crème fraîche

1 tablespoon chopped chives

IN ADVANCE Have the fishmonger gut and fillet the fish and remove the skin from the fillets. Be sure to save the fish heads and bones. When you get the fillets home, check them carefully and remove any bones.

MAKE a fish broth by soaking the fish heads and bones in cold water for 30 minutes, draining them, and combining them with the chopped onion, bouquet garni, and enough water to cover in a 4-quart pot. Bring the broth to a slow simmer and simmer for 30 minutes, skimming off any froth that floats to the top. Strain the broth through a medium-mesh strainer.

REMOVE any remaining bones from the fillets and cut them into 16 equal-sized pieces (2 pieces per bowl). Refrigerate until just before serving.

OVER medium heat, cook the sliced onions and potatoes in the butter in a 4-quart pot for about 15 minutes. Be careful not to let the onions brown. Add the fish broth and bring the soup to a slow simmer. Simmer the soup for 5 or 10 minutes to finish cooking the potatoes. Check the potatoes by pushing one of the cubes against the inside of the pot with a spoon—it should crush easily. Add the heavy cream and simmer for 1 minute.

AT THE LAST MINUTE Just before serving the chowder, bring it to a simmer and add the cut-up fish fillets. Simmer the soup with the fish for 5 to 10 minutes, about 8 minutes per inch of thickness.

LADLE the chowder into hot bowls and decorate each one with a pinch of chopped chives.

SUGGESTIONS AND VARIATIONS | Try using fish in the South American *chupe* on page 402 or the corn and crayfish chowder on page 412. It's also worthwhile to experiment with different herbs; fresh tarragon gives the chowder a whole new dimension. I also like to add a handful of shredded sorrel leaves to the chowder a minute or two before serving to give it an exciting tang.

IF you want to use bacon, which gives the soup a satisfying smoky flavor, cook ¼ pound bacon, until the bacon is beginning to get crisp, cut into thin strips, and cook the onions and potatoes in the bacon fat. Sprinkle the cooked bacon strips into the soup just before serving.

Mexican-Style Fish Chowder

I made this soup one afternoon when I was craving the flavors of Mexican chilies, tomatoes, and garlic and at the same time wanted fish.

In some parts of the country it's difficult to find a large selection of chilies to play around with, so feel free to change this recipe, substituting chilies and adding more or less of any of the ingredients to taste. If worse comes to worst, you can use red sweet peppers, roasted and peeled, and then give the soup the necessary wallop with cayenne pepper.

MAKES 8 FIRST-COURSE SERVINGS

5 pounds round fish such as sea bass or red snapper, filleted, heads and bones reserved

1 medium-size onion, chopped

4 garlic cloves, chopped

3 assorted fresh chilies such as poblano (sometimes mistakenly called pasilla), New Mexico, Anaheim, or 2 red bell peppers, roasted, peeled, seeded (page 207), and finely chopped

2 jalapeño chilies, halved lengthwise, seeded and finely chopped

4 medium-size tomatoes, peeled, seeded, and chopped or 2 cups canned, seeded and drained

juice of 2 limes

2 tablespoons finely chopped cilantro leaves

½ cup heavy cream

salt

pepper

cayenne pepper (optional)

sour cream

lime wedges

tortilla chips

IN ADVANCE Soak the fish bone and heads for 30 minutes. Make a fish broth by thoroughly rinsing the fish bones and heads in cold water and then combining them with the onion, garlic, and enough water to cover in a 4-quart pot. Bring the broth to a slow simmer and simmer for 30 minutes, skimming off any froth that floats to the top. Strain the broth through a medium-mesh strainer.

CUT the fish fillets into 1-inch chunks so that you end up with about 3 chunks per person. Reserve in the refrigerator.

COMBINE the fish broth with the chopped roasted chilies, chopped jalapeños, and chopped tomatoes in a 4-quart pot. Simmer gently for 10 minutes.

AT THE LAST MINUTE Stir the lime juice, cilantro, cream, and cubed fish into the hot soup and simmer for 5 minutes, until the fish is done. Season to taste with salt and pepper; add cayenne if desired. Ladle into hot bowls and pass sour cream, lime wedges, and tortilla chips at the table.

Assorted Fish in Japanese Broth

The universal Japanese broth—*dashi*—was a revelation to me the first time I made it at home. It was as satisfying as a long cooked and labor-intensive consommé—and I had made it in a few minutes with some seaweed and a bag of dried fish shavings. Once you learn to make a basic *dashi*, you can whip up elegant soups by lightly sautéing or poaching a piece of fish or shrimp and serving it right in the broth. Flavoring the *dashi* with *mirin*, soy sauce, or sake is simple and straightforward.

The chunks of fish in this soup are lightly sautéed before being added to the broth. If you want to simplify things, you can skip this step and just simmer the fish in the broth, but the fish will cloud the broth slightly.

MAKES 6 FIRST-COURSE SERVINGS

2 pounds fish fillets, up to 3 different types, bones carefully
    removed
salt
pepper
all-purpose flour
3 tablespoons vegetable oil
1 quart *dashi*
5 tablespoons mirin
5 tablespoons dark soy sauce
2 tablespoons sake (optional)
3 scallions, both white and green parts, finely sliced

CUT the fillets into 18 pieces (3 pieces per bowl). Season the fish, dredge it in flour, and pat it between your hands to get rid of any excess. In a non-stick sauté pan, sauté the fish in the oil over medium-high heat for 2 minutes, just enough to lightly brown the flour. Remove it with a slotted spoon and put it on a plate covered with paper towels to blot up excess oil.

COMBINE the liquid ingredients in a 4-quart pot, bring them to a slow simmer, and add the fish. Simmer the fish for a minute or two, depending on its thickness, and arrange it in soup bowls. Sprinkle the scallions over it.

SUGGESTIONS AND VARIATIONS | I like to serve this soup in lacquer bowls to give it a Japanese feel. The version presented here is designed for a simple yet elegant first course, but for a quick family dinner you can add Japanese noodles (ramen or soba, cooked separately and drained) to give more bulk. You can also add vegetables such as spinach (quickly blanched), carrot (thinly sliced or julienne, simmered in a little *dashi*), leeks (julienne, simmered in *dashi*), or mushrooms (sliced or whole, cooked along with the fish).

Grilled Mackerel Fillets with Soba Noodles and *Dashi*

Robert Courtine, food critic for the Paris newspaper *Le Monde*, once wrote a tongue-in-cheek article about a society where the best and most flavorful fish were given to the slaves while the aristocracy insisted on eating insipid white-fleshed fish such as Dover sole and turbot. Courtine went on to extol the virtues of tasty fish such as mackerel and herring and wondered why these fish had fallen into such disrepute. My own theory is that too many of us have had them less than perfectly fresh, after they've developed a strong fish aroma and taste. Mackerel fillets are delicious lightly marinated with sweetened soy sauce and quickly grilled.

Although most of the cooking for this soup should be done at the last minute, the flavored *dashi* can be prepared several days in advance.

MAKES 4 FIRST-COURSE SERVINGS

2 1-pound mackerel, gutted and filleted

6 tablespoons Japanese dark soy sauce

3 tablespoons mirin

2 quarts water

6 ounces dried soba noodles

6 cups *dashi*

2 scallions, both white and green parts, finely chopped

seven-spice mixture (*shichimi*)

IN ADVANCE Carefully go over the mackerel fillets and cut off any stray bones with a paring knife or pull them out with pliers. To prevent the fillets from curling, lightly score each one with a very sharp paring knife so there are 5 slashes diagonally crossing it. Cut each of the fillets in two crosswise.

MARINATE the mackerel fillets in half the soy and half the mirin for 30 minutes. Pat dry. Arrange the fish pieces in groups of 4 and skewer them crosswise with 2 skewers. If you're using wooden skewers, make sure the fillets are touching each other or the skewers will be exposed to the flame and burn. Refrigerate until needed.

BRING the water to a boil and cook the soba noodles in it until they soften, about 6 minutes. Drain them in a colander and rinse them in cold water.

AT THE LAST MINUTE Bring the *dashi* to a simmer with the remaining soy sauce and mirin. Grill the mackerel, skin side down first, over a hot charcoal fire. As soon as pearls of moisture start to form on the flesh side—after about 3 minutes—turn the fillets over and grill for about 2 minutes more. (Figure about 8 minutes of total cooking time per inch of thickness.)

SLIDE the cooked soba noodles into the simmering *dashi*. Turn the heat up to high and, as soon as *dashi* returns to a simmer, distribute the noodles among deep bowls (preferably Japanese lacquer) with a fork and spoon. Poke through the top of the noodles with a fork and turn until they form a mound in each bowl.

PUT the chopped scallions into the simmering *dashi*. Arrange 2 pieces of fish over each mound of noodles, sprinkle the fillets lightly with *shichimi*, and ladle the *dashi* around the fish and noodles.

Basque-Style Salt Cod Soup

The Basques, both on the Spanish and the French side of the Pyrenees, are aficionados of salt cod, whose full flavor makes it especially delicious in hearty soups containing peppers and tomatoes. Get the thickest salt cod you can for this soup.

Basque cooks use their own local variety of chili—piments d'Espelette—but I haven't been able to find them in the United States. Most recipes written in English recommend using sweet peppers and then suggest adding cayenne to give the soup a little punch. I always find that sweet peppers take over the flavor of whatever they're in, so I like to use either fresh or dried Mexican and New Mexico chilies.

MAKES 6 FIRST-COURSE SERVINGS

I pound salt cod, soaked in cold water in the refrigerator
for 24 to 48 hours, water changed every 6 hours

3 fresh poblano or New Mexico chilies or 4 dried chilies
such as ancho or guajillo

½ cup dry white wine

I tablespoon olive oil

I small onion, finely chopped

I leek, white part only, washed and finely chopped

2 garlic cloves, finely chopped

3 medium-size tomatoes, peeled, seeded, and chopped or
1½ cups canned, seeded and drained

I bouquet garni

slices of French bread, toasted

DRAIN the cod and put it in a 4-quart pot with just enough water to cover. Bring to a slow simmer and immediately turn off the heat. Let the cod cool in the water.

IF you're using fresh chilies, roast, peel, and seed them as described on page 207, and cut them crosswise into strips.

IF you're using dried chilies, cut them lengthwise, remove the stem and seeds, and cut them crosswise into strips. Soak the strips for 20 minutes in just enough hot water to cover. Taste the soaking water—if it's bitter, throw it out; if it tastes good, add it to the soup. Finely chop the softened chilies into a coarse paste or puree them in a blender with the white wine.

COMBINE the olive oil, onion, leek, and garlic in a 4-quart pot over medium heat. Stir the mixture until the onion turns translucent, about 10 minutes. Add the chilies, tomatoes, bouquet garni, and white wine if you're using fresh chilies. Simmer for 10 minutes.

POUR the liquid used to poach the cod (if there isn't at least 3 cups, add water to make up the difference) into the tomato mixture. Shred the cod with 2 forks or your fingers and stir it into the soup. Simmer for 2 minutes. Season to taste with salt and pepper. Arrange the toast slices in the soup bowls before pouring the soup over or pass the toast at the table.

Moroccan Fish Soup in the Style of a Tagine

I'm fascinated by soups that are finished with pungent mixtures of herbs and spices: the *rouille* and *aïoli* of the French Mediterranean, Indian *tadka*, and Thai curry pastes. Reading books about Moroccan cooking—Paula Wolfert's *Couscous and Other Good Food from Morocco* is a particularly good one—I started experimenting with *charmoula*, a pungent mixture that Moroccan cooks use to finish soups and stews. The mixture is so delicious and exotic that I went through a period of stirring it into just about everything I cooked, Moroccan or not.

MAKES 10 FIRST-COURSE SERVINGS

4 pounds firm-fleshed fish

3 medium-size onions, 1 coarsely chopped and 2 finely chopped

1 bouquet garni

3 garlic cloves, finely chopped

2 red bell peppers, roasted, peeled, seeded (page 207), and finely chopped

3 tablespoons olive oil

6 medium-size tomatoes, peeled, seeded, and chopped or 3 cups canned, seeded and drained

juice of 2 limes

for the charmoula:

1 tablespoon olive oil

¼ cup tightly packed cilantro leaves

¼ cup tightly packed parsley leaves, preferably Italian

4 garlic cloves

a ½-inch slice of fresh ginger, peeled and thinly sliced

½ teaspoon ground cumin

½ teaspoon cayenne pepper or to taste

UP TO 8 HOURS IN ADVANCE Up to 8 hours ahead, make the fish broth. Have the fishmonger gut and fillet the fish and remove the skin from the fillets. Be sure to save the fish heads and bones. When you get the fillets home, check them carefully and remove any bones.

SOAK the fish bones and heads in cold water for 30 minutes, drain them, and combine them with the coarsely chopped onion, bouquet garni, and enough water to cover in a 4-quart pot. Bring the broth to a slow simmer and simmer for 30 minutes, skimming off any froth that floats to the top. Strain the broth through a medium-mesh strainer.

CAREFULLY remove any remaining bones from the fillets and cut them into 20 equal-size pieces. Refrigerate until needed.

IN a 4-quart pot over medium heat, cook the finely chopped onion, garlic, and red peppers in olive oil. When the vegetables have softened, in about 10 minutes, add the tomatoes, lime juice, and fish broth. Simmer for 10 minutes.

TO prepare the *charmoula*, drizzle the olive oil over the cilantro and parsley leaves—it helps seal in their flavor—and chop them very finely. Chop the garlic and ginger and crush them to a paste in a mortar and pestle or with the side of a large chef's knife. Combine the chopped herbs, garlic and ginger paste, cumin, and cayenne.

AT THE LAST MINUTE Add the pieces of fish to the hot soup and poach them for 2 to 10 minutes, about 8 minutes per inch of thickness. Remove the fish with a slotted spoon and arrange the pieces in hot bowls. Add the *charmoula* to the hot soup and simmer it for 30 seconds. Ladle it over the soup.

Poached Salmon with Fermented Black-Bean-Scented Broth

Many Chinese recipes call for fermented black beans, but surprisingly few are soups. I decided that fermented black beans are simply too tasty to let slip by, so I put together this untraditional recipe, which I think is delicious.

Buy black beans with ginger and not the type that includes Chinese five spices. Yang Jiang is my favorite brand, but black beans from both Mee Chun and Koon Chun are also good.

MAKES 4 FIRST-COURSE OR LIGHT MAIN-COURSE SERVINGS

¼ cup fermented black beans, soaked for 2 minutes in cold
    water, drained, and soaked again for 2 minutes and
    drained
4 garlic cloves, chopped
a ¼-inch slice of fresh ginger, peeled and chopped
½ teaspoon cayenne pepper
I teaspoon dark sesame oil
¼ cup dry sherry or Chinese rice wine (Shaoxing)
I tablespoon dark soy sauce
I quart fish or chicken broth
½ pound fresh Chinese egg noodles or fresh linguine, or
    ¼ pound dried noodles
I tablespoon sugar
2 tablespoons finely chopped cilantro leaves
I pound salmon fillet, cut into ½-inch cubes
2 scallions, both white and green parts, finely chopped

COMBINE the black beans, garlic, ginger, cayenne, sesame oil, sherry, and soy sauce in a blender with ½ cup of the broth. Process the mixture for about I minute, until smooth.

FILL a 4-quart pot two-thirds full of water and bring to a boil. Five minutes before you're ready to serve, cook the noodles—bite into one to make sure they're done—and drain them in a colander.

BRING the remaining broth to a simmer in a 4-quart pot and whisk in the black bean mixture, sugar, and cilantro. Add the salmon cubes. Simmer for I minute, add the scallions, and simmer for I minute or more as needed to cook the salmon.

DISTRIBUTE the noodles among hot deep bowls—preferably Asian style—and ladle the hot soup over them.

Spanish Garlic and Almond Sauce for Finishing Fish Soups

PICADA

This thick Spanish sauce is used to thicken and flavor fish soups and stews. There are dozens of variations containing different proportions of garlic, peppers, and nuts. This version is made with almonds, but some versions also contain hazelnuts. If you fall in love with *picada* as I have, you might want to play around and try substituting hazelnuts for half the almonds.

MAKES ABOUT 1¼ CUPS

6 ½-inch slices of French-style baguette or 2 slices from a
    good-quality white bread, crusts removed

I cup extra virgin olive oil

I cup blanched almonds

I ancho chili

I cup boiling water

8 garlic cloves, chopped

I jalapeño chili, seeded and finely minced

salt

PREHEAT the oven to 350°F. Sauté the bread slices in half the olive oil in a skillet over medium heat until light brown on each side. Don't get the pan too hot or the olive oil will lose its flavor and the bread slices will burn.

TOAST the almonds in the oven for about 15 minutes, until they turn pale brown.

SOAK the ancho chili in the boiling water for 20 minutes. Drain, cut in half lengthwise, and remove the seeds. Chop coarsely.

COMBINE the remaining olive oil, the garlic, almonds, ancho chili, and jalapeño in the bowl of a food processor, a miniature food processor, or the processor attachment of a blender. (A mortar and pestle will also work, but count on at least 30 minutes of continuous grinding.) Process the mixture for 30 seconds, add the bread, and process for 4 minutes more. (This long grinding is needed to get a smooth paste.) Scrape the sides of the food processor as needed to get the mixture moving. If your food processor is too large for the blade to reach the mixture, add enough broth or soup to get the mixture moving. Season to taste with salt.

Garlic and Olive Oil Mayonnaise

AÏOLI

My appetite for *aïoli* has become a physical craving. One broke summer in Paris I practically lived on the stuff, dolloping it on boiled potatoes and string beans, smearing it over the occasional sautéed fish, mopping it up with bread. . . . Such excess isn't supposed to be good for you, but I always feel healthy and full of energy after *aïoli*, even when I've overdone it.

Aïoli is a mayonnaise made by stirring extra virgin olive oil into egg yolks and finely ground raw garlic. Although vegetable oil mayonnaise can be made easily in a blender or food processor, *aïoli* must be made by hand because extra virgin olive oil turns bitter if beaten too quickly or if overworked. The oil must be worked very gently into the egg yolks. Traditionally a mortar and pestle are used, but if you don't have these, the oil can be worked gently into the egg yolks with a wooden spoon.

When you're using *aïoli* to flavor soups, pour the hot soup into the *aïoli*; don't add the *aïoli* directly to the soup, or it may curdle. Pass the remaining *aïoli* at the table so your guests can add more to the soup and smear it on toasted French bread. If you have a mortar, pass the *aïoli* in it, but no matter how you serve it, *aïoli* is hard to resist, and your guests or family will surprise you by how much they eat.

Because *aïoli* is very rich, some chefs like to add a cooked potato to the mixture to thicken it without adding more oil.

MAKES 2 CUPS

3 large garlic cloves, peeled
coarse salt
2 egg yolks
1 tablespoon fresh lemon juice or vinegar
1¾ cups extra virgin olive oil

COMBINE the garlic cloves with the coarse salt in a mortar and pestle and work the mixture to a smooth paste; then add the egg yolks and the lemon juice or vinegar and slowly work in the olive oil. If you don't have a mortar and pestle, make the mayonnaise in a bowl: chop the garlic and crush it on the cutting board with the side of a chef's knife, put it in a bowl with the egg yolks, lemon juice or vinegar, and slowly stir in the olive oil with a wooden spoon.

IF the mayonnaise starts to thicken so much that it's difficult to work, thin it with a tablespoon of water.

SUGGESTIONS AND VARIATIONS | Mayonnaise can separate (chefs call it "breaking") if you stir the oil in too fast. Most recipes have you start out by dribbling the oil into the egg yolk drop by drop and then pouring a little faster once the mayonnaise starts to thicken. This is a nuisance because it means holding the bottle with one hand while stirring with the other. It's easier to pour about a tablespoon of oil to one side of the egg yolk in the mortar or bowl and then work it into the rest of the mixture gradually, being careful not to stir it together all at once. Once the mixture thickens, you can pour in 3 or 4 tablespoons of oil at one time.

IF the mayonnaise does separate—it suddenly thins and takes on a grainy look—put another egg yolk in a bowl and work the broken mayonnaise into the new yolk, taking the same precautions as if you were pouring in oil.

SAFFRON AND GARLIC MAYONNAISE The flavor of saffron and garlic is a magical combination, and a dollop of saffron and garlic mayonnaise does wonders when whisked into a fish soup. In fact I often substitute saffron and garlic mayonnaise for the traditional *rouille* served with a *bouillabaisse* or the *aïoli* served with a *bourride*. Making saffron and garlic mayonnaise is easy; just soak ¼ teaspoon saffron threads in I tablespoon warm water for 20 minutes and then stir the threads and the water into a cup or two of *aïoli*.

Note: These days many people hesitate to eat raw egg yolks because of the risk of salmonella. To be on the safe side, combine the egg yolk and lemon juice in a bowl and whisk it over a bowl of simmering water. As soon as the egg yolk starts to stiffen, remove the bowl from the heat and whisk it for 15 seconds longer to cool the yolk and stop the cooking. If you overcook the yolks, they'll curdle into scrambled eggs. Once you have the cooked yolk, add the olive oil and other ingredients in the same way as when using raw yolks.

Mediterranean Pepper, Garlic, and Bread Sauce for Thickening Soup

ROUILLE

This intensely flavored Provençal sauce is the classic finish for a *bouillabaisse*. Because it will turn the most insipid broth into a pungent and full-flavored soup, I also swirl it into less grandiose fish and vegetable soups as a final thickener. It's great smeared on toasted French bread.

Traditional versions of *rouille* are made with hot peppers, garlic, olive oil, bread crumbs, and sometimes saffron. Although traditional recipes don't contain egg yolks, most restaurant versions are actually *aïoli* with pureed red pepper added.

Sometimes finding the right kind of hot chilies for a *rouille* can be a nuisance. If you can't find them, just add Tabasco sauce or cayenne pepper to taste at the end.

MAKES 1⅔ CUPS

2 red bell peppers, roasted, peeled and seeded (page 207)

2 jalapeño chilies, cut in half lengthwise, seeded and finely
　　chopped

3 garlic cloves, chopped

I teaspoon coarse salt (see directions)

3 ½-inch slices of French baguette, crusts removed or I
　　slice standard white bread, crusts removed, 2 ounces

½ cup extra virgin olive oil

COARSELY chop the peeled red peppers and combine with the jalapeños, garlic, and
coarse salt in a mortar. Work the mixture to a smooth paste. Soak the bread for a
few seconds in the hot soup or in some water to soften it. Squeeze the excess liquid
out of the bread and add it to the mixture in the mortar. Work the mixture again
until it is smooth; gradually incorporate the olive oil.

IF you don't have a mortar and pestle, you can make *rouille* in a food processor or
blender. Simply combine all the ingredients except the olive oil (use fine salt instead
of coarse) and puree the mixture to a smooth paste. Transfer the paste to a bowl
and work in the olive oil with a wooden spoon (processing the extra virgin oil would
make it bitter).

SUGGESTIONS AND VARIATIONS | To use potato instead of bread crumbs as a
thickener, cook a medium-size waxy potato in simmering water until soft. Peel the
potato while it's still warm and work it with the other ingredients in the mortar and
pestle or in the food processor. If you're using a food processor, don't overwork the
potato, or it will make the sauce gluey.

ROUILLE is delicious flavored with saffron. Soak a small pinch of saffron threads in
a tablespoon of warm water for 20 minutes and add them to the recipe.

"Most bivalves can be
cooked into soups . . ."

Bivalve
Shellfish
SOUPS

Shellfish that have two hard shells hinged together with an animal living inside are called *bivalves*. The family include mollusks such as mussels, clams, scallops, oysters, and a host of less important varieties that are rarely eaten except by an adventurous beachcomber or shipwreck survivor.

Because most bivalves can be cooked into soups using the same techniques and similar ingredients, many of the recipes in this chapter are interchangeable, with only small differences in cooking times. Once you're comfortable working with these shellfish and a few basic ingredients, you can use different ingredients and techniques to make chowders, *ceviches*, Asian-style soups, and French-style *pots-au-feu*.

Steaming in a small amount of flavorful liquid is the best way to convert clams, mussels, and cockles into soups. When these bivalves cook, their shells open and juices are released into the surrounding liquid, which becomes the soup base. Some bivalves, such as oysters and scallops, are shucked ahead of time and poached in the soup at the last minute.

CLAMS AND COCKLES Although there are dozens of varieties of clams and cockles, only a few appear with any regularity in city fish markets. Most clams fall into one of two categories: soft-shelled and hard-shelled. Soft-shelled clams (also called *steamers*) are more difficult to find than hard-shelled types, and when they are available they're usually eaten steamed, baked, or on the half shell. Hard-shelled clams are more common and are the best for making soups.

Most of the hard-shelled clams in fish markets are named according to their size, even though they are all the same species, called *quahogs*. The smallest clams are called *littlenecks*, medium-size clams are called *cherrystones*, and the largest are called *chowder clams*.

Any size clam can be used for making soups, but the little ones usually have the best flavor. If you use little clams, you of course need more clams and more patience taking them out of the shells. Recently, tiny Manila clams—sometimes called *Japanese littlenecks*—have begun to appear in fish stores. They are very small—less than an inch wide—but their flavor is incomparable. Unfortunately they are not cheap.

Many recipes for clam soups and chowders call for first shucking the clams. This is an unnecessary nuisance. It is easier and just as effective to steam open the clams in a small amount of liquid in the same way as mussels. The only difference between cooking mussels and clams is that clams take longer to open. Clams cook in about 12 minutes—but there are almost always one or two stubborn ones that take longer and spring open just as you're about to swear them off as dead.

You can use almost any liquid to open clams or mussels. I usually use white wine, but fish or chicken broth, hard cider, beer, or even water will work.

Some people recommend canned clams or bottled clam juice for making soups. These are certainly helpful for making large quantities or in restaurants that have clam soups or chowders on the menu, but they are of course never as good as fresh. Bottled clam juice always seems to have an aggressive fishy taste, so I always opt for something else—even water—if I have to.

If you're lucky enough to find them, cockles can be used in any of the clam soup recipes. I first tasted cockles in a Paris fish restaurant a couple of years ago and then noticed them a few months later in a fancy food store in Manhattan. When I got them home, I steamed them open in a little wine, added a little cream, and devoured them along with most of a French-style baguette. Those cockles that I've been able to find are very small—about the size of a nickel—so when you use them, you may want to add them to the soup, shells and all. This relegates them to meals that are more convivial than formal, where people can reach in with their hands, slurp freely from their spoons, and not worry about making a mess.

In a pound there are about 16 medium-size clams, 20 small littlenecks, 35 Manila clams or cockles, and approximately 8 chowder clams.

MUSSELS Fresh live mussels are inexpensive and easy to prepare. When heated in a small amount of liquid, they release a savory, sealike broth that can be mopped up with crusty French bread or converted into a delicious soup.

The common mussel, or blue mussel, is available in many shapes and sizes. Buy small (about 2 inches long, about 20 to a pound) cultivated mussels, which consistently have the best flavor and the least sand. Larger mussels, which often have a rougher outer shell, are often sandy and can be so large that they can be unpleasant to eat. Sometimes they have a strong, gamey flavor.

Make sure the mussels haven't been allowed to open and dry out; they should be firmly closed. If they get lazy and open slightly after you get them home, make sure they are still alive by giving them a quick squeeze to see if they close. Be patient; sometimes they take their time. (I once threw a couple of pounds of half-opened mussels in the trash. When I glanced into the trash can a half hour later, they had all closed.) If you're uncertain about a slightly opened mussel, give it a good sniff; it should smell like the ocean and nothing else.

Be sure to use mussels within a day or two. If you're not using them right away, store them in the refrigerator in a bowl covered with a wet towel. Some cooks suggest storing mussels submerged in salt water to simulate the sea, but this is more trouble than it's worth. Never store them submerged in fresh water; it will leach out their flavor and cause them to die very quickly.

Cultivated mussels are already clean and need only a light scrubbing with a small brush before they are used. The best way is to brush them under cold running water to get rid of any grit. Most mussels have a small bunch of little hairs (called the *beard*) sticking out of the sides, which you should pull out. Tug on them while moving them quickly back and forth. If the beards are really stubborn, leave them for the time being and pull them off after the mussels are cooked.

In any batch of mussels there are usually one or two dead ones that must be thrown out or they will spoil a whole pot of soup. While you're washing the mussels, hold the shells between your thumb and forefinger and push the top and bottom shells sideways in opposite directions. Any dead mussels will fall apart in your hand.

Most soup recipes start with cooking the mussels in a small amount of liquid in a tightly covered pot. You don't need much liquid to get the mussels to open, because once they start cooking they release liquid of their own. You can use water to get the process started, but most recipes use something tastier, like wine, cider, beer, chopped tomatoes, or even rum. In addition to liquids, fresh herbs and chopped aromatic vegetables such as garlic and shallots are often included in the flavorful liquid used for steaming.

Once the mussels have cooked and released their flavorful juices, there's a delicious broth left at the bottom of the pot that can be served just as it is or finished in an almost infinite number of ways. French recipes sometimes add cream and egg yolks and flavor the broth with saffron or curry; Mediterranean mussel soups are often finished with pistou, *aïoli,* or *rouille;* and Asian versions often use coconut milk as both liquid and thickener.

Cultivated mussels rarely contain any sand, but if you're stuck with sandy mussels, it may be necessary after you steam them to strain the broth through a strainer lined with a triple layer of cheesecloth or a cloth napkin. Be sure to rinse out the cloth thoroughly first to eliminate traces of bleach or chemicals. Sometimes if the steaming liquid from the mussels contains a small amount of sand, I don't bother straining it but carefully pour it into another container, leaving the sand behind.

Count on 8 to 12 mussels per person, depending on their size, as a first course and twice as many if the mussels are being served as a main course.

OYSTERS As recently as 20 years ago East Coast bars and restaurants sold platters of oysters with steins of draft beer for little more than it would cost now to go out for a pizza. Unfortunately this joyful era is over—at least in New York—and oysters are sold individually in chic Manhattan restaurants for a price that not so long ago would buy a dozen.

Because oysters are expensive and extraordinary, an oyster soup or stew is always a special treat. Unlike clams and mussels, which are usually steamed open in white wine or some other flavorful liquid, oysters need to be shucked. For the inexperienced, this is a nuisance. If you're going to use the oysters within a few hours, have them shucked at the fish store, but if they need to wait overnight, you'll have to shuck them yourself. When storing unopened oysters, keep them in the refrigerator, arranged in a bowl so they stay flat. If thrown haphazardly into a bowl or bag, their liquid will drain and they will dry out.

The best way to shuck an oyster depends on the type. Although there are dozens of varieties, most oysters fall into one of two categories, elongated oysters which have a thick, heavy shell, and the less common Belons or "flat oysters," which are relatively thin and almost perfectly round.

To shuck an elongated oyster, hold it in a towel, making sure that the towel covers and protects your hand in case you slip with the oyster knife. Insert the oyster knife between the two shells next to the hinge—wiggle it slightly from side to side so that it starts to penetrate the shell—and twist it to separate the top and bottom shells. Once the shells separate slightly, slide the oyster knife under the top shell to cut through the muscle and detach the top shell. Be careful to keep the knife pressed against the underside of the lid so as not to damage the oyster. Some chefs recommend using a can opener wedged into the hinge to open oysters, but I always have better luck with an oyster knife. If the oyster knife doesn't work for you, try the can opener.

The best way to shuck a flat oyster is to hold it in a towel and slide a thin, flat (but not sharp) knife between the two shells starting from the side opposite the hinge. Once you get the knife in between the two shells, slide it against the underside of the top shell to cut through the muscle, holding the top shell in place.

When you get the tops off the oysters, hold the oysters over a bowl and detach the oysters by running the oyster knife firmly against the bottom shell. Be sure to catch any liquid that runs out of the shell in a bowl along with the oysters.

Before you put the oysters into a soup, check them carefully for grit. Strain the oyster liquid before adding it to a soup. If the oysters seem especially gritty, take them out of the bowl and spread them on a clean cotton towel, roll them around for a few seconds, and then take them off right away—any grit or pieces of shell will adhere to the towel.

When making oyster soups, it is important that the oysters not be cooked for more than a few seconds—just the time to heat them through. Though the basic soup has to be prepared completely in advance, it can include the liquid saved from the oysters, but the oysters themselves can be added only at the last minute.

Many different liquids can be used as the base for an oyster soup. American oyster stew recipes usually call for milk thickened with a little flour, while French versions often use fish broth finished with a little heavy cream. But other liquids can be used: hard cider, beer, white wine, and the cooking liquid from mussels all make excellent liquid bases.

SCALLOPS Several kinds of scallops are available in the United States and can be used to make wonderful soups. The largest scallops are sea scallops, delivered to fish markets already out of their shells. This is unfortunate because once the scallop is out of the shell it quickly dies and is never as fresh or as flavorful as a scallop shucked just before it is used. Fortunately, as the public becomes more demanding, scallops in their shell are starting to appear in fish markets.

If you can't find sea scallops in the shell and have to rely on the preshucked scallops usually found in fish markets, check them over carefully before you buy. Ask the fishmonger if you can give them a sniff. There shouldn't be any odor. Sea scallops should be almost perfectly white and slightly shiny. Sometimes it's possible to spot stale scallops—before going through the business of the sniffing—because they look slimy or even slightly brown. Beware also of scallops that are perfectly white with a matte appearance and no sheen at all. This probably means they have been left to soak or rinsed off because they are stale.

Sea scallops have a small strip—actually a muscle—that runs vertically along one side. Be sure to pull this off before cooking the scallops because it has a hard and unpleasant texture as soon as it gets hot. Sea scallops come in all different sizes, so you may need to slice some of the larger ones crosswise in half or even into thirds.

Bay scallops, which come from the northern Atlantic coast, are in season from November to March. They are about one-third the size of sea scallops, and although they are usually marketed out of the shell, they can occasionally be found in the shell in East Coast fish markets. It is worth the extra effort and expense to buy them in the shell because they'll be fresher and have a more lively flavor. Unlike clams and mussels, which should be firmly closed, bay scallops usually gape a bit, which doesn't necessarily mean they are old.

If you're lucky enough to find bay scallops in the shell, you'll need to have the fishmonger shuck them or shuck them yourself. Unlike mussels or clams, which can be cooked directly in the soup, eastern bay scallops contain an unsightly brown "rim" that wraps around the nugget of seafood and must be removed. Fortunately, this is easy, because unlike clams and mussels, bay scallops usually gape, making it easy to get the knife in.

Slide a thin knife along the underside of the top shell, detaching the scallop. Keep the knife flush with the shell so you don't leave the scallop attached. Cut and pull away the "mantle" surrounding the scallop (which is actually the small muscle in the middle, called the abductor muscle) and discard the mantle. (Although it is edible—I've had it in sushi bars—it's not to everyone's taste.) Slide the knife under the scallop and reserve.

The smallest scallop is the calico scallop which comes from Florida and the southern Atlantic coast. These are often sold as bay scallops, but they are much smaller—they look like tiny marshmallows—and rarely have as good a flavor. They are usually lightly cooked at the factory to make it easier to get them out of the shell.

In the Pacific Northwest, there is a small scallop—the pink and spiny scallop, sometimes called singing scallop—which doesn't need to be cleaned before it is cooked; it can be steamed open in the soup and served shell and all in the same way as simple clam or mussel soup.

Like most shellfish, scallops take poorly to long cooking and should be added to hot soups only at the last minute.

SEA URCHINS: Along with caviar and foie gras, sea urchins rank among my favorite luxury foods. When I lived in Paris in the 1970s, fresh sea urchins were such a delicacy that one sea urchin in the shell was almost the price of a dozen oysters—and oysters weren't cheap. When I returned to the United States to open a restaurant in Manhattan, I was delighted to find that sea urchins were so inexpensive I could buy a whole crate for the price of a dozen oysters. Now sea urchins have become a luxury because they are so popular in sushi bars, where their roe is sold as *uni*.

If you're lucky enough to find fresh sea urchins in the shell, cut off the top of the shell—the side with the hole in the middle—with a pair of heavy kitchen shears. Start by cutting into the hole and snipping your way to the side of the shell. Then, cut around the circumference of the shell and remove the entire top. Scoop out the golden-orange roe—the only part that is eaten—with a small spoon. If you can't find sea urchins in the shell, you may be able to order just the roe, which is sold on small wooden trays, at your fish store. If worse comes to worst, you can buy *uni* at a Japanese restaurant, but it will be expensive.

Improvising Shellfish Soups

Once you master a few basic methods for making shellfish soups, it's easy to invent a soup following a whim or to adapt your cooking plans according to what looks good in the market. I rarely have more than a vague idea of what I'm going to cook until I snoop around my favorite food stores or outdoor markets. Usually I spot one or two special looking foods and then build a meal around them.

There are two approaches to making a soup out of bivalves. One method, used for mussels, clams, and cockles, is to steam open the shellfish in a small amount of liquid, take the shellfish out of the shells, and then build a soup on the briny liquid left in the bottom of the pot.

Another method, used for oysters (which don't take well to steaming and are better shucked raw), is to prepare a flavorful soup completely independent of the oysters. The oysters are then cooked for only a few seconds in the soup base immediately before serving.

Whichever method you use, you must start with a flavorful liquid base. Some recipes suggest cooking aromatic vegetables and sometimes meat in a little fat before any liquid is added. When improvising, I use this method for Mediterranean soups containing tomatoes, saffron, and ham or for Asian-style soups where a base of strong spices needs to be cooked lightly in oil to release its flavor. A more straightforward method is to simmer the liquid directly with herbs or vegetables and then add the shellfish at the appropriate point (clams and mussels at the beginning; oysters at the end).

In some more elaborate soup recipes, a flavor base is prepared by gently sautéing aromatic vegetables and at times flavorful meats in a small amount of oil or fat before any liquid is added. Here are a few of the possibilities:

Oils or Fats:
  Olive oil
  Rendered bacon fat
  Butter
  Vegetable oil

Savory Meats:
  Bacon
  Prosciutto
  Pancetta

Liquids:

Water
White wine
Cider
Beer
Fish broth
Milk

Herbs:

Parsley (chopped)
Tarragon (chopped)
Chervil (chopped)
Marjoram (chopped or bouquet garni)
Thyme (chopped or bouquet garni)
Lemongrass (chopped)
Ginger

Aromatic Vegetables:

Tomatoes (peeled, seeded, chopped)
Onions (chopped)
Shallots (chopped)
Celery (diced)
Carrots (diced)
Leeks (diced)

FINISHES AND THICKENERS: Once the shellfish have been steamed open in the flavor base, additional liquids, flavorings, and vegetables are often added to the shellfish cooking liquid. Some of these liquids are designed to stretch the soup, while others are added to give it richness and a smooth texture.

Some recipes include flavorful mixtures that need to be whisked into the soup near the end.

Flavorful Liquids:

Tomato pure
Fish broth
Vegetables purees

Liquid Added to Enrich and Thicken:

Heavy cream
Crème fraîche
Sour cream (added just before serving)
Egg yolks
Yogurt

Flavorful finishes:

Aioli (page 349)
Rouille (page 350)
Picada (page 348)
Butter (plain or flavored)
Indian spices (tadka)
Herbs and spices

EXTRA INGREDIENTS: These are independent of the basic soup but can be added to make the soup more substantial and colorful. Using these ingredients is an easy and exciting way to convert a simple, tasty broth into a main course:

Spinach (blanched, whole leaves, or cut into chiffonade)
Sorrel (whole leaves or chiffonade, not blanched)
Wild or cultivated mushrooms (simmered in soup or sautéed in butter or olive oil and added at the end)
Pearl onions (peeled)
Leeks (julienne)
Carrots (julienne)
Celery root (julienne)

Mussels Steamed in White Wine

MOULES À LA MARINIÈRE

This is one of the best and easiest ways to cook mussels; and the result—bowls of steaming hot mussels, scented with herbs and white wine, is irresistibly satisfying. Be sure to pass French bread with the soup and set large bowls on the table for the finished shells; everybody happily slurps, dunks bread, and sips white wine. Mussels cooked this way make a delicious meal in themselves; they also provide the basic broth for more elaborate soup variations.

The process for steaming mussels is simple: washed and sorted mussels are put in a large pot with chopped shallots, a bay leaf, and white wine; the pot is then covered and the whole thing put on the stove until the mussels open. The mussels are then scooped out into soup bowls, chopped parsley is added to the liquid, in the pot, and the hot, briny broth is poured over the mussels.

MAKES 6 FIRST-COURSE SERVINGS

3 pounds small cultivated mussels, about 60
2 cups dry white wine
3 shallots, finely chopped
I bay leaf
2 tablespoons finely chopped parsley leaves
French bread

WASH the mussels and discard any dead ones.

BRING the white wine, shallots, and bay leaf to a simmer in a pot large enough to hold the mussels. Cover the pot with a lid and leave it at a slow simmer for 5 minutes so the shallots and bay leaf have time to flavor the wine.

ADD the mussels all at once, cover the pot tightly, and turn up the heat so the liquid comes to a rapid boil. After about 3 minutes, shake the pot to move the mussels around and help them cook evenly. Cook the mussels for 3 minutes more. Open the lid. All the mussels should be wide open. If some are still closed or only partially opened, put the lid back on the pot and steam them for 2 minutes more.

TAKE the mussels out of the pot and distribute them with a slotted spoon among hot bowls. Check the broth for sand. If there is none, add the parsley directly to the broth, bring it back to a simmer for I minute to cook the parsley, and ladle the hot broth over the mussels. If the broth is sandy, strain it into a saucepan through a triple layer of cheesecloth or a cloth napkin (rinsed first to eliminate bleach or chemicals), or pour it from one container to another, leaving sand behind in each one, before adding the parsley. Serve the mussels in their broth with slices of crusty French bread.

SUGGESTIONS AND VARIATIONS | You can give the mussel broth a completely different flavor by replacing the shallots with chopped garlic. Herbs such as fresh thyme or marjoram can also be added with the wine at the beginning. Or try making a spicy broth by replacing the parsley with chopped tomatoes and chopped fresh cilantro and adding cayenne or Tabasco to taste. Or finish with cream or coconut milk.

Cream of Mussel Soup

BILLI BI

Billi bi, along with *vichyssoise* and lobster bisque, epitomized elegance in French restaurants in the United States during the fifties and sixties. You don't see it around much anymore, but it's a soup worth remembering.

Legend has it that *billi bi* was invented by a chef for an American who loved the flavor of mussel broth but was squeamish about the mussels themselves. I've never seen *billi bi* on a menu in France, but then the French like their mussel soups with mussels in them.

This recipe contains heavy cream and egg yolks, which give the soup a lovely texture but also make it quite rich. You can easily eliminate the egg yolks and use less cream, but don't try to substitute milk for the cream. Milk may curdle and will at least make the soup very thin.

When the soup is done, you'll have a pot full of cooked mussels to eat on the spot without broth or to use for something else. Leftover mussels are wonderful when taken out of the shell and served cold, tossed with vinaigrette and sprinkled with chopped fresh chives, parsley, or tarragon, but I sometimes just reheat the shelled mussels in the soup.

Billi bi can be made a day or two in advance, but be careful when reheating it not to let it boil and curdle the egg yolks.

MAKES 4 FIRST-COURSE SERVINGS OR 6 WITH THE MUSSELS

3 pounds small cultivated mussels, about 60

2 cups dry white wine

3 shallots, finely chopped

1 bouquet garni: 2 fresh thyme sprigs, 1 small bunch of
   parsley, and 1 bay leaf

1 cup heavy cream

4 egg yolks (optional)

2 tablespoons finely chopped chives

freshly ground white pepper

French bread

WASH the mussels. Sort through them and throw out any dead ones. Combine the wine, shallots, and bouquet garni in a 6-quart pot. Cover the pot and simmer the mixture for 5 minutes to flavor the liquid with the herbs. Add the mussels, cover the pot, and turn the heat up to high.

STEAM the mussels until they open, after about 6 minutes, let them cool slightly, and scoop them out with a slotted spoon. Take out and discard the bouquet garni. If the liquid in the pot contains sand, strain it through a triple layer of cheesecloth or a cloth napkin (rinsed first to eliminate bleach or chemicals) or pour it from one container to another, leaving behind sand each time.

COMBINE the heavy cream with the egg yolks and whisk thoroughly to combine them. Bring the cooking liquid from the mussels to a simmer in a 2-quart pot. Whisk the simmering cooking liquid into the cream/egg yolk mixture and pour the mixture back into the pot. Put the soup over medium heat and stir with a wooden spoon. Be sure to reach into the corners of the saucepan and not to let the soup boil, or the egg yolks will curdle. The egg yolks thicken the soup very slightly, giving it a silky texture, but don't wait for any dramatic thickening, or you're liable to curdle the soup. (If you have a thermometer, it should read 175°F at this point.) If you've left out the egg yolks, just bring the soup to a simmer.

ADD the chopped chives and grind in fresh white pepper just before serving with slices of crusty French bread.

SUGGESTIONS AND VARIATIONS | *Billi bi* can also be made more substantial by adding vegetables. If you can find some sorrel—it's in season during the summer— a handful of the shredded leaves with the stems removed added to the soup at the end gives it a tangy accent and a little more substance. Peeled, seeded, and chopped tomatoes can also be added to round out the flavors and give the soup color.

IT'S easy to convert a *billi bi* into a curried mussel soup by gently cooking 2 teaspoons (or more to taste) good curry powder in a tablespoon of butter for 30 seconds and then whisking the mixture into the finished soup. A small pinch of saffron threads soaked in a little water also provides an exciting accent.

I sometimes use *billi bi* almost as a sauce for a main-course soup of salmon and mussels. I sauté salmon fillets, prop them in the center of wide bowls on a mound of fresh spinach, and surround them with the *billi bi* and shelled mussels. A couple of teaspoons of chopped fresh tarragon is a nice addition.

Saffron Mussel Soup

This soup combines the briny flavor of fresh mussels with garlic, fennel, and Mediterranean herbs. It is one of the deepest flavored fish soups I know—probably because fresh whole fish is used to make the basic soup which functions as a flavorful backdrop for the briny flavor of the mussels. Saffron threads tint it orange and give it a final pungent note of flavor.

This soup is complicated, but much of the work can be broken down into simple stages.

MAKES 12 FIRST-COURSE OR 6 MAIN-COURSE SERVINGS

8 pounds firm-fleshed fish such as red snapper, sea bass,
    striped bass, or grouper

2 medium-size onions, chopped

I bouquet garni

2 cups dry white wine

2 shallots, finely chopped

4 pounds cultivated mussels, well scrubbed and sorted,
    about 80

3 garlic cloves, chopped

I small fennel bulb, chopped

3 tablespoons olive oil

4 large tomatoes, cut in half crosswise and seeds squeezed
    out

I cup heavy cream

pinch of saffron threads, about a ¼ teaspoon, soaked in
    I tablespoon water for 20 minutes

salt

pepper

slices of French bread, toasted

HAVE the fishmonger fillet the fish and remove the skin, saving the heads and bones.

PREPARE a fish broth by soaking the fish heads and bones in a bowl of cold water for 30 minutes, changing the water once or twice. Drain and combine the fish heads and bones, onions, and bouquet garni in a 6-quart pot. Add enough water to barely cover the bones. Bring to a simmer over medium to high heat and then turn the heat down enough to maintain a slow simmer for 30 minutes. Use a ladle to skim off any froth that floats to the top. Strain through a medium-mesh strainer. You will end up with more broth than the quart needed for preparing the soup. Save the extra broth for another recipe (it freezes forever) or simmer the broth until it cooks down to a quart.

COMBINE the white wine, shallots, and mussels in a 6-quart pot. Cover the pot and place over high heat for about 10 minutes. When the mussels have opened, take them out and discard the shells. If the liquid from the mussels is sandy, strain it through a triple layer of cheesecloth or a cloth napkin (rinsed first to eliminate bleach or chemicals) or gently pour it from one measuring cup into another, leaving sand behind in each one until there is no sand left.

IN a 4-quart pot over medium heat, cook the chopped garlic and fennel in the olive oil until they soften, about 20 minutes. Add the tomato halves to the vegetables and pour in the fish broth and the cooking liquid from the mussels. Cut the fish fillets into 2-inch chunks and add them to the soup. Bring to a slow simmer, cover the pot, and keep the soup at a slow simmer for about 30 minutes, until the fish is completely cooked and starts to fall apart.

STRAIN the soup and reserve the liquid. Puree the fish and solids that won't go through the strainer in a blender or food processor. (You may need to add some of the liquid to get them moving.) Work the fish puree through a food mill with the finest disk. Discard what won't go through the food mill. Combine the fish puree with the reserved liquid.

ADD the cream, saffron and its soaking liquid, and cooked mussels. Season the soup with salt and pepper and serve in hot wide bowls. Pass slices of toasted French bread.

SUGGESTIONS AND VARIATIONS | This rich and flavorful soup can be served as a main course for lunch or the first course of a substantial dinner. Poach extra fish fillets, scallops, or shrimp in the soup at the end to make it more of a meal. You can also add vegetables such as braised fennel wedges, tomato wedges (peeled, seeded, and gently sautéed in olive oil for 5 minutes), pearl onions (gently cooked in olive oil until soft), whole garlic cloves (peeled and boiled until soft), and precooked baby artichokes.

IF you're serving the soup with extra ingredients, present it in the largest soup bowls you have. Or serve it in plates with deep rims so the different garnishes can be seen at their best.

Mussel and Shiitake Mushroom *Dashi*

This is one of many examples of how a simple Japanese *dashi* can be used as the base for an elegant—and fat-free—first-course soup. The mussels are steamed in a small amount of the *dashi*, the top shell is removed, and the mussels are served in the dashi with shiitake mushrooms and fine vegetable julienne. You can serve the soup in wide bowls, but I prefer Japanese-style black lacquer bowls with lids.

The *dashi* can be prepared a day or two in advance, and the mussels can be cooked earlier in the day the soup is served.

MAKES 8 FIRST-COURSE SERVINGS

2-inch length of daikon, peeled, or 1 leek, washed, white
    part only
1 large carrot
40 small cultivated mussels, about 2 pounds

5 cups dashi

12 shiitake mushrooms, stems removed, each cut into
  3 or 4 slices

2 scallions, both green and white parts, finely sliced

IF you're using leek instead of daikon, slit the leek down the middle and rinse out any sand, then slice 2 layers at a time into fine julienne with a chef's knife. If you're using daikon, cut the daikon, along with the carrot, into julienne strips with a sharp knife or a benriner cutter.

SCRUB the mussels, throw out any dead ones, and put them into a 4-quart pot with 3 cups of the *dashi*. Cover the pot and bring the broth to a rapid boil. After 5 minutes, start checking the mussels every 2 minutes to see if they've opened. As soon as they've all opened, remove them from the heat. Let them cool slightly and remove the top shells. If the broth is sandy, strain it through a triple layer of cheesecloth or a cloth napkin (rinsed first to eliminate bleach or chemicals) or pour it from one container to another, leaving sand behind in each one.

WHILE the mussels are steaming, simmer the vegetables and mushrooms for about 10 minutes in the remaining *dashi*. Combine the *dashi* used for cooking the vegetables with the liquid from the mussels and bring it to a simmer in a small pot.

ARRANGE the mussels, vegetables, and mushrooms in hot soup bowls, sprinkle with the chopped scallions, and pour the simmering *dashi* over all.

SUGGESTIONS AND VARIATIONS | This soup can easily be made more substantial by serving it over Japanese ramen or soba noodles that have been cooked separately in boiling water. You can also give it a more assertive flavor by whisking a tablespoon or two of miso into the *dashi*.

Clams with Cream and White Wine

This is the simplest way to prepare and serve small clams or cockles. Although most recipes for clam soup require a flavor base of herbs, onions, or other vegetables, the briny juice that clams release during cooking has such an intensely pure flavor of the sea that these other accents seem almost superfluous.

Baskets of crusty French bread are essential for convivial dipping and slurping.

MAKES 4 FIRST-COURSE SERVINGS

5 dozen littleneck clams, about 3 pounds, or 3 pounds
    cockles

2 cups dry white wine

1 cup heavy cream

1 tablespoon finely chopped parsley leaves

freshly ground pepper

French bread

RINSE the clams or cockles and brush off any grit with a small scrub brush. Place them in a 4-quart pot with the white wine, cover with a tight-fitting lid, and put the pot on high heat for 5 minutes. Turn the heat down to medium, grab the sides of the pot and lid with a kitchen towel, and toss the clams around to redistribute them. Simmer for 2 minutes more and then start checking every few minutes to see if the clams have opened.

WHEN all the clams have opened, scoop them into wide bowls with a slotted spoon. Check the liquid in the bottom of the pot to see if it contains grit or sand. If so, pour it carefully from one container to another, leaving sand in the bottom of each one, or strain it through a triple layer of cheesecloth or a cloth napkin (rinsed first to eliminate bleach or chemicals) into a clean saucepan. Add the heavy cream to the clam liquid. Bring the soup to a simmer, stir in the parsley, simmer for 1 minute more, and pour it over the clams. Grind fresh pepper over the bowls or just pass the pepper mill at the table.

SUGGESTIONS AND VARIATIONS | The heavy cream rounds out the soup's flavor, but you can leave it out or use less if you're worried about calories or fat; the broth is still delicious without it. Don't try to substitute milk or half-and-half, which will make the broth look grainy and give it a peculiar milky flavor that interferes with the sealike flavors of the clams.

THIS soup is hard to improve on, but a couple of fresh thyme sprigs added to the broth at the beginning or shredded sorrel or chopped chives added at the end will do no harm. If you want to serve this soup in a more formal setting, take the clams out of the shells before serving. To quickly turn this soup into a light meal, pour it over individual mounds of fettuccine or linguine.

YOU can also use this soup as a light sauce. Try poaching thin tuna or swordfish steaks in the broth and serving it as a main course in wide plates with deep rims. Garnish the plate with the clams.

New England Clam Chowder

Clam chowder is one of those dishes that Americans argue about in the way the French debate the right way to make a *bouillabaisse* or the Italians dispute how to make pasta. Everyone is expected to know that New England clam chowder is made with milk and that Manhattan chowder contains tomatoes, but those in the know argue over more refined issues—what ratio of clams to onions to potatoes, whether to use quahogs or soft-shells, and whether or not one or two tomatoes might be slipped into a New England version.

I've never been fond of arguments that try to establish the right or wrong way to cook a particular dish—if I've got good ingredients and they make good culinary sense, then in they go. At the same time, if I don't have some essential ingredient, I'll risk being "unauthentic" and substitute something else.

Even if you're willing to take a free-form approach to chowder making, a few guidelines can be helpful. It should never be necessary to use roux (cooked flour and butter) to thicken the soup because a chowder always contains something starchy—usually potatoes but sometimes corn—that gives it plenty of body. Most recipes for New England chowder call for milk, but I prefer to use heavy cream and less of it to give the chowder a smoother texture and a more forthright flavor. Authentic chowder starts out with salt pork, but since I usually don't have any around, I'll substitute butter or bacon—to some, heretical, but delicious nonetheless. If you're using bacon or salt pork, be sure to cut it up into cubes and blanch it for 5 minutes in boiling water first or its flavor will completely take over the chowder.

Clam chowder can be made a day or two in advance.

MAKES 8 FIRST-COURSE SERVINGS

5 dozen littleneck or cherrystone clams

1 quart water or fish broth

1 bouquet garni: 3 fresh thyme sprigs, 1 bay leaf and
    1 small bunch of parsley

¼ pound salt pork or bacon, cut into 1- by ¼-inch strips
    and boiled for 5 minutes, or 4 tablespoons unsalted
    butter

4 medium-size onions, chopped

3 medium-size waxy potatoes, peeled and cut into
    ¼-inch cubes

2 cups heavy cream

1 tablespoon finely chopped parsley

1 tablespoon finely chopped chives

salt

freshly ground pepper

French bread

soda crackers

SCRUB the clams and put them into a 4-quart pot with the water and bouquet garni. Cover the pot and bring it to a simmer to steam open the clams. When the clams have all opened, after about 12 minutes, take them out with a slotted spoon and transfer the broth from one container to another, leaving sand behind in each one, or strain the cooking liquid through a triple layer of cheesecloth or a cloth napkin (rinsed first to eliminate bleach or chemicals). Take the clams out of their shells. If they're large, cut them in half or in quarters. Keep them covered with plastic wrap in a bowl until needed.

IN a heavy-bottomed 4-quart pot, cook the salt pork or bacon for 10 minutes, until the fat is rendered, or simply melt the butter. Remove the pieces of salt pork or bacon with a slotted spoon, turn down the heat, and add the onions. Stir with a wooden spoon every few minutes to make sure the onions don't brown. When the onions start to soften and turn translucent, after about 10 minutes, add the potatoes and cooking liquid from the clams. Simmer the soup for about 10 minutes to cook the potatoes. Add the heavy cream, parsley, and chives and simmer for 1 minute more. Add the reserved clams, season with salt and pepper, and serve immediately in hot wide bowls. Because the chowder contains potatoes, it can be eaten without bread, but traditionally it is served with crackers. Small freshly toasted croutons also make a nice touch.

Manhattan Clam Chowder

Perhaps it's unfair to call this soup a Manhattan clam chowder. Most versions contain an array of aromatic vegetables, potatoes, and a large proportion of tomatoes, often canned. Much as I like the traditional Manhattan chowder, I usually end up tasting everything except the clams. This is a much simpler interpretation and one I find more exciting because the sealike flavor of the clams makes its way through the flavors of the other ingredients.

Don't be shocked by all the garlic; by the time it's cooked and pureed it is surprisingly mild and gives the soup a smooth texture and a flavor that, though assertive, doesn't mask the taste of the clams.

Manhattan clam chowder can be made a day or two in advance.

MAKES 6 FIRST-COURSE SERVINGS

4 dozen littleneck or cherrystone clams or cockles

1 head of garlic

3 fresh thyme sprigs or ½ teaspoon dried

3 cups fish or chicken broth or water

6 medium-size tomatoes, peeled, seeded, and chopped or
    3 cups canned, seeded and peeled

2 tablespoons finely chopped parsley leaves

slices of French bread, toasted

SCRUB the clams under cold running water with a small scrub brush. Break up the head of garlic to separate the cloves. This is easier if you wet the garlic first. Pull off the excess papery peel, but don't bother peeling each clove. Put the garlic cloves in a saucepan with the thyme and 2 cups of the broth. Cover the pot and simmer until the garlic cloves turn to mush when you squeeze them against the inside of the saucepan, about 20 minutes. If much of the broth or water evaporates, add water so you end up with the original amount.

STEAM open the clams in a covered pot in the remaining broth or water. When the clams have opened, take them out of their shells and discard the shells. If the liquid in the bottom of the pan contains sand or grit, transfer the liquid from one container to another, leaving sand behind in each one, or strain it through a triple layer of cheesecloth or a cloth napkin (rinsed first to eliminate bleach or chemicals).

WORK the garlic cloves and their cooking liquid through a small food mill or push them through a medium-mesh strainer with the back of a wooden spoon. Capture as much of the liquid and pulp as you can in a small bowl. Don't worry about the skins—the pulp squeezes right out when you press on it.

CHOP the tomatoes to any consistency you like. If they are particularly beautiful, leave them on the chunky side.

COMBINE the cooking liquid from the clams, the garlic pulp and strained cooking liquid, the tomatoes, parsley, and reserved clams. Bring the soup to a simmer and serve immediately in hot bowls. Pass thinly sliced French bread toasts at the table.

Clam or Cockle Soup with Borlotti Beans

ZUPPA DI VONGOLE

As with so many of my Italian food experiences, I first had this soup in New York. I would never have thought of combining beans and clams, but the association is delicate and intriguing. This recipe includes a fair amount of fresh parsley, which contributes to the freshness of the dish.

Use the smallest clams you can find—Manila clams are my favorite—or better yet, tiny New Zealand cockles, which are beginning to appear more regularly in fancy fish markets.

This soup is best finished at the last minute, but the time-consuming part, cooking the beans, can be done a day or two in advance. Whatever you do, don't chop the parsley until just before you add it to the soup or it will lose its freshness.

Borlotti beans (tongues of fire) are popular with Italian cooks because of their rich flavor and creamy consistency, but if you can't find them, use cannellini beans or any small white bean such as Great Northerns.

MAKES 4 FIRST-COURSE SERVINGS

I cup dried borlotti, cannellini, or Great Northern beans,
  soaked in water to cover for 3 hours

I bouquet garni

2 pounds small clams or cockles, about 40 to 50, scrubbed
  and rinsed

2 cups dry white wine

¼ cup finely chopped parsley leaves

salt

pepper

DRAIN the beans and put them in a 4-quart pot with enough water to cover by I inch. Nestle in the banquet garni. Bring the liquid to a slow simmer, cover the pot, and simmer until the beans are soft, about I-½ to 2 hours. You may need to add water from time to time to make up for evaporation.

PUT the clams in a 4-quart pot with the wine. Bring to a simmer, cover the pot, and continue simmering until all the clams have opened, about I0 minutes.

SCOOP the clams out of the pot and take them out of their shells, discarding the shells. Carefully pour the liquid left in the bottom of the pot into another container, leaving any sand behind. If the liquid is very sandy, strain it through cheesecloth (rinsed first to eliminate bleach or chemicals) or a fine-mesh strainer.

ADD the clam liquid, shelled clams, and parsley to the beans. Bring to a simmer, season with salt and pepper, and serve immediately.

SUGGESTIONS AND VARIATIONS | Spanish cooks make a similar but more assertive version of this soup called *fabes con almejas*. It is made almost the same way, but some chopped garlic and a good pinch of saffron and ground chili are cooked together with the clams.

ZUPPA di vongole has a light, brothlike texture that makes it a great dish for summer— it can even be served cold. If you want to thicken the soup slightly, puree about a third of the beans in a blender and stir them into the finished soup. In the winter I sometimes add a little heavy cream, which is magnificent.

Spanish "Quarter Hour" Clam and Shrimp Soup

SOPA AL CUARTO DE HORA

As its name implies, this Spanish soup is easy and quick to prepare, but I have to admit that a quarter hour is a bit exaggerated. Count on about 45 minutes from start to finish.

Much of the character for this soup comes from serrano ham, which unfortunately isn't available in the United States, but I make it with prosciutto and it's still wonderful.

This soup can be made a day in advance.

MAKES 6 GENEROUS FIRST-COURSE SERVINGS

18 large shrimp, about 1 pound, shelled, deveined, and cut into ½-inch pieces, shells reserved

40 small clams, about 2 pounds

1 quart fish broth or water

½ cup medium-dry sherry

2 ounces prosciutto, about 2⅛-inch-thick slices

1 medium-size onion, finely chopped

1 garlic clove, finely chopped

2 tablespoons olive oil

3 medium-size tomatoes, peeled, seeded, and chopped

1 bouquet garni

¼ cup long-grain rice

¼ teaspoon saffron threads, soaked in 1 tablespoon water for 20 minutes

juice of 1 lemon

2 tablespoons finely chopped parsley leaves

salt

pepper

COMBINE the shrimp shells, clams, fish broth, and sherry in a 4-quart pot with a tight-fitting lid. Cover the pot and put it on high heat. Turn the heat down and keep the liquid at a simmer for about 10 minutes. Check the clams, take out those that have opened, cover the pot, and boil for 5 minutes more. Repeat if necessary, but discard any clams that haven't opened after 20 minutes.

TAKE the clams out of their shells and discard the shells. Strain the cooking liquid through a triple layer of cheesecloth or a cloth napkin (rinsed first to eliminate bleach or chemicals) to eliminate the shrimp shells and any grit from the clams.

CUT the ham slices into strips ⅛ inch wide and 1 inch long.

COOK the onion, garlic, and ham in the olive oil in a 4-quart pot over medium heat until the onion turns translucent, about 10 minutes. Add the tomatoes, bouquet garni, rice, saffron with its soaking liquid, and strained clam-cooking liquid. Cover the pot and leave the soup at a slow simmer for about 15 minutes, until the rice has completely softened. (Spoon out a piece and bite into it.)

ADD the lemon juice, parsley, shrimp, and cooked clams and simmer gently for about 3 minutes to cook the shrimp. Season to taste with salt and pepper.

Bay Scallop Soup with Snow Peas

This Chinese soup is light, colorful, and takes just a couple of minutes to cook. A few simple ingredients—ginger, garlic, soy sauce, and sesame oil—give it a distinctive full flavor. And it's almost completely fat-free. It's a boon for lovers of snow peas, which are cooked very quickly in the soup so they retain their crunch.

MAKES 8 FIRST-COURSE SERVINGS

6 cups chicken broth

3 ¼-inch slices of fresh ginger

2 garlic cloves, peeled

2 tablespoons plus 1 teaspoon dark soy sauce

3 tablespoons medium-dry sherry

1 teaspoon dark sesame oil

¼ pound snow peas, ends and strings removed, cut in half crosswise

1 pound bay scallops

6 scallions, both white and green parts, finely sliced

pepper

COMBINE the chicken broth, ginger, and garlic in a 4-quart pot. Bring to a simmer, cover, and keep at a slow simmer for 15 minutes. Reach in with a slotted spoon and remove and discard the ginger and garlic.

FIVE minutes before you're ready to serve, stir in the soy sauce, sherry, and sesame oil. Bring the soup to a rolling boil and add the snow peas. Boil the snow peas in the soup for 1 minute and then add the bay scallops and scallions. Simmer the soup for 1 minute more. Season with pepper and, if needed, extra soy sauce.

SUGGESTIONS AND VARIATIONS | This soup is delicious served cold. Chill the soup over a bowl of ice as soon as you add the scallops.

Bay Scallop, Clam, and Sea Urchin Roe Soup

This soup is so intensely flavored that I serve relatively little of the rich sea urchin broth around the scallops. The base for the broth is made with the briny liquid released by the clams, which is then flavored with fresh thyme leaves and finished with cream and the sea urchin roe. I serve this soup at my fanciest dinners. The sea urchin and cream mixture and the clam and thyme broth can be made earlier the same day.

MAKES 4 FIRST-COURSE SERVINGS

2 dozen bay scallops, preferably in the shell (see pages 357 to 358)

½ cup dry white wine

1 cup basic fish broth (page 307) or basic white chicken broth (page 63)

½ teaspoon fresh thyme leaves

1 medium-size shallot, peeled and very finely chopped

18 littleneck clams, or 28 manila clams, or 36 cockles, well rinsed

6 whole sea urchins or 6 mounded teaspoons sea urchin roe

½ cup heavy cream

1 tablespoon finely chopped chives or parsley

pepper

salt, if needed

IF you're using bay scallops in the shell, shuck them as described on page 358. Put the wine, fish broth, thyme, and shallot in a pot large enough to hold the clams.

Cover the pot and simmer over low heat for 5 minutes. Add the clams, cover the pot, and turn the heat to high. Steam the clams for 3 to 10 minutes—cockles and Manila clams open much faster than littlenecks—until most if not all of them open. (Often one or two have to be coaxed open by sliding a thin knife between the shell on the opposite side from the hinge.) Take the clams out of the shells and gently pour the steaming liquid into a clean saucepan, leaving any grit behind.

IF you're using whole sea urchins, take the roe out as described on page 359. Combine the cream with the sea urchin roe and work the mixture through a strainer. Use your fingers, rubbing the roe against the inside of the strainer, to break it up and force it through. Reserve in the refrigerator until needed, but no longer than 12 hours.

SHORTLY before serving, put the scallops in the saucepan with the clam cooking liquid, cover the pan, and bring to a boil over high heat. As soon as the liquid comes to the boil, turn the heat down and transfer the scallops to heated soup plates with a slotted spoon. Whisk in the sea urchin cream and the chives, then whisk over low heat for 1 minute. If the clams have cooled, stir them into the creamy broth along with the chives to reheat them. Don't let the broth boil. Season the broth to taste with pepper and salt, if needed. Divide the clams evenly among the bowls and spoon over the broth.

Oyster Stew

They're dozens of sophisticated and lovely things you can do with oysters but nothing can beat a plain and simple oyster stew. My only suggestions are that you arm yourself with plenty of crunchy French bread and crisp white wine and that the bowls for the stew be piping hot.

MAKES 4 MAIN-COURSE SERVINGS

48 oysters
1½ cups heavy cream
salt
pepper

optional accompaniments:

French bread
croutons
oyster crackers

WITHIN a few hours of preparing the stew, shuck the oysters over a fine-mesh strainer set over a bowl or have them shucked at the fish store and slide them into the strainer when you get them home. Save the briny liquid that goes through the strainer. If you're not using it right away, keep it in the refrigerator. Roll the oysters on a clean kitchen towel—don't use paper towels—so that any grit attached to the oysters will come off onto the towel. If you're not cooking the oysters right away, don't leave them on the towel—reserve them in a small bowl in the refrigerator.

WHEN you're ready to cook, put the oysters in a small saucepan. Pour the strained oyster liquid over the oysters. Pour over the cream.

PLACE over medium heat. When the oysters curl up on the sides and the liquid in the pot feels hot to the touch—don't let the liquid come to a full boil—spoon the oysters into heated bowls, giving eight per person for a main course or four per person for a first course. Season the liquid left in the pan with salt (which may not be necessary) and pepper. Ladle the liquid over the oysters in each heated bowl and serve immediately.

Oyster Soup with *Fines Herbes*

Fines herbes (pronounced *feen zairb*) is a mixture of equal parts of chopped chives, chervil, parsley, and tarragon, but I usually use half as much tarragon as the other herbs because it is the strongest of the four and tends to take over. If you don't have all these herbs fresh, just use those you do have; don't substitute dried. In fact, most recipes calling for *fines herbes*, including this one, are perfectly good with chopped parsley alone.

MAKES 4 FIRST-COURSE SERVINGS

12, 16, or 20 oysters, depending on size
2 shallots, finely chopped
2 tablespoons unsalted butter
¾ cup dry white wine
¾ cup fish broth or water
½ cup heavy cream
I heaped tablespoon finely chopped parsley
I heaped tablespoon finely chopped chervil
I heaped tablespoon finely chopped chives
freshly ground white pepper
salt

SHUCK the oysters (or have the fishmonger do it) and save them in a bowl in the refrigerator. Reserve all the juice. Throw out the shells.

COOK the chopped shallots gently in butter in a 2-quart saucepan over medium heat. Be careful not to let them brown. When they start to smell fragrant—after about 5 minutes—add the white wine and fish broth. Leave the mixture at a slow simmer for 5 minutes to infuse the flavor of the shallots.

GENTLY take the oysters out of the bowl with a slotted spoon and spread them on a wet kitchen towel or cloth napkin; this eliminates any grit or particles of broken shell. Pour the oyster liquid through a fine-mesh strainer (or a regular strainer lined with rinsed cheesecloth) directly into the shallot/white wine mixture.

ADD the heavy cream and chopped herbs to the soup. Simmer the soup for 1 minute to cook the herbs. Add the oysters and poach for 30 seconds, being careful not to let the liquid boil. Stir the soup and grind in some white pepper. Taste the soup and add salt if the soup needs it.

POUR the soup into hot bowls, distributing the oysters evenly.

Oyster and Chicken Gumbo

What I love about this recipe, which comes from *The Picayune Creole Cook Book* (1928), is that it's relatively simple, so the flavor of the oysters isn't lost among too many other ingredients. Except for the chili pepper, this dish is almost identical to a dish popular in France in the 18th century.

You can serve this soup in two ways. The easiest—best for a main course—is just to give everyone a whole piece of chicken surrounded by the oysters and creamy broth. If you want to serve something lighter, as a first course, you'll have to take the chicken off the bone, cut it into cubes, and serve it in the broth.

If you're serving chicken and oyster gumbo as a first course, it can be made a day or two in advance and reheated—just be careful not to boil it, or the oysters will toughen.

MAKES 4 MAIN-COURSE OR 8 FIRST-COURSE SERVINGS

1 3- to 4-pound chicken, quartered

salt

pepper

all-purpose flour for dredging the chicken

4 tablespoons unsalted butter

¼ pound cured ham such as tasso, Smithfield, or prosciutto,
    cut into ¼-inch cubes

1 medium-size onion, finely chopped

2 jalapeño chilies, seeded and finely chopped

1 quart chicken broth

1 bouquet garni

2 dozen oysters

½ cup heavy cream

about ¼ cup finely chopped parsley leaves

SEASON the chicken with salt and pepper and roll the pieces in flour. Pat off any excess flour.

MELT the butter in a sauté pan or skillet just large enough to hold the chicken. Brown the chicken—skin side down first—in the butter over medium to high heat. If the butter starts to burn, turn down the heat. When the chicken is well browned on the skin side, after about 10 minutes, turn it over and brown it for 5 minutes on the other side. Take it out of the pan and place it on a plate.

POUR out all but 1 tablespoon of the cooked fat in the sauté pan and add the ham, onion, and jalapeños. Cook over medium heat for about 10 minutes, until the onion starts to turn translucent.

PUT the chicken back in the pan and add the broth and bouquet garni. Bring to a slow simmer. Cover the pan and simmer gently for 15 minutes or until the chicken is firm to the touch. (If you don't have a cover that fits, just turn the chicken over after 5 minutes so it cooks on both sides.)

WHEN the chicken is done, take it out of the pan with a slotted spoon. Use a ladle to skim off any fat that has floated to the top of the liquid in the pan and remove the bouquet garni. If you're serving the gumbo as a main course, just keep the chicken warm in the oven; otherwise, let it cool slightly, peel off and discard the skin, pull the meat away from the bone, and cut the meat into ½-inch dice.

SHUCK the oysters—or have the fishmonger do it—and scrape them into a bowl, being sure to save all their liquid. If the oysters seem gritty, gently take them out of the bowl with a slotted spoon and spread them on a wet kitchen towel or cloth napkin; any grit or particles of broken shell will cling to the towel. Pour the oyster liquid through a fine-mesh strainer (or a regular strainer lined with rinsed cheesecloth) into the gumbo.

IF you're using cubed chicken, put it back in the pan with the liquid, add the cream and the chopped parsley, and gently reheat the gumbo. Season with salt and pepper. Poach the oysters in the hot gumbo for about 30 seconds and serve immediately in hot wide bowls. If you're using whole pieces of chicken, arrange them in hot bowls and pour the simmering gumbo over them.

SUGGESTIONS AND VARIATIONS | The original recipe in the *Picayune Creole Cook Book* uses the traditional thickening of filé powder (ground sassafras leaves). I don't bother with it because I like soups with a light texture, but if you want to give it a try, whisk in 2 tablespoons filé powder along with the cream and parsley.

Oyster Ceviche

Even though a *ceviche* is traditionally fish or shellfish marinated in lime juice with herbs and seasoning, this is a soupy version that I can't resist including. Because the oysters are left raw, this *ceviche* captures the taste of the ocean in a way that's lost if the oysters are cooked. The ingredients in this recipe are the same as those in a traditional Mexican or South American *ceviche*—tomatoes, hot peppers, lime juice, and cilantro.

Use small but flavorful oysters because some people don't enjoy eating a bowl of large, fat raw oysters. Oysters from cold northern waters are best for this group. Belons from Maine, Blue Point oysters from California, Japanese oysters, and small Cape Cod oysters are especially good for this recipe; all are small and have an intense briny flavor.

The base for this soup—without the oysters—can be made a day or two in advance, but the soup is best eaten the same day once the oysters have been added.

SERVES 4

20 small oysters, shucked, liquid in the shells strained and
    reserved

4 medium-size tomatoes, peeled, seeded, and chopped

juice of 1 lime

1 small onion, finely chopped

1 clove garlic, chopped and crushed to a paste in a mortar
    and pestle or with the side of a chef's knife

3 jalapeño chilies, cut in half lengthwise, seeded, and finely
    chopped

1 tablespoon finely chopped cilantro leaves

3 tablespoons virgin olive oil

COMBINE all the ingredients in a stainless-steel or glass bowl. Cover with plastic wrap and refrigerate for 1 or 2 hours to chill the soup and give the flavors a chance to blend. Serve the soup in cold bowls, making sure everyone has 5 oysters. Pass a basket of tortilla chips or sliced crusty French bread at the table, or if you want to be more formal, serve 1 or 2 toasted French bread slices on a small plate at the side of each bowl.

SUGGESTIONS AND VARIATIONS | Try combining raw fish or shellfish with different vegetables, fruits, and herbs to invent an almost limitless number of variations. I sometimes make a French-style raw oyster soup by combining the oysters with 1 tablespoon finely chopped chives, 24 tarragon leaves (plunged into boiling water for 5 seconds, then rinsed in cold water), 2 peeled and seeded tomatoes, 4 drops Pernod, and a more or less generous drizzle of heavy cream.

Scallops in Light Broth with Chives

This is a lean and simple way to present scallops, and once you have the broth it takes only a minute or two to prepare. If you're using sea scallops, remember to pull off the small strip that runs up the side of each one.

MAKES 4 FIRST-COURSE SERVINGS

I pound bay or sea scallops, large scallops sliced crosswise
    into $\frac{1}{3}$-inch-thick disks
2 cups *dashi* or chicken or vegetable broth, simmering
2 tablespoons finely chopped chives
salt
freshly ground white pepper

SPREAD the scallops in a single layer in a wide pan. Pour in just enough of the hot broth to come up to the top of the scallops and put the pan over medium heat. Watch the scallops carefully and as soon as the tops start to turn white and opaque—usually about a minute after the broth comes to a simmer—take the scallops out of the pan with a slotted spoon and arrange them in a single layer in wide soup bowls.

ADD the chopped chives to the broth and simmer for 30 seconds to cook their flavor into the broth. Taste the soup and season with salt and freshly ground pepper. Ladle the broth over the scallops.

SUGGESTIONS AND VARIATIONS | The kind of broth you use will determine the flavor, sophistication, and difficulty of the finished dish. You can use fish broth for the poaching, but I often prefer chicken broth for shellfish because it has a more subtle flavor. The easiest route is to use canned low-sodium chicken broth, but almost equally simple is to make a quick vegetable broth. You can also use the cooking liquid from mussels or clams; a full-flavored meat, fish, or crustacean consommé; *dashi*; or a spicy Thai broth made with lemongrass and hot chilies.

ALTHOUGH this recipe uses chives, almost any chopped herb can be used to give the soup a special character.

Sea Scallop Soup with Green Curry

I first had this soup at the eclectic Duane Park Café in New York. The sous-chef, Richard Overholt, who likes to combine European techniques with Asian ingredients, came up with this exciting method of gently poaching sea scallops and then giving the poaching liquid a fiery jolt with Thai green curry. His version uses fish broth, but chicken broth works equally well.

MAKES 6 FIRST-COURSE SERVINGS

> 1 ½ pounds sea scallops, 5 small or 3 large scallops per
>   serving
> 5 cups fish or chicken broth
> 2 ½ tablespoons green curry paste (page 17)
> 3 tablespoons Thai fish sauce (*nam pla*)
> juice of 2 limes
> ¼ cup finely chopped parsley leaves
> salt
> pepper

REMOVE the small muscle running up the side of each of the scallops. If the scallops are large, cut them crosswise into halves or thirds. Rinse the scallops and arrange them in a sauté pan just large enough to hold them in a single layer.

BRING the broth to a simmer and pour it over the scallops. Gently simmer the scallops for about 2 minutes, until they lose their sheen. Use a slotted spoon to transfer the scallops to hot wide bowls.

WHISK the remaining ingredients into the simmering broth. Simmer for 1 minute, adjust the seasoning with salt and pepper (or more curry or fish sauce) and ladle the broth over the scallops.

SUGGESTIONS AND VARIATIONS | Try this soup with the red curry paste on page 18 or the mussaman curry paste on page 18. There is no need to restrict this soup to scallops. Any fish or shellfish or combination can be poached in broth and the broth finished with Thai curry.

Mixed Shellfish *Pot-au-Feu*

A traditional French *pot-au-feu* is a long-simmered pot of beef and vegetables with not a bit of fish in it. Naming this seafood soup after such a distant cousin may be carrying poetic license too far, but the two dishes do have certain similarities. Both contain a variety of ingredients simmered together and served in a light, unthickened broth.

I don't recommend making this soup for more than 4 people because there is a lot of last-minute cooking and arranging of shellfish in bowls. This soup can be served as a first course, but because it is so elaborate it makes more sense to serve it as a dramatic main course.

The recipe calls for 4 kinds of shellfish—mussels, clams, scallops, and oysters—but the soup can be made with as few as two. The important thing is to use the correct techniques for each one and to cook them in the right order.

MAKES 4 GENEROUS FIRST-COURSE OR LIGHT MAIN-COURSE SERVINGS

12 littleneck clams

12 cultivated mussels

½ pound sea scallops, 1 large or 2 small per person

8 large shrimp, preferably with heads, heads left on,
     bodies peeled (peeling optional)

12 oysters

1 cup dry white wine

¾ cup fish broth or water

2 shallots, finely chopped

¼ cup finely chopped parsley leaves

4 tablespoons unsalted butter (optional)

freshly ground pepper

salt

slices of French bread, toasted

IN ADVANCE Up to 24 hours ahead, wash the clams and mussels and discard any dead ones. Remove the small muscle from the sides of the scallops. If the scallops are more than ½ inch thick, cut them crosswise into 2 or even 3 disks. Shuck the oysters into a small bowl. Be sure to save any liquid that comes out of the shell. If the oysters seem gritty or have pieces of shell attached to them, roll them on a clean kitchen towel for a few seconds to pull off the grit. Strain the liquid. Combine the strained liquid and the cleaned oysters in a bowl. Reserve in the refrigerator.

AN hour or two before serving, combine the wine, fish broth, and shallots in a 4-quart pot. Bring the liquid to a slow simmer and cover the pot with a tight-fitting lid. After the liquid has simmered for about 10 minutes, add the clams. Replace the lid and simmer the clams for 8 minutes. Lift off the lid to see if any of the clams have opened. If none have opened, cook them for a minute more and check again. Keep doing this until the first clam opens, then add the mussels. Cover the pan and simmer over medium heat for 5 minutes more. Keep checking until all the clams and mussels have opened; remove the pot from the heat.

TAKE the clams and mussels out of the pot with a slotted spoon or skimmer. Let them cool slightly and pull off the top shells, leaving the clams and mussels in their bottom shells. If you're not serving the soup immediately, cover the clams and mussels with plastic wrap and keep them in the refrigerator.

IF the broth used for cooking the clams and mussels seems sandy, pour it carefully into another container, leaving the sand behind, or strain it through a cloth napkin or a triple layer of wet cheesecloth (rinsed first to eliminate bleach or chemicals). Reserve in the refrigerator until needed.

AT THE LAST MINUTE Just before serving, divide the broth equally between two 2-quart saucepans. Put the clams and mussels in one of the saucepans, cover it with a tight-fitting lid, and put it over low to medium heat for about 5 minutes, just long enough to reheat the clams and mussels. Bring the broth in the second saucepan to a simmer and add the shrimp. Simmer the shrimp for about 3 minutes, until they turn red, and add the scallops. Poach them for 30 seconds to a minute, then add the oysters with their liquid. Poach the oysters for 30 seconds.

TO serve, use a slotted spoon to distribute the shellfish among wide bowls. Combine the liquid in the two saucepans and add the chopped parsley and the butter if you're using it. Simmer the broth for 30 seconds to cook in the flavor of the parsley. Grind in a little pepper and taste to see if it needs salt; it usually doesn't. Pour the hot broth over the shellfish in the bowls. Pass a basket of toasted French bread or serve individual slices on side plates.

SUGGESTIONS AND VARIATIONS | This *pot-au-feu* is served with the flavorful broth that is the natural by-product of cooking the shellfish. By definition, the broth from a *pot-au-feu* is left alone except for garnishes such as herbs and vegetables and light seasoning. But if you want a richer broth, you can finish it with some heavy cream, whisk it into a full-flavored mayonnaise such as an *aïoli* or *rouille*, or finish it with a vegetable puree.

YOU can also make the *pot-au-feu* more colorful and substantial by arranging cooked vegetables with the shellfish in each of the bowls.

1. Combine the *pot-au-feu* broth with ½ cup heavy cream. At this point you can also flavor the broth with a pinch of saffron threads or a tablespoon of curry powder heated for 30 seconds in a tablespoon of butter.

2. Whisk the *pot-au-feu* broth into ¼ cup *aïoli* (page 349) or *rouille* (page 350) in a stainless-steel bowl. Return the broth to one of the saucepans and heat it slowly to cook the sauce. Don't allow it to boil, or the mixture will curdle.

3. The pot-au-feu can be converted into a summer stew by adding tomato puree or finely chopped raw tomatoes to the broth to give it more substance and an exciting flavor and color.

4. For an elegant winter version of the *pot-au-feu*, add ¼ cup heavy cream and the leaves from I bunch of watercress (cooked for 2 minutes in boiling water) to the hot broth. Puree the mixture for I minute in a blender and serve with the shellfish instead of the plain broth.

GARNISHES You can add almost any single vegetable or combination to the *pot-au-feu* to make it even more colorful and substantial. Try a mixture of carrots, leek, and turnip julienne cooked for 10 minutes in butter; fennel wedges braised in olive oil; little French string beans cooked for a couple of minutes in boiling water; spinach, boiled for I minute; or mushrooms—wild or cultivated—simmered in a covered saucepan with a little of the broth. You can also finish the broth with chopped herbs such as tarragon, chives, or parsley. Or try placing a few chervil sprigs over the soup just before serving.

"Crustacean soups
are made almost
everywhere . . ."

Crustacean

SOUPS

Crustacean soups are made almost everywhere: in inland areas with freshwater shrimp and crayfish as well as near the sea, where there is always some kind of walking shellfish. In America each region has its own particular version that makes the best use of the local shellfish—gumbo from Louisiana, chowder from New England, and crab *cioppino* from San Francisco.

Shrimp, lobster, crayfish, and crabs are all members of the crustacean family. Crustaceans, unlike mollusks, have jointed bodies and an assortment of legs and appendages to help them move around. Crustacean soups, especially when made with lobster or crayfish, are always a luxurious treat. Even though most crustaceans are expensive, they are available alive, so you're always sure they are impeccably fresh. And when you're using crustaceans to make soup, a little goes a long way.

Because much of a crustacean's flavor is contained in its shell, several special techniques are used for getting the most flavor out of the shells without over-cooking the flesh. The easiest and most often used is to partially cook the crustaceans with flavorful vegetables and remove them while they are still undercooked. The shells are then peeled off and returned to the pot with the vegetables. Softer shells—from shrimp and crayfish—are broken up with a food processor before they are returned to the pot, while harder shells, from crabs and lobsters, are crushed in the pot with the vegetables using the end of a cleaver, a wooden spoon, or a European-style rolling pin (without handles). Broth or water is then added, and the mixture is simmered to extract the flavor from the shells. The shellfish and any last-minute flavorings or gar-nishes are then heated in the strained broth just before serving.

A simple crustacean broth made from shells can be converted into a bisque, chow-der, gumbo, or lobster stew by using different thickeners and flavorings, but the basic techniques for preparing the broth remain the same. Almost all crustacean soups start with a flavor base of vegetables cooked lightly in an appropriate fat or oil. The vegeta-bles in the flavor base vary according to the style or origin of the soup. Indian versions are likely to contain garlic and ginger, gumbos invariably contain peppers and smoked ham, and classic French versions contain carrots, onions, and a little celery. Almost all crustacean soups use broth or water as the basic liquid, while soups from India and Southeast Asia often contain coconut milk, classic French versions contain wine and perhaps a little cognac, and Mediterranean variations may contain a large proportion of tomatoes. These full-flavored crustacean broths are then finished with thickeners that again vary from place to place; chowders are thickened with potatoes or corn, bisques with rice or bread crumbs, Spanish soups with *picada* or *romesco*—pungent purees of gar-lic, nuts, and peppers; and gumbos are given extra body with cooked okra.

Once you're used to working with a few basic ingredients, making flavorful crus-tacean soups is a straightforward process of substituting ingredients at different stages during the cooking. Most of the recipes given here contain only one crustacean, but once you're comfortable with techniques and cooking times you can come up with deli-cious combinations by adding more than one variety of crustacean to the same soup. The techniques remain essentially the same.

BISQUES These are the best known of the crustacean soups. An authentic bisque is prepared by cooking the shells of the crustacean to make an aromatic broth and then pureeing some of the crustacean meat to help give texture to the finished soup. Most recipes also include cooked rice or sometimes bread crumbs to give the soup extra body, but modern versions like the shrimp bisque in this section are thickened lightly with a puree of aromatic vegetables. The texture of a traditional bisque may strike contemporary palettes as a bit too thick; you may want to serve lighter, more brothlike versions instead.

CHOWDERS Occasionally, crustaceans are cooked into chowders. Chowders usually contain some starchy element—most often potatoes but sometimes corn—and either heavy cream or milk. South American shrimp chowder, called *chupe*, contains potatoes and cream but, unlike North American versions, starts out with a base mixture made with chilies and tomatoes.

GUMBO Like many crustacean soups, seafood gumbo is based on a broth made from shrimp and crayfish shells, but smoked ham, peppers, and Tabasco sauce give it a characteristic flavor all its own. Unlike bisques or chowders, gumbo is thickened with a dark, long-cooked roux and slowly cooked okra.

SOUTHEAST ASIAN SOUPS Unlike Western versions, Thai and Vietnamese crustacean soup recipes rarely call for cooking the crustacean shells to extract their flavor. They rely instead on savory mixtures of shallots, hot peppers, lemongrass, fish sauce, and other exotic ingredients to make a delicious and intensely flavored soup base. Light, Asian-style broth is then added. Relatively little seafood is needed to round out the flavor of the soup.

JAPANESE SOUPS Most Japanese soups are based on the light broth called *dashi*. Shrimp or lobster are then cooked separately and then added already cooked to the hot broth. Japanese cooks have a light touch; crustacean soup is likely to have only a small piece of lobster or shrimp tastefully arranged with other ingredients so the bright orange of the crustaceans is highlighted for maximum effect.

Tips for Buying and Preparing Crustaceans

LOBSTER For lobster soup you need live lobsters. Once dead, lobster meat deteriorates and becomes quickly unusable. Because most of the lobster's flavor is in the shell, tomalley, and coral, frozen lobster tails aren't much good for making soup unless you're preparing an Asian-style soup where the crustacean shells aren't needed for making the broth.

Until recently, live lobsters were difficult to find anywhere except on the East Coast, but now they are available in fancy supermarkets all over the country. People who live in large cities also have the advantage of being able to find surprisingly inexpensive lobster in ethnic markets; Chinese markets are usually the best source.

When you're buying lobster, look for culls, which have only one claw and are usually much less expensive. While the cost of seafood has soared in recent years, lobster prices have remained relatively stable so they no longer seem like quite such an extravagance.

Males and Females: If you're using a recipe that makes use of lobster coral—the dark green sac that contains the ovaries and eggs—select female lobsters. You can ask the fishmonger for only females, but it helps to know what you're doing. To tell the difference, turn the lobster over and notice the tiny legs that run along each side of the tail. Follow these up along the tail until you come to the pair right next to where the head and tail join. On a female lobster these are thin and flexible; on the male they are thicker, with a hard, shell-like texture.

Working with Live Lobsters: To make good lobster soups it is often necessary to cut up live lobsters before cooking. This is best done over a bowl so any escaping juices don't end up on the cutting board instead of in the pot. If you're squeamish, this can be a grisly job and may take some getting used to—the lobster parts love to hop around after you've cut them into sections.

To kill a lobster humanely, quickly cut the front half of the lobster's head in half by placing the lobster upright on the cutting board and holding a large chef's knife straight up and down on the middle of the head. Insert the knife quickly and rapidly bring it down toward the front of the head, cutting all the way through to the cutting board. Immediately hold the lobster, head down, over the bowl so as not to lose any of the juices. After a few seconds the juices will have drained out and you can be sure the lobster is dead. Twist off the tail and snap off the claws, still working over the bowl. Place the lobster head on a cutting board and cut it in half lengthwise. Pull out the gritty grain sac from each half of the head near the front. Be sure to add any of the flavorful lobster juices to the soup pot along with the parts themselves.

Using Lobster Coral: Lobster aficionados know that the tastiest parts are the tomalley and coral. The tomalley is the lobster's liver and is usually pale green or blue. The raw coral is very dark green—almost black—but turns bright orange once cooked. Some recipes have you take the coral and tomalley out of the raw lobster and add them to the soup just before serving. Even though this can be a bit of a nuisance, it's the best way to capture the flavor of the lobster.

To remove the coral and tomalley from raw lobster, place a strainer over the bowl you use to capture the juices and a teaspoon each of brandy and wine vinegar in the bowl (these prevent the juices from clotting). Kill the lobster as described earlier. Remove the tomalley and coral by reaching your finger into the base of the head and into the tail to scoop them out. Squeeze the head over the strainer to extract any juices. Use a small ladle or your fingers to work the tomalley and coral through the strainer. Be sure to keep the strained tomalley and coral in the refrigerator until you use it; it's very perishable and should be used the same day. Snap the claws off the lobster heads.

Removing the Meat: There are several simple methods for taking the meat out of cooked lobster. To take the meat out of the tail section, break back the flap at the end—it should snap right off—and grab the tail with a kitchen towel. Place the tail sideways on the work surface and gently lean on it with the heel of your hand until you feel it crack. Don't press too hard, or you'll crush the meat. Hold the cracked tail upside down in a towel and pull outward from each side of the shell. The tail will crack open so that you can then press the whole section of tail meat out from the end.

To remove the meat from the claws, hold the claw at the base and gently move the small pincer from side to side until you hear it snap in each direction. Then pull the pincer away from the claw while pulling it back. If you do it just right, the tiny strip of meat will stay attached to the claw, and the translucent piece of cartilage embedded in the claw will come away with the pincer. Turn the claw upside down (so the thorny part is facing up) and whack it with an old chef's knife or a cheap kitchen knife you don't care too much about. (Use the part of the blade closest to the handle, which is less likely

CRUSTACEAN BUTTER

Many sophisticated recipes for lobster soup suggest swirling a tablespoon of crustacean butter per serving into the broth just before taking the soup to the table.

Crustacean butter is time-consuming to prepare and by no means essential, but it's well worth it if you want to give extra flavor and color to your soups. A little crustacean butter goes a long way and will keep for at least a month in the refrigerator and indefinitely in the freezer.

To prepare crustacean butter, you need a sturdy mixer with a paddle blade. Save the shells from about five lobsters or 7 pounds of crayfish or shrimp with the heads (you can freeze them and use them when you've accumulated enough). Combine them in the electric mixer bowl with a pound of cold butter cut into large chunks. Leave the mixer on slow speed for 20 minutes, until the shells break apart and the butter turns pink.

Transfer the shell/butter mixture to a 4-quart saucepan and put it on the stove over very low heat for about 45 minutes. Watch it carefully so the butter doesn't burn.

Run about 2 quarts of hot tap water into the pot. Let cool and refrigerate overnight.

The next morning the bright red butter will have floated to the top of the liquid and congealed. Lift it off very carefully with a spoon and put it into a small saucepan. Discard the liquid and shells.

Melt the crustacean butter and strain it through a fine-mesh strainer. Store in the refrigerator or freezer.

to be damaged.) The knife should enter about ¼ inch into the shell. With the knife embedded in the shell, turn it sideways and the whole claw shell will break in half. Crack the two hinges at the base of the claw with the chef's knife and pull out the claw meat in one piece. Separate the small sections attached to the claw by leaning on the joints with the knife. Cut the little pieces on one side with scissors and pull out the little pieces of meat with a paring knife or your fingers.

Cooking Lobster: Most people overcook lobster. While it's almost impossible to *undercook* it, "fully" cooked lobster is almost always a disaster. When you're pre-cooking lobster parts for a soup, cook them only until the shell turns completely red and then let the parts cool. The lobster meat should have a slightly jellylike consistency and look slightly translucent. Remember, it's going to continue cooking once reheated in the soup.

For soups such as bisques or those in which the lobster is pureed or cut into small pieces, there's no way of avoiding overcooking it. But don't worry—the flavor of the lobster will end up in the broth.

SHRIMP   Shrimp range in size from tiny bay shrimp to giant prawns, 6 or even 8 inches long. The color of shrimp also varies from pale blue to orange and sometimes brown depending on species, origin, and time of year.

Buying Shrimp: Always buy shrimp with their shells and preferably with their heads (for the heads you'll probably need to shop in an Asian market). Although the flavor differs somewhat among species, the most important thing to look for is freshness. Because most of the shrimp available in the United States has been frozen and then thawed before being sold, it is often a good idea to buy frozen shrimp and thaw them yourself. Frozen shrimp usually come in 5-pound boxes; if you have room in your freezer, this is the least expensive way to buy it.

If you're buying thawed or fresh shrimp, the best indicator of freshness is smell. Don't hesitate to smell the shrimp before you buy them or open up the package and stick your nose in it. If there is any trace of ammonia, give it back and go somewhere else or make something different. Large shrimp, even though their flavor is no better, are usually more expensive than small ones. You need to buy larger shrimp only if you want them to look dramatic in the bowl or want fewer to clean.

Cleaning Shrimp: People often argue over whether or not to devein shrimp. In Mediterranean countries they don't bother, but Americans tend to be squeamish about these things. In general, the larger the shrimp, the more likely they are to have large, unsightly veins (actually intestines), so if you have large shrimp, devein a few and see what the vein looks like. Sometimes there is nothing in the veins and the process isn't worth the bother.

To devein shrimp, always start with raw shrimp and devein along the back. There is certainly no need to remove the little filament that runs along the inside of the shrimp. There is a gadget on the market (a shrimper) that you just slide under the shell so the shrimp is deveined at the same time you remove the shell. If you don't have one of these, peel the shrimp first and cut into the back of the shrimp with a paring knife. Then reach in and pull out the vein with your fingers.

CRAYFISH: Although crayfish are abundant in American streams and lakes, until recently, they were marketed only in Louisiana and a few outposts on the West Coast. Today crayfish are beginning to work their way into the culinary mainstream and are appearing in fancy food markets around the country.

To make good soup, you need live crayfish. They're useless if they're dead, because there is no way of telling if they died five minutes or a week ago. You can also buy packages of crayfish tails if you want extra tails for garnish, but to prepare a flavorful broth you'll need whole crayfish, shells and all.

Some markets set the crayfish out so you can pick through them and pick out the live ones. If the fish purveyor weighs them out for you, make sure he or she picks through them.

When you get the crayfish home, make sure they are all still alive. The easiest way to do this is to pour them out on a large table (lock the cat in another room) and quickly sort through them. If you're squeamish about handling them, use the handle of a long wooden spoon to separate out any dead ones. Put the live crayfish in a colander and rinse them with cold running water.

Many older recipes for crayfish insist that they be deveined while they are still alive, but this seems a needless nuisance—and inhumane—especially since the veins are easily removed after the crayfish have been cooked.

Unlike shrimp, which can be peeled raw, the meat from crayfish can be removed only after they are cooked. To get the meat out of the tails—the claws aren't worth the bother—just twist the tail off at the base of the head. Then give the tails a little pinch on the sides (you'll feel a little snap) and peel off the shells by pulling outward with your thumbs. The heads, claws, and the shells from the tails are then used to make the broth.

Like some shrimp shells, crayfish tails often contain an unsightly vein that most people like to remove. Take out the vein from the back of the crayfish tails by gently pressing along one side of the peeled tail with your thumb; a little flap of tail meat will fold over so the vein (actually the intestine) can be pulled out easily.

CRABS: There are many kinds of crabs on all three coasts of the United States. The most common Atlantic crab is the blue crab, sometimes called the Atlantic blue crab. Blue crabs are less expensive—sometimes ridiculously so—in part, no doubt, because it requires so much effort to get a small amount of meat out of the shells. They make wonderful soups. Blue crabs become soft-shell crabs for short periods in their lives each time they shed their hard outer shell. Soft-shells are rarely used to make soup because they are so expensive.

Blue crabs should always be bought alive. To get them ready for the soup pot, brush and clean them well. Rinse them under cold running water—hold them from behind so they don't pinch you—and scrub them with a small brush to eliminate grit and mud.

In *North Atlantic Seafood*, Alan Davidson suggests stabbing blue crabs in two places with an ice pick—on the bottom under the tail flap and just behind the eyes on the underside—to kill them quickly and humanely before cleaning them. To clean them, pull back and twist off the small flap on the bottom of each of the crabs and discard it. With the crab upside down, press against the body of the crab so that it snaps out of the outer shell. Pull off the outer shell—save it—and pull the gills off the section with the legs attached and discard them.

On the Pacific coast there is the famous Dungeness crab, which is not only far meatier than the Atlantic blue crab but also has a harder shell that is less willing to surrender its flavor in a pot of soup. To make a soup with Dungeness crab, lightly cook the crab, pull the meat out of the shell, and use the meat alone as the soup base. Although the results are wonderful, this is a time-consuming process. You can also buy crab meat already out of the shell—it comes in chilled containers—but it tends to be very expensive, best used as an accent in other soups.

Light Cream of Lobster Soup

This is a soup I often serve to out-of-town guests who delight in the flavor of lobster and love eating it in as many forms as possible. The soup has almost the same flavor as a bisque but unlike classic bisques, which are thickened with rice or bread crumbs, it has a lighter texture and a fresher taste.

Cream of lobster soup can be made up to 3 days in advance.

MAKES 8 FIRST-COURSE SERVINGS

I small carrot, chopped

I medium-size onion, chopped

I garlic clove, crushed

2 tablespoons olive oil

4 lobster culls, 1¼ pounds each

5 cups fish or chicken broth or water

10 medium-size tomatoes, rinsed, cut in half crosswise,
    seeds squeezed out and discarded

2 teaspoons chopped fresh tarragon leaves

2 tablespoons finely chopped parsley leaves

I cup heavy cream

salt

pepper

small croutons (page 595)

lobster butter (page 391)

COOK the carrot, onion, and garlic in the olive oil in a 4-quart pot over medium heat until the vegetables soften, about 10 minutes.

RINSE the lobsters in cold running water. Place each lobster on a cutting board and cut through each head with a large chef's knife to kill them quickly and humanely. Remove the tails and claws and cut the head in half. Remove and discard the grain sac. Tie the lobster tails together in pairs with string, with the insides of the tails facing each other. This prevents the tails from curling during cooking.

PUT the lobster parts in the pot with the vegetables along with any lobster juices that ran out onto the cutting board. Add 1 quart of the broth and bring it to a simmer. Cover the pot. Move the lobsters around with a wooden spoon every 2 minutes until the lobster shells have turned completely red, about 5 minutes.

LET the lobsters cool, then remove the meat from the claws and tails and reserve both the meat and the shells. Cut each of the tomato halves into four pieces. Put the shells back in the pot with the vegetables, the tomatoes and the broth used for cooking the lobsters. Break up the lobster shells and tomatoes by pressing down on them firmly with a large wooden spoon or with the end of a cleaver. Spend a couple of minutes breaking up the shells and then cover the pot and leave the mixture at a gentle simmer for 20 minutes.

STRAIN the mixture through a colander into another pot. Put the broken-up shells back in the pot and add the remaining broth. Stir the mixture around to extract more flavor from the shells and drain it again through a colander into the rest of the lobster broth. Throw out the shells (or save them for crustacean butter) and vegetables. Strain the liquid through a fine-mesh strainer to eliminate any pieces of shell.

ADD the tarragon and heavy cream, taste the soup, and season it with salt and pepper.

SLICE the meat from each lobster tail into 4 pieces. Carefully slice each claw in half lengthwise so it keeps its original shape.

TO serve, distribute the pieces of lobster among wide soup bowls. Just before serving, put the bowls in a warm oven. Ladle in the broth and serve with croutons and a dollop of lobster butter.

SUGGESTIONS AND VARIATIONS | This soup is flavored delicately so that nothing interferes with the flavor of the lobster, but you can invent subtle variations by accenting the broth with different herbs and spices. Finely chopping a large bunch of parsley or chervil and adding it to the soup just before serving adds a fresh flavor and an elegant green contrast to the orange broth.

SAFFRON and curry can also be used to give a tantalizing complexity to the broth. Add a pinch of saffron threads (soaked for 15 minutes in a tablespoon of water) or a tablespoon of curry powder. (Remember when using curry to cook it for 30 seconds to a minute in a little butter or oil before adding it to the broth to wake up its flavor.)

FOR a more elaborate main-course soup, increase the amount of lobster used for making the broth without increasing any of the other ingredients. A good trick is to put a mound of freshly creamed spinach in the center of each bowl, arrange the lobster on top of the spinach, and pour the broth around. In this way the lobster can be seen above the broth.

A decorative touch for a main-course version of this soup is to cut leeks, carrots, and turnips into fine julienne, lightly blanch them in boiling water or cook them gently in a little butter, and arrange them over the lobster just before serving.

ONCE you're used to the basic techniques for cooking lobster, it's easy to prepare other lobster soups and stews; usually it's a simple matter of replacing an ingredient here or there or, in the case of a stew, using less liquid. A much appreciated lobster stew from Menorca, *calderata de langosta menorquina*, is prepared exactly like the soup given here except that chopped green peppers are cooked at the beginning with the vegetables and less liquid is used so the mixture is thicker and more concentrated.

PROBABLY the most famous lobster dish, *homard â l'Américaine*, is prepared in the same way except that the lobster is sautéed with the vegetables and a couple of tablespoons per lobster of cognac are added along with the liquid ingredients.

Cold Tomato and Lobster Soup with Lobster Coral

I can't praise this soup enough: I simply don't know of any other dish that captures the flavor of lobster better. People who taste it for the first time are amazed; it's as if they've never really tasted lobster before.

The tomato soup can be made a day in advance, but the lobster must be prepared the same day because the lobster coral is very perishable.

MAKES 6 FIRST-COURSE SERVINGS

6 very ripe, medium-size tomatoes, peeled, seeded, and
    chopped

¼ cup finely chopped chives

6 tablespoons heavy cream or yogurt

salt

2 female lobsters, 1½ pounds each

juice of ½ lime

1 cup water

½ cup heavy cream

PREPARING THE TOMATO SOUP Combine the tomatoes with the chives, cream, and salt to taste. Chill for at least an hour in the refrigerator.

PREPARING THE LOBSTERS Prepare the lobsters as explained on pages 389–391, removing the coral and tomalley from the lobster head and tail as described. With your fingers, work the tomalley and coral through a fine-mesh strainer into a bowl containing the lime juice, which prevents the coral from clotting. Stir the ½ cup of heavy cream into the tomalley. Cover the bowl of strained coral with plastic wrap and keep it in the refrigerator until needed.

TIE the lobster tails together in pairs with string, with the insides of the tails facing each other. Put the lobster parts and water in a 4-quart pot with a tight-fitting lid. Cover the pot and put it on high heat.

WHEN the liquid comes to a full boil, turn the heat down and continue cooking the lobster for about 4 minutes. Remove the lid. The lobster parts should be completely red; if they aren't, cook them for a minute or two more. Take out the lobster and let cool.

WHEN the lobster parts have cooled, remove the meat from the shells and strain the cooking liquid into the chilled tomato soup. Discard the shells or save them for lobster butter. Carefully slice each lobster tail into 3 medallions and cut the lobster claws in half lengthwise.

LADLE the tomato soup into chilled bowls, arrange the lobster pieces over the soup, and spoon the coral sauce over and around the lobster pieces.

SUGGESTIONS AND VARIATIONS | Other shellfish such as crayfish, shrimp, or pieces of poached fish can also be added to this soup. Depending on how generous you are with other shellfish, or with extra lobster, this soup makes a great main course for lunch.

IF you absolutely can't stand the idea of eating raw lobster coral, whisk the coral sauce over medium heat in a small saucepan until it turns orange. Be sure not to let the mixture boil, or the lobster coral (eggs) will curdle.

Shrimp Bisque

Maybe it's because I grew up in the fifties and sixties, when making anything so sophisticated as a bisque occurred only to the most adventurous cooks, that I associate bisques with rather old-fashioned, stuffy French restaurants. Bisque—along with consommé—is one of those formal dishes that make me think I'd better dress up and be prepared for an onslaught of rich, classical cooking. But bisques are wonderful creations, particularly as the focal point for an intimate lunch.

Although bisques are traditionally thickened with rice or bread crumbs, this version uses a puree of vegetables gently cooked at the beginning with the shrimp shells. A small amount of the meat from the shrimp is also pureed in a food processor and stirred in to finish the soup. If you can find shrimp with the heads on—I usually look in Asian markets—so much the better; the heads give the broth an excellent flavor.

Shrimp bisque can be made in advance except for the last-minute cooking of the whole or diced shrimp which should be added just before serving.

MAKES 8 FIRST-COURSE SERVINGS

2 pounds shrimp, about 50 medium-size, or 2¾ pounds
    with heads

1 small carrot, chopped

1 medium-size onion, chopped

1 garlic clove, crushed and peeled

1 small turnip, peeled and chopped

4 fresh thyme or marjoram sprigs or ½ teaspoon dried

3 tablespoons unsalted butter

1 quart fish or chicken broth or water

4 medium-size tomatoes, halved crosswise and seeds
    squeezed out

½ cup heavy cream

salt

⅛ teaspoon cayenne pepper or more to taste

PEEL and devein the shrimp, saving the shells (and the heads if you have them) and reserving 24 shrimp (3 per serving). Put the shrimp shells, heads, and remaining peeled shrimp in a 4-quart pot with the vegetables, thyme, and butter. Cook the mixture on medium to high heat until the shrimp shells turn red and the vegetables soften, about 10 minutes.

ADD the tomatoes and 2 cups of the broth and simmer for 5 minutes. Transfer the contents of the pot to a food processor and process to a paste, about 2 to 3 minutes. Combine the pureed shrimp mixture with the remaining broth and strain the liquid through a food mill with a medium disk and then again through a medium-mesh strainer. If you want a finer consistency, or if you've used shrimp heads, which can make the soup murky, strain the mixture again through a fine-mesh strainer. Add the cream. If necessary, thin the soup with extra broth or water. Season with salt and cayenne.

CUT the reserved shrimp into ½-inch sections. Just before you're ready to serve, add the shrimp cubes to the hot broth and simmer gently for 1 minute. Serve immediately.

SUGGESTIONS AND VARIATIONS | If you have shrimp with their heads, you can prepare a broth with the heads and peels alone—leaving the peeled shrimp out of the puree mixture—and leave all the shrimp whole. The shrimp can then be poached in the flavorful broth just before serving and the whole thing served as a kind of shrimp stew with a bisquelike flavor. The finished stew can then be sprinkled with freshly chopped herbs such as chives, chervil, or parsley. Chopped, peeled, and seeded tomatoes can also be swirled into or dolloped onto the stew or bisque at the end.

IF you want a thicker, more traditional version, lightly toast 4 slices of white bread with the crusts removed and combine the bread with the soup before straining it through the food mill.

A tablespoon of curry powder or a pinch of saffron would be a wonderful flavoring for shrimp bisque.

Indian-Style Shrimp and Coconut Soup

For people who like curry (oddly, not everyone does) this soup can be highly addictive, both to drink and to cook. I find the sweetness of the coconut milk and the heat of the peppers an irresistible combination.

This recipe uses a standard *garam masala* with a little turmeric to give it an appealing color. Adventurous cooks will want to experiment with blending their own curries.

This soup can be made entirely in advance and kept for up to 3 days in the refrigerator.

MAKES 8 FIRST-COURSE SERVINGS

I pound medium-size shrimp, about 4 per serving, or
     1½ pounds with heads, peeled, deveined, and shells
     and heads reserved
I quart chicken or fish broth

2 large onions, finely chopped

3 garlic cloves, minced

a ½-inch slice of fresh ginger, peeled and minced

2 or 3 small fresh hot chilies such as jalapeños, seeded and minced

3 tablespoons unsalted butter

2 tablespoons *garam masala*

1 teaspoon ground turmeric

2 cups coconut milk

2 tablespoons chopped cilantro leaves

3 tablespoons fresh lime juice, from about 2 limes

salt

cayenne pepper

COMBINE the shrimp shells (and the heads if you have them) with the broth in a 4-quart pot, cover the pot, and slowly simmer the mixture for 20 minutes. (If the mixture includes the heads, break them up with a large wooden spoon or the end of a cleaver while they are simmering.)

MEANWHILE, cook the onions, garlic, ginger, and chilies in the butter over low heat in another 4-quart saucepan until they have softened, about 20 minutes. Add the *garam masala* and the turmeric and cook the mixture for 2 minutes more.

STRAIN the broth into the vegetable mixture and discard the shrimp shells. Add the coconut milk, whole shrimp, and cilantro to the soup. Simmer slowly for 5 minutes to poach the shrimp and infuse the flavors. Add the lime juice, salt if needed, and cayenne pepper if you want the soup to be spicier.

SUGGESTIONS AND VARIATIONS | As with so many soups, you can use the liquid as the basic broth for more elaborate soups and stews; try poaching pieces of fish, shellfish, or even chicken in the soup shortly before serving. It's also easy to convert this soup into a more substantial family meal by adding some cooked rice to the pot at the last minute.

IN this recipe the shrimp is added to the soup all at once at the end, but if you want to be sure that all your guests get the same amount of shrimp, try poaching the shrimp in a separate pan with just enough broth to cover, pouring the broth back into the rest of the soup, and then distributing the shrimp evenly among the bowls before pouring over the broth. You may also want to dice the shrimp.

Cajun Shrimp Soup with Smoked Salmon

The idea for this soup is inspired by a shrimp dish I had once at a dinner prepared in Manhattan by Paul Prudhomme. The shrimp was served in a spicy rich cream sauce with an underlying smokiness that came from tasso, a special kind of New Orleans ham. It occurred to me that smoked fish would be interesting to couple with shellfish, so after a series of experiments, here it is.

MAKES 6 FIRST-COURSE SERVINGS

18 large shrimp, preferably with heads, about I pound
    without heads, I½ pounds with

I medium-size onion, chopped

2 garlic cloves, chopped

3 jalapeño chilies

4 fresh thyme sprigs or I teaspoon dried

2 tablespoons rendered bacon fat or olive oil

3 cups chicken or fish broth or water

3 medium-size tomatoes, peeled, seeded, and chopped or
    I½ cups canned, drained and seeded

¼ pound smoked salmon or other smoked fish, thinly sliced
    and cut into ⅛- by I-inch strips

I cup heavy cream

cayenne pepper or Tabasco sauce

salt

pepper

PEEL and devein the shrimp. Save the shells and heads and reserve the shrimp.

IN a 4-quart pot over medium heat, cook the vegetables, shrimp shells (and the heads if you have them), and thyme in the bacon fat for about 10 minutes. If the shrimp have heads, break them up in the pot with a thick wooden spoon or the end of a cleaver. Add the broth and tomatoes, cover the pot, and simmer for 30 minutes, stirring every 5 minutes.

STRAIN the soup through a colander or a coarse sieve into a clean pot. Puree the cooked shells and vegetables in a food processor or blender and add the puree to the soup. Bring the soup to a simmer for 5 minutes to get all the flavor out of the puree and then strain it again through the fine disk of a food mill or coarse strainer. Discard the solids that won't go through the food mill or strainer. If you want the soup to have a finer texture, strain it again through a medium-mesh or even fine-mesh strainer.

ADD the smoked salmon, heavy cream, and reserved shrimp to the soup and simmer for 3 minutes while stirring. This soup is quite spicy, but if you want it hotter, add cayenne or Tabasco. Season with salt and pepper. Distribute the shrimp among hot bowls—3 per person—and ladle over the soup.

SUGGESTIONS AND VARIATIONS | If you want to make a more substantial dish out of this and serve it as a main course, try poaching a piece of fish in the broth before you add the cream and then serving the shrimp as a garnish over the fish and the broth around it as a kind of light sauce. A nice touch is to grill different-colored sweet peppers—yellow, red, and green—cut them into julienne, and lay them over the top of the fish as an additional garnish.

IF you don't want to run out and buy smoked fish, bacon makes a good substitute. Cut ¼ pound into I- by ¼-inch strips and cook the bacon gently in a sauté pan until it just starts to turn crisp. Stir the bacon instead of the smoked salmon into the soup.

South American Shrimp Chowder

CHUPE

I had never thought of combining spicy flavors like peppers and cilantro with potatoes until a few years ago, when I read a recipe for this soup. Since then I've been hopelessly addicted. A *chupe* (pronounced choopay) is a South American chowder that, in addition to potatoes and cream like its North American cousins, contains hot peppers, tomatoes, and cilantro. This version uses only shrimp, but other fish or shellfish can be added as well.

Shrimp *chupe* can be made entirely in advance and stored in the refrigerator for up to 3 days.

MAKES 8 FIRST-COURSE SERVINGS

2 medium-size onions, chopped

3 garlic cloves, chopped

3 jalapeño chilies, seeded and chopped

2 tablespoons olive oil

24 medium-size shrimp, preferably with heads, I pound without heads, I½ pounds with heads, peeled and deveined

8 medium-size tomatoes, peeled, seeded, and chopped or
    4 cups canned, seeded and drained

3 medium-size potatoes, peeled, ½ roughly cubed and
    ½ cut into ¼-inch cubes

3 cups fish or chicken broth or water

¾ cup heavy cream

3 tablespoons finely chopped cilantro leaves

salt

pepper

OVER medium heat, stew the onions, garlic, and peppers in the olive oil in a heavy-bottomed 4-quart pot until the vegetables soften, about 10 minutes. Don't let the vegetables brown. Put the shrimp peels (and the heads if you have them) in the pot with the vegetables and cook the mixture for 5 minutes more over medium heat.

ADD the tomatoes, roughly cubed potato, and 2 cups of the broth to the pot with the vegetables and shrimp trimmings. Cover the pot and simmer the mixture for about 20 minutes or until the potatoes have softened thoroughly. While the soup base is cooking, simmer the cubed potato in the remaining broth in a covered pot until it just begins to soften, about 20 minutes.

STRAIN the soup base through the fine disk of a food mill or puree it in a blender or food processor a little bit at a time and strain it through a medium-mesh strainer. If you want the soup to have a smoother consistency, strain it again through a fine-mesh strainer.

COMBINE the soup base and the cooked potato cubes with their cooking liquid in a pot with the heavy cream and the chopped cilantro. Bring the soup to a simmer and add the shrimp. Cook the shrimp for about 2 minutes. Season with salt and pepper and serve immediately in hot bowls.

SUGGESTIONS AND VARIATIONS | Different vegetables such as corn kernels or peas can be added to this *chupe*, as well as different fish and shellfish.

Thai-Style Hot and Sour Shrimp Soup

This irresistible soup is easy and fun to make because the basic ingredients are so flavorful that they seem to cover all the major tastes—sweet, sour, and hot—and you need only a little broth to round it out and give it body. Perhaps it is this combination of robust flavors served in a light soup that has made Thai cooking so popular.

For the soup to be authentic, you'll need a few unusual ingredients such as lemongrass and fish sauce (nam pla) but the joy of this soup is that you can use substitutes for practically all of these and still come up with something delicious: Tabasco sauce or Mexican peppers instead of the little Thai red chilies, scallions instead of the lemongrass, a strip of blanched lime zest instead of the lime leaves (though the leaves do give the soup an irresistible exotic flavor). The only essential ingredient is the fish sauce, and a bottle of it will last a year in the refrigerator.

As you prepare this soup you may want to vary the ingredients somewhat according to taste. If you're sure of your guests' sense of adventure, try using a little more fish sauce and lime juice.

This soup is best served the same day it is made, but you can make it a day or two in advance up to the point of adding the shrimp.

MAKES 6 FIRST-COURSE SERVINGS

18 large shrimp, about 1 pound, peeled and deveined

2 tablespoons safflower oil

2 shallots, finely chopped

3 garlic cloves, finely chopped

3 Thai red chilies or 4 jalapeño chilies, seeded and chopped,
    or Tabasco sauce to taste

a 3-inch length of lemongrass or scallion, finely chopped

3 Kaffir lime leaves, broken into quarters, or a 1-inch
    strip of lime zest blanched in boiling water for
    2 minutes

1 teaspoon sugar

¼ cup fresh lime juice

¼ cup Thai fish sauce (*nam pla*)

4 cups chicken broth

18 small cultivated mushrooms, quartered, button
    mushrooms, or canned straw mushrooms, drained

CUT the shrimp in half lengthwise and keep refrigerated until needed. Heat the safflower oil in a 3-quart pot. Add the chopped shallot and garlic and stir with a wooden spoon until they sizzle, but don't allow them to brown. Add the chopped chilies, lemongrass, lime leaves, and sugar. Stir for 2 minutes more. Add the lime juice, fish sauce, and I quart of the chicken broth.

HEAT the soup to a slow simmer and add the shrimp and the mushrooms. Simmer for 5 minutes more and serve in hot bowls.

SUGGESTIONS AND VARIATIONS | Try this soup with both shrimp and thinly sliced chicken breasts or with other seafood such as lobster, mussels, or clams.

WHEN you're using chicken, cut the raw breasts into narrow 3-inch strips and add them to the hot soup about 2 minutes before serving. Wash mussels or clams and plunge them into the hot soup for 5 to 10 minutes, until they open. The easiest way to deal with lobster is to poach it or steam it in advance, remove the meat from the shell, and arrange it in the bowls before pouring over the hot soup.

YOU can also turn this soup into a magnificent main course by using a combination of chicken and seafood and serving it in wide bowls.

If you want a slightly richer soup, add a cup of coconut milk to the finished soup.

Thai-Style Hot and Sour Blue Crab Soup

Getting the meat out of East Coast blue crabs may require more effort for people, myself among them, who lack the necessary dexterity and determination, than is justified by the result. It is, no doubt, for the likes of us that there's a market for frightfully expensive crab meat. But there are few things as luxurious as eating chunky pieces of crab with a fork or spoon, with no shells anywhere in sight. It was with this in mind that I thought up this soup (although there must be others like it), imagining the crab accented by the tang of lime juice and the lemony flavor of kaffir lime leaves and lemongrass. You can, of course, make the broth with fresh live crabs (see Blue Crab Soup with Picada, page 406), which will give the soup a much deeper flavor of crab, but unless you're an expert crab picker, I recommend being a little extravagant and using lump crab meat.

MAKES 6 FIRST-COURSE SERVINGS

I pound fresh lump crab meat

2 shallots, peeled and finely chopped

2 garlic cloves, peeled and finely chopped

4 Thai chilies or 6 small jalapeño chilies, steamed, seeded, and finely chopped

I stalk of lemongrass, white part sliced as thin as possible

3 kaffir lime leaves (optional)

3 ¼-inch-thick slices fresh or frozen galangal (optional)

¼ cup lime juice or more to taste

¼ cup Thai fish sauce or more to taste

2 teaspoons sugar

3 cups chicken broth or crab broth made as described on
    page 407

1 15-ounce can unsweetened coconut milk

salt (optional)

2 tablespoons coarsely chopped cilantro leaves

SORT through the crab meat and remove any pieces of shell.

COMBINE all the ingredients except the crab and cilantro and simmer gently for 10 minutes. Season to taste with salt, more fish sauce (Thai dishes that taste under-salted often need fish sauce instead of salt), and/or more lime juice. The soup should have a distinct tang. Immediately before serving, bring the soup to a boil over high heat and stir in the crab meat and the cilantro. Leave the crab meat over the heat for just 1 minute more to heat through. Serve immediately in hot bowls.

Blue Crab Soup with Picada

This recipe is inspired by those wonderful soups you find along the Mediterranean that are almost frighteningly pungent with garlic but that seem to satisfy some deep craving for foods with unreserved amounts of flavor.

This soup is flavored with *picada*—a powerful Spanish paste of garlic, bread, nuts, and olive oil—which can be used to finish any number of soups. Here it is used to finish an already tasty broth made from fresh blue crabs.

The soup can be made entirely in advance and kept in the refrigerator for up to 3 days.

MAKES 8 FIRST-COURSE SERVINGS

1 small onion, chopped

1 small carrot, chopped

½ celery rib, chopped

2 tablespoons olive oil

12 blue crabs

8 fresh or canned tomatoes, cut in half crosswise and seeds
    squeezed out

7 cups fish broth or water

I cup picada (page 348)

½ teaspoon cayenne pepper

5 tablespoons heavy cream or water

¼ teaspoon saffron threads, soaked in I tablespoon water
    for 20 minutes

slices of French bread, toasted

COOK the vegetables in the olive oil in a 4-quart pot over medium heat until soft, about 10 minutes.

MEANWHILE, clean and remove the inedible parts of the crabs (page 393) and crack the legs and bodies with a rolling pin. When the vegetables are soft, add the broken-up crabs and stir them over medium heat. When the crab parts have turned red, in about 15 minutes, add the tomato halves and fish broth. Cover the pot and simmer the mixture for 30 minutes, stirring and pounding on the shells every few minutes with a large wooden spoon or the end of a cleaver.

STRAIN the soup through a fine-mesh strainer into a clean pot. Whisk the hot soup into ¾ cup of the *picada* just before serving. Add the cayenne. Combine the remaining *picada* with the cream, to loosen it, and the saffron with its soaking liquid. Swirl this *picada*/saffron mixture on top of each bowl of soup just before serving or pass it at the table.

SUGGESTIONS AND VARIATIONS | You can use this soup as the basic broth for a fish soup or stew by poaching pieces of fish or shellfish directly in the soup just before serving it as a generous first course or a main course. Vegetables such as fennel wedges gently simmered in some of the crab broth until they soften or peeled tomatoes cut into small wedges with the seeds removed can be added to the soup just before it is finished with the *picada*. Or try adding chanterelles sautéed in olive oil as a last-minute sophisticated touch.

IN her book *The Cuisines of Mexico*, Diana Kennedy describes a crab soup similar to this one; the broth is flavored with a goodly amount of garlic, jalapeño peppers, tomatoes, and finished with sprigs of fresh epazote.

Callaloo

I've never tasted an authentic version of this Caribbean soup because I've never been able to find the taro leaves that provide the traditional greenery. But the flavors of bacon and crab or shrimp are so delicious with Swiss chard or spinach that I couldn't resist including it. It's also a snap to prepare.

Callaloo can be prepared completely in advance and stored for up to 3 days in the refrigerator.

MAKES ABOUT 12 FIRST-COURSE SERVINGS

¾ pound bacon, preferably slab, rind removed,
    sliced ¼-inch thick

1 large onion, finely chopped

2 garlic cloves, finely chopped

½ pound fresh okra or 1 10-ounce package frozen, stems
    removed, sliced ¼-inch thick

4 jalapeño chilies, seeded and finely chopped

7 cups chicken broth or water

¾ pound crab meat or 1 pound medium-size shrimp, peeled
    and deveined

1¾ cups coconut milk

1½ pounds Swiss chard or spinach, about 1 large bunch,
    stems removed, leaves rolled and cut into ⅛-inch-wide
    strips

salt

pepper

Tabasco sauce

CUT the bacon slices across the grain into ¼-inch-wide strips. In a 4-quart pot, cook the bacon strips over medium heat, stirring occasionally, until they just begin to turn crisp, about 10 minutes. Take them out with a slotted spoon and drain on paper towels.

POUR out all but 1 tablespoon of the bacon fat. Add the onion, garlic, okra, and jalapeños and cook over low to medium heat for 25 minutes, stirring every few minutes. Add the broth and simmer for 10 minutes more. Skim off any fat that floats to the surface.

ADD the Swiss chard, crab, and coconut milk and simmer for 4 minutes. Season with salt and pepper. Put a bottle of Tabasco sauce on the table.

SUGGESTIONS AND VARIATIONS | It's easy to play around with the ingredients in this soup. Substitute half as much heavy cream for the coconut milk or, for a leaner version, leave out both. I also fool around with the seafood—mussels are cheap and good (steam them open and add the liquid to the broth) or lobster if I'm being extravagant (precook the lobsters and arrange the medallions decoratively on top of each bowl).

Crayfish Broth

Even though crayfish have always been plentiful throughout the United States—the French have long envied us our almost limitless supply—until recently Louisiana was virtually the only place where crayfish were eaten. Admittedly it takes a lot of crayfish to make a substantial meal but the heads and claws have a wonderful flavor that's easy to extract for making soup.

MAKES 6 CUPS

3 pounds live crayfish, about 55

I small carrot, chopped

I medium-size onion, chopped

I garlic clove, crushed

3 fresh thyme sprigs or I teaspoon dried

2 tablespoons olive oil

I cup dry white wine

½ cup cognac or flavorful brandy

I quart fish or chicken broth or water

6 medium-size tomatoes, cut in half crosswise, seeds
     squeezed out, chopped

½ cup heavy cream

2 fresh tarragon sprigs, stems removed and leaves finely
     chopped

salt

pepper

SORT through the crayfish and throw out any dead ones. Rinse them under cold running water in a colander.

IN a 4-quart pot over medium heat, cook the vegetables and thyme in the olive oil until the vegetables begin to soften and smell good, about 10 minutes. Throw in the crayfish, turn up the heat, and stir the crayfish around in the hot oil until they turn completely red, about 5 minutes. Add the wine and cognac and simmer for 2 minutes to cook off the alcohol. Scoop the crayfish out of the pot with a slotted spoon and spread them out on a baking sheet to cool. Leave the liquids and vegetables in the pot.

TWIST off the crayfish tails, remove the meat (pages 392–393), and reserve both meat and shells. Twist the claws off the heads and reserve. (The claws have to be removed at this point because their hard shells will damage the food processor blade.) Put the heads and shells from the tails in a food processor and process for 1 minute. (You may need to add a little broth to get the shells moving.) Put the ground crayfish and the claws back in the pot and add the tomato halves and remaining broth. Cover the pot and gently simmer the mixture for about 20 minutes. While the soup is simmering, remove the veins from the peeled tails (page 393).

STRAIN the soup into a smaller pot through a coarse strainer and a second time through a medium- or fine-mesh strainer. Add the heavy cream and tarragon to the soup and season with salt and pepper.

JUST before serving, distribute the crayfish tails among hot bowls and pour the hot soup over them.

SUGGESTIONS AND VARIATIONS | This soup can be converted into a bisque—as can any shellfish broth—by thickening it with rice or bread crumbs and seasoning it carefully with cayenne pepper. To thicken it with bread crumbs, remove the crusts from 10 slices of good-quality white bread and process the bread in a food processor along with the heads and shells. Flavor the soup at the end with a small pinch of cayenne; classic bisques should be only mildly spicy.

CRAYFISH broth makes a wonderful light sauce for pasta. Cook the finished broth (don't add the crayfish tails yet) down to half its original volume, season it with salt and pepper, and pour it over small mounds of pasta in large, wide bowls. Arrange the crayfish tails around or on top of the pasta.

Cold Cucumber and Crayfish Soup with Dill

This elegant summer soup starts with a simple and spicy cucumber gazpacho and elevates it several notches with the flavor of fresh crayfish. The orange crayfish broth and tails against the pale green background of the cucumbers is irresistible; the flavors are deeply satisfying and complex.

MAKES 8 FIRST-COURSE SERVINGS

I recipe crayfish broth (preceding recipe) without the
    tarragon and cream
2 tablespoons chopped fresh dill
½ cup crème fraîche or yogurt
2 long hothouse cucumbers or 4 standard, 3 pounds)
2 tablespoons Tabasco sauce or cayenne pepper to taste
2 teaspoons salt
56 cooked crayfish tails reserved from the broth,
    7 per serving
8 small fresh dill sprigs

ADD the chopped dill to the crayfish broth and reduce the broth over medium heat until only a cup remains. Let the broth cool and stir in the crème fraîche. Put the mixture in the refrigerator to chill.

PEEL the cucumbers and cut them in half lengthwise. Scoop out the seeds with a small spoon. Finely dice the cucumbers by hand or in a food processor using the pulse mechanism. Whichever method you use, don't chop the cucumbers so finely that they turn into puree. Chill the chopped cucumbers and season with Tabasco and salt. The chopped cucumbers may seem dry, but as soon as you add the salt they will release liquid.

COMBINE the crayfish tails with the chilled and reduced crayfish broth. Ladle the cucumber soup into chilled bowls and spoon the crayfish tails and about 3 tablespoons of the broth into the center of each one. Decorate each bowlful with a sprig of dill.

SUGGESTIONS AND VARIATIONS | If you don't have any dill or don't like it, substitute tarragon, chervil, parsley, or even cilantro. The principle of taking a full-flavored crustacean broth and swirling it over a spicy gazpacho of raw chopped vegetables or fruits can be used as a model for other soups. If you have trouble finding crayfish, try using shrimp.

Corn and Crayfish Chowder

I always thought that taking the kernels off fresh corn would be hopelessly elaborate and messy until one day I just decided to try it. I stood the ears upright and cut along the sides with a sharp knife, and the kernels snapped right off without any problem. Since then I've started cooking corn in all manner of ways (stewed in cream is my favorite), and I came up with this soup. It's a bit like a traditional chowder—except it has corn and hot peppers instead of potatoes. If you don't like hot and spicy foods, leave out the cayenne.

Corn and crayfish chowder can be made in advance and kept for up to 3 days in the refrigerator.

MAKES 8 FIRST-COURSE SERVINGS

1 small onion, chopped

2 jalapeño chilies, seeded and finely chopped

3 tablespoons unsalted butter

Kernels from 8 ears of sweet corn or 3 10-ounce packages frozen, 6 cups

1 recipe crayfish broth (page 409) without the tarragon and cream

½ cup heavy cream

juice of 1 lime

2 teaspoons sugar if you're using frozen corn or fresh corn that isn't sweet enough

1 teaspoon cayenne pepper or more to taste

the cooked crayfish tails from the broth

salt

pepper

GENTLY cook the onion and jalapeños in the butter for 10 minutes in a heavy-bottomed 4-quart pot over medium heat. Add the corn, stir over medium heat for 10 minutes, then add the broth. Simmer the soup for 5 minutes, let it cool slightly, and puree it in a blender or food processor. (Don't fill the blender or food processor more than a third full of hot liquid.)

STRAIN the soup through a medium-mesh strainer (don't use a strainer with too fine a mesh unless you want the soup to be quite thin), bring it to a simmer on the stove, and add the cream, lime juice, sugar, and cayenne to taste. Heat the crayfish tails in the broth for about 1 minute. Season with salt and pepper.

SUGGESTIONS AND VARIATIONS | This principle—using a flavorful crustacean broth as the base for pureed vegetable soups—works with other vegetables such as watercress, spinach, potato, and even tomato. The corn gives this soup a fine texture and a delicate sweet taste that lends itself well to being finished with flavorful herbs such as chopped fresh thyme, marjoram, or cilantro. The soup can also be finished with a decorative swirl of chopped tomatoes or lightly stewed and strained tomatillos.

IF you can't find crayfish, you can also make this soup with crab, lobster, or shrimp. In very hot weather, serve it iced with a little bowl of finely chopped hot peppers passed at the table.

Crustacean Soup with Saffron and Morels

When I first tasted this dish—actually it's more like a stew than a soup—I was working in a 3-star restaurant in the French countryside. As a lowly apprentice I'd spend the mornings preparing the lobsters and langoustes that arrived every morning from Brittany, the live Bulgarian crayfish, and morels from the local forests—all for this amazing dish. The result was astonishing.

Before you set out to make this soup, be aware that it requires a major shopping trip and that all your organizational skills will be called into play. Fortunately, most of the work can be done ahead of time, with only last-minute heating.

Don't serve too much broth, or the shellfish and mushrooms will sink to the bottom of the bowl and much of the drama will be lost. Ideally, arrange the shellfish tails and morels in wide soup bowls or plates with deep rims and just enough broth poured in to come halfway up the sides.

MAKES 4 MAIN-COURSE SERVINGS

1 small carrot, chopped

1 small onion, chopped

1 garlic clove, crushed

3 tablespoons olive oil

20 live crayfish, about 1 pound

2 cups fish or chicken broth or water

2 1½-pound lobsters, preferably female

1 teaspoon white wine vinegar (for lobster coral)

1 teaspoon Cognac if you have lobster coral

12 large shrimp, preferably with heads

4 medium-size tomatoes, cut in half crosswise and seeds
squeezed out

20 fresh or dried morels

¼ cup Madeira if you're using dried morels

¼ teaspoon saffron threads, soaked in 1 tablespoon of
water for 20 minutes

¾ cup heavy cream

1 small bunch of chives, finely chopped

salt

pepper

UP TO 8 HOURS IN ADVANCE Up to 8 hours ahead, cook the carrot, onion, and garlic in the olive oil in a 4-quart pot, over medium heat until soft, about 10 minutes. Sort through the crayfish to make sure that none are dead. Rinse the live ones under cold running water and put them in the pot with the vegetables. Add the broth, turn up the heat, cover the pot with a tight-fitting lid, and steam the crayfish with the vegetables for about 5 minutes, until the crayfish turn bright red. Remove the pot from the heat, take out the crayfish, and reserve. Leave the liquid in the pot.

CUT up the lobsters alive (page 390) and save any coral and the tomalley, mixed with the vinegar and cognac, as a last-minute thickener and flavoring for the broth.

PUT the lobster parts in the pot used to cook the crayfish, cover the pot, and steam the pieces over medium heat for about 8 minutes, until they turn completely red. Take the lobster parts out of the pot and let them cool slightly. Remove the meat and reserve it in the refrigerator. Cover with plastic wrap. Save the shells.

RINSE the shrimp and poach them in the broth used to cook the crayfish and lobster for about 4 minutes, until they turn orange. Take them out of the pot and peel off the heads and shells. Devein and reserve the shrimp and put the heads and shells back in the pot with the broth.

TWIST the tails off the crayfish, remove the shells from the tails, and put both the heads and the shells from the tails in the pot. Put the lobster shells and the tomato halves in the pot and put the pot back on the stove over medium heat. Cover the pot and simmer for 20 minutes. Break up the shells every few minutes with a large wooden spoon or the end of a cleaver. Strain the broth through a colander and then through a fine-mesh strainer. Discard the shells and reserve the broth.

PUT the morels in a colander and rinse them quickly under running cold water. You don't always need to rinse fresh morels, but dried ones almost always contain grit. If you're using dried morels, put them in a bowl with the Madeira after rinsing. Toss them every 5 minutes or so until they soften, about 20 minutes.

ADD the saffron and its soaking water to the broth.

AT THE LAST MINUTE Cut the lobster tails in half lengthwise and arrange them in a single layer in a pan along with the shrimp, the crayfish tails, and the morels. Pour the broth over, cover the pan, and gently warm the shellfish. Don't let the broth boil, or the shellfish will curl up and dry out.

ARRANGE the shellfish and morels in wide bowls or on deep plates. Keep the bowls warm in a low oven while you're finishing the broth.

ADD the cream and chives to the broth and quickly reduce it until only 2 cups remain. Whisk the hot broth into the lobster coral and tomalley. Return the mixture to the pan and gently heat it to cook the coral and tomalley. As you're heating the broth, the coral will cause it to turn bright orange. Don't let the broth approach a boil, or it will curdle.

TASTE the broth; it has such an intense flavor that it's unlikely to need any seasoning, but have salt and pepper handy just in case. Carefully pour it into the plates or bowls so that it surrounds the shellfish and mushrooms.

SUGGESTIONS AND VARIATIONS | This intensely flavored stewlike soup can be used as a base for practically any combination of vegetables. The morels are particularly subtle tasting and elegant to look at, but the broth has such an intense crustacean flavor that it's unlikely that anything you use will overpower it. Asparagus tips, baby peas, or fresh fava beans first blanched in boiling water; julienne of carrots, leeks, or turnips lightly cooked in butter; braised fennel wedges, glazed pearl onions, sliced white or black truffles, and different wild mushrooms are just some of the possibilities. An especially beautiful presentation is to arrange the vegetables in a mound in the center of a deep bowl and then pour the broth around them.

Seafood Tomato Soup

CIOPPINO

When I was growing up in San Francisco, *cioppino*, made with Dungeness crab, was a treat reserved for church dinners and mildly raucous social gatherings. The dish wouldn't fit into a formal setting because the cracked crab was simmered, shell and all, in thick bright red tomato sauce—requiring everyone to wear a bib. The bibs always had cute little sayings on them, which made it impossible for the guests to take themselves seriously.

At the risk of spoiling the fun, this version is a lot easier to eat—everything is shelled beforehand—but delicious nonetheless. In San Francisco we always used crab, but the idea is to use whatever shellfish you have.

Cioppino should be served the same day it is made.

MAKES 8 FIRST-COURSE OR 4 GENEROUS MAIN-COURSE SERVINGS

2 medium-size onions, finely chopped

4 garlic cloves, finely chopped

1 teaspoon chopped fresh or dried thyme

1 teaspoon dried oregano or marjoram or 2 teaspoons
    chopped fresh

¼ cup olive oil

2 cups dry white wine

24 mussels, scrubbed and beards pulled off

4 live lobsters, 1½ pounds each

1 quart fish or chicken broth or water

3 pounds firm-fleshed round fish such as red snapper or
    sea bass, filleted, skin removed, heads and bones
    reserved

1½ pounds shrimp, preferably with heads, peeled, deveined,
    shells and heads reserved

8 medium-size tomatoes, peeled, seeded, and chopped or
    4 cups drained and seeded canned tomatoes, chopped

1 cup tightly packed fresh basil leaves

salt

pepper

slices of French or Italian bread

IN a 6-quart pot over medium heat, cook the onions, garlic, thyme, and oregano in 3 tablespoons of the olive oil until the onions turn translucent, about 10 minutes.

ADD the wine and mussels, bring to a rapid boil, and cover the pot to steam open the mussels.

START checking the mussels after about 8 minutes. When they have all opened, take the pot off the heat, scoop out the mussels, and take them out of their shells. Reserve the mussels, discard the shells, and leave the cooking liquid in the pot.

RINSE off the lobsters and tie them together with string so they are facing each other. Put them in the pot used to steam the mussels. Cover the pot tightly and put it over high heat. Start checking the lobsters after about 7 minutes; when they've turned completely red, turn off the heat. When the lobsters have cooled, remove the string and twist off the tails, holding the lobsters over the pot so that any liquid that runs out is not lost. Take the lobster meat out of the shells (page 391). Cut each of the tails lengthwise in two and reserve the tail and claw meat.

BREAK up the lobster shells with a heavy knife and add them to the mussel/lobster steaming liquid. Add the broth, the bones and heads from the fish, and the shrimp shells (and heads if you have them). Cover the pot and simmer gently for 25 minutes. Fifteen minutes into the cooking, break up the shells and fish bones with the end of a cleaver or a large wooden spoon.

STRAIN the lobster shell mixture into a 4-quart pot. If the strained liquid is sandy, strain it again through a triple layer of cheesecloth (rinsed first to eliminate bleach or chemicals). Add the tomatoes to the strained liquid and simmer gently for 10 minutes.

FINELY chop the basil with the remaining tablespoon of olive oil and reserve.

CUT the fish fillets into 8 pieces.

TEN minutes before serving, simmer the fish in the soup. Five minutes into the cooking, add the shrimp; 8 minutes into the cooking, add the reserved mussels and lobster meat.

ARRANGE the fish and shellfish in hot wide bowls. Whisk the chopped basil into the soup, season to taste with salt and pepper, and ladle it into the bowls. Serve with bread.

SUGGESTIONS AND VARIATIONS | If you want to make *cioppino* with Dungeness crab, heat the meat of 2 or 3 cooked crabs in the soup just before serving. If you're using crab, you can leave out the lobster.

Shrimp and Crayfish Gumbo

Although a gumbo can contain any amount or combination of seafood or poultry, my favorite version is made only with shrimp and crayfish.

Gumbo is made in much the same way as seafood soups and stews from all over the world, but it has several essential ingredients that give it an unmistakable character. After being flavored with tasso—a heavily smoked New Orleans ham—it is lightly thickened with a slowly cooked and deeply colored brown roux. Finally the soup gets its own special texture and body from chopped okra. As a final American touch, the gumbo is flavored with Tabasco and Worcestershire sauces.

This soup can be made the day before up to the point of adding the cooked crayfish and shrimp tails at the end.

MAKES 8 MAIN-COURSE SERVINGS

6 cups water

4 pounds live crayfish

2½ pounds shrimp, preferably with heads

1 large onion, quartered

1 medium-size carrot, chopped

1 bouquet garni: 5 fresh thyme sprigs, 1 small bunch of parsley, and 1 bay leaf

20 ounces fresh or 2 10-ounce packages frozen okra, sliced into ¼-inch pieces

⅔ cup vegetable oil

2 celery ribs, chopped

2 green bell peppers, seeds and stems removed, finely chopped

4 garlic cloves, finely chopped

¼ pound tasso, Smithfield ham, or prosciutto, finely diced

2 tablespoons all-purpose flour

6 medium-size tomatoes, peeled, seeded, and chopped or 3 cups canned, seeded and drained

2 tablespoons finely chopped parsley

2 tablespoons Tabasco sauce or to taste

2 tablespoons Worcestershire sauce or to taste

salt

pepper

4 cups cooked long-grain rice (optional)

BRING the water to a simmer in a 4-quart pot and add the crayfish. Simmer the crayfish for about 4 minutes or until they turn completely red. Remove the crayfish with a skimmer or slotted spoon and let them cool. Twist off and reserve their tails. Crush the heads with your hands or the side of a cleaver. Put the crushed heads back in the pot with the water. Peel the shrimp and add the shells and heads to the pot with the crayfish heads. Add the onion, carrot, and bouquet garni. Peel the crayfish tails and add the shells to the pot. Cover the pot and leave it at a slow simmer for an hour. Reserve the peeled shrimp and crayfish tails.

STEW the chopped okra in ⅓ cup of the vegetable oil in a heavy-bottomed pan for about 20 minutes. Stir the okra every few minutes to prevent it from sticking. Reserve until needed.

GENTLY stew the celery, green peppers, garlic, and tasso in the remaining oil in a 4-quart pot over medium heat for about 10 minutes, until the vegetables soften. Remove them from the oil with a slotted spoon and set them aside with the okra.

MAKE a roux by adding the flour to the oil used to stew the vegetables. Cook the roux over low heat for about 30 minutes, stirring every 5 minutes, until the flour turns brown. Add the tomatoes and simmer the mixture for a minute or two, until it thickens.

STRAIN the crayfish/shrimp broth through a colander and then through a fine-mesh sieve into the tomato/roux mixture. Bring it to a simmer and leave the soup at a slow simmer for 15 minutes. Skim off any froth or fat that floats to the top. Add the vegetable/ham mixture to the soup and simmer for 10 minutes more. Continue to skim off oil and froth that floats to the top.

FIVE minutes before serving, add the reserved shrimp and crayfish tails and the chopped parsley. Season the soup to taste with the Tabasco and Worcestershire sauces and the salt and pepper.

TRADITIONALLY, cooked rice is served in the gumbo, but I like to serve the rice at the table so people can serve themselves. I also put a bottle of Tabasco on the table for people who like their gumbo spicy.

"Meat is the perfect
starting point for
a flavorful soup . . ."

Meat
SOUPS

Meat is the perfect starting point for a flavorful and satisfying soup, and because meat is so nutritious and rich in protein, a generous helping of a well-made meat soup can provide the main course for a simple meal. Meat soups contain relatively little fat because most of the fat is rendered and skimmed off during long, slow cooking.

Meat soups are made in all parts of the world, in many different styles, and flavored using a seemingly infinite number of ingredients. There are, however, certain traditions and techniques that, once understood, help make sense out of what sometimes seems like endless variety and complexity.

European and American Meat Soups

In Europe and in most of North and South America meat soups are made by slowly simmering relatively large chunks of meat with vegetables and herbs. Up until this century the soup caldron suspended in the hearth was a constant presence in country kitchens. In European and early American farmhouses the hearth not only heated the home but slowly cooked dinner at the same time.

European and American meat soups are made in one of three ways:

NEW ENGLAND BOILED DINNER, POT-AU-FEU, BOLLITO MISTO The simplest and most fundamental method for making meat soups is to slowly simmer large chunks of meat in a large pot with vegetables. These are the great soups of the European and early American farm kitchen. The principle is simple: meat and vegetables are covered with water and simmered gently for several hours until the meat is tender. To serve a New England boiled dinner, a French *pot-au-feu*, or an Italian *bollito misto*, the broth is traditionally presented first, followed by a platter of the steaming meats. Assorted condiments and sauces are put on the table to eat with the meats.

HEARTY PEASANT SOUPS These are prepared in the same way as boiled dinners except that the meat is cut into smaller chunks and so many vegetables—usually cabbage, beans, or root vegetables—are crammed into the simmering pot that almost all the broth is absorbed.

STEWLIKE SOUPS It's sometimes hard to distinguish between a soup and a stew because the only real difference is the proportion of liquid to solid. The techniques for making certain kinds of soup are almost the same as for making stews, except that more liquid is added to the pot when making a soup.

Stewlike soups are cooked in almost the same way as the boiled dinners except that the meat is cut up into smaller pieces (usually bite size) and flavorful liquids such as wine, beer, or cider are more likely to be used than water. Vegetables such as mushrooms, pearl onions, carrots, or baby artichokes are sometimes cooked separately and added to the soup just before serving.

Unlike meat soups that are cooked uncovered, stewlike soups are cooked covered so the flavor of the cooking liquid melds with the herbs, vegetables, and meat. The meat for stewlike soups is often browned before liquid is added, whereas the meat in boiled dinners and hearty peasant soups is rarely if ever browned.

Once you've made one or two of these soups, it will be easy to convert any stew recipe into a lighter, soup version.

Asian-Style Meat Soups

In Asia, where heating and cooking fuel are scarce, the tradition of quick stir-frying—and subsequent soup-making—gave birth to cooking techniques still used today.

Asian soups are easy to make in only a few minutes because the meat is cut into very thin strips that cook very quickly. Sometimes the meat is marinated ahead of time and the soup is prepared at the last minute by simmering the meat for a few seconds in water or broth. For many of the best-known Asian soups the diners do this themselves.

For some Asian soups the meat is quickly stir-fried in hot oil with flavorful ingredients such as ginger and garlic until it browns slightly. Water or broth and flavorful ingredients are then added, the soup is brought to a simmer, and then it is served immediately.

Whereas European and American soups are best made with tough cuts of meat that break down slowly and contribute their savor to the surrounding broth, Asian soups—because of the short cooking time—are best made with more tender cuts or with meat that has been marinated to make it more tender.

Using Marinades

Marinades are used both to flavor and to tenderize meats before cooking. There is no need to tenderize the meat for American- and European-style soups, because the long cooking will break down the meat's fiber and tenderize it anyway, or for Asian-style soups that call for an already tender (and expensive) cut. But when an Asian-style soup recipe calls for an expensive cut of meat (many recipes just say "steak") you can replace it with a less expensive, tougher cut and tenderize it using some ingredient in the marinade to help break down the fiber and soften it. Finely chopped tropical fruits such as fresh mango, papaya, and pineapple are the best natural meat tenderizers. Acidic ingredients such as lime juice, wine, or vinegar are also effective tenderizers. Marinate the meat strips in a mixture containing 2 tablespoons finely chopped tropical fruit for about an hour.

In most boiled-dinner-style soups, a marinade is not used so that the natural

USING LEFTOVER MEATS

Although leftover cooked meats contribute little flavor to the surrounding broth, a few leftover strips of chicken or turkey or a few cubes of steak can turn a simple vegetable soup into something substantial enough for a small meal.

If you have leftover roasts, still on the bone, you can make a simple broth by simmering them in water for an hour or two—long enough to loosen any meat clinging to the bone—and then use both the broth and the meat clinging to the bone to enhance or start a simple soup.

If you have leftover meat and no bones, cut the meat into bite-size pieces and add it to a soup just a few minutes before serving. Added any sooner, the meat will dry out.

flavor of the meat stays intact. But much of the distinctive flavor of an American- or European-style stewlike soup or an Asian-style soup comes from first tossing the ingredients in a flavorful marinade. The marinade ingredients—tropical fruit and all—can then be included in the soup as additional flavoring.

Most European and American marinades contain herbs, wine, vinegar, aromatic vegetables, and a small amount of oil to prevent the meat from drying out. The exact ingredients used in the marinade depend on the country and the whim of the cook. In France the marinade will almost always contain the herbs later used in the bouquet garni—thyme, bay leaf, and parsley—while the meats going into an Italian soup may be marinated with a little marjoram, oregano, or rosemary.

Marinades from Asia are more varied than their European counterparts and are essential to the final flavor and character of the soup.

New England
BOILED DINNER,
POT-AU-FEU, AND
BOLLITO MISTO

New England Boiled Dinner

The word *boiled* has always disturbed me. Few dishes benefit from boiling—green vegetables are the exception—and most dishes described as boiled are actually poached. But of course Poached New England Dinner sounds as though the meat was stolen in the middle of the night.

A traditional New England boiled dinner, which dates from colonial times, is different from other meat soups because corned rather than fresh beef is used. Beef, usually brisket, is corned by being soaked in brine flavored with herbs and spices. In this recipe the corned beef is blanched to eliminate most of its salt; unlike traditional recipes, some of the hot broth is served with the meats.

MAKES 8 MAIN-COURSE SERVINGS

4 pounds corned beef brisket

1 bouquet garni

1 medium-size head of cabbage, preferably Savoy

3 medium-size beets

4 medium-size turnips, peeled and cut into 6 wedges each

4 medium-size carrots, split lengthwise and cut into 2-inch
    lengths

6 golf-ball-size white onions, peeled

6 medium-size waxy potatoes, peeled

freshly ground pepper

sour gherkins

horseradish

mustard

RINSE the corned beef and tie it up with string. Place it in a 6-quart pot and add enough cold water to cover the beef by I inch. Bring the water to a simmer over medium heat and keep the liquid at a simmer for 10 minutes. Drain the beef in a colander, rinse it again in cold water, and place it back in the pot. Cover the meat again with cold water, add the bouquet garni, and bring to a slow simmer. Cover the pot and simmer very gently for 2½ hours.

CUT the cabbage vertically into quarters; remove the core from each quarter and tie each quarter with string.

SIMMER the beets in enough water to cover until they have the texture of cooked potatoes when poked with a knife, usually 30 to 45 minutes. Drain, peel, and, unless the beets are quite small, cut them into quarters.

ADD the cabbage and all the vegetables except the beets to the simmering beef and cook for 30 minutes more, until the vegetables have softened.

TO serve, drain the corned beef and vegetables, saving the broth, and slice the beef. Divide each section of cabbage in half and slice the potatoes into I-inch-thick chunks. Arrange the beef and vegetables in wide soup bowls. Season the broth with freshly ground pepper and ladle enough into the bowls so it comes about ½ inch up the sides of the meat. Pass bowls of sour gherkins, horseradish, and mustard at the table.

French Boiled Beef and Vegetables

POT-AU-FEU

If the glory of French cooking can be summed up with one dish, it is a simple pot of simmered beef and vegetables—the *pot-au-feu*—(pronounced poe toe fuh) left on the corner of the farmhouse stove or, better yet, over the coals in the hearth. This dish is often a surprise to Americans, who usually think of French dishes as laden with butter and cream. *Pot-au-feu* is almost completely lean and contains no dairy products.

Although the French have romanticized *pot-au-feu* as a symbol of their rural past, the harried pace of life for French city dwellers has relegated the gently simmered dish to holiday feasting or prolonged Sunday lunches with the extended family.

A traditional *pot-au-feu* is prepared by very slowly simmering vegetables in water with 2 or 3 different cuts of beef and marrow bones tied in a packet with cheesecloth so the marrow doesn't seep out during the cooking. When the meat is done, the broth is served first, followed by plates of the meat and vegetables. Coarse salt, mustard, sour gherkins (cornichons), and occasionally tomato sauce are passed at the table.

Pot-au-feu can be made a day or two in advance and the meat gently reheated in the broth 30 minutes before serving.

MAKES 8 MAIN-COURSE SERVINGS

2 pounds beef short ribs, cut into 3-inch lengths,
    at least 1 per serving

1 2-pound beef brisket or chuck roast, tied up with string

2 pounds beef shank, cut into 2 1½-inch-thick slices

8 marrow bones, wrapped together in cheesecloth

1 large bouquet garni

3 large carrots, halved lengthwise and cut into
    2-inch lengths

4 leeks, white part and 1 inch of green, split in half
    lengthwise and washed

1 large turnip, peeled and cut into 8 wedges

16 golf-ball-size white onions, peeled

2 cloves, stuck into one of the onions

2 celery ribs, cut into 2-inch lengths

salt

slices of French bread, toasted

Dijon mustard

cornichons

coarse salt

PLACE the meats and marrow bones in a 6-quart pot. Add enough cold water to cover the meat by about 1 inch. Bring the liquid to a very gentle simmer over high heat. When it simmers, turn down the heat to low. Using a ladle, skim off any froth and scum that float to the top. After about 20 minutes, when scum has stopped floating to the surface, add the bouquet garni.

LEAVE the *pot-au-feu*, partially covered, for 1½ hours, skimming every 15 minutes, and then add the vegetables. Simmer slowly for 1½ hours more. Add liquid as needed to keep the meat covered.

CAREFULLY remove the meat, marrow bones, and vegetables from the pot with a slotted spoon. Discard the bouquet garni.

ARRANGE the meats and vegetables on a platter. Slice the brisket or chuck roast and arrange the slices, along with the beef shank, the marrow bones, and the vegetables, on the platter. Cover the platter tightly with aluminum foil and place it in a warm oven.

WITH a ladle, skim as much fat off the broth as you can and strain it into a clean pot. Bring it to a slow simmer and skim again. Season to taste with salt.

SERVE the broth in hot bowls, passing the toast in a basket at the table.

WHEN the bowls have been cleared, you can distribute the meat and vegetables on plates in the kitchen, but if you have the room, present the platter in the dining room and arrange it on the plates in front of your guests. Encourage your guests to spread the hot beef marrow on the toast. Pass bowls of mustard, cornichons, and coarse salt.

SUGGESTIONS AND VARIATIONS | I sometimes serve *pot-au-feu* as a single course by slicing the meats and serving them in wide bowls along with the broth and vegetables.

ALTHOUGH a *pot-au-feu* is almost always made with water, you'll get a dramatically delicious bouillon if you start out with broth. I like to begin a couple of days in advance and make a broth with beef bones and vegetables, then simmer the *pot-au-feu* in the broth.

TO make a basic broth with bones, buy 10 pounds of beef or veal knuckle bones (*not* marrow bones). Roast them in the oven at 400° for about an hour, until well browned, with 2 large onions, cut in half; 2 carrots, cut into sections; and one turnip, peeled and cut in half.

TRANSFER everything to a 10-quart pot, cover with cold water, and simmer slowly for 12 hours, skimming and replenishing evaporated water as needed. Strain the broth, let it cool for a couple of hours, and refrigerate until needed.

REGIONAL POTS-AU-FEU

Every region of France has its own *pot-au-feu* variation. *Le pot-au-feu berriaud* (from the Berry, a region of the Loire Valley) replaces some of the beef with veal shank and lamb shoulder. A version from the Auvergne contains little balls of stuffed cabbage; the Burgundian version simmers an oxtail with the other meats; and a recipe from Provence uses lamb and flavors the broth with juniper berries and dried melon rind. One of my favorite versions comes from Gascony and includes confit of goose and duck.

Poached Hen with Vegetables

POULE AU POT

In traditional French cooking, a *poule au pot* is prepared by submerging a stuffed hen in the simmering *pot-au-feu* about an hour and a half before serving. The hen is carved and served on the platter along with the other meats and vegetables.

Most of the hens you find today at the butcher's, should you be lucky enough to have a butcher, are old stewing hens who have laid too many eggs and are beginning to slow down. They make a great chicken broth, but no matter how you cook them, their flesh is always tough and dry. For this reason I like to use a plump roasting chicken instead of a hen.

There are also many times when I want to present slices of poached chicken surrounded with broth and I don't just happen to have a *pot-au-feu* simmering on the stove. The solution is to poach the chicken in chicken broth along with some carrots, onions, turnips, and leeks, then reduce the poaching liquid to concentrate its flavor. The carved chicken served in wide bowls surrounded with vegetables and broth makes an elegant and satisfying main-course soup.

If you do want to serve chicken as part of an elaborate *pot-au-feu*, just submerge the chicken in the hot *pot-au-feu* an hour before you want to serve. Because of the space taken up by the other meats, you may find it impossible to completely submerge the chicken in the broth, so you may need to temporarily take out some of the other meats (provided they are completely cooked) or add extra broth to cover the chicken.

If you don't have a *pot-au-feu*, follow this recipe. To make a stuffed chicken, use the recipe on page 431.

MAKES 4 MAIN-COURSE SERVINGS

I 4-pound chicken

4 quarts brown chicken broth or more or less to cover

12 golf-ball-size white onions, peeled

3 medium-size carrots, cut into 2-inch lengths

3 medium-size turnips, peeled and cut into wedges

3 leeks, white part only, cut in half lengthwise and washed

coarse salt

slices of French bread, toasted

RINSE the chicken in cold running water. Tie the drumsticks together at the ends with a short piece of string. Fold the wings backward so they stay in place against the chicken's back.

PLACE the chicken in a deep 6-quart pot. (Use as closely fitting a pot as possible so you don't need too much broth to cover the chicken.)

KNOWING WHEN
THE CHICKEN'S DONE

A 4-pound chicken is usually done in about an hour, but if you want to know for sure, lift the chicken out of the broth by sticking a wooden spoon in its cavity. Poke the thigh—at the point where the drumstick joins the rest of the thigh—with a metal skewer or sharp kitchen fork. Watch the juices that run out—if they are clear, the chicken is done; if they are pink, poach the chicken for 10 minutes more and check again.

ADD enough chicken broth to cover the chicken by about an inch (you may need more or less depending on the size of the chicken) and place the pot over medium heat. When the broth approaches the boil, turn down the heat to keep the broth at a slow simmer.

AFTER the chicken has simmered for 5 minutes, skim off any froth with a ladle, add the vegetables, and cover the pot with the lid ajar an inch or two.

POACH the chicken for 30 minutes. Check to see if any part of the chicken is protruding from the broth. If so, reach into the chicken's cavity with a wooden spoon and carefully turn the chicken around so that any part that was protruding is now submerged. Replace the lid and poach for 30 minutes more. Check the chicken for doneness (see box).

GENTLY lift the chicken out of the broth and place it on a plate. Cover it with foil to keep it warm.

BRING the broth to a slow simmer and skim off any fat and froth with a ladle. Strain the broth into a wide pan; put the vegetables in a covered bowl and keep them warm.

BRING the broth to a boil and then slide the pot to one side of the heat so it is boiling on one side only—this forces any scum to one side so it's easier to skim off. Continue boiling and skimming off fat with a ladle until the broth has reduced by half, about 30 minutes. (If you've used canned chicken broth, skip this step or the broth will end up being too salty.)

STRAIN the broth through a fine-mesh strainer into a clean pot. Don't season the broth—you may have some left over to use in another dish—but let your guests season the dish at the table.

CARVE the chicken and arrange it in hot bowls. Arrange the vegetables around each portion and ladle about ½ cup broth over each serving.

PASS the coarse salt and toasted French bread at the table.

SUGGESTIONS AND VARIATIONS | I sometimes add chopped fresh herbs such as parsley, chervil, thyme, or tarragon to the broth about 5 minutes before serving.

THERE'S no need to limit yourself to the vegetables suggested here; use practically anything you have around. Mushrooms, celery, peeled and seeded tomatoes, and garlic are just a few possibilities.

Stuffed Poached Chicken

In a traditional *poule au pot* the chicken is almost always stuffed before going into the pot. Stuffing a chicken is a good way to stretch a single chicken into a meal for more people; stuffings are also easy and fun to improvise.

To stuff a chicken, sew the neck closed with a trussing needle and some thin cotton string. Fill the cavity with the stuffing and either seal it off with a piece of aluminum foil or sew it closed. Don't pack the stuffing in too hard, because it will expand during the poaching and can cause the chicken to tear. If you don't want to bother with all this sewing, wrap the chicken in cheesecloth and tie the two ends with string.

MAKES ENOUGH FOR ONE 4-POUND CHICKEN

STUFFINGS FOR CHICKEN Stuffings are a great way to use leftover meats, especially long-simmered meats from *pot-au-feu*, stews, and meat used for making broth. If you don't have leftover meats, you can make a simple stuffing of chopped onions, celery, bread, and walnuts or a richer stuffing with meat. Pork is inexpensive and makes excellent stuffing. If you decide to use leftover roast meats, be sure to include some fat such as cubes of fatback or bacon, or the stuffing will be dry. On the other hand, leftover meats such as short ribs from a *pot-au-feu* or chunks of meat from a stew usually have enough fat of their own.

CUBES of toasted bread or bread crumbs are often used in stuffings to provide a softer texture and to keep the stuffing from turning hard and cakey once it is cooked. Bread crumbs are usually worked to a paste with milk or broth before being combined with the rest of the mixture.

Chicken, duck, or calf's liver as well as bacon or prosciutto (raw cured ham) gives the stuffing a rich deep flavor. If you're using bacon, be sure to cut it into strips or cubes and simmer it for about 5 minutes in water to remove some of the strong smoky flavor, otherwise it will overwhelm the flavor of the stuffing. If you can't find slab bacon, at least be sure to use a naturally smoked bacon (it will say so on the package) instead of "smoke-flavored" bacon.

I always include onions, garlic, and chopped fresh thyme in stuffings, but

GASCON-STYLE POULE AU POT

Food writers usually claim that *poule au pot* originated in Gascony. It's hard to imagine that something as obvious as poaching a chicken in an already simmering *pot-au-feu* should be limited to Gascony, but if you want to stick to the legend, use duck or goose confit as the meat in the stuffing and good prosciutto (in Gascony they use Bayonne ham, but it's not imported into the United States) instead of bacon.

During the holidays I sometimes take the Gascony fantasy further and go to extravagant extremes and gently fold cubes of foie gras and sliced raw truffles or cèpes sautéed in goose fat into the stuffing.

other herbs such as marjoram or rosemary and vegetables such as carrots, mushrooms, shredded chard leaves (blanched first), and spinach can also be thrown in.

Egg is added to stuffings to hold them together.

Simple Bread and Pork Stuffing

MAKES ENOUGH FOR ONE 4-POUND CHICKEN

2 chicken livers

meat from 1 large pork shoulder chop or ¾ cup leftover
    stew or *pot-au-feu* meat

2 ounces fatback if you're using lean leftover meat, cut into
    ¼-inch cubes, ½ cup

2 ounces slab bacon, rind removed, cut into ¼-inch cubes,
    simmered in 2 cups water for 5 minutes, ½ cup

4 slices of white bread, crusts removed, cut into ½-inch
    cubes

½ cup milk or broth

1 medium-size onion, finely chopped

2 garlic cloves, finely chopped

2 teaspoons fresh thyme leaves

1 egg, lightly beaten

salt

pepper

tiny pinch of freshly grated nutmeg

2 tablespoons pure olive oil

COMBINE the chicken livers in a food processor with the pork and fatback. Work the mixture until it has the consistency of hamburger meat. Stir in the bacon.

IN a mixing bowl, combine the bread cubes with the milk and work in the ground meats with your hands. Stir in the onion, garlic, thyme, and the egg. Season with salt, pepper, and the nutmeg.

TO test the seasoning, gently cook a 1-inch-diameter patty in vegetable oil and taste it.

FILL the chicken only two-thirds full of the stuffing—the stuffing expands when cooked—and then sew the chicken at both ends or tie it up with cheesecloth.

Poached Beef Tenderloin with Vegetables

BOEUF À LA FICELLE

To make *boeuf à la ficelle* the traditional way, tie a piece of string around a piece of beef tenderloin and then suspend it in a pot of simmering broth or, more authentically, in a *pot-au-feu* until the tenderloin is cooked rare. To a French person—and to a number of Americans, including me—an authentic *boeuf à la ficelle* represents the best of all possible worlds. The *pot-au-feu* broth and vegetables have benefited from long, slow cooking, but the tenderloin is as rare and tender as a good steak.

If you're making a *pot-au-feu* and want to jazz it up with added elegant flair, buy a section of beef tenderloin—about an inch of thickness per serving—and poach it in the *pot-au-feu* about 15 minutes before serving. Slice the tenderloin and serve it on the platter with the other meats and vegetables.

If you don't just happen to have a *pot-au-feu* simmering on the back of the stove, you can still serve a *boeuf à la ficelle* using the method that follows; all you need is some beef broth.

The vegetables for this recipe can be cooked in advance, but it's almost not worth the bother. If you have the broth, you can trim and wash the vegetables the morning before the dinner and then just add everything to the pot in stages.

In this recipe the broth, meat, and vegetables are served together, unlike a traditional *boeuf à la ficelle*, where the broth is served as a separate first course.

MAKES 6 MAIN-COURSE SERVINGS

2 quarts clear beef broth

1 bouquet garni

3 large carrots, cut into 2-inch lengths

3 leeks, white part and 1 inch of green, split in half
    lengthwise and washed

2 medium-size turnips, peeled and cut into 6 wedges each

12 golf-ball-size white onions, peeled

1 clove, stuck into one of the onions

1 celery rib, cut into 2-inch lengths

a 6-inch section of beef tenderloin, center cut or butt end,
    tied with a string

salt

slices of French bread, lightly toasted

coarse salt

HEAT the beef broth in a 4-quart pot over medium heat. When the broth reaches the simmer, turn the heat down to low. Leave the broth at a very slow simmer for 10 minutes and with a ladle skim off any froth that floats to the top.

ADD the bouquet garni and the vegetables to the broth and partially cover the pot. Gently simmer the vegetables for 30 minutes.

LOWER the beef into the simmering broth and vegetables. Make sure it's completely submerged. (If it isn't, add more broth or water.) Gently simmer for 15 minutes.

TRANSFER the beef to a cutting board and slice it into 6 thick slices. Arrange the slices in wide soup bowls and arrange the vegetables around each slice of beef. Season the broth with salt and ladle it *around* the beef slices. (Don't pour it *over* the slices, or they will lose their color.)

SERVE immediately. Pass the toast and the coarse salt at the table.

SUGGESTIONS AND VARIATIONS | A *boeuf à la ficelle* is prepared using a simple method of poaching lean meats in an already flavorful broth. The same method can be used for cooking lean and tender meats without fat and then serving them surrounded by a lean and flavorful broth instead of a rich sauce. The method is easy to adapt using other meats. Try poaching duck breasts (see recipe below), chicken breasts (remove skin), miniature game birds (Cornish hens, squab), lamb (leg, trimmed of most fat), and loin of veal.

YOU can also use other vegetables such as mushrooms (wild or cultivated), cabbage, and spinach. The vegetables can be cut into different shapes such as julienne or chiffonade.

Poached Duck Breast with Vegetables

CANARD À LA FICELLE

Poaching a duck breast in a rich broth is virtually the same process as poaching a whole tenderloin (see recipe page 433). Most recipes call for removing the fatty skin from the breast before poaching, but I like to sauté the duck breasts skin side down before poaching to render some of the fat and leave the skin crispy. The large mullard duck breasts (see Sources), which weigh about a pound each, are ideal for this—each breast makes two generous main-course servings—but breasts from the smaller Long Island ducklings (sometimes called Pekin ducks) also work.

MAKES 4 MAIN-COURSE SERVINGS

1 recipe, about 2 quarts, clear duck broth (page 79) or
   1 recipe, about 2 quarts, basic beef broth (page 74),
   or 2 quarts basic brown chicken broth (page 62)

1 bouquet garni

1 large carrot

2 leeks, white part and 1 inch of green, split in half
   lengthwise and washed

1 medium-size turnip, peeled and cut into 6 wedges

8 golf-ball-size white onions, peeled

1 celery rib, cut into 2-inch lengths

2 1-pound mullard duck breasts or 4 Long Island duckling
   breasts

salt

pepper

4 slices of French bread, about 1 inch thick, lightly toasted

coarse salt

HEAT the broth in a 4-quart pot over medium heat. When the broth reaches a simmer, turn the heat down to low. Leave the broth at a very slow simmer for 10 minutes and with a ladle skim off any froth that floats to the top.

ADD the bouquet garni and the vegetables to the broth and partially cover the pot. Gently simmer the vegetables for 30 minutes.

WHILE the vegetables are simmering, make a series of slits into the duck skin—about 20 going at a diagonal from side to side and another 20 going lengthwise on a diagonal. Cut as deeply into the skin as you can, but without exposing any of the meat. Season the skin with salt and pepper and cook the duck breasts in a skillet (without any additional fat), skin side down, over medium heat, for about 8 minutes for small duck breasts and 12 minutes for the large mullard breasts, until the skin is brown and crispy.

SUBMERGE the duck breasts in the simmering broth—you can tie a string around them and tie the other end of the string to a wooden spoon to make them easier to retrieve—for about 3 minutes for small duck breasts and 5 minutes for large breasts—the meat should remain rare or at most medium rare. Take out the breasts and

BROWN DUCK BROTH:

MAKES ABOUT 2 QUARTS

Coarsly chop two duck carcasses with a cleaver and brown them with a medium-size onion and carrot, chopped, in a tablespoon of oil over high heat. Add a bouquet garni and enough water or chicken broth, about 2 1/2 quarts, to cover by 1 inch and simmer for about 3 hours. Keep adding liquid—either more broth or water—to keep the duck carcass pieces covered.

cut into one to see if it is done enough. If not, continue poaching for a minute or two more.

TRANSFER the duck breasts to a cutting board and slice them, crosswise, as thinly as you can. Place a piece of French bread in the center of four heated wide soup plates and ladle the broth and vegetables around. Arrange the duck slices on top of the bread. Pass the coarse salt at the table.

Pot-au-Feu Dodin Bouffant

I first read about this dish in a funny little book called *The Life and Passion of Dodin Bouffant, Gourmet*, first published in French in 1925. Dodin is a mythical character living in the French countryside during the first half of the 19th century. There's a pretentious visiting prince in the region, and Dodin decides to teach him a lesson—that simple things can be great—and invites the prince to dinner. When the prince arrives with great pomp and ceremony, Dodin announces that the main course at dinner is a *pot-au-feu*—in that era, a dish for peasants. The Prince is affronted and tempted to leave but, remembering Dodin's reputation as a great gourmet, decides to stay. The *pot-au-feu* is of course sumptuous, and the prince is taught his lesson.

This recipe isn't straight out of the book—some of the suggestions such as a whole foie gras poached in Chambertin—seemed a little excessive. Here is a feasible but still luxurious version of the original.

This is a spectacular dish that will dazzle your guests, but be warned: count on a couple of days to get ready. The final arranging of the different meats is somewhat complicated and has to be done quickly, so it's a good idea to get someone to help in the kitchen.

The broth can be prepared 2 or 3 days in advance (or even longer if it's frozen), and the meats and foie gras can be prepared the morning of the dinner.

MAKES 8 GENEROUS MAIN-COURSE SERVINGS

a 4-inch section of beef tenderloin, center cut or butt end,
    tied with string

2 boneless breast halves from a large roasting chicken, skin
    removed

2 boneless duck breast halves, skin removed

1 pound foie gras bloc, preferably *mi-cuit*
    (optional)

salt

freshly ground white pepper

2 quarts clear beef broth

1 bouquet garni

3 large carrots, cut in half lengthwise and then cut into
2-inch lengths

3 leeks, white part and 1 inch of green, split in half
lengthwise and washed

1 large turnip, peeled and cut into 12 wedges

8 golf-ball-size white onions, peeled

1 clove, stuck into one of the onions

slices of French bread, lightly toasted

coarse salt

IN ADVANCE On the same day you plan to serve, trim the meats and remove the foie gras from the can or plastic wrapping. Slice the foie gras into 8 even slices. Season the meats with salt and pepper and keep them in the refrigerator tightly covered with plastic wrap.

AT THE LAST MINUTE Forty-five minutes before serving, heat the beef broth in a 4-quart pot over medium heat. When the broth reaches a simmer, turn the heat down to low. Leave the broth at a very slow simmer for 10 minutes and with a ladle skim off any froth that floats to the top.

ADD the bouquet garni and vegetables to the broth and partially cover the pot. Gently simmer the vegetables until they begin to soften, about 30 minutes.

FIFTEEN minutes before serving, arrange the slices of foie gras on a sheet pan and place them in a warm oven (you can use the same oven to heat the bowls).

LOWER the beef into the simmering broth and vegetables. Make sure it is completely submerged. If it is not, add a little more broth or water. Gently simmer for 5 minutes and then add the chicken breasts. Simmer for 5 minutes more and add the duck breasts. Simmer very gently for 5 minutes more.

SERVING Transfer the meats to a cutting board. Arrange the vegetables in the center of the warm soup bowls.

FOIE GRAS

This luxurious and expensive ingredient rarely makes it into soup. In the United States foie gras is the liver taken from ducks that have been allowed to overeat so that their livers have a high concentration of fat. Foie gras can be cut into small cubes and added to full-flavored consommés (see recipe for foie gras and truffle soup, page 546) or, as in the recipe given here, poached whole and sliced.

Foie gras is sold in several forms: the whole raw liver, the liver compressed into a block and partially cooked (labeled *bloc, mi-cuit*), completely cooked and canned, and pureed as a mousse. The best to use for soups is the partially cooked block foie gras, which has the most luxurious texture and deepest flavor.

SLICE the beef into 8 even slices. Slice the chicken and the duck breasts on an angle so you get 12 slices out of each half (3 slices per serving). Arrange the beef, chicken, duck, and foie gras slices in a circular pattern around the vegetables.

LADLE about ½ cup hot broth into each bowl. Sprinkle salt and pepper over each bowl.

SERVE immediately. Pass the toasted French bread and the coarse salt.

SUGGESTIONS AND VARIATIONS | This principle of poaching meat and vegetables in savory broth can be adapted to practically any ingredients. One refinement is to cut the vegetables into julienne, cook them in a small amount of broth, and then mound them in the center of the bowls. The poached and sliced meats can then be arranged on the vegetables.

WILD mushrooms or even truffles can also be simmered in the broth in addition to or instead of the traditional *pot-au-feu* vegetables.

Italian-Style Poached Meats in Broth

BOLLITO MISTO

A *bollito misto* is the Italian version of a *pot-au-feu*—a pot of slowly simmering meats and vegetables. Most traditional versions of French *pot-au-feu* contain only beef, while a *bollito misto* always contains at least two and as many as seven kinds of meat. And while a *pot-au-feu* is served with coarse salt and sour pickles, *bollito misto* is served with one or more traditional sauces.

The first time I tasted *bollito misto*, in a well-known Italian restaurant in New York, I was fascinated by the sauces, which were served cold. One of the sauces was a green mayonnaise with lots of herbs—sort of an Italian tartar sauce—but I had never seen anything like the other sauce, which was both sweet and savory and contained candied fruit. It was a *mostarda di frutta* from Cremona, from a recipe that dates back to the Renaissance.

This version of *bollito misto* contains veal shanks (*ossobuco*), beef tongue, beef brisket, short ribs, a veal foot, and fresh sausage, but you can get by using half as many meats—just adjust the quantities of the other meats accordingly. I sometimes make a version at home that contains only the veal shanks and the beef tongue. What makes *bollito misto* exciting is to use as many different sauces, both hot and cold, as possible to accompany the meat.

Aficionados of *bollito misto* insist that the meats be added to already boiling water, the idea being that this seals in the juices, but I've found that the broth is clearer and tastier if you start out with cold water. This recipe, unlike traditional versions, includes a handful of parsley leaves thrown in a minute before serving to give it color and a fresh flavor.

You'll have enough food for 16 people, but don't hesitate to make it for a smaller group so you'll have leftovers. One wonderful way of using the leftover meat is to slice it the next day, bread it with a little beaten egg and fresh bread crumbs, and then grill it—drizzling it all the while with butter or olive oil—or sauté it, just long enough to heat it through. You can also just reheat the meat in its broth and serve it the same way the next day. If you are planning to serve a *bollito misto* to a large crowd, be sure to get someone to help you in the kitchen, especially when it comes time to carve the meat and arrange it in the bowls.

To prepare *bollito misto* in advance, cook the meats until they are completely done. Let them cool for 15 minutes, wrap them tightly in plastic wrap, and refrigerate for up to 3 days. Let the broth cool, cover, and refrigerate. To reheat, skim any congealed fat off the surface of the broth and slowly reheat the meats in the broth placed over medium heat. The broth should take at least 30 minutes to come to a simmer—if not, the meats won't be heated all the way through.

MAKES 12 TO 16 SERVINGS

1 calf's foot, split in half lengthwise and then again
    crosswise (have the butcher do this)*

3 pounds beef brisket, second (angle) cut

2 garlic cloves, crushed to a paste

1 teaspoon chopped fresh thyme or marjoram or
    ½ teaspoon dried thyme

salt

pepper

1 beef tongue, about 5 pounds

6 2-inch-thick veal shanks

4 pounds short ribs

1 large bouquet garni, preferably including 5 fresh
    marjoram sprigs

5 carrots, cut into 1-inch lengths, 2 pieces per person

3 or 4 turnips, peeled and cut into 10 wedges each, 2 pieces
    per person

3 celery ribs, cut into 1-inch lengths

24 to 32 golf-ball-size white onions, peeled

1 clove, stuck into one of the onions

1 pound fresh sausage such as *cotechino, saucisse à l'ail,* or
    zampone

¼ cup tightly packed chopped Italian parsley leaves

thick slices of crusty bread, lightly toasted

*A pig's foot will work, too; lacking either, use 2 extra pieces of veal shank.

COVER the calf's foot with cold water in a 4-quart pot. Bring to a boil, turn down the heat and keep at a simmer for 10 minutes. Drain and rinse the calves' foot with cold water.

SMEAR the brisket with the garlic paste, sprinkle it with the chopped herbs, and season with salt and pepper. Roll it up into a large sausage shape and tie it with string.

PUT the calf's foot in a 12-quart pot along with the rolled brisket, beef tongue, veal shanks, short ribs, and bouquet garni. Add enough water (or broth) to cover and bring to a slow simmer over medium heat. For the first 30 minutes, carefully skim off any fat or froth that floats to the top.

PARTIALLY cover the pot and simmer the meats until they have almost completely softened (a knife should slide in with no resistance), about 3 hours. Add the vegetables and the sausage—you may have to add more water or broth at this point to keep everything immersed—and simmer for 45 minutes more, until the vegetables have softened.

FINISHING AND SERVING Carefully reach into the broth with a skimmer and pull out the meats and vegetables. Strain the broth through a medium-mesh strainer. Place the tongue on a cutting board and carefully peel off the skin. Let the sausage cool slightly and peel off the skin.

IF you're serving the *bollito misto* to a large gathering, it makes an impressive sight to bring all the meats out to the dining room on a large platter and serve them in front of your guests. The problem is that everything gets cold by the time everyone is served. I usually compromise by showing the guests a platter loaded with the meats, but then I rush it back into the kitchen and set up the bowls in there.

SLICE the tongue and brisket and pull the meat off the short ribs and veal shanks. Slice the sausage into 1-inch pieces. Discard the calf's foot (or trim off the gelatinous meat, cut it into cubes, and add it to the soup) and the bouquet garni.

BRING the broth back to a simmer and toss in the parsley leaves. Arrange the sliced meats and vegetables in wide soup bowls—give each person two of each vegetable and a slice of each of the meats—and ladle the broth over this. (You may need to reheat the sliced meats slightly in the simmering broth.) Pass the sauces and the bread slices at the table.

SUGGESTIONS AND VARIATIONS | In this recipe, the vegetables for the *bollito misto* are simmered along with the meats near the end of cooking. If you want to have more or different vegetables—or your pot's too small—simmer potatoes, leeks, carrots, turnips, or onions separately in some of the broth.

LIKE *pot-au-feu*, you can make *bollito misto* as simple or as elaborate as you like. Beef tenderloin can be poached in the simmering broth during the last 15 minutes of cooking, sliced and served rare in the bowls along with the other meats. In one elaborate variation skinned and boneless duck breasts are poached in the broth for the last 5 minutes and served along with the rest of the meats.

Green Sauce

BAGNET VERD

SERVE THIS COLD. MAKES 1 CUP

4 hard cooked egg yolks

6 tablespoons heavy cream or half-and-half

2 garlic cloves, finely chopped and crushed to a paste

1 cup tightly packed Italian parsley leaves

½ cup tightly packed fresh mint leaves

8 anchovies, soaked in cold water for 5 minutes, drained and chopped

¼ cup drained capers

2 tablespoons white wine vinegar

4 teaspoons sugar

½ cup extra virgin olive oil

salt

pepper

IF you're using a food processor, combine all the ingredients except the olive oil and the salt and pepper and puree them—using the pulse mechanism—for about 1 minute, until the mixture is smooth. Transfer the sauce to a mixing bowl and slowly work in the olive oil with a wooden spoon. Season with salt and pepper.

IF you're making the sauce by hand, work the egg yolks and heavy cream to a paste in a 2-quart mixing bowl. Finely chop the solid ingredients, stir in the garlic, and slowly work in the olive oil with a wooden spoon. Stir in the rest of the ingredients.

Cold Fruit Sauce

MOSTARDA D'UVA

Don't confuse this sauce with mustard or mustard fruits. Many Italian condiments are called mostarda even if they contain no mustard at all. *Mostarda d'Uva* is traditionally made around the time of the grape harvest, when there is plenty of fresh grape juice around. It's usually made with red grape juice, but I sometimes make it with bottled white grape juice because the red grape juice I find in the supermarket is made from Concord grapes and has too distinctive a flavor. If you have access to fresh red grape juice made from less assertive grape varieties, use that instead.

Because supermarket grape juice is made from table grapes, it's much sweeter than grape juice made from wine grapes, so this recipe contains vinegar. You may need to add more or less vinegar depending on the grape juice you use.

SERVE THIS SAUCE COLD. MAKES 2 CUPS

2 unripe pears, peeled, cored, and cut into ¼-inch dice

3 cups white or red grape juice, preferably not from
        Concord grapes

2 apples, peeled, cored, and cut into ¼-inch dice

1 clove

pinch of ground cinnamon

¾ cup walnut halves

¼ cup balsamic or other wine vinegar

SIMMER the pear cubes in the grape juice until they soften, but don't allow them to turn into mush. Transfer them to a bowl with a slotted spoon. Simmer the apple cubes in the grape juice for 10 minutes and combine them with the pears.

ADD the clove and cinnamon to the grape juice. Boil the grape juice until about ¼ cup is left; it should turn into a light syrup. Combine the fruit, syrup, walnuts and vinegar. Let cool.

Horseradish Sauce

SALSA DI CREN

There are many ways to make horseradish sauce, but this is my favorite.

2 apples, peeled, cored, and chopped

2 tablespoons unsalted butter

¼ cup freshly grated or bottled horseradish

⅔ cup heavy cream

salt

pepper

COMBINE the apple and butter in a 1-quart saucepan. Cook, covered, over medium heat for about 10 minutes, stirring every couple of minutes, until the apple softens. Remove the lid, stir in the horseradish, and continue cooking until you've obtained a thick applesauce. Refrigerate.

BEAT the cream to medium stiffness in a 2-quart mixing bowl. Fold the cream into the cold applesauce. Season to taste with salt and pepper.

Pepper and Eggplant Sauce

PEPERONATA

This saucelike mixture of tomatoes, peppers, and eggplant is seasoned with sugar and vinegar so it ends up tasting almost like a chutney. Serve it cold or warm.

MAKES 1½ CUPS

6 tablespoons extra virgin olive oil

I small eggplant, preferably thin Italian or Japanese type, peeled and cut into ½-inch cubes

2 medium-size onions, finely sliced

2 garlic cloves, finely chopped

4 red or yellow bell peppers or a combination, roasted, peeled, seeded (page 207), and sliced into thin strips

I teaspoon fresh or dried marjoram leaves (optional)

I cup dry white wine

6 medium-size tomatoes, peeled, seeded, and chopped or 3 cups canned, seeded and drained

2 teaspoons sugar

¼ cup balsamic vinegar

salt

pepper

HEAT the olive oil in a 4-quart pot over medium heat and add the eggplant, onions, and garlic. Stir until the vegetables soften, after about 10 minutes.

STIR in the peppers, marjoram, wine, and tomatoes. Simmer the mixture over low to medium heat, stirring every 5 minutes to prevent burning, until the sauce thickens. Add the sugar and vinegar. (You may need more or less to taste.) Season with salt and pepper.

SUGGESTIONS AND VARIATIONS | The sweet and savory *mostarda di cremona* that I had with my first *bollito misto* is difficult to make at home, but it's available in jars in Italian specialty shops. A similar version, *mostarda vicentina*, is a Venetian specialty and can be served in the same way as *mostarda di cremona*.

SOME recipes call for a hot tomato sauce made by stewing tomatoes with chopped garlic and onion until they thicken and then finishing the sauce with a generous amount of freshly chopped parsley and basil.

Asian Tabletop
MEAT SOUPS

Japanese Beef Fondue

SHABU-SHABU

Shabu-shabu is a Japanese meat and vegetable fondue; each of the guests cooks his or her own food in a pot of simmering liquid set in the center of the table. When all the meats and vegetables are gone, the diners drink the broth. Traditional recipes start out with water flavored with a little Japanese seaweed (konbu), but I like to use a full-flavored *dashi* or good chicken or beef broth.

Shabu-shabu is served with two sauces for dipping the cooked meats and vegetables—ponzu and sesame sauce (goma-dare)—which are served in little dishes placed in front of each diner. These sauces are easy to make, but sometimes I put together a makeshift version of *shabu-shabu* and just serve little dishes of soy sauce.

The best dish to use for *shabu-shabu* is a traditional Japanese casserole called a *donabe*, whose elegant shape helps set the mood, but you can fake it with a fondue set or a chafing dish. Or if aesthetics aren't important, just set a pot on a hot plate.

MAKES 6 MAIN-COURSE SERVINGS

3 pounds beef tenderloin or sirloin strip, sliced ⅛ inch
    thick (ask the butcher to do it using a meat slicer)

8 Napa or celery cabbage leaves

a 6-inch length of daikon, peeled

18 *shiitake* or cultivated mushrooms, stems removed

9 scallions, both white and green parts, cut into 2-inch
    lengths

1 bunch of chrysanthemum leaves (1 sprig per serving,
    optional)

3 cakes of Japanese tofu, cut into 1-inch cubes

2 quarts *dashi*

4 scallions, both white and green parts, finely chopped

CUT the sliced beef into rectangles measuring about 4 by 6 inches. Keep them covered with plastic wrap until just before serving.

BOIL the cabbage leaves in salted water for about 5 minutes. Drain the leaves and rinse them with cold water. Cut out any thick stalks that run up into the leaves. Roll the leaves into cylinders about 1 inch thick and cut each of these into 1-inch-thick rounds.

SHRED the daikon with a benriner cutter or by slicing and cutting into very fine julienne with a chef's knife.

ARRANGE the meat slices on a platter. Be sure to keep the slices spread out on the platter so they are easy to pick up with chopsticks or fondue forks.

ARRANGE the shiitake mushrooms, cabbage rounds, daikon, scallion sections, chrysanthemum leaves, and tofu on a second platter.

BRING the *dashi* to a simmer on top of the stove and then transfer it to the *donabe* or a fondue dish set over an alcohol lamp or a can of Sterno set up on the table.

ARRANGE little dishes of the two sauces (recipes follow) at each place setting and give each diner a bowl. Pass the two platters at the table so that guests can dip what they want into the simmering *dashi*. Because the meat cooks literally in about 3 seconds, it's best to hold on to it with a fork or with chopsticks while it sits in the simmering *dashi*. The vegetables, however, are best plunged into the *dashi* and retrieved in a minute or two.

WHEN all the ingredients have been used, add the chopped scallions to the *dashi*, wait 30 seconds, and ladle the hot *dashi* into the bowls.

SUGGESTIONS AND VARIATIONS | Almost any food can be thinly sliced, presented on a platter, and passed around the table for the guests to help themselves. Strips of chicken or duck breast (skin removed), little noisettes of lamb (center-cut lamb chops with the bone taken off), assorted wild mushrooms, zucchini, and asparagus tips are just a few ideas. I sometimes even combine fish and meat and include slices of raw tuna, swordfish, or salmon. Although traditional recipes don't call for them, noodles—shirataki or cellophane—are a great way to round out the dish.

IF serving *shabu-shabu* in the traditional way at the table seems like too much of a nuisance, go ahead and simmer the ingredients in the kitchen and serve everything in deep, wide bowls. To serve *shabu-shabu* for a light lunch, cut the portions in half.

Ponzu

Ponzu will keep in a tightly sealed jar in the refrigerator for up to a year. See the Ingredients chapter for more information on anything unfamiliar.

MAKES ABOUT 2 ½ CUPS

½ cup fresh lemon juice, from about 3 lemons
½ cup rice vinegar
1 cup dark Japanese soy sauce
3 tablespoons mirin
2 tablespoons tamari sauce
¼ ounce (about 1 cup) hana-katsuo
a 6-inch length of konbu

COMBINE all the ingredients in a saucepan and bring to a simmer over high heat. Turn off the heat and let sit for 3 minutes, then strain. *Ponzu* can be used right away, but it is best after it has been allowed to mature for a month.

Sesame Sauce

GOMA-DARE

Sesame sauce is best made the same day it is used, but it will keep for up to a week in the refrigerator.

MAKES ABOUT 3 CUPS

½ cup white sesame seeds
½ cup dark Japanese soy sauce
3 tablespoons mirin
2 teaspoons sugar
¼ teaspoon dark sesame oil

LIGHTLY toast the sesame seeds in an iron skillet over medium heat, stirring them constantly so they brown evenly. As soon as they're lightly browned, pour them out into a bowl.

GRIND the sesame seeds for 1 minute in a coffee grinder, food processor, or blender or use a mortar and pestle or a Japanese grinding bowl called a *suribachi*.

COMBINE the ground sesame seeds with the other ingredients.

Japanese Quick-Simmered Beef with Vegetables

SUKIYAKI

The first time I ever had *sukiyaki* (pronounced skee-ya-kee with equal accents on each syllable) was on the floor of a minuscule Tokyo apartment. After a 13-hour flight from California I had been up for 24 hours, but my hosts insisted we all sit and have dinner. I found out later that *sukiyaki* is something prepared only for special guests and occasions.

Sukiyaki is made with slices of beef tenderloin (even more of a luxury in Japan than in the United States), vegetables, and tofu that are quickly simmered at the table in a flavorful *dashi*. Everything is cooked at the table in front of the guests, so part of the pleasure comes from the conviviality—and sometimes confusion—of cooking and eating all at once. Unlike French soups such as *pot-au-feu*, where the broth is served first, followed by the meat and vegetables, in a *sukiyaki* the meat and vegetables are served first and the broth last.

In Japan a special skillet for making *sukiyaki* (logically called a *sukiyaki*) is sold but in the United States the easiest implement to use for cooking at the table is an electric frying pan or a regular iron skillet set over a hot plate. As the meat and vegetables simmer, the guests reach in with chopsticks (or fondue forks).

Traditionally each piece of meat or vegetable is dipped in raw egg just before it is eaten, but unless you're sure of your eggs, this probably isn't a good idea. I prefer to dip the meat and vegetables in *ponzu* (page 447) or just a little soy sauce placed in a little bowl next to each guest's place.

MAKES 6 MAIN-COURSE SERVINGS

6 cups *dashi*

1½ tablespoons sugar

½ cup mirin

1 cup dark soy sauce

6 ounces shirataki filaments or cellophane noodles

3 pounds beef tenderloin or sirloin strip, sliced ⅛ inch
    thick (ask the butcher to do it using a meat slicer)

12 scallions, both white and green parts, cut into
    2-inch lengths

24 fresh shiitake mushrooms, all but ½ inch of stem
    removed

4 cakes of Japanese tofu, cut into 1-inch cubes

2 tablespoons peanut oil

BRING the *dashi*, sugar, *mirin*, and soy sauce to a simmer in a 2-quart pot.

IF you're using shirataki filaments, soak them in hot water for about 5 minutes, until tender. If you're using cellophane noodles, soak them in warm water for 30 minutes. Drain either noodle just before serving.

ARRANGE the meat, vegetables, tofu, and noodles decoratively on a platter.

AT the table, heat the vegetable oil in a skillet and add the scallions and mushrooms. Stir for 5 minutes.

PUSH the scallions and mushrooms to one side of the skillet, add the tofu and the noodles, and pour in the hot *dashi* mixture. Wait for the *dashi* to come back to a simmer.

INVITE the guests to reach into the simmering skillet with chopsticks or fondue forks.

WHEN about half of the meat and vegetables has been eaten, ladle the hot broth into soup bowls. Pass a bowl of soup to each guest.

SUGGESTIONS AND VARIATIONS | Unless you and your guests eat very quickly, the thin slices of beef tend to dry out if they sit too long in the simmering *dashi*. So you may want to cook the *sukiyaki* in stages instead of all at once.

I frankly find it a nuisance to set up my dining room for serving *sukiyaki* at the table; I don't have all the bowls and serving dishes to make things look beautiful, so the event isn't as spectacular as I would like. But I love the flavors of the whole thing—especially the broth—so I sometimes prepare *sukiyaki* entirely in the kitchen and serve it in deep porcelain bowls. My guests seem no less impressed.

ONCE you get the feel for this technique of last-minute simmering in Japanese broth, you may want to experiment with adding different ingredients. I especially like *sukiyaki* made with chunks of fresh salmon, bamboo shoots, and those little grilled eels called *anago* sold in Japanese markets.

Hearty Peasant
SOUPS

Peasant soups sometimes contain so much meat and so many vegetables that a spoon plunged into the soup will stand straight on end. One of the best things about making these hearty soups is that the next day you can spread the leftover soup in a casserole and bake it for lunch.

These full-meal soups are usually made by first preparing a rich broth with meat—usually pork but sometimes other meats—and then simmering vegetables in the broth along with the meat. These are winter dishes, and the vegetables most likely to find their way into the pot are cabbage, dried beans, and root vegetables such as turnips, potatoes, beets, and carrots.

Even though these hearty soups are rustic, unadorned, and inexpensive to prepare, I never feel as though I'm eating cheap food but rather that I'm partaking in something primal and deeply satisfying.

French Pork and Cabbage Soup

POTÉE

This soup is one of many examples of what the French call *potées*—rough-and-tumble affairs in which various combinations of pork, cabbage, beans, duck, beef, sausage, carrots, turnips, onions, and potatoes are simmered slowly until the whole steaming pot is brought to the table and spooned out over slices of stale bread. In traditional *potées* the cooking broth has all but disappeared into the meat and cabbage; this version, although still a meal in itself, is a bit soupier.

When I tell my guests what we're having for dinner, they usually seem a little disappointed until I bring on the soup. And then they eat, almost in spite of themselves, as though they've forgotten what hearty simple food is like.

This recipe can be made entirely in advance and kept for 3 or 4 days in the refrigerator.

MAKES 10 LIGHT MAIN-COURSE OR 10 SUBSTANTIAL FIRST-COURSE SERVINGS

1 pork shoulder—5 pounds whole, 3 pounds trimmed
    boneless meat
½ pound bacon, preferably slab, rind removed
2 medium-size onions, finely chopped
5 garlic cloves, peeled

2 cups dry white wine

2 quarts pork, chicken, or beef broth or water

I large bouquet garni

I head of cabbage, preferably Savoy

I pound thick raw sausage, such as *saucisse à l'ail, cotechino,* or kielbasa

thick slices of country French bread, toasted

2 garlic cloves, peeled

TRIM off and discard the rind and any large pieces of fat from the pork shoulder. Cut the meat away from the bone. Save the bone. Cut the shoulder meat into I-inch cubes.

IF you're using slab bacon, cut it into I- by ¼-inch strips. If you're using presliced bacon, slice it across the grain into I-inch strips.

PUT the bacon in a 2-quart saucepan half-filled with cold water. Simmer the bacon for I0 minutes, drain it, and rinse under cold water (to eliminate its strong smoky flavor). Cook the bacon in a 6-quart pot over medium heat. When it just begins to turn crisp, take it out with a slotted spoon and reserve.

TURN the heat to high and brown the pieces of pork in the bacon fat. Don't add all the pieces at once, or they won't brown properly. Remove the pork with a slotted spoon and add the onion and garlic. Stir over medium to high heat for about I0 minutes, until the onions have softened slightly.

POUR the wine into the pot and boil it down for about 5 minutes to evaporate the alcohol. Put the pork back in the pot—including any juices that have run out—and pour in the broth. Add the bouquet garni, reserved bacon, and reserved bone from the pork shoulder.

BRING the broth to a very slow simmer, cover the pot, and cook on top of the stove or in a 275°F oven for about I½ hours. Check the pork every 30 minutes. If the liquid is nearly boiling, turn down the heat.

WHILE the pork is cooking, prepare the cabbage. Peel off and discard the outermost leaves and cut the cabbage into quarters through the core. Shred the cabbage by slicing the wedges as finely as possible with a chef's knife.

ADD the shredded cabbage to the pork, cover the pot, and simmer for 30 minutes more.

POKE 4 or 5 small holes in the sausage with a paring knife and add it to the pork. Simmer for 30 minutes to cook the sausage. The pork will have cooked for a total of 2½ hours.

WHEN the pork is done, discard the bone and the bouquet garni and skim off the fat. Let the sausage cool slightly and peel off the skin. Slice it into 1-inch chunks. Heat the pieces of sausage in the simmering broth. Season with salt and pepper.

RUB each slice of toast with the garlic cloves. Place a toast in the center of each of the soup bowls and ladle the soup over.

SUGGESTIONS AND VARIATIONS | You can make this soup even more substantial by adding vegetables such as beans, potatoes, carrots, or turnips at appropriate times during the cooking.

Stuffed Cabbage Soup

Stuffed cabbage comes in many guises, including one of my favorite versions, in which individual balls of flavorful pork mixture are wrapped in cabbage leaves and then simmered in a rich broth. The mixture I call for here contains juniper berries, which give it a lovely flavor that is a little reminiscent of gin.

MAKES 8 SUBSTANTIAL FIRST-COURSE SERVINGS OR LIGHT MAIN-COURSE SERVINGS

1 small head (1½ pound) Savoy cabbage (you'll need 16 whole leaves)

salt (for cabbage water)

2 large garlic cloves

1 small bunch of parsley (preferably flat Italian variety)

10 juniper berries

2 slices stale white bread, crusts removed and soaked in ½ cup milk

1 pound coarsely ground pork shoulder

¼ pound sliced bacon (preferably ¼ inch thick) cut into ¼-inch dice

1 egg, lightly beaten

1 teaspoon fresh thyme leaves or ½ teaspoon dried

1 teaspoon salt (for the stuffing)

½ teaspoon freshly ground pepper (for the stuffing)

6 cups full-flavored beef, chicken, pork, or turkey broth

BRING about 4 quarts of water to a rapid boil in a large pot, with extra room for submerging the cabbage.

CAREFULLY pull away the outer leaves from the cabbage, discarding the dark green outer ones. Plunge the cabbage in a pot of boiling water for about 1 minute, rinse with cold water, peel off as many leaves as you can, and keep repeating this process until you've removed all the leaves. Discard the core. Simmer the cabbage leaves in a large pot of boiling salted water for 5 minutes. If you plunged the cabbage into boiling water, you can use the same water—drain them in a colander and rinse them under cold running water. Cut any thick ribs or tough sections out of the leaves.

FINELY chop the garlic, parsley, and juniper berries. Crush the juniper berries first under the bottom of a pot or with the side of a cleaver. Work the soaked bread to a paste with your fingers and combine it with the juniper berry mixture, the ground pork, the diced bacon, the egg, the thyme, salt, and pepper. Work the mixture with your hands to evenly distribute all the ingredients but don't work it any longer than necessary or the mixture will be tough.

DEPENDING on their size, cut the cabbage leaves in halves or in thirds so you end up with 32 pieces, large enough to wrap the balls of stuffing. Divide the stuffing into 32 equal portions and roll up a ball of stuffing about the size of a small walnut and place it in each piece of leaf. Roll the leaves up around the stuffing.

ABOUT 15 minutes before serving, bring the broth to a gentle simmer and gently slide in the cabbage balls. Simmer the cabbage balls over low to medium heat for 10 minutes, with the pan partially covered (so the part of the cabbage that's not submerged gets cooked). Use a slotted spoon to place four of the cabbage balls in each of eight heated soup plates. Season the broth to taste with salt and pepper and ladle it into the soup plates.

Gascon Duck and Vegetable Soup

GARBURE

A *garbure* is a vegetable soup generously flavored with preserved duck or goose (*confit de canard* or *confit d'oie*) that, when well made, represents French country cooking at its best.

A *garbure* is a winter dish, best served late on a cold Sunday afternoon, preferably in the country—maybe after a day's skiing. If you don't want to spend the whole morning cooking, *garbure* can be made a day or two in advance (or even longer if it's frozen) and reheated. It's a complete meal, so you won't need to bother with much else except a green salad and perhaps a little fruit for dessert.

Garbure is one of those legendary dishes that French and American food fanatics like to argue about. It's unlikely that cooks in Gascony adhere rigidly to any one recipe; they probably adjust the ingredients according to what they have around. In any case, every time I make *garbure* it comes out differently—but it's always good. You will of course need a few essential ingredients to make *garbure*—cabbage, beans, and duck or goose confit (see Sources at the back of the book to order confit by mail). Most recipes also call for raw cured ham and salt pork. I'm not fond of salt pork, so I replace it with fresh pork shoulder or more confit.

MAKES 10 MAIN-COURSE SERVINGS

5 garlic cloves, peeled

2 pounds boneless pork shoulder, trimmed of fat and cut into ½-inch cubes (it's often easiest just to take the meat off 3 pounds shoulder pork chops)

¼ pound prosciutto, cut into ¼-inch cubes

1 medium-size onion, chopped

2 tablespoons duck or goose fat from the confit

1 cup dried white navy beans or cannellini, soaked for 3 hours in enough water to cover abundantly

1 bouquet garni, including 1 clove

2 quarts duck or chicken broth or water, or more as needed

1 small head of cabbage, preferably Savoy

1 turnip, peeled and cut into ¼-inch cubes

2 leeks, white part and 1 inch of green, washed and finely sliced

2 medium-size waxy potatoes, cut into ½-inch cubes

8 confit duck thighs or confit of 2 ducks, meat pulled away from the bone and left in large chunks

salt

pepper

COOK the garlic, pork, the prosciutto, and onion in the duck or goose fat in a 4-quart pot over medium heat until the onions turn translucent, about 10 minutes. Drain the beans and add them to the pot with the bouquet garni. Pour in enough broth to cover the ingredients by 4 inches. Bring to a simmer over medium heat and skim off any froth that floats to the surface. Cover the pot and simmer for about 2 hours, until the beans are tender. Stir gently every 30 minutes to be sure that nothing sticks to the bottom. If necessary, add more broth to keep everything covered.

PEEL away and discard the dark outer leaves from the cabbage. Cut the cabbage into quarters by cutting vertically through the core. Shred the cabbage by slicing each of the quarters as finely as possible.

WHEN the beans have softened thoroughly, add the shredded cabbage, turnip, leeks, and potatoes. Add more broth or water to cover—about 3 cups. Cover the pot and simmer for 15 minutes.

ADD the confit and simmer for 10 minutes more. Season with salt and pepper. You can serve the *garbure* directly in hot soup bowls or, if you have an earthenware pot, gently transfer the ingredients from the cooking pot into the earthenware pot, heat the whole thing in a 250°F oven for 15 minutes, and serve at the table.

Duck and Bean Soup

One evening I was experimenting with soups made with beans and confit. It started to get late, and I was expecting friends for dinner and didn't have time to wait for the confit to cook, so I came up with this shorter version. It captures all the flavor of the duck while using none of the fat. Although this soup involves several steps, the finished product looks very simple. But you'll be amazed by its taste.

Even though the soup contains surprisingly little fat, the beans make it quite filling, so it can be served as a light meal along with some good bread, maybe a little cheese, and a green salad. If you want to serve it as a first course in a more elaborate dinner, make sure not to follow it with something too rich.

This soup can be made 2 or 3 days in advance.

MAKES 8 GENEROUS SERVINGS

the duck broth:

I duck

I large onion, coarsely chopped

I large carrot, coarsely chopped

3 garlic cloves, unpeeled but cut in half

I bouquet garni

the beans:

>   2 cups dried cannellini, navy, or borlotti beans, soaked in
>   enough water to cover abundantly, for 3 hours
>
>   1 bouquet garni
>
>   1 medium-size onion, peeled
>
>   1 clove, stuck into the onion
>
>   3 garlic cloves, peeled
>
>   2 teaspoons salt
>
>   pepper
>
>   slices of French bread, lightly toasted

PREPARING THE BROTH AND THIGH MEAT Take the thighs and boneless breasts off the duck and set them aside (see box on page 498). Cut the wings off the duck and cut as much fat as you can off the remaining duck carcass. Discard the fat or save it for making confit. Break up the wings and carcass with a cleaver or a heavy knife.

HEAT the duck thighs, skin side down, in a 4-quart pot over medium heat for about 10 minutes, until they start to render fat. Add the broken up duck wings and carcass along with the onion, carrot, and the garlic. Brown the duck and vegetables over medium to high heat, stirring everything around with a wooden spoon, for another 10 minutes. Put in the bouquet garni and enough cold water to cover. Heat over medium heat until the liquid approaches a boil, then lower the heat to keep the liquid at a slow simmer. Meanwhile, start to prepare the beans.

WITH a ladle, skim off any froth or fat that floats to the top of the broth. After the broth has simmered for 45 minutes, reach in with a slotted spoon and take out the 2 duck thighs. When the thighs have cooled, peel off and discard their skin. Pull the meat away from the bone and cut it into ½-inch dice. Continue simmering the broth for an hour more. Strain it and reserve.

PREPARING THE BEANS Drain the beans and put them in a 4-quart pot with the bouquet garni, vegetables, and enough water to cover by about 2 inches. Bring to a slow simmer and skim off any froth that floats to the surface. After about 30 minutes, stir in the salt. Cover the pot and continue cooking for about 1½ hours, until the beans have softened thoroughly. Add water as necessary to keep the beans barely submerged in liquid. When the beans have cooked, take out and discard the bouquet garni.

COMBINE half of the cooked beans and the onion (pull out the clove) with a cup of the duck broth in a blender. Process for 1 minute.

COMBINE the bean puree and the remaining whole beans in a 4-quart pot.

PREPARING THE DUCK MEAT Place the duck breasts, skin side down, in a skillet or sauté pan. (You don't need any fat or oil; the breasts render their own.) Cook them for about 15 minutes over medium heat until the skin starts to turn brown and crisp. Turn the breasts over and cook them for 10 minutes more. Take out the breasts—leave the rendered fat in the pan—and peel off and discard their skin. Cut the breast meat into ½-inch dice.

PUT the cubed thigh and breast meat into the sauté pan with the fat and stir over medium heat until they brown slightly, about 5 minutes. Remove the cubes with a slotted spoon and discard the rendered fat in the pan. Add a cup of duck broth, bring to a simmer, and scrape up all the coagulated juices in the bottom of the pan.

FINISHING THE SOUP Bring the bean mixture to a simmer and add the duck meat, the duck broth in the pan used for browning the duck, and more duck broth to thin the soup to the consistency you like. (If there isn't enough broth, you may need to add some water.)

BRING the soup to a simmer, adjust the salt, season with pepper, and serve with the toast.

SUGGESTIONS AND VARIATIONS | If you're lucky enough to find fresh beans, be sure to use them. Fresh borlotti beans and sometimes fava beans can be found in Italian markets—but remember, if you're using fava beans, they have to be peeled twice. Use 2½ times the volume of fresh beans (after peeling) as you would dried. There is no need for preliminary soaking. Because fresh beans cook relatively quickly, simmer the water with the vegetables and the bouquet garni for about 20 minutes before you add the beans. The beans are done when they're soft, anywhere from 10 to 30 minutes.

Lamb and Bean Soup

This soup is an example of an apparently rich and very tasty soup that uses relatively little fat while somehow capturing all the flavor of lamb.

The best cut of lamb for this soup—it also happens to be very inexpensive—is the shank. The shanks don't have a lot of meat on them, but they provide natural gelatin that gives the soup a rich flavor and a creamy texture.

This soup can be made entirely in advance. Be sure to prepare the beans at the same time you're braising the lamb shanks.

MAKES 6 GENEROUS SERVINGS

the lamb shanks:

4 lamb shanks, cut in half crosswise

salt

pepper

3 tablespoons olive oil or duck fat

20 garlic cloves, unpeeled

1½ quarts chicken or beef broth or water

the beans:

2 cups dried cannellini, navy, or flageolet beans, soaked for
3 hours in enough cold water to cover abundantly

1 large bouquet garni

1 medium-size onion, peeled

1 clove, stuck into the onion

1 medium-size carrot

2 teaspoons salt

BRAISING THE LAMB SHANKS Trim any excess fat off the lamb shanks. Season them with salt and pepper and brown them in the olive oil in a heavy-bottomed pan with a tight-fitting lid over high heat. Add the garlic cloves to the shanks while they are browning.

WHEN the shanks are well browned, add 1 cup of the broth to the pan. Bring to a rapid boil and cook down until all the liquid evaporates and lightly browns on the bottom of the pan. (The shanks will release liquid, which then caramelizes on the bottom of the pan, enhancing their flavor.) Add the rest of the broth, cover the pan, and cook for 2 hours over very low heat (the liquid mustn't boil) or in a 300°F oven.

WHEN the shanks are done, put them on a plate to cool and strain the cooking liquid and garlic cloves into a 2-quart saucepan. Press on the garlic cloves to force the pulp through the strainer. Bring the cooking liquid to a slow simmer and skim off any fat that floats to the surface.

PULL the meat off the lamb shanks and pull it apart into shreds with your fingers.

PREPARING THE BEANS Drain the beans and put them in a 4-quart pot with the bouquet garni, the onion stuck with the clove, the carrot, and enough water to cover by 2 inches. Bring them to a slow simmer, cover the pot, and cook for about 2 hours, until the beans are completely soft. If necessary, add water from time to time to keep the beans barely covered. Add the salt 30 minutes into the cooking.

TAKE the carrot and bouquet garni out of the beans and discard them. Take the clove out of the onion. Combine the onion and about half of the beans in a blender. Pour in a cup of the lamb/garlic cooking liquid and puree the mixture until smooth. Combine the puree with the rest of the beans.

FINISHING THE SOUP Combine the bean puree, the rest of the lamb/garlic liquid, and the shank meat. Bring the soup to a slow simmer and thin it if necessary with broth or water. Season with salt and pepper.

SUGGESTIONS AND VARIATIONS | If you have trouble finding lamb shanks, substitute 2 pounds lamb stew meat, lamb shoulder, or leg of lamb cut into 1-inch chunks. This soup is also excellent made with venison.

Spanish Bean Soup

COCIDO

Spanish cooks make an amazing variety of hearty bean and sausage soups. The first recipe I read for one of these elaborate Spanish soups was in a French cookbook from the 17th century that described dishes served at the court of Louis XIV. The dish, an *oille*, was an elaborate mixture of simmered meats and vegetables. According to Alexandre Dumas's *Encyclopedia of Cuisine*, written in 1873, the now forgotten *oille* was a close relative to the Spanish *olla podrida*, a dish all but forgotten except in some obscure Castilian villages.

According to Penelope Casas in her book *The Foods and Wines of Spain*, olla podrida predated the now almost universal *cocido*. *Cocido* was originally a Sephardic Jewish dish that contained no pork, but modern versions of the dish are almost all based on pork, especially sausages, and chick-peas. Unfortunately the dish is only as good as the products that go into it, and there are few if any places that have pork products as good as Spain's. Every region of Spain has its own *cocido* variations; all use local vegetables and sausages, while others include ham hocks and still others miniature meatballs called pelotas. The basic techniques for making *cocido* are the same all over Spain. An assortment of meats is poached gently for several hours and combined with chick-peas, which are cooked separately in some of the meat broth. The *cocido* is then served in two courses: a bowl of soup, usually with some thin noodles added; and a groaning platter of sliced meats, cooked cabbage, chick-peas, and the vegetables cooked along with the meat. I prefer to serve the *cocido* in one course—broth and all—arranged in wide bowls. Most *cocidos* include chicken, but I always find that the chicken gets upstaged when it's served with all the other meats.

When preparing *cocido*, select the sausages carefully. Most recipes call for *chorizo* and *morcilla* or *botifarra*. *Morcilla* is Spanish blood sausage similar to the French *boudin noir*. If you live near a Spanish market, you'll probably be able to track some down but don't get hung up trying to find the same kind of sausages used in Spain. Sausage made in America is never going to taste like genuine Spanish sausage anyway. (Importation of genuine Spanish sausage into the United States is still not allowed.) Your best bet is just to use the best sausage you have available: kielbasa, *saucisson à l'ail*, *cotechino*, or Italian sausage (without fennel seeds) will all work.

This *cocido* is best and easiest to make over 2 days.

MAKES 12 MAIN-COURSE SERVINGS

2 pounds beef brisket

1 pound prosciutto end or 2½-pound ham hocks

2 pounds veal shoulder, tied with string

1 calf's or pig's foot, split

1 bouquet garni

5 leeks, including 1 inch of the green, cut in half
    lengthwise, well rinsed, tied in a bundle with string

4 carrots, cut into 1-inch lengths

2 turnips, peeled and cut into wedges

1 head of Savoy cabbage, quartered

1½ cups dried chick-peas, soaked for 3 hours or overnight
    in enough cold water to cover abundantly

1 pound sausage such as *chorizo, saucisson à l'ail, cotechino,*
    kielbasa, *botifarra,* or Italian sausage (without fennel)

1 pound blood sausage, *morcilla* or *boudin noir*

THE FIRST DAY Put all the meats except the sausages in a 6-quart pot.

ADD enough water to cover the meats by 2 inches and bring to a boil. Turn down the heat and simmer gently for 1 hour. Add water from time to time if needed to make up for evaporation. Skim off any fat or froth that floats to the surface. Add the bouquet garni and the vegetables, except the chick-peas, and simmer for 45 minutes more. Add more water if necessary to keep everything immersed. Take the pot off the heat, let cool, and refrigerate overnight.

THE SECOND DAY Skim off any fat that has congealed on top of the meat pot.

DRAIN the chick-peas, put them in a 4-quart pot, and add enough water to cover them by 2 inches. Bring the chick-peas to a boil, cover the pot, and simmer the peas until soft, about 1 hour. If necessary, add water from time to time to keep the chick-peas covered.

ABOUT 45 minutes before the chick-peas are done, poke three tiny holes in each of the sausages with a paring knife to prevent them from tearing open during cooking. Add the sausages to the pot with the meats and vegetables and bring the whole thing to a simmer. Simmer gently for 30 minutes to cook the sausages.

SERVING Slice the beef, veal, prosciutto end, sausages, and cabbage. Place a small ladleful of beans in each wide bowl, arrange the vegetables and sliced meats over the beans, and ladle the broth over all.

SUGGESTIONS AND VARIATIONS | If you like tripe, you might want to simmer it with beans and vegetables as in Galicia. (See the recipe on page 544 for preparing tripe and then cook the tripe along with a prosciutto end, beans and vegetables.)

Spanish Bean Soup with Beef and Kale

CALDO GALLEGO

Once you get into the habit of making bean soups, you'll find it easy to switch from one to the other, adding ingredients as you go, until you develop your own favorite soups and a personal style. *Caldo gallego* is a justifiably well-known dish, and although much of its greatness comes from using genuine serrano ham and the freshest vegetables, I've had good luck making it in the United States with slab bacon and a prosciutto end.

MAKES 6 MAIN-COURSE SERVINGS

¼ pound bacon, preferably slab, rind removed, cut into 1-
    by ¼-inch-strips
I cup cannellini or Great Northern beans, soaked for 3
    hours or overnight in enough cold water to cover
    abundantly
I prosciutto end (3¼ to I pound)
3¼ pound beef chuck or brisket
I medium-size onion, peeled, chopped
I bouquet garni
2 quarts beef or chicken broth or water, or more as needed
2 teaspoons salt
3 medium-size waxy potatoes, peeled and cut into
    I-inch-thick slices
2 medium-size turnips, peeled, cut into 6 wedges each
2 pounds Swiss chard, stems removed
pepper
slices of crusty bread or toast

PLACE the bacon in a 2-quart pot half-filled with cold water. Simmer the bacon for 10 minutes to eliminate some of its smoky taste. Drain and reserve the bacon.

IN a 6-quart pot, combine the bacon, the drained beans, the prosciutto end, beef, onion, bouquet garni, and broth. The broth should cover the solid ingredients by at least 3 inches. Bring to a slow simmer over medium heat and use a ladle to skim off any froth or scum that floats to the top.

COVER the pot and simmer slowly for 30 minutes. Add the salt and simmer for about 1½ hours more, until the beans are almost tender. Add more broth or water as needed to keep the solids covered by at least 3 inches. Add the potatoes and turnips, simmer for 15 minutes more, and then add the Swiss chard. Simmer for 15 minutes more, until all the vegetables are soft. Season to taste with salt and pepper.

SERVE in deep, wide bowls.

SUGGESTIONS AND VARIATIONS | Penelope Casas describes a bean soup from Valencia that is almost like a *caldo gallego* except that it contains saffron, rice, and best of all, tiny snails.

Russian-Style Cabbage Soup

SHCHI

Most of what I've learned about Russian cooking come from the writings of 19th-century French chefs who cooked for the czar. At that time the Russians and French went through a period of mutual admiration; traditional Russian dishes were refined by French cooks and sometimes even exported back to France. Needless to say, my reading taught me little of how the Russian people ate or eat day to day.

I've since been able to read about Russian cooking from more firsthand (and modern) sources. Anya von Bremzen and John Welchman's *Please to the Table* is a particularly interesting book on Russian cooking. Their recipe for *shchi* includes dried porcini—an excellent idea.

Except for an occasional sprig of dill tied into the bouquet garni or a dollop of sour cream added just before serving, most recipes for *shchi* are indistinguishable from a French country *potée* of cooked cabbage, vegetables, and beef or pork. But the version given here contains not only fresh cabbage but sauerkraut, which gives the soup a satisfying tang.

I'm lucky to live near a Russian market where they dish homemade sauerkraut out of big earthenware crocks. If you don't have this luxury, buy sauerkraut in jars or in sealed plastic bags (in the refrigerator section), but avoid canned versions, which usually have a metallic taste.

This soup can be made entirely in advance.

MAKES 8 SERVINGS

the beef broth:

    4 pounds beef shank, cut into 2-inch-thick rounds,
        or 4 pounds beef brisket

    1 large onion, cut in half

    2 carrots

    1 celery rib

    1 bouquet garni

the soup:

    12 dried porcini, soaked in 1 cup water for 1 hour

    4 tablespoons unsalted butter

    1 large onion, finely chopped

    1 turnip, peeled and cut into ½-inch dice

3 medium-size carrots, cut in half lengthwise and chopped

3 garlic cloves, peeled

1 small head of cabbage, preferably Savoy

2 cups sauerkraut, 1 pound, rinsed

salt

pepper

sour cream

chopped fresh dill

PREPARING THE BROTH Combine the beef, vegetables, and bouquet garni in a 4-quart pot. Pour over enough cold water to cover by about 1 inch. Bring the pot to a slow simmer. Use a ladle to skim off any froth and fat that floats to the surface. Simmer for 2 to 3 hours, until the meat is completely tender, so that a knife inserted into the meat offers no resistance. Strain and reserve the cooked meat and broth. Discard the vegetables and the bouquet garni. Cut the cooked meat into 1-inch cubes. If you used shanks, discard the bones.

PREPARING THE SOUP Drain the mushrooms and reserve their soaking liquid. If they seem gritty or dirty, rinse them quickly under cold water. Chop the mushrooms coarsely. If the soaking water contains grit or sand, pour it carefully into another container, leaving the grit behind, or strain it through a fine-mesh strainer.

HEAT the butter in a 4-quart pot over medium heat. Add all the mushrooms and all the vegetables except the cabbage and sauerkraut and stir the mixture until the onions start to turn translucent, after about 10 minutes. Add the strained beef broth and the mushroom-soaking liquid to the vegetables and bring to a simmer.

SHRED the cabbage by first cutting it into quarters vertically through the core, trimming the white core from the center of each quarter, and then finely slicing the quarters. You should end up with about 4 cups chopped cabbage. Add the cabbage to the soup, simmer gently for 10 minutes, and add the sauerkraut and cubes of meat. Simmer for 15 minutes more. Season with salt and pepper.

DOLLOP each bowl with sour cream and sprinkle with fresh dill or pass the sour cream and dill at the table.

SUGGESTIONS AND VARIATIONS | As in a French *potée* the meats and vegetables for *shchi* can be varied almost endlessly. I sometimes substitute pork shoulder for the beef or if I'm in a hurry I simmer the cabbage, sauerkraut, vegetables, and bouquet garni in an already-made broth and just sauté pork chops to add to the soup as I serve it. I also like to fill this soup out with sausages—kielbasa, French garlic sausages, *cotechino*—added along with the cabbage. If I'm being fancy, I sauté duck thighs (I often have some left over in the freezer from other duck dishes) and add them to the soup at the same time as the cabbage.

Borscht

THERE ARE DOZENS OF RECIPES FOR BORSCHT—FROM SIMPLE VEGETABLE SOUPS WITH a couple of chopped beets thrown in to complicated whole-meal affairs made with pork, beef, sausages, and even ducks. More traditional recipes also call for a few tricky ingredients. Some of these recipes call for fermenting the beets a couple of days in advance, while others call for *kvass,* a kind of rye beer that means a trip to a Polish or Russian market or making it yourself. In Polish markets *kvass* is called *zur naturalny.*

Two recipes are given here, a simple peasant version that you can prepare in half an hour and cook for an hour more and a grandiose version that you should start thinking about 3 or 4 days in advance.

Simple Version of Borscht

MAKES 6 SERVINGS

3 tablespoons unsalted butter

2 medium-size onions, finely chopped

4 leeks, white part only, finely chopped

I celery rib, cut into ¼-inch dice

I medium-size turnip, cut into ¼-inch dice

2 garlic cloves, finely chopped

I pound fresh trimmed or 3¼-pound drained canned beets, cut into ¼-inch dice, 2 cups

5 cups beef broth

6 tablespoons white wine vinegar or to taste

salt

pepper

sour cream or crème fraîche

chopped fresh dill (optional)

slices of black bread

MELT the butter in a 4-quart pot over medium heat. Add the vegetables and cook for 15 to 20 minutes, until the vegetables soften. (If you're using canned beets, add them after the other vegetables have softened.)

ADD the beef broth and bring the soup to a simmer. Simmer slowly for 10 minutes. Reach in with a spoon and sample a few of the vegetables to make sure they have softened thoroughly.

SPRINKLE in the wine vinegar to taste. Season with salt and pepper.

SERVE in hot bowls. Pass the sour cream, chopped dill, and sliced black bread at the table.

SUGGESTIONS AND VARIATIONS | You can turn this simple borscht into a puree or a simple cream soup by putting it in a blender and straining it—and, if you like, finishing it with a cup of heavy cream. In the summer, cold pureed *borscht* makes a delightful cold soup. (See also the cream of beet soup on page 159.)

Grand Version of Borscht

Some versions of borscht, such as the preceding recipe, are prepared with a simple beef broth, while other versions contain chunks of pork *and* beef. For this recipe, use any combination of the meats suggested. Just make sure that you have between 6 and 8 pounds total.

This soup takes a long time to prepare, so you may want to make it in stages. The meats can be simmered the day before and kept in the refrigerator with their broth. If you're using fresh beets, they can also be prepared the day before.

MAKES 12 MAIN-COURSE SERVINGS

the meat:

2 1-pound smoked ham hocks

3 pounds beef brisket or chuck, 1 or 2 large chunks

3 pounds pork shoulder, trimmed of rind and excess fat, in 2 or 3 large chunks

2½ quarts beef broth or water

1 bouquet garni, including 3 marjoram sprigs if available

the vegetables:

1½ pounds fresh or 2 10-ounce cans whole beets, drained

1 small head of cabbage, preferably Savoy

1 large onion, finely chopped

4 leeks, white part only, finely chopped

1 cup white wine vinegar

salt

pepper

garnishes:

sour cream

finely chopped fresh dill

PREPARING THE MEATS Place the meats in an 8-quart pot and cover them by about 2 inches with the beef broth. Add the bouquet garni and set the pot over high heat. As soon as it approaches a boil, turn down the heat and cover the pot. Keep at a slow simmer for 3 hours. Every 30 minutes or so, with a ladle, skim off any froth or fat that floats to the surface.

STRAIN the soup and reserve the broth. Take the meat off the ham hocks and discard any rind, gristle, or bone. Break the meat from the ham hocks into ½-inch chunks. Slice the beef and cut the pork into ½-inch chunks. Put the meats back in the broth.

PREPARING THE BEETS Preferably the day before serving, if you're using canned beets, just rinse them, slice them, and cut them into strips 1 to 1½ inches long and ¼ inch on each side.

IF you're using fresh beets, which will give the soup a deeper flavor, preheat the oven to 375°F, wrap the beets in aluminum foil, and roast them for about an hour, until they can be pierced easily with a fork. Let them cool, peel them, and cut them into strips as for canned beets.

PREPARING THE CABBAGE Peel off and discard the tough outer cabbage leaves. Cut the cabbage vertically into quarters and cut away the strip of core running along the side of each quarter. Slice the quarters as thinly as you can, shredding the cabbage.

FINISHING AND PRESENTING THE SOUP Add the chopped onion, leeks, cooked beets, and cabbage to the soup and simmer gently for 25 minutes. Stir in the wine vinegar and season to taste with salt and pepper.

LADLE the soup into hot bowls. Put a small dollop of sour cream on each bowl and sprinkle with the chopped dill.

SUGGESTIONS AND VARIATIONS | There are 19th-century descriptions and recipes for borscht that call for princely ingredients and portions. If you love the flavors of borscht—the special taste of rich broth simmered with beets and cabbage—it's easy enough to make a feastlike version by adding different meats.

SOME recipes call for sausages such as kielbasa, *saucisse à l'ail, cotechino,* or *chipolata;* simmer the sausage in the broth at the last minute, peeled, sliced, and served atop the soup with the other meats.

YOU can also make an especially luxurious version by serving slices of well-roasted duck or goose sliced at the last minute and served with the other meats.

Kentucky Burgoo

A burgoo contains a variety of meats simmered together until the meats start to fall off the bone. Vegetables are then added and the whole thing simmered again until the vegetables soften. Although burgoo is a solidly American invention, it's made using the same techniques as European hearty soups and *potées*. Native ingredients such as corn, lima beans, okra, and Tabasco sauce give it an unmistakable American character.

Most recipes for burgoo call for several kinds of meats and are meant for a large crowd. At the risk of offending anyone used to more authentic versions, I've simplified this recipe slightly so you can make it for a small crowd of 12. If the idea of cooking rabbit puts you off, use 2 chickens instead.

MAKES 12 MAIN-COURSE SERVINGS

2 4-pound rabbits

3 pounds short ribs, cut into 2-inch lengths, or 3 pounds beef brisket

3 pounds 2-inch-thick veal shanks

1 bouquet garni

3 quarts chicken or beef broth or water or enough to cover

3 medium-size onions, chopped

3 waxy potatoes, peeled, and cut into ½-inch dice

3 carrots, cut into ¼-inch dice

2 red bell peppers, seeded and cut into thin strips

1 cup peeled fresh lima beans, or 1 10-ounce package frozen

1 cup fresh corn kernels, from 2 large ears, or 1 10-ounce package frozen

2 celery ribs, chopped into ¼-inch dice

7 medium-size tomatoes, peeled, seeded, and chopped or 1 quart drained and seeded canned tomatoes

4 jalapeño chilies, seeded and finely chopped

salt

pepper

Tabasco sauce to taste

¼ cup finely chopped parsley leaves

corn bread

Worcestershire sauce

CUT each rabbit into 8 pieces by first cutting the thighs and forelegs away from the body. Divide the rest of the body in half by cutting crosswise between the second and third ribs.

COMBINE the rabbit, the rest of the meats, and the bouquet garni in a 12-quart pot. Add the broth, bring to a simmer, and continue simmering for about 2½ hours, skimming off any fat or froth, until all the meat is very tender and falling off the bone. Add more liquid as needed to keep the meats covered.

TAKE the meats out of the broth and separate the meat from the bones. Discard the bones and put the meat back in the broth.

ADD the vegetables and simmer until soft, about 30 minutes.

SEASON with salt, pepper, and Tabasco. Add the parsley, simmer for 1 minute more, and serve, passing corn bread and Worcestershire at the table.

Chicken

EVEN THOUGH I EAT IT AT LEAST ONCE A WEEK, I NEVER GET TIRED OF CHICKEN. AND unlike so many of my favorite foods, there's nothing exotic or extravagant about it. Chicken is so versatile that once you've mastered a few of its basic principles you'll be able to improvise literally dozens of soups. Chicken is also inexpensive. Even the so-called free-range chickens, which cost about twice as much as mass-produced varieties, are inexpensive when compared with other meats.

Buying Chicken

Several kinds of chicken are available in supermarkets and butcher shops throughout the United States. The most common are broilers or small roasters, which weigh from 3 to 4 pounds, are good, inexpensive, and all-purpose birds for making soups. The best chickens for making soup—or anything for that matter—are free-range chickens. The difference in flavor and texture between a free-range chicken and a supermarket chicken is striking.

Stewing hens are good for making broth but not much else. There was a day when an old hen provided passable flesh after a few hours of cooking, but the hens available now are specially bred for egg laying, and their meat is always tough and dry.

Techniques for Making Chicken Soup

Chicken soups can be approached in one of three ways. The most direct method is to poach a whole chicken in broth or water with some chopped-up vegetables such as onions, carrots, turnips, garlic, or leeks thrown in for flavor. When the chicken is done, you can then cut off the meat, slice it or cut it into cubes, and serve it in its own broth. You can also use the broth as a base for another soup and use the poached chicken for making chicken salad or other cold chicken dishes.

A second method for cooking chicken, more popular with Asian cooks, is to take the meat off the raw chicken and make a broth with the leftover bones. The chicken meat is then cut into strips or dice, usually marinated, and then combined with the simmering broth and other flavorful ingredients. Sometimes the chicken strips or cubes are stir-fried before the broth is added.

A third method for making chicken soup is to quarter the chicken (see box, page 472), simmer it in water or some flavorful liquid until it has completely cooked, and then take the chicken off the bones. Although this is similar to the first method, it requires less liquid and therefore produces a fuller-flavored soup. Almost any recipe in the Vegetable Soups can be converted to some variation of chicken soup by simply simmering a cut-up chicken in the soup, taking the meat off the bones, and then adding both the cut-up chicken meat and the cooking liquid to the soup.

Here are outlines of the three basic methods for making chicken soups.

USING A WHOLE CHICKEN

1. *Truss the chicken.* You may also stuff the chicken at this point.

2. *Place the chicken* in as close-fitting a pot as possible so you'll need a minimum of water or broth.

3. *Add chopped aromatic vegetables and herbs* (herbs tied into a bouquet garni) to the pot with the chicken.

4. *Pour enough water or broth* into the pot to completely cover the chicken or just enough water or broth to come halfway up the sides of the chicken and then turn the chicken over halfway into the cooking so that any part that was not in the liquid is submerged.

5. *Bring the water or broth* to a gentle simmer. Partially cover the pot to prevent too much of the poaching liquid from evaporating.

6. *Simmer for about an hour,* until the chicken is done—clear juices will run out of the thigh when poked with a fork or skewer. If the juices are pink, cook the chicken for 10 minutes more and check again.

7. *Remove the chicken.* Skim and strain the broth. Serve the carved chicken in wide bowls surrounded with the vegetables and broth. If you wish, you can cook down (reduce) the broth to concentrate its flavor.

USING RAW CHICKEN (ASIAN METHOD)

1. *Remove the chicken flesh from the bones.* The easiest way to do this is to cut off the wings and thighs and then cut down along each side of the breastbone and remove the breast meat. Cut the bones out of the thighs. Discard the skin, prepare a broth with the bones and the wings (page 62), and cut the chicken meat into cubes or 1-inch-long strips, depending on the recipe.

2. *Marinate the chicken (optional).* Most Asian cooks marinate chicken and other meats with flavorful ingredients for 1 or 2 hours. The marinade ingredients are then added to the soup along with the chicken. The choice of marinade ingredients depends on the type of cuisine, but you're likely to encounter ginger, garlic, scallions, soy sauce, fish sauce, hot peppers, rice wine, mirin, sake, dark sesame oil, and many others.

3. *Stir-fry the chicken pieces (optional).* Most Asian cooks stir-fry in smoking hot oil in a wok, but a heavy iron skillet works almost as well. Heat a tablespoon of peanut oil in a

When a chicken is "quartered," it is actually cut up into more than four pieces. In addition to the two half-breasts and two thighs with the drumsticks attached, there is also the back and the two wings. Thus the chicken is really cut into seven pieces instead of four. The back contains so little meat that it's best used for making broth or cut in half or thirds and added to the sauté pan with the rest of the chicken to keep the bottom of the pan covered (to prevent it from burning in those areas left uncovered) or to augment the flavor of an eventual soup. The wings, while meatier, can be used in the same way. In most soup recipes calling for quartered chicken, I recommend removing the meat from the bone after the chicken has cooked to make the soup easier to eat. However, in some cases, you may want to leave the chicken on the bone and cut the quartered chicken into smaller pieces to make sure every serving of soup has a piece of chicken in it. You can convert four pieces into six simply by cutting the drumsticks away from the rest of the thighs and you can cut the half-breasts in half again so that you end up with eight pieces in addition to the wings and back.

To quarter a chicken, pull any large chunks of fat out of the inside of the chicken (I discard them but they can be rendered and used as cooking fat). Turn the chicken breastside down and pull away a wing. Cut the wing off where it joins the body. Repeat with the second wing. Fold the wing tips under the thickest part of the wing, forming a kind of triangle, so the wings hold their shape during cooking. Turn the chicken over and pull one of the thighs forward. Cut into the loose skin between the thigh and breast, cutting toward the thigh (so enough skin is left to cover the breast) and then slide the knife down to the joint where the thigh joins the back. Fold the thigh back away from the chicken and snap the ball out of the joint, dislocating the thigh. Slide the knife—I use a medium chef's knife—along the back, following its contours so you leave any meat attached to the thigh instead of the back, and detach the thigh from the back. Repeat with the second thigh. Cut the back away from the double breast by holding the chicken on end so the larger opening is facing upward. With a large chef's knife, cut through the rib cage all the way down to the bottom and open up the chicken, separating the back from the breast. Cut the back away from the double breast. Cut the double breast in half by resting it, skin side down, on a cutting board and forcing a knife into the bone in the middle of the two halves. Pull the knife toward you while pressing down. Turn the breast around and repeat in the other direction to separate the two halves. You should now have two thighs (with drumsticks), the back, two wings, and two half-breasts.

wok or skillet until it just starts to smoke. Add the chicken pieces and stir them quickly over high heat for about 3 minutes. Add the marinade ingredients and stir for 1 minute more. Vegetables, chopped or cut into thin strips (julienne), can also be added at this stage.

4. *Add liquids.* Usually the best and most obvious liquid to use is the broth you made from the chicken bones, but some recipes use *dashi* or water. Pour the liquid over the chicken and bring it to a simmer. If the skillet isn't large enough to hold all the ingredients, pour everything into a larger pot.

5. *Add quick-cooking ingredients.* Some ingredients, such as tofu, bamboo shoots, and finely chopped herbs and vegetables, need only to be heated through for a few minutes. These are added to the soup a minute or two before serving.

USING A QUARTERED CHICKEN (SEE BOX, PAGE 472)

1. *Quarter the chicken* (1 chicken makes from 4 to 8 bowls of soup). Season with salt and pepper.

2. *Sear the chicken in a sauté pan in unsalted butter or oil.* Usually chicken develops a better flavor when it is well browned, but if you want a very pale soup, such as the chicken soup with apples and leeks on page 476, the chicken should be cooked gently in the fat so that it doesn't brown. Cook the chicken for about 8 minutes with the skin side down, then turn the chicken pieces over and cook them for 5 minutes on the other side. You can also just bake the chicken pieces in a 350°F oven for 25 minutes.

3. *Take the chicken out of the pan and add chopped aromatic vegetables such as chopped onions, leeks, carrots, or turnips.* Cook the vegetables for 5 or 10 minutes in the butter or oil left in the pan or, if the butter has burned, replace it with fresh. Green vegetables should be added at a later stage (see Step 5). If they are added too soon, they will turn gray.

4. *Put the chicken pieces back in the pan with the vegetables and add enough liquid—such as broth, water, cider, or wine—to cover completely.* Simmer the chicken for 15 minutes. Take the chicken parts out of the pan and pull the chicken meat off the bones. Discard the skin and cut the meat into bite-size pieces. Simmer the broth for about 10 minutes with the pan moved to one side of the heat source. Skim off any fat or froth that floats to the surface.

5. *Add green vegetables or precooked vegetables.* Green vegetables should be added just long enough before serving to cook them through. Some green vegetables, such as spinach or sorrel leaves, will cook in about 30 seconds, whereas tougher green vegetables such as string beans may need 5 to 10 minutes.

6. *Return the chicken cubes to the soup.* Simmer them for a minute or two, just long enough to heat them through.

7. *Flavor, enrich, or thicken the soup with vegetable purees (optional).* At this point the soup can be finished with cream, finely chopped herbs, garlic mayonnaise *(aïoli)*, and, of course, salt and pepper. Vegetable purees such as leftover mashed potatoes or spinach puree can also be whisked into the soup at this stage.

INGREDIENTS FOR SOUP MADE WITH A WHOLE POACHED CHICKEN (See recipe for poached hen with vegetables, page 429)

Liquids for Poaching Chicken:
broth, water, cider

Aromatic Vegetables Simmered with Chicken:
    carrots (cut into 2-inch lengths or sliced)
    pearl or small onions (peeled)
    turnips (peeled and left whole or cut into wedges)
    leeks (greens removed, tied with string)
    garlic (whole peeled or unpeeled cloves)
    tomatoes (chopped, peeled, seeded)

Flavorful Ingredients Simmered with Chicken:
    bouquet garni (can contain any combination of herbs)
    cloves (stuck into one of the onions)

Flavorful Finishes and Thickeners for Broth:
    finely chopped herbs (parsley, chervil, tarragon, basil, etc.)
    aïoli (page 349)
    rouille (page 350)
    picada (page 348)
    cream
    butter
    pureed vegetables such as mashed potatoes, pureed spinach, and root vegetable purees
    curry
    saffron

POSSIBLE INGREDIENTS FOR CHICKEN SOUP USING A RAW CHICKEN CUBED OR CUT INTO STRIPS (ASIAN METHOD):

    1 chicken (meat removed, cut into ½-inch cubes or 1- by ¼-inch strips), skin discarded, broth prepared with bones (optional)

Marinade Ingredients:
    ginger, garlic, soy sauce, fish sauce, sesame oil, sake, rice wine, kiwi fruit (as a tenderizer), hot peppers, etc.

Oil for Stir-Frying:
    peanut or vegetable

Flavorings Added Just Before or at the Same Time as the Liquids:
    the marinade, fish sauce, soy sauce, Thai curry pastes, Indonesian *bumbu* (Indonesian spice mixture)

Liquids:
    broth (probably the broth made from the chicken bones), *dashi*, water

Quick-Cooking Ingredients:
    spinach, watercress, mushrooms, tofu, bamboo shoots, chopped herbs such as cilantro, mint, and basil

Starchy Fillers:
   rice, noodles, dumplings, wontons

SOME POSSIBLE INGREDIENTS FOR CHICKEN SOUP USING A QUARTERED
CHICKEN (SEE BOX, PAGE 472):
   1 chicken (quartered)
   salt and pepper

Fat for Browning:
   unsalted butter
   olive oil
   vegetable oil
   rendered fat such as duck, goose, chicken, or lard

Slow-Cooking Vegetables:
   leeks (chopped or cut into fine julienne)
   onions (chopped or thinly sliced)
   pearl onions (peeled)
   carrots (sliced or cut into cubes)
   garlic (peeled and chopped, or peeled and left whole)
   mushrooms (cultivated or wild, left whole, sliced or
      quartered
   turnips (peeled, cut into cubes)
   potatoes (peeled, cut into cubes)

Liquids:
   water
   broth
   white wine
   red wine
   sherry, port, or other fortified wines
   brandy
   (a bouquet garni can be added at this
      point)

Green Vegetables and Precooked Vegetables:
   spinach (whole or shredded leaves)
   sorrel (whole or shredded leaves)
   green beans (whole or sliced)
   broccoli (cut into florets, cooked first for
      2 minutes in boiling salted water)
   asparagus tips
   beans (cooked separately)

COMBINING CHICKEN
AND SHELLFISH

Eighteenth-century French cooks often combined shellfish with poultry. Some of these recipes, such as squab with crayfish and duck with oysters, have fallen into obscurity and are prepared only occasionally by France's more eccentric chefs. A few of these dishes have survived—chicken with crayfish is the best known—and continue to be well-loved French regional dishes.

Chicken is especially suitable for combining with shellfish because its flavor so willingly settles into the background. Making chicken and shellfish soups is also an excellent method for stretching the flavor of expensive ingredients such as oysters and lobster.

Flavorings, Enrichments, and Vegetable Purees:

finely chopped herbs (parsley, chervil, tarragon, basil, etc.)

aïoli (page 349)

rouille (page 350)

picada (page 348)

cream

butter (plain or flavored, pages 593–594)

pureed vegetables such as mashed potatoes, pureed spinach, and root vegetable
    purees

curry

saffron

Chicken Soup with Apples and Leeks

This full flavored winter soup balances the sweetness of apples and the tang of cider vinegar against an earthy background of gently simmered leeks. The flavor of the apples can be
accentuated by adding a tiny amount of Calvados (see box) just before serving, but the
soup is still wonderful without it. Instead of disguising the flavor of the chicken, the apples
and leeks seem to accentuate it and bring it into focus. This delicious soup never fails to
get a rise out of my guests, especially if they've just come in from the cold.

MAKES 8 SERVINGS

I 4-pound chicken, quartered

salt

pepper

2 tablespoons unsalted butter

3 leeks, including I inch of green, cut in half lengthwise,
    washed, and finely sliced

2 Golden Delicious, Granny Smith, or tart local baking
    apples, peeled and cut into ½-inch cubes

I cup apple juice

½ cup apple cider vinegar

3 cups white chicken broth

3 tablespoons Calvados (optional)

½ cup heavy cream

slices of French bread, toasted

SEASON the chicken with salt and pepper. Melt the butter over medium heat in a
sauté pan just large enough to hold the chicken. Add the chicken, skin side down,

and cook for about 8 minutes over medium heat. If the butter in the pan starts to brown, lower the heat slightly. Turn the chicken and lightly sauté in the same way for 5 minutes more.

REMOVE the chicken from the pan and place it in a bowl. If the butter in the sauté pan has burned, pour it out and replace it with 2 tablespoons fresh butter. Add the leeks and cook them for 10 minutes over medium heat. Stir the leeks every couple of minutes; they should soften but not brown.

PUT chicken back in the pan with the leeks. Add the apples, apple juice, vinegar, and broth. Bring the liquids to a slow simmer and with a ladle skim off any fat or froth that floats to the top. Cover the pot and simmer the chicken very gently for 10 to 15 minutes, until it is completely cooked (the breast meat should feel firm to the touch).

REMOVE the chicken and let it cool. Remove and discard the skin and pull the meat away from the bones. Cut the meat into ½-inch chunks.

USE a ladle to skim off any fat that has formed on the surface of the liquid in the sauté pan. Add the Calvados and the heavy cream. Bring to a simmer and season to taste with salt and pepper. Heat the chunks of chicken in the soup for 2 minutes and serve immediately in hot bowls. At the table, pass a basket of lightly toasted French bread slices.

CALVADOS

The Normans make a brandy, Calvados, by distilling hard cider and aging it for varying lengths of time in oak casks. When well made, Calvados is not only a delightful drink (after dinner or in the middle of the meal as the infamous *trou normand*) but also can be added to soups, stews, and sauces cooked with cider to accentuate the flavor of the apples.

SUGGESTIONS AND VARIATIONS | Try adding a cup of sliced mushrooms along with the apples. The mushroom flavor goes well with the other ingredients, and the mushrooms make the soup more substantial. This soup is also delicious with curry, which can be added by gently cooking a tablespoon of curry powder in a tablespoon of butter and stirring it into the soup shortly before serving.

Chicken Soup with Garlic, Saffron, Basil, and Tomatoes

This is another one of those soups that I use to squelch my sporadic but overwhelming cravings for garlic. It is very similar to a Mediterranean *bourride* except that chicken is used instead of fish.

You can make this soup as simple or as complicated as you like. When I'm home alone, I quickly simmer a cut-up chicken in a little broth and whisk in some garlic mayonnaise that I throw together while the chicken is cooking. The version given here is really an elaborate vegetable soup—similar to the pistou on page 258—with chicken simmered in it during the last few minutes of cooking.

Except for the final whisking with the garlic and saffron mayonnaise and the basil cream, this soup can be prepared 2 or 3 days in advance.

MAKES 8 FIRST-COURSE OR 4 MAIN-COURSE SERVINGS (10 CUPS)

I small fennel bulb, trimmed and chopped, about 1½ cups

I leek, white part only, washed and chopped

I medium-size carrot, chopped

I small turnip, peeled and chopped

6 medium-size mushrooms, sliced

I bouquet garni

I quart chicken or vegetable broth

5 medium-size tomatoes, peeled, seeded and chopped or
    2 ½ cups canned, seeded and drained

I 4-pound chicken, quartered

I cup tightly packed fresh basil leaves

I tablespoon olive oil

½ cup heavy cream

½ cup fresh, cooked dried, or canned cannellini, Great
    Northern, or borlotti beans

I bunch of spinach, stems removed, I cup packed leaves,
    shredded (chiffonade)

salt

pepper

2 cups garlic and saffron mayonnaise (page 350)

slices of French bread, lightly toasted

COMBINE the fennel, leek, carrot, turnip, mushrooms, and bouquet garni with the broth in a 4-quart pot. Simmer gently over medium heat until the vegetables barely begin to soften, after about 10 minutes.

ADD the tomatoes and chicken to the simmering soup. Make sure the chicken is completely submerged and simmer for about 20 minutes more. Take the chicken out of the soup with a slotted spoon and let it cool. Peel off the skin. If you're serving this soup as a main course, you may want to leave the chicken pieces whole; otherwise, pull the chicken away from the bone and cut it into chunks.

SPRINKLE the basil leaves with olive oil to keep them from turning dark and chop them finely with a chef's knife or in a blender. If you use a blender, you may have to add a little more olive oil to get the leaves moving. Combine the chopped basil with the heavy cream.

PUT the chicken back in the soup along with the beans and spinach and simmer the soup for about 2 minutes. Season with salt and pepper.

PUT half the garlic and saffron mayonnaise in a mixing bowl and whisk in the hot soup. Place a slice of French bread toast in the bottom of each wide soup bowl and ladle the soup over it. If you've left the chicken pieces whole, prop the chicken up on the toasts and ladle the soup over that. Drizzle the top of each bowl with a tablespoon of garlic mayonnaise and a tablespoon of the basil cream. Pass the remaining mayonnaise and basil cream at the table.

SUGGESTIONS AND VARIATIONS | Almost any vegetable soup can be turned into a chicken soup by poaching pieces of chicken in the simmering soup about 15 minutes before serving. If you don't want to deal with the last-minute skinning and boning of the chicken, bone the chicken in advance—if you have time, make the broth with the bones—and then just add the boneless chicken meat to the soup about 5 minutes before serving.

Chicken and Tomato Soup with Olives and Capers

I've developed a rather compulsive habit of envisioning almost everything I eat as some kind of soup. The idea for this soup came from puttanesca sauce, popular in Southern Italy as a sauce for pasta. While you can make this soup without anchovies, if you don't like olives, which are the heart and soul of this dish, make something else. When buying the olives, look for as many varieties—both black and green—as you can find. The different flavors of olives are intriguing, and the palette of colors is great to look at. The preserved lemons (see box, page 481), a Moroccan touch, while optional, add an exotic note. This soup can be prepared almost entirely ahead of time. Only the capers, anchovies, preserved lemons, and olives should be added just before serving, or they'll make the broth too salty.

MAKES 4 MAIN-COURSE OR 6 FIRST-COURSE SERVINGS

I 4-pound chicken, quartered

pepper

I tablespoon olive oil

I medium-size onion, finely chopped

4 garlic cloves, finely chopped

I teaspoon ground cumin

2 teaspoons paprika

3 cups chicken broth

4 ripe tomatoes, peeled, seeded, and chopped, or
    I 28-ounce can, drained, seeds squeezed out, and
    pulp chopped

I teaspoon saffron threads or ¼ teaspoon powdered saffron

6 anchovy fillets, packed in olive oil, patted dry, and finely
    chopped (optional)

3 tablespoons small nonpareil capers

I preserved lemon quarter, cut into ¼-inch dice (optional,
    see box page 481)

I cup olives (6 ounces), preferably a mixture of dark and
    green, pitted (squeeze the olive on both ends between
    thumb and forefinger to force out the pit), chopped
    coarse (don't use canned olives)

SEASON the chicken parts with pepper (don't salt the pieces because the broth is salty) and brown them for about 8 minutes on the skin side and 5 minutes on the flesh side, over high heat, in olive oil, in a heavy-bottomed pot just large enough to hold them in a single layer. Transfer to a plate and reserve.

POUR all but I tablespoon of fat out of the pan, lower the heat to medium, and stir in the onion and garlic. Cook over medium heat, stirring every couple of minutes until the onion turns translucent but doesn't brown. Stir in the cumin and paprika, and stir over medium heat for 30 seconds more, until you smell the cumin. Pour in the broth, nestle the chicken in the pot, and add the tomatoes and saffron. Cover the pot and bring to a gentle simmer over medium heat. Simmer the chicken for about 15 minutes after the broth has reached the simmer—once the chicken pieces feel firm to the touch, don't cook them any more. Take the chicken out of the broth with tongs to let cool. Simmer the broth for 10 minutes more, skimming off any fat with a ladle. Take the chicken off the bones in strips and reserve. Discard the skin and bones. Just before serving, stir the anchovies into the broth and sprinkle in the capers and preserved lemon. Put the meat in the broth, bring back to the simmer, and ladle into heated bowls. Sprinkle over the chopped olives and serve.

PRESERVED LEMONS

If you get a last-minute impulse to use preserved lemons, you can usually find them in gourmet stores, but with a little forethought, you can save money and make your own. Preserved lemons seem to last forever—I once had a jar in the back of the refrigerator for over two years. Most recipes (including this one) call for curing the lemons for a minimum of 2 weeks, so they develop the distinct flavor of preserved lemons. Recently I encountered "confit" lemons in a restaurant and after a little experimentation realized that they were simply lemons that had been salted for a day or two. If you want to make confit lemons, slice the lemons into thin rounds, pack them in juice and salt as described below, but only cure them for 2 days. Confit lemons retain much more of the delicate lemon fragrance than do preserved lemons and can be used as a garniture for soups and chicken and seafood dishes.

MAKES 2 CUPS (ENOUGH TO FILL A PINT MASON JAR)

9 lemons, preferably Meyer
5 tablespoons coarse salt

SCRUB 5 of the lemons, cut out and discard the brown part where the stem joined, and cut them into four wedges each. Stack them in a mason jar, sprinkling each layer with salt. You may have to press down on the lemons to get them to all fit. Squeeze the rest of the lemons and pour the juice over the lemons in the jar so the lemons are completely covered with juice. Seal the lid on tightly. Store it upside down in the refrigerator for a couple of days, turn it over for a couple of days more, repeating this process a couple of times during the first week to make sure the salt dissolves and is distributed evenly among the lemons. The lemons are ready to use after 2 weeks.

Chicken and Tomatillo Soup

One thing I miss about living in California is going out for inexpensive and wonderful Mexican food. I suppose a lot of it wasn't totally authentic, but I'll never forget the chicken enchiladas with green tomatillo sauce and sour cream. I think I've managed to capture the same tart flavor in this soup.

MAKES 6 SERVINGS

1 4-pound chicken, quartered

salt

pepper

3 tablespoons unsalted butter or olive oil

1 medium-size onion, finely chopped

3 garlic cloves, finely chopped

1 pound fresh tomatillos, papery husk removed, coarsely chopped, or 2 cups drained canned tomatillos, coarsely chopped

2 jalapeño chilies, seeded and finely chopped

3 cups chicken broth or water

2 tablespoons finely chopped cilantro leaves

cayenne pepper

sour cream

grated Monterey Jack or Cheddar cheese

SEASON the chicken with salt and pepper, then brown it on both sides in the butter or olive oil over high heat in a sauté pan just large enough to hold it in a single layer. When the chicken is well browned, after about 8 minutes on the skin side and 10 minutes on the flesh side, take it out of the pan and lightly sauté the onion and garlic in the fat left in the pan. (If the fat has burned, pour it out and add 2 tablespoons fresh oil or butter.)

RETURN the chicken to the pan along with the tomatillos, jalapeños, and broth. Cover the pan and simmer gently until the chicken is done—it will be firm to the touch—about 15 minutes.

TAKE the pan off the heat, remove the chicken, and let it cool for 10 minutes. Remove and discard the skin, pull off the chicken meat, cut it into bite-size pieces, and discard the bones. Skim off any fat or froth that has floated to the top of the soup.

WORK the ingredients in the pan through a food mill with a medium disk or puree them in a blender and strain through a medium-mesh strainer.

COMBINE the pureed tomatillos with the cilantro and chicken. Thin the soup with a little broth or water if it's too thick. Season with salt and pepper, or cayenne if it needs more heat. Serve sour cream, grated cheese, or both.

SUGGESTIONS AND VARIATIONS | I sometimes add a cup of corn kernels to Mexican soups because they go well with almost any Mexican ingredient. Just add the corn kernels along with the tomatillos and puree the mixture together.

SHELLED and toasted pumpkin seeds (½ cup pureed in a blender with a little of the soup, added before straining) are also a typically Mexican touch; they'll give the soup a distinctive flavor and also make it considerably thicker.

You may also want to experiment with adding dried chilies (see Ingredients chapter) to the soup shortly before serving.

Chicken and Red Mole Soup

When most of us think of moles, we have rather bizarre associations of stewed meats combined with chocolate. While many moles do contain chocolate, they have relatively small amounts, so its flavor stays in the background. The character of moles is far more determined by other ingredients, especially chilies, than it is by chocolate.

Moles are amazingly diverse and sophisticated (to say nothing of delicious) and often contain an array of dried chilies and various herbs, nuts, seeds, and spices. If you want to learn more about them (a very worthwhile effort), I highly recommend Rick Bayless's book, *Authentic Mexican*. Here I have simplified and lightened a traditional recipe so it becomes a soup. If you don't have all three chilies, just substitute more of the others. This soup is perfectly delicious with ancho chilies alone, but its flavor won't be as intriguingly complex.

MAKES 4 MAIN-COURSE SERVINGS

4 dried ancho chilies

2 dried mulato chilies

2 dried guajillo chilies

I 4-pound chicken, quartered (see box on page 472)

salt

pepper

2 tablespoons olive oil or vegetable oil

I medium-size onion, peeled and chopped

2 large garlic cloves, peeled and chopped

4 medium tomatoes, stemmed and coarsely chopped
   (don't bother seeding or peeling), or 1 28-ounce can
   whole tomatoes, drained and coarsely chopped

4 cups chicken broth or water

1 bouquet garni containing 1 small bunch parsley, 1 bay
   leaf, and 5 sprigs of fresh thyme

½teaspoon dried oregano, finely chopped

¼ teaspoon ground cloves

1 teaspoon ground cinnamon

3 tablespoons white raisins

3 tablespoons peanut butter (all natural—contents should
   read "peanuts, salt")

juice of 1 lime or more to taste

sour cream

WIPE the dust off the chilies with a damp towel and toast them in a hot skillet for about 1 minute on each side, until you smell their fragrance. Cut off the stems, cut the chilies in half lengthwise, and brush out their seeds. Put the chilies all together in a bowl and cover with about 2 cups of boiling water. Let soak for 20 minutes or until the chilies are soft and feel pliable and leathery. Drain and discard the soaking liquid; coarsely chop and reserve.

SEASON the chicken on both sides with salt and pepper. Brown it on both sides for about 8 minutes on the skin side and 5 minutes on the flesh side, in oil, in a pan just large enough to hold the parts in a single layer. Take out the chicken and pour out all but about a tablespoon of the fat in the pan. Add the onion and garlic to the pan and stir over medium heat, using a wooden spoon, until the onion turns translucent, about 10 minutes. Put the chicken back in the pan with any juices that accumulated on the plate and add the tomatoes and the broth or water, and nestle in the bouquet garni. Bring to a very gentle simmer and simmer, covered, for 15 minutes, or until the chicken feels firm to the touch.

TAKE the chicken out of the liquid and let it cool enough so you can handle it. Use a ladle to skim off any fat that has risen to the top of the soup. Peel off and discard the skin and pull the meat away from the bone. Shred the meat by pulling it apart with your fingers. Reserve the chicken. Discard the bouquet garni. Puree about 1 cup of the tomato broth with the reserved chilies, the oregano, spices, raisins in a blender (use only quick pulses at the lowest setting, see blenders, page 3). Combine this puree with the rest of the broth and whisk in the peanut butter. Work the soup through a food mill or push it through a large strainer with the back of a ladle into a small pot. Skim off any fat that floats to the top.

SHORTLY before serving, bring the strained soup to a simmer and whisk and add the shredded chicken. Season to taste with salt and lime juice. Pass the sour cream at the table for guests to help themselves.

Thai Chicken and Coconut Soup

GAI TOM KA

Thai restaurants have become such a fixture in American cities that it's hard to imagine that until about 10 years ago most Americans had never tasted Thai food. This soup, along with the hot and sour shrimp soup on page 404, is one of my favorite dishes in the Thai repertoire.

The only disadvantage of making Thai soups is that some of the ingredients are too exotic to be found at the local supermarket. Fortunately there are substitutes for many of the ingredients; others can be left out entirely. (see the Ingredients chapter for more information.) The results won't be authentically Thai, but the soup will be delicious nonetheless. The easiest way to find out where to shop for Thai ingredients is to wander into a Thai restaurant and ask them where to shop. You can also order from one of the sources listed at the back of this book.

MAKES 6 FIRST-COURSE SERVINGS

3 cups chicken broth

4 kaffir lime leaves, cut into thin strands

a 3-inch length of lemongrass, finely chopped, or zest of
     ½ lemon, cut into fine julienne

6 ⅛-inch-thick slices of galangal or 2 ⅛-inch-thick slices of
     fresh ginger

¼ cup Thai fish sauce (*nam pla*) or more to taste

½ cup fresh lemon or lime juice

2 red Thai chilies or 3 jalapeño chilies, seeds removed, finely
     chopped

2 skinless and boneless chicken breasts, cut into
     1- by ¼-inch strips

1½ cups coconut milk

2 tablespoons finely chopped cilantro leaves

salt

COMBINE the chicken broth, lime leaves, lemongrass, galangal, fish sauce, lemon juice, and chilies in a 4-quart pot. Bring to a slow simmer and add the chicken breasts, coconut milk, and cilantro. Simmer long enough to cook the chicken—about 3 minutes—and, if necessary, season to taste with salt or additional fish sauce.

SUGGESTIONS AND VARIATIONS | This soup, along with a bowl of jasmine or basmati rice, makes a perfect simple meal. If you want to turn it into something more elegant and substantial, add whole peeled shrimp, mussels, pieces of filleted fish, or even lobster medallions. Be sure to serve elaborate versions in wide bowls so everyone can see all the different elements. You can also turn this into a main-course soup by doubling the chicken.

WHEN I've encountered this soup in Thai restaurants in New York, it usually includes straw mushrooms. Since I've been able to find only canned versions—which don't have much taste—I'm not terribly enthusiastic. Chinese (soaked for 3 hours in warm water) or fresh shiitake mushrooms— thickly sliced and simmered in the soup for 5 minutes—are beautiful to look at and have a lovely flavor.

Chicken Vatapa

Although traditional Brazilian recipes usually describe chicken *vatapa* as a stew, this version is considerably lighter and makes an amazingly subtle and delicious soup. This recipe reflects my terrible weakness for coconut milk and is quite rich, but you can get by using half the coconut milk called for.

Traditional Brazilian recipes often call for dried shrimp, which, although certainly not essential, gives depth of flavor and a distinctive character to the soup.

This soup contains some jalapeño chilies, but I've purposely left the recipe a bit underseasoned so you can spice it to taste at the end with a little cayenne pepper or Tabasco.

Vatapa can be made 2 or 3 days in advance and kept in the refrigerator.

MAKES 10 SERVINGS

1 4-pound chicken, quartered

salt

pepper

¼ cup safflower oil

1 medium-size onion, finely chopped

4 garlic cloves, finely chopped

2 jalapeño chilies, seeded and finely chopped

6 medium-size tomatoes, peeled, seeded and chopped,
    or 3 cups drained and seeded canned tomatoes,
    chopped

3½ cups chicken broth

¾ cup roasted peanuts

½ cup dried shrimp (optional)

2 cups coconut milk

½ cup tightly packed cilantro leaves, finely chopped,
    2 tablespoons

2 tablespoons white wine vinegar

cayenne pepper or Tabasco sauce

SEASON the chicken with salt and pepper. In a skillet or sauté pan that fits the chicken as closely as possible, sauté it in 3 tablespoons of the safflower oil over medium to high heat for about 8 minutes on the skin side and 5 minutes on the flesh side.

PLACE the chicken on a plate and pour the cooked oil out of the sauté pan. Put the remaining tablespoon of oil in the sauté pan and add the onion, garlic, and jalapeños. Stir over medium heat until the vegetables soften, about 10 minutes.

PUT the tomatoes, chicken, and chicken broth in the sauté pan and bring everything to a slow simmer. Simmer for about 15 minutes.

IN a food processor or blender, grind the peanuts with the dried shrimp and enough broth to get them moving for about 2 minutes, until you obtain a smooth paste.

TAKE the chicken out of the sauté pan and let it cool. Peel off the skin and discard it. Take the meat off the bones and cut it into ½-inch cubes. Skim off any fat and froth that have floated to the top of the broth.

WHISK the coconut milk and the peanut/shrimp paste into the simmering broth/tomato mixture. Add the cilantro and season with salt and pepper and cayenne or Tabasco if you want the soup spicier. Add the chicken meat and reheat it for 2 minutes in the simmering soup.

ARRANGE a chicken piece on each plate and spoon the sauce over.

SUGGESTIONS AND VARIATIONS | In this recipe the chicken is taken off the bone and cut into cubes, but if you like, leave the chicken quarters whole and serve this as a main course for 4. Place a piece of chicken in the center of 4 wide soup bowls and pour the soup over.

YOU can also make this soup more substantial by cooking ½ cup rice and stirring it into the soup just before serving.

Chicken or Turkey Velouté with Sherry

When I was growing up, during the Christmas holidays my mother would roast the largest turkey she could find so we would have plenty of leftovers. The week following, there was a standard repertoire of dishes made from the leftovers—creamed turkey, turkey sandwiches, turkey broth with vegetables, and this soup. When I make roast chicken, even if it's just for two, I roast a big one and make this soup the day after.

MAKES 6 SERVINGS

3 tablespoons unsalted butter

1 medium-size onion, finely chopped

3 tablespoons all-purpose flour

½ cup dry sherry or ¾ cup dry white wine

1 quart broth made from a turkey or chicken carcass

1 bouquet garni

1 cup milk, half-and-half, or heavy cream

2 cups cubed meat from a leftover roast turkey or chicken

salt

pepper

MELT the butter in a 4-quart pot over medium heat and add the onion. Cook the onion, stirring every couple of minutes with a wooden spoon, until it turns translucent, 5 to 10 minutes. Do not let it brown.

STIR in the flour and cook it over medium heat for 3 minutes, until it has a pleasant, toasty smell.

POUR in the sherry and broth and whisk the soup for 30 seconds to get rid of any lumps of flour. Add the bouquet garni and bring the soup to a slow simmer. Simmer gently for 20 minutes. Use a ladle to skim off any froth or fat that floats to the surface. Discard the bouquet garni.

ADD the milk or cream and the leftover turkey or chicken meat and simmer the soup for 1 minute more. Season with salt and pepper.

SUGGESTIONS AND VARIATIONS | This is one of those catchall soups that's perfect for using whatever vegetables happen to be sitting in the refrigerator. When you add the broth to the soup, go ahead and add any chopped vegetables you like. Sliced mushrooms are especially good, but carrots, celery, leeks, potatoes, and leftover green vegetables (added just a few minutes before serving) can all be used.

I also like to add a couple of spoonfuls of chopped herbs such as parsley, chives, or tarragon along with the milk or cream to freshen the soup's flavor and to give it a lively color. This soup is also wonderful flavored with curry (gently cook a tablespoon of curry powder with the flour at the beginning) or saffron. (Soak a good pinch in water for 20 minutes and stir this into the soup 5 minutes before serving.) If you want to make the soup more substantial, stir in some cooked rice just before serving.

Chicken Gumbo

This version is lighter than a traditional Louisiana gumbo, but it still captures the spicy, smoky flavors of the original. Older recipes usually recommend browning the chicken in bacon fat, which is an excellent way of giving a subtle smokiness to the broth. Although very little bacon fat will find its way into the finished soup, you can substitute vegetable oil if the idea bothers you.

Gumbo can be thickened in three ways: with roux, okra, or filé powder. This version uses okra because it's relatively easy to find (you can use frozen okra), and it gives a special texture to the soup that roux will not. Filé—a powder made from dried sassafras leaves (the flavoring for root beer)—works as a thickener by whisking in a tablespoon at the very last minute, after you've taken the soup off the heat. Filé gives gumbo a distinctive, pine-like flavor.

A good gumbo should always have a mild smoky flavor that I like to introduce by adding slivers of the smoked Cajun ham, tasso. If you can't find tasso, use another smoked ham such as Black Forest or Westphalian.

Gumbo can be made a day or two ahead of time and kept in the refrigerator. It will keep frozen for a month. This version is quite thick, especially when you reheat it, so feel free to thin it with broth or water.

MAKES 8 FIRST-COURSE SERVINGS OR 4 MAIN-COURSE SERVINGS

1½ pounds fresh okra or 2 10-ounce packages frozen, cut
   into ¼-inch slices

6 tablespoons melted bacon fat or vegetable oil

2 medium-size onions, finely chopped

1 celery rib, cut into ¼-inch cubes

3 garlic cloves, finely chopped

1 red or green bell pepper, seeded and cut into ¼-inch cubes

¼ pound tasso or smoked ham, thinly sliced and cut into
   1- by ⅛-inch strips

2 teaspoons fresh thyme leaves or 1 teaspoon dried

6 medium-size tomatoes, peeled, seeded, and chopped, or
    3 cups drained, seeded, and chopped canned tomatoes

3 cups chicken broth

1 4-pound chicken, quartered

salt

pepper

1 pound *andouille* sausage, 2 links, or smoked kielbasa, cut
    into ½-inch slices

Tabasco sauce

1 cup rice, cooked

IN a 4-quart pot over medium heat, cook the okra in 3 tablespoons of the bacon fat or oil for about 15 minutes, until it's covered with a shiny glaze. Add the onions, celery, garlic, pepper, ham and thyme leaves. Cook gently for 15 minutes more, until the onions and celery are shiny and translucent.

ADD the tomatoes and broth and cook at a bare simmer for 10 minutes more.

WHILE the vegetable mixture is cooking, season the chicken and brown it for about 8 minutes on the skin side and 5 minutes on the flesh side, in the remaining bacon fat or vegetable oil in a skillet or another 4-quart pot. Drain out the cooked fat and cover the chicken with the vegetable/tomato mixture. Add the sliced sausage.

COOK the chicken and sausage at a gentle simmer for 15 minutes. Take out the chicken and let it cool. Remove and discard the skin and remove the meat with your fingers.

PUT the meat back into the soup and season the soup to taste with Tabasco and salt.

BRING the gumbo back to a simmer and serve it in wide soup bowls with a mound of rice in the center of each one. If the gumbo is too thick, thin it with broth or water.

SUGGESTIONS AND VARIATIONS | Once you make the gumbo base, you can easily expand the soup into something more elaborate by adding seafood (shrimp is easy and can be simmered in the soup at the last minute) or slices of smoked meats such as duck or goose (this isn't authentic, but the smoky flavor is a natural).

YOU can also follow the advice of some writers and add corn kernels to the soup at the last minute.

GUMBO thickens if left overnight in the refrigerator, so you may need to thin it if you're reheating it the next day.

Spicy Chicken Soup from Borneo

SOTO BANJAR

This is a simplification of an elaborate traditional soup from Borneo that Copeland Marks wrote about in his book *The Exotic Kitchens of Indonesia*. The original version is served with hard-cooked eggs and fritters made from beef and potatoes. Like many soups from Southeast Asia, *soto banjar* is made by first preparing a paste of aromatic vegetables and spices, called a *bumbu*, and then stir frying the *bumbu* with meat or chicken before any liquid is added. For more information on the Asian ingredients, see the Ingredients chapter.

MAKES 8 SERVINGS

5 shallots, peeled

3 garlic cloves, peeled

⅛ teaspoon freshly grated nutmeg

⅛ teaspoon ground cardamom

½ teaspoon ground cinnamon

¼ teaspoon ground cloves

2 Thai chilies or 4 jalapeño chilies, seeds removed

a ½-inch slice of fresh ginger, peeled

2 tablespoons soy sauce or kecap manis

12 macadamia nuts

7 cups chicken broth or water

1 tablespoon vegetable oil

3 boneless chicken breasts, cut into ⅛- by 2-inch-long strips

a 6-inch length of lemongrass, thinly sliced

2 scallions, both white and green parts, thinly sliced

a ¼-inch slice of galangal (optional)

2 tablespoons tamarind paste combined with 6 tablespoons
    boiling water, strained

COMBINE the shallots, garlic, spices, chilies, ginger, soy sauce, macadamia nuts, and about ⅓ cup of the broth in a food processor. Process for about 1 minute, until the mixture is worked to a smooth paste.

HEAT the vegetable oil over high heat in a heavy iron skillet or wok. When the oil just begins to smoke, add the strips of chicken breast and stir for 1 minute. Add the spice/macadamia nut mixture and stir for about 2 minutes more.

KECAP MANIS

The word *kecap* (sometimes spelled *ketjap*) has the same Chinese origins as our beloved ketchup, although the actual products are entirely different. Javanese *kecap manis* is a specially flavored and sweetened soy sauce. Since I couldn't find *kecap manis* in even the most exotic markets, I've provided a recipe but have run up against two other exotic ingredients, salam leaves (a kind of tropical bay leaf—*Eugenia polyantha*) and palm sugar. If you're still determined, both the salam leaves and the palm sugar can be found in Asian markets or by mail order (see Sources). Or you can substitute curry leaves, which are somewhat easier to find (try an Indian grocery) and granulated sugar.

Kecap manis can also be used as a marinade for stir-fried, roasted, or grilled meats.

MAKES 2 CUPS

I 22-ounce bottle light Chinese soy
    sauce
4 salam leaves or 8 curry leaves
a ¼-inch slice of galangal, chopped
4 star anise, crushed
I clove garlic, sliced
2 cups granulated or palm sugar

IN a mixing bowl, combine all the ingredients except the sugar. Cook the sugar over medium heat in a heavy-bottomed 4-quart saucepan. Stir constantly until the sugar has completely melted and turns to a light caramel. Add the ingredients in the mixing bowl to the sugar. Bring the mixture to a simmer and simmer for 15 minutes. Remove from the heat and let cool. Strain. Store in a bottle in the refrigerator for at least a year.

ADD the remaining chicken broth, the lemongrass, scallions, tamarind, and galangal if you're using it and bring to a simmer. Simmer gently for 5 minutes and serve.

SUGGESTIONS AND VARIATIONS | If you want to make this soup more substantial or if the next day you have a few cups of soup left over that you want to stretch, you can heat cooked rice or raw cellophane noodles (soaked for 10 minutes in cold water) in the soup. I also like to add green vegetables such as spinach, briefly boiled watercress, or zucchini.

DON'T feel you have to stick to chicken in this recipe. The *bumbu* is so flavorful that it works well with pork, beef, or even shrimp.

INDONESIAN cooks would probably scream in dismay, but I sometimes finish this soup with a cup of coconut milk.

MOST Indonesian soup recipes are made using similar techniques: a *bumbu* is stir-fried with sliced meats or seafood, water or broth is added, and the mixture simmered with vegetables such as cabbage, bamboo shoots, cucumbers, chilies, and carrots. In addition to the ingredients listed here, an Indonesian bumbu may contain ground cumin, coriander seeds, fresh or ground turmeric, ground peanuts, or salam leaves.

Colombian Potato, Corn, and Chicken Soup with Capers

AJIACO DE POLLO BOGOTANO

This hearty soup is substantial enough for a main course and in many ways (the large proportion of chicken, the thickness of the surrounding liquid) is more like a stew. But in Colombia it's called soup, so soup it shall remain. Traditional recipes call for cutting the corncob in several chunks, but eating corn this way is messy, so I've taken the liberty of cutting the kernels off the cob. The chicken, also, is traditionally served in pieces on the bone, but here I suggest shredding it to make the soup easier to eat. This soup contains potatoes in two forms: pureed, to give body to the broth, and whole new potatoes for substance. I use fewer potatoes in the puree than are called for in traditional recipes, so the broth in this version is thinner but still substantial. The chicken can be browned and the basic broth (before the corn is added) made earlier the same day or the day before.

MAKES 4 MAIN-COURSE SERVINGS

I 4-pound chicken, quartered (see box, page 472)

salt

pepper

3 tablespoons butter

2 medium-size onions, peeled and finely chopped

2 garlic cloves, peeled and finely chopped

2 teaspoons cumin seeds

I heaping tablespoon chopped fresh ginger (don't bother peeling the ginger)

6 cups basic brown chicken broth (page 62)

I pound large Yukon Gold, Yellow Finn, or small Russet potatoes (total weight 10 ounces), peeled and kept in cold water to prevent darkening

4 medium-size tomatoes, coarsely chopped (don't bother peeling or seeding)

2 ears of corn, shucked, or I 10-ounce package frozen corn

4 small (about ¼ pound each) fingerling or new potatoes, simmered until soft, peeled while warm, and cut in half

I cup heavy cream

2 tablespoons coarsely chopped cilantro leaves

3 tablespoons capers (preferably nonpareil)

COLUMBIA'S OTHER GREAT SOUP: *SANCOCHO*

Many of South America's best-known dishes are derivatives of Spanish cooking but are given there own special twist by including local ingredients. A *sancocho,* a soup from Columbia, Ecuador, and Venezuela (where it is called *hervido*), is similar to the Spanish *olla podrida,* vaguely translatable as a "mixed pot" or the French pot-au-feu (see recipe, page 426), but often contains corn, sweet potatoes, tomatoes, and peppers, all completely unknown to the Spanish before the discovery of the New World. If you want to make a *sancocho,* you can simmer any or all of the meat cuts described in the recipe for pot-au-feu but include 2 or 3 peeled, seeded, and chopped tomatoes, a grilled and peeled red bell pepper or two cut into strips, a few sections of corn on the cob, plenty of peeled garlic cloves, and a finish of cilantro leaves. All of these ingredients should, of course, be added according to their cooking times—the sweet potatoes about 30 minutes before serving and everything else 5 minutes or so before the soup is done. I don't know if it's authentic or not, but I like to pass finely chopped jalapeno chilies at the table for guests to use as a condiment in the same way they might use mustard for a pot-au-feu.

SEASON the chicken pieces with salt and pepper. Melt the butter over medium-high heat in a sauté pan just large enough to hold the chicken in a single layer (if your pan is too large, you can include pieces of the chicken back to take up room). Put the chicken, skin side down, in the pan and brown it for about 8 minutes on the skin side and 5 minutes on the flesh side. Transfer the chicken to a plate or bowl and pour all but a tablespoon of the fat out of the sauté pan. Stir in the onions, garlic, cumin seeds, and ginger, and cook over medium heat until the onions turn translucent, about 10 minutes; pour in the broth. Slice the potatoes as thin as you can—ideally like potato chips—with a plastic vegetable slicer or a chef's knife—and add them to the sauté pan. Add the tomatoes to the sauté pan. Add the chicken and simmer until the potatoes and tomatoes are completely soft and the chicken firm to the touch, about 15 minutes. Remove the chicken with tongs—if it cooks before the vegetables, don't wait until the vegetables are done—and reserve and let cool. Use a ladle to skim off any fat that has risen to the top of the soup. Work the soup through a food mill or a large strainer with the back of a ladle into a clean pot.

PULL the skin off the chicken pieces and discard. Pull the meat off in strips and reserve. Discard the bones.

CUT the kernels off the corn by holding each ear at an angle with one hand and cutting along the side of the ear with a sharp knife. Discard the cobs and put the kernels in the soup. Put in the cooked fingerling potatoes, pour in the cream, and add the cilantro, capers, and the chicken. Bring to the simmer—simmer about 5 minutes to reheat the chicken and cook the corn—and season to taste with salt and pepper. Ladle the soup into heated soup plates.

Chicken Tagine with Apricots, Raisins, and Almonds

When I'm traveling around Manhattan and develop a sudden hunger, I drop into one of my favorite corner restaurants where they serve, along with good hamburgers and salads, delicious North African specialties. While most tagines—traditional North African stews—are long-simmered affairs, usually made with lamb, this version made with chicken is lighter and takes less time to prepare. The secret to its flavor is the juxtaposition of sweet dried fruits, almonds, and gentle spices such as cinnamon and saffron. Another secret to this soup is harissa (see box, page 496), one of my favorite of all spicy sauces (you can use it as a condiment for just about any North African soup or stew) passed at the table so guests can use as little or as much as they like. I often make a meal out of this soup, with a bowl of couscous served on the side for guests to spoon into their soup.

MAKES 4 MAIN-COURSE SERVINGS

I 4-pound chicken, quartered (see box, page 472)

salt

pepper

2 tablespoons olive oil

I medium-size onion, finely chopped

2 garlic cloves, finely chopped

I teaspoon ground turmeric or 2 teaspoons finely chopped fresh

2 tablespoons finely grated fresh ginger

I teaspoon ground cinnamon

¼ teaspoon ground cloves

5 cups chicken broth

I cup dried apricots cut into ¼-inch dice

½ cup white raisins

I teaspoon saffron threads or ¼ teaspoon powdered saffron

half of I 10-ounce box plain couscous

½ cup sliced almonds, toasted in a 350°F oven for 10 minutes, until they turn pale brown and smell fragrant

harissa (see box page 496)

SEASON the chicken parts with salt and pepper and brown them for about 8 minutes on the skin side and 5 minutes on the flesh side, over high heat, in olive oil, in a heavy-bottomed pot just large enough to hold them in a single layer. Transfer to a plate and reserve.

POUR all but I tablespoon of fat out of the pan, and stir in the onion and garlic. Cook over medium heat, stirring every couple of minutes, until the onion turns translucent but doesn't brown, about 10 minutes. Stir in the turmeric, ginger, cinnamon, and cloves and stir over medium heat for I minute more—until you smell the fragrance of the spices. Pour over the broth and scrape against the bottom of the pot to dissolve any caramelized juices. Sprinkle over the apricots, raisins, and saffron, and put the chicken back in the pan. Cover the pot and bring to a gentle simmer over medium heat. Simmer the chicken for 15 minutes after the broth has reached the simmer—once the chicken pieces feel firm to the touch, don't cook them any more. Take the chicken out of the broth with tongs to let cool. Use a ladle to skim off any fat that has floated to the top of the broth. Turn the heat off under the pot. Take the chicken off the bones in strips and put it in the pot with the broth. Prepare the couscous according to the directions on the package. Sprinkle

HARISSA

On a recent trip to Tunisia, I saw a cooking demonstration in which harissa was prepared in several different ways. Frankly, I came away in a state of confusion and have since done my best to decipher the ingredients in versions I've tasted in New York, and have consulted the works of my favorite North African food experts, Paula Wolfert (*Mediterranean Grains and Greens*), Kitty Morse (*North Africa: The Vegetarian Table*), and Habeeb Salloum and James Peters (*From the Lands of Figs and Olives*). Like so many recipes, nobody seems to agree on everything, but certain ingredients appear with sufficient frequency that I feel confident they're authentic. Most surprising are caraway seeds (something I associate with rye bread and aquavit), but the other ingredients are typical of cooking throughout the Mediterranean. Lest I lead you to think that making harissa is an entirely straightforward process, I must warn you that another spice mixture—*tabil*—enters into its preparation and that, in order to grind the *tabil* in the blender (although if you use a coffee grinder, you can make less), you'll need to make enough to last you a rather long time. You may, however, find yourself an harissa addict—I smear it on toast and dollop it on just about any stewlike dish of meat or fish. First the *tabil*:

To make $1/3$ cup, combine 2 tablespoons caraway seeds, 2 tablespoons coriander seeds, and $1\frac{1}{2}$ teaspoons good quality curry powder in a coffee grinder (if you're using a blender, you'll need to double these quantities) and puree to a powder, about 2 minutes. (Most recipes for *tabil* call for red pepper, but since we add it later to the harissa, there's no need to use it here.) The *tabil* will keep in a small jar in the freezer for up to a year.

Now the harissa:

Most recipes for harissa in American cookbooks call for New Mexico chilies, but I prefer anchos, which have a bit more heat and a more complex flavor. Paula Wolfert calls for sun-dried tomatoes, but since I like my harissa to have more the consistency of a sauce rather than a spread, I use a fresh tomato to thin it. Her version, however, will keep longer in the refrigerator—fresh tomatoes make it more perishable. This recipe makes $1\frac{2}{3}$ cups—more than you'll need for one batch of soup, but harissa will keep for at least a week in the refrigerator and for months in the freezer.

over the almonds and bring the soup back to the simmer. Season to taste with salt and pepper, and serve. Serve the couscous at the table or put a mound in each bowl of soup. Pass the harissa at the table.

6 ancho chilies, dust wiped off with a damp towel

2 garlic cloves, peeled, finely chopped and crushed to a paste with the side of a chef's knife

I teaspoon salt

I tablespoon *tabil* (see above)

I ripe tomato, peeled, halved crosswise, seeds squeezed out, and coarsely chopped

¼ cup pure (not extra virgin) olive oil or vegetable oil

¼ cup extra virgin olive oil

CUT the stems off the chilies and then cut the chilies lengthwise in half. Brush out the seeds. Put the chilies in a bowl and pour over 2 cups of boiling water. Let the chilies soak until they become pliable and leathery, about 30 minutes. Drain, squeeze out the excess water, and discard the soaking liquid. Coarsely chop the chilies.

COMBINE the chilies and the rest of the ingredients except the extra virgin olive oil in a blender and puree until smooth. Spoon the mixture into a bowl and work in the extra virgin olive oil a tablespoon at a time. (I don't put the extra virgin olive oil in the blender with the rest of the ingredients because it sometimes turns bitter.)

Duck

MY GUESTS ARE DELIGHTED WHEN I SERVE DUCK BECAUSE IT'S HARD TO GET IT WELL prepared in restaurants and people rarely serve it at home. Duck is also a delicious compromise between chicken and red meat.

Many cooks are afraid to prepare duck because they don't know what to do with the thick layer of fatty skin. The advantage of cooking duck into a soup is that either the fat can be removed ahead of time or the soup can be cooked long enough so that the fat is rendered and can be skimmed off.

Although duck can be cut up and cooked in the same way as chicken, I prefer to use different methods for cooking the thighs and breasts. The thighs are somewhat tough and need to be cooked thoroughly or soaked in a marinade containing tropical fruits to tenderize them. The techniques for cooking a quartered chicken (see box, page 472) or the Asian method (page 471) will work for cooking duck thighs. Duck thighs are also used to prepare hearty peasant soups with beans and cabbage. (See Gascon duck and vegetable soup, page 454, and duck and bean soup, page 455)

Unlike the thighs, duck breasts are tender and are best when cooked only to a pink medium-rare. I like to use duck breasts for a main course—usually sautéed with some kind of sauce—and then save all the bones, giblets, and thighs for making soup. Usually I make a broth right away with the bones—they take up too much room in the freezer—and then freeze—the thighs and broth and wait until I've saved enough to make soup. One of my favorite ways to cook duck breasts is to sauté them skin side down to get them to render their fat, poach them in broth, and serve them sliced, surrounded with the broth and vegetables (see recipe, pages 89–91).

Some elaborate soups such as the sautéed or grilled duck breast in savory broth on page 89 use both the duck thighs and breasts. First a broth is prepared with the duck bones and thighs; the duck breast is cooked shortly before serving and added to the soup only at the last minute. In this way the breasts can be kept slightly pink.

HOW TO BUY A DUCK

Usually ducks are sold only whole, so you'll need to have the butcher cut them up or do it yourself. You should end up with two thighs, two breasts, two wings, and a large back and rib cage section, which is mostly bone. Some butchers sell boneless duck breasts, but two single breasts usually cost as much as a whole duck. When you get the cut-up duck home, you may want to do what I do and make a broth with the wings and the rib cage section, use the thighs in soup, and freeze the duck breasts to use as an elegant entrée.

Vietnamese Duck Soup with Noodles

I first read a duck recipe similar to this one in Nicole Routhier's *The Foods of Vietnam*. I like duck in almost any form, but this soup is one of my favorites because the duck skin ends up sweet, spicy, and crispy while the meat inside is tender and juicy without being over-cooked. Another thing I love about this soup is that it uses only the legs from the duck, leaving me the breasts for other dishes.

Normally duck thighs are tough and need longer cooking than the 20 minutes suggested here to make them tender. The secret is to include a tropical fruit such as kiwi, mango, papaya, or fresh pineapple in the marinade; the fruit's enzymes soften the meat.

MAKES 6 SERVINGS

6 duck thighs

the marinade:

¼ cup sugar

½ cup dark soy sauce

I cinnamon stick or I teaspoon ground cinnamon

a ½-inch slice of fresh ginger, peeled and thinly sliced,
    or I teaspoon ground ginger

4 star anise

4 cloves

I teaspoon coriander seeds

2 cups water

I kiwifruit, peeled and finely chopped

the soup:

I cup peanut oil

salt

I½ quarts chicken broth

6 tablespoons Vietnamese (*nuoc mam*) or Thai fish sauce
    (*nam pla*) 16 dried Chinese mushrooms, soaked in hot
    water for 3 hours, stems removed, sliced, or 16 fresh
    shiitake mushrooms, stems removed, sliced

¾ pound thin fresh Chinese or Italian egg noodles or
    ½ pound dried

6 scallions, both white and green parts, finely chopped

2 tablespoons finely chopped cilantro leaves

½ cup marinade, strained

IN ADVANCE Use a paring knife to take the bone out of each of the thighs. Starting on the inner, flesh side of each thigh, cut along each side of the bone until it remains attached only at the drumstick joint. Cut through the joint and pull out the bone. Leave in the drumstick bone.

COMBINE all the marinade ingredients except the kiwifruit in a 2-quart saucepan. Cover the pan and simmer the mixture slowly over low heat for 30 minutes. Strain the mixture into a bowl, let it cool until you can comfortably hold your finger in it, and add the kiwifruit and the duck thighs. Toss the duck legs in the marinade so they are well coated. Let sit for 3 hours or overnight in the refrigerator.

AT THE LAST MINUTE Heat the vegetable oil in a heavy-bottomed pot or skillet until the surface ripples. If the oil starts to smoke, turn down the heat. Dry the duck legs with paper towels, season them with salt, and fry them for about 5 minutes on each side in the hot oil, until both sides are brown and crisp.

PUT the fried duck thighs in a 4-quart pot. Pour in the chicken broth and fish sauce and add the mushrooms. Simmer gently for 20 minutes, carefully skimming off any froth that floats to the surface with a ladle.

TAKE the duck thighs out of the soup with a slotted spoon and cut the boneless part of each thigh into 4 slices.

COOK the egg noodles until they are *al dente* in a pot of boiling water. (This can range from 30 seconds for just-made fresh noodles to 15 minutes for dried noodles.) Using a large spoon and a fork, drain the noodles and arrange them to one side in the hot soup bowls.

ARRANGE the sliced duck thighs and drumsticks next to the noodles. Add the chopped scallions, cilantro, and reserved marinade to the broth, simmer for 1 minute, and ladle the broth over the duck and noodles.

SUGGESTIONS AND VARIATIONS | I sometimes add a small bunch of chopped mint or basil near the end of cooking in addition to the cilantro. If you can find Asian basil, it has a more intense licorice flavor that goes with the other flavors in this soup.

Duck and Sherry Soup

A word of warning right away—this soup is complicated, expensive, and you end up with some shredded duck floating around in broth. The taste, however, is well worth the effort. I love the mildly disappointed look on my guests' faces when they see a bowl of simple broth set in front of them. But when they taste!

Although Chinese versions of this recipe call for whole duck, I usually use duck thighs because sautéed or grilled duck breasts are a part of my regular dinner fare and the leftover thighs accumulate in my freezer. However, if you need duck broth, you'll need to buy a whole duck and make the broth with the bones.

Be sure to use authentic Spanish sherry. My favorite is Manzanilla, which is light and perfectly dry, but if you can't find it, use a good dry fino. Don't use cream sherry. Give yourself at least 2 days to prepare this soup.

MAKES 6 SERVINGS

1 5-pound duck

2 tablespoons vegetable oil

1 medium-size onion, chopped

1 medium-size carrot, chopped

2 garlic cloves, crushed

1 bouquet garni

2½ cups dry sherry

9 Chinese mushrooms, soaked overnight in water to cover and sliced

2 scallions, both white and green parts, finely chopped

salt

pepper

PREPARING THE DUCK BROTH A day or two before serving, remove the boneless breasts and the thighs from the duck or have the butcher do it. Reserve the breasts and thighs in the refrigerator and break up the remaining bones and wings with a heavy knife (I have an old carbon steel knife I keep around for such things) or a cleaver. In a 4-quart pot, brown the bones in vegetable oil with the onion, carrot, and garlic over high heat. Put in the bouquet garni and add enough water to cover. Simmer gently for 3 hours, skimming off fat and scum every once in a while. Add water as needed to keep the bones immersed.

STRAIN the broth into a clean 2-quart pot and reduce it at a slow simmer until 2½ cups remain. Reserve in the refrigerator.

COOKING THE DUCK MEAT The day before serving, remove any congealed fat that has formed on top of the chilled duck broth.

PEEL the skin off the duck breasts and thighs, using a paring knife to cut carefully between the meat and the skin.

PLACE the duck breasts and thighs in a 2-quart pot with a tight-fitting lid. Pour in the sherry and reserved duck broth and cover.

FIND a second pot with a cover that will completely contain the pot with the duck. Put about 2 inches of water in the larger pot and bring it to a rapid boil. Gently place the pot with the duck in the water and put the lid on the larger pot. Turn the heat down under the larger pot so the liquid in the larger pot stays at a slow simmer for 4 hours. Check the water in the larger pot every 30 minutes and add more as needed to make up for evaporation. Don't open the smaller pot.

AFTER 4 hours, take the whole apparatus off the stove and let it cool to room temperature. Take out the smaller pot—still don't open the lid or some of the soup's delicate aroma will be lost—and place it in the refrigerator overnight.

FINISHING THE SOUP Take the lid off the pot and use a spoon to carefully remove the tiny layer of congealed fat that has formed on the surface of the broth. Take the pieces of duck out of the pot and remove the meat from the bones. Separate the meat into fine shreds with your fingers. Discard any leftover pieces of skin or fat.

STRAIN the cold broth through a fine-mesh strainer. It might be slightly gelatinous, but this shouldn't prevent it from going through the strainer. Wash out the small pot and put in the shredded duck, the strained broth, and the Chinese mushrooms with their soaking liquid.

Just before serving, bring the soup to a simmer, add the scallions, and season with salt and pepper. Serve in small Chinese bowls.

Chinese Duck and Orange Soup

I got the idea for this soup from a wonderful crispy duck I once ate at Susanna Foo's Chinese restaurant in Philadelphia. Ms. Foo first braises the duck, coats it with water chestnut flour, and then deep-fries it. I've eliminated the deep-frying, cut the duck into smaller pieces, and use more broth, but I've retained the delicious combination of orange, star anise, and Szechuan peppers that I tasted in Philadelphia.

MAKES 6 FIRST-COURSE OR 4 LIGHT MAIN-COURSE SERVINGS

1 5-pound Long Island duck

salt

pepper

1 medium-size onion, peeled and quartered

1 medium-size carrot, peeled and cut into ½-inch-thick
    slices

2 quarts basic brown chicken broth or more as needed
    (page 62)

2 tablespoons Szechuan peppercorns (page 32)

6 large garlic cloves, peeled and chopped

8 scallions, both green and white parts, finely chopped

8 star anise

½ cup naturally brewed Japanese soy sauce

2 tablespoons sugar

2 navel oranges

¼ cup Grand Marnier or Cointreau (optional, don't
    substitute triple sec or orange curaçao, which have an
    artificial taste)

2 tablespoons balsamic vinegar or to taste

¼ cup Cognac

CUT up the duck as described in the box on page 494. Score the skin on the breasts by quickly sliding a very sharp chef's knife, held diagonally, along the surface of the skin. Cut as deeply as you can into the skin, but don't cut all the way down to the meat. Score 20 times in one direction, turn the duck 90°, and score 20 more times going in the other direction. This exposes the fat under the skin so it will render and the skin will turn crisp more quickly in the sauté pan.

SEASON the duck thighs and breasts on both sides with salt and pepper. Brown the duck parts, skin side down, over medium heat in a sauté pan just large enough to hold them in a single layer. When the skin is brown and crispy and the duck parts have released a lot of fat, after about 20 minutes, turn the parts flesh side down and sauté for 5 minutes more. If the duck skin is browning too quickly, turn down the heat. If you cook it over too high a heat the skin will brown without releasing its fat. Remove the duck, let it cool, and reserve in the refrigerator. Pour all but 2 table-spoons of the duck fat out of the sauté pan.

BREAK up the duck carcass into inch-wide pieces with a cleaver or heavy knife and put the pieces in the sauté pan with the onion and carrot. Brown the carcass and vegetables, stirring every few minutes, over medium heat, about 20 minutes. Use

SUPREMING AN ORANGE

To cut an orange into perfect wedges without any membrane attached—a method called supreming—cut the ends off the oranges, just deep enough in so you see the flesh, and set them on one end. Cut away the peel with a sharp knife, following the contour of the orange, leaving no membrane attached to the oranges. While holding the peeled orange over a bowl, cut along the thin membrane that separates the wedges down to the center of the orange, cutting out each of the wedges so that none of the membrane is left attached. Squeeze what's left in your hand—the membranes without any orange pulp—over the oranges, to extract the juice.

tongs to transfer the pieces of duck carcass and vegetables to a narrow pot and pour out and discard the fat from the sauté pan. Deglaze the sauté pan with 2 cups of the broth by simmering the broth for about 3 minutes over medium heat, while scraping the bottom of the pan with a wooden spoon. Pour this and the rest of the broth over the duck pieces. Bring to a simmer over high heat and turn the heat down to maintain the broth at a gentle simmer. Skim off any fat and scum with a ladle. Simmer for 3 hours with the cover ajar. If the broth evaporates, leaving some of the duck bones uncovered, add more broth or water from time to time to keep the duck carcass pieces covered. Put the Szechuan peppercorns in a small, heavy-bottomed skillet over medium heat and cook for about 20 minutes until they brown slightly and release their fragrance; shake the pan every few minutes so they brown evenly. About 10 minutes before you're ready to strain the broth, add the garlic and scallions and toasted Szechuan peppercorns. Crush the star anise by leaning on it with the corner of a saucepan and add it to the broth. Simmer for 10 minutes, then strain through a fine-mesh strainer or triple layer of cheesecloth. Discard the duck carcass and vegetables and wash out the pot.

PUT the browned duck pieces in the pot and pour over the strained broth. Stir in the soy sauce and sugar and simmer, partially covered (to prevent too much evaporation), very gently for 30 minutes, skimming off any foam and fat with a ladle.

CAREFULLY slice the zest off one of the oranges with a sharp knife, doing your best not to leave any white pith attached to the zest. Slice the zest into fine julienne. You can also use a zester—they have five tiny holes on one end—to peel away the zest in julienne. "Supreme" the oranges (see box, this page). Blanch the julienned zests by stirring them into a cup of boiling water, simmering for 30 seconds, and immediately draining through a strainer.

REACH into the duck broth and gently remove the duck pieces. Strain the broth into a clean pot. Pull the skin away from the duck pieces and discard it. Shred the duck meat with your fingers or cut it into cubes. Discard any bones. Put the duck into the simmering broth along with the orange zests, the Grand Marnier, vinegar, and Cognac. Simmer for 3 minutes and adjust the seasoning, adding more salt (usually not necessary because of the soy sauce) or Grand Marnier. Ladle the soup into hot bowls. Decorate the bowls with the orange wedges.

CUTTING UP A DUCK

Cut off any excess fat and skin including the large flap of skin attached to the neck end of the duck.

Turn the duck with the breasts facing down on the cutting board and cut off the wings where they join the body. Be sure to cut carefully around the joint so as not to damage any of the breast meat.

Turn the duck over with the drumsticks facing you. Make a 3-inch slit in the skin between the thigh and the breast. Reach in with your two thumbs and snap the thigh to dislocate the joint. Cut along the skin all the way to the back of the duck. Cut along the back, pulling the thigh as you go until it pulls off. Repeat with the other thigh.

To remove the breasts, cut down along one side of the breast bone which separates the two breasts. Keep the knife against the bone so you don't cut through the meat. Slide the knife along the bone around the side of the duck until the breast comes off. Repeat with the other breast.

You should now have two thighs, two breasts, two wings, and the remaining carcass with the rib cage and back. When making broth, break the rib cage and the back into smaller pieces with a cleaver or old knife.

VARIATIONS | Because this is such a time-consuming dish, I sometimes turn it into a main course by adding vegetables such as blanched spinach leaves (or Chinese spinach) or Swiss chard, other Chinese greens (see box, page 117), and/or soaked rice noodles or cooked soba noodles.

Smoked Duck and Wild Rice Soup

Because wild rice has a natural affinity for game and smoked foods, I like to pair it with smoked duck, chicken, pork, or goose. It also works well with leftover barbecued chicken or pork, and I've even paired it with duck confit. I also infuse the broth with a little bacon to reinforce the smoky flavor and use onions, port, and vinegar to add a sweet and sour dimension.

MAKES 8 FIRST-COURSE OR 4 MAIN-COURSE SERVINGS

2 teaspoons salt, for cooking rice

¾ cup wild rice, well rinsed

¼ pound thick-sliced bacon, cut into ¼-inch cubes

2 large red onions, peeled, as thinly sliced as possible
   (a plastic vegetable slicer is good for this)

¼ cup port (optional)

6 cups basic brown chicken broth (see page 62) (or duck
     broth (see page 89)

I pound smoked duck, chicken, turkey, duck or goose
     confit, or pork, skin removed (from poultry) and
     discarded, meat cut into ¼-inch cubes (or, if you're
     using confit, pulled away in shreds)

salt

pepper

2 tablespoons red wine vinegar or more to taste

BRING 6 cups of water to a rapid boil in a large pot with the 2 teaspoons salt. Add the wild rice, turn down the heat to maintain the water a gentle simmer, and partially cover the pot. Cook the rice for about 45 minutes (wild rice takes much longer to cook than regular white rice), but don't overcook it or it will burst open. It should still have some texture when you bite into a piece. (Start tasting the grains after 30 minutes of cooking.)

WHILE the rice is simmering, cook the bacon cubes for about 10 minutes in a large (large enough to hold the sliced onions) heavy-bottomed pot over medium heat until they render their fat and barely begin to turn crispy. Add the onions to the pot, turn the heat up high, and stir the onions around until they release their liquid. If they start to brown, turn down the heat. When the onions have released liquid and it begins to caramelize on the bottom of the pot after about 20 minutes, scrape the bottom of the pot with a wooden spoon. Stir in the port and continue simmering until it evaporates. Add the chicken broth, simmer for 5 minutes, and stir in the cubes of smoked duck or chicken or other meats. Drain the rice and add it to the soup. Add the vinegar to taste and bring back to the simmer. Season to taste with salt and pepper and, if it needs it, more vinegar.

Squab

SQUABS, ONCE A RARE DELICACY SERVED ONLY IN THE MOST EXPENSIVE RESTAURANTS, are now available at most fancy grocers or butchers, but, unfortunately, they're not cheap. Like duck, I prefer to cut squabs, which are really pigeons (but not from the park), into pieces and cook each part using the cooking method that best suits it. I quickly sauté or grill the boneless breasts, leaving them rare, and use the rest of the bird for making broth, the base for sauces and, of course, soup.

Squab Soup

Venetian recipe books often include recipes for squab (pigeon) soup made by simmering the squabs gently and then baking them, stacked between layers of bread and Parmigiano. The idea of a squab soup has always appealed to me—squabs, I think, are the tastiest farm-raised game birds—but a long stewing never has seemed appropriate for the tender (and expensive) domesticated squabs I've found in the United States. So I've played around with the recipe a bit by making a broth out of the squab thighs (which are always tough) and carcasses, sautéing the breasts at the last minute, finishing the soup with the pureed livers from the squabs (much like a giblet gravy), and then placing the sliced breasts on a piece of toasted bread in the middle of the soup. You can serve this soup as a first course, serving the breast from 1/2 squab per person, or as a main course, giving everyone the two half-breasts from a whole squab. The most time-consuming part of this soup, making the squab broth, can be done up to a day ahead.

MAKES 4 MAIN-COURSE OR 8 FIRST-COURSE SERVINGS

4 squabs, preferably with livers, lungs, and hearts

salt

pepper

1/2 cup unsalted butter

1 medium-size onion, coarsely chopped

1 garlic clove, crushed

2 cups full-bodied red wine

8 cups basic brown chicken broth (page 62)

bouquet garni including 5 fresh thyme sprigs
    (or 1/2 teaspoon dried), 1 bunch of parsley, and
    1 bay leaf

4 slices of French bread, ½ inch thick and 4 to 5 inches in
    diameter, large enough to hold 2 squab breasts
    (2 breasts per squab), or 8 smaller slices, large enough
    to hold a single breast
3 tablespoons olive oil or clarified butter (for browning
    breasts)
2 tablespoons chopped parsley (chopped at the last minute)

REACH into the squabs and pull out and reserve the livers, lungs, and hearts. Cut off the wings where they join the body of the squab and cut off the thighs, keeping the knife pointed against the inside of the thigh. It's important that the breast meat remain covered with skin. Remove the breasts by sliding a small sharp knife along the breast bone and then down along the rib cage until the boneless breasts are completely detached so that each squab gives you two breasts. Season the skin on boneless breasts on both sides with salt and pepper and keep refrigerated until needed.

CHOP up the thighs, wings, and carcasses with a cleaver or heavy knife and brown them in 2 tablespoons butter with the onion and garlic over medium to high heat in a small heavy-bottomed pot, stirring every few minutes, for about 15 minutes. Pour in the red wine, turn the heat up to high, and boil the wine until it evaporates. Pour in the chicken broth, scrape the bottom of the pot with a wooden spoon, nestle in the bouquet garni, and simmer gently—don't let the broth come to a hard boil—for 2 hours, using a ladle to skim off fat and froth that floats to the top. Strain the squab broth, discard the bones and bouquet garni, and reserve the broth.

IF you have a miniature food processor, puree the livers, lungs and hearts with 4 tablespoons butter. Otherwise, chop them together—with the butter—by hand to the consistency of a paste. Reserve in a medium-size heatproof mixing bowl. If you don't have any innards (or don't want to use them), reserve just the butter for finishing the broth.

BROWN the bread slices, in a frying pan, on both sides in the remaining 2 tablespoons butter and keep warm.

BRING the broth to a gentle simmer.

SAUTÉ the squab breasts, skin side down first, in the olive oil or clarified butter over very high heat for about 3 minutes. Turn them over and sauté them for about 1½ minutes on the flesh side; they should be well browned but rare in the middle. Slice them lengthwise into about six slices per breast and arrange them on the toasts in the middle of heated soup plates. Keep warm in the oven while finishing the broth.

Combine the parsley with the liver/butter puree and whisk in half of the hot broth. Pour this mixture into the pot with the rest of the broth—don't let the soup come to a boil at this point or it will curdle—and season to taste with salt and pepper. Ladle the broth around the toasts in each bowl and serve immediately.

Rabbit

IT DOESN'T OCCUR TO MANY OF US TO EAT RABBIT, MUCH LESS MAKE A SOUP OUT OF it. But once you get over any anxiety about eating it—we Americans seem to be alone in our distaste for rabbit—you can cook it virtually the same way you would chicken. An easy way to use rabbit in soup is to cut it up and brown it, simmer it in broth until the meat is cooked through, pull the cooked meat away from the bones, and reserve it. You can then continue simmering the bones in the broth to make it more concentrated and then add the cooked meat shortly before serving. Virtually any of the recipes for chicken soup (see page 470) can be converted to rabbit soup by using this method. The recipe given below is somewhat more sophisticated, since it involves boning the saddle, which makes it easier to eat and more elegant to look at.

Rabbit Soup with Foie Gras Stuffed Saddle

I've never had an aversion to rabbit (if something's got flesh on it I'll eat it) but rabbit frustrates me for other reasons. The front section—the rib cage and forelegs—doesn't have enough meat on it to make decent servings and the hindquarter, other than the two hind legs, has a complicated bone structure that most people can't figure out while trying to get at the meat. My solution is to make a concentrated broth with most of the rabbit and bone out the hindquarter ahead of time. I then serve the hindquarter, rolled up and tied, stuffed or not, sliced into rounds that I arrange on a small mound of pasta surrounded with the broth. Depending on how much you serve, this soup makes an elegant first course or a light main course.

The first task is to track down a couple of rabbits—they often come frozen—weighing 2 to 3 pounds each. Don't buy a rabbit that's any heavier or it will be tough.

MAKES 6 FIRST-COURSE SERVINGS OR 4 LIGHT MAIN-COURSE SERVINGS

2 2- to 3-pound rabbits

1 medium-size onion, peeled and quartered

1 medium-size carrot, peeled and cut into 1-inch sections

2 quarts brown chicken broth or more as needed to cover
    bones

bouquet garni containing 5 fresh thyme sprigs or
    ½ teaspoon dried thyme, 1 medium bunch of parsley,
    and 1 bay leaf

salt

pepper

4 ounces terrine of foie gras (optional)

2 tablespoons unsalted butter

½ pound fresh egg noodles such as fettuccine or linguine

2 tablespoons finely chopped parsley

1 tablespoon olive oil

BONING A SADDLE

To bone a saddle, turn the saddle on its back and notice the two thin muscles that run along its length, next to the backbone—these are the tenderloins. Slide a knife under these muscles, scraping them away from the underlying bone as you go. Slide the knife under the toothlike range of bones that were laying under the tenderloins and continue, following the bones' contours, until you detach the thicker—loin—muscles that run along the backbone closer to the back of the saddle. Continue in this way until you reach the small cartilaginous bones that poke through the outside membrane along the back. As you approach these bones, you may make a harmless tear or two but try to keep the skin as intact as possible. At this point, don't try to cut completely around the bones or you'll cut through the membrane. When you've practically detached the backbone—the skin should hang from the bone only along the very thin ridge of bones that practically protrude through the back—turn the saddle over with the back facing up. Gently pull the outer membrane back, and cut through the cartilaginous bones, one by one, while peeling back the membrane. You'll have to leave a tiny bit of bone embedded in the outer membrane—if you try to cut it out of the membrane you'll tear it. Continue in this way until you've cut through all the bones and the backbone comes away in one piece. Season the inside of the saddles with salt and pepper and reserve in the refrigerator.

CUT the head off the rabbit if it has one, and reserve. Cut off the forelegs—this is easy because there are no joints to cut through—and separate the front part of the rabbit by cutting crosswise between the second and third ribs (starting from the back) all the way down to the spinal column. Cut away the front part by giving the spine a whack with a heavy knife or cleaver where the two cuts you made join. Cut the rib cage into several pieces with a cleaver and reserve. Cut the two hind legs away from the rabbit by sliding a knife against the pelvis and through the joint that joins the legs to the body. This will leave you with the saddle—the hind section (the back)—with a piece of bone protruding out where you cut away the thighs. Hack the bone off with a cleaver or heavy knife. Reserve all bones and bone the two saddles.

COMBINE the reserved bones, the bones from the saddles, the two hind legs, and the head with the vegetables in a roasting pan just large enough to hold everything in a single layer, and roast the bones, hind legs, and heads, in a 450°F oven, stirring every 20 minutes with a wooden spoon, until all the bones and thighs are well browned, about an hour.

PLACE a bouquet garni in a small pot, arrange the rabbit bones, hind legs, and vegetables in the pot on top of the bouquet garni (the bouquet garni goes in first so it doesn't float to the top and interfere with skimming), and deglaze the pan with 2 cups of broth. Put the pan on the stove with the broth and scrape it with a wooden spoon to dissolve the caramelized juices. Pour the deglazing liquid over the bones, thighs, and head in the pot and pour over the rest of the broth. Bring to a gentle simmer and simmer for 2 hours, using a ladle to skim off fat and scum. Strain the broth and reserve. Discard the bones but reserve the whole thighs. Pull the meat off the thighs in shreds and reserve.

PREHEAT the oven to 400°F.

Cut the foie gras into 2 long pieces about the same length as the reserved saddles. Put the foie gras in each of the saddles, fold over the flaps, and tie the saddles together in about four places with string. Season the outsides with salt and pepper and brown the saddles in butter over medium heat for about 6 minutes, turning them after 3 minutes so they are evenly browned. Place the saddles in a small roasting pan or skillet and roast them for about 15 minutes, until an instant-read thermometer reads 125°F when slid into the center of the saddle.

WHILE the saddles are roasting, bring about 2 quarts of water to a rapid boil for cooking the pasta. Bring the rabbit broth to the simmer, add the shredded thigh meat, the parsley, and season to taste with salt and pepper. Add a small handful of salt and a tablespoon of olive oil to the pasta water. Cook and drain the pasta and season the rabbit broth to taste. Take the string off the saddles and slice them crosswise into six slices each. Place a small mound of pasta in the center of four or six heated soup plates. If you're serving the soup as a first course, arrange two saddle slices on each serving; if you're serving it as a main course, arrange three saddle slices on each serving. Ladle the rabbit broth with the shredded thigh meat around each mound of pasta.

Pork

THERE ARE BASICALLY TWO KINDS OF PORK SOUPS: EUROPEAN LONG-SIMMERED SOUPS that usually contain large chunks of pork, cabbage, beans, root vegetables, and sometimes sausages and Asian soups featuring thinly sliced strips of pork that are sometimes marinated and then usually stir-fried with flavorful ingredients.

Most European-style pork soups are hearty farmhouse concoctions and can be full meals in themselves. For these long-simmered soups, pork shoulder is the best cut. A whole shoulder, which weighs about 5 pounds, can be hard to find on the spur of the moment, so unless the recipe calls for very large pieces of meat that are sliced after being cooked, it's easier to buy pork shoulder chops and just cut off the bones. You can also use center-cut rib or loin chops, but because these contain less fat they tend to dry out during prolonged cooking. They are also more expensive than shoulder.

When you're selecting pork for an Asian-style soup, buy loin of pork that is relatively lean and easy to trim of excess fat and cut it into strips or cubes. You can also use pork tenderloin, the leanest of all pork cuts, but it's more expensive. Supermarkets may not have whole large pieces of loin of pork or pork tenderloin, and you'll have to buy pork chops and cut off the bones yourself. Center-cut rib chops or loin chops work best.

Tomatillo and Sorrel Soup with Hominy

POZOLE VERDE

The word *pozole* means hominy, the large white kernels of dried corn that have been treated with calcium hydroxide, also called *slaked lime*. A *pozole* is also any soup or stew made with hominy. You can use canned hominy, which just needs to be rinsed and added to the soup at the end, but the soup is far tastier and prettier to look at when you make it with dried hominy.

Mexican and Latin cooks make dozens of *pozoles,* but this version—a variation of Diana Kennedy's recipe in *The Art of Mexican Cooking*—is my favorite because it contains not only chilies but also sour things such as Mexican tomatillos and sorrel. Then, best of all, it is sprinkled with avocado, oregano, chopped onions, and my own addition (probably heretical), sour cream.

MAKES 8 GENEROUS FIRST-COURSE SERVINGS

2 cups whole dried hominy or 1 30-ounce can, drained

1 large white onion, chopped

2 garlic cloves, peeled

2 pounds boneless trimmed pork from shoulder or rib
    chops, cut into ½-inch cubes

6 cups chicken broth

3 cups quartered husked tomatillos or 2 18-ounce cans,
    drained

¾ cup pumpkin seeds, hulled and lightly toasted in a 350°F
    oven

30 large sorrel leaves, stems removed (optional)

1 to 3 serrano or jalapeño chilies, seeded and finely
    chopped

2 tablespoons fresh lime juice

salt

the toppings:

1 medium-size white onion, finely chopped

dried oregano, preferably Mexican

1 or 2 avocados, peeled, pitted, and cut into small cubes

2 limes, cut into wedges

sour cream

IF you're using dried or homemade hominy, rinse it in a colander and place it in a clean 4-quart pot. Add the onion, garlic, pork, and chicken broth. Bring to a simmer, cover the pot, and cook until the corn is tender and each of the kernels has burst open so that it looks like a small flower, about two hours.

IF you're using canned hominy, don't cook it at this stage; just simmer the pork in a covered pot with the onion, garlic, and chicken broth for two hours. You may need to add extra chicken broth or water from time to time to make up for evaporation.

DRAIN the hominy/pork mixture or the pork mixture into a colander and save the liquid.

COMBINE the tomatillos with the strained cooking liquid in a 4-quart pot. Cover the pot and bring to a slow simmer for about 20 minutes, until the tomatillos are completely soft.

GRIND the toasted pumpkin seeds to a fine powder in a spice or coffee grinder. Add them to the tomatillos along with the sorrel and chilies and simmer the mixture for 10 minutes more.

STRAIN the tomatillo mixture through the fine disk of a food mill and then a medium-mesh strainer or skip the food mill and puree the ingredients in a blender before straining.

BRING the strained soup to a simmer in a clean pot and add the hominy and pork mixture or just the pork and the canned hominy along with the lime juice. At this point you may want to thin the soup by adding water or broth. Simmer the soup for 15 minutes more, add salt to taste, and serve. Pass the toppings at the table.

SUGGESTIONS AND VARIA-TIONS | Diana Kennedy's version calls for a sprig of fresh epazote simmered with the soup for the last 10 minutes. Epazote adds a unique, subtle flavor but can be difficult to find.

MAKING YOUR OWN HOMINY

Hominy is prepared by soaking dried corn kernels in a solution of slaked lime (calcium hydroxide or pickling lime), sold at drugstores, Mexican grocery stores, or specialty stores that sell pickling products.

Place 2 cups dried white field corn in a 4-quart non-aluminum pot with enough water to cover it by 2 or 3 inches. Combine 2½ teaspoons slaked lime with 1 cup cold water in a small bowl and strain into the corn. Bring the corn to a simmer and cook gently over low to medium heat for about 20 minutes. Take the pot off the heat and allow the corn to cool in the cooking liquid.

Drain the corn in a colander, rinse it, and place it in a large mixing bowl. Cover the corn with cold water. Rub the kernels between your hands to detach the skin from the kernels. Skim off any skins that float to the top of the water and rinse off the corn in a colander. Remove and discard the hard point on each of the kernels with a thumb nail or a sharp paring knife. The kernels should be perfectly white with no husk attached.

AFICIONADOS of Mexican food will probably blanch, but I sometimes skip the hominy and cut the kernels off 4 ears of fresh corn and simmer them in the soup for the last 10 minutes of cooking.

Szechuan Pork and Pickle Soup

Once you have the ingredients, this soup takes about 10 minutes to cook, and it's delicious, light, and exotic enough to provoke plenty of dinner conversation.

After reading *Bruce Cost's Asian Ingredients*, I became totally fascinated with—and confused by—Chinese preserved vegetables. There are several types made from different varieties of cabbage, turnip, or radish and cured in a variety of flavorful mixtures. Other than the Szechuan preserved vegetable (actually a kind of cabbage called "mustard" cabbage) called for here, there are also *tientsin* vegetable (a kind of preserved cabbage like Korean *kimchee*), and pickled and dried mustard greens called *gan-cai-sun*.

I later found a recipe similar to the one given here in Barbara Tropp's fat and fascinating book, *The Modern Art of Chinese Cooking*.

MAKES 4 SERVINGS

2 pork chops, bone and fat removed, about ½ pound
    trimmed meat

1 tablespoon dry sherry

1 tablespoon dark soy sauce

½ teaspoon dark sesame oil

freshly ground pepper

3 ounces Szechuan preserved vegetable

1 quart chicken broth

2 scallions, both white and green parts, finely chopped

SLICE the pork meat as thinly as you can; shreds about ⅛ by 1 inch are ideal. Toss the pork in a bowl with the sherry, soy sauce, and sesame oil. Grind in some fresh pepper and let sit for 30 minutes to an hour.

RINSE the red paste off the preserved vegetable and cut the vegetable into shreds the same size as the meat.

BRING the broth to a simmer and add the vegetable and the pork mixture—stir it quickly to break apart the meat and disperse the shredded vegetable. Simmer for about 3 minutes, add the scallions, and simmer for 30 seconds more.

IF necessary, season the soup with more soy sauce.

SUGGESTIONS AND VARIATIONS | If you want to make this soup more substantial, do as Barbara Tropp does and add 3 ounces cellophane noodles (soaked for 10 minutes in warm water) at the same time as the shredded meat and vegetable. You can also add a bit more pork and turn this into a main-course soup.

Lamb

MOST CUTS OF LAMB ARE TOO EXPENSIVE FOR SOUP AND WOULDN'T MAKE GOOD culinary sense anyway. My favorite cut for making lamb soups is the shank, which is inexpensive, stays moist during cooking, and provides a delicious broth. Its only disadvantage is that it often needs to be ordered a day in advance from the butcher—a damper for the spontaneous cook. If you're using shanks to make a small amount of soup, have your butcher cut them in half crosswise so they'll fit into the pot. You can also use lamb shoulder, neck, or even, for the extravagant, leg.

Spicy Moroccan Soup of Lamb and Chick-Peas

HARIRA

Moroccan cooks have such a knack for using spices that I sometimes consult Moroccan recipes just to come up with new flavor combinations. When I was researching French medieval cooking, I discovered many of the same combinations in books written more than 500 years ago. Saffron, lemon, turmeric, mint, ginger, anise, cumin, and both the seeds and leaves (cilantro) of the coriander plant are all used to create exotic and surprising flavors.

Another interesting component of Moroccan cooking is *smen*—butter cooked in the same way as *ghee* (page 592). Because *smen* has all the liquid cooked out of it, it can be stored for long periods without turning rancid. Although *smen* has a characteristic flavor, most Moroccan soups can be made using whole butter.

MAKES 12 FIRST-COURSE OR 6 MAIN-COURSE SERVINGS

4 1-pound lamb shanks or 1¼ pounds lamb shoulder or
    stew meat, cut into ¾-inch cubes

2 tablespoons *ghee* (page 592) or 3 tablespoons whole butter
    or more as needed

2 medium-size onions, finely chopped

1 celery rib, finely chopped

1 teaspoon ground turmeric or 2 teaspoons finely chopped
    fresh

1 teaspoon finely chopped fresh ginger

1 teaspoon ground cinnamon

pinch of saffron threads

¾ cup dried chick-peas, soaked overnight in just enough
  water to cover

2 quarts water or meat broth

¾ cup dried lentils

6 medium-size tomatoes, peeled, seeded, and chopped, or
  3 cups drained and seeded canned tomatoes, chopped

2 tablespoons finely chopped parsley leaves

½ cup packed cilantro leaves, finely chopped

1 cup yogurt

salt

pepper

IN a 4-quart pot, lightly brown the lamb in the *ghee* or butter. If you're using *ghee*, use high heat, but if you're using whole butter use medium heat or the butter will burn. Take the lamb out of the pot. If the butter has burned, pour it out and replace it with fresh. Add the onions and celery. Stir over medium heat for about 5 minutes and then add the turmeric, ginger, cinnamon, and saffron. Stir for 5 minutes more.

RETURN the lamb to the pot and add the chick-peas, a cup of the chick-pea-soaking liquid if it hasn't been absorbed, and the water. Cover the pot and simmer gently for an hour. Add the lentils and tomatoes and simmer for an hour more or until the meat offers no resistance when you poke it with a fork and the lentils are completely soft. Use a ladle to skim off any fat that has floated to the top of the soup. If you're using lamb shanks, take them out of the soup and pull the meat away from the bones. Shred the meat or cut it into cubes and return it to the rest of the soup. Stir in the parsley, cilantro, and yogurt. Season the soup with salt and pepper.

SUGGESTIONS AND VARIATIONS
I sometimes simmer cubed potatoes in the broth about 20 minutes before serving or add cooked rice to the *harira* just before serving to convert it into a substantial meal. Some recipes also suggest adding vermicelli noodles.

USING LEFTOVER ROAST LAMB

I eat lamb in practically every form—roast leg of lamb for a quick-to-prepare substantial dinner that provides plenty of leftovers, rack of lamb if I'm showing off or just want a special treat, and braised lamb shanks if I want something cozy and old-fashioned. All of these lamb dishes leave me with plenty of bones and little pieces of meat for making soup.

To prepare a simple lamb soup with the trimmings from a leg of lamb, trim all the meat off the bone and simmer the bone for a couple of hours to make a broth. Discard the bone, skim off any fat and froth, and strain the broth into a clean pot. Cut any leftover meat into ½-inch cubes and add it to the broth along with 1 cup dried beans that have been soaked for a couple of hours, a chopped carrot and onion, and a fresh bouquet garni. Simmer until the beans are soft, about an hour.

Moroccan-Style Lamb Soup with Dried Apricots

Another delicious lamb soup from Morocco. The techniques for making this soup are very similar to those used in French cooking, but the herbs and spices used are completely different. I particularly like the exotic combination of dried fruit and almonds.

This recipe uses lamb shanks, which never seem to overcook and dry out, but cubes of lamb shoulder or lamb stew meat will do in a pinch.

MAKES 12 FIRST-COURSE OR 6 MAIN-COURSE SERVINGS

4 lamb shanks, cut in half crosswise by the butcher,
     trimmed of fat, or 1¼ pounds lamb shoulder, cut into
     ¾-inch cubes

¼ cup olive oil

4 garlic cloves

2½ quarts chicken, beef, or lamb broth or water

I medium-size onion, finely chopped

2 garlic cloves, finely chopped

I teaspoon ground turmeric or 2 teaspoons finely chopped
     fresh

a ¼-inch slice of fresh ginger, peeled and finely chopped, or
     ½ teaspoon ground

pinch of saffron

I 4-inch cinnamon stick or I teaspoon ground

6 medium-size tomatoes, peeled, seeded, and chopped or
     3 cups canned, seeded and drained

I cup dried apricots

30 pearl onions, peeled

½ cup slivered almonds

I tablespoon finely chopped cilantro leaves

I tablespoon finely chopped fresh mint leaves

salt

pepper

¼ cup white wine vinegar

IN a 4-quart pot over high heat, brown the lamb in half the olive oil. Turn down the heat and drain off the burned fat. Add the unpeeled garlic cloves and broth. Bring to a slow simmer, cover, and simmer the lamb for 2½ to 3 hours. Use a ladle to skim off any fat or froth that floats to the top. If there isn't enough liquid to cover the shanks, turn them around in the liquid halfway into the cooking. You may also need to add more broth or water from time to time to make up for evaporation.

IN a 4-quart pot over medium heat, cook the onion and finely chopped garlic in the remaining olive oil for about 5 minutes. Add the turmeric, ginger, and saffron and cook the mixture for 5 minutes more.

ADD the cinnamon, tomatoes, dried apricots, and pearl onions to the spice mixture and strain in the liquid from the lamb shanks. Simmer gently for about 20 minutes.

REMOVE the meat from the lamb shanks, discarding any pieces of fat, bone, or cartilage. Cut the meat into small cubes and add it to the soup.

PREHEAT the oven to 375°F and lightly toast the slivered almonds for about 15 minutes.

A minute before serving, remove and discard the cinnamon stick, stir the chopped cilantro and mint along with the vinegar into the soup, and season with salt and pepper. Ladle the soup into wide bowls and sprinkle the toasted almonds over it.

SUGGESTIONS AND VARIATIONS | This is a generous soup that can easily be turned into the focal point of a simple meal. Serve it with a plate of couscous and a green salad to follow.

BY all means play around with the spices in the spice mixture. If you have fresh marjoram or thyme, tie it into a bouquet garni and cook with the lamb.

Indian Curried Lamb Soup

This fragrant soup is a revelation to anyone who has never tasted a curry made with an assortment of ground spices rather than a commercial curry powder. For the best results you can grind your own spices using a coffee or spice grinder, but I use ground spices that I keep in the freezer.

This soup is inspired by Indian *kormas*, which are finished with cream and yogurt, but you can substitute extra yogurt for the cream.

MAKES 10 SERVINGS

> 4 1-pound lamb shanks, cut in half crosswise by the
> butcher, trimmed of fat, or 1¼ pounds lamb shoulder,
> cut into ½-inch cubes
> 3 tablespoons vegetable oil
> 2 quarts broth or water

8 garlic cloves

2 tablespoons unsalted butter or *ghee* (page 592)

2 medium-size onions, finely chopped

a ¼-inch slice of fresh ginger, peeled and finely chopped

I teaspoon ground cumin

I teaspoon ground mace

½ teaspoon ground cinnamon

2 teaspoons ground coriander

I teaspoon ground cardamom

½ teaspoon cayenne pepper

3 medium-size tomatoes, peeled, seeded, and chopped or
   I ½ cups canned, seeded and drained

I cup heavy cream

I cup yogurt

2 tablespoons finely chopped cilantro

salt

cayenne pepper

juice of 2 limes

IN a 4-quart pot over high heat, brown the lamb in the vegetable oil. Drain off the burned fat. Turn down the heat, add the broth, and bring to a slow simmer. Cover the pot and simmer the lamb for about 1-½ hours, using a ladle to skim off any fat or froth that floats to the top. If the shanks aren't completely covered with liquid, turn them over halfway into the cooking. You may need to add liquid from time to time to make up for evaporation.

ADD the unpeeled garlic cloves and simmer for ½ to 1 hour more, until the meat can easily be pulled away from the bones.

WHEN the lamb is done, heat the butter in a 4-quart pot over medium heat. Add the onions and stir gently for about 15 minutes, until they brown slightly, but don't allow them to burn. Add the ginger and spices and stir for 5 minutes more.

STRAIN the lamb broth into the spice mixture. Push the garlic cloves against the strainer so their pulp goes through into the soup. Remove the lamb shanks, let them cool slightly, and pull the meat away from the bone. Discard any pieces of fat or bone and cut the meat into small cubes.

ADD the tomatoes to the spice mixture and simmer for 10 minutes. Add the cubes of lamb and whisk in the cream, yogurt, and cilantro. Bring the soup back to a simmer, add the lime juice, and season with salt and cayenne pepper if you want it hotter.

SUGGESTIONS AND VARIATIONS | Although this soup has a thin texture and a delicate flavor, it is quite rich. Usually I serve it with a bowl of basmati rice as the main course, but if you want to show it off as the first course in a more elaborate dinner, follow it with something light—perhaps a grilled fish.

IF you don't want to wait for 2 hours for the lamb to cook, use a chicken, quartered, browned, and cooked the same way as the lamb. Add the garlic at the same time as the chicken and cook for only 30 minutes.

Malaysian Lamb, Red Lentil, and Eggplant Soup

BAHMIA

This is one of those traditional stews that enters my kitchen and comes out a soup. My fascination with soup has reached obsessive dimensions, and my more frequent dinner guests have gotten used to sitting down to a succession of liquid and semiliquid courses.

In the original version the split peas remain whole and the eggplant is served in slices. In this soup version the eggplant is pureed, contributing its texture to the soup; fresh or frozen peas and tiny cubes of lamb are the only ingredients left solid.

MAKES 12 FIRST-COURSE OR 6 MAIN-COURSE SERVINGS

4 1-pound lamb shanks, cut in half crosswise by the
    butcher, trimmed of fat, or 1¼ pounds lamb shoulder,
    cut into ½-inch cubes

3 tablespoons vegetable oil

4 garlic cloves, crushed

2 quarts beef, chicken, or lamb broth or water

3 tablespoons unsalted butter

2 medium-size onions, finely chopped

2 garlic cloves, finely chopped

3 Thai chilies or 6 jalapeño chilies, seeded and finely
    chopped

2 teaspoons ground coriander

1 teaspoon ground cardamom

½ teaspoon ground cloves

1 teaspoon fennel seeds

a ½-inch slice of fresh ginger, peeled and finely chopped

1 cup red lentils, checked for pebbles, rinsed

3 medium-size tomatoes, peeled, seeded, and chopped or
    1½ cups canned, seeded and drained

2 small eggplants, about 5 ounces each, preferably Asian
    type, peeled and sliced crosswise ½-inch thick

1¾ cups coconut milk

1 bunch of fresh mint leaves, stems removed,
    about 6 tablespoons

salt

pepper

¼ cup white wine vinegar

IN a 4-quart pot over high heat, brown the lamb in the vegetable oil. Drain off the burned fat.

TURN down the heat, add the unpeeled garlic cloves and broth, and bring to a slow simmer. Cover the pot and simmer the lamb for 2 hours. Use a ladle to skim off any fat or froth that floats to the top. If the lamb is not completely covered with liquid, turn it over halfway into the cooking. You may need to add water to the pot from time to time to make up for evaporation.

HEAT the butter in a 4-quart pot over medium heat and add the onion, freshly chopped garlic, and chilies. Stir for about 5 minutes, add the ground spices and ginger, and stir for 5 minutes more.

STRAIN the lamb broth into the spice mixture. Remove the lamb shanks, let them cool slightly, and pull the meat away from the bone. Discard any pieces of fat or bone and cut the meat into small cubes.

ADD the lentils, tomatoes, and eggplant to the spice mixture and simmer gently until the lentils are soft, about 30 minutes. Puree the soup by working it through the fine disk of a food mill or puree it in a blender and strain it through a medium-mesh strainer into a clean pot.

STIR in the lamb, coconut milk, mint, and vinegar. Season with salt and pepper.

SUGGESTIONS AND VARIATIONS | The method of gently cooking onions and garlic and then adding lamb broth and simmering the mixture with vegetables can be applied to almost any national cuisine. The red lentils can also be replaced with practically any kind of fresh or dried bean—yellow split peas work especially well with lamb—but slower-cooking beans should be simmered separately until they start to soften before being added to the rest of the ingredients.

Scotch Broth

I always thought of Scotch broth as an overly thick and definitely stodgy sort of soup until I began researching it and experimenting. I've since realized that a well-made Scotch broth is really a rich lamb broth with vegetables to give it freshness and a small amount of barley to give it substance and a little texture.

I've adapted this recipe to my own tastes: it contains less barley than the standard versions and no thickener, but I find it eminently satisfying and not stodgy at all.

MAKES 10 SERVINGS

3 pounds lamb shoulder or stew meat, cut into
    ½-inch cubes

1 bouquet garni

½ cup pearl barley, soaked in cold water for 2 hours

3 medium-size carrots, sliced

1 medium-size turnip, peeled and cut into ½-inch cubes

1 large onion or 3 leeks, white part only, finely sliced

1 celery rib, finely sliced

3 garlic cloves, peeled

salt

1 small bunch of parsley, stems removed, finely chopped

PLACE the meat in a 6-quart pot and enough water to cover the meat by 3 inches. Bring to a simmer over medium to high heat. Turn the heat down and skim off any froth that floats to the top. Add the bouquet garni and barley and simmer slowly for 1½ hours, adding water as needed to make up for evaporation. Continue to skim off fat and froth during the cooking.

ADD the vegetables and more water if necessary to cover. Simmer the soup for 1 hour more.

JUST before serving, take out the bouquet garni, season with salt and add the finely chopped parsley. Ladle the soup into hot bowls.

SUGGESTIONS AND VARIATIONS | There's no need to limit yourself to the vegetables given here. I like to take the same free and easy approach I would if I were making a simple vegetable soup and just add fresh vegetables—pearl onions, mushrooms, spinach, green beans, baby carrots and turnips, or sorrel—just long enough before serving to cook them through.

TO make this soup suitable as a main course, cook the lamb in one chunk (tied up with string) and then slice and present it in wide bowls in the broth. Even fancier: prepare a lamb broth using lamb stew meat and then gently poach a well-trimmed small leg of lamb in the broth for about 30 minutes. Slice the lamb—it should still be rosy—and serve it in wide bowls surrounded by broth.

Arabian Lamb and Tomato Soup

MEZZA BISHURBA

This simple lamb and tomato soup from Saudi Arabia can be made into a substantial meal by adding extra rice. It can also be kept light and served either hot or cold as a summer soup. Although older recipes specify simmering the lamb with the tomatoes for several hours, in this version the lamb is cooked in water and the tomatoes are added near the end so they keep some of their texture and their fresh flavor.

If you want a more stewlike version with meatier chunks, use lamb shoulder instead of shanks.

MAKES 10 SERVINGS

3 lamb shanks, cut in half crosswise by the butcher,
     trimmed of fat, or 2 pounds lamb shoulder, cut into
     ¾-inch cubes

2 tablespoons olive oil

4 garlic cloves

I quart chicken or beef broth or water

12 vine-ripened medium-size tomatoes, peeled, seeded, and
     chopped

I bunch of fresh mint or cilantro, stems removed,
     ¼ cup coarsely chopped

salt

pepper

IN a 6-quart pot over high heat, brown the lamb in the olive oil. Drain off the burned fat.

TURN down the heat, add the unpeeled garlic cloves and enough broth to cover the meat by I inch, and bring to a slow simmer. Simmer the lamb for 2½ to 3 hours. Use a ladle to skim off any fat or froth that floats to the top. You may need to add water to the pot from time to time to make up for evaporation.

IF you're using lamb shanks, take them out of the cooking liquid, remove the meat, and discard the bones. Cut the meat into cubes or strips and add it to the broth.

ADD the tomatoes and bring to a simmer. Simmer for 10 minutes. Stir in the mint or cilantro, season with salt and pepper, and serve.

SUGGESTIONS AND VARIATIONS | It's easy to give this soup a completely different character by adding a few different ingredients. For a Mexican-style soup, add 1 or 2 finely chopped jalapeño peppers and use chopped cilantro, not mint. You can make it Italian by adding chopped oregano and maybe some precooked white beans. A pinch of saffron will give it a Spanish character.

TO make the soup more substantial, add ½ cup rice about 20 minutes before adding the tomatoes. You can also stir a cup of yogurt into the soup just a minute before serving.

Beef

BEEF HAS SUCH A FULL FLAVOR THAT WE DON'T NEED TO EAT A THICK STEAK TO APPRE-
ciate it—a little will go a long way.

Beef is used in soups in one of two ways. In American and European soups the beef
is cut into relatively large pieces and simmered slowly in water or a flavorful liquid until
tender. In Asian soups the beef is cut into small strips or cubes. Typically it is then marinated and quickly stir-fried before liquid and other ingredients are added, or it is thinly
sliced for tabletop meals such as *sukiyaki* so that it will cook almost instantly.

Which cut of beef to use depends on the style of the soup. Use the less expensive,
tough cuts such as chuck, short ribs, and shank for slow-cooked soups; the long cooking
will tenderize the meat. Don't use expensive steak or roasting cuts in a slow-cooked soup,
or the meat will dry out and the broth won't have as good a flavor.

For Asian soups, the choice of beef depends on whether you're using a marinade. If
the diners will cook strips or slices of beef themselves—for *sukiyaki* or *shabu-shabu*—a
marinade will spoil the appearance of the raw meat on the platter. For these dishes it's
important to use a tender steak cut that will cook very quickly. If you're preparing an
Asian soup where the meat is marinated before cooking, you can use a lean but slightly
tough cut such as round, eye of round, chuck, or rump.

Oxtail Soup

This is one of those elegant 19th-century soups that I love to serve at a special dinner
party. It's not difficult to make, but it can be time-consuming because you have to start
with a full-flavored beef broth. I think it's worth the work and it's something that your
guests are unlikely to have had recently (if ever). This soup also has the advantage of being
almost fat-free.

Unlike traditional French and English recipes, which leave the sections of oxtail whole
in the soup, for this version you take the meat off the oxtails after they are cooked so the
soup is easier to eat. But if you're having a group of friends over who don't mind reaching
into their bowls to gnaw on the bones, just arrange the whole oxtail sections in each bowl.
In case your guests are curious, most oxtails come from steers raised for their meat, not
plow-dragging oxen—but somehow the name has stuck.

Because it takes as much time to make this soup for 2 people as it does for 20, the
recipe given here is for 12. If this is more than you need, you can freeze the rest for up to 6
months.

MAKES 12 SERVINGS

4 pounds oxtail, cut into sections at each vertebra
    (most oxtail is already sold this way, or you can
    have the butcher do it)

½ cup vegetable oil

2 medium-size onions, sliced

2 medium-size carrots, sliced

1 bouquet garni

3 quarts brown beef broth

½ cup port wine or medium-dry sherry, such as
    amontillado

salt

for decorating the soup:

2 leeks, including 1 inch of green, cut into fine julienne

2 carrots, cut into fine julienne

2 medium-size turnips, peeled and cut into fine julienne

¼ cup tightly packed Italian parsley leaves

thin slices of French baguette, lightly buttered and browned
    in the oven

COOKING THE OXTAIL Trim any large clumps of fat off the outside of the oxtail sections. In a sauté pan over high heat, brown the oxtail sections on both sides in half the oil. Take out the oxtail and throw out the oil left in the bottom of the pan.

ADD the remaining oil to the sauté pan and sauté the onion and carrot slices over medium heat for about 10 minutes, until the onions turn limp.

PUT the cooked onions and carrots and the bouquet garni in a 6-quart pot. Arrange the oxtail on top. Rinse any caramelized juices out of the sauté pan with a cup of the broth and pour it over the oxtails with the remaining broth.

BRING the oxtails to a simmer over medium heat. Turn down the heat to keep the broth at a slow simmer and cover the pot. Simmer—either on the stove or in a 300°F oven—for 3 to 4 hours, skimming off froth and fat every 30 minutes, until the meat pulls easily off the bone. You may need to add water or additional broth to the pot from time to time to make up for evaporation.

FINISHING AND SERVING Pour the oxtails with their broth through a colander set over another 6-quart pot or bowl. Spread the oxtails over a sheet pan and let them cool. Discard the vegetables and bouquet garni.

STRAIN the broth a second time through a triple layer of cheesecloth or a clean cloth napkin or towel that has been well rinsed to eliminate traces of soap. Bring the broth to a slow simmer in a clean 6-quart pot and skim off any remaining fat or froth that floats to its surface. Add the port and salt to taste.

PULL the meat away from the oxtails. Discard the bones and any remaining pieces of fat or gristle. With your fingers, break the meat into shreds about 1 inch long and ¼ inch thick.

SIMMER the vegetable julienne in the broth for about 15 minutes, until they have almost completely softened; they should have just a slight crunch.

PUT the oxtail meat back in the simmering broth with the vegetables. Ladle into hot bowls and serve.

SUGGESTIONS AND VARIATIONS | Most traditional recipes for oxtail soup suggest clarifying the broth with egg white and raw beef in the same way as a consommé. I've found that if you're very careful not to let the broth come to a boil at any point, and carefully skim the simmering broth, the broth will be perfectly clear if it is simply strained through cloth or cheesecloth.

OXTAIL is enhanced by something sweet added to the broth—hence the port or sherry. I once worked with a chef who made a delicious oxtail stew by adding a couple of bunches of grapes along with the broth. To do this here, add 2 cups of red grapes along with the oxtails at the beginning. Leave the grapes in a bunch and put them under the oxtails in the pot so they don't float to the top and interfere with skimming. When it comes time to strain the soup, take out the oxtails and push against the strainer to extract all the grape juice and eliminate the seeds and skins. Sprinkle a few peeled whole grapes into each bowl just before serving.

THERE is a fairly well-known Chinese version of oxtail soup that is prepared almost in the same way as this version except that a good amount of garlic, star anise, and cloves is simmered along with the oxtails. In most Chinese recipes water is used for simmering the oxtails instead of broth. To make this version, cook 6 whole garlic cloves with the onions and carrots that are added to the broth. Leave out the bouquet garni and instead add 2 whole star anise and 3 whole cloves. Use sherry instead of port. Decorate the bowls of soup with peeled garlic cloves, blanched in boiling water until soft, and finely chopped scallions. Season to taste with soy sauce instead of salt.

Oxtail Soup with Grapes

I once worked in a corner bistro in Montmartre where one of the specialties was an oxtail stew made with grapes. The braised oxtails created a rich broth, but the effect was lightened by the gentle sweetness of the grapes. I add a little vinegar or verjuice (the juice of underripe grapes; see Sources) to balance the sweetness of the grapes and create a sweet-and-sour effect, but if the grapes are sour, I add a sweet ingredient such as port or sugar instead. This soup will be all the better if you use a beef broth to moisten the oxtails, but it's less important than it is for the version on page 526 because the grapes provide their own flavorful juices. Look for the sweetest and most aromatic grapes you can find, such as muscat or concord. For an elegant effect, reserve about five grapes per serving and pull away the peel between your thumb and a small paring knife.

MAKES 8 FIRST-COURSE SERVINGS

6 pounds oxtail, cut into sections at each vertebra (most oxtail is already sold this way)

2 medium-size onions, peeled and quartered

2 medium-size carrots, peeled and cut into 1-inch sections

bouquet garni containing 5 fresh thyme sprigs or ½ teaspoon dried thyme, 1 medium bunch of parsley, 1 imported bay leaf

4 pounds sweet green or red grapes, preferably muscat or concord, stemmed

1 quart beef broth (page 74) or basic brown chicken broth (page 62), or water, or more as needed

¼ cup sherry wine vinegar or verjuice, or more to taste

¼ cup port wine or 2 teaspoons sugar, or more to taste (optional)

salt

pepper

40 peeled grapes (optional)

PREHEAT the oven to 450°F. Spread the oxtails, onions, and carrots in a single layer in a heavy-bottomed roasting pan and roast for about 1 hour, turning over the vegetables and oxtails after a half hour, until they are well browned on all sides. Take the oxtails out of the roasting pan and reserve.

PLACE the bouquet garni, the vegetables from the roasting pan, and the green or red grapes in a large pot. Place the oxtails over the ingredients in the pot (the other ingredients are added first so they don't float to the top and interfere with skimming) and pour out and discard any fat in the bottom of the roasting pan. Put the pan on top of the stove and pour in 2 cups of broth or water and simmer over high heat while scraping the bottom of the pan with a wooden spoon. When all the caramelized juices have dissolved, pour the liquid over the oxtails. Pour over the rest of the broth or enough to completely cover the oxtails.

BRING to a gentle simmer over medium heat, turn the heat to low, and cover the pot, leaving the lid ajar. Simmer very gently for 1 hour and remove the lid. (This initial simmering, partially covered, is to soften the grapes and get them to release their liquid.) Simmer gently, using a ladle to skim off froth and fat that floats to the top, for 3 hours. Add broth or water every hour to make up for evaporation—the oxtails should be covered with liquid at all times.

USE tongs to take the oxtails out of the pot and then strain the soup through a large strainer or colander into a clean pot. Press down on the ingredients in the strainer to extract as much liquid as possible and discard what doesn't go through. Pull the meat away from the oxtails and throw out the bones and pieces of fat and sinew. Bring the broth to a gentle simmer, skim off any fat and froth left on top, and add the oxtail meat. Taste the broth. If it seems sweet, add vinegar or verjuice to taste; if it seems sour, add port or sugar to taste. Season to taste with salt and pepper, ladle into heated bowls, and garnish each serving with five peeled grapes.

Burgundian-Style Beef and Red Wine Soup

My favorite part of a good stew is always the rich concentrated broth that surrounds the meat. To satisfy my craving, I've converted several traditional stews into soups. This soup is identical to a *boeuf sauté à la bourguinonne*, the classic red wine beef stew from Burgundy, except that more liquid is used and the herb- and red-wine-scented broth, instead of being thickened at the end, is served as a soup. You can apply this method to any of your favorite stews—just use more liquid at the beginning and don't add any flour or other thickeners.

This is a hearty soup best served as a main course. It can be made 2 or 3 days in advance.

MAKES 4 MAIN-COURSE SERVINGS

the soup:

3 pounds beef stew meat, such as shank, brisket, or chuck, cut into 1-inch cubes

5 cups full-bodied red wine, 1½ fifths

3 garlic cloves, crushed and peeled

1 teaspoon fresh or dried thyme leaves

    5 tablespoons safflower or olive oil

    3 medium-size carrots, cut into 1-inch lengths

    3 medium-size onions, coarsely chopped

    2 cups beef broth or water

    1 bouquet garni

the garnish:

    30 pearl onions, peeled

    1 tablespoon unsalted butter

    1 teaspoon sugar

    salt

    pepper

    ½ pound bacon, preferably slab, rind removed

    ½ pound button mushrooms or larger cultivated
        mushrooms cut into quarters

    ¼ cup finely chopped parsley leaves

COMBINE the stew meat, 2 cups of the red wine, the garlic, and the thyme in a stainless-steel or glass mixing bowl. Cover with plastic wrap and leave at room temperature for 3 hours or overnight in the refrigerator.

DRAIN the meat, saving the marinade, and dry it thoroughly on paper towels.

IN a 4-quart pot, heat 3 tablespoons of the safflower oil until it is smoking. Add half the stew meat and brown it on one side. Turn it over with tongs and add the rest of the meat. Continue until all the meat is well browned.

TAKE the meat out of the pot with a slotted spoon. Discard the hot oil in the pan and add the remaining safflower or olive oil. Put in the carrots and onions and stir over medium heat until they brown slightly, about 10 minutes. Be careful not to burn the caramelized meat juices on the bottom of the pan.

PUT the beef back into the pot and pour the marinade over it. Add the remaining red wine, the beef broth, and the bouquet garni. Bring to a simmer over medium heat, cover, and

BROWNING CUBES OF MEAT

Meat must be browned over a very high heat. If the heat is too low, the meat will release liquid and end up boiling in its own juices instead of forming a crisp and delicious brown crust.

Because home kitchen stoves do not always produce enough heat, it is best to add the meat in stages instead of all at once; otherwise the cold meat may cause the pan to cool momentarily. When you see that the first batch of meat is browning, go ahead and add more. For the same reason, when you're turning the pieces of meat, turn only a few pieces at a time.

turn the heat down very low or put the pot into a 300°F oven. Open the pot every 30 minutes to make sure that it isn't boiling—turn the heat down if it is—and skim off any fat or froth with a ladle.

PREPARING THE GARNISH Put the pearl onions in a sauté pan or small pot just large enough to hold them in a single layer. Add the butter and sprinkle in the sugar and salt and pepper. Add enough water to come halfway up the sides of the onions and set the pan over medium heat. Shake the pan every 5 or 10 minutes so the onions cook evenly. They should be done in about 20 minutes. Add more water as needed. If water is left in the pan when the onions are done, place the pan over high heat until all the water evaporates and the onions are covered with a shiny glaze and their juices have caramelized on the bottom of the pan. Add 2 tablespoons water to the hot pan to dissolve the juices into a glaze. Move the pan back and forth to coat the onions with the glaze. Set the onions aside until you're ready to serve.

CUT the bacon into 1- by ¼-inch strips and cook it gently in a skillet over medium heat until it barely begins to turn crisp, about 10 minutes. Drain the strips on paper towels. Reserve 3 tablespoons of the fat.

FINISHING THE SOUP After 2½ hours, poke a piece of the beef with a fork. The fork should penetrate the meat with no resistance. If the meat still clings to the fork, cook the soup for another 30 minutes and check again. Keep doing this until the meat is tender.

STRAIN the soup over a 4-quart pot and spread the solid ingredients on a sheet pan. Bring the liquid to a slow simmer on top of the stove and skim off any fat or froth. Take the meat off the sheet pan and put it into the liquid, discarding the carrots, onions, and bouquet garni. Keep the soup hot on the stove while you're finishing the garnish.

FINISHING THE GARNISH AND SERVING Sauté the mushrooms over high heat in the reserved bacon fat until well browned. Sprinkle with salt and pepper. Reheat the pearl onions.

LADLE the soup into hot bowls and divide the pearl onions, mushrooms, and bacon strips over each serving. Sprinkle with parsley. Serve with slices of crusty French bread.

SUGGESTIONS AND VARIATIONS | If you want the soup broth to be slightly thicker, in a blender, puree the carrots and onions that were cooked along with the meat. Stir the puree into the red wine broth before adding the meat, bring the broth to a slow simmer, and skim off any fat. Strain through a medium-mesh strainer to eliminate chunks of vegetable. Heat the meat in the thickened broth.

THE garnish of pearl onions, bacon, and mushrooms is the classic accompaniment to French red wine stews. I like to take a free and easy approach and add briefly boiled green beans (preferably the thin French variety), briefly boiled spinach, chopped fresh herbs (basil, marjoram), peeled, seeded, and chopped tomatoes, wild mushrooms, truffles, julienne-cut carrots and turnips, and so on.

I like to serve well-buttered fresh fettuccine noodles on the side with this soup.

Goulash Soup

GULYÁSLEVES

Hungary has a rich tradition of making soups and stews in enormous variety and according to strict edicts. George Lang, in his thorough book *The Cuisine of Hungary*, says about goulash (*gulyás* when a stew; *gulyásleves* when a soup) that one must "Never use any flour. Never use any spice besides caraway [although his recipe also calls for paprika]. Never Frenchify it with wine. Never Germanize it with brown sauce. Never put in any other garniture besides diced potatoes or galuska [little dumplings]. But . . . you may use fresh tomatoes, tomato puree, garlic, sliced green peppers, hot cherry peppers." I'm not fond of bell peppers in meat, soups, or stews, so I leave them out and use a high quality paprika (see box) to provide a more intriguing pepper flavor.

The goulash soup given here is made much like a beef stew except that more liquid is used. George Lang includes a beef heart in his recipe, but I use beef chuck or, if I can find them, beef cheeks, which develop a moist melting consistency. I serve this hearty soup as a main course.

MAKES 8 MAIN-COURSE SERVINGS

3 pounds beef chuck or beef cheeks, cut into 1-inch cubes

salt

pepper

2 tablespoons pure olive oil or vegetable oil (for browning the meat)

2 tablespoons butter or olive oil (for cooking the onions and garlic)

2 medium-size onions, peeled and chopped

3 garlic cloves, peeled and chopped

1 teaspoon caraway seeds, finely chopped or ground in a coffee grinder

1 tablespoon hot Hungarian paprika (see box, page 535)

I tablespoon mild Hungarian paprika (see box, page 535)

2 quarts basic beef broth (page 74), basic brown chicken broth (page 62), or water

4 tomatoes, peeled, seeded, and chopped, or I 28-ounce can whole tomatoes, drained

bouquet garni containing 4 thyme sprigs (or ¼ teaspoon dried), I small bunch of parsley, and I bay leaf

I ½ pounds waxy red or white potatoes, peeled, kept in cold water until needed

I recipe miniature dumplings (see box; optional)

2 tomatoes, peeled, seeded, and diced (optional garniture)

I pint sour cream (optional garniture)

SEASON the meat liberally with salt and pepper and let it sit for 3 hours so the salt can penetrate inside. Heat the oil in a heavy-bottomed pot (large enough to hold all the meat) over high heat. Pat the meat dry with paper towels (but don't let the meat sit on the towels or they'll stick and tear) and brown it, only several pieces at a time (if you add too much to the pan at once it won't brown) on all sides. Set the meat aside and discard the cooked fat in the pot. If the bottom of the pot is burned, rinse it to eliminate any bitterness.

PUT the butter in the pot, add the onions and garlic, and sweat them over medium heat while stirring, until they turn translucent, about 10 minutes. Add the caraway and paprika and stir over the heat for I minute more so the spices release their aroma. Add the broth and the tomatoes, and scrape the bottom of the pot with a wooden spoon to dissolve any caramelized juices. If you're using canned tomatoes, push your thumb through the side of each one and then gently squeeze them (wear an apron, the seeds like to squirt out) to get rid of the seeds. Chop them coarse. Put the bouquet garni in the pot and put the meat and any juices it has released on top.

BRING the soup to a gentle simmer, partially cover the pot (so too much liquid doesn't evaporate), and simmer for 2 hours.

CUT the potatoes into manageable-size pieces—about an inch on each side. Skim off any fat that has floated to the top of the broth

DUMPLINGS

Whisk together 4 large eggs with ¾ cup of flour and 1 teaspoon of salt in a mixing bowl. Stir in 2 tablespoons of melted butter. Let the batter rest for 30 minutes in the refrigerator. Spoon the batter, a teaspoon at a time, into a pot of simmering salted water. Simmer the dumplings for 3 to 5 minutes and scoop them out with a slotted spoon. Dumplings can be prepared earlier the same day—so you're not stuck making them in the soup just before serving—and allowed to drain on a sheet pan. (Don't cover the sheet pan with paper towels, as I once did, because the dumplings stick.)

Paprika, like all other chilies, is a member of the species *Capsicum annum*. The chilies used to make paprika are grown, of course, in Hungary but also in California (where the chilies tend to be on the mild side) and in Spain, where the chilies are smoked before they are ground, to produce *pimentón*. When making goulash, I prefer to use Hungarian paprika, which can be found, both hot and mild, in most supermarkets. If you're looking for a very high quality paprika or want to start experimenting with different brands to appreciate their nuances, look under "spices" or "Spanish Ingredients" in the source list on page 611.

and add the potatoes to the soup. Continue simmering until the potatoes are done (a knife slides easily in and out of each one), about 20 minutes more.

ADD the pre-cooked dumplings to the pot—simmer them for five minutes if they've grown cold—or heat them for 10 minutes in a 250°F oven and sprinkle them over each serving.

HEAT the optional diced tomatoes. Ladle the soup into heated bowls, and arrange the dumplings on top of each serving (unless you've made them directly in the soup). Sprinkle the diced tomatoes over each serving. Pass the sour cream at the table.

Korean Soybean Paste Soup

TWOENJANG-TCHIGAE

Korea is the only country in Asia—except for regions of northern China—that uses beef as part of the regular diet. This delicious soup starts out with strips of steak marinated in soy sauce, sesame oil, garlic, and *kimchee*—Korean preserved cabbage. The Koreans eat *kimchee* with almost every meal, and once you've tasted it you'll find it easy to understand why. *Kimchee* is easy to find in any grocery that sells Korean food products, or you can make it yourself.

Another staple of the Korean diet, and an essential flavoring in this soup, is *twoenjang*—fermented soybean paste. *Twoenjang* is the Korean equivalent of Japanese miso, which in a pinch can be used as a substitute.

MAKES 8 SERVINGS

½ pound steak such as sirloin strip or tenderloin, sliced into
strips about 1 by ⅛ inch thick

2 garlic cloves, peeled, finely chopped, and crushed to a
paste with the side of a chef's knife

¼ cup dark Japanese soy sauce

2 teaspoons dark sesame oil

1 tablespoon peanut oil

¾ cup *kimchee*, sliced into strips the same size as the beef

3 tablespoons *twoenjang* or dark miso

5 cups water or beef or chicken broth

2 green Thai chilies or jalapeño peppers, seeds removed,
finely chopped

2 cakes of tofu, preferably firm Chinese type, cut into ½-
inch cubes

12 dried Chinese mushrooms, soaked in just enough water
to cover for 3 hours and quartered, or 12 fresh shiitake
mushrooms, stems removed, quartered

½ pound *daikon*, about a 4-inch length, peeled and cut into
fine julienne

4 scallions, both white and green parts, finely sliced

salt

pepper

IN a 2-quart mixing bowl, toss together the steak, garlic, soy sauce, and sesame oil.
Leave the steak in this marinade for 30 minutes to an hour.

DRAIN the steak and quickly dry it in paper towels—don't leave it in the paper towels for more than a minute or two, or it may stick. Discard the marinade.

HEAT the vegetable oil in a skillet until it just begins to smoke. Add the beef strips
and gently stir them around for about 3 minutes, until they brown slightly. Turn the
heat down to medium, add the *kimchee* and the *twoenjang*, and stir for a few seconds,
until the *twoenjang* coats the pieces of beef.

ADD the water, chilies, tofu, mushrooms and daikon. Simmer the soup gently for
about 10 minutes.

ADD the scallions and simmer for about 30 seconds more. Season the soup with salt
and pepper.

Vietnamese Spinach, Beef, and Tofu Soup

What I like most about this soup is that it takes only a couple of minutes' cooking time and it's made with my favorite vegetable, spinach. The soup contains just enough meat to off-set the spinach with a savory broth. And the technique, a quick sautéing of marinated strips of beef with a little water, fish sauce, and vegetables, is good to remember for last-minute, improvised Asian soups.

If you live near an Asian market, you might want to experiment with Chinese spinach or water spinach. Chinese spinach, which has slightly fuzzy leaves, pink roots, and little twisted stems, is wonderfully tender and even more nutritious than what we're used to in the West. Water spinach—originally from India, where it grows in swamps—is also worth experimenting with even if it is less tender than Chinese or so-called Western varieties. ("Western" spinach is also eaten in Asia.) Water spinach is sold in large bunches in Chinese markets. It has thin pointed leaves and long stems. If you're using ordinary spinach with large leaves, tear the leaves into pieces about the size of a quarter.

MAKES 8 SERVINGS

¾ pound tender beef such as sirloin strip or tenderloin, cut
into 1- by ⅛-inch strips

the marinade:

2 garlic cloves, peeled, finely chopped, and crushed to a
paste with the side of a chef's knife

a ¼-inch slice of fresh ginger, peeled and finely chopped

1 teaspoon sugar

1 tablespoon Vietnamese (*nuoc mam*) or Thai fish sauce
(*nam pla*)

the soup:

1 tablespoon peanut oil

2 Thai chilies or 3 jalapeño chilies, seeded and finely chopped

5 cups water or beef or chicken broth

1 bunch of spinach, water spinach, or Chinese spinach,
stems removed, 1 cup tightly packed leaves

5 tablespoons Vietnamese (*nuoc mam*) or Thai fish sauce
(*nam pla*)

2 cakes of tofu, preferably firm, cut into ¾-inch cubes

juice of 2 limes

salt

TOSS the beef strips with the marinade ingredients. Cover and let sit for 30 minutes to an hour.

DRAIN the beef strips, saving the marinade.

HEAT the vegetable oil in a heavy pot or skillet until it starts to smoke. Toss in the beef strips and chilies and stir over high heat for 2 to 3 minutes, until the beef starts to brown.

POUR in the marinade and stir until the beef strips are coated with a light glaze, about 30 seconds. Add the broth and bring to a simmer. Stir in the rest of the ingredients except salt. Wait for about 1 minute, until the spinach is completely wilted. Season with salt and serve in hot bowls.

Vietnamese Spicy Soup with Rice Noodles

PHO BO

When I wrote the first edition of *Splendid Soups* in the early '90s, no one seemed to have heard of *pho*, pronounced like *foot* without the *t.* Now *pho*, at least in New York and Los Angeles, has become the food *du jour*, served in hip little restaurants and corner places made to look like Vietnamese noodle stands. *Pho*, which literally means noodle, is simply a more or less rich broth surrounding an abundance of rice noodles. Though there are dozens of variations, all of them can be derived by changing the basic broth or flavoring it with different herbs and spices (such as cinnamon and star anise) and by garnishing the soup immediately before or at the time it is served. The most common garnitures, usually offered at the table for guests to help themselves (or, at a noodle stand, requested), are sprigs of herbs, usually mint, cilantro, and basil; mung bean sprouts; lime wedges; fish sauce (*nuoc mam*), chopped scallions, and chopped fiery chilies. The broth itself can be a simple chicken stock, pork stock, rich oxtail soup (see page 526), or other beef broth made from beef short ribs or other slow-cooking cuts that might show up in a French *pot-au-feu*, a reminder of Vietnam's history as a French colony. I recommend serving *pho* for a crowd so everyone can have fun passing the condiments back and forth and to make the preparation of the slow-simmered broth worth the time and effort.

MAKES 6 MAIN-COURSE SERVINGS

the broth:

10 cups basic brown chicken broth (see recipe page 62,
pork broth (see recipe page 65), the basic beef broth
(not clarified) from the consommé recipe on page 75,
or oxtail soup (page 526)

4 star anise

1 2-inch length cinnamon stick

2 whole cloves

1 2-inch piece fresh ginger, cut into about 8 slices
    (don't bother peeling)

2 teaspoons sugar

1 medium-size onion, peeled and quartered

1 teaspoon white peppercorns

the noodles:

2 pounds rice noodles (*banh pho* or just *pho*; see page 538)

the garnitures (use as many or as few as you like):

cilantro leaves

mint leaves

basil leaves (preferably Thai basil or holy basil)

finely chopped Thai chilies (or other milder chili such as
    jalapeño if you're worried about the heat)

fish sauce (*nuoc mam*)

lime wedges

chopped scallions (including green parts)

hot chili sauce (see page 11)

hoisin sauce (see page 21)

mung bean sprouts

shredded meat or poultry used to prepare the broth

shredded leftover pieces of meat or poultry

PREPARING THE INFUSED BROTH Bring the broth to a gentle simmer. Crush the star anise by placing them on a cutting board and rocking over them with the corner of a saucepan, using most of your weight to push down on the pan. Crush the cinnamon into splinters and crush the cloves in the same way. Add the anise, ginger, cinnamon, cloves, sugar, and onion to the simmering broth and simmer gently, covered, for 20 minutes. Just before you're ready to strain the broth, crush the peppercorns and stir them into the broth. Simmer for 1 minute. Strain the broth through a fine-mesh strainer or a triple layer of cheesecloth.

PREPARING THE NOODLES Soak the noodles for 30 minutes in cold water. Bring about 4 quarts of water to a simmer. Just before you're ready to serve, plunge the noodles in the water, let sit for 30 seconds, and immediately drain in a colander. Use immediately.

SERVING THE SOUP Spoon a mound of noodles into each heated bowl and ladle over the broth so it comes about halfway up the sides of the noodles. Pass the garnitures at the table.

VARIATIONS | For a more luxurious and filling pho, add very thinly sliced strips of tender beef (such as sirloin strip or tenderloin) to the hot broth just before serving.

Veal

ORIGINALLY VEAL WAS TAKEN FROM CALVES WHO HADN'T YET HAD A CHANCE TO graze on grass and whose only sustenance was their mother's milk. Because their diet was naturally low in iron, the flesh of the calves remained pink and had a delicate fragrance of fresh milk. Today most commercial veal is raised under artificial conditions on specially formulated feed. The calves are allowed little freedom of movement and are fed antibiotics to prevent illness in the overcrowded conditions.

It's worth searching for veal that has been raised under healthy and humane conditions, preferably on a small farm. In some parts of the country veal can be difficult to find and even more so if you start getting fussy about how the veal was raised. The best way to find farm-raised veal is to call around to local butchers, health food stores, or restaurants known to serve organic foods. You can also use the mail-order sources at the back of this book.

By far the most flavorful cut of veal is the shank, often called by its Italian name, *ossobuco*. Veal shank is quite tough, but after an hour and a half to two hours of cooking it becomes meltingly tender and releases a delicious broth.

Veal Shank in Savory Broth with Vegetable Julienne

This hearty main-course soup is prepared in the same way as many soups and stews, where aromatic vegetables such as carrots, onions, and celery are cooked slowly with the meat to give it a deep, complex flavor. The trick to this recipe is to cut the vegetables into julienne strips so that by the time the veal is ready they have formed a melting, savory tangle. The combination of the rich broth, tender meat, and mixture of vegetables is irresistible.

You'll need to cook this soup in a large pot with a tight-fitting lid that will hold the veal shanks in a single layer and with plenty of room left on top for the vegetables.

MAKES 4 MAIN-COURSE SERVINGS

4 2-inch-thick veal shanks

salt

pepper

3 tablespoons olive oil

5 cups veal or chicken broth or water

1 bouquet garni

2 medium-size leeks, white part only, cut into fine julienne

2 medium-size carrots, cut into fine julienne

1 turnip, peeled and cut into fine julienne

1 fennel bulb, cut into 8 wedges

SEASON the veal shanks with salt and pepper. In a pot just large enough to hold the shanks in a single layer, brown them over high heat on both sides in the fat, about 8 minutes on each side.

TAKE the shanks out of the pan and pour out the burned fat. Put the shanks back in the pan along with the broth and bouquet garni. Bring to a slow simmer, cover the pan, and leave it at a slow simmer on top of the stove or in a 300°F oven for 45 minutes.

PUT the vegetables in the pot and continue cooking for 45 minutes more. Poke the veal with a paring knife; it should slide in with no resistance. If the veal still feels firm, continue cooking it for 30 minutes more.

CAREFULLY remove the veal shanks with a slotted spoon or skimmer—they're very fragile—and arrange them in the center of hot bowls with the vegetables heaped on top. Discard the bouquet garni and season the broth to taste with salt and pepper. Ladle the broth over the vegetables. Serve with coffee spoons or oyster forks for scooping the marrow out of the bones.

Tripe

WHEN IT COMES TO TRIPE, THE WORLD SEEMS DIVIDED INTO TWO CAMPS—THOSE who can't get enough of it in all its myriad forms and those who loathe the stuff. My own fondness for tripe falls somewhere in between, but my favorite version is the Mexican *menudo* with poblano chilies and hominy that I first tasted in a Mexican restaurant in New York.

In the United States, where tripe is not very popular, honeycomb tripe is the easiest to find. In Europe and in Latin countries (and neighborhoods), thick-seam and blanket tripe are also eaten. If you manage to find either of these less common varieties, try using more than one type; each kind of tripe has a slightly different texture.

Even though tripe purchased in the United States has almost always been cleaned and partially precooked, tripe still takes from two to five hours to finish cooking. And the only way to make sure it's done is to reach in and bite into a piece.

Tripe is often cooked with a calf's or pig's foot to augment the natural gelatin in the broth, but tripe contributes so much gelatin of its own—which gives the soup a rich, satiny texture—that if need be you can dispense with the feet.

Mexican Tripe Soup

MENUDO

Like *pozole verde, menudo* contains hominy. But if you don't want to bother cooking hominy, whole corn kernels added at the end make an acceptable substitute (see Suggestions and Variations). This recipe also uses poblano chilies, which give the soup a characteristic Mexican flavor.

MAKES 10 MAIN-COURSE SERVINGS

I calf's foot, split lengthwise, then cut in half crosswise

3 pounds honeycomb or assorted types of tripe, well rinsed
    in cold water and cut into I-inch squares or triangles

I large onion, cut into quarters

2 carrots, thickly sliced

6 garlic cloves, peeled

4 cups cooked or drained canned hominy (page 514)

8 poblano chilies

2 tablespoons finely chopped cilantro leaves

salt

jalapeño chilies, seeded and finely chopped

flour tortillas

PLACE the calf's foot and tripe in a 4-quart pot. Add enough cold water to cover by about 4 inches. Bring to a simmer over medium heat and keep at a simmer for 10 minutes. Pour everything into a colander and thoroughly rinse the calf's foot in cold water to eliminate any froth or scum.

PLACE the blanched foot and the tripe in a 6-quart pot with the onion, carrots, and garlic. Add enough cold water to cover the ingredients by 3 inches.

BRING the pot to a slow simmer and use a ladle to skim off any froth that floats to the top. Cover the pot and continue simmering for 3 hours.

SPOON out and taste a piece of tripe to make sure it is completely tender—if not, simmer for 30 minutes more and keep checking until it's done.

STRAIN the soup into a wide colander, saving the broth. Let the solids cool slightly and then sort through, discarding the vegetables, throwing the pieces of tripe into the broth, and setting the pieces of calf's foot aside on a cutting board.

NOT everyone likes the gelatinous flesh attached to the calf's foot, but if you do, cut it into ¼- to ½-inch cubes and add it to the broth.

BLACKEN the poblano chilies in the flame of a gas burner or under a broiler. Peel off the blackened skin with your fingers and scrape off the remainder with a paring knife. Cut the chilies lengthwise and remove the stem and seeds. Chop the chilies finely or puree them in a food processor and add them to the broth.

ADD the cooked hominy and bring the soup to a simmer—thin the soup with water if it seems too thick. Add the cilantro and salt to taste.

PASS around the chopped jalapeños and plates of hot tortillas.

SUGGESTIONS AND VARIATIONS | It's really the hominy and the last-minute cilantro and hot chilies that make this soup *menudo*. The technique for cooking tripe—the slow simmering with a blanched calf's foot and aromatic vegetables—is almost universal, so it's easy to prepare tripe soups (or stews) with a completely different national character by substituting different ingredients at various stages of the cooking.

FRENCH versions would most likely contain a bouquet garni, a clove stuck into the onion, and instead of water and hominy-cooking liquid may contain cider (*tripes à la mode de Caen* from Normandy) or tomatoes (*pieds et paquets* from Provence). A Milanese version contains beans, onions, leeks, and cabbage all cooked separately with a little bacon and added at the end. One delicious Caribbean version I discovered adds corned beef to the tripe near the end of cooking, and the whole dish is simmered for the last 30 minutes with potatoes, sweet potatoes, green olives, capers, raisins, and chilies.

A Few Less
COMMON INGREDIENTS

ONCE YOU HAVE A FEEL FOR WORKING WITH MEATS AND POULTRY, ADAPTING YOUR recipes and cooking style to more unusual ingredients shouldn't be difficult. Many people are reticent to experiment with foods not because of squeamishness but because they have no idea how even to begin. Rabbit, pheasant, partridge, and frog legs, for example, can be made into soup in the same way as chicken. Squab can be cooked in the same way as duck—saving the breasts for an elegant main course and using the carcasses and thighs for soup—or you can make the elegant squab soup on page 507. Venison can be prepared in the same way as pork or beef.

Foie Gras and Truffle Soup

Once a year around the holiday season, a couple of my closest friends and I splurge and buy ½ pound of truffles and spend an evening preparing a truffle feast. Our other friends are dismayed by the extravagance, but after all, we probably spend less than if we went out to dinner at a French restaurant.

At one recent feast we set out to duplicate a foie gras and truffle soup I first had years ago at Paul Bocuse's restaurant just outside Lyons. At the time, I was living in Paris washing dishes at the corner bistro, setting aside stray francs for meals in France's finest restaurants. A friend and I hitchhiked to Lyons, stayed in an airless room in the old section of town, and the next morning hitched a ride *chez Bocuse* from a driver perplexed by the disparity between our tattered coats and our destination.

Our long and luxurious lunch began with this soup.

MAKES 6 SERVINGS

2 quarts clear and rich brown beef or chicken broth or
    consommé

salt

pepper

¾ pound duck foie gras bloc, well chilled

2 or more whole black truffles

1 egg plus 1 egg yolk

6 puff pastry circles, homemade or frozen,
    well chilled

IF the broth is cold, heat it just long enough to melt it, season it to taste with salt and pepper, and distribute it among 6 deep, 2-cup soup crocks.

CUT the foie gras into ¼-inch cubes with a sharp knife. If the foie gras sticks, keep dipping the knife into a bowl of cold water. Distribute the cubes among the soup bowls.

PEEL the truffle with a sharp paring knife. Chop the peelings finely and distribute them among the soup bowls. Slice the truffle as thinly as you can with a sharp paring knife or a benriner cutter (see Equipment chapter) and distribute the slices among the bowls.

MAKE an egg wash by beating together the egg, egg yolk, and 1 teaspoon salt with a fork until the mixture darkens slightly and becomes very runny, about 2 minutes.

USE a sharp paring knife to make a series of decorative arcs on one side of the pastry circles, moving from the center to the outer edge. Be careful not to cut through the pastry.

TURN the pastry circles over and brush the undecorated side with the egg wash. Place the circles, egg side down, over each of the bowls. Press the pastry firmly all around the sides of the bowls to form an airtight seal.

BRUSH the top of each of the pastry circles with egg wash.

THE finished bowls of soup can be kept in the refrigerator for up to 12 hours before they are baked.

PREHEAT the oven to 400°F and bake the bowls on a sheet pan 25 minutes before serving. The pastry should rise into a dome shape. If it has completely browned before the 25 minutes is up, turn the oven down to 300°F.

SUGGESTIONS AND VARIATIONS | I sometimes prepare a more modest version of this soup with wild mushrooms and leave out the foie gras and truffles. The puff pastry domes and the full-flavored broth still make a dramatic and delicious soup. Fresh wild mushrooms should be sautéed in olive oil, butter, or, best of all, goose or duck fat before they're distributed in the bowls. Use a total of 1½ pounds assorted mushrooms for 6 servings. You can also use dried mushrooms, but the only dried mushrooms I find worth using are dried porcini (cèpes) and morels. Count on a total of 3 ounces for 6 servings. Rinse them off quickly under cold running water and then soak them for about 15 minutes—until they soften—in some of the warmed broth. Be sure to use the mushroom broth in the soup but be careful to leave behind any sand or grit the mushrooms may have released during soaking.

I occasionally make a kind of updated chicken pot pie by lightly precooking pieces of chicken breast, baby vegetables such as pearl onions, carrots, turnips, zucchini, and button mushrooms, combining them in the bowls with fresh tarragon leaves, chicken broth, and cream, covering everything with the pastry circles, and then baking in the same way.

Frog Leg Soup

Just to dispel a myth: the only thing frog legs have in common with chicken is that they are white; they have a delicate taste all their own—completely different from chicken.

My favorite way to eat frog legs is to toss them in flour, quickly sauté them in butter or olive oil, and eat them with my fingers. But less experienced frog leg eaters may like them a little more disguised. This soup is a perfect way to capture their flavor and make them easier to eat, both physically and psychologically.

Frog legs usually come frozen, which is fine; neither their flavor nor their texture seems to suffer. They are usually sold in pairs, which should be separated to make them easier to cook. Just cut through the joint at the top of each leg and discard the little bone that connects them at the top.

This soup calls for fresh parsley, chervil, and chives. If you can't the find the chervil—in some parts of the country it's hard to find—just use a little more parsley and chives.

MAKES 6 SERVINGS

36 frog legs (18 pairs), pairs separated at the top joint
salt
pepper
¼ cup all-purpose flour
4 tablespoons unsalted butter
2 shallots, finely chopped
½ cup dry white wine
1 quart vegetable broth
1 medium-size bunch of parsley, stems removed and leaves finely chopped
1 bunch of chives, about 20 strands, finely chopped
1 bunch of fresh chervil the size of a fist, finely chopped
1 cup heavy cream

SEASON the frog legs with salt and pepper and roll them in the flour. Pat the floured legs thoroughly to get rid of excess flour.

HEAT the butter in a wide sauté pan—preferably wide enough to hold all the legs in a single layer—over medium heat. When the butter starts to foam, add the legs. Turn up the heat and stir or toss the legs until they just begin to brown, about 5 minutes. If the butter starts to brown, turn the heat down to medium.

TAKE the legs out of the pan with a slotted spoon and place them on a large plate to cool. Throw out the cooked butter in the sauté pan. Add the shallot and wine and simmer for 5 minutes. Pour in the broth and transfer the liquid to a 4-quart pot.

PULL the meat off the frog legs, trying to keep the pieces as large as you can. Reserve the meat and put the bones in the liquid in the pot. Bring the liquid to a slow simmer, cover, and simmer for 30 minutes. Strain into another pot and add the herbs, cream, and frog leg meat. Simmer for 1 minute and season to taste with salt and pepper. Serve in hot bowls.

SUGGESTIONS AND VARIATIONS | If you want to try a watercress-flavored version from Alsace, blanch the leaves from 2 bunches of watercress for 2 minutes in boiling salted water, strain them, and rinse under cold water. Just before serving, puree the watercress in a blender for 2 minutes with just enough of the hot soup to get it to move around. Stir the watercress puree into the soup.

"I always serve soup
with some kind of
starch . . ."

Bread
SOUPS

Unless I'm serving a very formal dinner (which is rare) with delicate little cups of cream soup or consommé to lead into more substantial fare, I always serve soup with some kind of starch. Occasionally rice or noodles sneak into or around the soup, but more often than not a crusty loaf of French bread—which I like to slice in front of the guests—is resting on a cutting board somewhere on the table.

A European tradition is to put a thick slice of stale bread in the center of the bowl and then pour the soup over. I usually approach it somewhat differently and keep a slice of bread on the side, which I tear into sections and dip into the soup—hunched over inelegantly to keep the mess to a minimum. A French dinner partner once remarked that this habit was acceptable only *à la maison*; elsewhere the pieces of bread should be delicately—almost surreptitiously—stuck on the end of a fork before being plunged into the soup.

Bread and soup lore also dictates that the bread should be stale. This is difficult for me because I don't have access to fresh bread—unless I bake it myself—and I always finish the loaf by the second day, long before it's stale enough to qualify. If I want crunchy or dry bread, I toast the slices—usually in the broiler because the slices are too thick for the toaster. Sometimes I butter the slices or sprinkle them with olive oil, but more often than not I leave them alone.

Panades are soups that already have the bread in them. There are a number of traditional *panades*—such as the onion soup on page 200 and the roast pumpkin soup on page 218—but cooking a soup with bread is more often an excellent way to use soup and other leftovers from the night before. My own *panades* are winter dishes, really more crunchy and gratinlike than soupy; I usually serve them (often only to myself) for lunch or dinner the day after. Typically I slice some bread, toast it slightly, and spread it in a single layer in a gratin dish or individual soup crocks. Just enough of last night's soup (it's often vegetable) is poured over to cover the bread by about half an inch. Then the soup is sprinkled with grated cheese—this is important: the *panade* will only be as good as the cheese you use. I usually rely on Swiss Gruyère and authentic Parmesan. Whatever cheese you use, make sure it's dry and hard (or it will turn stringy) and don't grate it too coarsely (or it will turn hard).

The bread you use is also important. I like to use firm country-style sourdough bread with a hard crust and a firm texture so it doesn't turn to mush once cooked.

The consistency of your own *panades* will depend on your own tastes, which will make themselves felt as soon as you begin experimenting. On one end of the *panade*-thickness spectrum are soups such as French onion that have a few slices of toasted bread floating on a bowl (or crock) of broth. On the other end of the scale are soups like casseroles; the bread has absorbed all available liquid, and the "soup" is served on plates.

Mexican cooks have their own version of *panades*, called *sopas secas*—literally dry soups—which often contain cream and cheese. It's usually rice, not bread, that gives *sopas secas* their body and substance.

Vegetable Soup Panade

This is really more a casserole than a soup, but it's a great way to convert leftover soup from the night before into a main course for a simple lunch or a first course or side dish for the next day's dinner.

This recipe works best with leftover vegetable soup with chunky vegetables still in it—pureed soups, because they don't have much texture, make the consistency of the panade a little monotonous.

MAKES 6 FIRST-COURSE OR LIGHT LUNCH SERVINGS

4 cups leftover chunky vegetable soup

18 1-inch-thick slices of French baguette, preferably slightly stale

¼ cup olive oil or unsalted melted butter (optional)

1 cup grated Swiss Gruyère or ¾ cup grated Parmesan

2 tablespoons olive oil or unsalted melted butter for sprinkling on top

BRING the vegetable soup to a simmer in a 2-quart pot. Preheat the oven to 350°F.

IF the bread is relatively fresh and soft, toast it on both sides in the broiler; the slices should be too thick to fit into the toaster.

DRIZZLE the olive oil or melted butter on each slice if desired, then spread the slices in a single layer in an oval gratin dish or a square casserole or individual 2-cup soup crocks.

SPRINKLE the bread slices with half the cheese, pour over the hot soup, spread it evenly around, and sprinkle over the remaining cheese and the olive oil or melted butter reserved for sprinkling on top.

BAKE until the soup is bubbling and the top is golden brown, about 30 minutes. If the top of the casserole browns before 15 or 20 minutes, turn down the oven. Serve on hot plates.

SUGGESTIONS AND VARIATIONS | When I make this dish for a crowd, I sometimes make a double layer of bread with extra cheese and soup in between. You can put almost anything in the middle layer: cooked leftover spinach; sautéed mushrooms; peeled, seeded, and coarsely chopped tomatoes; stewed sorrel; freshly chopped fresh herbs such as thyme, rosemary, marjoram, basil; leftover roast meats (especially chicken or turkey).

Summer Basil and Tomato Bread Soup

PAPPA AL POMODORO

There are many versions of this Italian soup, all with varying proportions of tomatoes, bread, and broth. Once you start adding a lot of bread, it's hard to tell what it is—soup, casserole, or salad. Like all soups that rely on tomatoes for most of their character and flavor, I make this dish only in summer. You can serve this soup either hot or cold.

MAKE 6 SERVINGS

12 1-inch-thick slices of French or Italian baguette,
   preferably slightly stale

½ cup extra virgin olive oil

8 vine-ripened tomatoes, peeled, seeded, and very coarsely
   chopped

2 cups chicken broth or water

about 40 basil leaves, shredded (chiffonade)

2 teaspoons sugar (optional)

2 tablespoons balsamic vinegar

salt and pepper

IF the bread is fresh and still soft, toast it on both sides under the broiler. Cut the bread slices in half into semicircles. In a mixing bowl, toss the bread cubes in half the olive oil.

COMBINE the bread cubes, tomatoes, and broth in a 4-quart pot. If you're serving the soup cold, stir in the rest of the ingredients, let sit in the refrigerator for an hour, and serve in cold bowls.

IF you're serving the soup hot, bring it to a simmer, then stir in the remaining ingredients. Season with salt and pepper and serve immediately in hot bowls.

SUGGESTIONS AND VARIATIONS | Authentic versions of *pappa al pomodoro* never seem to suggest it, but I like to serve freshly grated Parmesan at the table for friends to sprinkle on the soup. I also sometimes just combine all the ingredients cold, toss in twice as much basil, and serve this "soup" chilled.

ANOTHER trick is to leave the bread in slices and layer them in the same way as the casserole version on page 553, sprinkle the whole thing with cheese and olive oil, and bake it.

Saffron-Scented Panade from the Périgord

MOURTAYROL

In the Perigord region of France, *mourtayrol* soup is sometimes served instead of broth as the first course of a *pot-au-feu*. It's easy to make; simply add saffron to a rich meat broth and then pour the broth over slices of crusty French bread and bake. For this recipe I've committed a sacrilege by suggesting sprinkling the whole thing with grated Parmesan.

MAKES 4 SERVINGS

24 1-inch-thick slices of crusty French baguette, preferably sourdough and stale

1 quart brown beef or chicken broth

about 1 teaspoon saffron threads, soaked in 1 tablespoon water for 30 minutes

salt

pepper

½ cup grated Parmesan cheese

IF the bread is still fairly fresh, toast it on both sides under the broiler.

PREHEAT the oven to 350°F, Arrange the bread slices in individual soup crocks that are large enough to hold both bread and broth, about a 2-cup capacity. You can also bake the soup all at once in an oval casserole, preferably one large enough to hold the bread slices in a single layer.

BRING the broth to a simmer and add the saffron. Let simmer for 5 minutes, season to taste with salt and pepper, and pour it over the bread slices in the bowls or casserole.

SPRINKLE the *mourtayrol* with the grated cheese and bake for 20 to 30 minutes—until it's covered with a golden brown crust.

TAILLEVENT'S MENJOIRE

Until recently, when French chefs began experimenting with unusual ingredients, saffron was rarely used in French cooking except near the Mediterranean. In medieval cooking, however, saffron and other spices were used in practically everything.

One of the first French cookbooks, *Le Viandier* (1380) by Taillevent, describes a soup called a *menjoire* that contains broth thickened with bread crumbs and spiced not only with saffron but with ginger, cinnamon, and cloves. The whole thing is then simmered with *hypocras*, a sort of mulled red wine.

PANADES: MORE HATED THAN LOVED?

Nowadays when we set out to make a *panade*, we have plenty of tasty ingredients on hand—good broth, good cheese, herbs, and perhaps saffron. But in years past, *panades* were often desperate affairs designed to convert a paucity of ingredients into something resembling (often poorly) a meal.

At times they were little more than bread heated with water, and understandably they induced a loathing roughly the equivalent to the gruel or mashed turnips of Dickensian boarding schools. Madame Saint-Ange, in her 1920s French classic, *La Cuisine de Madame Saint-Ange*, says, (roughly translated) that you either love them or you hate them and goes on to explain that they need something sharp flavored (such as sorrel) to make up for their "caractère insipide." She also goes on to suggest that you use good broth instead of water and that you take great care to brown the bread if it isn't stale—suggestions that still hold true today.

SUGGESTIONS AND VARIATIONS | Meat broth flavored with saffron is delicious and inspired, but sometimes the flavor and texture of a *mourtayrol* becomes a bit monotonous. In summer I like to spread a layer of coarsely chopped tomatoes on top of the bread slices before baking, and the rest of the year the *mourtayrol* model becomes fair game for all kinds of improvisations—chopped fresh herbs, cheese, cooked vegetables (fennel is wonderful with the saffron), spices (ground cumin, cayenne) sprinkled in between two layers of bread before baking.

Leftover Fish Soup Panade

This is a great method for using leftover fish soup and chunks of leftover fish that would be too fragile and would fall apart if reheated in broth. Any Western-style fish soup will work as long as it doesn't contain too much starch to begin with (I don't recommend leftover clam chowder). I particularly like this dish made with leftover Mediterranean-style soups such as *bouillabaisse* or *bourride*.

MAKES 6 FIRST-COURSE OR LIGHT MAIN-COURSE SERVINGS

24 1-inch-thick slices of crusty French baguette, preferably
    stale
1 quart leftover fish soup
1 cup *aïoli* (page 349)
½ cup finely grated Parmesan cheese

IF the bread is still fairly fresh, toast it on both sides under the broiler.

PREHEAT the oven to 350°F. Take any pieces of fish or vegetables out of the soup and bring the liquid from the soup to a simmer. Arrange any pieces of fish or vegetables from the soup in individual soup crocks or in an oval casserole. Spread on a thin layer of *aïoli* and arrange the bread slices on top.

POUR the simmering soup over the bread and sprinkle the parmesan on top.

BAKE until the soup starts to bubble and the *panade* is covered with a golden crust, 20 to 30 minutes. Serve with the remaining *aïoli*.

Her Majesty's Chicken and Almond Soup

POTAGE PURÉE DE VOLAILLE À LA REINE

This luxurious soup captures the essence of chicken and delicately teams it with almonds. *Purée à la reine* is traditionally a luxury soup because it contains cooked chicken breasts worked to a fine puree. At one time this meant hours bent over a mortar and pestle, but a blender or food processor works almost as well in about one-fiftieth of the time.

In my home library, I have recipes for *purée à la reine* that date back to the 17th century. The recipes change little over the centuries except that early versions are garnished with pistachios and pomegranate seeds—typical medieval touches. Most earlier versions contain bitter almonds to give this soup its characteristic flavor, but in this recipe sweet almonds and almond extract or Chinese "bitter almonds" are used, since bitter almonds contain traces of cyanide and are illegal in the United States.

Bread is used as a thickener along with almonds, pureed chicken breasts, and hard-cooked egg yolks. Instead of being left in large chunks or slices—as for a typical panade—the bread is pureed with the chicken breasts and almonds and then strained to give the soup a rich, creamy texture.

Although traditionally served hot, this soup can also be served cold.

MAKES 6 SERVINGS

3 skinless and boneless chicken breast halves

2 tablespoons unsalted butter

3 thin slices of white bread, crusts removed

4½ cups chicken broth

24 blanched almonds

4 hard-cooked eggs

6 drops of almond extract

¾ cup heavy cream

salt

white pepper

PREHEAT the oven to 350 °F. In a small sauté pan over medium heat, sauté the chicken breasts in butter until firm to the touch, about 4 minutes on each side. Let cool and cut into ½-inch cubes.

SOAK the bread slices in enough chicken broth to soften them.

TOAST the almonds in the oven until pale brown, about 15 minutes.

TAKE the yolks out of the hard-cooked eggs and discard the whites. Combine the yolks with the chicken breast meat, almonds, almond extract, bread, and half the chicken broth in a blender or food processor. Puree the mixture for about 2 minutes, until smooth.

TRANSFER the mixture to a 4-quart pot and combine it with the rest of the broth and the heavy cream. Bring the soup to a slow simmer.

STRAIN the soup through a medium-mesh strainer into a clean pot. Press firmly with a wooden spoon or the back of a ladle to work through as much of the solid mixture as possible. If you have one, you can also use a drum sieve to strain the solids.

SEASON the soup to taste with salt and white pepper and serve.

"Yogurt is used
as a healthy finish for
soups . . ."

Yogurt, Cheese, and Buttermilk

SOUPS

Traditionally, buttermilk was the liquid that remained after butter was churned. Today most of our butter is sweet butter, but in other times (and today in other places), butter was made with cream that had been allowed to ferment slightly from its own bacteria or, more likely nowadays, cultured with a laboratory bred bacteria. This caused the liquid released by the butter—as the fat congealed in the churn—to have a distinctly sour flavor. Today, buttermilk is made simply by inoculating milk with a culture of mixed bacteria. If you find the flavor of buttermilk too aggressive, you might try using keefer, available in health food stores, which more closely resembles tangy liquid yogurt.

Yogurt Soups

Yogurt is used widely in the Middle East, India, Eastern Europe, and Russia as a light and healthy finish for soups. It's also being seen more in the United States and Western Europe as a refreshing substitute for heavy cream. One particular favorite throughout the world is cucumber soup finished with yogurt and flavored with mint, onion, garlic, dill, or other seasonings, depending on the country (see recipe on page 179).

When yogurt is used in hot soups, it must be stirred in at the very end (or passed as a topping at the table), and it mustn't be allowed to boil, or it will curdle. However, if the soup is thickened with starchy ingredients such as split peas or lentils, these will prevent the yogurt from curdling. Some yogurt-finished broths contain cornstarch or flour to stabilize the yogurt so it won't curdle.

Yogurt, Spinach, and Sorrel Soup

DOVGA

This soup is derived from one given in Anya von Bremzen and John Welchman's book on Russian cooking, *Please to the Table*. Their version contains rice and yellow split peas, which you should feel free to add if you want a heartier version. What I love about this soup is the unusual combination of herbs—mint, sorrel, dill, and cilantro! This soup can be served either hot or cold.

MAKES 6 SERVINGS

I quart chicken or vegetable broth

2 cups yogurt

1½ tablespoons all-purpose flour

I cup tightly packed spinach leaves

2 cups tightly packed sorrel leaves

3 scallions, white part only, finely chopped

2 tablespoons finely chopped fresh dill

2 tablespoons finely chopped cilantro

3 tablespoons finely chopped fresh mint

pinch of cayenne pepper or more to taste

salt

pepper

I tablespoon finely chopped chives or dill

BRING the chicken broth to a simmer in a 4-quart pot.

WHISK the yogurt and flour together until smooth.

SHRED the spinach and sorrel by rolling the leaves over themselves and then slicing the rolled leaves into ⅛-inch-thick shreds.

WHISK a cup of the simmering broth into the yogurt mixture and then return the yogurt mixture to the rest of the broth.

ADD the rest of the ingredients and simmer for 1 minute. Serve hot or cold. Garnish each bowl with a dollop of yogurt and a sprinkling of chives or dill.

Yogurt and Cucumber Soup with Garlic

TARATOR

This is one of those recipes that can double as a soup or a salad depending on the amount of liquid in the cucumbers and on whether or not you add water. In either form this is a wonderfully cool and refreshing dish for summer. This version is designed for lovers of garlic and shouldn't be eaten before the theater or any other social gathering involving tight spaces.

Most versions of *tarator* are made with walnuts but it's also good with hazelnuts or almonds—the final decision is up to you. The mint and dill are also interchangeable.

MAKES 6 FIRST-COURSE SERVINGS

½ cup walnut halves, blanched almonds, or blanched hazelnuts

3 garlic cloves, peeled

4 cups plain yogurt (6 tablespoons reserved for decorating bowls)

3 tablespoons extra virgin olive oil

2 regular cucumbers or 1 long hot house variety cucumber, seeded, finely chopped

2 tablespoons freshly chopped mint or dill

salt and pepper

mint or dill sprigs for decoration

TOAST the nuts in a 350°F oven for 10 to 15 minutes until they turn pale brown and smell toasty. Let the nuts cool and grind them in a food processor with the garlic cloves until finely chopped. You may have to scrape the sides of the food processor a couple of times to get the mixture to move around.

COMBINE the nut/garlic mixture with the yogurt (except that reserved for decorating) and olive oil in a mixing bowl. Stir in the chopped cucumbers and the chopped mint or dill, and season to taste with salt and pepper. If the soup seems to thick, thin it with a little cold water.

SERVE ice cold in chilled bowls. Decorate each bowl with a tablespoon of the reserved yogurt and a sprig of mint or dill.

Cheese Soup

Cheese soup comes in various forms. In European *panades*, bread is layered with grated cheese, broth, and other ingredients such as cabbage, preserved goose, or stewed onions and the whole thing is baked, almost like a casserole. In American versions—one from Vermont is the most popular—broth or milk is thickened with flour, and Cheddar cheese is stirred in at the end. In a cheese fondue, in fact, a kind of soup, the cheese is melted with wine, and each diner dips pieces of bread into the simmering soup.

This recipe represents a variation on all three. I love cheese, but there's something monotonous about a cheese soup with no bread. In this version cubes of French bread are arranged over the top of individual soup crocks, a little more soup is sprinkled over, and more grated cheese goes over the top.

Lovers of cheese soup usually insist that Vermont Cheddar be used, but paradoxically authentic farmer's cheese from Vermont is harder to find than well-made European cheeses. So this recipe includes several alternatives. English Cheddars are wonderfully good, especially the cylindrical farmers' "truckle." Other good cheeses, to use here include Swiss Gruyère, aged Gouda, or blue cheese such as Stilton, Gorgonzola, or Roquefort.

It's important to serve this soup in small crocks rather than bowls with rims; otherwise the rims will get too hot in the oven.

This soup can be prepared a day or two in advance and baked just before serving.

MAKES 8 SERVINGS

3 tablespoons unsalted butter

1 medium-size onion, finely chopped

3 tablespoons all-purpose flour

7 cups milk, broth, water, or a mixture

1 bouquet garni

1½ pounds firm cheese, coarsely grated or crumbled*

6 1-inch-thick slices of French bread from a thick loaf,
        toasted and cut into 1-inch cubes

*If you're using strong-flavored cheeses such as Roquefort or other blue cheeses, the soup may require much less. Add only eight ounces of the cheese and then add more if necessary, to taste.

MELT the butter in a 4-quart pot over medium heat. Add the onion and stir the mixture for 5 minutes. Add the flour and stir for 5 minutes more, being careful not to let the butter burn.

WHISK in the liquid, add the bouquet garni, and bring to a boil. Simmer gently for 10 minutes, turn off the heat, and whisk in the cheese.

LADLE the soup into the serving crocks, reserving 1 cup. Arrange the bread cubes over each crock, ladle the remaining soup over the bread, and sprinkle with the remaining cheese.

IF you're serving the soup right away, bake the crocks in a 400°F oven until they start to bubble and brown on top, after about 10 minutes. If you've made the soup in advance and it's cold, bake in a 325°F oven for about 25 minutes.

Cheese Fondue Soup

I first tasted cheese fondue when my aunt Jane returned from a trip to Switzerland. Aunt Jane's many trips to Europe were invariably followed with a series of theme dinners accompanied by appropriate music and drink. Some of those lovely dinners I've forgotten, but the Swiss dinner—complete with yodeling music on the phonograph and plenty of kirsch and crisp white wine—have remained family traditions. Aunt Jane is one of the few people I know who still has her original fondue set.

Anyone who eats cheese fondue will remember that it goes through a series of phases as it sits in the pot. First there's the soup phase—the one I'm replicating here—followed by the stringy and crusty phases. Kirsch (or, as it's called in Germany and parts of Switzerland, kirschwasser) is a dry, very alcoholic cherry brandy. Don't confuse it with "cherry-flavored brandy," which is grape brandy flavored with cherry syrup and loads of sugar and tastes like cough syrup. Good kirsch is expensive—the best comes from Switzerland, but French brands from Alsace are decent—so don't be shocked and don't buy an inexpensive American brand, many of which seem to be made from cherry pits (which give the kirsch a distinctly almond flavor) rather than the fruit. Don't scrimp on the cheese either—authentic Gruyère and Emmentaler are essential. (And don't be taken in by packages that say "imported Swiss cheese" which can be imported from anywhere but never from Switzerland.) I suggest serving this soup with dry white wine and a little glass (or more as needed) of kirsch.

MAKES 6 FIRST-COURSE SERVINGS

1 French baguette, cut into cubes about ½ inch on each side

6 ounces authentic Swiss Gruyère

6 ounces authentic Swiss Emmentaler

2 teaspoons cornstarch

6 cups dry white wine

¼ cup good quality kirsch (optional)

salt

white pepper

SPREAD the bread cubes on a sheet pan and bake them in a 350°F oven for about 15 minutes, turning them over every 5 minutes, until they're lightly browned and crispy.

GRATE the cheese. Combine the cornstarch with a tablespoon of the wine and bring the rest of the wine to a simmer in a heavy-bottomed saucepan. Simmer the wine for about 7 minutes to cook off its alcohol and whisk in the cheese, the cornstarch mixture, and the kirsch. Stir over medium heat until the cheese dissolves and the soup returns to the simmer. Season to taste with salt and pepper, and ladle into heated soup plates. Sprinkle each bowl with a few bread cubes and pass the rest of the cubes in a basket at the table. This soup is thinner than an authentic fondue, so you can eat it with a spoon.

Buttermilk Soup

This simple soup is easy to play around with and alter to suit your own tastes. I serve it cold or hot and sometimes add cayenne pepper or curry powder, different herbs (especially tarragon), and even shrimp.

MAKES 6 FIRST-COURSE SERVINGS

COOKING WITH BUTTERMILK

Buttermilk can be substituted for the liquid in almost any soup. If you decide to use it as the base for a hot soup, you must first combine it with a light roux—flour and butter cooked to a smooth paste—to thicken it and prevent it from curdling. You can then add fish, vegetables, or even meats, following your own tastes.

The tangy flavor of buttermilk is well suited to cold summer soups. When serving it in a cold soup you don't have to worry about curdling, of course, but you may want to puree some of your soup ingredients with the buttermilk to give it some texture.

2 tablespoons unsalted butter

2 tablespoons all-purpose flour

I quart buttermilk

3 cucumbers, peeled, seeds scooped out, sliced

2 tablespoons finely chopped fresh dill or I tablespoon
    dried

juice of I lemon

salt

white pepper

fresh dill sprigs

COMBINE the butter and flour in a 4-quart pot over medium heat and stir for 3 minutes. Add the buttermilk while whisking and bring to a slow simmer. Add the cucumbers and chopped dill and simmer for 15 minutes more.

LET the soup cool for 10 minutes. Puree in a blender and strain through the fine disk of a food mill. Stir in the lemon juice and season with salt and pepper. Serve hot or cold garnished with fresh dill sprigs.

"Fruit soups served as dessert are light alternatives . . ."

Fruit Soups and Dessert
SOUPS

Fruits are particularly intriguing in soups when they're combined with spices and savory ingredients, as they are in the first three recipes in this section. Savory summer soups have a wonderfully refreshing quality.

Fruit soups served as dessert are light alternatives to rich pastries and sweets. A fruit soup can be a simple "broth," a medley of smooth purees swirled together in colorful combinations, or a chunky fruit salad bathed in coconut milk.

Instead of following any particular recipe, you'll have more fun mastering a few of the basic liquid components to dessert soups and then inventing and improvising, depending on what you feel like eating and what looks good at the market.

Fruit Purees

Making a fruit puree is one of the easiest and least expensive ways to come up with an elegant dessert soup. Puree the fruits in a food processor or blender and then strain them through a fine- or medium-mesh strainer or food mill. In winter, when fresh berries are expensive and those you can find don't have much taste, use thawed frozen whole berries. Avoid frozen berries that have been packed in syrup.

If you're stuck with hard, underripe fruit, you may need to cook it with a little sugar and water to soften it before straining, but avoid this if you can; cooking fruit, even for a minute or two, takes something away from its bright, fresh flavor.

Sometimes after you've prepared a fruit puree from seemingly sweet and ripe fruit, the puree will taste too sour and you'll need to add sugar. The easiest method is to make a sugar syrup by dissolving sugar in twice the amount of water—you may have to heat the mixture a little to get the sugar to dissolve—and then stir the sugar syrup into the puree, tasting as you go.

Fruit purees are almost always improved by adding a tablespoon or two of lemon juice. Surprisingly, this is true even with fruits that are already somewhat acidic.

Most fruit purees are too thick to use directly in a dessert soup, so you will have to dilute them with a little water. You'll probably have to play around with the ingredients—sugar syrup, lemon juice, water—to get the flavor and consistency you want.

Note: Sometimes the word *coulis* is used to describe a fruit puree. Although the meaning of the two words is similar, there is a real but sometimes subtle difference between the two—a coulis has been strained to eliminate seeds, a puree has not.

Chilled Indian Pear Soup

I've always appreciated the Indian habit of serving a slightly sweet and spicy dish at the beginning of a meal. The first time I had this soup was on a blistering August day; I started out with no appetite, but somehow the sweetness of the pears and the spiciness of the curry revived me, and we all ended up spending several hours eating a rather large meal.

MAKES 6 FIRST-COURSE SERVINGS

9 sweet ripe pears

1 quart light chicken broth

1 medium-size onion, chopped

2 tablespoons unsalted butter

1 tablespoon curry powder, preferably *garam masala*

1 cup heavy cream

salt

cayenne pepper

½ cup heavy cream, beaten until barely stiff

RINSE the pears, slice them in half lengthwise, and remove the cores with a spoon or melon baller. There is no need to peel the pears since the peels will be strained out anyway. Slice each pear half into several pieces. Put the sliced pears in a mixing bowl with the chicken broth. (The broth covers the pears and prevents them from turning brown.)

IN a 4-quart pot over medium heat cook the chopped onion in butter until it softens and turns translucent, about 10 minutes. Stir in the curry powder and cook for about 2 minutes until the smell starts to fill the room.

POUR in the pears and all the remaining chicken broth. Simmer the soup for about 15 minutes, until the pears are soft. If the pears are underripe, you may need to simmer them longer.

STRAIN the soup through a food mill with the finest disk or puree the pears in a blender or food processor and strain the soup through a medium-mesh strainer.

CHILL the soup and 1 cup heavy cream (see note). Season the soup to taste with salt and cayenne pepper. Decorate each bowl with a swirl of the lightly beaten cream.

Note: If you plan to store the soup overnight, bring the cream to a simmer before adding it to the soup. This sterilizes it and prevents it from souring. The cream can also be added the next day, shortly before serving.

SUGGESTIONS AND VARIATIONS | This soup also works with apples—in fact the idea came from an Indian hors d'oeuvre—*murgh chat*—made with cold chicken, potatoes, and apples spiced with curry and chopped cilantro. You can also add chopped cilantro to this soup just before chilling to accentuate the flavor of the curry.

ONE interesting version is cold pear soup with watercress, which chef Jeremiah Tower serves at Stars restaurant in San Francisco. Prepare the soup as directly, but leave out the curry. Take the leaves and small stems off 2 bunches of watercress and boil them for 1 minute in a pot of boiling salted water. Strain the watercress, rinse it with cold water, and combine it with a cup of the cold soup in a blender. Blend at high speed for 1 minute. Strain through a medium-mesh strainer into the remaining soup.

Chilled Puree of Seasonal Mixed Fruits

MARAK PERAT KAR

This is a wonderfully refreshing soup from Israel that can range from good to magnificent, depending on the quality of the fruit you track down.

The recipe here is really only a model. Feel free to increase, decrease, eliminate altogether, or add completely different fruits, depending on what you find. In midsummer I make this soup almost entirely with the little soft strawberries I find at the farmer's market; later in the summer I use Concord grapes instead of the white ones listed here as well as peaches if I can find good ones. As fall approaches I use plums, and later I experiment with old-fashioned varieties of apples that drift down from upstate New York.

I usually serve this soup as a refreshing dessert, but I always try to make extra so I'll have a little left the next day for breakfast. And sometimes I sneak in a little rum for a summer afternoon drink.

MAKES 8 DESSERT OR BREAKFAST SERVINGS

I medium-size honeydew or other ripe melon, peeled, seeds
    removed, cut into I-inch chunks

I quart strawberries or other berries, stems removed

I medium-size bunch of grapes, skins removed

3 ripe pears or apples, peeled, cored and sliced

juice of 3 lemons

3 cups fresh orange juice, from about 6 oranges

½ cup sugar

4 cups water

crème fraîche, sour cream, whipped cream, or
    yogurt

8 small fresh mint sprigs

PUREE the fruits together in a blender or food processor. You'll need to do this in several stages because the fruits won't all fit in at once. Add the lemon juice and enough of the orange juice to get the fruits moving while they're being pureed.

STRAIN the pureed fruit through the fine disk of a food mill or a medium-mesh strainer using a ladle or a wooden spoon to push the mixture through. If there's some stubborn pulp that won't go through, work it some more in the blender or food processor.

ADD any remaining lemon juice or orange juice to the fruit puree.

DISSOLVE the sugar in the water and stir the water into the fruit puree a cup at a time until the soup has the consistency you want. If the soup needs to be sweeter or tarter, adjust it with either sugar dissolved in water or lemon juice.

SERVE in chilled wide bowls with a dollop of cream or yogurt in the middle and a sprig of mint.

Spicy Tropical Fruit and Barbecued Chicken Soup

This soup started out as a salad when I was experimenting one especially torrid summer with tossing still-warm barbecued meats and fish into a freshly made fruit salad. This salsa-like soup version is hot and spicy, and everyone I've ever served it to has loved it. It looks best served in wide bowls so everyone can see the colors of the tropical fruits. I usually serve it as a main course on the hottest summer evenings.

The fruits can all be chopped and combined in advance, but the soup is best if the fruits are prepared the same day. You can chop the fruits in a food processor, but process them separately—so they don't end up exactly the same size—and use the pulse mechanism so you don't turn everything into a puree. The chicken can be barbecued in advance but if you can handle some last-minute work, it's best to serve it hot off the grill. Either way, don't combine the chicken with the slightly chilled tropical fruit base until just before serving; the enzymes break down the chicken's texture so that in a few hours it will have turned to mush.

If you can't find all the tropical fruits listed, just substitute more of those you can find.

MAKES 8 MAIN-COURSE SERVINGS

I small pineapple

I Hawaiian papaya, peeled, halved, and seeded

3 kiwifruits, peeled

2 mangoes

3 poblano chilies or 2 red bell peppers

4 jalapeño chilies, seeded and finely chopped, plus more to
    pass at the table

I cup tightly packed cilantro leaves, finely chopped,
    3 tablespoons

salt

pepper

½ cup water

4 whole chicken breasts, split in half

¼ cup extra virgin olive oil

I tablespoon white wine vinegar

I teaspoon chopped fresh marjoram or thyme

I Bermuda onion, finely chopped

CUT the leafy top and the base off the pineapple. With the pineapple standing on the cutting board, cut off the peel with a chef's knife. The easiest way to cut out the little pieces of peel that remain embedded in the flesh is to cut around the pineapple in a spiral pattern along the top of the pits and then turn the pineapple upside down, do the same thing again, and pull off the strips. Cut the pineapple vertically into 6 segments and cut off the strip of core that runs along each. Thinly slice the segments. Reserve the pieces of pineapple along with any liquid that runs out in a large mixing bowl.

CUT the papaya halves into strips, chop them into ¼-inch cubes, and combine them with the pineapple.

CUT the kiwifruits lengthwise into quarters and thinly slice. Combine with the other fruits.

CUT the mangoes in half vertically, cutting around the pit to detach each half. Make two rows of cuts into the flesh—down to but not through the skin of each half. Press against the skin so it inverts and the flesh is concave, facing out. Slice along the skin so the cubes detach. Reserve with the rest of the fruits.

THOROUGHLY blacken the poblanos or bell peppers over a gas flame or under a broiler. Rinse quickly under cold water and pull the skin off with your fingers. Scrape any stubborn pieces of skin with a paring knife. Cut in half and remove the seeds and stems. Slice into thin strips and combine with the fruits.

STIR the jalapeños and 2 tablespoons of the cilantro into the fruits. Season to taste with salt and pepper.

PUREE about a fourth of the fruit salad in a blender with the water for about 30 seconds and combine this puree with the rest of the salad. Reserve in the refrigerator.

BARBECUE the chicken breasts until their skin is crispy and they feel firm to the touch, about 10 minutes on each side. Let cool slightly and then pull the flesh away from the bone and cut it into thin strips. Toss the strips with the olive oil, vinegar, and marjoram. Season with salt and pepper.

LADLE the fruits into chilled wide bowls and arrange the strips in the center of each one. Sprinkle the strips with the remaining cilantro. Serve the chopped onion and chilies at the table.

Dried Fruit Soup

NORWEGIAN FRUKTSOPPA

As I child I adored tapioca pudding, but after years of indulging in decadent desserts, my jaded taste buds seek more contrast and my old childhood favorite now seems monotonous. Recently, I discovered this Swedish soup made with tapioca, dried fruits, and fresh apples, which give a tart accent to the soothing backdrop of the tapioca. Traditional versions leave the dried fruits whole, but I prefer to dice them.

MAKES 6 DESSERT SERVINGS

I vanilla bean, cut lengthwise in half

I cinnamon stick, about 3 inches long

⅔ cup sugar

3 tablespoons quick-cooking tapioca (minute tapioca)

I cup dried apricots cut into ¼-inch dice

I cup pitted prunes cut into ¼-inch dice

grated zest of I lemon

I large apple such as Golden Delicious, suitable for baking (don't use Granny Smiths or McIntoshes; they'll turn to mush), peeled, cored, and cut into ¼-inch dice

4 tablespoons yellow raisins

2 tablespoons dried currants

2 pints vanilla ice cream (optional)

PUT the vanilla bean, cinnamon stick, sugar, and tapioca in a pot with 6 cups of water. Bring to a simmer, stir until the sugar dissolves, and remove from the heat. Stir in the fruits and lemon zest and cover the pot. Let cool for about I hour and then refrigerate for at least 3 hours more.

REMOVE the cinnamon stick and vanilla bean halves. Scrape the tiny seeds out of the vanilla bean halves with a small knife and stir them into the soup. Chill. Stir the soup just before serving to redistribute the fruits, since the apples tend to float to the top. If you like, put a scoop of vanilla ice cream in the middle of each bowl.

DICING DRIED FRUITS

Cutting dried fruits into small cubes can get tedious since they get sticky and cling to the knife. If this starts to drive you crazy, try rubbing the knife with a little vegetable oil every few minutes to help prevent the sticking.

SUGGESTIONS AND VARIATIONS | Other dried fruits such as cranberries, blue-berries, and cherries can also be added to this soup, but because of variations in sweetness or tartness, you may have to adjust the amount of sugar. I like to stir a couple of tablespoons of good kirsch into the soup after it has chilled.

Cold Rhubarb and Strawberry Soup

Scandinavians eat a lot of cold fruit soups, seemingly concocting a soup out of any fruit, fresh or dried. Rhubarb soup is a classic, but I've Americanized it somewhat by adding strawberries. You can use it as a backdrop for any fruit, especially red berries. I like to serve this with a scoop of vanilla ice cream in the middle.

MAKES 6 DESSERT SERVINGS

I pound rhubarb, cleaned and trimmed, cut into
¼-inch-thick slices, or I 12- or 14-ounce package
frozen rhubarb

½ cup granulated sugar, or more as needed

I vanilla bean, split in half lengthwise

6 scoops vanilla ice cream, or I cup of cream whipped with
I tablespoon confectioners' sugar and a teaspoon of
vanilla extract (optional)

2 pints strawberries, stemmed and quartered vertically

COMBINE the rhubarb, granulated sugar, and vanilla bean in a pot with 4 cups of water and bring to a gentle simmer. Simmer with the cover ajar until the rhubarb is soft, about 15 minutes, then let cool, with the pot covered so the vanilla flavor infuses in the soup. Take out the vanilla bean halves and scrape the tiny seeds out with a small knife and reserve. Strain the puree, pushing down hard on the strainer with the bottom of a ladle to extract as much liquid as you can. Discard the pulp that doesn't go through the strainer and put the seeds back in the pot with the rhubarb. At this point you may need to add more sugar if you find the soup too tart, but keep in mind if you're serving ice cream that ice cream is very sweet and a tart soup will provide a welcome contrast . . . Chill the soup in the refrigerator and serve in chilled bowls. Put a scoop of ice cream in the middle of each bowl. Top with the strawberries. If you're serving the soup with whipped cream, put a dollop on each bowl or pass it at the table.

Berry Broth

A fruit broth is simply a puree that has been thinned with water, sugar syrup, or lemon juice until it has a souplike consistency. I sometimes combine fruit broths with other liquids such as custard cream.

Fruit broths can be made a day or two in advance and kept covered in the refrigerator. Because some fruits contain a lot of pectin, the purees may set in the refrigerator and will need to be quickly whisked or whirled in the blender just before serving to get them to liquify.

MAKES 2 CUPS

3 half-pints fresh berries or 1 16-ounce package frozen
(whole, not in syrup), thawed

½ cup sugar

½ cup water

juice of 1 lemon

PROCESS the berries in a blender or food processor for about 30 seconds. You may need to add ½ cup water to get the berries to move around. Strain the puree through a food mill or a medium- or fine-mesh strainer, working the mixture through with the back of a ladle.

HEAT the sugar with the water in a saucepan just long enough to dissolve the sugar. Slowly stir this syrup into the strained berry puree until it has the consistency and flavor you like. Stir in the lemon juice. If the broth seems too thick, thin it with water.

SUGGESTIONS AND VARIATIONS | Simple fruit broths can be made with almost any fruit including peaches, apricots, plums, and tropical fruits. Almost all fruit purees are best flavored with a little sugar syrup to give them the necessary sweetness. Lemon juice is also helpful to give the fruits a refreshing tang.

PEACH BROTH Substitute 4 ripe peaches, peeled and pitted, for the berries and reduce the sugar to ¼ cup. Proceed as directed.

Cold Cherry Soup

This is a purely summer interpretation of the traditional Hungarian soup, *meggykeszöce*. In some traditional versions the cherries are cooked with cinnamon, lemons, and sometimes cloves. I always find that the spices distort the flavor of the cherries, and in any case I associate the flavor of these spices with winter and such things as mulled wine and hot cider. Traditional cherry soups are also prepared with sour cherries (usually Morellos), but I use whatever is in season and then flavor the soup with lemon juice or sugar to get the flavor I want; height-of-the-summer Bing cherries are my favorites.

MAKES 4 SERVINGS

2 pounds fresh cherries

2 cups water

½ cup sugar

juice of 1 lemon

2 tablespoons imported kirsch (optional)

1 cup crème fraîche, heavy cream, lightly whipped,
    or sour cream

PIT the cherries, reserving 18 cut in half for decorating the soup. You can pit cherries by cutting them along each side with a paring knife, but it's much more efficient to use a cherry pitter (they also work for olives).

IN a mixing bowl, stir together the water and sugar until the sugar dissolves.

PUREE the cherries in a food processor using some of the sugar/water mixture to get them moving around or strain them through the fine disk of a food mill. Strain the pulp through a medium-mesh strainer.

COMBINE the sugar/water mixture, lemon juice, and kirsch, if you're using it, with the strained cherries. Taste the soup. If it's too tart, add two or three tablespoons sugar dissolved in ½ cup water. If it needs to be tangier, add more lemon juice.

SERVE in chilled bowls. Decorate with the reserved cherry halves and serve with the cream.

Melon Soup

It's essential to have ripe, sweet melons for this soup, something which oddly isn't easy, even at the height of summer. When I make this soup, I must always give some to my cat, who is nuts for melon but indifferent to fish.

MAKES 6 FIRST-COURSE OR DESSERT SERVINGS
(IF YOU'RE USING SOME OF THE VARIATIONS, SEE BELOW)

2 medium cantaloupes, about 1½ pounds each, or the same
   weight of French Cavaillon melons or other orange-
   fleshed melon

4 tablespoons sugar

3 cups water

1 tablespoon Cointreau or Grand Marnier, or more to taste
   (optional)

4 tablespoons lemon juice or more to taste

HALVE and seed the cantaloupes and scoop out the flesh into a blender or food processor. Stir the sugar with the water until it dissolves. Puree the cantaloupe in batches in the blender, adding enough of the sweetened water to each batch to get the mixture to turn around. Stir in the Cointreau and then the lemon juice to taste. Ladle into chilled glass bowls.

SUGGESTIONS AND VARIATIONS | Many recipes for melon soups contain spices (ginger, curry powder, cardamon, and saffron alone or in combinations are a few possibilities) or fruit juice instead of the sugar water I'm using here. I prefer the sugar water because it leaves the delicate flavor of the melon intact, but if your melon is less than perfect, chop some ginger, wring it out in a towel to extract the juice, and stir the juice into the soup. You can also replace the sugar water with fresh-squeezed orange juice or melon juice extracted with a juicer. I also like to garnish melon soup and other fruit soups by simmering some cream with a little curry powder, and then swirling the mixture—either hot or cold—over the soup in each bowl. Another savory addition are little shreds of finely sliced prosciutto. Diced fruits, such as kiwis or papayas, or berries, such as raspberries, also make an attractive and tasty garnish, as does ice cream if you're serving the soup as a dessert.

Bellini Soup

When sightseeing in a European city, my carefully planned hours of museum and cathedral visiting are often thwarted by a sudden thirst and a gnawing hunger that set in as soon as I've paid my liras or francs for the entrance ticket. Having grown wiser over the years, I now prepare myself for this phenomenon by researching bars and restaurants near the important tourist sites so I can break up my dutiful art gazing at any given time with a bite and a little nip. Venice is a perfect tourist city, because it has not only an abundance of architecture and painting but also plenty of bars, cafes, and restaurants. Harry's Bar is the most famous bar in Venice and possibly on the planet, and for the wandering sybarite is as important a stop as the Basilica St. Marco. How it acquired this fame I'm not sure (Hemingway drank there, but he also drank in a lot of other places), but it does have a particular charm for which one pays dearly. The bar's signature drink is the Bellini, named after Giovanni Bellini, whose paintings can be seen in the nearby Academia. The traditional Bellini is made with white peach puree fortified with the local sparkling wine, Prosecco. The result is a little like a mimosa in which peaches replace the orange juice, and it is perfectly lovely at a Sunday brunch but hardly adequate after a day of museum going when something more bracing is definitely called for. Fortunately, Harry's Bar also makes an excellent martini.

But because the Bellini seems more like food than drink, it occurred to me that it would make a wonderful dessert soup. The trick to success is, of course, the peaches, which aren't easy to find in decent shape these days even at the height of their season. Arrigo Cipriani (the owner of Harry's Bar) insists that only white peaches be used (see Sources) and that they must never be pureed by machine. But the situation isn't as grim as it sounds, because an excellent French brand of white peach puree can be mail-ordered, and despite Mr. Cipriani's insistence on white peaches for the Bellini, this soup is delicious with the more common yellow peaches.

MAKES 8 REFRESHING DESSERT SERVINGS

I 500 gr. package frozen white peach puree (see Sources) or
  I ½ pound ripe peaches
I tablespoon confectioners' sugar or more to taste
  (optional)
2 cups Prosecco or other good quality (but not extravagant)
  sparkling wine
2 ½-pint containers of raspberries, or blackberries, or
  I 1-pint container blueberries, or a combination
mint leaves

IF you're using frozen puree, simply let it thaw. If you're using fresh peaches, cut them in half and remove the pits. Put them in a food processor, in batches, and pulse them just long enough to puree them. Work the pureed peaches through a drum sieve or large strainer by rubbing them through with your fingers. If the puree seems tart, sweeten it to taste with sugar. Chill for at least 2 hours in the refrigerator.

JUST before serving, gently (so you don't work out the bubbles) stir the Prosecco into the puree and ladle the soup into chilled bowls. Sprinkle each serving with the berries and decorate each bowl with a mint leaf or two.

Hot Peach Soup with Crème Fraîche

I concocted this soup one summer while staying with relatives in California, where I had access to plenty of juicy, ripe peaches. It has since become one of my staple summer desserts.

MAKES 8 SERVINGS

12 ripe peaches, peeled, halved, and pitted
1 cup confectioners' sugar
2 teaspoons vanilla extract or ½ cup dark rum
2 cups white wine, preferably slightly sweet such as Riesling or Chenin Blanc
1 egg plus 1 egg yolk
1 teaspoon salt
6 puff pastry circles, homemade or frozen, well chilled
crème fraîche, whipped cream, vanilla ice cream

CUT the peach halves into ¼-inch-thick slices and toss them in a mixing bowl with the sugar and the vanilla. Let sit for at least 15 minutes and up to 4 hours.

ARRANGE the peaches in 12-ounce individual soup crocks or ramekins. Pour the wine over the peaches.

PREPARE an egg wash by combining the egg, egg yolk, and salt in a small bowl. Beat the mixture with a fork for about 2 minutes, until the egg is completely broken up and the mixture is runny.

PLACE the pastry circles on a work surface. Use a sharp paring knife to cut a series of decorative arcs starting from the middle of the circles and going out to the edges. Be careful not to puncture the pastry at any point.

TURN the pastry circles over and brush the plain side with egg wash. Place the circles, egg side down, on top of the soup crocks or ramekins and press the overlapping part of the circles against the sides of the bowls to form an airtight seal. Brush the top and sides of the pastry with egg wash.

REFRIGERATE the bowls for 30 minutes. Preheat the oven to 425°F for 20 minutes. If the pastry is completely browned in less time, turn the oven down to 300°F.

SERVE a bowl of crème fraîche, whipped cream, or ice cream at the table for guests to dollop into their hot soup as soon as they've broken through the puff pastry crust.

SUGGESTIONS AND VARIATIONS | I also like to prepare this dish with apricots, and if I'm being fancy I like to use Sautérnes or Muscat de Beaumes de Venise as the wine and leave out the vanilla or rum.

IF you and your guests like prunes, they make a delicious winter variation. Combine 3 dozen pitted prunes (6 per serving) with ½ cup sugar and 1 cup water in a 2-quart saucepan. Cover the saucepan and simmer the prunes for 20 minutes to soften them. Remove the lid, pour in a cup of Armagnac, replace the lid, and let the prunes cool.

ARRANGE the prunes and their steeping liquid in the bowls and bake as you would for the peaches.

Coconut and Tropical Fruit Soup

This is one of my summer favorites—a sort of tropical fruit salad surrounded with a piña colada-like mixture of pineapple and chilled coconut milk. The choice of fruits for the salad is up to you; I end up buying what I can find that looks ripe. If you have trouble finding tropical fruits, this soup is still delicious when made with just bananas and pineapples.

To make the pineapple-coconut broth, you'll need a cup of pineapple wedges. You can used canned pineapple but I always prefer to cut up a whole pineapple and use some of the wedges for the broth and some for the salad.

MAKES 6 SERVINGS

the piña-colada broth:

1¾ cups coconut milk

1 cup fresh pineapple wedges

the fruit salad:

4 of the following fruits (if you use more or fewer of the
  varieties listed, adjust the quantities accordingly)

Bananas: 2 large bananas, sliced within an hour of serving

Pineapple: 1 pineapple, peeled, core removed, cut into
  ¼-inch-thick wedges (page 574) 1 cup reserved
  for broth

Kiwifruit: 2 kiwifruits, peeled and sliced

Papaya: 1 Hawaiian papaya, peeled, seeded, and cut sideways
  into crescent shapes

Mango: 1 mango, peeled, seeded, and cut into chunks
  (page 574)

PREPARING THE BROTH Puree the pineapple wedges in a blender with the coconut milk for about 1 minute. Reserve, covered, in the refrigerator.

PRESENTING THE SOUP Ladle the broth into each bowl and arrange the fruits on top. The tropical fruits make this a very colorful soup, but if you like, decorate each bowl with a mint leaf or a pinch of shredded coconut.

SUGGESTIONS AND VARIATIONS | I sometimes flavor the coconut milk with ground spices such as ginger, cardamom, cloves, cinnamon, coriander, or saffron. You can also make this into ice cream: flavor 3 cups coconut milk with ½ teaspoon ground cardamom and ¼ teaspoon of saffron. Let the spices sit in the coconut milk for 30 minutes to infuse before freezing.

A shot of dark rum is delicious in the coconut/pinapple broth.

Fruit Soup with Spice Broth

This soup is delicate and intriguing because the fruits are served in a light syrup scented with exotic spices. I like to make this soup with unusual tropical fruits to keep guests conversing about what's what, but use whatever fruits you have available.

MAKES 6 SERVINGS

1 vanilla bean, cut in half lengthwise

1 ¼-inch-thick slice of fresh ginger

1 star anise, crushed

1 2-inch cinnamon stick or ½ teaspoon ground cinnamon

½ cup sugar

1 quart water

juice of 1 orange, about ⅓ cup

1 mango, pitted and cut into ¼-inch dice (page 574)

2 kiwifruits, peeled and cut into ¼-inch dice

1 Hawaiian papaya, peeled, seeded, and cut into ¼-inch dice

1 cup red berries such as raspberries, red currants, wild strawberries, or small strawberries

½ pineapple, peeled, cored, and cut into ½-inch dice (page 574)

COMBINE the vanilla bean, ginger, star anise, cinnamon, sugar, water, and orange juice in a 4-quart pot with a tight-fitting lid. Bring the mixture to a slow simmer, cover the pot, and simmer for 5 minutes. Remove from the heat and let cool. Remove and reserve the vanilla bean. Strain the mixture through a fine strainer, discarding the spices. Scrape the tiny seeds from the inside of each half of the vanilla bean and stir them into the strained syrup. Discard the halves of the vanilla bean.

COMBINE the fruits with the syrup in a mixing bowl and chill in the refrigerator for an hour. Serve in chilled bowls.

Hazelnut and Fresh Raspberry Soup

In July and August I practically live on fruit and tomatoes. I never tire of eating fresh raspberries with my fingers as my only dessert (except for perhaps a glass of chilled dessert wine), but I've found that guests like something a bit sweeter and more elaborate, so for their benefit I prepare this soup. Be sure to serve it in front of the guests—you'll get lots of *oohs* and *ahs*.

MAKES 6 SERVINGS

1½ cups milk
6 tablespoons hazelnut praline paste (recipe follows)
1½ cups heavy cream
1½ pints raspberries or as many as you want

IN a 2-quart mixing bowl, slowly whisk the milk into the praline paste until the mixture is completely smooth. Whisk in the heavy cream, but don't beat for too long or you'll end up with whipped cream. Cover and refrigerate for 30 minutes.

BRING the praline cream and the raspberries to the table. Ladle the praline cream into the bowls and sprinkle over the raspberries.

SUGGESTIONS AND VARIATIONS | Obviously any berry or combination of berries can be used for this soup. Crème anglaise can also be used. In the winter I serve hot caramelized pear halves in the praline cream and then top the whole thing with a pear-flavored butterscotch.

CARAMELIZED PEAR HALVES WITH PEAR-FLAVORED BUTTERSCOTCH Peel 6 pears, cut them in half lengthwise, and remove the core with a paring knife, a melon baller, or a spoon. Put the pear halves in a heavy-bottomed pan just large enough to hold them in a single layer. Sprinkle the pears with 1 cup sugar and ½ cup (1 stick) unsalted butter, cut into ½-inch cubes. Bake the pears in a 375°F oven until a brown caramel begins to form on the bottom of the pan and the pears have softened thoroughly. This takes from 20 to 45 minutes depending on the ripeness of the pears.

GENTLY take the pears out of the pan with a slotted spoon and keep them warm. Prepare the pear butterscotch by adding 1 cup heavy cream to the pan used to cook the pears. Bring the cream to a simmer in the pan. Stir for a minute to dissolve the caramelized pear juices.

HEAT the praline broth and ladle it into hot bowls. Arrange a pear half in the center of the bowls and ladle the pear butterscotch over it. A sprinkling of fresh berries and a sprig of mint are nice touches.

Hazelnut Praline Paste

Europeans love hazelnuts and use them as almost universal flavorings for chocolates and pastry. Americans are less accustomed to hazelnuts and almonds in their sweets but, once introduced, tend to become addicted.

It can be difficult to find good praline paste but with a little patience (and a food processor) you can make it yourself. Praline paste will keep indefinitely in a tightly covered container in the refrigerator.

MAKES 2 CUPS

1¼ cups (½ pound) hazelnuts or almonds
1 cup sugar
vegetable oil

TO remove the dark, papery skin from the hazelnuts, preheat the oven to 300°F and bake them on a baking sheet for 10 to 15 minutes (they'll start to smell good), then rub them in a dry towel. Inevitably a few are stubborn and impossible to peel completely; a few specks of peel are fine.

CHOP the nuts in a food processor using the pulse mechanism, until they're about the size of baby peas.

MAKE a caramel by melting the sugar in a heavy-bottomed 2-quart saucepan over medium heat. Stir continuously with a wooden spoon until all the lumps have melted. When the caramel has turned a deep reddish brown, add the coarsely chopped hazelnuts and stir for about 2 minutes off the heat.

LIGHTLY coat a rolling pin and a sheet pan with vegetable oil. Turn the gluey hazelnut/caramel mixture out onto the sheet pan, let it cool for about 2 minutes, and hammer the mixture with the rolling pin to flatten it into a rough sheet about ¼-inch thick. (Pastry chefs call these sheets nougatine.) If the mixture keeps sticking to the rolling pin, let it cool a minute or two more.

WHEN the mixture has cooled, cut it up into coarse chunks with a chef's knife. Grind the chunks in the food processor for about 5 minutes, stopping every minute or so to scrape the insides of the processor bowl with a rubber spatula. (Although this sounds like a long time, don't be tempted to stop sooner. It really does take 5 minutes to get the right consistency.) Store the praline paste in a tightly covered container in the refrigerator.

Blueberry Soup with Vanilla Custard Cream

Although it can be made with frozen blueberries, I usually make this soup only at the height of the season, when fresh blueberries are cheap and plentiful. This is my absolutely favorite way to eat blueberries.

Each of the components for this soup can be made a day or two in advance. But one thing to look out for: because of the pectin in the blueberries, the puree gels after about an hour in the refrigerator so you'll need to put it in the blender just before serving to liquefy it again.

MAKES 8 SERVINGS

½ cup sugar

½ cup hot water

2 pints fresh blueberries or 2 16-oz packages frozen, thawed

2½ cups custard cream (page 588)

8 fresh mint sprigs

MAKE a light sugar syrup by stirring the sugar with the hot water until the sugar dissolves.

RESERVE 30 whole blueberries for decorating the bowls and puree the rest of the blueberries with the sugar syrup in two batches in a blender.

STRAIN the puree through the fine disk of a food mill or a medium-mesh strainer. Chill.

LADLE the chilled blueberry puree into wide bowls, then slowly ladle the vanilla custard cream over it with a circular motion so it forms a decorative round pattern on top of the puree.

SPRINKLE the soup with the whole blueberries. Decorate each bowl with a sprig of mint.

SUGGESTIONS AND VARIATIONS | This method will work for almost any berry. The custard cream can also be flavored with different fruit brandies such as kirsch, framboise, poire william, etc.

Custard Cream

CRÈME ANGLAISE

Many fruit soups are enhanced when a few tablespoons of custard cream are swirled over the fruit broth and solid fruits.

MAKES 2½ CUPS

2 cups milk
1 vanilla bean or 2 teaspoons vanilla extract
¼ cup sugar
5 egg yolks

COMBINE the milk with the vanilla bean (see box) in a 2-quart saucepan. Bring to a slow simmer over medium heat.

WHISK the sugar and egg yolks together in a mixing bowl for about 2 minutes, until the yolks turn pale yellow.

POUR half the simmering milk into the egg yolk/sugar mixture while gently whisking. Return the mixture to the saucepan and place the pan over low heat. Stir continuously with a wooden spoon—be careful to reach into the corners of the saucepan—until the cream thickens slightly and coats the spoon. If you have an accurate thermometer, it should read 175°F. Immediately remove the pan from the heat and stir for 1 minute more to cool the mixture. Do *not* allow the cream to boil, or the yolks will curdle.

STRAIN the cream through a medium mesh strainer into a clean bowl, cover with plastic wrap, and place it in the refrigerator to cool. (It will keep 2 days, covered with plastic wrap.)

SUGGESTIONS AND VARIATIONS | Although it's hard to improve on such a good thing, custard cream can be flavored with chocolate, coffee, hazelnut, almonds, spices, spirits, even truffles.

TO make chocolate custard cream, follow the recipe but whisk ¼ cup unsweetened cocoa powder into the egg yolks with a little of the hot milk or melt ¼ pound bitter or 6 ounces

USING VANILLA BEANS

Most dessert recipes call for vanilla extract because it is convenient, easy to find, and relatively inexpensive. Whole vanilla beans, at least until recently, were hard to find and seemed to some like an exotic affectation. But in fact fresh vanilla beans have an alluring depth of flavor that never comes through in vanilla extract.

One of the best ways to take advantage of the subtle flavor of fresh vanilla beans is to use them to prepare a vanilla custard cream. When using vanilla beans, split them down the middle with a sharp knife, exposing the tiny flavorful seeds. Combine the vanilla bean halves in the milk and bring to a simmer. Take the vanilla beans out of the milk, scrape out the tiny seeds, and stir them into the hot milk. Discard the bean husks.

bittersweet chocolate in the hot milk as soon as you remove it from the heat and before you whisk it into the yolks.

TO make coffee custard cream, dissolve 2 tablespoons instant espresso (dark roast style such as Medaglia d'Oro) directly into one recipe of the vanilla custard cream. You can also get a more subtle effect by simmering 3 heaped tablespoons of finely ground dark roast coffee into the milk before cooking it with the yolks.

CUSTARD cream can also be flavored with spirits such as brandy or whiskey. Spirits should be added to crème anglaise only after it has cooled; otherwise their flavor will evaporate. The best way to flavor crème anglaise is to add the liquor a few tablespoons at a time unti the crème anglaise tastes right. Usually I end up adding about ¼ cup spirits to one recipe of vanilla custard cream. (Incidentally, I make my Christmas eggnog by flavoring crème anglaise with a hefty dose of brandy and then folding in whipped cream.)

IF you like the flavor of crème anglaise with spirits, don't hestitate to try all sorts of different flavors; fruit brandies such as kirsch, framboise, mirabelle, and poire william are especially delicious.

CUSTARD cream can also be flavored with spices such as cinnamon, cloves, ginger, and even a mixture of saffron and cardamom.

TWO approaches can be used for making spice-flavored custard cream. The easier is to combine ground spices with the egg yolks befote pouring in the simmering milk. The other method, which produces a brighter flavor, is to simmer spices in the milk before pouring it into the egg yolks. These quantities work well for one batch of custard cream:

2 teaspoons ground ginger or ½-inch segment fresh ginger root, peeled and
    grated
or
¼ teaspoon ground cloves or 6 whole cloves
or
I teaspoon ground cinnamon or 4 cinnamon sticks, broken up with a knife
or
½ teaspoon ground cardamom or 4 cardamom pods, peeled and combined with
    ¼ teaspoon saffron threads

Mango and Orange Soup with Cardamom and Saffron Custard Cream

I first tasted this magical combination of spices in an ice cream served at an Indian restaurant in New York. I've since been experimenting and have come up with this soup. If you can't find ripe mangoes, try it with oranges alone.

Each component of the soup can be made a day in advance and held in the refrigerator.

MAKES 6 SERVINGS

2 cups milk

5 egg yolks

½ teaspoon ground cardamom

small of pinch saffron threads

¼ cup sugar

I cup fresh orange juice

3 ripe mangoes, peeled and cut into ¼-inch cubes
    (page 574)

4 navel oranges

MAKE a custard cream as directed on page 588, bringing the milk to a simmer and combining the egg yolks, spices, and sugar; proceed as directed in the recipe.

CHILL the custard cream on a bowl of ice or in the refrigerator. Stir the fresh orange juice into the custard cream, cover with plastic wrap, and keep in the refrigerator until needed.

PUREE half the diced mangoes in a blender or food processor and strain the mixture through a medium-mesh strainer. If the puree is very thick, thin it with about ¼ cup water. Reserve in the refrigerator until needed.

SLICE off the top and bottom of each of the oranges just enough to expose their flesh. Set an orange on end and with a sharp knife cut off the peel down around the orange so that no membrane remains. Hold the orange over a bowl and cut carefully between the membranes separating the wedges so that each section falls off into the bowl. Chill the wedges until needed.

LADLE the custard cream into chilled wide bowls. Swirl the mango puree around the center of the bowls. Stack the orange wedges in the center of the bowl and arrange the reserved diced mango in a decorative pattern around the sides.

Chocolate Broth

This is a little like the best hot chocolate you've ever had, but when served in a bowl it makes a satisfying soup to serve as a dessert. Sometimes I swirl chocolate broth in a wide bowl with one or more fruit purees and then decorate the bowl with berries—a half-pint of raspberries does the trick—and/or sliced fruit such as skinless orange wedges cut into supremes (to do this, see instructions on page 504). Little brioche croutons add crunch.

Chocolate broth will keep for at least 2 weeks in the refrigerator.

MAKES 4 DESSERT SERVINGS

I cup heavy cream

8 ounces bittersweet chocolate, broken into almond-size chunks with a chef's knife

I cup warm water

I teaspoon vanilla extract

4 ¼-inch-thick slices brioche or all-butter pound cake

3 tablespoons butter

BRING the cream to a simmer in a 2-quart saucepan, remove from the heat, and add the chocolate. Let the chocolate sit in the hot cream for 5 minutes and then stir the mixture until the chocolate has completely dissolved. Add the water and vanilla extract and stir until the mixture is smooth. Keep covered in the refrigerator.

CUT the brioche or pound cake into ¼-inch cubes and toss them in melted butter over medium heat until they're golden brown and crispy. Bring the broth to a simmer, ladle it into hot bowls, and sprinkle the brioche croutons on top of each serving or pass them at the table.

CHOCOLATE broth can be flavored with coffee, brandies, whiskeys, or praline paste (page 586).

Basic Preparation

Indian-Style Clarified Butter

GHEE

A staple of Indian cooking, *ghee* is made by slowly cooking whole sweet butter until the water contained in the butter evaporates and the milk solids turn golden brown, giving the butter a rich, nutty aroma and flavor. Surprisingly little *ghee* can be stirred into soups just before serving to give them a rich, buttery flavor.

Because butter is about 25 percent water, it takes about a pound (2 cups) of butter to make 1½ cups of *ghee*. If you use *ghee* with any regularity, it's worth using at least a pound of butter and keeping the *ghee* in a plastic container in the refrigerator, where it will keep well for at least 6 months; in the freezer it will keep indefinitely.

Although *ghee* can be used alone as a flavorful finish for Indian and other soups (it's especially good in bean soups), most Indian cooks flavor it by using it to fry spices and flavorings such as garlic, onions, ginger, and chilies. This aromatic spiced *ghee*—called *tadka*—is then stirred into soups and other dishes as a last-minute flavoring.

MAKES 1½ CUPS

I pound unsalted butter

PUT the butter into a I- or 2-quart saucepan over medium heat. After about 5 minutes the butter will start foaming. You may have to turn the heat down at this point to keep it from boiling over. In about 10 more minutes the foam will subside and you'll see that the butter fat has separated from the white milk solids.

CONTINUE cooking the butter for a minute or two until the white milk solids separate into sandlike grains and the grains turn golden brown and adhere to the bottom of the pan. Be careful at this stage because it is easy to burn the butter.

IMMEDIATELY pour the butter through a fine-mesh strainer or through a regular strainer lined with a triple layer of cheesecloth or a sheet of muslin (rinsed first to eliminate bleach or chemicals) or a coffee filter.

STORE the butter in a plastic container with a tight-fitting lid.

Flavored Butters

It's amazing what a small slice of butter will do for a bowl of soup. In fact, when I order soup in cheap restaurants I usually put the butter in the soup instead of on the bread.

The French in their inimitable way have invented a whole collection of herb and flavored butters designed for dolloping on grilled meats and fish and also for serving atop bowls of soup. Most of these butters are prepared by working chopped herbs or other flavors such as garlic with a chunk of butter using a wooden spoon, an electric mixer with a paddle blade, or a food processor. Flavored butters can be rolled into a cylinder in wax paper—making it easy to slice into attractive disks—and stored indefinitely in the freezer.

There are no hard and fast rules about which butters to use on which soups. But don't use a strong-flavored butter in a delicate soup, such as garlic butter in artichoke soup. I usually add them as a last-minute whim—they look pretty floating in the middle of a bowl of soup—or slice the cylinders and pass them at the table for my guests to help themselves.

Herb butters also offer a good method of preserving herbs if you have a garden and find yourself with a year's supply of some herb.

One trick when making herb butters is to chop the herbs with a small chunk of butter and then combine this mixture with the rest of the creamed butter. This prevents certain herbs—such as tarragon and basil—from turning black.

Here are a few suggestions, but feel free to make up your own combinations.

PARSLEY BUTTER: Combine two tablespoons chopped parsley with one stick (4 ounces) of sweet butter by hand with a wooden spoon, in an electric mixer using the paddle blade, or in a food processor.

Place the butter along one side of a 1-foot square of wax paper. Use a rubber spatula to shape the butter into a cylinder about 6 inches long, then roll it in the wax paper. Twist the wax paper in opposing directions until the butter comes together in a tight cylinder. You can keep the butter like this for up to 2 weeks in the refrigerator. If you want to freeze the butter, wrap it—wax paper and all—in aluminum foil.

MINT BUTTER: Combine the chopped leaves of 1 bunch of mint with 1 stick of butter the same way as parsley butter.

BASIL BUTTER: Sprinkle 1 tightly packed cup of basil leaves with a tablespoon of olive oil and then chop finely. (The olive oil prevents the leaves from blackening.) Combine the chopped leaves with one stick (4 ounces) of unsalted butter in the same way as for parsley butter.

TARRAGON BUTTER: Prepare tarragon butter in the same way as parsley butter, but substitute the leaves from 10 fresh tarragon sprigs for the parsley. Combine a tablespoon of the butter with the leaves while chopping to prevent them from turning black.

CHERVIL BUTTER: Chervil has delicate leaves—it looks a little like miniature Italian parsley—and a subtle flavor, reminiscent of tarragon but more delicate. Chervil butter is excellent for delicately flavored soups such as artichoke or white bean.

Prepare chervil butter in the same way as parsley butter—chervil won't turn black when chopped—using 2 tablespoons chopped chervil for a stick of butter.

GARLIC BUTTER: Finely chop 2 garlic cloves, peeled, and crush them to a paste with the side of a chef's knife or in a mortar and pestle. Combine with 1 stick of butter.

GINGER BUTTER: Peel and finely grate a ½-inch segment of fresh ginger and combine it with a stick of butter. If you want to eliminate the tiny specks of ginger, work the butter through a strainer.

TOMATO BUTTER: Peel, seed, and chop 3 fresh tomatoes or chop 1½ cups drained canned tomatoes. Cook the tomatoes in a 2-quart saucepan over medium heat, stirring regularly with a wooden spoon, until the sauce is almost the texture of tomato paste, about 30 minutes. Let cool.

Work the tomato mixture with a stick of butter. Season to taste with salt and pepper.

Bread and Croutons

If I'm home alone or with close friends, I sometimes just place a thick slice of French bread—preferably a little stale or lightly toasted—in the center of each bowl before ladling in the soup. But not everyone likes their bread already in the soup, so when I'm having company I usually pass sliced bread at the table.

One of my favorite accompaniments to a bowl of soup is a simple basket of toasted French bread slices passed at the table. Depending on how diet-conscious my guests are, I sometimes smear the toasted bread with butter or brush it with extra virgin olive oil. If I want garlic bread—delicious with hearty Italian or southern French soups—I rub the toasted slices with a peeled garlic clove before rubbing them with butter or drizzling them with olive oil.

I also like to prepare miniature croutons for sprinkling in the center of the bowls. The croutons are especially welcome in puree soups because they provide a little crunch. And they look pretty, especially if sprinkled over a dollop of herb butter melting in the center of the bowls. Pass a bowl of extra croutons at the table.

Some traditional French soups and stews are served with elongated heart-shaped croutons, dipped in chopped parsley, arranged around the serving dish or around each individual bowl. Many people find this contrived and overly elaborate, but I like the old-fashioned charm of a red wine fish or meat soup surrounded by the croutons.

Italian cooks like to serve rustic soups with *crostini* made by covering well-buttered or olive-oil-drizzled slices of toast with grated Parmesan cheese and baking the *crostini* in a 375°F oven for about 10 minutes until the cheese melts. These are a bit filling if you're serving soup as a light first course, but a bowl of soup, some *crostini*, and a green salad have resulted in many a perfect lunch or light supper.

SMALL CROUTONS (ABOUT 8 SERVINGS): Cut 4 slices of white bread into ½-inch cubes. Melt a stick (½ cup) of unsalted butter or ½ cup extra virgin olive oil in a wide sauté pan over medium heat. Toss the bread cubes in the butter until crispy and golden brown. Drain the croutons on paper towels.

HEART-SHAPED CROUTONS (8 SERVINGS, 3 PER SERVING): Remove the crusts from 12 square slices of white bread. Cut the slices in half diagonally. Use a sharp knife to round off two of the corners so that each half-slice looks like an elongated heart.

Gently sauté the croutons in 1 stick of unsalted butter or ½ cup extra virgin olive oil until they are golden brown on each side. Drain on paper towels.

Dip the tips of the croutons in very finely chopped parsley and place them on the edges of bowls or serving platters with the tips pointing outward.

Patterns for
IMPROVISING SOUPS

One-Pot Meat Soups

Some soups contain so many ingredients that they can be served as the entire meal. Once you feel comfortable with the basic techniques for making meat soups, it's easy to prepare an unusual or unfamiliar recipe using the same techniques but substituting different ingredients. This chart shows a small sampling of one-pot meat soups from around the world.

COUNTRY	TITLE	DESCRIPTION	PRINCIPAL INGREDIENTS
ARGENTINA	*Puchero*	Poached beef and hen with *chorizos*	Beef brisket Stewing hen
BELGIUM/FRANCE	*Hochepot*	Poached beef, lamb, veal, and pork	Beef brisket Veal shank Lamb breast Pig's foot Sausages
BOLIVIA	*Chairo*	Beef (originally dried llama meat) simmered with vegetables and grains	Beef brisket Reconstituted potatoes (chuño)
BRAZIL	*Cozido*	Poached beef, ham hocks, and Portuguese sausages	Beef brisket Ham hocks *Paio* Linguiça Kielbasa *Saucisse à l'ail*
CHINA	Lion's Head Hot Pot	Poached cabbage and pork meatballs	Cabbage Pork

VEGETABLES, STARCHY INGREDIENTS, NUTS, ETC.	FLAVORINGS	SPECIAL CHARACTERISTICS	SERVING STYLE AND ACCOMPANIMENTS
Cabbage Carrots New potatoes Onions Leeks	Chilies Parsley	Hot and spicy interpretation of Spanish *cocido*	Meats served on a platter, broth served at same time Bread
Celery Onions Carrots Parsnips Turnips Leeks	Juniper berries Cloves Bouquet garni	*Pot-au-feu* with mixed meats	Broth served first; meats presented on a platter Bread
Garlic Celery Onions Chuño New potatoes Barley Hominy	Chilies Cumin Parsley	The use of dried and reconstituted potatoes (chuño) Hominy and barley	Served all at once Bread Rice
Garlic Onions Leeks Carrots Celery Cabbage Yucca Plantains Corn	Ginger Chilies Cumin Cloves Cilantro	Highly flavored with corn and plantains	Bread Rice
Cabbage	Ginger Sesame oil Soy sauce	Small cooked clams are added at the end	Rice Fried rice

COUNTRY	TITLE	DESCRIPTION	PRINCIPAL INGREDIENTS
ECUADOR	*Sancocho*	Poached beef or mixed meats with vegetables	Usually beef, but sometimes pork, chicken, or seafood
ECUADOR	*Caldo de Bolas*	Dumplings poached in broth	Spicy plantain dumplings
FRANCE	*Pot-au-Feu*	Poached beef with vegetables	Beef brisket, shank, short ribs, etc.
	Poule au Pot	Poached hen with vegetables	Stewing hen
	Boeuf à la Ficelle	Poached beef tenderloin	Beef tenderloin
	Petite Marmite	Miniature *pot-au-feu*	Oxtail Stewing hen Lean cuts of beef
ITALY	*Bollito Misto*	Poached mixed meats	Beef tongue Veal (shank or shoulder) Beef brisket Chicken Sausage Calf's foot
JAPAN	*Sukiyaki*	Quick-simmered beef	Thinly sliced beef Grilled bean curd

VEGETABLES STARCHY INGREDIENTS, NUTS, ETC.	FLAVORINGS	SPECIAL CHARACTERISTICS	SERVING STYLE AND ACCOMPANIMENTS

Carrots
Potatoes
Onions
Plantains
Leeks
Corn
Cabbage
	Bouquet garni with:
	   Mint
	   Parsley
	   Rosemary
	   Thyme
	Jalapeño
	Chopped cilantro added before serving
		Corn and plantains	Broth served first; meat and vegetables presented on a platter
			Bread

Plantains Garlic Carrots Onions	Ginger Chilies Parmesan cheese Parsley	Dumplings made with plantains and ground meat or shellfish	Dumplings served in hot broth Bread Parmesan cheese
Carrots Onions Celery Leeks Turnips	Bouquet garni	Long-simmered in water or broth	Traditionally, broth served first, meats and vegetables after Cornichons Coarse salt Mustard Bread
Carrots Onions Celery Leeks Turnips Stuffing	Bouquet garni	Hen simmered in water, broth, or *pot-au-feu*	Coarse salt Bread
Carrots Onions Celery Leeks Turnips	Bouquet garni	Tenderloin lightly poached in broth or in a *pot-au-feu*	Coarse salt Fresh ground pepper Tomato sauce Bread
Carrots Onions Celery Leeks Turnips Cabbage balls	Bouquet garni	Meats and vegetables served at the same time as broth	Served in individual crocks Croutons
Carrots Celery Onions	Bouquet garni with marjoram and/or mint		Potatoes, carrots, turnips, and onions boiled separately Assorted sauces Bread
Shiitake mushrooms Scallions Bean sprouts Bamboo shoots	Scallions Soy sauce Sake Trefoil		Cooked in a skillet at the table Rice

COUNTRY	TITLE	DESCRIPTION	PRINCIPAL INGREDIENTS
JAPAN	*Shabu-Shabu*	Tabletop braised beef	Thinly sliced beef Tofu
	Mizutaki	Tabletop-simmered chicken	Young chicken
KOREA	*Tubujongol*	Tofu hot pot	Tofu Ground beef
	Chongol	Beef and vegetable hot pot	Beef strips *Konnyaku* Tofu
	Shinsollo (Sin Sul Lo)	Elaborate meat and fish hot pot	Strips of sirloin Chicken breasts Calf's liver Fish fillets
MOROCCO	*Harira*	Hearty lamb stew with spices	Lamb shoulder
PARAGUAY	*Bori-bori*	Beef broth with cornmeal and cheese dumplings	Beef brisket Cornmeal Cheese dumplings
PERU	*Sancochado*	Poached, spiced, and rolled beef brisket	Beef brisket

VEGETABLES STARCHY INGREDIENTS, NUTS, ETC.	FLAVORINGS	SPECIAL CHARACTERISTICS	SERVING STYLE AND ACCOMPANIMENTS
Shiitake mushrooms Chinese cabbage Shredded white radish Wheat gluten (fu)	Edible chrysanthemum leaves Scallions Kelp (konbu)	Meats and vegetables are dipped in raw egg after cooking	Cooked at the table in Japanese casserole (donabe) Ponzu Sesame Sauce Rice
Chinese cabbage Shiitake mushrooms Sliced carrots Harusame filaments	Kelp (konbu) Trefoil Sliced scallions	Ingredients are simmered in konbu-flavored water or broth	Cooked at the table in donabe Ponzu Red maple radish Slivered yuzu citron or lemon zest
Mushrooms White radish Bamboo shoots	Sesame oil Soy sauce Garlic Chilies Scallions	Tofu "sandwiches"	Served in hot pot at the table Rice
Shiitake mushrooms Bamboo shoots Chinese cabbage Onions Spinach	Sugar Soy sauce Rice wine (or sherry)	Cooked in batches like sukiyaki	Cooked at the table Rice
Carrots Chinese mushrooms Ginkgo nuts Pine nuts	Ginger Soy sauce Garlic Scallions	Meats are coated with egg and fried before being layered and simmered in broth	Cooked at the table in a traditional shinsollo pot Rice
Bean sprouts Onions Celery Lentils Chick-peas Tomatoes	Saffron Ginger Cinnamon Turmeric	Unusual spice combinations	Served together in bowls
Onions Garlic Celery Carrots	Bay leaf Cloves Saffron Parmesan cheese Parsley	Italian-style flavors	Broth, meat, and dumplings served together in a tureen Parmesan cheese Bread
Carrots Turnips Yucca Chayotes Onions Leeks	Cloves Bouquet garni Oregano Garlic Ginger	Beef is coated with spices and rolled; corn beer is sometimes used for liquid	Hot chili sauce Aïoli Cilantro sauce

COUNTRY	TITLE	DESCRIPTION	PRINCIPAL INGREDIENTS
SPAIN	*Cocido*	Long-simmered pot of mixed meats and vegetables	Chicken Beef *Chorizo* Veal *Morcilla* (blood sausage) Meatballs
	Escudella i Carn d'Olla	Long-simmered pot of mixed meats and vegetables	Veal Chicken Ground pork or *Botifarra sausage* Botifarra negra sausage
	Olla Podrida	Old-fashioned simmered meats and vegetables	Beef brisket Lamb shoulder Pork Calf's foot Chicken *Chorizos* Game
UNITED STATES	New England Boiled Dinner	Simmered corned beef with vegetables	Corned beef Cabbage
VENEZUELA	*Hervido*	Poached beef or mixed meats with vegetables	Usually beef, but sometimes pork, chicken, or seafood
	Cruzado	Mixed beef, chicken, and seafood	Beef brisket Whole chicken Shellfish (clams or mussels) Fish fillets

VEGETABLES STARCHY INGREDIENTS, NUTS, ETC.	FLAVORINGS	SPECIAL CHARACTERISTICS	SERVING STYLE AND ACCOMPANIMENTS
Onions Leeks Garlic Carrots New potatoes Noodles Chick-peas	Bouquet garni		Bread
Cabbage Celery Carrots Turnips Noodles	Bouquet garni	Contains homemade sausages	Served in two courses Bread Olive oil
Carrots Leeks Onions Cabbage Potatoes Chick-peas	Garlic Bouquet garni		Served in two courses
Potatoes Beets Onions Carrots	Parsley	Because corned beef contains brine, the broth is not served	Meat and vegetables served together on platter Mustard Pickles Horseradish

Carrots
Potatoes
Onions
Plantains
Leeks
Corn
Cabbage
	Bouquet garni with:
	    Mint
	    Parsley
	    Rosemary
	    Thyme
	Jalapeño
	Chopped cilantro added before serving
		Corn and plantains	Broth served first; meat and vegetables presented on a platter

Onions Garlic Celery Carrots Cabbage New potatoes Corn	Jalapeño Chopped cilantro	Hot chilies Corn Combination of meat and shellfish	Meats served on a platter, broth served at the same time in individual bowls Bread Rice

Fish Soups

	ORIGIN	FLAVOR BASE
Anguille au Vert	Belgium Flanders	Onions Bouquet garni
Bouillabaisse	Provence	Onions Leeks Fennel Tomatoes Saffron Bouquet garni with: oregano, thyme, etc. Dried orange rind Garlic
Bourride	Provence	Onion Fennel Thyme Bay leaf Orange zest
Bourride Sétoise	Languedoc	Leeks Onions Swiss chard Bouquet garni
Caldeirada	Portugal	Onions Green sweet peppers Garlic Tomatoes Thyme
Calderata Asturiana	Spain	Olive oil Onions Red peppers Nutmeg
Caudière	Flanders	Onions Clove Bouquet garni Garlic
Chaudrée	Charente	Bouquet garni Pepper
Chirinabe	Japan	

MOISTENING LIQUID(S)	TYPES OF FISH	FINISH	GARNISH
Fish broth made with trimmings White wine	Eels and freshwater fish	Egg yolks Cream Herbs	Croutons
Fish stock made with trimmings Pastis (Pernot, etc.	Mediterranean	*Rouille*	Croutons
Fish stock made with trimmings	Mediterranean	*Aïoli*	*Aïoli*
Fish stock White wine	Monkfish	*Aïoli*	*Aïoli*
Fish broth made with trimmings White wine	Saltwater fish: sea bass, cod, monkfish, etc. Squid Bay scallops	None	Basil cut in strips
Sherry Water	Cod, sea bass, monkfish, etc.	None	None
Fish stock made with trimmings and water White wine Mussel cooking liquid	Small Atlantic fish; baby sole, flounder, conger eel	Cream	Mussels
White wine Water	Squid or cuttlefish Baby skate Eel Mullet	Butter	Buttered croutons
Konbu-flavored water	White firm-fleshed fish		Chinese cabbage Spinach Enokidake mushrooms Wheat gluten *(fu)* White radish Tofu

	ORIGIN	FLAVOR BASE
Chowder	North America	Onions Salt pork Bacon Potatoes
	Mexico	Roasted chilies Jalapeño
Cotriade	Cornwall (England)	Onions Sorrel Potatoes
Indian-Style Coconut Curry	India	Ginger Onions Hot chilies
Matelote Alsacienne	Alsace	Leeks Carrots Onions Bouquet garni
Matelote à la Bourguignonne	Burgundy	Onions Garlic Bouquet garni
Matelote à la Canotière	Alsace	Leeks Carrots Onions Bouquet garni
Matelote Normande	Normandy	Onions Garlic Bouquet garni
Pochouse	Burgundy	Onion Garlic Clove Bouquet garni
Romesco	Spain	Onions Leeks
Soupe de Poisson Niçoise	Nice (France)	Olive oil Onions Garlic Saffron Tomatoes
Ttorro	Basque Country	Olive oil Onions Garlic Red bell peppers Hot chilies Saffron Bouquet garni

MOISTENING LIQUID(S)	TYPES OF FISH	FINISH	GARNISH
Milk Fish broth	Cod White firm-fleshed ocean fish	Cream	Crackers
Fish broth made with trimmings	Firm-fleshed round fish	Cream	Tortilla chips Sour cream
Water Vinegar	Conger eel Mackerel Cod	Butter	Stale bread
Fish broth made with trimmings Tomatoes	Firm-fleshed fish	Coconut milk Cilantro	Rice
Fish broth made with trimmings and vegetables Riesling	Freshwater fish: carp, eel, perch, etc.	Cream Egg yolks *Beurre manié*	Buttered croutons
Red wine, Marc de Bourgogne	Freshwater fish: trout, eel, perch, etc.	*Beurre manié* Butter	Garlic-rubbed croutons
Fish stock made with trimmings and vegetables Riesling or Sylvaner	Carp and eel only	Butter	Mushrooms Crayfish
Cider Calvados	Saltwater fish: sole, flounder, Conger eel	*Beurre manié* Cream	Croutons Mussels
White wine (Bourgogne Aligote)	Freshwater fish: trout, perch, eel, pike, etc.	*Beurre manié* Cream	Pearl onions Bacon Mushrooms Croutons
Fish broth made with trimmings Sherry	Mediterranean	Romesco *(picada)*	None
Fish broth made with trimmings	Mediterranean	*Rouille*	French bread
Stock made with trimmings and vegetables	Saltwater fish and shellfish; mussels, langoustines, monkfish, conger eel, shrimp, lobster, etc.	None	Croutons cooked with olive oil Chopped parsley

	ORIGIN	FLAVOR BASE
Vatapa	Brazil	Onions Hot chilies Tomatoes Ginger
Waterzooï	Belgium	Butter Onions Bouquet garni Sage
Zarzuela	Catalonia	Onions Red sweet peppers Green sweet peppers Garlic Ham Tomatoes Saffron Bouquet garni

MOISTENING LIQUID(S)	TYPES OF FISH	FINISH	GARNISH
Coconut milk Water	Small ocean fish Shrimp	Coconut puree Peanut puree Rice	Chopped cilantro
Stock made with trimmings and vegetables	Freshwater fish: trout, eel, perch, pike, etc.	Butter Heavy cream	Chopped parsley Croutons
White wine	Lobster Large shrimp Mussels Bay scallops Sea scallops	None	Almonds Chopped parsley

Metric Conversion Chart

CONVERSIONS OF OUNCES TO GRAMS

OUNCES (OZ)	GRAMS (G)
1 oz	30 g*
2 oz	60 g
3 oz	85 g
4 oz	115 g
5 oz	140 g
6 oz	180 g
7 oz	200 g
8 oz	225 g
9 oz	250 g
10 oz	285 g
11 oz	300 g
12 oz	340 g
13 oz	370 g
14 oz	400 g
15 oz	425 g
16 oz	450 g
20 oz	570 g
24 oz	680 g
28 oz	790 g
32 oz	900 g

*Approximate. To convert ounces to grams, multiply number of ounces by 28.35.

CONVERSIONS OF POUNDS TO GRAMS AND KILOGRAMS

POUNDS (LB)	GRAMS (G) KILOGRAMS (KG)
1 lb	450 g*
1¼ lb	565 g
1½ lb	675 g
1¾ lb	800 g
2 lb	900 g
2½ lb	1,125 g; 1¼ kg
3 lb	1,350 g
3½ lb	1,500 g; 1½ kg
4 lb	1,800 g
4½ lb	2 g
5 lb	2¼ kg
5½ lb	2½ kg
6 lb	2¼ kg
6½ lb	3 kg
7 lb	3¼ kg
7½ lb	3½ kg
8 lb	3¾ kg
9 lb	4 kg
10 lb	4½ kg

*Approximate. To convert pounds into kilograms, multiply numbers of pounds by 453.6.

CONVERSIONS OF QUARTS TO LITERS

QUARTS (QT)	LITERS (L)
1 qt	1 L*
1½ qt	1½ L
2 qt	2 L
2½ qt	2½ L
3 qt	2¾ L
4 qt	3¼ L
5 qt	4¼ L
6 qt	5½ L
7 qt	6½ L
8 qt	7½ L
9 qt	8½ L
10 qt	9½ L

*Approximate. To convert quarts to liters, multiply number of quarts by 0.95.

CONVERSIONS OF FAHRENHEIT TO CELSIUS

FAHRENHEIT	CELSIUS
170°F	77°C*
180°F	82°C
190°F	88°C
200°F	95°C
225°F	110°C
250°F	120°C
300°F	150°C
325°F	165°C
350°F	180°C
375°F	190°C
400°F	205°C
425°F	220°C
450°F	230°C
475°F	245°C
500°F	260°C
525°F	275°C
550°F	290°C

*Approximate. To convert Fahrenheit to Celsius, subtract 32, multiply by 5, then divide by 9.

Sources

Ingredients Sources

Cheese: 3, 5, 19

Chilies: 3, 15 (for ñova chilies)

Chinese Ingredients: 1, 4, 6, 13, 17

Demi-glace, concentrated Broths: 1, 2, 3, 10

Dried Mushrooms (wild and cultivated): 3, 5, 18

European Ingredients (olives, olive oils, vinegars, fleur de sel, etc.): 1, 3, 5

Frozen French Fruit Purees:
http://www.feast.com (fruit purees not listed on site but can be obtained through this site's concierge service, which will order fruit purees for you): 5

Game Birds, Duck, Mullard Duck Breasts, Geese, Foie Gras, Confit, Duck Fat: 2, 3, 5

Indian Ingredients: 1, 8, 12, 13, 17

Indonesian Ingredients: 1, 4

Japanese Ingredients: 1, 3, 4, 9, 13, 17

Korean Ingredients: 4

Mexican Ingredients: 1, 3, 4, 15

Rice (specialty): 3, 7

Sea Salt: 1, 3, 5, 13

Smoked Fish: 3, 5

Spanish Ingredients: 3, 16, 19

Spices (whole and ground): 3, 13

Thai Ingredients: 1, 4, 13, 17

Truffles: 3, 5, 18

Vanilla Beans: 3, 5

Verjuice: 3, 5

Vietnamese Ingredients: 1, 13

1. **The CMC Company**
   P.O. Box Drawer B
   Avalon, New Jersey 08202
   1-800-262-2780
   http://www.thecmccompany.com

2. **D'Artagnan**
   39-419 St. Paul Avenue
   Jersey City, New Jersey 07306
   1-800 Dartagn
   http://www.dartagnan.com

3. **Dean and Deluca**
   560 Broadway
   New York, New York 10012
   http://www.deandeluca.com

4. *http://www.ethnicgrocer.com*
   Customer Service: 1-800-523-1961

5. *http://www.feast.com*

6. *http://www.gongshee*
   Customer Service: 1-800-523-1962

7. **Indian Harvest**
   P.O. Box 428
   Bemidji, Minnesota 56619
   1-800-346-7032
   http://www.indianharvest.com

8. **Kalustyan's**
   123 Lexington Avenue
   New York, New York 10016
   1-212-683-1691
   http://www.kalustyans.com

9. **Katagiri**
   224 East 59th Street
   New York, New York 10022
   212-755-3566
   http://www.katagiri.com

10. **More Than Gourmet**
    115 West Barges Street
    Akron, Ohio 44311
    1-800-860-9385
    FAX: 330-762-4832
    e-mail: *demi-glace@worldnet.att.net*

11. http://www.namaste.com
    Customer Service:1-800-803-1183

12. **The Oriental Pantry**
    423 Great Road
    Acton, Massachusetts 01720
    1-800-828-0368
    http://www.orientalpantry.com

13. **Penzey's Spices**
    P.O. Box 933
    Muskego, Wisconsin 53150
    http://www.penzeys.com

14. *http://www.querico.com*
    1-800-523-1963

15. **The Spanish Table**
    1427 Western Avenue
    Seattle, Washington 98101
    1-206-682-2827

16. **Spice Merchant**
    P.O. Box 524
    Jackson Hole, Wyoming 83001
    1-307-733-7811
    http://www.email.com/spice/

17. **Urbani USA**
    29-24 40th Avenue
    Long Island City
    New York, New York 11101
    1-800-281-2330
    http://www.urbani.com

18. **Zingerman's**
    1220 Jewett
    Ann Arbor, Michigan 48104
    1-888-636-8162
    http://www.zingermans.com

Index